*Japan: A Modern History*

Also by James L. McClain

*Kanazawa: A Seventeenth-Century Japanese Castle Town*
*Edo and Paris: Urban Life and the State in the Early Modern Era*
*Osaka: The Merchants' Capital of Early Modern Japan*

# Japan

## JAMES L. McCLAIN

# A MODERN

# HISTORY

**W.W. NORTON & COMPANY**   NEW YORK  LONDON

The text of this book is composed in Weiss
with the display set in Ruach.
Composition by Matrix Publishing Services
Manufacturing by Maple-Vail Book Group
Book design by Martin Lubin
Copy editor: Pearl Hanig

Library of Congress Cataloging-in-Publication Data

McClain, James L., 1944–
    Japan, a modern history / by James L. McClain.
        p.  cm.
    Includes bibliographical references and index.
    **ISBN 0-393-04156-5**
    I. Japan—History—1868     2. Japan—History—Tokugawa period, 1600–1868.
I. Title.
    DS881.9 .M34  2001
    952.03—dc21                                                    2001034545


W. W. Norton & Company, Inc., 500 Fifth Avenue, New York, N.Y. 10110
                         www.wwnorton.com

W. W. Norton & Company Ltd., Castle House, 75/76 Wells Street, London W1T 3QT

 2  3  4  5  6  7  8  9  0

To Anne and Katie

# Contents

## I   TRADITIONAL JAPAN

### 1 *The Tokugawa Polity*   5

The Origins of the Japanese State and the Appearance of the Samurai 11 ◘ Tokugawa Ieyasu and the Office of Shogun 16 ◘ Securing the Realm 20 ◘ Extending Authority Vertically 28 ◘ Legitimations of Power 30 ◘ Symbols and the Substance of Power 36 ◘ Japan and the World 39

### 2 *Cities, Commerce, and Lifestyles*   48

An Urban Revolution 50 ◘ Cities and Commerce 54 ◘ Commercial Agriculture and Protoindustrialization 60 ◘ Foreign Trade 64 ◘ Class, Status, and Standards of Living 69

### 3 *Self and Society*   76

*Bushidō* and Samurai Ethics 77 ◘ Merchant Reflections on Neo-Confucianism 83 ◘ Parallel Ways: Merchant Codes and Peasant Sages 89 ◘ Genders and Realities 93 ◘ Self and Community 98 ◘ The Shared Sense of Being Japanese 103

## II  JAPAN IN REVOLUTIONARY TIMES

## III    JAPAN IN THE NEW CENTURY

## IV    JAPAN AT WAR

## V  CONTEMPORARY JAPAN

# Maps

# Preface

My first view of Japan came from the decks of the USS *President Wilson* as it steamed into the headwaters of Tokyo Bay on a lovely autumn morning in October 1966. It took several hours for the ship to make its way to its berth at Yokohama, and as I looked out over Mount Fuji and the lush countryside, rich with the fall harvest, I had ample opportunity to ask myself what in the world I was doing in Japan. I had just graduated from the University of Michigan, but I had majored in American history and had not studied anything about Japan. Nor had I ever been outside of the United States. I had come to this faraway and unfamiliar place simply because a classmate had told me that his family in Tokyo would look after me if I wanted to visit his home country. I had come to Japan on a lark, and much to my surprise, the adventure would change the course of my life and eventually lead to a career as an historian of Japan.

I may have known almost nothing about Japan when I first stepped ashore there, but I did have a few stereotypes tucked away in my bags. Among other things, I carried with me the notion that Japan was a consensus society. The population, so the argument went back then, was very homogeneous; people looked alike and thought alike, and they easily achieved national agreement about any issue. It did not take long to realize how erroneous this line of thinking was. All around me I found people separated from one another by age, gender, education, and economic class, and they expressed very different convictions about almost everything— whether women belonged in the home or the workplace, whether Japan should be allied with the United States or pursue a course of neutrality, and whether big business should be praised for contributing to the country's postwar affluence or condemned for spewing pollution everywhere. To be certain, I realized, harmony and consensus were desired ideals, but in reality the Japanese were sharply divided about the major questions that confronted them.

What I learned during my initial stay in Japan influenced how I conceptualized that country's history. If heated debates and dissenting opinions were so readily apparent in modern Japanese society, it stood to reason that the country's history also was the story of its people and how their clashing points of view provided the dynamic that moved events forward. As with any society, megatrends clearly have been important; urbanization, industrialization, and globalization, to name just three great casual factors of the last two centuries, obviously have influenced the flow of Japan's history by shaping how individuals perceive themselves and their world and by placing limits around that which is possible. Nevertheless, within those great historical currents, the Japanese people, in all their great diversity, made their own history. Consequently, this narrative is built on the premise that our first duty is to understand how different individuals and social groups defined what was important to them and then struggled to construct a way of life that gave meaning to their dreams, values, beliefs, and ambitions.

I also came to realize, as I shared conversations with my new friends and colleagues over the years, that most Japanese feel closer to their past than do most Americans I know. Perhaps that is natural in a country that has been a unified political entity for more than a millennium. Japan is also a place where one easily can hop off a modern subway train and duck into the quiet of an ancient temple or sit in a coffee shop enjoying a cup of French Roast and listening to the latest jazz release only to look out the window and see an elderly woman walk by, dressed in traditional kimono and carrying a shamisen, the three-stringed lute heard everywhere in the "floating world," the demimonde of theater and prostitution districts found in Japan's early modern cities. The coverage given in this volume to that early modern era (1603–1868) reflects the importance of the linkages between the present and the past. Among other things, *Japan: A Modern History* examines how a political culture that permitted ordinary Japanese to participate in the self-governance of their villages and urban neighborhoods nurtured the growth of a modern citizenry that believed itself entitled to critique government policies, organize political movements and parties, and play an important role in the parliamentary system created in the Meiji period (1868–1912); how the growth of commerce and protoindustrialization in the eighteenth and early nineteenth centuries made rapid industrialization possible after 1868; and how traditional ways of thinking about family and gender have affected patterns of behavior throughout the modern era.

My experiences in Japan also conditioned me not to view that society or its history as a success story. When I first went to Tokyo in the late 1960s it was difficult not to be impressed with the affluence that I saw around me, with the towering new buildings and clean streets, or with the fact that everything seemed to work so well. Yet, newspaper editorials and television documentaries were quick to point to what many considered as shortcomings and failures in Japan's modernizing efforts: too many people still lived in substandard housing, the education system placed more emphasis on the rote memorization of facts than on developing each student's innate talents and abilities, and middle managers in major corporations worked such long hours that they had little time for a family life, or even a life at all.

The problems plaguing Japanese society in the last half of the twentieth century made it clear, even to an initiate like myself, that Japanese history could not be construed as a simple succession of events that led inevitably to a better and brighter future. Indeed, many of my Japanese friends spoke discouragingly about the cheerless aspects of certain historical continuities, such as the way in which prejudice against native outcast communities and a contemptuous attitude toward neighboring Ainu and Koreans in the early modern period congealed into a pattern of discrimination that endures today. Moreover, at times in the past, whenever the country reached a crucial historical crossroad, the Japanese had to make decisions that would move their country and society in new directions. Sometimes their choices produced outcomes that most people found rewarding, but at other times they plotted a course that led to what, in retrospect, almost everyone agreed were tragic consequences. One need only contrast the social and intellectual vitality of the 1920s with the repressive atmosphere of the war years at the end of the 1930s and beginning of the 1940s to realize that Japanese history has held its fair share of cruel twists and turns.

Over time I also came to realize that Japanese culture and history are not exceptionalist. Japan is clearly unique, in the sense that all national cultures and histories are distinctive from one another, even though they might share certain commonalties. Accordingly, while Japanese act in particular ways, both now and in the past, those modes of conduct are just as commonsensical as those of other peoples, as long as we understand the values that inform those patterns of behavior. Being distinct, to put it another way, is not the same thing as being inscrutable. After I returned from my first trip to Japan and entered graduate school at Yale, I read an essay by the anthropologist Clifford Geertz that helped me pull together my own thoughts about cultural distinctiveness.* He had studied Moroccans, and the more he comprehended, Geertz wrote, the more the Moroccans seemed both logical and singular. "Understanding a people's culture," he concluded, "exposes their normalness without reducing their particularity."

*Clifford Geertz, "Thick Description: Toward an Interpretational Theory of Culture," in his *The Interpretation of Cultures* (New York: Basic Books, 1973), pp. 3–30.

As I have pursued my career as an historian, the thoughts assembled above have provided me with a set of guides: to abandon stereotypes and attempt to understand the values and ways of thought that inspired various Japanese to act as they did; to appreciate the legacies of the past while always remembering that history constantly forces people to make decisions that can propel their futures in radically new directions; to assess the outcomes of past actions by taking into account the judgments of the people who lived through the events; to remember that as strange as things might seem at times, the Japanese and their past are comprehensible; and always to bear in mind that there is no single model for doing things, and that other peoples can find satisfaction and value in life in ways that are very different from our own.

Understanding another people's culture and past is not always easy. Geertz realized that as well when he cited the tale of an Englishman who, having been told that the world rested on a platform that rested on the back of an elephant which, in turn, rested on the back of a turtle, asked what that turtle rested on. Another turtle. And that turtle? "Ah," his Indian friend replied, "after that it is turtles all the way down." Similarly, we may never fathom all the depths of Japanese history; rarely have I understood anything as completely as I would like. But Geertz has another thought to comfort all of us: It is not necessary, he wrote, "to know everything in order to understand something." Applied to my own study of Japan, I have taken that to mean that history, at its very innermost essence, is the art of guessing at people's motives and assessing the significance of their actions, evaluating our observations, and then drawing conclusions from our better insights. In that sense, for the beginner as well as the experienced scholar, exploring Japanese history and pushing out the boundaries of our knowledge is rich in its rewards.

Although the themes that run through this volume are my own, I am deeply indebted to countless individuals for making this book possible. Steve Forman, vice president and editor at W. W. Norton, conceived of this project and helpfully read drafts of many chapters. Most of all, though, I am thankful to Steve for all his words of encouragement throughout the years and for enduring more delays than he could ever have imagined possible when we first set to work. Were it in my power, I would immediately enshrine him as the foremost Confucian paragon of patience. Steve's assistant, Lory Frenkel oversaw production of the book. I especially appreciate her assistance in helping to select illustrations and for the gentle manner she employed as she nudged and shepherded me toward important deadlines. I also am beholden to the eagle-eyed Pearl Hanig, whose tough copy editing vanquished many errors from the manuscript, and to Norton's entire staff of indexers, designers, and layout artists.

A host of other people also read drafts and helped to prepare this volume for publication. Many students—Atsuko Aoki, Andrew Bell, Betty Chung, Andrea Damon, Brian Fong, Lisa E. Hartmann, Shiho Imai, Ricky Wong, and Rachel Zimet—graciously shared their thoughts with me about earlier versions of the manuscript. In a more general sense, I am obliged to students in all my classes who consistently have insisted that I scorn simplicity and make my analyses more complex, and thus, for them, more genuine and true to life. Many colleagues took time from their own busy schedules to comment on various chapters, and I particularly wish to express my appreciation to Andrew Barshay, John Dower, Alexis Dudden, Jerome Grieder, Kerry Smith, Constantine Vaporis, Brett Walker, Akio Yasuhara, and Louise Young for their valuable suggestions about how to improve the narrative. Thanks as well go to Smith and to my friend and colleague Roger Keyes for the hours they spent helping me choose and locate illustrations. Not least, I am grateful to all scholars working on Japanese history, and the entries in "Further Readings" can only begin to suggest how indebted I am to them.

There is an old Asian proverb, at least I have always heard it as an Asian proverb, "May you live in interesting times." My wife and daughters, Chang, Anne, and Katie, have done that for my life, and made it worthwhile as well.

# Reader's Guide

A t first glance, written Japanese may intimidate, but it is an easy language for most Americans and Europeans to speak. There are five vowels (*a,i,u,e,o*), and they are pronounced more or less as in Spanish. A macron represents a double-length sound. Syllables are formed from single vowels or from a combined consonant and vowel. In addition, a nasal *n* functions as an independent syllable; that sound is transcribed simply as *n* before a consonant or at the end of a word but as *n'* before a vowel to distinguish it from such syllables as *na* and *ni*. Thus, the name Ise is pronounced as "i-se"; Kōbe as "ko-o-be"; Honshū as "ho-n-shu-u"; and *Chōnindō* as "cho-o-ni-n-do-o." In accordance with standard practice, we have deleted the macron from well-known place-names; thus Japan's capital is spelled Tokyo, even though it is pronounced as "to-o-kyo-o."

Personal names take their native form: surname following given name for Americans and other Westerners, family name preceding personal name for East Asians (except for scholars who prefer the Western order when writing in English). In a few instances, individuals are referred to by their personal name (e.g., Ieyasu for Tokugawa Ieyasu) in order to distinguish them from others with the same surname. In addition, certain artists and writers (e.g., Andō Hiroshige and Natsume Sōseki) commonly went by their personal names, while some writers (including the poet Bashō) adopted a literary name. Finally, this volume follows the general Japanese preference of referring to emperors by their reign names, as in Emperor Meiji and the Meiji emperor.

Japan's calendar system will interest those who are making their initial voyage into that country's history. The Japanese adopted the Gregorian calendar on January 1, 1873. Before that date, they employed a calendar of consecutively numbered years based on era names known as *nengō*. Customarily, the imperial court declared a new *nengō* after an emperor or empress ascended the throne, or whenever calamity struck or danger seemed to present itself, in the hope that decreeing a propitious new name might assure future peace and prosperity. The year after Kōmei became emperor in 1847, for instance, he chose the era name Kaei, which implied a long and auspicious reign, but seven years later, after American gunboats under the command of Matthew C. Perry forced Japan to abandon its traditional seclusion policy, the court switched to Ansei, composed of ideographs that denote an era of peaceful and stable government. Only after 1868 did Japan adopt the practice of retaining an era name for the entire reign of an emperor.

Each traditional year began near the midway point between the winter solstice and spring equinox and was divided into twelve months of twenty-nine or thirty days each, with an intercalary month inserted from time to time to keep the passage of the years in rhythm with the journey of the earth around the sun. Thus, any particular year in a *nengō* cycle overlapped in large part with a Western solar-based year, so that Kaei 1 corresponded roughly to 1848 and Kaei 2 to 1849. Japan's lunar-based years were not exactly cotermonous with their Western counterparts, however, and dates falling in the final two months of a Japanese year might find their equivalent in the following Western year. Since Tokugawa Yoshinobu, the last member of his family to hold the position of shogun, took office on the fifth day of the Twelfth month of Keiō 2, for instance, his date of appointment often is given as 1866, whereas the exact correspondence is January 10, 1867. In *Japan: A Modern History*, dates before January 1, 1873, are given according to the traditional Japanese calendar, with a conversion of the era year to the nearest corresponding Western year. For important events involving Western nations, both Western and Japanese dates are provided.

Wherever appropriate, I have followed the guidance of the *Kodansha Encyclopedia of Japan* in providing translations of Japanese terms and names. Romanization follows the practices of that work and *Kenkyusha's New English-Japanese Dictionary*. Other reference works that guided the definition of terms, the dating of events, and the reading of personal and place-names include the historical dictionary *Kokushi daijiten*, the chronological tables included in *Nenpyō: Nihon rekishi* (Chikuma Shobō), and the gazetteer *Nihon rekishi chimei taikei* (Heibonsha).

For the most part, Chinese is romanized according to the pinyin system. Introduced by the Chinese government in the 1950s, pinyin largely has displaced the former Wade-Giles practices and the place-name readings found in the *Postal Atlas of China*. Thus, the founder of the People's Republic appears in *Japan: A Modern History* as Mao Zedong rather than Mao Tse-tung, and the Chinese capital is spelled Beijing throughout (in opposition to Peking, used before 1928, and Peiping, generally used between 1928 and 1949). I have made a few exceptions for names in dialect or that are difficult for Western readers to recognize in pinyin; thus Mao's leading opponent is Chiang Kai-shek rather than Jiang Jieshi and Canton remains Canton (rather than Guangzhou). The index includes the older equivalents of the pinyin forms for personal and place-names.

To complicate matters, many cities and regions had variant Chinese, Japanese, and Western names or went by different appellations in different periods. In general I have favored the version most suited to a particular chapter's subject matter. Thus, Edo is used to designate the shogunate's home city and Tokyo appears after that name was adopted in 1868. Similarly, I have tended to retain certain colonial names so as to capture the flavor of the past (e.g., Port Arthur rather than Lüshun).

Since this volume is intended for students and interested general readers, we have included chronologies at the beginning of each major division of the book, translations for technical terminology wherever appropriate, and a glossary of terms and persons that appear on several occasions in separate parts of the text. Some entries in the "Notes" include the expression "(modified)" to indicate that a particular quotation was shortened or altered so as to conform to the stylistic practices for this volume.

# Traditional Japan

# Chronology

## PART I  TRADITIONAL JAPAN

**646**

◻ *First Month, first day* Leaders of the Yamato family purportedly issue the Taika Reform Edict and eventually establish their authority as an hereditary line of Heavenly Sovereigns

**712**

◻ Scribes in the service of the Yamato Line finish compiling the *Kojiki* ("Record of Ancient Matters")

**794**

◻ The Heavenly Sovereigns establish their capital at Heian (Kyoto)

**1192**

◻ Minamoto Yoritomo is appointed shogun and establishes his "tent government" at Kamakura

**1274** and **1281**

◻ Typhoon gales known as *kamikaze,* "divine winds," ravage Mongol fleets and save Japan from invasion

**1333–1338**

◻ Ashikaga Takauji overthrows the Minamoto shogunate and is appointed shogun

**1467–1477**

◻ The Ōnin War leads to the Sengoku era, a century when Japan is "A Country at War"

**1543**

◻ Portuguese traders land on the island of Tanegashima, south of Kyūshū

**1549**

◻ Francis Xavier inaugurates the first Christian mission to Japan

**1571**

◻ The daimyo Ōmura Sumitada opens Nagasaki to Portuguese shipping

**1573**

◻ The warlord Oda Nobunaga drives the Ashikaga shogun into exile and burns most of Kyoto

**1575**

◻ Nobunaga scores a major victory at the Battle of Nagashino after arming his troops with new Western-style firearms

**1580s**

◻ Following Nobunaga's death in 1581, Toyotomi Hideyoshi hammers the daimyo into submission

**1590**

◻ Ieyasu transfers his domain to the Kantō region and begins to construct Edo Castle

**1592**

◻ Hideyoshi's armies land at Pusan

**1598**

◻ Hideyoshi dies, and Japanese armies retreat from Korea

**1600**

◻ Tokugawa Ieyasu prevails at the Battle of Sekigahara

**1603**

◻ *Second Month, twelfth day*  The Heavenly Sovereign appoints Tokugawa Ieyasu as shogun

**1604**

◻ The shogunate recognizes the Matsumae family as the daimyo of a domain on the southern coast of Hokkaidō and confirms their right to trade with the Ainu in Ezochi

**1607**

◻ Ieyasu normalizes relations with Korea

**1611**

The Ryūkyū Islands become a dependency of Satsuma domain while nominally retaining their autonomy

**1615**

◻ *Fifth Month*  Tokugawa forces overwhelm Toyotomi loyalists at Osaka Castle

◻ *Seventh Month, seventh day*  Ieyasu issues the Regulations concerning Warrior Households

◻ *Seventh Month, seventeenth day*  Ieyasu and Hidetada issue the Regulations concerning the Royal Court and Nobility

**1617**

◻ Ieyasu's remains are interred at Nikkō, and he is deified as Tōshō Dai Gongen, "Illuminator of the East, August Avatar of Buddha"

**1622**

◻ *Eighth Month, fifth day*  The shogunate's persecution of Christians begins with the execution of fifty-five believers at Nagasaki

**1623**

◻ The shogunate begins to appoint allied daimyo as senior councillors

**1629**

◻ Ieyasu's granddaughter ascends the throne as the Heavenly Sovereign Meishō

**1633–1639**

◻ The shogunate issues the so-called seclusion laws proscribing Christianity, forbidding Japanese to travel abroad, and regulating foreign trade

**1634**

◻ *Seventh Month, eleventh day–Eighth Month, fifth day*  Iemitsu makes a grand visit to Kyoto

**1635**

◻ The shogunate undertakes a major revision of the Regulations concerning Warrior Households

**1643**

◻ The first printed guide to the daily foods of commoners, *Ryōri monogatari* ("Tales of Cooking"), is published

◻ Miyamoto Musashi is said to have retreated to a cave this year to write *Gorin no sho* ("The Book of Five Rings")

**1649**

◻ *Second Month, twenty-sixth day*  The shogunate issues the Instructions of the Keian Era

**1656**

◻ Yamaga Sokō expounds his version of *Bushidō* in his *Bukyō yōroku* ("Essentials of the Warrior Code")

**1669**

◻ The Ainu leader Shakushain launches attacks on Japanese settlements in Ezochi

**1673**
◫ The Mitsui family opens a dry goods store, the Echigoya, in Edo

**1689**
◫ Bashō completes his *haikai* collection *Oku no hosomichi* ("The Narrow Road to the Deep North")

**1700**
◫ By this date Edo probably is the world's largest city

**1702**
◫ The first manual on sericulture appears

**1716**
◫ *Onna Daigaku* ("Greater Learning for Women") is published
◫ Yamamoto Tsunetomo completes *Hagakure* ("In the Shadow of Leaves")

**1724**
◫ The Kaitokudō opens in Osaka

**1729**
◫ Ishida Baigan begins to give public lectures about the essentials of Shingaku (Learning from the Heart)

**1785**
◫ The shogunate establishes the Baled Goods Office at Nagasaki

**1802**
◫ Jippensha Ikku begins the serialized publication of *Tōkaidōchū hizakurige* ("Shanks' Mare")

**1832**
◫ Hiroshige travels from Edo to Kyoto and back and begins work on the wood-block print series entitled *Fifty-three Stations of the Tōkaidō Highway*

**1839**
◫ By this date at least three hundred private academies and three thousand *terakoya* are in operation

**1842**
◫ The shogunate employs Ninomiya Sontoku to plan several village revitalization projects

**CHAPTER 1**

# The Tokugawa Polity

On the afternoon of the twelfth day of the Second Month 1603, Tokugawa Ieyasu donned a scarlet mantle of ceremony and settled himself on a dais in Fushimi Castle, a Tokugawa fortress just south of Kyoto. Soon a herald appeared, bowed deeply, and struck together two wooden clappers to announce the arrival of high-ranking envoys dispatched by the Heavenly Sovereign, the emperor of Japan. Alighting from their carriages, the imperial representatives approached the dais and, in an elaborate, precisely orchestrated ceremony, presented Ieyasu with an Edict of Appointment naming him the shogun of Japan, the military general entrusted with maintaining order throughout the realm. To show his gratitude, Ieyasu hosted a banquet for the delegates and sent them home to Kyoto with tokens of his appreciation: bags of silver and gold and a horse sporting a raised gold saddle embossed with his crest.

The investiture of Tokugawa Ieyasu as shogun was a seminal event in Japanese history, and the pageantry surrounding his elevation to the highest military office in the land reflected the power and glory of the samurai estate at the end of the sixteenth century and beginning of the seventeenth. Across Japan at that time, some 250 mighty daimyo lords ruled over autonomous domains, and their majestic citadels, many exceeding in size the largest castles built in medieval Europe, loomed over the countryside as awesome symbols of their prodigious strength. No daimyo family stood on a par with the House of Tokugawa, however, and its fortress at Fushimi was among the grandest in the land. Built between 1592 and 1596 by a fellow warlord, Fushimi's invulnerable stone walls and broad moats protected a towering donjon, residences for a garrison force of two thousand samurai, of-

*Fushimi Castle*

fice compounds, and warehouses for food and weapons, all distributed among a half dozen spacious enceintes, each protected by its own internal walls and fortified gates.

Like other daimyo fortresses, Fushimi Castle was as much a palace as a military redoubt. Ever mindful that rituals and symbols added immeasurably to the substance of power, Japan's overlords designed alcazars that dazzled with their opulence and aesthetics as well as their impregnable might. At Fushimi, Ieyasu flaunted his wealth and paraded his cultural aspirations in a manner that exuberantly proclaimed the ability of the House of Tokugawa to command the material and human resources of the land. When daimyo allies visited, Ieyasu greeted them in an expansive reception chamber that measured nearly one hundred feet on each side. There, while discussing affairs of the day, Ieyasu could direct his guests' admiring eyes to graceful wooden transoms richly decorated with carvings of sage rulers of antiquity and sliding petitions adorned with paintings of auspicious birds and flowers executed by leading artists of the day. Out-of-doors, the warrior elite could take its leisure in a handsome landscape garden and even appreciate classical noh drama performed on the castle's own stage.

The riches and splendor on display at Fushimi recalled the previous grandeur of Kyoto. Several centuries earlier, at the start of a new millennium, the emperor's capital was one of the greatest cities the world had known. Following East Asian ideals of imperial urbanism, streets and avenues laid out in meticulous geometric order crisscrossed the metropolis, creating rectangular neighborhoods that were home to more than 100,000 people. Intersecting the very center of the city, a magnificent boulevard lined with willow trees ran nearly three miles south to north, leading from the main entry gate, the famous Rashōmon, to the Imperial Palace. On occasion, Kyoto's residents might catch sight of the Heavenly Sovereign, seated in an ornate ox-drawn carriage and accompanied by hundreds of gaily costumed outriders, as he progressed down that thoroughfare on his way to visit famous sites in the pleasant countryside around the capital. Mostly, however, the imperial figure remained inside his vast palace compound, where he performed sacred rituals that honored Japan's protective deities and simultaneously identified him as the ultimate source of moral and political authority. Also cloistered inside that sanctuary was the emperor's personal residence, a deceivingly simple building whose unpainted timbers, raised wood floors, and graceful shingle roofs defined the epitome of Japanese architectural preferences and offered subtle testimony to the majesty of the Heavenly Sovereign.

At the height of Kyoto's glory in the early eleventh century, nearly two thousand aristocratic households arced necklacelike to the east and south of the palace. The grander noble estates spread over an acre or more and included a main house, expansive gardens filled with carefully selected trees and flowering plants, an artificial lake, dwellings for servants, and numerous storage and service buildings. Dressed in delicately embroidered silks, the courtiers enjoyed the finest crafts produced in Kyoto's artisanal workshops. Narrative scrolls depicting daily life show the early use of tatami mats, spread out on wooden floors for seating purposes, and sliding partitions decorated with exquisite paintings of the changing seasons and the passage of human life. In that refined setting, Kyoto's nobles created a sophisticated cultural tradition that transcended the bonds of time and space. Murasaki Shikibu's fictionalized diary of court romance and intrigue, the renowned *Tale of Genji*, belongs to that moment, an era when haughty aristocrats considered themselves the only legitimate patrons and practitioners of tanka poetry, courtly gagaku music, and the other patrician arts that for them represented the apogee of Japan's cultural accomplishments.

*Aristocrats in Kyoto*

The envoys who conveyed the title of shogun to Ieyasu in 1603 returned to a capital where the emperor and many dispirited aristocratic families lived in penury. Over the centuries the emperor and courtiers saw their wealth erode steadily, and in the 1470s the city was devastated in fighting that touched off a long civil war that was only reaching its denouement with Ieyasu's appointment as shogun. Impoverished, his palace in disrepair, one emperor had to postpone his coronation ceremonies for nearly two decades at the beginning of the sixteenth century, and many once-proud nobles moved into humble back-street tenements or sought refuge in temples. Kyoto's merchants and artisans also faced precarious times; warfare destroyed their neighborhoods, thieves roamed the streets, and in 1573 one daimyo set fires that ravaged the better part of the city once again. It was a sad decade when aristocrat and commoner alike might well remember the opening lines of a famous warrior epic:

> The sound of the bell at Gion Shōja echoes the impermanence of all things;
> The hue of the teak-tree flowers reveals the truth that the prosperous must decline.

The proud do not endure; they are like a dream on a spring night;
The mighty fall at last, they are as dust before the wind.[1]

Life in the middle of the sixteenth century also was filled with tribulations for the overwhelming majority of Japanese who lived their entire lives in self-contained hamlets. For those families the outside world began just a few steps down the village lane, and everywhere the emphasis was on self-sufficiency. Some households owned enough land to live comfortably, but most men and women worked long hours through endless days growing their own crops, sewing their own clothes, and making and repairing the tools necessary for their survival. For them, living in houses made of thatch and mud plaster and clothed in crude garments fashioned from hemp and other local fibers, life was short and usually did not rise much above subsistence level. Seasonal festivals—to ask the gods' favor at the spring planting and to thank them for the autumn harvest —broke the solitary passage of the months, and occasionally a peddler might make his way into the village, bearing curious stories about mysterious happenings in far-off Kyoto and offering for sale or barter seaweed, salt, and other valued commodities that villagers could not grow or produce for themselves.

For all the despair wrought by warfare, sprouts of renewal were pushing their way to the surface when Europeans first journeyed to the Japanese islands in the decades surrounding the turn from the sixteenth century into the seventeenth. Jorge Álvares, a Portuguese merchant who produced the earliest European eyewitness report after visiting Japan in 1546, found "a beautiful and pleasing country, with an abundance of trees, such as the pine, cedar, plum, cherry, laurel, chestnut, walnut, oak, and elder. There is also much fruit not to be found in our country; they grow the vegetables which we have in Portugal, except lettuces, cabbages, drills, corianders, and even mint; all the rest they have. They also cultivate roses, carnations and many other scented flowers, as well as both sweet and bitter oranges, citrons, pomegranates and pears."[2] A half century later the Florence native Francesco Carletti agreed that "[t]he country is very pleasing to the eye and produces large crops of rice and corn and all sorts of cereal crops, vegetables and fruits," while Alessandro Valignano, a Jesuit born in Naples, praised the ordinary men and women of Japan when he visited from 1579 to 1582 and again from 1590 to 1592. "They are very capable and intelligent," Valignano wrote, and "cultured" as well: "Even the common folk and peasants are well brought up and are so remarkably polite that they give the impression that they are trained at court. In this respect they are superior not only to other Eastern peoples but also to Europeans as well."

No less than the countryside, the merchant quarters of Kyoto appeared on the road to recovery by the time Ieyasu received his Edict of Appointment. A genre of elaborately painted screens depicting *Scenes in and around the Capital* reveal a lively city of plentitude at the end of the sixteenth century and beginning of the seventeenth. In one rendition, men and women, the young and the old—aristocrats, samurai, priests, merchants, artisans, beggars—have swarmed onto Kyoto's streets to admire a procession of magnificent floats decorated with memorable incidents drawn from Japanese history and mythology. The floats are the highlight of the Gion'e, a festival honoring a deity who protected the city from plague, and the crowds have settled into every nook and cranny of the parade route. On the banks of the Kamo River some samurai gentlemen unpack a picnic lunch; along Shijō Avenue a merchant family—father, mother, three toddlers, and a grandfather—admire the pageant of floats from their prosperous street-level shop; farther along, refined aristocratic ladies view the proceedings from the ornate entry gate to their estate. All across the cityscape people stop to chat with friends and neighbors and pause to enjoy something to eat: The picnicking samurai buy melons from a peddler, a kneeling servant dispenses tea and snacks to the guests of a temple priest, and a man clad only in a loincloth smiles to himself as he fillets a plump sea bream.

The revitalization of Kyoto calls to mind the tenacity of Japan's past. Just as the city survived the warfare of the sixteenth century, so the imperial line endured as the impervious, eternal locus of political legitimation, and in 1603 the throne's powers of appointment conferred upon the House of Tokugawa both the duty to return peace to the realm and the prerogative to help rule the country. But while history's influence was persistent, the patterns of the past did not merely replicate themselves, for Ieyasu and his successors as shogun presided over what contemporaries came to call the *Taihei*, a "Great Peace" that made subsequent economic, social, and cultural innovations possible. Initially, Ieyasu had only a tenuous hold on power, but during the seventeenth century the Tokugawa shoguns moved decisively to strengthen their hand, shape order out of chaos, and create sophisticated mechanisms of governance that gave them unparalleled civil authority even while permitting the country to flourish. As they did so, they created an environment in which all of Japan's social classes could contribute to unprecedented changes, and by the time the last Tokugawa stepped from office in 1868, Japan had become a very different country from what it had been in 1603. During those two and a half centuries, farm production multiplied severalfold, hundreds of cities sprang up across the countryside, new social classes came into existence, commerce flourished, and the Japanese came to enjoy one of the world's most advanced standards of living. At the same time, scholars and teachers formulated news codes of social behavior, and the merchant and artisan families in Japan's urban centers popularized new amusements and artistic accomplishments—Kabuki, haiku poetry, and wood-block printmaking—that now are heralded as the quintessential elements of Japanese culture.

## The Origins of the Japanese State and the Appearance of the Samurai

The evolutionary appearance of the warrior class in Japan was an unanticipated by-product of the formation of a centralized polity in the late seventh and early eighth centuries. Prior to that time, chiefdoms comprised of numerous village hamlets and presided over by ascendant lineage groups dominated most of the central and western portions of the island of Honshū and spread across Kyūshū and Shikoku as well. Such clans were highly independent; each functioned as an autonomous entity that ruled itself, determined its own codes of behavior, protected its homes and fields against rapacious neighbors, and produced the food and crafts necessary for continued existence. In addition, the paramount of each chiefdom conducted rituals of worship that honored the supposed progenitor deity of the lineage, thus combining in a single leader powers that were sacred as well as secular.

By the late fifth century one powerful family had asserted a recognizable, though decidedly fragile, hegemony over several other chiefdoms around its headquarters in the Yamato region, at the eastern end of the Inland Sea. Known alternatively as the Yamato Line or Sun Line, after its progenitor deity, Amaterasu Ōmikami (the Sun Goddess), that family subsequently used diplomacy, marriage alliances, patronage, and occasionally brute force to buttress its claims to power in central Japan and then extend a degree of authority over other clans to the south and west. By the beginning of the seventh century the Sun Line had emerged as primus inter pares among paramounts, ruling somewhat precariously over a federation of subordinate allies and satellite chiefdoms.

Dissatisfied with their still-incomplete grasp on power, enterprising Yamato leaders searched for new ways to augment their strength and influence. In the Sixth Month of 645, the most daring of the inner circle invited prominent rivals to a lavish banquet and then massacred them in the drunken hours of the late evening. Several months later, on New Year's Day

646, according to traditional accounts, the head of the Yamato Line announced the epochal Taika Reforms. Inspired by sophisticated concepts of statecraft that the Japanese had observed on embassies to Tang China, the goal of the reform program, implemented in steps over the next several decades, was to break the power of the remaining chieftaincies and transform the Sun Line into a powerful monarchy that possessed uncontested and direct authority over the people and resources of the Japanese islands. Emblematic of the momentous changes at hand, the Yamato chieftain became the country's *tennō*. Historians typically have translated that newly coined term as "emperor" to signify the *tennō*'s ambitions to wield absolute power. The more literal rendering of Heavenly Sovereign, however, better captures the notion that the Yamato family used its mythological descent from the Sun Goddess to validate its claims to rule as a "sacred and inviolable" sovereign in a dynasty that would reign forever, in a line "unbroken for ages eternal." The legends included in the *Kojiki*, the legendary "Record of Ancient Matters" commissioned by the Taika reformers and completed in 712, depicted Amaterasu as an especially influential deity who in the murky depths of the prehistoric past had entrusted a mirror, jewel, and sword—the blessed Three Regalia—to her grandson Ninigi no Mikoto when she sent him down from the High Celestial Plain to pacify the Japanese archipelago. Jimmu, Ninigi's great-grandson and the scion of mixed mortal and divine parentage, completed the conquest of Japan, the "land of luxuriant rice fields," in 660 B.C.E. according to the canons of mythohistory, which fictitiously anointed him as the islands' first ruler. In that manner, the Yamato monarchs conjured up the hoary traditions of the religious past and played on their supposed divinity to sanction their new and expanded claims to worldly kingship.

More concretely, the Taika reformers created elaborate central and provincial bureaucracies to manage affairs of state on behalf of the Heavenly Sovereign. At the apex of the new administrative hierarchy stood the Grand Council of State, or Dajōkan. Directed by a grand minister, the Dajōkan oversaw the activities of more than seven thousand officials assigned to eight principal ministries (Central Affairs, Personnel, Civil Affairs, Popular Affairs, Military Affairs, Justice, Finance, and the Royal Household). To extend the new polity's authority over all the Japanese islands, the Taika Reforms further divided the country into sixty-six provinces and assigned a civil governor and support personnel to each. In a move designed to win the allegiance of former rival chieftains and simultaneously to create a pool of administrators to staff the new organs of government, the Yamato monarchy converted the former clan lineages into a hereditary aristocracy, with those highest in the social hierarchy made eligible for appointment to the

**MAP 1.1** *The Traditional Provinces of Japan*

more important government posts. A series of legal and administrative edicts, most notably the Taihō and Yōrō Codes of 702 and 757 respectively, helped anchor the new monarchy by reinforcing the proposition that authority derived singularly from the Heavenly Sovereign and by meticulously spelling out the duties of all officeholders.

Still other measures rounded out the Taika Reform effort. Recognizing the necessity of securing a sound financial base, the fledgling monarchy claimed all Japan's agricultural land as its own, specified procedures for distributing paddy to farm families as tabulated in periodically conducted censuses, and decreed that those families pay annual taxes to the government. To provide a home for itself and the attendant aristocracy, the Yamato Line constructed a succession of capital cities. In 710 the court occupied Heijō (present-day Nara), and then in 794 the monarch and nobles moved their palaces and homes permanently to newly founded Heian, "Capital of Peace and Tranquillity," today's Kyoto.

With the machinery of state functioning smoothly, the Heavenly Sovereigns increasingly retreated from participation in routine decision making and filled their days conducting sacred rituals and sacerdotal acts considered essential to the well-being of the country. Thus, before the planting season each spring, the *tennō* instructed his ritualist staff to distribute offerings to priestly subordinates in the provinces, who would then lead a prescribed prayer: "Before the mighty ancestral gods and goddesses who augustly reside on the High Celestial Plain, we humbly raise our words of praise even as we bring choice offerings from the divine descendant at this moment of the majestic and brilliant dawning of the morning light. Before the presence of the deities who govern the crops we do humbly speak, praying that they will grant a late-ripening harvest of grain."[3] In such a manner, over time the Heavenly Sovereign came to be considered the personification of religious morality and the fount of political legitimacy, the semidivine monarch who reigned while aristocratic officeholders managed affairs of state in his name.

Viewed in the long sweep of Japanese history, the Taika Reforms established important philosophical norms, legal principles, and fundamental institutions that continued to shape the nature of governance in meaningful ways throughout Japan's premodern history. They also ushered in an era of stability when the court and aristocracy flourished. As the nobles settled into the routine of officeholding and policy making, they acquired titles to private landed estates, or *shōen*, that brought them enormous incomes. Blessed with wealth and power, aristocratic men and women of Kyoto built their palatial mansions, patronized the arts, and created what many have hailed as the golden age of Japanese high culture.

Despite the best efforts of the new monarchy, not all reform efforts worked as intended. Conspicuous in that regard was the stillborn attempt to create a permanent conscript army. In the early eighth century the new government asserted its authority to induct all males, sons of aristocrats excepted, into provincial military regiments, which the monarch could call up in rotation for guard duty in provincial capitals or in Kyoto. But many young men were reluctant to abandon their families, and women were just as sad to see their sons and husbands go. As one pair of poems from the *Man'yōshū,* the oldest anthology of Japanese verse, put it:

A frontier-guard
I set out in the morning;
And at the door—
How she wept, my darling wife,
Unwilling to let go my hand!

I will think of you, love,
On evenings when the grey mist
Rises above the rushes,
And chill sounds the voice
Of the wild ducks crying.[4]

With desertions making it impossible to recruit a dependable conscript army, the young regime began calling on certain local families that had trained themselves to be skilled fighters to maintain law and order. At first, such bands of warriors, known interchangeably as *bushi* or samurai, were family-based and took up their swords and bows only occasionally, when officials in Kyoto deputized them to preserve peace in provincial capitals and quell outbreaks of banditry in the countryside. By the eleventh century, however, the legions of warriors had evolved into large-scale, permanently armed organizations allied under the umbrellas of the Minamoto and Taira families. Adorning both family trees were the offspring of various Heavenly Sovereigns, surplus sons cut off from the royal line in order to reduce the possibility of succession disputes in an age when primogeniture was not the standard practice. In compensation for having to leave Kyoto, those transplanted offshoots received land and official appointments in the provinces that permitted them to thrive and attract adherents to their banners. By the twelfth century the Minamoto family (sometimes referred to as the Seiwa Genji) had made their headquarters in the Kantō region in eastern Japan, while the Taira (or Heike) nestled along the Inland Sea to the west of the capital.

## Tokugawa Ieyasu and the Office of Shogun

In the second half of the twelfth century a standoff between feuding claimants to the throne brought the *bushi* into Kyoto and eventually propelled the Minamoto family into the ranks of the country's ruling elite. As tensions between rival cliques in the capital deepened in the 1150s, one faction prevailed upon the Taira family for support, and the other side countered by asking the Minamoto to move their samurai into the city. After bitter fighting in 1160, forces commanded by Taira Kiyomori prevailed, and the Minamoto beat a sad retreat back to eastern Japan. With peace at hand, the court expected the Taira to return to its Inland Sea homeland, but to the chagrin of the aristocracy, Kiyomori settled down in Kyoto, had himself and many of his kin appointed to high office, appropriated titles to hundreds of the nobles' *shōen* estates, married his daughter into the royal household, and in 1180 even had his infant grandson enthroned as the Heavenly Sovereign. Increasingly frustrated with Kiyomori's power play, disgruntled courtiers asked the revitalized Minamoto to reenter the fray, and in the bloody Genpei War of 1180 to 1185, Minamoto Yoritomo and his followers dealt a stunning blow to their old adversaries, wiping out the Taira virtually to the last man.

Sensitive as never before to the need for dependable military support, in 1192 the court named Minamoto Yoritomo as the *seii tai shōgun* ("Great Barbarian-Subduing Field Marshal"). The position was an ancient one, dating back to the last half of the eighth century. At that time peoples known as Emishi, a word written with ideographs signifying "Eastern Barbarians," continued to resist the imposition of Yamato rule in northern Honshū, and the Kyoto government from time to time commissioned certain nobles as *seii tai shōgun*, instructing them to muster forces and subdue the recalcitrant inhabitants of the frontier. Although the title fell into disuse after Kyoto officially declared the remote northern regions secure early in the ninth century, the court resurrected the position after the Minamoto victory in the Genpei War. Rather than require Yoritomo to subdue barbarians, however, the monarchy henceforth entrusted the shogun and his descendants with heading a *bakufu* ("tent government") that wielded military and police powers designed to complement civil authority everywhere in Japan.

Among other responsibilities, the Heavenly Sovereign delegated to the *bakufu*, commonly rendered as "shogunate," standing authority to take up arms against anyone posing a threat to the monarchy. In addition, the Kamakura shogunate, so called because the Minamoto settled into that seaside town in eastern Japan, was supposed to maintain discipline over the samurai estate, adjudicate disputes involving conflicting claims to landownership, and ensure that public tax receipts and *shōen* rents flowed from the rural countryside into the state bursary and aristocratic coffers in Kyoto. So that the shogun could discharge his responsibilities competently, the court authorized its new police deputy to appoint higher-ranking warrior followers as military governors, assigned to serve alongside traditional civilian counterparts in the provinces, and to post vassal samurai as land stewards throughout the country.

Although the Kamakura shogunate worked in tandem with the civil bureaucracy in Kyoto to provide domestic stability for more than a century, eventually certain powerful military governors, supported by growing numbers of disaffected land stewards, came to believe that Kamakura did not sufficiently recompense them for their services. The warriors' sense of injustice suffered further aggravation when the shogunate dispensed few rewards to the samurai it stationed along Kyūshū's beaches to fend off invasion attempts by Kublai Khan in 1274 and again in 1281, when the Mongol leader set sail more than four thousand ships bearing nearly 140,000 men to lend meaning to his demand that the Japanese acknowledge his suzerainty. On each of those two occasions the Mongols gained a toehold on Japanese soil, but then *kamikaze*, a "divine wind" supposedly stirred up by Japan's protective deities, ravaged the invasion fleets and forced the Mongols back to their continental bases. However fortunate the appearance of those typhoon gales, the enormous cost of erecting fortifications and maintaining a defense alert for twenty years thereafter brought great economic distress to the warrior estate. With frustrations mounting, in 1333 Ashikaga Takauji, a military governor and distant clansman of the Minamoto's, raised the banner of rebellion and destroyed the Kamakura shogunate.

In 1338 the Heavenly Sovereign appointed Takauji shogun, and the Ashikaga family established its tent government in Kyoto. Despite their pedigree and imperial sanction, however, the Ashikaga shoguns never were able to muster sufficient wealth and prestige to keep other major warrior families at heel. Increasingly, military governors began to amass titles to lands and to act autonomously, obeying or disregarding Kyoto's injunctions as they pleased. In the mid–fifteenth century a factional dispute over shogunal succession upset the delicate balance between the Ashikaga family and its military governors and provided the excuse for ambitious rivals to fall upon one another in a struggle for military supremacy. Fought between 1467 and 1477, the frightfully destructive Ōnin War brought about the downfall of nearly all provincial military governors, left Kyoto smoldering in ashes, and ushered in a century of disunity known as the Sengoku age, an era when Japan was "A Country at War."

**TABLE 1.1** *Japan's Three Shogunates*

| SHOGUNAL FAMILY | HEADQUARTERS | DATES OF SHOGUNAL RULE |
| --- | --- | --- |
| Minamoto | Kamakura | 1192–1333 |
| Ashikaga | Kyoto (Muromachi district) | 1338–1573 |
| Tokugawa | Edo | 1603–1868 |

Although the royal court and shogunate survived the Ōnin War, they were left as empty shells, a government in name only with scant ability to influence events beyond the confines of the devastated capital. Outside Kyoto, local military lords referred to as daimyo gathered samurai around themselves and staked out control over tightly organized domains that they ruled with savage independence. Aggressively, daimyo built rustic forts and then imposing castles, taxed the peasants on their holdings, and fended off other marauding lords even while attacking neighbors in the hope of expanding their territorial holdings. The period of political decentralization reached a peak in the middle of the sixteenth century, when hundreds of daimyo domains blanketed most of the Japanese archipelago.

Despite the extreme fragmentation and chaos of the Sengoku age, the ideal of a centralized sovereign polity remained alive, and in the latter half of the sixteenth century three powerful warlords knitted Japan back together. The first to dream of national reunification was Oda Nobunaga. The son of a minor daimyo based in Owari Province, Nobunaga burst into prominence in 1560, when his armies overwhelmed those of a vastly stronger neighbor. Eight years later he led his samurai into Kyoto, the sovereign center, and installed Ashikaga Yoshiaki as a puppet shogun. When the usually weak-willed Yoshiaki had the temerity to oppose him, Nobunaga in 1573 burned much of Kyoto and chased the unfortunate Yoshiaki into exile, thus bringing the Ashikaga shogunate to a formal end.

A brilliant tactician and tireless campaigner, Nobunaga kept his armies constantly in the field, ever expanding his circle of authority. He also was among the first to grasp the potential of firearms, introduced by Portuguese traders when they landed on the small island of Tanegashima to the south of Kyūshū in 1543. Within a few years Japanese merchants were importing the new arms, artisans were busy turning out replicas of the "Tanegashima musket," and in the early summer of 1575 Nobunaga's newly organized corps of three thousand musketeers brought him a spectacular victory in the Battle of Nagashino, which extended his control to the north and east of Kyoto. By 1582 Nobunaga had brought some twenty-two provinces in central and eastern Japan under his domination when suddenly a treacherous vassal ambushed him at the Honnōji temple in Kyoto. Wounded, Nobunaga withdrew to the depths of the main hall of worship, and as flames consumed the building, he disemboweled himself rather than suffer the indignity of death at the hands of another.

Toyotomi Hideyoshi quickly avenged his master's death and then turned to the task of hammering the remaining daimyo into submission. Born of humble parentage, the son of a foot soldier in the service of the Oda family, according to the most likely account, Hideyoshi rose through the ranks to become one of Nobunaga's leading generals. When Hideyoshi assumed the mantle of unifier in 1582, he had more than 250,000 samurai, musketeers, pikemen, archers, and foot soldiers under his command, one of the largest armies known to the contemporary world. Boldly he led those battalions into Shikoku and Kyūshū, wiping out some daimyo and winning over others by intimidation and persuasion. After securing hegemony over those two islands in 1587, Hideyoshi wheeled to the north, taking the Kantō provinces in the fall of 1590 and accepting the surrender of daimyo in the far north of Honshū soon thereafter. The military reunification of Japan was

*Samurai using Western firearms in the Battle of Nagashino, 1575*

then complete: Hideyoshi either held all territory directly or entrusted it to surviving daimyo, who submitted oaths of loyalty to Japan's new hegemon in return for documents of enfeoffment.

Hideyoshi's death in 1598 opened the doors of opportunity for Tokugawa Ieyasu. A resolute campaigner himself, Ieyasu traced his origins back to a warrior family that by the early sixteenth century had fought its way to control over portions of Mikawa Province in central Japan. After Ieyasu inherited the family headship, he continued to wage war against neighboring daimyo, teamed occasionally with Nobunaga, and by the end of 1582 had emerged as one of the dozen or so largest daimyo of the land, with a fast grip over Mikawa and four adjoining provinces. From the mid-1580s Ieyasu allied himself with Hideyoshi, and in 1590 some thirty thousand Tokugawa troops joined the push into the Kantō region. Hideyoshi rewarded his supporter handsomely by more than doubling the size of Ieyasu's holdings, assigning to the House of Tokugawa most of the expansive Kantō Plain, Japan's greatest rice-producing region and the historic homeland of the samurai class. Ieyasu quickly transferred his samurai to their new domain, and as summer turned to fall in 1590, he began construction of an enormous new castle headquarters at the tiny village of Edo along the upper reaches of the bay with the same name.

Just before he died in 1598, Hideyoshi made five major daimyo, Ieyasu among them, swear to manage affairs on behalf of the House of Toyotomi until his infant son Hideyori, resident at Osaka Castle, came of age. The pull of ambition and the lure of national hegemony, however, quickly seduced Ieyasu and the other great overlords, who fell into bickering and plotting that pitted Tokugawa and his followers against an alliance of daimyo from western Japan. The two sides collided in the climactic Battle of Sekigahara, fought in the middle of the Ninth Month 1600. Ieyasu's army of seventy thousand men promptly routed its foes, and on the afternoon of his triumph Ieyasu donned a special ceremonial helmet to view the severed heads of thousands of enemy troops slain in battle. The next month the victorious warlord began to accept pledges of loyalty from daimyo across Japan. Less than three years later, in the Second Month of 1603, the Heavenly Sovereign recognized Ieyasu's feat by elevating him to the office of shogun.

## Securing the Realm

Following Ieyasu's appointment as shogun, the House of Tokugawa created a new and vastly more powerful kind of tent government than had existed in the past. Like their predecessors, the Tokugawa shoguns shouldered an obligation to supervise the warrior estate and preserve domestic tranquillity. But Ieyasu and his immediate successors, Hidetada and Iemitsu, also asserted the supreme right to proclaim laws, levy taxes, and adjudicate disputes. When the process of state building reached completion in the second half of the seventeenth century, the Tokugawa shogunate embraced an imposing assemblage of new duties that made it the center of national governance.

The House of Tokugawa built its superstructure of power on twin cornerstones: unassailable armed strength and an unquestioned monopoly over the office of shogun. To ensure the office would remain within his own family, Ieyasu officially retired in 1605 and arranged to have the Heavenly Sovereign confirm his son Hidetada as the new shogun. A decade later, in 1614 and 1615, Ieyasu and Hidetada led their armies in a final campaign against Hideyori and nearly 100,000 Toyotomi loyalists who had taken refuge with him at Osaka Castle. In some of the bloodiest fighting in an era that already had seen more than its share of unrestrained violence, the Tokugawa regiments reduced the great fortress and its surrounding merchant community to ashes, exterminated the defenders of the Toyotomi name, and drove the hapless, desperate Hideyori to suicide. The following year Ieyasu went peacefully to his grave, content that he had laid the foundation for an enduring regime.

The acquisition of wealth also helped the Tokugawa line of shoguns tighten their grasp on power. Victory on the battlefield permitted the House of Tokugawa to confiscate the holdings of many opponents, and by the time of the third shogun, Iemitsu, the family claimed for its own about one-quarter of all agricultural land in Japan. The annual rice production on shogun-

**TABLE 1.2**  *Tokugawa Shoguns*

| | | | |
|---|---|---|---|
| Ieyasu, ruled | 1603–1605 | Ieshige | 1745–1760 |
| Hidetada | 1605–1623 | Ieharu | 1760–1786 |
| Iemitsu | 1623–1651 | Ienari | 1787–1837 |
| Ietsuna | 1651–1680 | Ieyoshi | 1837–1853 |
| Tsunayoshi | 1680–1709 | Iesada | 1853–1858 |
| Ienobu | 1709–1712 | Iemochi [a] | 1859–1866 |
| Ietsugu | 1713–1716 | Yoshinobu (Keiki) [b] | 1867–1868 |
| Yoshimune | 1716–1745 | | |

[a] Appointed shogun on Ansei 5.12.1 (January 4, 1859).

[b] Appointed shogun on Keiō 2.12.5 (January 10, 1867); removed from office on Keiō 3.12.9 (January 3, 1868).

al lands amounted to approximately 6.8 million koku (with koku being a dry measure equal to approximately five bushels, theoretically enough unhulled rice to feed one adult male for one year). The shogunate used the taxes levied on that output to finance its operations and to pay annual stipends to its approximately twenty-two thousand direct retainers, the five thousand bannermen and somewhat more than seventeen thousand housemen who supervised thousands upon thousands of lower-ranking warriors. In addition, shogunal officials directly administered such important ports and emerging cities as Nagasaki and Osaka, and they also controlled the mines that produced the gold, silver, and copper used for the nation's coinage.

As part of the effort to ensure the supremacy of their house, the Tokugawa shoguns maneuvered to extend their authority horizontally over other elites—the monarch and courtiers, the Buddhist clergy, and daimyo overlords—whose cooperation was crucial to the survival of the new regime. Although Kyoto's nobility had suffered grievously during the long decades when Japan was A Country at War, the semidivine Heavenly Sovereign remained the primal source of political legitimation. Consequently, the Tokugawa shoguns understood that they could enhance their own reputations by refurbishing the prestige of the throne and its attendant aristocracy. To that end the shogunate rebuilt long-neglected palaces and mansions and set aside sustenance lands for the royal family and courtiers.

But if Ieyasu enriched, he also enchained. In the Seventh Month of 1615, fresh from crushing the last Toyotomi holdouts at Osaka Castle, Ieyasu and Hidetada issued the Regulations concerning the Royal Court and Nobility. The seventeen clauses in that document represented an audacious attempt by the military hegemons to regulate the behavior of the Heavenly Sovereign and his court and to isolate them from other elites. Pointedly, several clauses instructed the courtiers on the finer points of proper decorum, prescribing a lifestyle devoted to ceremonial pursuits so that the aristocrats would behave like the dignified custodians of traditional culture that they were supposed to be. Article 1 even went so far as to tell the monarch how to spend his time: "The Heavenly Sovereign is to be engaged in the arts, the first of which is scholarship."[5] Lest there be any misunderstanding about the court's subordination to the military overlords, the Tokugawa shoguns already had stationed a military deputy in Kyoto and garrisoned samurai in the massive, newly constructed Nijō Castle located in the middle of the city.

The same blend of patronage and coercion characterized the Tokugawa shogunate's relationship with the Buddhist establishment. Buddhism had made its way to the Japanese archipelago in the sixth century, after having spread from India across the Asian continent to China and Korea. Japanese embassies to Tang China in the seventh century could see the physical manifestations of Buddhism's universal appeal: networks of awesome temples and monasteries, volume upon volume of scripture that pointed the way to salvation, and a corpus of magnificent art and iconography. In addition, Japan's Taika reformers realized that the Chinese emperors had harnessed the influence of the Buddhist priesthood behind the government by lavishing patronage on individual sects in exchange for the recitation of prayers and the performance of rituals intended to enhance imperial rule and grandeur. Not surprisingly, when the Japanese monarchy settled into Nara at the beginning of the eighth century, it encouraged several major denominations to build extravagant temples there, making the new capital a major center of world Buddhism.

Although royal patronage of Buddhism declined after the monarchy moved to Kyoto, two sects founded at the beginning of the ninth century became leading centers of religious training and scholarship. One, the Tendai sect, built its home monastery of Enryakuji on Mount Hiei, just to the northeast of Kyoto, while the other, the Shingon sect, located its central temple on Mount Kōya in Kii Province. Later the Kamakura shogunate helped sponsor the introduction of Zen sects into Japan, and in the thirteenth century spellbinding evangelists associated with such popular denominations as the Pure Land and the True Pure Land sects fanned out from Kyoto, searching for converts in villages and country marketplaces across Japan. Many warriors became Zen adherents, while both warriors and common people flocked to the popular sects after hearing the simple message that heartfelt trust in the mercy of Amida, the Buddha of the Western Paradise, would bring salvation to the faithful.

In time certain Buddhist sects became secular powerhouses. Even before Minamoto Yoritomo founded the Kamakura shogunate, Tendai's clerics had taken advantage of their influence at court to gain proprietary control over vast numbers of *shōen* estates and had organized a militia of "rowdy monks" to protect their economic interests. In the late fifteenth and early sixteenth centuries, adherents of the Honganji branch of the True Pure Land denomination seized control of several provinces in central Japan and along the coast of the Sea of Japan. From their great temple-fortress of Ishiyama Honganji, near the center of modern-day Osaka, the sect's abbots ruled over a far-flung religious confederation that was as wealthy and powerful as the domains of many leading daimyo.

Oda Nobunaga saw the great Buddhist sects as a formidable obstacle to his efforts to reunify Japan. When the clerics at Enryakuji opposed his intrusion into Kyoto, the warlord in 1571 unleashed his samurai against Tendai's monastery on Mount Hiei, putting the torch to some three thousand buildings and slaughtering thousands of monks. He then turned his troops against Honganji and, after nearly a decade of often savage fighting that claimed tens of thousands of lives, accepted the surrender of the sect's fortress headquarters in 1580. With the secular power of the major sects broken, Tokugawa Ieyasu and his successors moved swiftly to consolidate political and economic control over the Buddhist establishment. In a series of regulatory directives issued between 1610 and 1614, the new regime established its right to intervene in the administration of the major sects and limited priests strictly to the study of religious doctrine and the maintenance of monastic discipline, even while it endowed important temples with landholdings sufficient to sustain themselves as centers of religious devotion and learning.

The House of Tokugawa also strove to impose its will over the two hundred or so daimyo who survived the wars of reunification. Learning from the practices of Hideyoshi, Tokugawa Hidetada in 1617 established the principle that upon succession each and every daimyo would swear a pledge of fealty to the House of Tokugawa, in return for which the national hegemon bestowed upon the regional lord a patent of investiture that defined his holdings and entitled him to rule. Thus, while the old provinces continued to exist on paper, the effective unit of local administration became the daimyo domain. At the same time, the shogunate asserted the right to transfer daimyo to different territories, reduce or even confiscate the domains of troublesome or incompetent lords, and reward worthy followers with new or expanded holdings. The first five Tokugawa shoguns were especially intrusive, depriving 213 daimyo of all or a portion of their holdings for some offense real or imagined, promoting 172 trusted followers to daimyo status, and ordering 281 transfers from one domain to another. As a consequence, some 540 different warrior families held the rank of daimyo during the early modern period, with roughly 250 to 280 coexisting at any given moment.

The shogunate sorted the various daimyo into categories that corresponded to the lord's relationship to the Tokugawa family. Closest to the head of the House of Tokugawa were twenty-three daimyo descended by birth or adoption from Ieyasu and known as *shinpan* ("cadet families"). Three of those, the lords of Kii, Mito, and Owari domains, constituted the *gosanke* ("Three Successor Houses"), whose offspring could be named as shogun in the event that some hegemon died without a suitable direct heir. Assured of their absolute loyalty, the shogunate assigned the cadet houses to domains in the Kantō region or at other strategically important locations. The average cadet daimyo ruled over a substantial domain whose villages col-

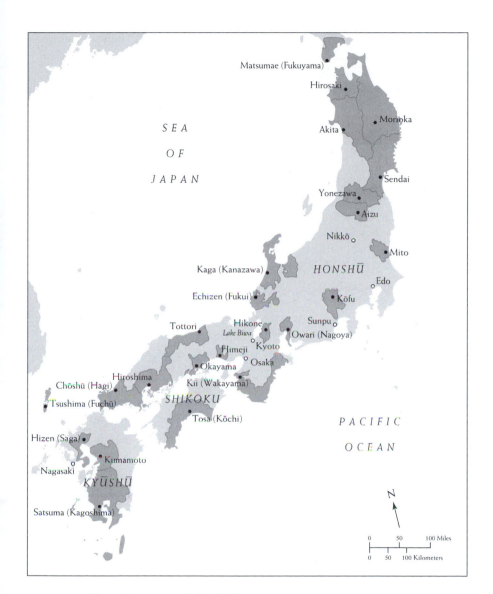

**MAP 1.2** *Major Domains and Castle Towns, circa 1660*

lectively produced approximately 50,000 koku of rice a year, while the Three Successor Houses administered larger territories assessed at 619,000 (Owari), 555,000 (Kii), and 350,000 (Mito) koku respectively.

Next in status came 150 or so *fudai* daimyo, "house" or "allied" lords, who attained that rank under Tokugawa patronage and who, for the most part, had taken the field with Ieyasu at Sekigahara. The majority of *fudai* domains were assessed between 10,000 and 100,000 koku, and the shogunate situated its trustworthy allied daimyo at critical places across the country where they could parry any potential threat against shogunal interests. In contrast, the 100-odd *tozama* ("outside") daimyo, many with domains in excess of 100,000 koku, had achieved their status independently or under the aegis of Oda Nobunaga or Toyotomi Hideyoshi, and most did not swear allegiance to the House of Tokugawa until after 1600. Assuming them at best to be neutral and at worst hostile to Tokugawa authority, the shogunate generally left them in their traditional homes on the periphery of the Japanese islands.

Whatever their status, all daimyo were subject to various expressions of Tokugawa authority. Although it did not tax the daimyo directly, the shogunate expected military service from the various lords upon demand, and whenever the national overlord saw fit, he obligated the daimyo to contribute manpower, material, and money to construct and maintain Tokugawa castles and to carry out public works projects, such as building and repairing roads. In pace with the regulatory measures imposed on the nobility and priesthood, in 1615 the shogunate issued the Regulations concerning Warrior Households. "Law," the code stated, "is the foundation of the social order," and it made daimyo marriages, inheritance, and castle construction or renovations subject to shogunal approval.[6] Other decrees restricted daimyo to a single castle and specified the exact number of samurai and other troops each lord could maintain.

Even while the shogunate moved aggressively to assert paramount authority over the daimyo, the regional lords preserved as best they could the prerogative of managing the internal affairs of their domains. Indeed, most daimyo preferred to conceive of their holdings as autonomous principalities; there they proudly commanded a body of loyal samurai, policed their own borders, oversaw religious institutions, and were free to levy taxes of their own choosing upon peasants and merchants, issue legal codes whenever they saw fit, enforce laws with whatever rigor they deemed necessary, encourage commerce enterprises that benefitted the local economy, and interfere at will in the personal lives of the inhabitants of the domain in order to preserve peace. Within that context, each daimyo had the unilateral right to forbid people to travel outside the domain, move away from their native villages, or even hold festivals or religious celebrations that he considered unacceptable, for whatever reason.

The daimyo were figures of formidable stature, but as one scholar has noted, their "discretionary power was discretionary only up to a point."[7] By demanding pledges of fealty, confiscating and reassigning domains, promulgating codes of expected conduct, and placing limits on the size of armies and the use of force, the first three Tokugawa shoguns made it abundantly clear that the daimyo existed only at their sufferance. Moreover, however much latitude the daimyo enjoyed in governing their domains, the shogunate increasingly expected them to rule in a manner consistent with its practices. The regional lords, as a second version of the Regulations concerning Warrior Households put it in 1635, were to "follow the laws of Edo in all things." Consequently, while daimyo autonomy was to remain a vital and legitimate part of the political system in the early modern era, by the middle of the seventeenth century the regional lords "were no longer absolute masters of their own house."

The daimyo had good reason to take their cues from the House of Tokugawa. By paying allegiance to the shogun and following his guidance, the regional lords received confirmation of their existence and realm-wide recognition of their territorial borders. Tokugawa rule also provided the daimyo with security—after generations of warfare, no lord any longer had to fear aggression from a neighbor—and the shogunate usually provided food, loans, and other aid to domains struck by typhoons, earthquakes, and other natural disasters. The shogunate too obviously profited from the bifurcated nature of governance during the early modern era. First and foremost, the regime in Edo could not have ruled successfully without the cooperation of the daimyo, whose domains covered nearly three-quarters of the country. Similarly, pledges of armed support permitted the shogunate to maintain peace, just as financial contributions enabled it to build castles and carry out public works projects. As ultimately crafted, mutual advantage and interlocking interests undergirded the complex, multidimensional shogun-daimyo relationship.

Reciprocity also formed part of the shogunate's interactions with the court and clergy. To be certain, obvious risks discouraged any shogunal leader from acting too arbitrarily or perhaps even letting his thoughts drift toward pushing Japan's other elites off history's stage. Just as the daimyo almost certainly would have united against any move to abolish them as a class, potential popular opposition cautioned against further suppression of Buddhist sects that had won millions of adherents at all levels of society. Beyond any fear of resistance, however, Ieyasu and his successors foresaw the positive benefits that would flow from choosing to live in symbiotic harmony with Japan's other national elites. Only the Heavenly Sovereign, after all, could appoint someone shogun, with all the privileges of authority that implied, and by providing proper incentives, the shogunate could hope to shepherd the Buddhist clergy back to their traditional role of mustering spiritual support for the nation and its leaders.

## Extending Authority Vertically

The complementary, interdependent nature of rule by shoguns and daimyo became more clearly defined during the early decades of the seventeenth century as both components of government initiated policies that penetrated downward into society, securing control over the people and resources of their respective realms. One of the key concerns of the overlords was to fashion a dependable form of taxation that would permit them to claim a share of the annual rice crop. Consequently, the shogunate and daimyo carefully honed extractive mechanisms designed to maximize tax revenues: Officials conducted censuses, dispatched cadastral survey teams to measure the land and assess its output, and imposed systems of taxation that put a third or more of the crop into the hands of the government.

The shogunate and regional daimyo also issued a steady stream of ethical admonitions, practical advice, and legal proclamations intended to serve as guides to everyday conduct for the people on their holdings. The shogunate's Instructions of the Keian Era constituted one of the more famous compilations of such ordinances. Directed specifically toward farmers and issued in 1649 by Iemitsu, the code's thirty-two clauses admonished people that "shogunal law must be observed in everything," lauded such virtues as frugality and self-reliance, exhorted farm families to work industriously, and made it clear that everyone had to submit the annual tax assessment promptly and in full. "As long as he pays his taxes," the document intoned, "no one's life is as carefree as that of a peasant."[8]

In addition to resting their authority on a mix of military might and legal codes, the leaders of the new regime developed sophisticated bureaucracies to help them maintain peace, guide agricultural development and other forms of economic activity, and generally rule more effectively. For advice and assistance in policy making, the shoguns relied on two major advisory boards. First appointed in 1623, the senior councillors were middle- and high-ranking *fudai* daimyo who met in Edo Castle during their tenure in office. As the chief advisers to the shogun the senior councillors exercised authority over matters national in scope, including defense against foreign attack and supervision of the court in Kyoto, as well as over the people, land, villages, and towns and cities within the shogunate's own domain. The junior councillors, also stationed in Edo and named from among *fudai* daimyo of lesser status beginning in 1633, handled the more domestic aspects of shogunal life and at the same time took responsibility for the peacetime training and assignment of military guard units, as seen in Figure 1.1.

Several other officials also reported directly to the shogun. Selected from middle-ranking allied lords beginning in the 1630s, the commissioners of temples and shrines regulated religious establishments and maintained law and order on certain shogunal lands lying outside the Kantō region. First appointed in 1619, the keeper of Osaka Castle was also a middle-size *fudai* daimyo, typically with a domain assessed in the range of fifty to sixty thousand koku. During his tour of duty, each keeper of Osaka Castle resided in the imposing fortress that the Tokugawa shoguns rebuilt in Osaka following their victory over Toyotomi forces in 1614 and 1615 and functioned as the shogun's senior military officer in central Japan, standing watch against potentially troublesome daimyo. The grand councillor, by way of contrast, was a ceremonial figurehead, and the post often went unfilled.

**FIGURE 1.1** *Selected Offices in the Tokugawa Shogunate*

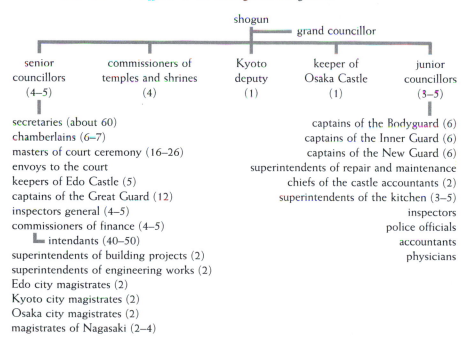

shogun

grand councillor

| senior councillors (4–5) | commissioners of temples and shrines (4) | Kyoto deputy (1) | keeper of Osaka Castle (1) | junior councillors (3–5) |

secretaries (about 60)
chamberlains (6–7)
masters of court ceremony (16–26)
envoys to the court
keepers of Edo Castle (5)
captains of the Great Guard (12)
inspectors general (4–5)
commissioners of finance (4–5)
  └ intendants (40–50)
superintendents of building projects (2)
superintendents of engineering works (2)
Edo city magistrates (2)
Kyoto city magistrates (2)
Osaka city magistrates (2)
magistrates of Nagasaki (2–4)

captains of the Bodyguard (6)
captains of the Inner Guard (6)
captains of the New Guard (6)
superintendents of repair and maintenance
chiefs of the castle accountants (2)
superintendents of the kitchen (3–5)
inspectors
police officials
accountants
physicians

Among subordinate officials within the shogunate, the various city magistrates and the commissioners of finance were especially notable. The shogun generally assigned two *fudai* daimyo or bannermen of some consequence as magistrates to oversee the activities of the merchants and artisans in each of the larger cities that the shogunate administered directly. The commissioners of finance (who, like the city magistrates, reported to the senior councillors) supervised tax collection and attended to civil administration within the villages on the shogun's direct landholdings. Assisting them were dozens of intendants, appointed from among the shogun's bannermen, who generally resided in Edo while traveling periodically to the villages under their jurisdiction to ascertain that all was in order.

Although local conditions spawned considerable regional variation, daimyo generally created bureaucratic structures similar in nature to those of the shogun, with high-ranking and trusted retainers advising the lord and making policy, while lesser vassals served as the functionaries who looked after tax collection, policing, and the day-to-day management of affairs. The pervasiveness of the new bureaucratic tradition held great significance. Remarkably, within one or two generations at the beginning of the seventeenth century, the samurai transformed themselves from fierce warriors into learned and competent civilian administrators. More than that, however, the shogun and daimyo, who had risen to power through brute strength and conquest, came to base their mandate to rule on the attributes of law, regulation, precedent, rationality, and eventually even public interest.

## Legitimations of Power

The Tokugawa shoguns went to great lengths to articulate an ideology of legitimacy that validated their new form of governance. According to the *Tokugawa jikki* ("True Records of the Tokugawa"), a documentary compilation that paid homage to the accomplishments of the first ten shoguns, "Ieyasu had conquered the nation on horseback, but being an enlightened and wise man, realized early that the land could not be ruled from a horse. He wisely decided that in order to govern the land and follow the path proper to man, he must pursue the path of learning."[9] Ieyasu and his successors did far more than tread a scholarly path; they chased after social status, manipulated religious images, and even turned to an imported set of ethical and philosophical teachings in order to persuade the daimyo, samurai, and ordinary people to accept—without question or reservation—the control mechanisms and instruments of governance that they were imposing on the country.

The House of Tokugawa began to spin a web of legitimacy by constantly reinforcing its close relationship with the Heavenly Sovereign, and the first three shoguns personally journeyed to Fushimi Castle to receive investiture as the *seii tai shōgun*. In addition, Hidetada visited Kyoto in 1617, in the company of "innumerable daimyo," and again in the autumn of 1619 to pay respects to the reigning monarch, Go-Mizunoo. Less than a year later the shogun wed his daughter Kazuko to the monarch, and when Go-Mizunoo abdicated in 1629, an offspring of that particular union of court and camp ascended the throne as the Heavenly Sovereign Meishō, the first woman to reign since the eighth century.

In the Sixth Month of 1634 Iemitsu swept into Kyoto at the head of a grand processional of nearly forty thousand persons. Many daimyo brought their own large retinues of family and samurai retainers into the city for the occasion, pushing the total number of visitors to Kyoto over the 300,000 mark. With great pomp and circumstance, the shogun basked in the image of legitimacy that Meishō's ascension had wrought, made lavish displays of wealth, and seized every opportunity to remind the court and assembled daimyo that the nation's destiny did not stand separate from the fate of the Tokugawa family itself. Although Iemitsu's memorable journey was the last in the tradition of personal visits to Kyoto, every future shogun reaffirmed the blueness of Tokugawa blood by procuring wives and consorts from the royal family and from high-ranking Kyoto nobility.

Proximity to the royal line, however, offered no ironclad guarantee that the Tokugawa line could hold the office of shogun in perpetuity. After all, the Minamoto and Ashikaga shogunates had fallen after losing their martial dominance, and should the Tokugawa somehow falter, the monarch might well sprinkle his favors on some other warrior family capable of providing stable rule. Conscious of their vulnerability, Ieyasu and his successors pulled a religious shroud around their shoulders. Ieyasu developed a keen interest in Buddhism after taking up residence in his retirement castle at Sunpu (modern-day Shizuoka) in 1607, according to Tenkai, a Tendai monk and the ex-shogun's spiritual adviser. One afternoon, while on an outing in nearby mountains, Ieyasu strayed from his companions and, as nightfall approached, overheard a hermit muttering, "This day has passed. My life has lessened. We are like fishes in shallow water. What pleasure could this be?"[10] Ieyasu suddenly realized the vanity of life, in Tenkai's account of events, and in 1614 the holy man supervised the warlord's conversion to the Tendai faith.

Shortly before his death in the Fourth Month of 1616, Ieyasu confided to his priestly mentor: "After I die, I first shall be buried on a mountain near Sunpu, and then, after one full year has passed, be moved to Nikkō, where my spirit will abide, forever able to protect my country and my descendants."[11] Located in a mountain range some seventy-five miles north of the shogunate's Edo headquarters, Nikkō reputedly was the abode of numerous benevolent deities, and Tenkai had established a small temple there some time earlier. In accordance with Ieyasu's wishes, in the spring of 1617 his body was disinterred from its original grave and transported in an elaborate processional across the Kantō provinces to the mausoleum prepared for it at Nikkō. On the first anniversary of the great warlord's death, Tenkai presided over a solemn consecration ceremony, and a proclamation issued by the Heavenly Sovereign in Kyoto deified Ieyasu, bestowing upon him the posthumous title Tōshō Dai Gongen ("Illuminator of the East, August Avatar of Buddha").

Japan's Buddhist sects asserted that Buddha could assume different forms: the historic Gautama Siddhārtha (Sākyamuni), who supposedly lived from 563 to 483 B.C.E. and founded the religion in his native India; the universal, eternal, all-embracing Buddha known in Japanese as Dainichi; and *nyorai*, transcendent figures, such as Amida, the Buddha of the Western Paradise, and Yakushi, the Buddha of Healing. Ranking just below the Buddhas were bodhisattvas, beings of great spiritual virtue and boundless compassion who had achieved enlightenment but refrained from entering paradise so they could help others find salvation. As Tōshō Dai Gongen the canonized Ieyasu became an avatar of Yakushi, able to illuminate the pathway to enlightenment for the people of the Japanese islands.

Ieyasu's transformation to Tōshō Dai Gongen also gave his consecrated spirit a place within the pantheon of native Shinto deities. Often referred to as Japan's indigenous religion, Shinto beliefs began to coalesce around an organized set of practices in the sixth and seventh centuries, just as Buddhism was being introduced into the country. The core values that made up the "Way of the Gods" were much older, however, and centered on a deep reverence for *kami*, spirits or deities that animistically inhabit nature. Written with the same ideograph as the *shin* in Shinto (whose second ideograph means "way"), the term *kami*, in the formulation of one prominent eighteenth-century scholar, denoted "the deities of heaven and earth that appear in the ancient texts [such as the *Kojiki*] and also the spirits worshipped at shrines; furthermore, among all kinds of beings—including not only human beings but also birds, beasts, trees, grass, seas, mountains, and so forth— any being whatsoever which possesses some eminent quality out of the ordinary, and is awe-inspiring, is called *kami*."[12]

*Kami* were omnipresent across the Japanese islands, and all had the capacity to intrude upon events in the material world. The scope and potency of their interventions varied considerably, however. A great goddess like Amaterasu possessed powers that extended nationwide and could affect the lives of everyone, while lesser *kami*, venerated at local shrines, made their presences felt only within a single village or urban neighborhood. Moreover, since each *kami* had a potentially malevolent side as well as a serene, altruistic one, humans had to devise rituals and ceremonies that would induce them to use their powers in a manner beneficial to the human community. For that reason, the Heavenly Sovereigns left the day-to-day management of political affairs in the hands of others so that they might concentrate on conducting elaborate rituals to Amaterasu and other important deities. Similarly, farm families periodically hosted festivals at village shrines, at which they offered special foods, set out casks of sake, and arranged performances of music and dance to persuade the local deity to provide an abundant harvest, protect the community against disease, keep natural disaster at bay, or otherwise help people overcome the travails of daily life.

If Shinto creed rested on the assumption that people could be happy and perhaps even prosper in this life if they worshiped *kami* properly, Buddhist doctrine promised a world of inevitable sadness and profound sorrow. Common to the teachings of all Buddhist sects was the uncompromising proposition that humankind's painful and often perplexing existence stemmed from people's emotional attachments, to others and to material possessions. But since everything—emotions, the physical world, existence itself—is transitory, ephemeral, and in constant flux, it is extremely difficult to acquire what one desires, and virtually impossible to keep what one does manage to possess: Beauty fades; fortunes dissipate; death awaits. Moreover, the doctrine of karma ("idea and effect") held that acts in previous existences enmeshed people tightly in a web of desire and suffering, thus frequently condemning them to repeated cycles of rebirth and sorrow. Against the bleakness of that message, Buddhism held out the ultimate hope: By extinguishing desire and individual consciousness, by accepting impermanence and realizing the ultimate oneness of the universe, a person could break the chain of desire, suffering, and karma and enjoy the eternal beatitude of nirvana. For adherents of the Tendai sect, intense study of the Lotus Sutra, purportedly Gautama's last sermon, would light the pathway to enlightenment, while the Zen sects stressed seated meditation as a way to stifle one's ego and overcome acquisitiveness, and the popular faiths urged followers to call on the mercy of the compassionate Amida Buddha.

Whatever their metaphysical and cosmological differences, Shinto and Buddhism coexisted peacefully throughout Japan's premodern history. One reason for that perhaps had to do with the complementary nature of the two systems. Since Shinto rituals, by and large, focused on openhearted supplications to *kami* for assistance in this world, whereas Buddhism dealt with the fate of one's soul after death, a person could participate in both faiths. Moreover, most Japanese seemed to possess a relaxed tolerance for alternative versions of religious truth, as revealed in attempts to harmonize the two traditions. In the centuries after Buddhism had been introduced into Japan, religious authorities and lay followers alike came to view *kami* as incarnations of specific Buddhas and bodhisattvas. In that regard, Amaterasu, the Sun Goddess and central figure in the Shinto pantheon, became equated with the cosmic Buddha, Dainichi, whose Sanskrit name, Mahāvairocana, meant "Great Sun," and well before the Tokugawa period, most major religious institutions contained both Buddhist and Shinto chapels.

The enshrinement of Ieyasu at Nikkō transformed him from a mortal warlord into a powerful deity whose brilliance shone from the east and cast its protective aura over all the Japanese islands. As an avatar of Yakushi he was a leading Buddha who would work for the salvation of fellow Japanese, and his final resting place recalled that connection, for Nikkō was the name of an important bodhisattva who often appeared beside Yakushi. Drawing upon Shinto beliefs, Ieyasu also was venerated as a *shinkun*, a "divine ruler." Written with the ideographs for *kami* (and, again, pronounced *shin* as in Shinto) and "master" or "ruler," the term implied that Japan's gods vouchsafed the temporal authority of the House of Tokugawa and that Ieyasu's Shinto spirit would protect his descendants, the Heavenly Sovereign and court, the samurai estate, and the entire nation. In a culture that attached great significance to the meaning of names, Tōshō Dai Gongen brought together various prized connections: Ieyasu was a "divine ruler," and he was Buddha Incarnate, the great Illuminator of the East, whose title, for good measure, contained a character, *shō*, that also appeared as the *terasu* in Amaterasu.

The Tokugawa political elite also turned to Confucianism to legitimate further their claims to authority. A Chinese contemporary of the Indian Gautama Siddhārtha, Confucius constructed an ethical system that in his calculations would enable humans to create stable, orderly, and gratifying patterns of living in this world. Subsequent reinterpretation and modification of the original construct brought to the fore two fundamental propositions that later drew the attention of Japanese scholars: Society was divided into hierarchical strata of rulers, peasants, artisans, and merchants, and everyone, regardless of status, was enmeshed in one or more of the basic Five Relationships—ruler and subject; husband and wife; father and son; older brother and younger brother; friend and friend. Moreover, social harmony could prevail only when each person carried out his assigned social function (the ruler to govern, peasants and artisans to produce goods, merchants to bring commodities to market) and faithfully discharged the obligations inherent in the dualistic pairings (the subject to obey the ruler, the wife to honor her husband, the son to be filial to the father, and so forth). Thus, it was the responsibility of each individual to cultivate his own moral and intellectual capabilities by acquiring knowledge of rituals, poetry, and music, thereby becoming "a person of virtue" who contributed to the greater good of all by understanding and fulfilling his duties.

During the Song dynasty (960–1279), philosophers in China began to emphasize certain metaphysical concepts that elaborated upon Confucianism's traditional concern with practical ethics. Neo-Confucianism, as the new doctrines were called, drew particular attention to the ri-ki dualism. Ki was "ether" or "material force," a kind of vapor capable of metamorphosing itself into the five elements (wood, fire, earth, metal, and water). Moreover, ki could combine with ri, and when that happened, ki was condensed, producing living beings as well as physical objects. Similarly, when ki and ri separated, things ceased to exist. While ki acted as the life-giving force, ri remained forever as "principle," an elusive abstraction that contained within itself natural law and social norms. Further, ri endowed man with his nature, determined the property of things, and steered the course of worldly events. By comprehending ri, people could replicate on earth the social hierarchy and personal relationships that defined the perfect moral order.

At the dawn of the early modern period, Japanese intellectuals began to pay close attention to Neo-Confucianism. In particular, the establishment of a new polity and the inauguration of the Great Peace heightened interest in questions about the nature of society and government and the most desirable relationship between the two. Fujiwara Seika, a Kyoto monk and cultured recluse, usually is credited as being the first Japanese to teach Confucianism openly as an independent philosophy, and his student, Hayashi Razan, explicated its doctrines for Tokugawa Ieyasu.

During the course of the seventeenth and eighteenth centuries, Neo-Confucian thought won considerable backing from Japan's political elites. Hayashi first lectured to Ieyasu in 1605 and two years later became a permanent adviser to the shogunate. As he moved closer to the center of political affairs, Hayashi drafted official documents, counseled shoguns on ceremonial rituals, participated in historiographic projects, and authored the 1635 revision of the Regulations concerning Warrior Households. In return for his services, Tokugawa Iemitsu helped Hayashi establish a school of Neo-Confucian studies in Edo. In 1797 that academy was reorganized and named the Shōheikō, which served thereafter as the official college for sons of bannermen and housemen, the shogun's direct retainers. Concurrently, most daimyo also established domain schools to provide a Confucian-based education for their samurai. By the nineteenth century there were more than two hundred such institutions nationwide, and nearly all sons of samurai spent several years learning the Confucian ABCs and such martial skills as archery and horsemanship.

The appeal of Neo-Confucianism to Japan's shoguns and daimyo seems self-evident. After a century of warfare and chaos, the doctrine's emphasis on order, obedience, duty, and service to the family, community, and state arrived as welcomed concepts. So too did the notion that a universal moral order required all subjects to be loyal to their rulers. Moreover, in China scholars schooled in the Confucian classics served as state officials and belonged to the category of "rulers," the highest rung of the social hierarchy. As warriors turned bureaucrats, the new samurai of the early modern era could equate themselves with the scholar-officials who served the state in China, privileged as a social class and entitled to rule simply by the very nature of things.

Neo-Confucianism, however, was a double-edged instrument that also made good governance an expectation. If subjects were to be obedient, they likewise were entitled to hold their officials to high moral standards. As Confucius himself once averred, worthy men need not serve unworthy rulers. Accordingly, the shogunate and daimyo were obligated to be righteous, moral, and benevolent governors who exercised their considerable powers on behalf of the people of the realm. Any daimyo who failed the litmus test of virtuous action might have his domain reduced in size or even confiscated. By extension, shoguns who did not rule in a manner that enhanced the well-being of the people ran the risk of dismissal. A corollary observation rounded the circle: Exemplary rulers deserved unswerving loyalty. Articulated in that manner, Neo-Confucianism added another underpinning to Tokugawa legitimacy, combining with the moral authority derived from serving as the delegate of the Heavenly Sovereign and the religious sanction of Ieyasu's deification to create a compelling ideological structure that otherwise would have rested merely on the proposition that might made right.

## Symbols and the Substance of Power

The Tokugawa shoguns crafted symbols that added an aura of tangible visibility to their legitimacy. With deliberate forethought, the new regime invented ceremonies that honored its founders, created rituals that added tensile strength to the ties running between Kyoto and Edo, and set in motion a culture of movement that made palpable to the court and regional lords the pre-eminent position held by the House of Tokugawa. The regalia of power gave physical, concrete substance to claims to authority that otherwise would have remained abstract and theoretical, and they furnished compelling evidence about the durability of the shogun's mandate to rule. In that context, the new symbols of legitimacy were not mere ornaments or decorations; rather, ritual and ceremony became an integral part of the praxis of rule itself.

Between 1634 and 1636 Tokugawa Iemitsu rebuilt and expanded his grandfather's mausoleum at Nikkō. That tribute to the twentieth anniversary of Ieyasu's death became one of the most expensive architectural projects undertaken during the early modern period, consuming an amount equal to nearly four years' output of the country's gold and silver mines. Only those invited by the House of Tokugawa could visit the grand new Nikkō, and they approached the site through a Shinto torii, or gateway, and then walked gently uphill along a pathway that brought into view a sacred stable and three storehouses containing the shrine's most precious treasures. After admiring those buildings, guests passed through a second torii and paused to pray at the Honchidō, a hall of worship that enshrined Yakushi, Ieyasu's Buddhistic manifestation.

Looming ahead was the enormous and extravagantly ornamental Yōmei Gate, the highlight of any pilgrimage to Nikkō. Replete with carvings of auspicious birds and flowers, teeming with sculptures of fearsome dragons and protective gargoyles, and finished with gold leaf and glittering metalwork, Yōmei Gate inspired the famous expression "Do not utter the word 'magnificent' until you have seen Nikkō." Of greater symbolic note, as visitors shifted their gaze to the lintels immediately above the gate's main doors, twenty-two figures celebrating painting, calligraphy, music, and the other accomplishments of Confucian gentlemen-scholars came into view, together with thirty scenes of Chinese children at play illustrating parables that taught moral values. No guests, whatever their rank or distinction, could proceed beyond Yōmei Gate—only mausoleum priests and members of the Tokugawa family enjoyed that privilege—but they could catch a glimpse of another, inner gate that featured a sculpture of the "Duke of Zhou," extolled by Confucius as the paragon of virtuous rule. Beyond that gate stood a Shinto hall dedicated to Ieyasu's *kami* spirit, and to the right a pathway led up the mountain to his funeral urn.

The largess that Iemitsu expended on Nikkō was an act of conspicuous piety that redounded to his political advantage. Beginning with the reconsecration ceremony in 1636, the shogunate periodically required daimyo to join grand processionals to Nikkō, where the regional lords bowed in hum-

*Yōmei Gate at Nikkō*

ble obeisance in front of Yōmei Gate. Moreover, in 1645 the court in Kyoto recognized Nikkō as having the same status as Ise Shrine. Located about as far to the southeast of Kyoto as Nikkō is to the north of Edo, Ise is the abode of Amaterasu, and shogunal envoys to Kyoto annually stopped at Ise to offer respects to the Sun Goddess. Beginning in the late 1640s, the monarch reciprocated by dispatching emissaries to Edo and Nikkō. Each year, as the Heavenly Sovereign's delegation gathered at the Honchidō and then at the steps to Yōmei Gate, priests chanted sutras, burned incense, and offered prayers in a solemn ritual that exalted the apotheosis of Ieyasu and reaffirmed the sanctity of Tokugawa rule.

Ritualized movement, such as that seen in the pilgrimages to Nikkō, had great symbolic importance in early modern Japan, and it acquired additional prominence when Iemitsu regularized the *sankin kōtai* system of "alternate attendance." From the very early days of the shogunate, some daimyo visited Edo from time to time to pay homage to the House of Tokugawa, and by the 1610s a few even had constructed residences near Edo Castle, where they spent their sojourn. The 1635 revisions to the Regulations concerning Warrior Households, however, instructed all *tozama* daimyo to reside in Edo every other year, and the shogunate extended that requirement to all daimyo in 1642. Subsequently, the shogunate divided the lords into different groups so that approximately half the *tozama* and a like proportion of *fudai* daimyo resided in Edo in any given year.

The regional lords made the best of the situation, progressing back and forth to Edo in grand cavalcades that permitted them to vaunt their wealth and grandeur. A major daimyo traveled with a thousand or more warriors and servants. Typically, flag bearers and pikemen carrying tall halberds decorated with exotic animal furs marched at the front of the column, followed by mounted samurai, porters bearing handsome lacquered boxes emblazoned with the daimyo's crest, high-ranking domain officials, the daimyo seated in his own palanquin and attended to by valets and other personal attendants, and a rear guard of warriors and servants. With the *tozama* daimyo moving in and out of Edo during the Fourth Month, and different groups of allied lords filling the country's roadways in the Second and Eighth months, ordinary Japanese had ample opportunity to admire what one observer called the "pomp and magnificence" of daimyo processions.[13]

However gratifying parades across Japan may have been for lordly egos, ultimately the rhythmical coming and going of the processionals affirmed Edo's political centrality. As everyone knew, the daimyo were moving about because the shogunate had ordered them to do so. Moreover, the shogunate required the lords to perform various ritualized acts of service and homage while in Edo, including periodic visits to Edo Castle or to Hidetada's mausoleum, a short distance away in the southern part of the city. Gifts too entered the equation. Upon arrival in Edo, the lords presented to the shogun carefully bred horses, exceptional swords, finely crafted suits of armor, and other tokens of gratitude for having received the Original Gift of a domain and for enjoying the benefits of the Great Peace that had settled over the land. Finally, as part of the alternate attendance system, each regional lord had to maintain a lavish residential estate in Edo, where he left a permanent staff and, as a surety of good behavior, his principal wife and heirs.

## Japan and the World

The Tokugawa shoguns claimed for themselves the prerogative of acting as the arbiter of Japan's foreign relations, and, in doing so, again mixed symbols with substance to reinforce further their domestic political legitimacy.

Japan's longest and richest ties were with its continental neighbors, China and Korea. During the era of the Taika Reforms, Japanese learned key principles of statecraft from China, and later generations of Kyoto aristocrats took great delight in Chinese art and poetry. The cultural debt to Korea was no less great. Even before the Taika coup d'état of 645, Koreans helped introduce Buddhism to Japan. Moreover, during the fifth and sixth centuries many scribes, potters, weavers, and metalworkers moved from the peninsula to the islands. Those migrants brought with them advanced technical skills and new forms of knowledge, and some became heads of powerful chiefdoms that supported the Yamato Line when it fashioned its hegemony over other clans. Indeed, so important were the migrants' contributions to the formation of the Taika polity that perhaps a third of the newly created aristocratic families that populated Nara and Kyoto had roots that extended back to the peninsula.

Japan lived in peace with its nearest neighbors for a thousand years, until Hideyoshi decided to extend his power beyond Japan's borders. To this day no one understands his motive. Perhaps it was to acquire additional lands to distribute to daimyo loyal to him, or perhaps it was just an insatiable thirst for power, megalomania run wild. After all, in one letter to the king of Korea, Hideyoshi wrote that he was conceived when the Wheel of the Sun entered his mother's womb in a dream, an unequivocal sign that the glory of the Toyotomi name should illuminate the Four Seas, just as the sun shone throughout the universe. He had pacified Japan and demonstrated his invincibility there, Hideyoshi signaled, and now he would invade Korea and China, even India, and introduce Japanese customs and values to those countries.

Hideyoshi's expeditionary army of nearly 160,000 men landed at Pusan in southern Korea on the twelfth day of the Fourth Month 1592 and took that city in a single day. The Japanese sped up the peninsula, arriving at the gates of Seoul in just three weeks and reaching the Tumen River by summer's end. The farther north the invasion force ventured, however, the more trouble it found. Korean fleets kept Japanese supply ships out of the Yellow Sea, forcing Hideyoshi's quartermaster corps to carry arms and food on the backs of men and horses up the entire length of the peninsula over unsecured roads that merely led from one hostile village to the next. Guerrillas harassed the troops every step of the way, disrupting supply efforts and driving the Japanese into fortified garrison towns. By the end of the year Hideyoshi's armies were bogged down and dared not venture outside their forts in bands of fewer than three hundred; north of Seoul, it was said, five hundred were needed for safety. Massive Chinese intervention in the First Month of 1593 overwhelmed the Japanese armies, which retreated to enclaves around Pusan. Hideyoshi renewed the war in the Seventh Month of 1597, and the new expeditionary force fought its way to within forty-five miles of Seoul. After key losses on land and sea demoralized Japanese forces, however, they again retreated to the Pusan redoubt and then returned to Japan after Hideyoshi died in the Eighth Month of 1598.

Little good came of the conflict. Looted scholarly texts pirated to Japan stimulated interest in Neo-Confucianism, while Korean craftsmen taken captive and resettled in Japan began to manufacture Arita (Imari) and Hagi pottery, still famous today. More overwhelming, however, was an enduring legacy of mutual bitterness. Nearly one-third of Japan's 150,000-man army perished in the winter of 1592–1593, killed by guerrillas or dead from exhaustion, hunger, cold, and disease. Koreans suffered almost beyond imagination. Japanese troops burned Seoul to the ground in 1593, and when Hideyoshi renewed the invasion in 1597, he ordered his generals to kill anyone who resisted them—combatants and noncombatants; men, women, and children alike—and to hack off and pickle their noses for shipment to Japan. In Kyoto, Hideyoshi piled tens of thousands of those grisly trophies into a sizable hill beside his mausoleum. Planted with cherry trees, the misnamed Mound of Ears remains today a favorite site for springtime picnics and blossom viewing.

A different testimonial to the horrors of the 1590s came from the diary of Keinen, a Buddhist priest and physician who accompanied his daimyo lord to Korea. Keinen's *Chōsen hinikki* ("Korea Day by Day") presented an intense, distraught portrayal of soldiers infected with what he called the Three Poisons: covetousness, anger, and the ignorance of right and wrong. "The very fields have been put to the fire," he wrote one day, "not to speak of the forts. People are put to the sword, or they are shackled with chains and bamboo tubes choking the neck. Parents sobbing for their children, children searching for their parents—never before have I seen such a pitiable sight." To that observation he attached a poem:

The hills are ablaze
with the cries of soldiers
intoxicated
with their pyrolatry—
the battleground of demons.

Keinen watched aghast as slavers rounded up "men and women, young and old alike," part of the fifty to sixty thousand Koreans forcibly taken to Japan. "Having tied these people together with ropes about the neck, they drive

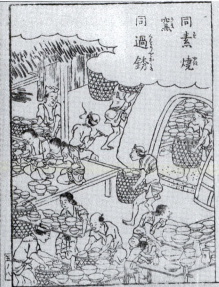

*Men and women potters at Arita*

them along before them; those who can no longer walk are made to run with prods or blows of the stick from behind." When the priest witnessed the brutal attack on Namwŏn he sadly noted, "All in the fortress were slaughtered, to the last man and woman. No prisoners were taken." With such scenes burned into his memory, Keinen concluded: "Hell cannot be in some other place apart from this."[14]

Despite the agonies of the time, considerable numbers of Westerners began to arrive in Japan during the last half of the sixteenth century, carried there on the last wave of Europe's great maritime explorations. Just six years after the Portuguese came ashore at Tanegashima in 1543, the Jesuit apostle Francis Xavier inaugurated the first Christian mission to Japan, and by the time Ieyasu became shogun, Portuguese, Spanish, Italian, Dutch, and English traders and adventurers had become common sights in port towns in central and western Japan. Impressed by physical differences, many Japanese tended to refer to the English and Dutch as Red Hairs. Since the Iberians sailed to Japan from the south, in particular Macao and the Philippines, they got lumped together as *nanban* ("Southern Barbarians"), a term sometimes applied to all Europeans and their customs and products.

Initially, most Japanese gave the Europeans a hospitable reception. In part, of course, some simply were curious about the external aspects of different, far-off civilizations, such as the exotic clothes Westerners wore and the strange but intriguing foods they ate. Indeed, at this time the Japanese came to enjoy unfamiliar fruits and vegetables, such as watermelon and sweet potatoes, and, it is said, learned how to make bread and tempura from the Portuguese. New knowledge that the Europeans possessed about geography, cartography, shipbuilding, and navigation attracted others. For daimyo still fighting to secure a place in the emerging political order, access to muskets and other military technology was reason enough to greet European arms dealers warmly. Finally, a few intrepid Japanese traders themselves were venturing abroad to establish trading outposts and small "Japan towns" as far afield as the Philippines, Cambodia, and Siam, and they were happy to exchange goods for a profit with their European counterparts.

Japanese also listened attentively to the proselytizing of Francis Xavier and other Christian missionaries. By 1600 Jesuit, Franciscan, and Dominican apostles claimed to have converted 300,000 Japanese. Doubtless, many Japanese sincerely believed in the message of Christ, but faith and trade were intimately interwoven. Some Portuguese sea captains dropped anchor only at ports where the local daimyo welcomed Christianity. That message was clear too, and a few daimyo had every person in their domains embrace the Christian God in order to attract Portuguese shipping. Perhaps the most prominent Christian daimyo was Ōmura Sumitada. Baptized in 1563, that warlord took the name Dom Bartolomeu and opened his port at Nagasaki to Portuguese trade in 1571.

It did not take long, however, for Japan's unifiers to become suspicious of a foreign religion whose First Commandment demanded exclusive loyalty to a jealous God. As early as 1587 Hideyoshi issued a decree instructing all Jesuit missionaries to leave "within twenty days." Although the warlord did not enforce the order immediately, a decade later he accused six Franciscan friars, three Jesuits, and seventeen converts of subversion and had them publicly executed upon the cross in Nagasaki. In explanation of his anti-Christian attitude, Hideyoshi wrote to the governor of the Philippines that he could not allow missionaries to propagate a foreign creed in his realm any more than the kings of Spain and Portugal would tolerate Shinto or Buddhist priests moving about their countries.

Even with the example of the Twenty-six Martyrs fresh on their minds, Roman Catholics continued to spread the faith until the Tokugawa shoguns stepped up the persecution of Christians. In 1614 Ieyasu again ordered all missionaries to depart the country. The "pernicious doctrine" of Christianity, his decree read, merely taught people to "contravene governmental regulations, traduce Shinto, calumniate the True Law, destroy righteousness, corrupt goodness."[15] When many foreign apostles ignored the shogun's rage and continued to proselytize under cover, the shogunate launched a merciless persecution, executing fifty-five Christians at Nagasaki in 1622 and hunting down Catholic priests and their followers everywhere. By the time the attack on the Catholic Peril ended in the late 1630s, as many as four thousand believers had met their deaths, and Christianity survived only in isolated rural hamlets on Kyūshū, far from the zealous eyes of shogunal officials.

Iemitsu made the persecution of Christianity part of a broader exclusionary ban on Europeans in Japan. In the mind of the third shogun, the West was synonymous with Christianity, and the propagation of the foreign faith constituted not only a threat to Tokugawa attempts to anchor its legitimacy in the Shinto and Buddhist creeds but also an assault on all native traditions, just as his grandfather's decree had stated. Moreover, trade was a consideration: Shogunal advisers remained aware that in the past daimyo in southwestern Japan had used foreign trade as a means to build strength. In addition, unrestrained trade drained the country of its precious gold and silver reserves. Its mines yielded considerable amounts of silver, perhaps one-third of the world's output annually at the beginning of the seventeenth century. At the same time, however, Portuguese traders in Japan were loading as much as twenty tons of silver a year onto their galleons for shipment to their headquarters in Macao. "Had the Portuguese enjoyed the trade to Japan but twenty years longer," one foreign observer later wrote, "such riches would have been transported out of this Ophir to Macao, and there would have been such a plenty and flow of gold and silver in that town, as sacred writ mentions there was in Jerusalem in the time of Solomon."[16]

Consequently, between 1633 and 1639 the shogunate issued five so-called seclusion edicts that totally proscribed Christianity, forbade Japanese to travel abroad, banned Portuguese ships from entering Japanese ports, and strictly regulated foreign trade. When the Portuguese sent an embassy from Macao in a futile attempt to get trading privileges reinstated, the shogunate ordered "that the ship shall be consumed by flames and the principal ambassadors shall be put to death along with their companions so that nothing may remain of this harbinger of evil."[17] A sixth edict, issued in 1641, confined the Dutch to Dejima, an artificial island constructed in the middle of Nagasaki Bay, and effectively authorized only Dutch and Chinese traders to operate in Japan.

Apart from the Chinese and Dutch, the only other outsiders permitted to enter Japan during the Tokugawa period were diplomatic envoys periodically dispatched by the kings of Korea and the semi-independent monarchy that ruled over the Ryūkyū Islands. In 1607 Ieyasu agreed to normalize relations with Seoul, and the Korean king sealed the negotiations by promising to send ambassadorial missions to Edo on appropriate occasions. In addition, the Ryūkyū Islands became an "emissarial country" during the early modern era. The Shō dynasty had reigned over that archipelago from the fourteenth century, but the daimyo of Satsuma domain invaded the islands with fifteen hundred samurai in 1609 and overran the headquarters of the Ryūkyūan king. A treaty concluded in 1611 nominally preserved the kingdom's autonomy but in reality made the islands into a dependency of the Shimazu daimyo family, lords of Satsuma domain. On fifteen occasions between 1634 and 1806, the Shō monarchs dispatched embassies to Edo to confirm the suzerainty of the Shimazu daimyo and the Tokugawa shogunate.

The seclusion edicts and the treaties with Korea and the Ryūkyū Islands augmented the shogunate's arsenal of powers. The Minamoto and Ashikaga shoguns had been anointed as the defenders of the country, but the Tokugawa rulers moved beyond that to claim exclusive responsibility for formulating foreign policy. Symbolically, the shogunate employed the ritual of movement to represent its ascent to the apex of national affairs. Significantly, most corteges of foreign ambassadors rushed through Kyoto without stopping to pay respects to the Heavenly Sovereign. Their arrival in Edo, in contrast, was a grand event marked by lavish ceremonials, special performances of classical orchestral music, and exhibitions of mounted archery and other martial skills. There was also considerable symbolic gift giving; from the Korean ambassadors, the shogun could expect to receive bolts of silk, catties of ginseng, jugs of refined honey, and the skins of tigers hunted in the peninsula's rugged mountains.

Moreover, on several occasions between 1636 and 1655 many of the foreign delegations from Korea and the Ryūkyū Islands proceeded to Nikkō, suggesting that Ieyasu had become a universal god whose authority extended even beyond the shores of Japan. That notion received visual representation in 1643, when the king of Korea shipped a large bronze bell to Nikkō. An inscription on the gift celebrated Ieyasu's splendor: "The Hall of Religious Practices at Nikkō was constructed for Tōshō Dai Gongen, the August Avatar of Buddha. Possessed of infinite merit and virtue, the August Avatar receives infinite reverence. The filial piety inherent in succeeding to his work and expanding thereupon increasingly glorifies the illustrious deeds of this ancestor. Our king has heard of this and, overjoyed, has caused this bell to be cast."[18] Officials constructed a belfry just to the right of Yōmei Gate, where each daimyo and royal envoy who made the pilgrimage to Nikkō could read this tribute to the sweeping, irresistible majesty of the Tokugawa shogunate.

Starting in 1633, representatives of the Dutch trade mission stationed in Nagasaki also traveled yearly to Edo. The shogun did not always treat those merchants with dignity, however, preferring to make his point about shogunal eminence with blatant crudeness. One member of a Dutch delegation in 1691 recalled waiting "upwards of an hour while the shogun seated himself in the Hall of Audience."[19] Finally a chamberlain ushered the foreigners into the presence of the shogun, where, according to one, "we all had to show our submission in Japanese fashion with heads to floor and crawl in the direction" of the overlord. With the pecking order firmly established, "the farce began." After posing "a number of meaningless questions," the shogun instructed his guests "to take off our *kappa*, or ceremonial robes, and sit upright so that he could inspect us; had us now stand up and walk, now pay compliments to each other, then again dance, jump, play the drunkard, speak Japanese, read Dutch, draw, sing, put on our coats, then take them off again." In the end, one young man noted resentfully, " I join'd to my dance a love-song in High German."

---

The capacity to dictate foreign policy added to the growing number of governing prerogatives exercised by the Tokugawa shogunate. During the first half of the seventeenth century the new regime in Edo made the Heavenly Sovereign and his court dependent on its favors, subordinated the Buddhist establishment to secular discipline, and tamed the daimyo. As it compelled the regional lords to participate in the alternate attendance system and claimed the right to speak for all Japanese in dealing with the outside world, the shogunate emerged as the focal point of central governance in Japan. Moreover, its ability to dominate other elites and formulate policies that affected the entire nation eclipsed the powers previously exercised by the Heavenly Sovereign and Dajōkan in Kyoto and by the earlier Kamakura and Ashikaga shogunates.

Initially, the House of Tokugawa relied on brute strength, on the coercive power of its armed might and economic wealth, to advance its claims to rule the country. By the time of Iemitsu's death in 1651, however, the image of a ruler on horseback had given way to a new ideological legitimacy that derived moral authority from Buddhism and Shinto and drew additional philosophical support from Neo-Confucianism. At the same time, new structures and techniques of authority came to the fore. By mid-century it was not an individual shogun but, rather, the shogunate, an organization of trained officials, that managed affairs, and it did so in accordance with legal codes, bureaucratic regimentation, and recorded precedent.

The regional lords also maneuvered to tighten their grips over their individual domains during the first half of the seventeenth century. Daimyo were not deified in the manner of Ieyasu, but they did augment their claims to authority by patronizing local religious institutions and sponsoring schools that propagated Neo-Confucian doctrine. Furthermore, by participating in the Tokugawa rituals of power—by residing alternately in Edo and swearing an oath of fealty in exchange for a document of investiture—daimyo announced their inclusion in a realm-wide system in which legitimacy ultimately flowed from the Heavenly Sovereign. As the daimyo became strong civil governors, they began to intrude more visibly into the lives of the inhabitants of their domains. Just like the shogunate on its direct holdings, the daimyo on their domains issued legal codes, imposed taxes, and crafted administrative systems that brought their authority into every village and each household. In that regard the early seventeenth century was an important epoch in Japanese history when state control—both the ability of the center in Edo to dominate other elites and the ability of shogun and daimyo to impose their will on their subjects—became more evident and pervasive than ever before in Japanese history.

As powerful as the Tokugawa shoguns and regional lords became, however, they were not autocrats. For all of their pretensions to power, the Japanese hegemons and their officials did not have unlimited resources, and sometimes they found that their reach exceeded their grasp. At other times, as improbable as it might seem, samurai bureaucrats showed little appetite for dictatorially controlling economic and social developments. As much as it might appear on the surface as the Age of the Samurai, in many significant ways the early modern period eventually became as well the Age of the Commoner, an era when the ordinary men and women of Japan—peasant, merchant, and artisan alike—shaped the character of Japan's commercial, social, and cultural life in a multitude of significant ways.

# Cities, Commerce, and Lifestyles

A bout the time that Tokugawa Ieyasu became the shogun of Japan, the Mitsui family decided to pack away its swords and become merchants. For several generations, heads of the Mitsui house faithfully had served the Sasaki daimyo of Ōmi Province, and by the middle of the sixteenth century Mitsui Takayasu, also known by his honorary title of Lord of Echigo, was ensconced in a branch castle near Lake Biwa. When Oda Nobunaga launched his campaign to consolidate control over central Japan in the late 1560s, he obliterated the Sasaki family, and Takayasu beat a quick retreat to the small marketing center of Matsusaka in Ise Province. From that location, Sokubei, Takayasu's son and successor to the family headship, watched the House of Tokugawa rise to a position of military dominance. Sensibly, according to an official family history compiled long after the fact, Sokubei soon concluded that an era of lasting peace was about to settle over Japan, and he further reasoned that the Mitsui family would enjoy a brighter future as shopkeepers than as warriors. Scraping together the necessary capital, he opened a brewery, which he named Echigo Dono no Sakaya (The Lord of Echigo's Sake Shop).

Sokubei's timing was providential, for the sake business brought in enough for the young man to marry and begin to raise a family. He was even more fortunate to take as his wife the young Shuhō, the daughter of a fellow merchant. Wed when she was just twelve years old, Shuhō eventually bore Sokubei a dozen children and still found time to contribute to the family's business success. With an eye to earning more than just an income from brewing, Shuhō persuaded her husband to use some of their savings to open a combination pawnshop-moneylending business. The profits from that endeavor quickly overshadowed the proceeds from the Lord of Echigo's Sake Shop, and the Mitsui family became one of the leading merchant houses in Ise Province.

After Sokubei died in 1633, Shuhō sent her eldest son to Edo with enough capital to open a branch shop. Two years later she dispatched her youngest son, Takatoshi, to assist him, and not long thereafter Takatoshi took over the Edo operations from his older sibling. An adroit businessperson, Takatoshi also became a rice broker and turned the profits from the various Mitsui enterprises into a sizable sum before deciding in 1673 to open a draper's shop in Edo, which he named the Echigoya (The Echigo Shop). At first, this was a small operation, employing a dozen or so clerks who took samples of fine silks to the residences of well-to-do samurai, negotiated a price that varied according to the depth of the customer's purse, and accepted orders on credit.

When a fire destroyed his shop in 1673, Takatoshi reopened the Echigoya at Nihonbashi, where its direct descendant, the main Mitsukoshi Department Store, stands today. There Takatoshi revolutionized retailing practices when he hung out the famous signboard, still preserved in the Mitsui Museum, announcing GENKIN, KAKENE NASHI ("Cash Only, Fixed Prices"). That is, the Echigoya began to carry a line of textiles that ordinary merchant and artisan families, as well as wealthy samurai, could afford, and Takatoshi expected customers to come directly to his store, where they paid cash for goods whose prices were openly advertised and marked the same for everyone. As sales expanded dramatically, Takatoshi spread the Echigoya's fame by lending customers oiled-paper umbrellas on rainy days, each gaily emblazoned with the store's trademark, and by befriending playwrights and poets who furthered enhanced Mitsui's public image in their writings. By 1700 the Echigoya had become Japan's largest store, and Takatoshi had opened branches in Kyoto and Osaka.

The Mitsui were not typical merchants; few others could match their successes, and not many family histories accorded their women as many accolades as Shuhō received. Nonetheless, Sokubei was only one of thousands of warriors who chose to become merchants at the beginning of the early modern era, and it was not uncommon for a wife and mother to share the responsibility of running a family business, even though the husband and father stood as the official household head. Together with the Mitsui household, many of those families participated in the three great revolutions that

*The Echigoya at Nihonbashi in the early nineteenth century*

swept across Japan during the early modern era. A country of villages and largely self-sufficient farm families when Ieyasu received his appointment as shogun, Japan within a century became highly urbanized, and countless children of farmers, as well as the offspring of former samurai, moved into the emerging cities in search of better lives as merchants and artisans. There, as they struggled to provide for themselves and hoped even to prosper, they created a commercial economy, as exemplified by the appearance of dry goods emporiums such as the Echigoya. In turn, vast numbers of families across the entire country enjoyed substantially improved standards of living—better housing, food, and clothing—as that urban-centered economy gathered momentum and brought a diverse range of new goods to market.

## An Urban Revolution

The appearance of dozens of castle towns at the end of the sixteenth and beginning of the seventeenth centuries ignited an urban revolution in Japan. As daimyo consolidated their grasp over increasingly larger domains during those decades, they began to construct enormous moat and tower fortresses in the fashion of Fushimi Castle to serve as their military and administrative headquarters. In general, the regional lords located their new citadels at strategic points where they could dominate the surrounding agricultural villages that provided them with tax revenues and necessary foodstuffs. Almost immediately, new communities began to sprout up around the castles as the daimyo required their samurai to build residences near the massive stone ramparts and as prospective merchants and artisans migrated to the emerging towns to make their livings by supplying the warrior estate with a variety of everyday goods and services.

With dramatic suddenness, Japan became a remarkably urban country. In the brief span of years between 1580 and 1610, nearly half of today's largest cities came into existence as castle towns—from Sendai and Fukushima in the north, to Kanazawa, Kōfu, Shizuoka, and Nagoya in central Japan, and on to Hiroshima, Okayama, Kōchi, and Kumamoto in the south and west. The sizes of the castle towns were as impressive as their numbers. Generally, about 10 percent of all people living within a particular domain eventually congregated in the new communities. In all, approximately 140 castle towns had populations of at least 5,000 persons, and the giants Kanazawa and Nagoya topped the 100,000 mark.

The layout of the castle towns followed a common logic that adhered closely to the needs of the daimyo and their samurai retainers. In principle, each overlord situated his castle at a militarily defensible point, such as along the ocean's shore, as at Kagoshima, or on a rise of land between two rivers, as at Kanazawa and Hiroshima. The lord and his family lived inside the central enceinte, safely sheltered by the soaring walls and a concentric network of moats and canals. The daimyo settled his major retainers on estates adjacent to the castle. That was a location of considerable prestige and security, and convenience as well since those higher-ranking samurai increasingly spent their working hours in administrative offices inside the castle ramparts. Next came a belt of residential quarters for merchants and artisans, who made up 50 percent or so of the population in most castle towns. The families of foot soldiers and other low-ranking samurai lived farther away, in an outer ring of barracks-style apartments. Finally, most daimyo instructed Buddhist sects to locate their temples at strategic approaches along the perimeter of the city. The daimyo could garrison the expansive halls of worship in case of attack, and the graveyards created open spaces that an advancing army could cross only at risk.

Kyoto, Osaka, and Edo—three national cities administered directly by the shogunate—hovered above the network of regional castle towns. A city of sovereignty, nobility, and cultural achievement for hundreds of years, Kyoto added a commercial dimension to its silhouette during the early modern era as daimyo, upper-level samurai, and other people of means began to prize the luxury handicrafts produced by its artisans. A population register dated 1685 reflects the diversity and richness of Kyoto's inhabitants. Alongside physicians, dentists, poets, men of letters, and "masters" of the tea ceremony, flower arrangement, and noh acting, the document lists hundreds of famous shops whose owners enjoyed national reputations for making and selling fine silks, porcelain, folding fans, writing paper, and fixtures for Buddhist household altars. By the date the register was completed, Kyoto's total population numbered well over 300,000 persons, many of whom made a living producing and selling high-quality crafts across Japan.

Nearby Osaka had a storied and sometimes tragic past. As early as the sixth and seventh centuries, a settlement on the shores of magnificent Osaka Bay served as a terminus for diplomatic and trade missions arriving from the continent via the Seto Inland Sea, and the new monarchy settled there briefly after the Taika coup d'état in 645. In subsequent centuries a thriving port and marketing community grew up slightly inland on the banks of the Yodo River, which ran from Kyoto to the ocean. A much larger merchant settlement came into being in the sixteenth century, after the prelates of the Honganji branch of the True Pure Land sect had established their temple-fortress, the Ishiyama Honganji, on the site. Those families suffered greatly when Oda Nobunaga overwhelmed the temple-fortress in the 1570s, and although the merchant community enjoyed a renaissance after Hideyoshi built majestic Osaka Castle in 1584, it nearly was obliterated once again in the ferocious battles of 1614 and 1615.

Aware of the military and political significance of the Osaka region, the House of Tokugawa rebuilt the castle to serve as its defense anchor in western Japan. By the end of the seventeenth century, the merchant and artisan population of the surrounding community had soared to approximately 365,000, rendering nearly invisible the 1,000 or so samurai stationed at the castle. As Osaka underwent a metamorphosis from military redoubt into a bastion of commercial activity, it emerged as the country's leading center of production for many goods used in daily life. By 1700 Osaka's artisans were famous for squeezing rapeseeds into lamp oil, fashioning raw cotton into finished cloth, and refurbishing used household goods for resale in secondhand stores. By that date the Sumitomo family and other copper smelters were among the city's largest employers; with seventeen refineries in the city, approximately ten thousand households depended on the copper trade for their livelihoods.

It was inevitable that Osaka, home to so much manufacturing, would become a major shipping and distribution center, a transition encouraged by its proximity to the Inland Sea. By the 1710s more than two thousand ship's carpenters resided in the city, as did thousands upon thousands of wholesalers, distributors, jobbers, and forwarding agents. Somewhat later one respected city official wrote that Osaka "lies at the intersection of the great sea routes of the country and is congested with goods and traffic. Thus, people commonly say that Osaka is the 'country's kitchen,' a store-house of provisions for all Japan. Indeed, the eaves of the affluent and of wealthy merchant families line the streets of the city, and ships from many provinces always lie at anchor in the harbor. Rice, the necessities of daily life, even goods from abroad; all are brought to this place and put on sale. The people lack nothing."[1]

The shogun's direct retainers, the bannermen and housemen, provided the nucleus for Edo's growth. Most of those twenty thousand or so families employed attendants, valets, and households servants, jobs that drew tens of thousands of rural immigrants to the shogun's capital. After Iemitsu institutionalized the system of alternate attendance in the 1630s, the members of the daimyo's immediate families who resided permanently in Edo together with their extensive entourages added perhaps another one-third of a million to the city's population, bringing the total warrior count to approximately 500,000. Like Rome, Edo was built on seven hills, and the elite daimyo located their estates on verdant hillsides that rolled away to the south of the castle. The shogunate settled its trusted bannermen and their families on Kōjimachi Rise, to the west of the castle. Military considerations entered that decision since the area fronted onto the Musashi Plain, a natural avenue of attack on the castle. Still, the undulating hilltop was considered a choice location since most bannermen could find sunny spots upon which to situate their homes and gardens.

Throughout the seventeenth century, construction workers, craftspeople, and dealers in all manner of goods poured into Edo to cater to the needs of its burgeoning samurai-administrator population. The heart of merchant Edo was Nihonbashi, about halfway between the shores of Edo Bay and the main entry gate to Edo Castle. From that center, artisan and merchant neighborhoods spread out, nestling in the valleys that twisted through the sun-lit hillsides dominated by daimyo estates and samurai residences. By the 1720s, as many merchants and artisans resided in the city as did samurai, and with a total population well in excess of one million, Edo had become the world's largest city.

With Edo leading the way, Japan became one of the most urbanized countries in the world. At the beginning of the early modern era, Kyoto

*Construction crews build merchant houses in the Nihonbashi area*

was the only Japanese city with more than 100,000 residents. By 1700 Edo, Osaka, Nagoya, and Kanazawa also exceeded that mark, and approximately 5 to 7 percent of all Japanese lived in such large metropolises. That compared with a figure of 2 percent in Europe, where only fourteen cities were as large, and where only the Netherlands and England-Wales had urban concentrations greater than Japan's. It was a period of urban construction unparalleled in world history, and Japan's remarkable century of urban growth profoundly affected the country's economic and social development.

## Cities and Commerce

The robust vitality evident in the Three Metropoles of Edo, Osaka, and Kyoto helped spark a great commercial revolution that swept across the entire country. Although the daimyo and shoguns originally conceived of the regional castle towns and the cities of Edo and Osaka as defensive enclaves, the mass migration of merchants and artisans transformed those communities into pulsating nodes of consumption and production, so that ultimately their commercial significance exceeded by far their original military purpose. In turn, the geometrically expanding volume of handicraft production and trade depended on the development of a highly integrated nationwide marketing system, the elaboration of reliable transportation facilities, and the creation of an infrastructure of banking, insurance, and other business services. Japan entered the early modern period as an agrarian society; by the nineteenth century nearly every Japanese family to some extent was participating in the urban-based commercial economy, and all felt the touch of its consequences.

Ironically, the extraordinary commercial expansion achieved during the era of the Great Peace originated in the crucible of sixteenth-century warfare. Armies required provisions, and even in the midst of widespread destruction and turmoil, farmers sought to boost yields by improving their tools, devising new strains of seeds, and formulating richer fertilizers. At the same time, innovative engineering techniques enabled daimyo and rural communities to undertake major irrigation, flood control, and land reclamation projects that nearly doubled the amount of land under cultivation between 1550 and 1650. The enhancements to the country's productive capacity supported an accelerating growth in population, so that in the century and a half after 1550 the total number of Japanese leaped from approximately ten or twelve million to thirty-one million and simultaneously made it possible for many children to leave the farm and seek their futures as merchants and artisans in the city.

The inexhaustible consumption demands of the mushrooming urban population for food, clothing, and building materials stimulated the rapid growth of interregional trade and the development of a nationwide marketing system. Clearly, no one domain could produce all the different goods and foods gobbled up by the residents of its castle town, and it took the entire nation to supply the nearly insatiable appetites of the men, women, and children of Edo and Osaka. Responding to the call of the urban market, producers in different regions became famous for certain specialties: Camphor and shiitake mushrooms from southern Kyūshū, lumber and charcoal from Tosa domain, Toyama medicines, and Kōfu grapes were only a few of the many items that fetched handsome prices in the Three Metropoles.

Daimyo policies contributed to the expanding exchange of goods nationwide. The regional lords needed considerable sums of cash: to keep their castles in good repair and carry out irrigation and land reclamation projects within their own domains, to pay the periodic levies imposed by the shogunate, and to finance their annual journeys back and forth to Edo and to cover the costs of maintaining residential estates and supporting the retinue of relatives and retainers living permanently in the city. Since daimyo derived the overwhelming proportion of their income from agricultural taxes paid in rice, they needed to convert the collected grain into cash in order to pay all the bills that came their way. Beginning in the 1620s, the lords from central and western Japan began to ship their tax rice to Osaka, where rice brokers arranged to have it sold in various urban centers. In the beginning, perhaps one million koku of rice annually passed through Osaka's warehouses, a figure that increased more than fourfold by the 1720s. The flow of such enormous amounts of grain—the nation's principal dietary staple—into and out of Osaka helped transform that city into the economic hub of Japan, the "country's kitchen" in the parlance of the day.

In their quest for revenue, many daimyo eventually enacted policies designed to promote the development of cash crops and local specialty products that could be marketed in consumer centers such as Edo and Osaka. Such schemes assumed a variety of forms. The Maeda daimyo paid a handsome stipend to a famous Kyoto potter to spend a year training local craftspeople at kilns in the villages of snowy Kaga domain. Farther to the north, in Yonezawa, the Uesugi daimyo house brought in experts from other parts of the country to establish indigo plantations, used to produce one of Japan's favorite dyes, and to teach techniques of weaving cotton cloth to local farmers. In the final decades of the eighteenth century, domain officials again invited outside specialists to Yonezawa, this time to advise farmers about planting groves of mulberry, whose tender, young leaves were fed to silkworms. The lord of Yonezawa also funded the establishment of twelve nurseries to propagate mulberry seedlings and published handbooks to teach rural families the secrets of raising and marketing silkworms.

The daimyo hoped to profit from the domain-sponsored enterprises in several ways. In some instances, the officials authorized only certain merchants or villages to participate in the new endeavor and then charged them an annual licensing fee for that privilege. In other cases, the regional lords levied new taxes, such as a set payment for each mulberry tree grown or bale of ceramics shipped out of the domain. In still other instances, officials compelled producers to sell their output to designated wholesalers, who then shipped the goods to dealers in Osaka and turned over a portion of the proceeds to domain coffers. In addition to increasing domain revenues, most daimyo hoped that successful intervention in the economy would work to the advantage of ordinary people and contribute to the perception of benevolent lordship. As one early-nineteenth-century manual on sericulture explained, "The immediate benefit which silk farming brings to society is that it enables unused land along river banks, in the mountains and by the edge of the sea to be planted with mulberries, and silk spinning and weaving to flourish. Needless to say, when the products of the region are exported to other areas, the domain will become rich and its people prosperous."[2]

The shogunate further facilitated the flow of goods across the country by encouraging the standardization of weights and measures and by establishing a national currency. With most of the nation's mines under its control, the shogunate began to operate mints in several cities, and the silver mint, or *ginza*, in Edo reached such prominence that the term eventually became used as the place-name for the section of the city where it was located. Quickly the shogun's coins became the country's currency; while most daimyo issued paper money valid for business dealings within individual domains, merchants calculated payments for commodities that crossed domain borders and for transactions consummated in Edo, Osaka, and other major marketing centers in terms of the gold, silver, and copper coins issued by the shogunate.

The shogunate aided the development of transportation and communication facilities. Since overland transport was difficult in mountainous Japan, most merchants preferred to trust their goods to oceangoing barges and cargo boats. To aid waterborne commerce, the shogunate commissioned Kawamura Zuiken, a wealthy Edo lumber merchant, to institute measures that would reduce existing dangers to coastal vessels. Kawamura immediately set about charting dangerous waters, erecting beacons and lighthouses, and providing lifesaving and rescue facilities from Edo to ports along the northern Pacific coast. He then did the same for the entire coastline along the shores of the Sea of Japan, through the Shimonoseki Strait, and up the Seto Inland Sea to Osaka. When the Kamigata Circuit completed the gap between Osaka and Edo in the 1670s, the so-called Eastern and Western Shipping Circuits linked the most remote regions of Japan to the country's major consumption centers.

The shogunate also undertook a systematic program of road improvement, with an emphasis on the Five Highways that radiated outward from Nihonbashi, the hub of merchant Edo. The most heavily traveled of the great roads was the Tōkaidō, which generally followed the Pacific for nearly three hundred miles from Edo to Kyoto, with an extension continuing to Osaka. The graded roadbed, a deep layer of crushed gravel covered with packed-down sand, averaged nearly twenty feet in width. Markers placed atop mounds planted with pine trees showed travelers how far they had journeyed from Nihonbashi, or how much farther they still had left to go, and stone guideposts kept them from turning the wrong way at crossroads. Strung out along the Tōkaidō Highway were fifty-three post towns where weary travelers could replace their sandals, enjoy a snack and cup of tea, and check into an inn for dinner and a night's lodging.

Since most bulk cargo went by sea, the daimyo processions that filled the Tōkaidō Highway encountered only a few packhorses, shod in straw leggings and led by hostlers who often as not appeared as ornery as their animals. Express couriers, in contrast, sped up and down the road in great numbers. From the very beginning of the seventeenth century the shogunate dispatched official messengers three times a month between Edo and Osaka. In 1664 merchants in Edo, Osaka, and Kyoto established express services for the private sector, and runners carrying small packages, business documents, and cash departed each city almost daily. At first, it required six days for couriers to complete the run between Edo and Osaka, but by the beginning of the nineteenth century expensive superexpress operations had cut the time to just two days. By then couriers had extended the communications network to cities like Nagasaki, Kanazawa, and Sendai.

Japan's leading merchant houses created a host of other business services that enabled economic expansion to continue. In Osaka the Kōnoike family and its wealthy colleagues started to operate what amounted to banks. At times the Ten Exchange Houses, as they were known collectively, advanced substantial loans to daimyo to cover current budget deficits, meet the costs of the alternate attendance obligations, and finance development projects. On other occasions the financiers made loans to individual wholesalers. Those entrepreneurs, in turn, re-lent the money to rural families that needed the funds to cover the cost of planting commercial crops or producing textiles and crafts for sale to urban customers. In addition, bankers in Osaka and elsewhere offered insurance to shippers, held cash on deposit, issued promissory notes secured by real estate, and issued letters of credit and bills of exchange to expedite transactions between merchants based in different cities.

Japan's commercial revolution changed the face of the country's cities. If the castle towns and the great metropolises of Edo and Osaka began as cities of lords and samurai, by the end of the early modern era they had become the domain of commoners. That transformation can be seen clearly in wood-block prints that celebrated life in the merchant quarters. Hiroshige, often considered Japan's finest print artist, produced more than a thousand scenes of Edo, and he began his most famous work, *Tōkaidō gojū-santsugi* ("Fifty-three Stations of the Tōkaidō Highway") with a view of Nihonbashi, the center of merchant Edo. In similar fashion, popular guidebooks, such as *Naniwa suzume* ("The Naniwa Sparrow") and *Edo meisho zue* ("An Illustrated Guide to Places in Edo"), depicted shops in Osaka and Edo overflowing with customers contemplating the purchases of an almost endless variety of goods.

The guidebooks also directed the curious to the Kabuki theaters that flourished in the Three Metropoles and to the puppet theaters that were especially popular in Osaka from the end of the seventeenth century until well into the eighteenth. Since authorities placed the theater districts off limits to samurai, who were supposed to satisfy themselves with the more refined and edifying productions of noh drama, playwrights for the popular theaters concentrated on topics that excited the imagination of well-to-do merchants and artisans. One genre known as *sewamono*, or domestic plays, showcased semifictional accounts of horrendous murders or other spectacular scandals, such as the double suicide of a prostitute and her merchant lover, who lacked the money to buy out her contract with the brothel. In contrast, period pieces, or *jidaimono*, dealt with historic events, especially the heroic struggles of the Taira and Minamoto in the twelfth century, and with the warriors involved in the more recent wars of reunification, whose ex-

*A packed house enjoys a Kabuki production in Edo*

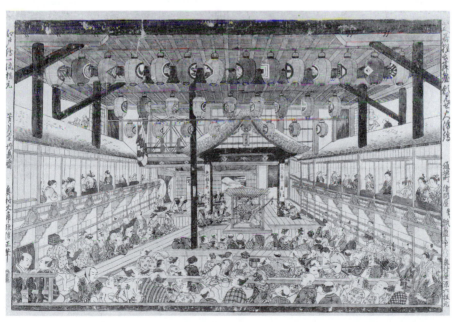

ploits exemplified values, such as loyalty and bravery, that everyone could appreciate.

## Commercial Agriculture and Protoindustrialization

Japan's commercial revolution also changed patterns of agricultural production in the countryside. In every region of the country, farm families turned to cultivating tea, tobacco, and a wide range of fruits and vegetables for sale to the emerging urban population. In some cases, commercial crops could be grown successfully on marginal land not suited for rice production. In other instances, farmers planted a second crop after the rice harvest. Early in the seventeenth century, to take one example, merchants in Osaka discovered an inexpensive method for pressing lamp oil from rapeseed, and urbanites across the country began to enjoy the comfort provided by dependable oil lamps, whose light reassured and enchanted even as it enhanced security by discouraging thieves and other ne'er-do-wells. With demand soaring, farmers in the villages surrounding Osaka grew so much rape as a second crop that fields in early spring seemed to be dyed a brilliant yellow.

Rural industries appeared in increasing numbers throughout the Tokugawa period. By the beginning of the nineteenth century, country workshops were turning out an extensive list of commodities: from silk and cotton fabrics to straw hats, paper, tatami mat facing, charcoal, nails and tools, and lacquerware and crockery, as well as such food products as salt, sugar, vinegar, soy sauce, and miso. In some places, domain officials took the lead in founding businesses in rural areas, as in the production of pottery and crockery in Kaga domain. More often, prosperous urban merchants and peasant families who had accumulated a nest egg from engaging in commercial agriculture supplied the capital and organizational know-how for such enterprises. In all instances, however, the spread of rural-based production of marketable commodities represented the protoindustrialization of the Japanese economy. That is, the emerging rural industries reflected a nascent entrepreneurial spirit in which individuals risked their capital to establish ventures that produced for distant markets in hopes of realizing a profit on their investment. In that sense, protoindustrialization differed both from ordinary household production, in which families made for themselves the clothing and tools they needed in daily life, and from traditional artisanal trades, where craftspeople fabricated goods for sale locally and seldom contemplated expanding their operations or earning more than was needed to support their families.

The new rural firms varied enormously in size. At one extreme were large-scale workshops that brought together as many as six or seven hundred men to brew soy sauce or to smelt iron and forge tools. Small village enterprises employing five to twenty workers were common in the production of charcoal, sugar, salt, tea, and textiles. Sometimes there might not even be a central workshop at all; in various parts of Japan village women wove cotton cloth at home in the evenings and turned it over to wholesaler-distributors who had advanced them money to purchase looms and thread.

Some workers, such as the rural women who stole a few hours or days from farm chores whenever they could to do their weaving, labored irregularly. Others spent considerable lengths of time away from home. Women from villages scattered along a mountainous peninsula in Chōshū domain in western Japan often worked at seaside salt fields in the summer months, returning home to resume their roles as wives and mothers only when the salt-making season was over. In northern Japan it was not uncommon for all the men from an entire village to spend the snowbound winter months at a distant sake or soy sauce brewery. In all those diverse cases, however, the workers had begun to sell their labor in exchange for some form of wage, another defining characteristic of protoindustrialization.

Silk production was an especially prominent form of protoindustrial activity in the early modern era. The manufacture of finished silk cloth was a complicated process that began with hatching and rearing silkworms, which farm families cultivated on flats spread out across ceiling rafters in their houses. After boiling the resultant cocoons, workers pulled away gossamer-thin fibers of silk, twisted them together to form long strands, and reeled the filaments onto bobbins. Operatives then plaited several filaments together in a variety of patterns to create different kinds and grades of thread, a process known as throwing. At that point, dyers and weavers turned the silk thread into finished cloth ready to be cut and sewed into kimonos and other forms of apparel.

At the beginning of the early modern era only a smattering of Japanese households produced a limited amount of low-grade silk cloth for their own use or sale locally, and the single major center of production was located in Kyoto, where weavers in the Nishijin section of the city turned out high-quality silk for aristocrats and wealthy daimyo. From the middle of the seventeenth century, profit-minded entrepreneurs began to encourage sericulture, rationalized the manufacturing process, improved the quality of finished cloth, and started large-scale production for markets nationwide. Innovators first focused on the earliest stage of production, growing silkworms from eggs. Those creatures were vulnerable to disease and sensitive to even slight changes in temperature. After decades of experimenting with selective breeding, farmers developed hardier strains, and by the early eighteenth century prized silkworm eggs from the Fukushima region in northern Japan were in demand across the country. At the same time, other farmers found ways to produce hybrids whose fibers had just the right hue and luster to meet current fashion trends. As an index of how busy and successful the experimenters were, the first manual on sericulture, dated 1702, described five varieties of silkworm, while an encyclopedia published in the mid-1860s listed nearly two hundred. Moreover, a comparison of various texts on silk farming shows that the amount of usable fiber on each cocoon had increased by some 25 percent.

One of the most striking technological advances was the introduction of water-powered throwing machines. In the second half of the eighteenth century, about sixty years after the first silk mills opened in England, a Japanese wheelwright named Iwase Kichibei devised a means of applying waterpower to the large multispindled wheels used to throw silk. Although few others adopted Iwase's breakthrough, it made his hometown of Kiryū, located in a rugged area of Kōzuke Province to the northwest of Edo, a leading center of silk production. Tinkerers also improved the reeling process. At first silk producers relied on simple equipment that required reelers to twist silk filaments together by hand and then wind them around a wooden roller or frame. In the middle of the eighteenth century, however, reeling devices employing gears and drive belts started to appear in various parts of the country, and in some places the new machines were driven by waterpower rather than by hand.

The advances in reeling and throwing increased productivity enormously and facilitated the development of large-scale weaving workshops. Kiryū and surrounding communities emerged as a national center of silk production in the 1760s, after local weavers had mastered the refined dying techniques that famous textile houses in Kyoto's Nishijin district previously had kept as family secrets. As Kiryū silk gained a national reputation for its fine quality, other master weavers moved into the area, purchased additional looms, and employed upward of one hundred workers each. According to one document dated 1835, "Weavers who came to make a living hired women operatives to spin and weave, and people came crowding into the town from other provinces, renting houses there and even in surrounding hamlets."[3]

The functional specialization of the productive process, maximizing output for sales to regional and national markets, and the use of wage labor and rudimentary machines also came to typify the manufacture of cotton cloth. Although the Japanese grew some cotton from ancient times, hemp and associated fibers, such as flax and ramie, provided the most important clothing materials for ordinary men and women until soldiers returning from Hideyoshi's invasion of Korea brought home with them a type of cotton plant that was specially suited for cultivation in the Osaka region. Durable, cool in summer, comfortable in winter, and increasingly affordable, cotton quickly became the clothing material of choice for most ordinary Japanese during the first half of the seventeenth century. So fashionable did it become that farm families in the provinces around Osaka dedicated as much as 70 percent of their acreage to cotton, alternating that crop with rice on one- or two-year rotations.

Although cultivation was concentrated in central Japan, entrepreneurs in even far-off regions purchased raw cotton or thread, which they turned over to weaving specialists for finishing into cloth. In many areas, farm women wove at home in their spare hours and received their pay on a piece-work basis. As consumer demand and the scale of production increased, however, weaving specialists began to work full-time at their craft. Some of them remained independent producers, but other master weavers employed wage labor in workshops that contained twenty, thirty, or even more looms. As was the case with the processing of silk, innovators introduced a host of technical improvements: Selective breeding increased the varieties of cotton plants, new spinning machines produced stronger thread, more efficient looms boosted productivity, and developments in weaving and dying resulted in an amazing array of patterns, textures, and colors.

As commercial agriculture and rural industry took hold across the countryside, scores of villages grew into rural towns that functioned as nodes of industry, trade, and transport. Kiryū, for example, tripled in size between 1757 and 1855, when nearly all its households worked at some aspect of the silk trade. Similarly, in 1843 only 14 percent of the 277 households in Uda-ōtsu, a village in Osaka's hinterland, still farmed, whereas 46 percent held jobs related to the cotton industry, and a census of the village Okashi in Owari Province taken two years later found that 20 percent of its 262 households were engaged in agriculture, 31 percent had jobs involving cotton production, and 22 percent worked in transportation-related occupations. The transformation of tiny, dusty settlements into bustling communities of several thousand inhabitants fleshed out Japan's urban hierarchy and formed new links in the production-distribution network that tied together the rural hinterland with Japan's ports, post towns, castle towns, and the Three Metropoles.

## Foreign Trade

When the shogunate promulgated the so-called seclusion edicts in the 1630s, its goals were to affirm its prerogative to direct Japan's foreign relations, exert control over the conduct of foreign trade, and rid the country of what it saw as a sinister religion. That accomplished, the government in Edo did not intend to terminate all relations with the outside world. Rather, throughout the early modern period the shogunate continued to receive ambassadorial embassies from Korea and the Ryūkyū Islands, and its officials oversaw what sometimes was a brisk trade with Chinese and Dutch merchants, conducted under the general oversight of shogunal officials stationed in Nagasaki. In addition, the shogunate allowed the daimyo and merchants of Satsuma, Tsushima, and Matsumae domains to trade with the Ryūkyū Islands, Korea, and territories to the north of Japan.

The Nagasaki Meeting Office, a semiofficial merchant organization licensed and regulated by the shogunate, organized and conducted the Nagasaki trade. Formed in 1604 and granted a monopoly after the promulgation of the seclusion edicts, the Meeting Office took orders for various domestic commodities desired by foreign traders and purchased goods off-loaded from Chinese and Dutch vessels at Dejima, the artificial island in Nagasaki Harbor where officers of the Dutch East India Company resided year-round and maintained a permanent trading station. Japanese merchants were es-

*A Portuguese ship arrives at Nagasaki*

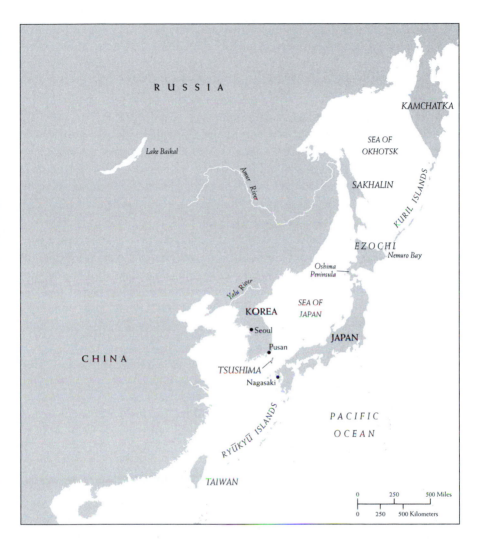

**MAP 2.1** *Japan and Its Neighbors*

pecially happy to import silk thread and fabrics, herbs, spices, sugar, and medicines, and they filled the outgoing ships with copper, camphor, sulfur, swords, pottery, and lacquerware.

The total volume of the Nagasaki trade swung back and forth during the late seventeenth century, but the Japanese often bought more than they sold. The severing of relations with Portugal in the 1630s temporarily halted the hemorrhaging of precious metal that had so worried Tokugawa Iemitsu and his advisers, but the renewed outflow of bullion to cover trade imbalances at the end of the seventeenth and beginning of the eighteenth centuries once again alarmed the shogunate, which in 1715 issued the New Regulations on Ships and Trade. Provisions in that ordinance specified that only thirty Chinese and just two Dutch ships could dock at Nagasaki annually and limited the value of trade to the equivalent of 11.3 metric tons of silver for the Dutch and 22.5 metric tons for the Chinese annually.

After Satsuma domain exerted its suzerainty over the Ryūkyū Islands in 1611, the shogunate authorized the daimyo of Satsuma to resume what already had become lucrative trade relations with the islanders and through them with private merchants along the coast of China. The trade between Satsuma and the Ryūkyūans flourished for several decades, until the shogunate imposed restrictions on the amount of silver that Satsuma could export in the 1680s. Trade flows shrank markedly after that date, but the islands remained an important source of sugarcane and refined sugar, which the domain marketed in Osaka and other major cities.

In the seas between Kyūshū and Korea, the Sō daimyo ruled over Tsushima. Long entrenched on that rugged island, the Sō family had maintained amicable relations with Korea from the fifteenth century and regularly dispatched trading missions to the peninsula. After Sō Yoshitomo brokered the peace settlement between Edo and Seoul in 1607, the shogunate authorized the resumption of commercial relations. Trade accords permitted the Sō to send twenty ships a year filled with goods to be sold to the Korean government and also allowed the Japanese to staff a trading station at Pusan, where they negotiated private deals with Korean merchants. Eventually the volume of trade reached considerable proportions, with the Japanese exchanging bullion principally for silk and ginseng, as well as lesser amounts of tin, buffalo horn, pepper, sappanwood, and such artistic wares as ceramics and ink paintings. In the middle of the eighteenth century, however, the old problem of silver outflows prompted the shogunate to impose restrictions that crippled official trade between Tsushima and Korea.

To the north, the Japanese also traded with the Ainu. The origins of that culturally and linguistically distinct indigenous people are lost in the mists of time, but by the ninth century two discrete cultures flourished on what is modern-day Hokkaidō. One, the Satsumon people, occupied most of the island, while the bearers of Okhotsk culture lived along the northeastern coastline of Hokkaido and on nearby islands of the Kuril chain and on southern Sakhalin. By the thirteenth century a more inclusive Ainu culture had evolved out of the Satsumon tradition, and the indigenes included in their number former Emishi peoples who had fled north to escape Japanese rule. Since the Japanese had come to refer to the Emishi as Ezo, an alternative reading for the ideographs used to signify "Eastern Barbarians," it is perhaps natural that they called the Ainu homeland Ezochi, or the Land of the Ezo.

When Tokugawa Ieyasu received his appointment as shogun, the Ainu numbered about thirty to forty thousand. Although they spoke different dialects and displayed some regional cultural variations, the Ainu shared a common lifestyle and material culture. Living in permanent villages that usually consisted of a dozen or so households, Ainu families cooperated to support themselves by hunting deer, bear, and other game, fishing Ezochi's rivers and harvesting kelp and other bounty of the coastal waters, gathering fruits and vegetables, and cultivating sorghum, millet, and a variety of edible plants in riverside gardens. The Ainu took pleasure in a rich oral tradition that centered on epic poems, and they worshiped phenomena of the natural world that they personified as *kamuy* ("deities").

The rich hunting and fishing grounds of Ezochi yielded a surplus of furs and sea products, which the Ainu for some time had traded with the Japanese to the south and shipped to the Asian continent through Sakhalin and the Kurils. As the volume of trade expanded during the sixteenth century, Japanese established trading communities along the shores of the Oshima Peninsula, on the extreme southwestern tip of Hokkaidō. Eventually the Kakizaki family of warriors emerged as the leader of the Japanese on Oshima, and in 1599 they took the surname Matsumae. Five years later the shogunate recognized the head of the Matsumae family as the overlord of a domain on the southern half of the peninsula and confirmed his right to control all trade with the Ainu.

From their castle town headquarters at the tip of Oshima Peninsula, the Matsumae samurai set up a chain of trading posts scattered along the coast of Ezochi, where they swapped rice, sake, tobacco, clothing, ironware, and other household utensils for salmon, trout, kelp, and such exotic items as bear gallbladders, the pelts of sea mammals, and live falcons used for sport hunting. Many Ainu resented the intrusion of the Japanese samurai-traders since the natives lost their political autonomy and their former prerogative to trade freely with whomever they pleased. Ainu ballads expressed a growing sense that their neighbors had betrayed them. "I had heard the Japanese called honorable people, people with truly good hearts," ran one set of lyrics, "but how evil your hearts must be!"[4] Such resentment turned into violence in 1669, when a sizable force commanded by the regional leader Shakushain attacked Japanese settlements in Ezochi and prepared to march on Matsumae domain.

A startled shogunate mustered an army of samurai and musket bearers drafted from several domains on northern Honshū, and several hundred Japanese settlers and probably even more Ainu died before hostilities ended. Defeated in Shakushain's War, the Ainu ultimately found themselves subjected to even greater economic exploitation. In 1717 merchants from the Japanese mainland began to pay the Matsumae lord an annual fee in exchange for charters giving them the right to manage specific trading outposts. By century's end new trading districts had spread across the lower Kurils and onto Sakhalin, and as they advanced further into Ezochi, some Japanese merchants created commercial empires that dominated fishing operations in the bountiful northern seas. Eventually herring-meal fertilizer became the region's greatest revenue producer. Venturous entrepreneurs from the ranks of the Japanese merchant community spearheaded the development of that industry by introducing advanced fishing methods that hauled in great catches of herring, building processing plants and barracks for Ainu workers (who generally received meager wages and lived in poverty), and shipping the cakes of fertilizer to rice-growing villages on the main Japanese islands.

The shogunate became involved in the northern trade in the eighteenth century. As Japanese officials at Nagasaki searched for substitutes for silver and copper, they were delighted to find a market in China for sharks' fins, dried abalone, tangle, sea slugs, and other marine products used in cooking. Since the merchants who ran the trading outposts in Ezochi packed such goods in straw bags, those commodities commonly went by the name of baled goods. After experimenting with several different kinds of marketing arrangements, in 1785 the shogunate established a Baled Goods Office at Nagasaki to collect the marine delicacies from merchants in Ezochi and northern Honshū and sell them to Chinese traders.

According to most assessments, the grand total of the combined trade with the Ainu, Ryūkyūans, Koreans, Dutch, and Chinese did not represent a significant proportion of the Japanese economy at any time during the early modern era. Nonetheless, export opportunities provided employment for many Japanese, including the potters in Kyūshū, whose wares sold well in Holland, and the Sumitomo and other copper merchants and artisans in Osaka, who by the beginning of the eighteenth century were shipping nearly their entire output to Nagasaki. Moreover, some imported goods contributed to the expansion of agricultural output; by 1740 herring-meal cakes from Ezochi were fertilizing nearly half of all rice paddies in western Japan. Other imports enriched lives and improved living standards. The well-to-do prized Korean art objects and luxury silks from China, and many Japanese enjoyed healthier lives because the Nagasaki Meeting Office transferred all medicines imported from Asia to an association of pharmacists in Osaka that assessed their content, relabeled them with Japanese names, and sold them in conveniently sized packages to druggists throughout the country.

## Class, Status, and Standards of Living

Squid, eels, and octopus; sardines and mackerel; rice and barley; sugar, salt, vinegar, and soy sauce; burdock, turnips, and lotus root; tangerines and persimmons; tea and sake; fine silks and durable cottons; footwear, umbrellas, and rain gear; hair decorations and all sorts of personal accessories; tools and lumber to build new houses and keep them repaired; books and woodblock prints; pots, pans, and lacquered bowls and chopsticks: Even a cursory glance at guidebooks to Japan's larger cities and decorative screens portraying the merchant quarters in various castle towns reveals the abundance of food and other goods found in urban markets by the late seventeenth century.

Families from different economic classes reaped the benefits of the growing commercial economy in contrasting ways. It was common in major cities to see the servants of upper-level samurai and merchant barons like the Kōnoike poke the sea bream to test for freshness, sniff the tea leaves to judge their quality, and pick out only the finest brocaded silks for their masters' pleasure. At the opposite extreme, unskilled artisans, day laborers, and tenant farmers lived in a far different world; they got their protein from tofu instead of fish, drank plain water with their meals, and could afford only the cheapest cottons, often acquired from dealers in secondhand clothing.

Social status too was a consideration. Throughout the seventeenth century the shogunate and regional daimyo governments sought new ways to create more meaningful and readily evident distinctions among the four status groups that made up the Neo-Confucian social order. Several motives inspired that attempt to institute a system of rule by status. Among other things, officials believed that placing people in segregated containers would make it impossible for them ever to mount a unified challenge against the hegemonic order. Moreover, the process of defining more precisely the social order provided the government with ample opportunities to lecture people about the formal obligations that accompanied membership in any particular social estate. In that regard, officials seemed especially determined to impress upon Japan's commoners—the peasant, artisan, and merchant statuses—the need to obey laws, pay taxes, and enrich society by consuming little and producing much. Finally, by finding ways to privilege the samurai as society's elites, the overlords hoped to win the warriors' eternal gratitude and ensure their service as loyal, unquestioning agents of state authority.

The shogunate and daimyo regimes enforced the concept of rule by status in numerous ways. The construction of castle towns at the end of the sixteenth and beginning of the seventeenth centuries created geographical distinctions, with farmers dwelling by themselves in the countryside while in the newly emerging communities the samurai lived in exclusive neighborhoods separate from the merchants and artisans. In addition, a series of decrees initiated by Hideyoshi and elaborated upon by the Tokugawa hegemons instructed people to follow the occupations of their parents, forbade marriage between offspring of samurai and the other estates, and gave warriors the sole right to bear arms. As the new polity took shape, the shogunate and daimyo conferred upon the samurai the prerogative of serving as policy makers and important government functionaries. Further, only the samurai carried surnames; peasants generally assumed just personal names, and merchants customarily were known by their occupation or shop names, such as Tabakoya Shichibei, "Shichibei the Tobacconist."

Beginning in the middle of the seventeenth century, the shogun and individual daimyo domains issued a stream of edicts that regulated consumption patterns as a means of further reinforcing status distinctions. In that spirit, a decree promulgated by the Maeda daimyo of Kaga domain in 1660 specified that upper-level samurai could wear thirteen kinds of silk, which it defined with minute precision, and limited lower-ranking warriors to four lesser grades of silk, such as pongee. The same statute, as was becoming common practice everywhere, collapsed the merchants and artisans into a single category of *chōnin* ("townsperson") and restricted them to plain silks and cotton. Similarly, a shogunal ordinance of 1683 instructed Edo's *chōnin* to use only pongee, cotton, and ramie as clothing materials. Nor did officials ignore the peasants. The 1649 Instructions of the Keian Era admonished villagers to wear clothing made only of cotton, a provision repeated in the prohibitions circulated in Kaga domain eleven years later and in similar decrees issued by daimyo across Japan.

The historical record has left contradictory accounts about how people observed the regulations. Clearly, disobedience was not uncommon. Reports from Kanazawa, the castle town of Kaga domain, suggest that well-to-do townspeople, happy to pay a small fine or sit through an official's sermon about social responsibility in exchange for the satisfaction of showing off their finest to admiring neighbors, often disregarded the regulations about clothing. Even in Edo, according to Buyō Inshi, a keen observer of life in the shogun's capital at the beginning of the nineteenth century, "The shogun's proclamations and ordinances are called 'three-day laws.' No one fears them, and no one pays any attention to them. They are disregarded after that short period of time. Since everyone knows that the government merely issues laws whenever it feels it needs them, it is no wonder that the lower orders do not take the time to learn them, do not obey them."[5]

Buyō's cynicism notwithstanding, other evidence indicates that the combination of status regulations and economic wherewithal did shape lifestyles of individual families to a considerable degree. Not only did the affluent dine on fresh sea bream, but they also sampled such delicacies as crane, goose, pheasant, wild boar, and venison. In Kanazawa some samurai became such gourmands that the daimyo feared they might lose their martial spirit. Consequently, in 1663 the domain issued a proclamation that began "Recently there have been reports of samurai holding lavish parties," and then limited meals on holidays and ceremonial occasions to two soups, a fish, five vegetable side dishes, two flasks of sake, rice, pickles, and cakes and green tea.[6] Merchant families, the Maeda lord continued, should serve more modest meals befitting their status: one soup, three side dishes, two decanters of sake, rice, pickles, and tea with a sweet.

As might be surmised from the guidelines in Kanazawa, a diet of steamed rice accompanied by soup, side dishes, and tea was becoming the preferred style of dining for many during the early modern era. Still, for persons of middling economic means—people, that is, judged to be neither wealthy nor poor by their contemporaries—daily fare could vary considerably, depending on region, the time of year, and just how well-off one felt at any particular time. Entries for 1837 in the diary of one middle-level samurai from Kaga domain indicated that he ate fish daily and had steamed rice with every meal, while a journal kept by another samurai from western Japan revealed that his family in the 1830s and 1840s typically ate rice mixed with barley, a vegetable or tofu, and miso soup, with fish appearing on the dinner table only a few times each month. Some years before that, in the Second Month of 1817, one scholar traveling along the Tōkaidō Highway fondly recorded in his travel diary exactly what he ate each day. At noon on the nineteenth, he stopped at an inn with a view overlooking Lake Biwa and enjoyed a meal of clear soup, a dish of finely sliced carrots tossed with burdock and kelp, and trefoil dressed with a white sesame sauce. Toward evening, as thick snow began to fall, he checked into a hostelry at the post town of Kusatsu and warmed himself with a supper consisting of a soup of greens and dried bean curd; a dish of daikon, persimmon, and greens flavored with vinegar; a small bowl of mixed vegetables served with slices of boiled and molded fish paste; and grilled salted mackerel.

Whatever their preferences, peasants had to endure a barrage of injunctions about what they might eat and drink. In a series of decrees issued in the 1640s, the shogunate banned the consumption of sake and tea in farm villages and further instructed rural families to consume less rice and more wheat, potatoes, and millet. The effectiveness of such laws remains unclear, but many farm families made do with a coarse diet. "Peasants who reside in areas with rice paddies," noted one official in the 1720s, "sometimes eat rice, but only as a porridge containing other edibles. Many who live in the mountainous regions or where other grains are grown cannot even eat rice during the three festive days of the New Year. Even when cooking millet or wheat, they mix in so many turnips, potato and bean leaves, and other greens that one can hardly see the grain. Moreover, they eat such food only once a day and supplement their meal with watery gruel."[7]

As described earlier, the built environment of Edo and Japan's castle towns—monumental fortresses that proclaimed the preeminence of shogun and daimyo, preferential locations for the residences of elite samurai, and neighborhood segregation—physically embodied the chief principles underlying the concept of rule by status. So too did housing styles vary according to status and economic standing. Wealthy samurai employed skilled carpenters and used the finest building materials to construct their spacious residences. The grandest samurai home typically sat behind a wall and elaborate gate, whose size and decorative features accorded with the owner's place within the samurai hierarchy. The house itself usually included a formal entry where people removed their footwear, a sitting room for entertaining guests, and several other rooms where family members could gather for conversation during the day and sleep in the evening. Tatami covered the floors of most rooms, which were separated by shoji partitions and *fusuma*, sliding doors consisting of wooden frames covered with thick paper. In the best of homes, paintings adorned the *fusuma*, and the sitting room featured a built-in writing desk, shelves for displaying books and ceramics, and a tokonoma, the alcove designed to accommodate a hanging scroll, an arrangement of flowers, or some valued art object. The families of lower-ranking samurai lived in houses that were similar but smaller, shedding rooms and decorative features as one moved down the scale of income and prestige.

Merchant and artisan houses typically had a shop in front, opening onto the street, where business was conducted, with living quarters for the family and employees located to the rear. Most such shop-residences were simple, unadorned structures featuring few interior amenities; at the beginning of the early modern era, for instance, nearly all families sat and slept on plain wooden floors with only bags filled with straw to ease their discomfort. Later in the period townspeople with the means to do so laid down tatami, copied the embellishments found in the homes of well-to-do samurai, and added second and even third floors where local ordinances permitted. At times affluent merchants found creative subterfuge a necessary evil if they wished to construct the home of their dreams. In Kanazawa and many other cities, regulations stated that the façades of merchant and artisan residences be no higher than one and a half stories, thus prompting some townspeople to build houses whose roofs measured exactly that height in front but then slanted steeply upward to permit full second floors in the rear. When it came to furnishing such a home, even outright deception was not out of the question; how else was a successful merchant to deal with annoying regulations that forbade someone of his status from using gold and silver leaf for decoration or from having household possessions finished in gold lacquer?

Many poorly paid artisans and day laborers lived in back-alley tenements known as *nagaya* ("long houses"). The front door to each apartment usually opened onto a cramped earthen-floored kitchen equipped with a clay stove for cooking, a bin to store firewood, pegs driven into the wall to hang pots and pans, and not much else. The individual, or family, lived and sometimes even worked in a single tatami room measuring approximately nine feet by nine feet. The apartment dwellers sweltered in Japan's hot and humid summers and in winter drew what warmth they could from the cooking stove. No running water was piped into the individual units, and the residents shared a well, an outhouse, and a garbage bin.

Although farmhouses varied considerably in size and design, most contained distinct sections for living and working. The family used the earthen-floored work space for farm tasks and sometimes sheltered animals there. Commonly, that room also contained a clay stove for cooking and a sink for cleaning up after meals. In the homes of the poorest farmers, the living sections had plain earthen floors, covered with bagged straw and separated from the work spaces by low dividers. Families with more income added rooms, built raised wood floors, and gathered around interior hearths for meals and for warmth in winter. As might be surmised, the residences of village elites boasted several rooms and many of the amenities found in the houses of well-to-do merchants and samurai.

In general, material well-being and living standards improved substantially during the early modern period. Reliable statistics are a scarce commodity, but sufficient evidence exists to conclude that merchant and artisan families in the early nineteenth century dressed better, ate a more interesting variety of food, and lived in more spacious dwellings than their ancestors had two hundred years earlier. Houses also became more comfortable as people increasingly sat on tatami rather than wooden floors, slept on futon stuffed with cotton wadding, stored their bedding in built-in closets, and placed their other belongings in chests specially crafted to hold spare clothing, medicines, writing implements, cosmetics, business papers, and cash. Diets changed considerably as sweet and white potatoes, squash, carrots, green beans, watermelon, and other foods introduced from the West became more widely available. Restaurants featuring tempura, grilled eels, and other specialties appeared in Edo, Osaka, and other leading cities in the eighteenth century—another sign of rising levels of prosperity—and sushi became all the rage after a chef in Edo invented the dish at the beginning of the nineteenth century.

Similar trends were evident in the countryside. Largely self-sufficient at the beginning of the seventeenth century, even families in remote villages could purchase a variety of food and clothing, and sometimes small luxuries as well, by the midway point of the early modern period. At first peddlers crisscrossed the countryside, hawking such items as dried fish, kitchen utensils, and hoes and other farm implements. Later the demand for goods expanded to the point that many villages began to sport permanent "general stores," where local residents could buy a full range of what they had come to consider daily necessities: bean paste and tofu, kelp, noodles, *senbei* ("rice crackers"), lamp oil and candles, thread and needles, zori, geta, and straw sandals, tobacco and pipes, and paper, ink, and writing brushes. As one observer noted in the early nineteenth century, "Year after year the retail trade in country districts increases. Sake, dyes, dry goods, toilet articles, hardware, lacquerware—everything you can think of—are sold in villages."[8]

Of course, not every individual or family prospered: Merchants and artisans who were incompetent or simply unlucky slipped down the scale of well-being, while farm families unprepared to take advantage of the opportunities offered by commercial agriculture and protoindustrialization continued to live in substandard housing and eat rice gruel for generation after generation. Samurai faced a different problem: They received fixed annual stipends from their lords that generally did not increase after being set at the beginning of the seventeenth century. Since status regulations prohibited them from participating in the commercial economy, most samurai did not benefit from rising standards of living to the same degree as other Japanese.

Like most exceptions, however, such observations confirm the general rule: For most Japanese, lifestyles and standards of living improved significantly between 1600 and 1850. Indeed, living conditions for most Japanese families in the middle of the nineteenth century probably were comparable to those in England and the United States on the eve of their Industrial Revolutions. In that context, it is worth noting that the life expectancy for Japanese born at the end of the early modern era seems to have been nearly the same as for western Europeans born in 1840 (39.6 years for men; 42.5 for women) and somewhat better than for Americans born in 1850 (37 years for men; 39 for women).

Certainly, the impressions that the intrepid globe-trotter Isabella Lucy Bird recorded in her *Unbeaten Tracks in Japan* after she traveled nearly fifteen hundred miles on horseback from Tokyo to northern Honshū in 1878 stack up favorably against her experiences twenty years earlier in the United States. When the Englishwoman visited Chicago in the 1850s, her innkeeper first tried to stick her into a room containing four beds, five women, and a sick child. After registering a strong complaint, Bird settled for a tiny chamber but was dismayed to discover that the single narrow bed was covered with a "dirty buffalo-skin" that played host to "swarms of living creatures." Later the filth in the dining room appalled her, and Bird had little appetite for the "boiled legs of mutton, nearly raw," the "antiquated fowls, whose legs were the consistence of guitar-strings," or the baked pork "swimming in grease."[9]

In contrast, when Bird visited Nikkō, she stayed at a "middle-class" rural home that "delighted" her. "I don't know what to write about my house," she began. "It is a Japanese idyll; there is nothing within or without which does not please the eye." After admiring the polished stairs, tatami mats ("so fine and white that I almost fear to walk over them"), and the painting of "a blossoming branch of the cherry on white silk" that hung in the tokonoma, she confided, "I almost wish that the rooms were a little less exquisite, for I am in constant dread of spilling the ink, indenting the mats, or tearing the paper windows." For her meals, Bird thoroughly enjoyed trout, eggs, rice, and tea served in "fine Kaga porcelain."

# CHAPTER 3

# Self and Society

In "Shanks' Mare" (*Tōkaidōchū hizakurige*), the best-selling novel published serially beginning in 1802, Yaji and Kita set out from their native Edo to travel the Tōkaidō Highway. The pair were happy-go-lucky artisans who lived out the stereotype that lowly Edo commoners spent money without care and seldom planned for the future. Lighthearted bachelors, Yaji and Kita were fascinated by the endless variety of people they encountered on their journeys, some of whom rubbed the irrepressible rogues the wrong way. In a series of mischievous adventures, Yaji and Kita heckled pompous samurai, ridiculed priests who sold dispensations, poked fun at the thick dialects spoken in the provinces, and saw the country girls who worked at restaurants and inns as little more than potential conquests.

As comic and exaggerated as the encounters with their fellow Japanese may have been, the reactions of Yaji and Kita were grounded in the realities of the day. After all, many Japanese did identify strongly with the village, town, and domain where they had been born. In addition, Japan was a status-divided society, and samurai, townspeople, and farmers lived in distinct communities and neighborhoods and wore clothing made from different materials. Moreover, during the early modern period the various social estates articulated separate Ways, ethical codes of conduct that overlapped to a great extent but at points also emphasized divergent standards and principles. Finally, the various Ways tended to subordinate women to men, thus condoning the predatory attitude displayed by Yaji and Kita.

In sequels published over two decades, Yaji and Kita extended their travels to other parts of Japan, eventually journeying as far afield as the great Konpira Shrine on the island of Shikoku. As they wandered about, Yaji and

Kita became more familiar with their country and their fellow Japanese. Among other things, they found out the hard way that women made up their own minds about things and that true romantic fulfillment was based on choice, not compulsion. In addition to developing a tolerance for difference, Yaji and Kita discovered an elemental Japaneseness. "Naturally," they noted, "one is curious about the people who are travelling the same roads," and since people out to see the world "are not tied by convention as when they live in the same row of houses, they can open their hearts to each other and talk until they are tired."[1] As people chatted at inns, restaurants, and teahouses, they learned that they shared a history, had experienced parallel life events, knew the same myths and legends, worshiped the same deities, possessed a similar sense of right and wrong, appreciated certain emotions and sentiments, read the same books, and enjoyed the same wood-block prints. From that came friendships and a shared sense of being Japanese, or as Yaji and Kita happily saw it, "The Edo man can make acquaintance with the Satsuma sweet potato."

The collective sense of Japaneseness bred a satisfying contentment with one's self, one's countrymen, and the natural environment that everyone shared. "You can go as if you were taking part in a picnic," Yaji and Kita felt, "enjoying all the delights of the road. You can sit down in the shadow of the trees and open your little tub of sake, and you can watch the pilgrims going by ringing their bells. Truly travelling means cleaning the life of care. With your straw sandals and your leggings you can wander wherever you like and enjoy the indescribable pleasures of sea and sky."

## Bushidō *and Samurai Ethics*

Medieval warrior tales first delineated an idealized code of behavior for samurai. In times of warfare, such as the Genpei War of the late twelfth century and the turbulent Sengoku era, samurai were expected to be brave, tough-willed individuals who were skilled riders and swordsmen, proud of their family name, loyal to their lord, and willing to face death at any moment. Some of the most eloquent expressions of that ethos appeared in *Heike monogatari* ("The Tale of the Heike"), an epic account of the fighting between the Taira and Minamoto families during the late twelfth century. In one of the most famous episodes, Kumagai Naozane, a samurai in the service of the Minamoto family, spotted a lone horseman. "It is dishonorable to show your back to an enemy!" Kumagai called out. "Come on back." The warrior, Taira Atsumori, wheeled his horse about, and the foes fell upon each other. Kumagai quickly hurled his opponent to the ground and, holding Atsumori motionless, "pushed aside his helmet, intending to cut off his head, and saw that he was only sixteen or seventeen years old." Struck by the resemblance between Atsumori and his own son, Kumagai decided to set the young man free. Just then, fifty Minamoto samurai appeared on the horizon. "I would like to spare you," Kumagai exclaimed, "but there are Minamoto warriors everywhere. You can't possibly escape. It will be better if I'm the one to kill you, because I'll offer prayers for you." Replied Atsumori, "Just take my head; don't waste time."[2]

In real life, as might be imagined, many samurai did not always live up to such lofty ideals. Some broke and ran when the tide of battle turned against them, and many remained loyal to their lord only so long as he protected them and bestowed rewards and favors on them. In other cases, samurai sold their services to the highest bidder or even changed sides in the middle of battle simply to advance their own self-interests. Nevertheless, with the cherry blossom as their symbol—because just as that flower suddenly might be blown away, scattered by the wind while still in majestic full bloom, so too might a warrior lose his life at the peak of his glory— the codes expressed the ideals against which most samurai measured themselves.

During the seventeenth century, samurai watched the epic days of battlefield adventures recede into the distant past. As the *bushi* mutated from fierce warriors into lusterless bureaucrats, living in thriving cities and surrounded by a prosperous urban consumerism, many began to contemplate seriously what it meant to be a samurai in the new age of peace. Neo-Confucianism, with its stern emphasis on obligation and accountability, provided some guidelines to comportment, and the Regulations concerning Warrior Households, issued by the shogunate in 1615, drew attention to the dual nature of the samurai's mission in the new polity. "The study of letters," that injunction began, "and the practice of military arts, including archery and horsemanship, must be cultivated diligently." But exactly how one might embrace the new civic responsibilities while still honoring older cultural idioms sparked a lively discourse that produced the concept of *Bushidō*, the Way of the Warrior.

One of the first depictions of the new ethics appeared in *Gorin no sho* ("The Book of Five Rings") by Miyamoto Musashi. Born in central Japan in 1584, Miyamoto later claimed that he killed for the first time when he was thirteen years old. Just three years later he followed his lord into the Battle of Sekigahara, and like other warriors whose masters died fighting for the losing side, Miyamoto was left a *rōnin* ("masterless samurai"). Wandering Japan, he became a devotee of Zen and a highly accomplished callig-rapher and painter. He also developed a new two-sword style of fencing and, according to his own count, prevailed in more than sixty sword fights during his travels around the country. In 1640, Miyamoto became a fenc-ing instructor for the daimyo of Kumamoto domain in southwestern Japan, and in 1643 he retreated to a mountain cave, where he wrote "The Book of Five Rings."

For all his bravado, Miyamoto opened his tract by denouncing the cult of death and declaring that warriors always must strive for success. "The Way of the Warrior frequently is said to lie in the resolute acceptance of death," Miyamoto began. "However," he continued, "warriors have no mo-nopoly on this virtue: monks, women, and peasants, too, can confront death bravely out of a sense of duty or shame. The true distinction of the samu-rai lies in applying military strategy to overcome other men, thus gaining glory for his lord and himself."[3] That overarching principle stated, Miyamoto then proceeded to explain how warriors could prevail over their opponents. Much of his advice was technical—how to grip the sword, the importance of footwork when parrying and thrusting, and so forth—but he also placed great emphasis on mental preparation. Study "your opponents' traditions," he admonished in one chapter, "observe the personal character of adver-saries, find out people's strengths and weaknesses, maneuver in ways con-trary to opponents' expectations, determine opponents' highs and lows, ascertain the rhythms in between, and make the first move; this is essen-tial." Once you gain the upper hand, he urged, press your advantage; "the main thing is to see that adversaries feel defeated from the bottom of their hearts. As long as opponents still have hope, they will hardly collapse. But if you knock the heart out of them, you do not have to pay attention to them anymore."[4]

Consequently, while "The Book of Five Rings" always circled back to the art of sword fighting, ultimately Miyamoto's message unfolded into a more universal abstraction: The Way of the Warrior is to prevail, and any individual must order his life so that he can accomplish whatever objective he sets for himself. For Miyamoto, that was the heart of *Bushidō*—one did not embrace death but, rather, attempted to achieve conquests and glory in this world, in the present time, as a way of fulfilling one's role in life. That goal in turn required a warrior always to be prepared, to know his enemy and to understand himself, and to be ready to act decisively at the moment of prime opportunity.

Yamaga Sokō had a different perspective about the ethical standards the samurai ought to adopt. Yamaga was born in northern Japan in 1622 and in his youth traveled to Edo to study with the Confucian savant Hayashi Razan. After serving as a scholarly adviser and military instructor to the daimyo of Akō domain, near Hiroshima, Yamaga returned to Edo and opened his own school of Confucian and military studies in 1660. He authored several works concerning Confucian studies, military science, and Japanese history but is best remembered for advancing concepts that helped define the Way of the Warrior.

In his *Bukyō yōroku* ("Essentials of the Warrior's Creed") and *Shidō* ("The Way of the Samurai"), Yamaga struggled with the question of what samurai should do to justify their existence in a world where they no longer had to fight but did not contribute to the economy of production and distribution. As a man of letters Yamaga was drawn to early texts in the Chinese Confucian tradition, such as the "Book of Changes" (*Yi jing*) and the "Spring and Autumn Annals" (*Chun qiu*), which presented a vision of an ideal gentleman-scholar learned enough to serve the Chinese state and so virtuous that his personal conduct raised the level of popular morality. With the Great Peace settling over the country, Yamaga argued in his various writings, Japan's *bushi* should emulate the Confucian sages of the past and devote themselves to moral and political leadership.

In order to discharge that responsibility, Yamaga continued, samurai had to dedicate themselves to the "study of letters," just as the shogunate's Regulations concerning Warrior Households stated, and they were obligated to become proficient in music, poetry, and the other arts, as had the ideal Chinese gentlemen-scholars of the past. In addition, he urged the samurai to cultivate a sense of personal virtue based on the concept of *makoto* ("sincerity"). In Chinese Confucianism, "sincerity" was considered both the cardinal virtue that underpinned all other forms of goodness and the principle that ought to govern relationships between individuals. In the Shinto tradition, *makoto* developed its own cluster of nuances, signifying that which was true, genuine, pure, and honest.

The most noble expression of the warrior's creed, in Yamaga's view, was to shine as a moral exemplar while serving one's lord as a warrior and an official. "The business of the samurai," he wrote in *Shidō*, "consists in reflecting on his own station in life, in discharging loyal service to his master if he has one, in deepening his fidelity in associations with friends, and, with consideration of his own position, in devoting himself to duty above all."[5] Yamaga did not forget that the fulfillment of one's obligations to daimyo and shogun had a martial component. After all, the *bushi* of the early modern era were heirs to a centuries-long legacy of battlefield legends, and the Heavenly Sovereign continued to entrust them with safeguarding the country; thus, they should stay fit, practice military arts, and study tactics and strategy. Nevertheless, Yamaga reminded them, the samurai had entered a new era when their civil responsibilities predominated, and that placed different concerns at the forefront.

First of all, samurai must infuse their service with *makoto*. That is, the samurai-official should never act in his own narrow self-interest. Rather, he must be motivated only by "sincere" and "pure" intentions so that he could govern benevolently, in accordance with moral ideals and public values. Moreover, Yamaga's logic called upon the *bushi* to redefine the object of their loyalties. Previously, warriors swore personal fealty to an individual lord. In the seventeenth century, however, daimyo no longer were merely commanders of bands of armed fighters but, instead, had become governors of domains with the attendant responsibility to rule on behalf of the people who lived within that territory. Accordingly, samurai too had moved into a more impersonalized world. Since he held his rank permanently in the early modern era, a samurai pledged his allegiance to the house of his lord, rather than to the specific individual who happened to be the daimyo at any particular time, and even more abstractly to the domain, whose people he served. Finally, since the head of each samurai family usually held office for generation after generation, it followed that loyalty must be absolute and unconditional.

In 1700, some years after Yamaga had reworked the *bushi* code of ethical behavior, the samurai Yamamoto Tsunetomo expressed a strong, almost uncontrollable desire to commit ritual suicide after his master, Nabeshima Mitsushige, daimyo of Saga domain in Hizen Province, died at the age of seventy-three. Although self-immolation upon the death of one's lord, known as *junshi*, never had been especially common, in the medieval period warriors occasionally chose to die on the battlefield with their lord or to disembowel themselves when their leader fell to the enemy, and some retainers brought the ultimate expression of loyalty into peacetime by committing *junshi* when their daimyo died of natural causes. In the middle of the seventeenth century, self-sacrifice acquired a faddish popularity, and samurai who had received some special favor from their lord increasingly seemed to consider *junshi* the natural way to end their lives. Some of those retainers surely were acting out the traditional imperative of loyalty. "It is the fashion in contemporary society to cut one's belly after the death of the master," one daimyo noted in the 1630s. "They consider such an action a meritorious deed."[6] Others, however, were more calculating, sacrificing themselves in the knowledge that their heirs would be rewarded handsomely. Still others killed themselves out of grief; male-male liaisons between daimyo and younger retainers were a normal, accepted part of the warriors' lifestyle, and the former lovers of a lord often followed him to death with a sad willingness.

As incidents of *junshi* mounted in the middle of the seventeenth century, so too did criticism of the custom. Yamaga Sokō condemned it as an emotional, selfish act that undermined efforts to define a new norm of rational, institutionalized loyalty directed toward the domain and the house of the lord. At the same time, the shogunate and many daimyo governments regretted the unnecessary loss of men of talent, and when twenty-six samurai followed his own father to death, Nabeshima Mitsushige banned the practice in Saga domain in 1661. Three years later the shogunate followed suit, adding a prohibition against *junshi* to the Regulations concerning Warrior Households. Thus, when Mitsushige died, Yamamoto put aside his desire to commit suicide, resigned his commission as a samurai, and retired to a small hermitage several miles north of Saga Castle.

Between 1710 and his death from illness in 1716, Yamamoto recorded his reflections about life and duty in some thirteen hundred anecdotes that he bundled together under the title *Hagakure* ("In the Shadow of Leaves"). Unabashedly, *Hagakure* rejected the efforts of ruling authorities and intellectuals like Yamaga to tame the samurai. Yamamoto had little use for the injunction to cultivate "the study of letters," as stated in the shogunate's Regulations concerning Warrior Households. "Learning is a good thing," he conceded at one point, "but more often it leads to mistakes," and "for the most part, we admire our own opinions and become fond of arguing." To his anti-intellectualism, Yamamoto coupled a disdain for the arts. "A person who is said to be proficient at the arts is like a fool," he proclaimed. "The saying, 'The arts aid the body,' is for samurai of other regions. For samurai of the Nabeshima clan the arts bring ruin to the body. In all cases, the person who practices an art is an artist, not a samurai."[7]

In contrast with the sterility of contemporary society, Yamamoto praised the ancient ideal of personal loyalty. "If one were to say in a word what the condition of being a samurai is," one story began, "its basis lies first in seriously devoting one's body and soul to his master." In affirmation of the deep emotional bonds between lord and retainer, Yamamoto recalled that Mitsushige once had given him warm words of appreciation accompanied by the gift of the daimyo's own futon and nightgown. "Oh," he cried, "if only it were the olden days, I would have cut my belly beside this futon, covered my body with this nightgown, and followed my master."[8]

In addition to its emphasis on absolute fealty, *Hagakure* contained many episodes that glorified death. "The way of the samurai," the book opened, "is found in death." For Yamamoto, the key to being a true samurai was to learn how to die honorably:

One should expect death daily so that, when the time comes, one can die in peace. Calamity, when it occurs, is not so dreadful as was feared. It is foolish to torment oneself beforehand with vain imaginings. Tranquilize your mind every morning, and imagine the moment when you may be torn and mangled by arrows, guns, lances, and swords, swept away by great waves, thrown into a fire, struck down by thunderbolts, shaken by earthquakes, tumble from a precipice, fall victim to disease, or meet an unexpected accident: die every morning in your mind, and then you will not fear death.[9]

Hagakure did not circulate widely beyond the boundaries of remote Saga domain, and Yamamoto's near obsession with death unsettled most of his fellow samurai. Nevertheless, his prescriptions resonated with enough bushi that they survived as part of the code of the warrior class. Samurai first used the word Bushidō in the seventeenth century, when they wrestled with the problem of making sense of their existence in a rapidly changing society. The samurai in the early modern era clung to the traditional notion that courage, fealty, and willingness to confront the terror of death still held meaning, but they added new ideals to the older ethos to construct a contemporary Way of the Warrior: Success was a virtue, and one should study and prepare for the opportunities that eventually came one's way; the purity of one's motives was paramount; and one could honor the obligations inherent in one's status by serving the government of one's domain and contributing to the well-being of its residents.

## Merchant Reflections on Neo-Confucianism

During the early modern period, commoners too had to decide which values they held dear, mold a self-identity, and carve out places of dignity for themselves within society. In the end, townspeople and farmers alike developed ethical canons that gave direction to their lives and drew attention to their contributions to the larger community around them. As was the case with samurai, contemporary experience and precepts drawn from Buddhist and Shinto religious traditions profoundly influenced how merchants, artisans, and farmers thought about themselves. So too did Neo-Confucianism. Commoners learned about that moral philosophy in a variety of settings, and by the middle of the eighteenth century most ordinary Japanese had at least a passing familiarity with its fundamental principles. By that time as well, moralists and scholars from merchant backgrounds were combing through Confucian doctrine, busily looking for clues to shape a code of ethical conduct that would suit the needs of Japan's urban commoners.

From the mid–seventeenth century well-known scholars began to open private academies in the Three Metropoles and the regional castle towns that enrolled as, full-time students, the offspring of affluent townspeople and wealthier rural families from nearby villages. Another kind of school, known as *terakoya* ("temple schools"), catered to children from the local neighborhood or village. Some *terakoya* in fact were run by Buddhist or Shinto priests. Frequently, however, a single teacher or married couple set up a so-called temple school in their home and lived on the fees collected from the students, who attended for perhaps an hour or so a day as best they could.

*Children studying at a* terakoya

The number of private academies and local *terakoya* increased dramatically at the end of the eighteenth and beginning of the nineteenth centuries. Even as early as 1750 in Edo, according to one account, "Tuition has become extremely inexpensive, and school-registration procedures simplified. It amounts to a bargain sale on education, and as a result, even people of low status have enrolled in *terakoya*, to the point that *muhitsu*, 'brushless people' who cannot write, are a rarity."[10] By the 1830s at least three hundred private academies and as many as three thousand *terakoya* were in operation. By some estimations, nearly every adult in Edo and Japan's other major cities could read and write by the end of the early modern era, while other tallies suggest that in 1850 about 40 to 50 percent of all boys and 10 to 15 percent of all girls in Japan received some formal schooling at one kind of school or another. In all, literary rates in Japan at the middle of the nineteenth century probably were higher than for any other country in the world, with the possible exceptions of England and the Netherlands.

The typical curriculum at a private academy introduced entering students to the Confucian classics and provided advanced tutoring to those who stayed on for several years. Teachers in *terakoya* drew on a wider variety of texts, such as the *Shōbai ōrai* ("A Guide to Commerce") and *Hyakushō ōrai* ("A Course Book for Farmers"), to impart to their students the language and math skills they needed to understand official pronouncements, prepare invoices, keep accurate accounts, read agricultural manuals, maintain tax records, and so forth. Weaving its way through all instruction at most *terakoya*, however, was an emphasis on duty, obligation, filial piety, and community responsibility—values that resided at the heart of Confucian ethical norms.

While commoner children digested the basics of Neo-Confucianism, they sometimes encountered texts that denigrated them as being far less worthy than the privileged samurai elite. In 1719 Nishikawa Joken, a Confucian moralist and astronomer who lectured to the shogun, published his widely read *Chōnin bukuro* ("The Merchant's Satchel"). The title suggested that Nishikawa had a bagful of advice to offer townspeople, and he admonished them, "*Chōnin* are at the bottom of the four classes. Being at the bottom, they should not exceed their superiors. They should not be envious that others have prestige and majesty. They should keep to simplicity and plainness and be content with their status. If they keep to their kind, like oxen enjoy being with other oxen, they will achieve lifelong enjoyment."[11]

As merchants became wealthier and better educated, some began to rethink certain Neo-Confucian precepts and eventually challenged the intellectual bias that likened them to beasts of burden and located them on the lowest rung of the hierarchy of social-occupational estates. Scholars at the Kaitokudō, a private academy in Osaka, played a particularly important role in reformulating older ideas. Founded in 1724 by five Osaka businessmen, the school admitted some samurai but essentially served well-to-do merchant youths of the city who wished to receive enough education in the Chinese classics to enable them to move about easily in the upper reaches of Osaka society, where some familiarity with the accumulated wisdom of the past and the ability to versify in Chinese were considered useful assets and a convenient social lubricant. Moreover, there was some hopeful expectation that time spent at the Kaitokudō might yield practical lessons, guides to ethical and moral conduct that would enable them to succeed in business.

At the beginning, the founders of the Kaitokudō based the curriculum on standard Neo-Confucian orthodoxy. While the students diligently studied their texts, however, a succession of brilliant teachers, chiefly from merchant backgrounds, reworked Confucianism so that it accorded virtue to merchants as well as to samurai. The crowning achievement in the long course of reinterpretation came in the first decade of the nineteenth century, when Yamagata Bantō completed his *Yume no shiro* ("In Place of Dreams"). Born Hasegawa Yūkyū in Harima Province, Yamagata came to Osaka at the age of thirteen to serve as a clerk in the house of his uncle, the prominent merchant Masuya Kyūbei. The young Bantō studied at the Kaitokudō merchant academy for a time, before succeeding his uncle as household head. A remarkably shrewd financier, Yamagata steered the Masuya businesses to new levels of prosperity. Near the end of his long life of achievement, he wrote his famous compendium of knowledge, *Yume no shiro*, in which he set forth his ideas about how to understand the past and bring succor to the ordinary people of his world.

Yamagata built his epistemology around the proposition that all objective knowledge and human values proceed from the universality of science. In particular, he was drawn to astronomy, which he learned from Chinese translations of Western books, and he began "In Place of Dreams" with the observation "The universe exists prior to all else. The earth follows, and after that come human beings and moral norms. Compassion, righteousness, propriety, filial piety and loyalty are all parts of the way men order society and do not exist prior to the universe."[12] From there Yamagata went on to discuss geography, people and creatures in prehistoric times, the dawn of Japan's recorded history, the formation of a political order within that history, and the current state of Japan's political economy. Finally, in an overall conclusion to *Yume no shiro*, he reaffirmed the rationality of all phenomena and dismissed superstitions, by which he meant religion, speculation about the divine origins of the Japanese people, and tales of the occult, all of which he labeled "dreams."

Two fundamental themes wound their way through Yamagata's monumental treatise. The first was the assertion that knowledge was objective and verifiable, thus accessible to all human beings who took the trouble to study the world around them. The second was his insistence that "the way men order society," indeed all human experience, was grounded in the nature of the universe. That judgment in turn led to a series of axioms. If Copernicus taught that the earth was not the center of the universe, reasoned Yamagata, then similarly no geographical location was the center of that globe. Thus, it followed that human culture, which was inseparable from the physical and cosmic order, did not privilege members of one status group over their countrymen.

Finally, Yamagata coupled his conviction that no social estate held sway over others to the notion that any individual acquired knowledge by examining things located within his immediate environment. From that proposition, the businessperson-scholar concluded that each status group had a certain relative expertise that enabled it to contribute to the welfare of society in general. Thus, samurai "knew" politics, and that made them capable of governing. Peasants comprehended the complexities of agricultural production, and they could feed the country. Merchants understood the economy; only they grasped the nature of money, the reality of the marketplace, and the universal law of supply and demand. Consequently, the knowledge that merchants possessed had virtue; indeed, their wisdom about economic matters was just as crucial to improving the lives of fellow Japanese, in Yamagata's formulation, as was the political sagacity attributed to the nation's samurai leaders.

Ishida Baigan also made significant contributions to the construction of a coherent set of ethics that attributed virtue to townspeople. The son of a farmer in Tanba Province, Ishida in his youth moved to Kyoto, where he apprenticed himself to a merchant family. Later he began to study Neo-Confucianism, and in 1729, shortly after the founding of the Kaitokudō, the forty-five-year-old Ishida began to lecture publicly on a moral philosophy commonly known as Shingaku (Learning from the Heart). His ideas won immediate favor with merchants and artisans in Kyoto and then spread rapidly across the country; at one point in the early nineteenth century his disciples held forth at Shingaku lecture halls in dozens of cities and taught at more than one hundred Shingaku schools that enrolled a total of more than thirty thousand students.

A belief in the potential moral perfectibility of human beings constituted the core tenet of Shingaku. Ishida and his followers accepted the Confucian assertion that an individual needed to comprehend *ri*, the elusive "principle" that embodied natural law and social norms, if he wished to become a moral person and help society function properly. But while most Japanese Neo-Confucian scholars saw *ri* as an immutable cluster of dicta fixed at the beginning of time, Ishida held that moral virtue was internal, alive within each person's heart. Thus, he had little use for objective scholarship of the sort prized by Yamagata. Rather, the founder of Shingaku averred, the most effective way to fathom the nature of the cosmos was to comprehend one's spiritual nature. Moreover, Ishida argued, active engagement with the world, in particular devotion to one's work, constituted the most direct path to understanding one's inner self and releasing the goodness that guided an individual along the path of proper behavior.

Later Ishida's disciples drew more fully upon Japan's religious traditions for insights into how to unlock the knowledge of one's "true heart." From Zen Buddhism they borrowed the technique of meditation as a means of looking deeply into one's spiritual center. Another way, they suggested, was through the practice of austerities associated with certain Buddhist and Shinto ascetics. Shingaku leaders did not mean that the ordinary person ought to leave human society and go stand under a waterfall, but they did advocate observing frugality in one's daily life. Indeed, Ishida himself, or so he said, ate sparingly and did his own cooking for years in order to transcend the demands of daily life and nurture a serenity that allowed him to penetrate his inner heart.

Merchants and artisans flocked to Shingaku lecture halls because Learning from the Heart vigorously reconfirmed their inherent worth as merchants. For Ishida, as for Yamagata Bantō, heaven endowed each status group with unique and honorable responsibilities that advanced the well-being of everyone. "If there were no trade," Ishida wrote in the merchants' defense, "the buyer would have nothing to buy and the seller nothing to sell. If it were thus, the merchants would have no livelihood and would become farmers and artisans. If the merchants all became farmers and artisans, there would be no one to circulate wealth and all the people would suffer."[13]

Moreover, the status groups had complementary functions. "The samurai, peasant, artisan, and tradesman all together bring happiness to the country," Ishida declared. "If any of the four statuses ceases to exist there shall be no hope of seeing the country prosper." Specifically, he continued, "To rule over the whole country is the duty incumbent upon the shogun and daimyo." Assisting the rulers, he went on, "is the role of the four classes.

The samurai is the retainer who has the rank from old. The farmer is the retainer of the countryside. The merchant and artisan are retainers of the town. All of those estates are bound in duty to assist the lords. By their acts of buying and selling," he repeated for good measure, "tradespeople help society." In addition, since all status groups contributed to the country's general welfare, they were entitled to parallel rewards. Each samurai family received an annual stipend in exchange for serving its lord; similarly, Ishida reasoned, "The payment of the price is the stipend of the artisan. Giving the harvest to the farmer is like the stipend of the samurai. The profit of the merchant too is equivalent to the stipend."

## Parallel Ways: Merchant Codes and Peasant Sages

As scholars like Yamagata and Ishida reinterpreted Neo-Confucianism in a manner that bestowed virtue upon merchants, they helped elaborate a code of practical ethics known as Chōnindō. Rendered as the "Way of the Townsperson," the term generally applied to artisan as well as merchant families, but because prominent merchants took the lead in formulating Chōnindō, it frequently is translated as the "Way of the Merchant." Ishida himself defined the core values of Chōnindō when he wrote that knowing one's heart would produce a particular syndrome of behavior that was anchored in respect for the integrity of the Five Relationships and unqualified devotion to one's obligations and occupation. "First," he admonished, "behave prudently, serve your lord with righteousness and serve your parents with love, treat your friends with faithfulness, love men at large and have pity on poor people. Though you have merit, do not be proud. Maintain economy with respect to such things as clothing, furniture, and the like and do not seek elegance. Do not neglect the family business, and as for wealth, measure what comes in and be aware of what goes out."[14]

Household codes spelled out those ideals with greater specificity. Increasingly throughout the eighteenth century, many of Japan's well-to-do merchants, sometimes with advice and tutoring from Shingaku and Kaitokudō scholars, wrote narratives reflecting upon their lives and setting forth their secrets for success. Some compilations were brief, while Mitsui Takafusa's formulation, completed in the late 1720s, ran to several dozen pages. Written primarily to provide subsequent generations with practical advice about how to manage a business, the codes contained a wealth of accumulated professional acumen and frequently commented on a businessman's familial obligations and social responsibilities. Taken as a whole, the household codes presented a far-reaching discourse about merchant propriety and enucleated the ethical prescriptions of *Chōnindō*.

According to most household codes, hard work was an absolute prerequisite for success. "Rise early," counseled Shimai Sōshitsu, a prominent sake brewer in Hakata (modern-day Fukuoka) and one of the first to set down precepts for his successors, "and in matters of business and money-making work harder than anyone else."[15] Itō Chōjirō, whose family dry goods shop in Nagoya became the modern-day Matsuzakaya chain of department stores, countered by exhorting his workers to rise "earlier than others in the world." Moreover, he warned, "Sloth is never good," and so "even if kneading cow or horse dung be your family business, do it enthusiastically." Less imaginatively, the laconic Mitsui Takafusa told his family and employees, "One who keeps working will never be poor."[16]

Worldly success, moreover, depended on winning the goodwill of customers. One way to do that, according to the household code of one famous brewer, was to "make absolutely certain that you are honest regarding everything." In a similar vein, another merchant wrote, "Charge the standard market price for an article, and do not add an unfair profit to the price." Courtesy was also essential. "Deal politely with all who enter or leave the shop," wrote one merchant patriarch, "whether they be young or old, male or female." Added the household head of the Shirokiya drapers, a Mitsui rival in Edo, "It is natural to be polite to those who make large purchases," but, he continued, the surest way to keep your clientele was to "be polite to all customers, regardless of the size of their purchases."

Business leaders stressed that the purpose of working hard and adhering to ethical business practices was not to increase one's own personal profit but, rather, to benefit the *ie*. As conceived in the early modern period, the *ie* was a multigenerational household that included one's ancestors, the current living generation, and successors yet unborn. Members of the household strove for success in order to safeguard what they had inherited from past generations and to enhance it for the betterment of those family members still to come. "Everyone," Itō Chōjirō wrote, "has inherited a family name from his parents, and everyone will have descendants. A house—one cannot ignore the fact—continues forever." Thus, he warned, "Should you become poor because of your own misjudgment, your ancestors will have labored in vain; your descendants, your wife, and you yourself will suffer, and people will mock you." That sentiment was repeated in the code of the Kōnoike family, one of Osaka's leading merchant houses: "Not to keep intact the estate inherited from one's ancestors is to behave unfilially toward those ancestors and to jeopardize the prosperity of one's descendants as well."

Many household heads knew from personal experience that money was hard to earn but easy to spend. Consequently, they urged all family members and shop employees to be prudent and frugal in order to preserve the business and estate for generations to come. "Be always careful and cautious in your work or your business will fail," the Mitsui code warned. The parsimonious Shimai Sōshitsu admonished his heirs against going on flower-viewing excursions or becoming devotees of the tea ceremony, and he instructed them to find some good use for leftover scraps of paper, rope, and plaster. Mitsui Takafusa made his point by writing about the example of some Edo merchants who "wore elegant clothes" when they "went sightseeing or on pilgrimages to temples. Their wives and daughters," he noted ominously, "rode around in palanquins, and even their ladies' maids and menservants were the height of fashion, making a splendid show. Before they knew where they were, their houses and storehouses were broken up and sold off, the masters were without servants, their ladies went on foot, and their belongings were auctioned off." In the end, Mitsui noted with a certain smugness, they were reduced to "making a living by turning out miserable paper lanterns."

Finally, most household codes endorsed the legitimacy of shogunal rule. The Mitsui family code included the injunction "All laws and ordinances issued by the government should be faithfully followed by all, from the master to the lowest of employees." Just as forthrightly, another famous merchant wrote, "Obey exactly all regulations established by the authorities." The corollary that followed from acknowledging the validity of Tokugawa authority was that merchants should accept their place within the system of rule by status. That was another reason Mitsui Takafusa stuffed his compilation with stories recounting the sad consequences that befell merchants who tried to emulate samurai or otherwise lived in a manner inappropriate to their status. Such aphorisms were grounded in the fear of reality: At the beginning of the eighteenth century authorities denounced Osaka's most prominent merchant, Yodoya Tatsugorō, for extravagant living, banished him from the city, and confiscated the family fortune.

Yet, if merchants observed the basic principles of Chōnindō—if they were honest and diligent, preserved their inheritance from the past and added to it for the sake of their descendants, and lived in harmony with government and their fellow Japanese—they would bring honor to themselves and justify their place in the social order. "Samurai study the martial arts and work in the government," read one household code, echoing the thoughts of Shingaku moralizers. "Farmers till their lands and pay their taxes. Artisans labor at their family industries and pass on to their children the family traditions. Merchants have trading as their duty. Each of the four classes has it own

Way and that Way is its true Way." Or, as Mitsui Takafusa put it, "To make one's own house prosperous, to nurture one's family properly, to have a long life and to pass away with a clear conscience is to be a living Buddha."

As suggested in warrior memoirs and merchant household codes, farmers too shouldered a set of obligations and responsibilities that summed up to a Way. For Miyamoto Musashi, that Way was rather simple: to "spend the years attending to the changes in the four seasons."[17] Ishida Baigan, who characterized the farmer as "the retainer of the countryside," sketched out a more romantic image of a dutiful Japanese peasant: "He goes out to the fields in the morning before dawn and returns home in the evening by starlight. In spring he ploughs, in summer he weeds, and in the fall he harvests, never forgetting to produce as much as possible from the fields, even to a single grain of rice."[18] In that manner, according to Ishida, like the samurai and townsperson, the farmer "exhausted" himself for the sake of others and thus was virtuous and worthy of respect.

Ninomiya Sontoku exemplified those ideals. Born to a prosperous farm family in Sagami Province, Ninomiya was orphaned in 1802 after floods destroyed his family's fields. Just fifteen years old at the time, he cared for his two younger brothers and by dint of untiring effort restored the family fortunes. Impressed by the young man's deeds, the local daimyo asked him to organize a program to improve productivity in the domain's villages following a ruinous famine. Ninomiya's accomplishments there led to appointments in other domains in northern Japan, where he supervised the construction of irrigation facilities, roads, and housing after cold and stormy weather had brought devastating famines into that region in the 1830s. Eventually he earned a national reputation, and in 1842 the shogunate employed him to plan several village revitalization projects.

By the end of his long career Ninomiya had filled thirty-six volumes with practical and moral lessons for success. His prescription for getting ahead in life, he wrote, contained "one spoon of Shinto and a half-spoon each of Neo-Confucianism and Buddhism."[19] Even so, his creed rested on the simple, and familiar proposition, "The root of virtue is found in labor, and the loss of virtue comes from idleness." The Shinto deities provided humankind with a potentially abundant natural environment, Ninomiya believed, and labor was the worthiest human activity because it brought to fruition the promise of that bounty. No matter how fertile nature was, he proclaimed, "paddies and ploughlands are useless fields without peasants. It is the effort of human beings that brings about crops."

Ninomiya also emphasized the need to plan. If nature was kind, it also could be cruel, and famines and poor harvests were part of earth's inexorable

rhythms. Necessarily, people had to prepare if they were to prosper in ordinary years and overcome the calamities that surely would occur from time
to time. Thus, Ninomiya advocated a kind of scientific agriculture. Farmers, he claimed, needed to calculate how much irrigation water and fertilizer would maximize yields. Further, they should study seed types to learn
which performed best under different conditions and accurately record crop
yields over ten-year periods to verify their hypotheses. Families also ought
to keep household accounts so that they did not overspend their incomes,
and he showed them how to budget their time by making diagrams of the
daily tasks they had to perform in each season.

Japan's Peasant Sage, as Ninomiya became known, also urged villagers
to band together to help themselves. In his conception, the welfare of the
individual and the community moved in unison. If some suffered, ultimately
all would be negatively affected, while if each household progressed, the
benefits would accrue to everyone in the community. In response to the
teaching of Ninomiya and his disciples, some villagers in the 1840s began
to organize communal associations that helped sick or disabled neighbors,
convened monthly meetings to discuss agricultural practices, repaired roads
and irrigation canals in the off-season, and sometimes even established a
pool of funds that they lent at little or no interest to fellow villagers who
had fallen on difficult times.

Predictably, the targeted beneficiary of hard work, planning, and communal cooperation was the multigenerational household. "The wealth of our
parents depends on the achievements of their forebearers," Ninomiya intoned, and just as "our wealth depends on the accumulated goodness of our
parents," so too does "the wealth of our children and grandchildren depend
on our labor and effort." Beyond that, Ninomiya believed that each person
had to "repay virtue." That is, each individual, each family, had received the
blessings of the gods and nature, and all were morally obligated to return
that benison by working hard, being frugal and honest, and helping others.
The phrase Ninomiya used to convey the idea of repaying virtue was *hōtoku*,
and that idea become so deeply embedded in the rural consciousness that
village mutual aid associations typically called themselves Hōtoku Societies.

## Genders and Realities

Most samurai ideologues and authors of household codes wrote principally
for a male audience, the fathers and sons whom, they assumed, headed the
*ie*, served in bureaucratic office, ran shops, and tilled the family farms. Symp-

tomatic of the indifference for the women in their lives was the comment in *Hagakure* that daughters "are a blemish to the family name and a shame to parents. The eldest daughter is special, but it is better to disregard the others." Despite the dismissive attitude of Yamamoto's language, other writers paid close attention to the role they expected women to play in the home and family. As might be expected, moralists tended to view life through gendered glasses and relegated women to the private sphere of the household. That position, however, did not always square with reality.

One of the most widely circulated tracts concerning the moral training of women was *Onna daigaku* ("Greater Learning for Women"), published in 1716. The authorship of the text is unknown; scholars frequently attribute it to Kaibara Ekken, a prominent Confucian scholar who wrote influential treatises on health and medicine and dozens of moral essays aimed at specific groups in society, although some speculation also has centered on Kaibara's wife. Whatever its pedigree, the nineteen chapters that make up the "Greater Learning for Women" encapsulated a mode of thought that subordinated women to men and cooped them up within the home, where the woman's world consisted chiefly of housework, reproduction, and child rearing.

*Onna daigaku* repeatedly hammered home the point that women shouldered a lifetime of endless responsibility. When she was young, the primer intoned, "The chief duty of a girl living in the parental house is to practice filial piety towards her mother and father." Once married, the new wife "must look to her husband as her lord, and must serve him with all worship and reverence. When the husband issues his instructions, the wife must never disobey them."[20] One section of the text elevated the male even higher, stating: "A woman should look on her husband as if he were Heaven itself." The arrival of children multiplied the number of wifely and motherly duties: to "fix meals, wash and fold clothing, sweep the floor," and never "weary of weaving, sewing, and spinning." At the same time, the model wife learned that she was to "honor her father-in-law and mother-in-law beyond her own parents" and "perform any task they may require of her." While carrying out those obligations, the text continued, women must "avoid extravagance" and "never give way to luxury." Wives and daughters-in-law were to cultivate proper demeanor as well, behaving in a manner that was "courteous, humble, and conciliatory, never peevish and intractable, never rude and arrogant."

Although hopeful that girls would grow up to be virtuous women, the author of *Onna daigaku* sadly predicted that "seven or eight of every ten" will be "disobedient, inclined to anger, slanderous, envious, or stupid." Those congenital "blemishes in her nature" made women "inferior to men" and could disrupt a marriage. Consequently, "Greater Learning for Women" empowered men with the moral license to divorce their wives for any of seven reasons: if they were disobedient to their fathers- or mothers-in-law; failed to bear children; acted lewdly; were jealous persons; contracted leprosy or "any like foul disease"; disturbed the harmony of the households; or were addicted to stealing.

A number of theorists disseminated similar ideas. First at his own school in Edo and later as a lecturer to the samurai of Yonezawa and Owari domains, the noted savant Hosoi Heishū repeated the message he delivered to a crowd of commoners in Nagoya in 1783: "When she is young, a girl must obey her parents. When she is married, she must obey her husband. When she grows old, she must obey her sons."[21] Shingaku scholars also ignored status and class distinctions and regarded all women—samurai, peasant, and townswoman alike—as a single mass constituency sorely in need of moral guidance. In seminars and lectures specially tailored for female audiences, Shingaku teachers castigated women as having "constricted hearts, making them easily prone to stinginess and vain pride."[22] Thus, each woman had to search her original heart to discover the "six Confucian virtues for women"—obedience, purity, goodwill, frugality, modesty, and diligence—all of which she could realize best in the context of marriage.

Such sermonizing was not without effect. Generations of merchant and peasant daughters became dutiful wives, and when daimyo began to anoint certain women as role models of proper behavior, they usually could choose from a number of moral exemplars, such as the young woman from Kanazawa who postponed her marriage to care for her ailing widowed father, saved the family's life savings one night by pushing a burglar into the outhouse latrine, and then, just before her father's death, gratefully married the man he had selected to be his adopted son and successor as household head. When Yamakawa Kikue, a prominent socialist and feminist in the early twentieth century, compiled the memoirs of her ancestral family, samurai in the service of the lord of Mito domain, she wrote of women in the 1840s and 1850s "whose unremarked lives were confined to the domestic sphere," where they "had to cope with hardships, silently doing their best to keep their households going and raise their children."[23] Not all women, of course, found such family-centered life objectionable. The novelist Suzuki Bokushi wrote, "My beloved mother had great integrity and quarreled with no one. Indeed, she never got angry but devoted herself to my father, and they worked together like two wheels of a cart."[24]

More often than the rhetoric of Confucian theorists suggested, however, the lived experiences of merchant and peasant women diverged significantly from the idealized codes of behavior presented in scholarly tomes. For one thing, women were not as housebound as *Onna daigaku* and other texts made them out to be. Urban women helped their husbands tend shop and keep accounts. Moreover, in Osaka and some other cities in western Japan, a woman could even serve as the head of a household, although it was considered preferable to have a male do so. In the countryside, men and women worked together closely. Wives and daughters tended vegetable gardens, picked and dried fruits, and even toiled alongside men in rice paddies; in the springtime they helped transplant seedlings from the nursery beds to the main fields, and in the fall they hackled the rice, pulling the harvested stalks through a toothed device that plucked out the eatable grains.

Many women of nonsamurai status worked outside the house, especially before marriage. Encyclopedias published at the end of the seventeenth century and beginning of the eighteenth listed more than one hundred kinds of work performed by women. Occupations ranged from seamstress to field hand, shellfish diver, laundress, carpenter, strolling book lender, teahouse waitress, bathhouse attendant, prostitute, nun, masseuse, wet nurse, cook, and peddler of incense sticks, straw sandals, flowering plants, and tofu. The greatest number of women found work as maids and household servants in well-to-do samurai and merchant households and as spinners, weavers, and dyers in the emerging textile trades. It is impossible to know what proportion of women worked, but some calculations suggest that one-quarter to one-half of the females in various neighborhoods in Kyoto and Osaka at the beginning of the eighteenth century were servants.

Moreover, women were not always the "gentle, obedient, chaste, and quiet" persons that the author of *Onna daigaku* wanted them to be. "The most ill-tempered people," went one proverb, "are packhorse hostlers, ship's captains, and wet nurses."[25] Servants who did not get along with their employers were notorious for complaining in public about mistreatment, spreading rumors about what went on inside the masters' family circles, pilfering household goods, or simply absconding with valuable belongings. In extreme cases, servants violently attacked their employers, and arson by maidservants appeared frequently in the police records of most towns. In the 1660s one maid in Kanazawa worked for six samurai families in succession, embezzled money from the household accounts of each, and set their houses on fire in order to conceal her crimes before authorities finally caught her (and boiled her in a cauldron for her misconduct).

Women trapped in unhappy marriages struggled to find ways to survive. Some stayed with their mates but made life miserable by constantly scolding them and calling them disrespectful names, while others built a wall of silence and withheld sexual favors. Samurai woman had few other strategies available to them since divorce was essentially a male prerogative. A warrior wishing to shed his spouse simply had to write her a letter to that effect. Such a document usually followed a short, standardized form, and "three and a half lines" became the popular term for an instrument of divorce. The woman then received the dowry she had brought to the union and returned to her natal household. Any children remained with the husband, and Confucian orthodoxy frowned on remarriage for divorcées, just as it did for widows. "A woman, once married and then divorced," the author of *Onna daigaku* lamented, "has wandered from the 'way' and is covered with great shame."

Women from peasant and merchant backgrounds had more choices. Some escaped troubled marriages by fleeing to an *enkiridera*, or divorce temple. After a woman had served in such a convent-temple for two full years, government officials declared her free from all marital entanglements. Statistics do not record how many distraught wives sought refuge in such *enkiridera*, but the most famous, the Temple Tōkeiji in Kamakura, took in about two thousand women between the 1720s and the end of the early modern era. More commonly, a merchant or peasant woman simply walked out of her husband's home, often taking the children with her. In some villages around Osaka in the early nineteenth century, for instance, it appears that at least 15 percent of all marriages ended that way. Moreover, divorced commoner women often wed again, and remarriage did not carry the same stigma as in samurai society. After the author Suzuki Bokushi sent his young wife, Mine, back to her parents, apparently because she was not particularly skilled at managing the household, she wed a second and then a third time. Suzuki continued to show interest in Mine's welfare; he spoke glowingly on her behalf at her second marriage and even thought of remarrying her after her third try at marital bliss ended in failure.

Some women preferred the single life. Yamakawa Kikue recalled that when her great-great-grandfather Ichinoshin could not father a child by his wife, he arranged to have the young daughter of a prosperous merchant family from the nearby port of Minato come to the castle town of Mito to be his "second wife." Minato was a thriving, flamboyant entrepôt in the coastal trade between Edo and Ezochi, and people dubbed it Little Edo. Just as soon as she bore Ichinoshin a son (Yamakawa's great-grandfather), the young woman ran away and returned to her family in Minato. There she "resumed the lighthearted lifestyle of a townsman daughter," for whom "the pleasures of learning the polite accomplishments or going to the theater were taken for granted."[26] When envoys from Mito sought to bring her back, she simply replied, "Thank you very much, but I've had enough of living in a samurai house. I left with the intent of never returning, so please just let me be. Whatever consideration my son might show me, I'd rather stay as I am now here in Minato."

The life choices of the young woman from Minato serve as a strong reminder that all Ways were descriptions of ideal conduct, not depictions of reality. Just as some samurai in the past had been fierce warriors, and others timid cowards, so too in the early modern period some turned out to be enlightened, skilled administrators, while sitting next to them were men scarcely competent enough to rubber-stamp documents before shuffling them from one pile to the next. Similarly, some farmers turned soil to ashes even as green-thumbed neighbors prospered and gathered enough capital to start side businesses that made them even more well-off. Some shopkeepers established rock-solid enterprises, but enough businesses failed that prosperous merchants saw the need to compile household codes that provided their successors with guides to success. If their sons and daughters did not obey their prescriptions, mothers and fathers of all status groups could take some solace in knowing that while most youth tried to follow the proper Way, a great many others simply chose to tread their own paths.

## Self and Community

In addition to being the basic unit of social organization, the *ie* linked individual commoners to the local political community and to higher forms of state authority. Within Japan's villages and cities, the most influential families were property holders—that is, households that enjoyed the prerogative, sanctioned by daimyo in their domains and by the shogunate on the territories it administered, to possess, rent out, sell, and bequeath specific fields or parcels of business and residential land. In exchange for recognition of their property rights, such families paid a variety of taxes and assumed many important functions designed to promote social control and to ensure that life in their urban neighborhoods and farming communities remained orderly and peaceful.

Within each urban neighborhood, government officials divided propertied families into clusters typically referred to as *goningumi* ("five-person groups"). In actuality, the organizations consisted of households, each represented by its head, and the number of families included in any one *goningumi* varied from fewer than five to a dozen or more. Whatever their number, the members of the five-household groups performed several important functions on behalf of higher authorities. First and foremost, governing officials instructed the household representatives to make absolutely certain that all family members and employees, as well as each renter and tenant, understood and obeyed officialdom's laws, injunctions, and decrees. To add steel to its bluster, officials held every household within a group accountable for transgressions committed by any member of the cluster.

The five-household groups discharged a number of other important civil functions on the neighborhood level. Responsibilities varied from place to place, but generally the member families helped one another through hard times, took care of snow removal, kept local streets and bridges in good repair, maintained fire-fighting equipment and stood ready to extinguish blazes that threatened their corner of the city, and settled minor spats that ruffled neighborhood tranquillity. In addition, the propertied families in each residential quarter contributed funds to establish and staff guardhouses at intersections with adjoining neighborhoods. Each evening the guards closed the gates that separated neighborhoods in order to inhibit burglars and other mischief-makers from moving about and then patrolled the streets, keeping an eye out for strangers and, in the winter months, banging together a pair of wooden clappers to remind residents to exercise care with their cooking and heating fires.

To act as a liaison with the household groups, daimyo and shogunal governments appointed some prestigious merchants to serve as city and neighborhood elders under the supervision of samurai-level city magistrates. The city elders (three in Edo) transmitted laws and proclamations from government agencies to subordinate neighborhood elders (approximately 260 in Edo), each of whom oversaw dozens of *goningumi* scattered across several residential quarters. Working in unison, the city and neighborhood elders also ascertained that people paid their taxes in a timely manner, identified residents who exhibited exceptional filial piety, verified transfers of title to property, and safeguarded census records and other important documents. Furthermore, they helped resolve nonviolent disputes among townspeople, such as disagreements about property lines, complaints about the quality of goods someone purchased, and defaults on loans.

Similar collective arrangements prevailed in rural areas. Since there were more than twenty thousand villages in the early modern era, practices differed considerably from region to region, but as in the cities, the trend was toward a system that held households jointly responsible for honoring their obligations to higher authority while delegating to them a considerable degree of self-management over local affairs. Thus, propertied villagers formed themselves into *goningumi* whose household heads were to ensure that family members and all tenants who rented fields from them obeyed the lord's laws. Together, the groups looked after neighbors who became ill, maintained roads and bridges, helped one another thatch roofs, and rebuilt the dikes around rice paddies after storms and earthquakes.

The village headman, who sometimes served on a hereditary basis and sometimes was chosen by consensus of property-holding families, functioned as the linchpin between the household groups and samurai officials of the daimyo or shogunate. With the assistance of a small number of village elders, the headman kept the village census, helped mediate disagreements, and so forth. Unlike his counterpart, the city elder, the village head played an important role in apportioning taxes. In urban centers, each property holder generally paid an annual tax that was calculated according to the street frontage occupied by his shop. In rural areas, however, the shogunate and daimyo simply assigned each village an aggregate tax bill and left it to the headman, working with the advice of the elders and perhaps other prominent household heads, to divide it among propertied families according to whatever method seemed to work best in a particular village.

Governments in the early modern era also spun a web of authority over outcast communities while simultaneously permitting them to manage their own internal affairs. "Lowly persons of five kinds," to use an ill-defined phrase from legal documents compiled shortly after the Taika Reforms, had experienced discrimination since the beginning of Japan's recorded history. In general, such individuals usually were associated with pollution. Fundamental Shinto beliefs equated goodness and godliness with purity and cleanliness, and they further held that impurities could cling to things and persons, making them evil or sinful. Unavoidably, some amount of blood and other unsanitary matter attached itself to every individual in the course of daily life, and therefore, everyone periodically had to perform acts of ritual purification to clean away the corruption. But a person could become seriously contaminated by habitually killing animals or committing some hideous misdeed that ripped at the fabric of the community, such as engaging in incest or bestiality. Such persons, custom decreed, had to be cast out from the rest of society, condemned to wander from place to place, surviving as best they could by begging or by earning a few coins as itinerant singers, dancers, mimes, and acrobats.

During the early modern era, discrimination became a matter of state policy. In general, the shogunate and regional daimyo categorized outcasts as *eta* ("pollution in abundance") or as *hinin* ("nonhumans"). *Eta* (or *kawata*, "leather workers," as they preferred to call themselves) were families that knew how to strip hides from animals and then tan and fashion them into saddles, harnesses, bindings for armor, and other equipment used by samurai. Daimyo had struck up relationships with *eta* during the great age of warfare, and as the lords settled into their domains at the end of the sixteenth and beginning of the seventeenth centuries, they began to sequester the leather workers in specific communities, often located on agricultural land along the outskirts of the castle town. There the *eta* farmed and enjoyed a government-sanctioned monopoly on animal processing and the production of leather goods, which they sold to the lord and his warriors. Like other rural communities, most *eta* settlements had their own headman and exercised a considerable degree of self-management over their own internal affairs. But they suffered several restrictions that divided them from fellow Japanese. During the seventeenth century the shogunate and regional daimyo governments made the status hereditary and prohibited *eta*, whose total population numbered perhaps a quarter of a million in the 1850s, from leaving the communities of their birth.

Early modern rulers tended to refer to Japan's several other outcast groups as *hinin*. A heterogeneous collection of beggars, street performers, and other economically marginal "nonhumans," *hinin* included both persons who inherited the label by birth and those who forfeited commoner status because they had committed some crime or because they had fallen into poverty and could not be counted on to be responsible members of their communities. In either case, officials prohibited *hinin* from engaging in commerce, artisanal enterprises, or even manual labor. Rather, the government assigned to them such unsavory tasks as cleaning execution grounds and caring for victims of contagious diseases. *Hinin* also were free to beg and to amuse people with street performances, for which they could accept offerings from the crowds they attracted.

The shogunate and daimyo governments followed the conventional pattern of permitting the "nonhumans" considerable autonomy over their internal affairs while holding them accountable to higher authority. In Edo, for instance, *hinin* rented lodgings by the day or month at any of several hundred outcast rooming houses scattered around the city. An "outcast headman" presided over each lodge, and for a fee (customarily a portion of a day's take) he assigned "begging space" to outcasts who stayed with him. In turn, each headman was responsible for making certain that his renters obeyed the law and through regional headmen reported to Danzaemon, the name taken by successive heads of a family the shogunate entrusted with overseeing the activities of all outcasts in Edo.

The structure of accountability that linked the individual and *ie* with the shogunate and domain governments had a dual nature. Looked at from above, the integrated chain of command, which originated with policy-making officials and ran through city magistrates and rural intendants to the city elders and village headmen and finally to the *goningumi* and propertied households, greatly augmented the ability of the national hegemon and regional lords to exercise their will on the village, neighborhood, and even family and individual level more decisively and forcefully than any previous regime in Japanese history. When the organization of power is viewed from below, however, it is equally clear that ordinary people played an important role in supervising their own communities. Moreover, as townspeople and villagers took up their responsibilities during the seventeenth century, they came to feel that a social covenant bound together all members of society, a notion that intertwined itself tightly around the proposition, advanced by Neo-Confucian scholars, that government must be benevolent and conduct itself in a manner that enriched the lives of all. The conception of society as an organic whole that functioned best when all parts worked in unison reinforced the twin ideas that ordinary people had a rightful participatory role to play in government and that they could hold officials to high standards of performance.

As ordinary people accepted new assumptions about the nature and purpose of government, they did not hesitate to voice their disapproval when governing authorities failed to carry out their obligations satisfactorily. During the seventeenth and eighteenth centuries, commoners complained frequently about official malfeasance, the imposition of new or higher taxes, and sudden upward spikes in the price of rice, the nation's basic staple. Standard procedures called for someone with a grievance to submit a written statement to his village headman or neighborhood and city elders. Those local officials verified the facts and, if they found sufficient grounds to support the complaint, forwarded the case to samurai officials, such as the rural intendants or city magistrates, who would conduct a further examination if necessary before issuing a binding decision.

Political authorities were able to resolve most objections routinely, but when they did not, otherwise peaceful men and women held mass demonstrations. On nearly three thousand occasions during the early modern era, people in various regions of the country put down their tools and ledgers to join some sort of protest movement. In 1686, for example, two thousand peasants in Matsumoto domain in central Japan converged on the castle town and remonstrated for five days after the lord introduced new methods of taxation. Similarly, when the retail price of rice reached unacceptable heights in the summer of 1736, neighborhood elders in Osaka showered city officials with a blizzard of petitions on behalf of unhappy merchant households. Finally, on the sixth day of the Sixth Month, nearly twelve hundred neighborhood elders and representatives from every residential quarter within the city converged on the offices of the magistrates to voice their objections to government policies that contributed to excessively high rice prices. Officials in Osaka got off easy; when the shogunate and local daimyo governments did not initiate relief programs promptly after poor harvests drove up rice prices in 1783, people rioted in some thirty major cities, including Kōfu, Sunpu, Nara, Hiroshima, Nagasaki, and Edo, where protesters smashed the shops of nearly a thousand rice dealers.

Even in the passion of violent demonstrations, people did not challenge the legitimacy of the shogunate and daimyo regimes. Rather, protesters criticized government officials for falling down on the job and harangued them to fulfill their responsibilities as defined by the social covenant. As was typical of their genre, protest documents submitted to city magistrates in Osaka in 1736 opened with an expression of deference ("With due reverence, we submit the following letter"), pointed out that ill-conceived policies had brought hardship to ordinary men and women ("at this time, the people of the city are suffering through a period of profound distress and poverty"), suggested specific measures to cure problems, and closed by reaffirming the ability of the lord and officials to right wrong ("We shall be extremely grateful to receive the blessing of your generous benevolence").[27]

During the seventeenth century the shoguns and daimyo put forth a concerted effort to persuade people that they did not govern from horseback but, rather, were entitled to rule because they presided over a just and humane social order. In time, townspeople and villagers came to accept that justification of authority, and they crafted Ways and accepted a place in the political order that acknowledged the legitimacy of the Tokugawa hegemony. Concurrently, however, the emerging social covenant and the Neo-Confucian emphasis on benevolence set perimeters around the exercise of political power. When Uesugi Harunori, daimyo of Yonezawa, retired in 1785, he left his heir a short epistle on statecraft. "The domain," Uesugi began, "is inherited from one's ancestors and passed on to one's descendants: it should not be administered selfishly. The people," he continued, "belong to the domain: they should not be administered selfishly. The lord," he concluded, "exists for the sake of the domain and the people: the domain and the people do not exist for the sake of the lord."[28]

## The Shared Sense of Being Japanese

Ruler and ruled, rich and poor, male and female, young and old, merchant and farmer: The Japanese differentiated themselves from one another in numerous ways as they lived out their separate fates in their individual domains and self-contained villages and urban neighborhoods during the early modern period. So obvious was the partitioning of society that one prominent interpreter of his country's history later noted, "The millions of Japanese at that time were closed up inside millions of individual boxes. They were separated from one another by walls with little room to move around. The four-level class structure of warriors, farmers, artisans, and tradesmen froze human relations along prescribed lines."[29]

Although distinctions based on occupation, gender, wealth, and social class shaped lives in significant ways, important commonalties also bound people together, creating a shared cultural identity and an enduring sense of Japaneseness. A common political geography contributed to an emerging cultural synthesis during the early modern era. The imposition of the Tokugawa hegemony produced boundaries that identified who was Japanese and who was not. No matter how much they might differ from one another, Japanese lived on shogunal lands and in daimyo domains, and that fact distinguished them clearly from neighbors in China and Korea, who were subject to other rulers; from the peoples of the Ryūkyū Islands, who shared some cultural traits with the Japanese but preferred to claim an independent political standing; and from the indigenes of Ezochi, who seemed to acknowledge no supreme temporal authority.

The people who lived under the shogun and daimyo also shared a common religion and used a mutually intelligible language. Thousands of local shrines dedicated to a myriad deities dotted the countryside, but everywhere Japanese drew religious sustenance from a distinctive blend of Buddhist and Shinto beliefs, and they considered themselves living in the Land of the Gods. Moreover, people bounded over linguistic hurdles. "It is very difficult for me to understand the Edo dialect," complained one samurai from Tosa domain when he attended a scholarly talk shortly after he arrived in the city as part of his lord's alternate attendance retinue.[30] Nevertheless, he adjusted quickly to his new language environment, partly with the help of published guides to the peculiarities of Edo speech, and within a month he "could understand well" other lectures he went to hear. Likewise, even though they spoke a variety of local dialects, when people from different regions met, as "Shanks' Mare" and other travel novels make clear, they could "open their hearts to each other and talk until they are tired," and if romance happened to fill the air, "the man from Edo" found few barriers to making "acquaintance with the Satsuma sweet potato."

Food and material culture reinforced the notion of cultural unity. Local specialties flavored menus everywhere, but increasingly all Japanese ate, or hoped to enjoy on a regular basis, meals consisting of steamed rice accom-

*The Kawasaki Mannen'ya, a popular Edo eatery in the early nineteenth century*

panied by certain soups, particular side dishes, and a piece of fish. That was especially so after cookbooks began to appear in the middle of the seventeenth century. Published in 1643, *Ryōri monogatari* ("Tales of Cooking"), the first guide to the daily foods of commoners, gave instructions on preparing some twenty different soups, a variety of vinegared dishes, broiled fish, and a great deal else, while *Edo ryōri-shū* ("A Collection of Edo Cooking"), printed in six volumes in 1674, introduced that city's cuisine to the country. In like fashion, people increasingly dressed in clothing of similar design and styling, and while they might delight in local architectural flourishes, they lived in post-and-beam houses that featured shoji partitions, tatami flooring, and tokonoma alcoves.

Travel nurtured the concept of Japaneseness. Increasingly during the early modern era, daimyo processions and government officials shared the Tōkaidō Highway and other roads with itinerant merchants, troupes of wandering players, solitary poets, bands of religious pilgrims bound for Ise Shrine and famous Buddhist temples in western Japan, well-to-do women off to enjoy the waters at famous hot springs, Edoites headed for celebrated natural sites in remote corners of the country, and rustics on their way to experience for themselves the pleasures of the Three Metropoles. By the early eighteenth century travel had become a national mania, and each year as the warmth of spring spread over the land, millions of Japanese hit the road. The development of a highly integrated transportation system stimulated recreational travel, as did the growth of post towns filled with inns, restaurants, teahouses, and guide services. Indeed, by the early nineteenth century, one could even prepay for lodging and meals with regional networks of inns that then provided the traveler with a combination identification–credit card valid at any member hostelry.

The emergence of a culture of travel had important consequences for the production of a national identity. As men and women sailed past the misty islands of the Inland Sea, gazed upon snow-capped Mount Fuji, appreciated the gnarled pine trees along the sandbar at Amanohashidate, strolled the beach where Kumagai Naozane sadly took the head of Atsumori, crossed battlefields where daimyo clashed when Japan was A Country at War, crowded into the sanctuary at Ise to pay their respects to the Sun Goddess Amaterasu, or climbed the thousand steps to Konpira Shrine on Shikoku, they created an inventory of places and scenes that gave concrete

*Travelers stay at an inn at Akasaka, a post town on the Tōkaidō Highway, circa 1830s*

expression to the traditions, legends, and historical experiences that infused the national consciousness.

Travelers spread the national culture in other ways. During the eighteenth century touring players wandered from town to town and village to village, performing abbreviated renditions of Kabuki and the puppet dramas that were first popular with audiences in the Three Metropoles. In time farmers who visited Edo or Osaka brought home librettos and costumes, which they used to stage amateur productions in their villages. Similarly, travelers marveled at local products: pottery from Kanazawa, Uji tea, *senbei* rice crackers from Amanohashidate, religious charms from Ise. Happy to snap up such objects as souvenirs, travelers carried them home and, in doing so, added them to the catalog of Japan's shared material culture. Finally, Yaji, Kita, and other travelers talked and talked and talked some more as they shared meals and rooms at inns, and in so doing, they discovered a commonality of values and lived experiences that transcended barriers of region, class, and gender.

Eventually one did not have to leave home to experience the pleasures and educational broadening of travel. In the 1830s the well-known print designer Hokusai completed his celebrated "Thirty-six Views of Mount Fuji," and Hiroshige, perhaps the most famous of all wood-block artists, quickly sold out his "Fifty-three Stations of the Tōkaidō Highway." Hiroshige's prints were so popular with armchair travelers that he designed twenty additional series of Tōkaidō scenes, more than a thousand depictions of famous places in Edo, and several sets of famous sites in Osaka, Kyoto, and Ōmi. The production of wood blocks was only one part of a flourishing print culture. By the beginning of the nineteenth century, there were hundreds of bookstores and rental libraries in Edo and Osaka and substantial numbers in provincial towns. To meet burgeoning demand, publishers churned out thousands of new titles every year, ranging from serious works of scholarship and religious tracts to anthologies of verse, commentaries on theatrical productions, light fiction, historical novels, and travel guides. Relatively inexpensive, the books and wood-block prints reached a wide audience of samurai, townspeople, and villagers alike. In total, the print culture put together a universe of scenes and themes, heroes and villains, ethical dilemmas and spiritual resolutions, values and beliefs that were particular to the Japanese of the early modern era and the property of large groups of people at every level of society.

Written accounts of encounters with foreigners presented another way to gauge Japaneseness. As might be anticipated, narratives frequently highlighted the exotic features of the newly arrived aliens. "In the reign of Go-Nara [1526–1557], a Southern Barbarian trading vessel came to our shores," began one anonymous chapbook written in 1639. "From this ship emerged an unnamable creature, somewhat similar in shape to a human being, but

*A Korean embassy arrives in Edo*

looking rather like a long-nosed goblin. Upon close investigation, it was discovered that this was a being called a 'Padre.' The length of the nose was the first thing which attracted attention: it was like a conch shell attached by suction to his face. His head was small; on his hands and feet he had long claws; his teeth were longer than the teeth of a horse. What he said could not be understood at all: his voice was like the screech of an owl. One and all rushed out to see him, crowding all the roads."[31]

Koreans and Ryūkyūans also excited the popular imagination. The arrival of each foreign embassy was a major event that attracted hordes of curious sightseers. "A million onlookers swarmed like ants on the riverbanks," wrote one Korean when he passed through Osaka in 1682, "pontoon bridges spanned the water, and countless thousands lined up on them to watch us."[32] Japanese artists who documented the coming and going of ambassadorial entourages called attention to the physical characteristics and clothing styles that made the visitors different from Japanese. Thus, Koreans typically were bearded, plume-hatted, frill-collared, trousered, and booted, in contrast with their Japanese escorts, who sported shaven pates, wore formal pleated skirts or simple kimonolike robes, and walked around barefooted or shod in zori.

Images of Ainu celebrated differences in a way that implicitly underscored the more refined, advanced nature of life in Japan. Descriptions of Eastern Barbarians often began with comments about the men's flowing locks and beards and the facial tattooing common among Ainu women and then moved on to quizzical observations about a diet that included much game and fish but little rice. Those stock accounts created the impression that the Ainu lived not only outside the Japanese social order but even beyond the pale of civilization. "They know not the moral way," wrote one Japanese in 1710, "so fathers and children marry indiscriminately. They do not have the five kinds of grain and eat the flesh of birds and fish. They gallop around the hills and dive into the sea and are just like some kind of beast."[33]

Ordinary Japanese did not merely ingest the images contained in the new print culture; rather, men and women from diverse backgrounds also joined together to popularize new literary forms that gave voice to a sense of shared Japaneseness. Matsuo Bashō, the son of a minor samurai living in central Japan, legitimated *haikai*, a forerunner to modern-day haiku. After moving to Edo in 1672, Bashō published several poetic diaries filled with verse that recorded his thoughts and emotions as he traveled through famous provincial areas. The most popular such work was his *Oku no hosomichi*

*Bashō on the Narrow Road to the Deep North*

("The Narrow Road to the Deep North"), completed in 1689 after a five-month journey that took Bashō north to Sendai, west across the mountains to the Sea of Japan, south to Kanazawa, and then back across the mountains to Lake Biwa before he returned to Edo.

Included in *Oku no hosomichi* are some of Bashō's best-remembered *haikai*.[34] When he came across a ruined castle in the far north, he wrote:

> A thicket of summer grass
> Is all that remains
> Of the dreams and ambitions
> Of ancient warriors.

A few days later darkness overtook Bashō as he approached a mountain pass, and he sought shelter in a small hut. When a storm brewed up and kept him there for three days, he complained:

> Bitten by fleas and lice,
> I slept in a bed,
> A horse urinating all the time
> Close to my pillow.

Bashō fared better a few days later when a well-to-do merchant with a "truly poetic turn of mind" put him up:

> I feel quite at home.
> As if it were mine,
> Sleeping lazily
> In this house of fresh air.

Reinvigorated, Bashō was in a more pensive frame of mind when he visited a tranquil temple located deep in a mountain recess. "The silence was profound," he confided to his diary, and "feeling my heart begin to open," he wrote:

> In the utter silence
> Of a temple,
> A cicada's voice alone
> Penetrates the rocks.

The emotions expressed in *haikai* resonated strongly with all Japanese, and by the time Bashō died in 1694, people everywhere were madly engaged in turning out the short, seventeen-syllable poems that combined clever wordplay and an appreciation for classical literature with earthy humor and a melancholy fondness for nature's beauty. So popular did the genre become that more than 700 *haikai* teachers resided in Kyoto at the end of the seventeenth century, and one Osaka literary figure noted, "Formerly *haikai* verses were the pastimes of those who had retired from active life in the world, or the wardens of Shinto shrines, or of the samurai class. Recently, however, *haikai* have grown so popular in our society that every last apprentice and scullery maid tries his or her hand at them."[35] As that observer suggested, persons from all social estates were joining *haikai* clubs, and when *Kawachi no kuni meisho kagami* ("A Mirror of Famous Places in Kawachi Province") was published in 1679, it included contributions from nearly 180 men and women who lived in eighty-nine different towns and villages in the Osaka area.

When Westerners first stepped ashore on the Japanese islands in the latter half of the sixteenth century, they found A Country at War. Yet even in the midst of bitter fighting and extreme political fragmentation, they also discovered the promise of renewal and growth. Wherever the traders and missionaries from the West traveled, they encountered a "cultured" people and eulogized a "beautiful and pleasing countryside" bursting forth with an abundance of "rice, vegetables, and fruits." In the early seventeenth century, as part of a lengthy and strenuous effort to promote domestic stability, the Tokugawa shoguns expelled from their country all Europeans except the Dutch. As a consequence, most Westerners at best had only a rudimentary understanding of the great changes that transformed life in Japan during the next two centuries.

As the *Taihei*, the Great Peace, descended over Japan during the seventeenth century, men and women from all levels of society lent their talents to bringing to fruition the promise of prosperity and ordered well-being sensed by the European visitors. For much of the early modern era, Japan was capably administered, agriculture flourished, cities grew, and a thriving commercial sector carried improved standards of living to households in every corner of the land. At the same time Neo-Confucian scholars, samurai thinkers, merchant philosophers, and peasant sages devised codes of social behavior and ethical conduct that profoundly changed how Japanese conceived of themselves, their professions, their families, and their communities. New ideas redefined political relationships by calling on rulers to be benevolent as well as lordly and by entitling ordinary people to expect just governance in exchange for obedience. Concurrently, new cultural activities, from popular theater to *haikai* poetry and recreational travel, created a sense of cultural cohesion, of being Japanese, that cut across natural divisions of region, gender, status, and class.

In the early decades of the nineteenth century, Westerners returned to Japanese waters. The military commanders, traders, and government officials who plunged into Asia at that time were very different from the Europeans who first arrived in Japan in the sixteenth century. Beneficiaries of scientific and industrial revolutions, Westerners in the nineteenth century were boldly self-assured, supremely confident that their self-evident military and economic prowess sprang from political systems and religious values that were far superior to anything found in Asia. Possessed of very little knowledge about Japan, and even less respect, the Americans, British, and Russians who stormed into the Pacific were harshly critical of the "backward" ways of Asians, and many expressed an aggressive determination to bring the supposed blessings of their civilization to a torpid, barbarous part of the globe.

The bellicose attitude of the Euro-Americans dismayed many Japanese, who came to fear that awesome powers such as the United States, Britain, and Russia did have the ability to overwhelm their island country—militarily, economically, and culturally. To complicate matters, the Westerners showed up on Japan's doorstep just as the shogunate and daimyo were struggling to find solutions to a series of domestic problems caused by decades of accumulated economic and social change. By the middle of the nineteenth century, the combination of threats from without and troubles from within produced a crisis of confidence. Despairing for their very survival, many Japanese concluded that it was necessary to jettison the past and embrace Western-style political, economic, and social practices. That quest for modernity seemed to promise a world where everything would be new and different, but as their country moved into its future, Japanese discovered that the legacy of the early modern era—from the creation of a centralized polity and professional bureaucracy to the development of a highly commercialized economy and the articulation of cultural values—would continue to shape their lives in profound ways.

PART II

# Japan in Revolutionary Times

# Chronology

## PART II   JAPAN IN REVOLUTIONARY TIMES

**1774**

☐ Sugita Genpaku and his colleagues complete their *Kaitai shinsho* ("A New Text on Human Anatomy")

**1792**

☐ *Ninth Month, third day* The Russian naval lieutenant Adam Laxman sails into Nemuro Bay

**1798**

☐ Motoori Norinaga completes his *Kojiki den* ("A Commentary on the *Kojiki*")

**1804**

☐ *Ninth Month, sixth day* The managing director of the Russian American Company sails into Nagasaki

**1808**

☐ *Eighth Month, fifteenth–sixteenth days* The captain of the English frigate *Phaeton* threatens Nagasaki

**1814**

☐ *Eleventh Month, eleventh day* Kurozumi Munetada experiences a "divine union" with the Sun Goddess and begins his ministry

**1823**

☐ *Fifth Month* More than one thousand villages around Osaka protest in favor of open trade for ginned cotton and vegetable oils

**1825**

☐ *Second Month, eighteenth day* The shogunate issues the Order for the Repelling of Foreign Ships

☐ Aizawa Seishisai completes his *Shinron* (New Theses)

**1833**

☐ Beginning of the Tenpō famine, which triggers violent demonstrations in 1836 and lasts into 1838

**1837**

☐ *Second Month, nineteenth day* Ōshio Heihachirō initiates a rebellion in Osaka

**1838**

☐ *Tenth Month, twenty-sixth day* Nakayama Miki experiences a divine revelation and begins a ministry that will result in the founding of the Tenri sect

**1841**

☐ *Fifth Month, fifteenth day* The shogunate launches its Tenpō reform program

**1842**

☐ *Seventh Month, twentieth-fourth day* China and Britain settle the Opium War, begun in 1839, by signing a peace treaty that establishes the treaty port system

**114** ☐

## 1844

⬚ *Ninth Month, twenty-second day* The shogunate receives a letter from King William II of Holland warning of trouble from without

## 1853

⬚ *Sixth Month, third day (July 8)* Commodore Matthew C. Perry arrives at the entrance to Edo Bay and six days later goes ashore to deliver President Fillmore's letter to shogunal authorities

## 1854

⬚ *First Month, seventeenth day (February 14)* Perry returns to Japan
⬚ *Third Month, third day (March 31)* Perry and shogunal representatives sign the Treaty of Peace and Amity between the United States and Japan

## 1858

⬚ *Sixth Month, nineteenth day (July 29)* Harris and Ii Naosuke sign the United States-Japan Treaty of Amity and Commerce
⬚ *Seventh Month, fifth day* Ii begins his purge by placing Tokugawa Nariaki and several other daimyo under house arrest

## 1859

⬚ *Tenth Month, twenty-seventh day* The shogunate executes Yoshida Shōin

## 1860

⬚ *Second Month, twenty-sixth day* First shogunal embassy departs for the United States
⬚ *Third Month, third day* Shishi assassinate Ii Naosuke

## 1862

⬚ *Second Month, eleventh day* Princess Kazu is wed to Iemochi at Edo Castle
⬚ *Eighth Month, twenty-first day* Samurai from Satsuma domain murder Richardson
⬚ *Intercalary Eighth Month, twenty-second day* The shogunate relaxes the alternate attendance requirements

## 1863

⬚ *Second Month, twenty-fifth day* Shishi desecrate statues of the Ashikaga shoguns in Kyoto
⬚ *Third Month, fourth day* Shogun Iemochi's procession enters Kyoto
⬚ *Fifth Month* Activists in Chōshū fire shore batteries at Western ships
⬚ *Seventh Month, second–fourth days* British ships bombard Kagoshima
⬚ *Eighth Month, eighteenth day* Shishi loyalists are driven from Kyoto after plotting a coup

## 1864

⬚ *Seventh Month, eleventh day* Shishi assassinate Sakuma Shōzan
⬚ *Seventh Month, nineteenth day* Proshogunal forces rout *shishi* putschists in the Battle of Hamaguri Gate
⬚ *Seventh Month, twenty-third day* Chōshū is branded as an enemy of the court
⬚ *Eighth Month, fifth–sixth days* Western ships pound shore batteries in Chōshū domain and send landing parties ashore
⬚ *Eleventh Month* The shogunate organizes a punitive expedition against Chōshū

## 1866

⬚ *First Month, twenty-first day* Satsuma and Chōshū conclude a secret alliance
⬚ *Fifth Month, twenty-ninth day* Edo's commoners riot over food prices
⬚ *Sixth Month, seventh day* The shogunate launches its second punitive expedition against Chōshū
⬚ *Sixth Month* Large-scale "world renewal" riots erupt across the country

## 1867

⬚ *First Month, ninth day* Crown Prince Mutsuhito, teenage son of Kōmei, ascends the throne
⬚ *Seventh Month* The *ee ja nai ka* phenomenon begins near Nagoya

**1868**

🔲 *January 3 (Twelfth Month, ninth day, of the previous lunar year)* Rebels seize the imperial palace and the emperor proclaims the restoration of imperial rule

🔲 *Third Month, fourteenth day* The new government issues the Charter Oath

🔲 *Third Month, twenty-eighth day* The new government orders the separation of Shinto and Buddhism

🔲 *Fourth Month* Fukuzawa Yukichi reorganizes his former school for Dutch Learning as Keiō Academy

🔲 *Fourth Month, second day* Edo falls to loyalist armies

🔲 *Intercalary Fourth Month, twenty-first day* The government promulgates the Constitution of 1868

🔲 *Seventh Month, seventeenth day* Edo is renamed Tokyo

🔲 *Ninth Month, eighth day* Meiji is declared as the new reign name

**1869**

🔲 *Third Month, twenty-eighth day* Tokyo becomes Japan's capital

🔲 *Fifth Month, eighteenth day* Final pro-Tokugawa forces surrender, ending the Boshin Civil War

🔲 *Sixth Month, seventeenth day* The emperor announces that he will accept the return of the documents of enfeoffment from all daimyo and appoints diamyo as "imperial governors"

🔲 *Sixth Month, seventeenth day* The government abolishes the traditional status groups and reclassifies the population as nobility, ex-samurai, and commoners

🔲 *Seventh Month, eighth day* The government founds the Hokkaidō Colonization Office

**1870**

🔲 *January 24 (Twelfth Month, twenty-fifth day of the previous lunar year)* Telegraph service is opened between Tokyo and Yokohama

🔲 *Intercalary Tenth Month, twentieth day* Ministry of Public Works is established

🔲 Fukuzawa Yukichi completes his *Seiyō jijō* ("Conditions in the West")

**1871**

🔲 *Third Month, first day* Postal service begins between Tokyo and Osaka

🔲 *Fifth Month, tenth day* The New Currency Regulation establishes the yen as the national currency

🔲 *Seventh Month, fourteenth day* The government abolishes daimyo domains and creates prefectures

🔲 *Seventh Month, eighteenth day* The government establishes the Ministry of Education

🔲 *Eighth Month, twenty-eighth day* The government issues the Emancipation Proclamation reclassifying outcasts as ordinary citizens

🔲 *Eleventh Month, twelfth day* The Iwakura Mission departs for the United States

🔲 Nakamura Masanao publishes his translation of Samuel Smiles's *Self Help*

**1872**

🔲 *Second Month, twenty-sixth day* Fire rages through the Ginza district and the government commissions a British engineer-architect to construct a neighborhood of Western style brick buildings

🔲 *Eighth Month, third day* The government issues the Fundamental Code of Education, divides the country into new school districts, and mandates four years of compulsory education for all children

🔲 *Ninth Month, thirteenth day* A grand opening ceremony is held to christen the railroad line from Shinbashi Station in Tokyo to Yokohama

🔲 *Tenth Month, fourth day* The Tomioka model filature begins production

🔲 *Eleventh Month, fifteenth day* The National Bank Ordinance is promulgated

🔖 Japan adopts the Gregorian calendar, with the third day of the Twelfth Month becoming January 1, 1873

## 1873
🔖 *January 10* The Conscription Ordinance is promulgated
🔖 *July 28* The government issues the Land Tax Reform Law
🔖 *August 1* The government charters the First National Bank
🔖 *September 13* The Iwakura Mission returns to Japan
🔖 *October 24–25* Emperor Meiji announces his opposition to proposals to invade Korea; Saigō Takamori and other advocates of war resign from government
🔖 *November 10* The Home Ministry is established

## 1874
🔖 *January* Itagaki Taisuke founds the Public Party of Patriots and issues the Tosa Memorial, demanding the immediate establishment of a national assembly
🔖 *February 1* Etō Shinpei launches the Saga Rebellion
🔖 *February* The Meirokusha is founded
🔖 *April 10* Itagaki and his followers establish the Self-Help Society

## 1875
🔖 *February 11* Kido and Ōkubo convene the Osaka Conference to discuss representative government
🔖 *February 22* Members of Itagaki Taisuke's Self-Help Society organize the Society of Patriots
🔖 *April 14* An imperial rescript announces the establishment of a Chamber of Elders and promises to implement constitutional government "in gradual stages"
🔖 *June 28* The government issues the Press Ordinance of 1875
🔖 *November 29* Niijima Jō opens the gates to his new school, Dōshisha

## 1876
🔖 *March 28* Samurai are deprived of the right to wear swords
🔖 *March 31* Mitsui Bank is chartered as Japan's first private commercial bank
🔖 *July 29* Mitsui Trading Company is established
🔖 *August 5* The government announces its intention to replace the ex-samurai's hereditary stipends with bonds
🔖 Fukuzawa Yukichi completes his *Gakumon no susume* ("An Encouragement of Learning")

## 1877
🔖 *January 4* The government announces a reduction in the land tax, effective July 1
🔖 *February* Satsuma Rebellion begins
🔖 *March* Furukawa Ichibei acquires the Ashio Copper Mine
🔖 *April 12* Tokyo University is established
🔖 *August 18* The First National Industrial Exposition opens in Tokyo
🔖 *September 24* Saigō Takamori dies

## 1878
🔖 *May 14* Ōkubo Toshimichi is assassinated

## 1880
🔖 *March 17* The Society of Patriots reorganizes itself as the League for Establishing a National Assembly
🔖 *April* The government issues the Public Assembly Ordinance

## 1881
🔖 *April 7* The government establishes the Ministry of Agriculture and Commerce
🔖 *October 1–2* Itagaki reorganizes the League for Establishing a National Assembly into the Liberal Party
🔖 *October 11* Government leaders suspend the planned sale of the assets of the Hokkaidō Colonization Office and expel Ōkuma from office

☐ *October 12* An imperial rescript announces that a national assembly will open within ten years

☐ *October 21* Matsukata Masayoshi becomes finance minister and implements deflationary policies

☐ *November 11* Private investors found the Nippon Railway Company

**1882**

☐ *January 4* The emperor issues the Imperial Rescript to Soldiers and Sailors

☐ *March 14* Itō departs for Europe to consult with constitutional experts; Ōkuma announces his intention to establish the Constitutional Reform Party

☐ *March 18* Fukuchi Gen'ichirō and other leading journalists form the Constitutional Imperial Rule Party

☐ *May 3* Shibusawa Eiichi founds the Osaka Spinning Mill

☐ *November 28* More than a thousand protesters march on a police station at the height of the Fukushima Incident

**1884**

☐ *July 7* The government promulgates the Peerage Act

☐ *September 23–24* Police suppress the insurgency at Mount Kiba

☐ *October 29* The Liberal Party dissolves itself

☐ *October 31–November 10* Farmers sack the homes of moneylenders and storm government offices in the Chichibu Incident

**1885**

☐ *July Jogaku zasshi* ("The Magazine of Women's Learning") begins publication

☐ *September 29* Mitsubishi absorbs rival shipping firms and establishes the NYK

☐ *December 22* The Dajōkan is abolished and a cabinet system inaugurated

**1887**

☐ *December 26* The government issues the Peace Preservation Law, and two days later the Tokyo chief of police exiles more than five hundred suspected political activists from the capital

**1888**

☐ *April 30* The Privy Council is established with Itō as its first president

**1889**

☐ *February 11* Emperor promulgates the Constitution of the Empire of Japan

☐ *July 1* The Tōkaidō trunk line providing rail service from Tokyo to Kōbe is completed

**1890**

☐ *October 30* The emperor issues the Imperial Rescript on Education

☐ *December 26* Telephone service begins in Tokyo and Yokohama

☐ By this year the Ashio Copper Mine has become the largest mining and refining complex in Asia, and its effluents are poisoning the Watarase River Valley

**1896**

☐ *June 12–16* Women at the Amamiya filature in Kōfu launch Japan's first industrial strike

**1897**

☐ *May* The government orders pollution control devices installed at the Ashio Copper Mine

**1898**

☐ *July 16* The Meiji Civil Code becomes law

**1899**

☐ *August* Kikuchi Yūhō begins the serial publication of *Ono ga tsumi* ("My Sin")

**1903**

☐ *April 13* The Ministry of Education stipulates that all elementary schools must adopt texts compiled and distributed by the ministry

# CHAPTER 4

# The Meiji Restoration

I i Naosuke, the shogunate's chief policy maker, emerged from his home at midmorning on the third day of the Third Month 1860, and climbed aboard a palanquin for the short trip to his office inside Edo Castle. As his entourage neared the Field of Cherry Trees Gate, a main entry into the citadel, a nondescript band of young samurai, seventeen of them from Mito domain and one from Satsuma, emerged out of the swirling snow. The innocent-looking men approached the palanquin deferentially, then suddenly pulled their swords and swarmed over Ii's escort. Surprise on its side, the gang fought its way to the palanquin; having pried open the door, the terrorists shot and hacked at Ii before pulling him out and slashing off his head.

The assassins' outrage sprang from their conviction that Ii and his immediate predecessors within the shogunate had mishandled a series of domestic crises and a growing foreign threat. *Naiyū gaikan* ("troubles from within and without") was an ancient East Asian phrase, invoked at chaotic times when the course of a nation's history seemed to be cascading toward a major watershed. Samurai impoverishment and declining martial spirit; arrogant merchants who lived "beyond their status and financial means"; famine and dearth; peasant uprisings and urban riots; ideological ferment and mystical religions; failed reform: Troubles from within seemed to be sprouting up everywhere during the first half of the nineteenth century. Troubles from without arrived full force in 1853, when Commodore Matthew C. Perry sailed into Edo Bay and demanded that Japan open itself to full intercourse with the Western world. Believing that trade might benefit his country, and convinced that Japan was not strong enough to reject Perry's ultimatum, Ii broke with established tradition in 1858 and signed treaties establishing diplomatic and commercial relations with the United States and several European nations.

To the young samurai from Mito and Satsuma, Ii was a coward and traitor for having submitted so meekly to outside pressure, and the appearance of "foreign barbarians" on Japanese soil seemed to portend the demise of traditional Japanese culture. Ii's ruthless suppression of his critics—he had placed under house arrest their own mentor, the former lord of Mito domain—fueled their bitterness and triggered their decision to carry out the assassination. As they perhaps anticipated, nearly all the men involved in the attack on Ii met their own deaths, either critically wounded during the skirmish or captured and executed later. Their action, however, marked a significant turning point in Japanese history. In the years following Ii's assassination, other young samurai, "men of high purpose," as they styled themselves, erupted in equally dramatic acts of violence against the despised foreigners and the shogunal officials who tolerated the barbarians' presence. As discord raged across Japan, the shogunate became less confident of itself and less able to assert its prerogatives; in a snowballing manner, its opponents multiplied, and so did their dissatisfactions, until ultimately they decided to topple a regime that had ruled for nearly two and a half centuries.

## Economic Woes, Social Dissidence

In the early nineteenth century many samurai families in Kanazawa, the relatively prosperous castle town headquarters of the Maeda lords of Kaga domain, ripped the shrubbery from their gardens in order to plant plums, apples, and apricots for sale in the city's markets. Other warrior families in the city began to supplement their incomes by setting up home workshops and producing such items as straw sandals, umbrellas, decorative hair ribbons, oil lamps, and the festive items used in the New Year's celebration: clay dolls, papier-mâché tigers, and self-righting toys. Kanazawa's martial families turned to those commercial pursuits because they believed their standard of living was declining. The economic distress experienced by Kanazawa's samurai estate was not unusual; in most castle towns across Japan, an increasing number of samurai households, 70 percent and more in some domains, took up similar by-employments or worked part-time in merchant and artisan shops. With increasing frequency, many once-proud warriors pawned their swords and armor, sent daughters away to work as household servants, or even resorted to infanticide in order to fend off a slide into poverty.

In some measure, the samurai's sense of growing impoverishment was psychological. The daimyo and the shogun fixed the stipends paid to their retainers in the early seventeenth century and rarely increased them thereafter. Since the stipends usually were denominated in rice, the income that the samurai received when they marketed their stipend rice probably rose slightly in the seventeenth and eighteenth centuries as the price of that grain increased. But such gains, if contemporary accounts are accurate, were not sufficient to permit the ordinary samurai family to keep up with its more well-to-do merchant and artisan neighbors, whose incomes generally were growing at a more rapid pace. Moreover, the commercial revolution of the Tokugawa period made available a variety of wonderful new consumer goods. The most desirable of them, however, were priced beyond the pocketbooks of many samurai, reinforcing the notion that warrior families could no longer enjoy a lifestyle appropriate to their elite status. Many warriors took out their frustrations by execrating wealthy merchants and farmers. "Among the households of urban commoners," wrote one high-ranking samurai in Kanazawa, "are many who no longer observe the status regulations, spend too much money, and have a poor sense of social responsibility." Those "audacious" merchants, he continued, purchased splendid clothing, "coveted the houses of families of higher social standing," and indulged in "expensive banquets at weddings, beyond their status and financial means."[1]

To compound their jealousy and grievances, the real incomes of warrior families actually shrank at times in the early nineteenth century as the shogun and daimyo occasionally cut samurai stipends. In Kanazawa the Maeda daimyo reduced stipends by 10 percent in the 1820s and by a staggering 50 percent in the 1830s. Daimyo in other domains required similar financial sacrifices from their retainers because like the Maeda, they were struggling to escape from a morass of growing budget deficits. By the opening decades of the nineteenth century, most daimyo were spending three-quarters or more of their revenues on meeting the obligations of the alternate attendance system. At the same time, they faced escalating costs for social obligations, such as weddings and funerals, as well as unrelenting demands from the shogunate for funds to maintain roads and bridges and to rebuild its cities after periodic fires. Such expenditures threw most domain budgets into the red, and with few options available to them, many daimyo slashed their retainers' stipends.

Many samurai did not take kindly to such treatment. In Kanazawa, one official rued that "in recent years the policy of cutting stipends has caused hardships for the retainers, especially those of low rank. Many do not behave appropriately and refuse to observe domain laws."[2] A leading official in Chōshū domain voiced a similar lament: "For years now, the samurai have suffered poverty and their minds are preoccupied with making a living. 'Buy this, sell that,' 'pawn this to pay for that' have become all of their lives. Inevitably, even those dedicated to their duties debase themselves and engage in unsavory conduct. They live from day to day, eating only rice gruel morning and night. Their life dissipated, their spirit and their manners have grown shameful and mean. They have become accomplished liars and cheats."[3]

The rigidity of the political system exacerbated the discontent of lower samurai. Everyone paid lip service to the principle that merit ought to constitute the most important factor in deciding who would be appointed to office. In practice, however, a family's social rank within the warrior hierarchy chiefly determined which position, if any, a samurai might be eligible to hold. As a consequence, by the nineteenth century higher-ranking samurai were staffing most offices of significance, and in many domains elite families monopolized key posts for several successive generations. The gap between ideal and praxis galled ambitious young men from poorer families. Those sons of lower samurai often sat next to their social betters in domain schools, and they realized that high birth easily could make one as proud as a peacock and just as often as muddy-headed as a mule. Some lower samurai reacted by disparaging their superiors as weak-minded and incompetent, unable, in the pet phrase of the day, even to referee an archery contest. Others, desperate to win appointment to office so that they might work out solutions to the economic problems confronting their families, began to call for the appointment of "men of talent," a code word for politically aware young men of intellectual promise, regardless of their social standing within the warrior estate.

Many rural and urban commoners also became less deferential to authority in the early nineteenth century, especially after a series of substandard harvests caused the devastating Tenpō Famine, which lasted from 1833 until 1838 and took the name of the contemporary calendrical era. It is impossible to verify the number of persons who succumbed to starvation and disease in those years, but officials in northern Japan reported 100,000 dead in 1836 alone, and the specter of deserted villages, unburied corpses, and even cannibalism haunted every corner of the region. "Corpses were thrown into wells and there was a report of a woman who ate her children," one man confided to his diary. "The starving and dead were all over; some chose to stone children to death instead of letting them suffer death by starvation. Robbery, burglary, and stealing were the order of the day. Masterless samurai attacked the old and children. The world was without order."[4]

Individual acts of random violence against the weak were part of the chaos of famine, but patterns of protest also reveal how most people brought a shrewd political consciousness to their search for a solution to the crisis. For one thing, commoners did not merely blame natural disasters for their misfortune; rather, they organized protest movements and demanded that government authorities implement policies that would alleviate suffering. In that spirit, farmers beseeched authorities to defer temporarily the collection of rice taxes, open the doors to daimyo storage granaries, and interdict the shipment of grain to cities. In urban centers, starving people harangued the shogunate or local daimyo to provide relief supplies from government warehouses, to halt price gouging, and to compel rice dealers to sell at a "reasonable price" any grain that they were hoarding in anticipation of being able to charge higher prices as the crisis worsened. If officials refused to respond, the demonstrators might break into the lord's granary and loot rice shops, tossing the grain onto the street, where they sold it to all comers at what they claimed was a fair and morally just price. Moreover, by the early nineteenth century people had learned from previous experience that organized collective action impressed the authorities: Defiance had forced the government to implement relief measures during earlier subsistence crises, and the approximately four hundred peasant uprisings and urban riots recorded in the 1830s totaled more than had occurred during the entire seventeenth century. In addition, the irate protesters maximized their strength by organizing on an unprecedented scale: In 1836 an estimated ten thousand demonstrators threw Mikawa Province into an uproar, and to the north of Mount Fuji thirty thousand hungry protesters rose in anger.

The most sensational act of dissidence in the 1830s was led by Ōshio Heihachirō, a samurai and former government official, who urged villagers around Osaka to rise up and sack the city. Ōshio's rebellion repeated the common demand for popular justice. "We must first punish the officials, who torment the people so cruelly," he wrote in a manifesto issued in 1837; "then we must execute the haughty and rich Osaka merchants. Then we must distribute the gold, silver, and copper stored in their cellars, and the bales of rice hidden in their storehouses."[5] On the nineteenth day of the Second Month 1837, Ōshio led a raid against government offices and set fire to parts of the city in hope of touching off a massive peasant revolt. After two days of confused fighting, authorities routed the attackers, Ōshio took his own life, and the poor of Osaka were left to mourn the loss of more than three thousand of their homes and approximately fifty thousand koku of rice, consumed in Ōshio's conflagration.

Other contentious events, many related to protoindustrialization, scarred the early decades of the nineteenth century. In many regions farm families that had grown prosperous from their commercial endeavors organized protests against incumbent village leaders whose families had held local office for generations by virtue of inheritance. Occasionally, as happened in Chōshū domain in the 1830s, the discontent even launched violent demonstrations to urge governing authorities to abolish inherited office-holding in favor of new procedures that would empower the upwardly mobile. Other collective movements energized persons from many villages. In 1823 commercial farmers and local merchants who produced ginned cotton and vegetable oils in 1,007 villages around Osaka used all available legal means to protest a long-standing government policy that granted wholesaling and distribution rights for those commodities to a select group of Osaka merchants. Such monopolies, the producers complained, were unethical since political control over the market advanced the interests of a privileged few while threatening the livelihoods of many. "Trade," they declared, "should be unrestricted."[6] As was happening elsewhere, the voices of protest caught the ears of officials who were sensing a new vulnerability, and authorities in Osaka sanctioned free trade.

## New Discourses, New Religions

New intellectual discourses and modes of religious expression also filled the air as the eighteenth century gave way to the nineteenth. For some time scholars associated with Kokugaku, or the school of National Learning, had been returning to Japan's earliest texts to rediscover the distinctive characteristics of Japanese culture. On the basis of their research, major figures in the National Learning movement came to believe that antiquity represented a golden past, a repository of values and moral lessons that could serve the needs of contemporary society. Writing in the middle of the eighteenth century, one of the foremost National Learning scholars, Kamo no Mabuchi, focused his attention on the *Man'yōshū*, the anthology of poetry compiled nearly one thousand years earlier. Mabuchi revered those verses because in his estimation, they captured the essence of an original Japanese personality that took shape before being overlain, and even corrupted, by the "artifice" of such foreign doctrines as Buddhism and Neo-Confucianism. According to Mabuchi, the virtues that distinguished the Japanese from other peoples, as revealed in the *Man'yōshū*, were "sincerity (*makoto*), directness, vitality, manliness, and elegance of the heart."[7]

Motoori Norinaga, Mabuchi's successor as the leading figure in the Kokugaku movement, went a step farther to declare that not only were

Japanese values distinctive, but they were also more praiseworthy than the life principles espoused by other peoples. Norinaga spent decades immersed in reading the *Tale of Genji* and the *Kojiki*, and he emerged from his studies persuaded that ancient Japanese had lived happily under the reign of Heavenly Sovereigns. Moreover, as he argued in his life's work, the forty-four–volume *Kojiki den* ("A Commentary on the *Kojiki*"), which he finished in 1798, those monarchs governed according to inspirations communicated from the Sun Goddess Amaterasu and other Shinto deities. For Norinaga, that divine linkage was key to understanding the admirable nature of Japanese society. "This grand country of our Heavenly Sovereign is the home of the august and awesome divine ancestress, the great goddess Amaterasu," he once wrote, "and this is the primary reason why our country is superior to all others." In contrast, he noted, "Other lands are not the home of the great goddess Amaterasu, and so they have no established principle of rulership. There, men's hearts are evil, and their behavior is unruly."

Scholars of Dutch Learning, or Rangaku, turned their curiosity outward. In 1720 the shogunate lifted an earlier ban on the importation of Western books, excepting those on Christianity, in the hope that Western scientific and technical knowledge could be used to improve domestic agriculture and commercial production. Thereafter Chinese translations of Western books, together with a smaller number of Dutch renditions of important works on mathematics, astronomy, and botany, began to trickle into Japan. Increasingly, Japanese physicians took an especially close interest in books on anatomy and pharmacology. Most of those doctors had been trained in the Confucian tradition, and in an age when the government forbade autopsies and when knowledge about the exact effect of traditional herbal medicines on specific organs was imperfect, their quest for new information honored the Confucian ideal that one should deploy knowledge to help those who suffered the depredations of this world. As one intellectual wrote, "The work of the physician is only to help other human beings and not to promote the self. Not seeking idleness or thinking about fame, one must simply abandon the self and pledge to save others."[8]

Respect for Western medicine increased noticeably after 1771, when Sugita Genpaku and a coterie of other inquisitive physician-scholars observed the illegal dissection of the body of a female criminal executed in Edo. Sugita's group compared what they witnessed with diagrams and anatomical tables contained in a Dutch translation of *Tabulae anatomicae: in quibus corporis humani* . . . , written by the German physician Johann Adam Kulmus in 1722. Impressed by the accuracy of the foreign text, Sugita and his colleagues set out to translate the Dutch version of that classic work on anatomy into Japanese. Unfortunately, they did not know Dutch, and at the time there were no dictionaries or language primers to guide them. Painstakingly, and equipped only with a manual that discussed the general principles of how to translate Chinese into Japanese, Sugita's group unlocked the Dutch text word by word, sentence by sentence. "We sometimes stared at each other blankly from morning to dusk, unable to decipher a single line," Sugita later recalled, and once "we spent a long spring day puzzling over such simple lines as 'An "eyebrow" is hair growing above the eye.' "[9] After a year or so, he continued, "our command of vocabulary gradually increased," and in one of the great triumphs of Japanese intellectual history, Sugita and his colleagues completed their *Kaitai shinsho* ("A New Text on Human Anatomy") in 1774.

In addition to energizing interest in Western medical practice, the appearance of *Kaitai shinsho* stimulated the preparation of Dutch-Japanese dictionaries and other reference aids for translators. As a result, Japanese scholars began to roam more widely through the corpus of Western arts and sciences, especially after the shogunate opened a translation bureau in 1811 and several daimyo subsequently sponsored academies of Dutch Studies and established repositories for scholarly translations of Western works on geography, cartography, physics, chemistry, natural history, and military science. In his 1815 reminiscences, Sugita expressed satisfaction that new translations were appearing annually and that interest in things Western had spread like "a drop of oil, which, when cast upon a wide pond, disperses to cover its entire surface."

Scholars of National Learning and Dutch Studies did not intend their work to be politically or socially subversive. Sugita and others who pursued the secrets of Western medicine were not rejecting their own society; rather, they saw themselves as following the traditional ethic that one learned as much as one could in order to promote the well-being of fellow humans. In that context, even Yamagata Bantō, whose analysis of human society *Yume no shiro* rested on the author's understanding of Copernican astronomy, upheld the legitimacy of a polity that recognized the virtue of merchants. In similar fashion, although Norinaga lavished praise on the monarch rather than the shogun as the agency of benevolent rule, he was a scholar immersed essentially in an academic exploration of the origins of Japanese culture. Nonetheless, by the middle of the nineteenth century the intellectual ferment generated by the original advocates of Dutch Studies and National Learning would encourage a new generation of Japanese to debate the utility of a Confucian-based social hierarchy, pose tough questions about the role of the shogunate in a country where there were so many "troubles" and where the rosy memory of direct rule by the Heavenly Sovereign offered the vision of an alternative political arrangement, and examine critically the potential dangers as well as advantages posed by engaging foreign cultures.

A more immediate challenge to the existing political and social order came from millennial religious movements. Kurozumi Munetada, a Shinto priest from Bizen Province, organized one of the earliest of the so-called new religions after he experienced a "divine union" with the goddess Amaterasu Ōmikami while contemplating the rising sun during the winter's solstice in 1814. Kurozumi soon recovered from infectious tuberculosis, which had taken the lives of his parents, and, believing himself blessed, began a ministry devoted to improving the lot of the ill and downtrodden. The central tenet of the new Kurozumi sect was faith in the Sun Goddess, who as the pivotal creation deity could both guarantee eternal bliss and relieve people of evil in the here and now. Worshiping Amaterasu, according to Kurozumi, would release the essential goodness contained within each human being, bring about a reign of peace and prosperity, and offer all believers cures from disease, the prolongation of life, an abundance of children, bountiful harvests, and success in trade and business.

The Tenri sect also promised the construction of a new moral order that would free people from the temporal miseries fostered by incompetent officials, an unfair polity, and a cruel political economy. In 1838 Nakayama Miki, who experienced only hardship and suffering as a maltreated farmer's wife after her marriage at the age of thirteen, received a divine revelation that she was possessed by the deity Tenri Ō no Mikoto, self-identified as the "true and original god who has descended from Heaven to save mankind."[10] Released from her trance, Nakayama abandoned her family and began to preach the deity's "divine wisdom" (tenri): Faith will cleanse human beings of the "eight dusts" that produce selfish behavior and, in their place, nurture a new ethic of selflessness and mutual aid.

Like other new religions, the Kurozumi and Tenri sects placed a spotlight on the economic and social discord of the early nineteenth century, and they recruited the bulk of their believers in localities where famine and the economic dislocations associated with protoindustrialization were greatest. Faith, their prophets claimed, offered the sole means of escape from dearth and earthly sorrows. Since "Deity and man are the same" in the words of the founder of one new religion, faith would enable people to behave as if they themselves were saints on earth.[11] Ultimately the new autonomous communities of faithful, according to the believers, would overcome the social evils of the times and "renew the world" by introducing an earthly paradise where everyone would know plenty and be free from pain, suffering, and fear.

## Failed Reform, Failed Expectations

Authorities were not oblivious of the social and economic turmoil of the early nineteenth century, and the shogunate and several daimyo responded by initiating reform programs in the 1830s and 1840s. Mizuno Tadakuni, who by 1841 had emerged as the shogun's chief policy maker, crafted an elaborate set of proposals that relied on traditional recipes of moral rearmament, frugality, and agrarian fundamentalism. In quick order he punished allegedly corrupt officials, trimmed government expenditures, instructed samurai to practice austerity and self-discipline, rolled out familiar sumptuary regulations, directed merchants to reduce prices, and abolished certain merchant associations whose monopolistic practices were deemed guilty of fueling inflation. In rural areas, Mizuno issued bans against commercial agriculture and cottage industries so that farmers would concentrate solely on growing crops. With an eye to augmenting the shogunate's revenues, he extracted monetary contributions from merchants, unveiled plans for new taxes on agriculture, and announced a momentous scheme that would turn over to the shogunate all arable lands surrounding Edo and Osaka that currently were in the possession of individual daimyo or the shogun's bannermen.

Numerous domains also undertook reform programs in the Tenpō period, the years from 1830 to 1844. The attempts were a mixed and diverse lot: Some repeated Mizuno's emphasis on economic retrenchment and the revival of moral rectitude, while others struck off in new directions by setting up domain-sponsored enterprises and monopolies over certain products that could be marketed in Edo and Osaka in order to capture profits that would turn budgetary red ink into black. A few domains enjoyed modest success. In Chōshū, which kicked off a reform program in 1838, authorities balanced the domain's budgets for several years by reducing official expenditures, repudiating the daimyo's debts to merchants, and peddling monopoly rights on such commodities as salt, sake, and cotton to newly formed merchant associations. Satsuma domain followed very different tactics but was even more successful than Chōshū in balancing its budget and accumulating reserves in its treasury. Boldly, officials from Satsuma resolved the domain's debt crisis in a single stroke by unilaterally declaring that all outstanding loan repayments to merchants would be stretched over a 250-year period with interest reduced to 0.5 percent per annum. Officials also encouraged expanded production of cane sugar and introduced new commercial crops that farmers sold to the domain for subsequent marketing in Japan's urban centers.

In contrast with Chōshū and Satsuma, most daimyo reform programs ended inconclusively. One reason was that reforming lords tended to treat symptoms, not causes. Too many daimyo relied on traditional prescriptions—sumptuary decrees, stipend cuts, and debt repudiation—that at best provided only temporary solutions to the domains' fiscal woes. Moreover, reformers who boldly intervened in the political economy to create new domain monopolies usually lacked experience and expertise. As a consequence, their innovative experiments more often than not simply ended up promoting chaos, shortages, and higher prices, the very economic dislocations that they had hoped to overcome. On the national level, Mizuno was no more successful. His policies did not halt inflation, permanently reduce deficits, or create economic prosperity, and his plan to confiscate daimyo land around Edo and Osaka caused an uproar that ended with his dismissal from office in the autumn of 1843.

The Tenpō reform era left two enduring legacies. Among the daimyo, many lords began to distrust a shogunate that seemed inept yet stubbornly determined to impose its authority over the lords by threatening to confiscate their holdings. In the popular mind, a pervasive sense of "failed expectations" indicated an incipient loss of confidence in government among the commoners, a nascent disbelief that the shogunate or the daimyo could ever formulate solutions to the social and economic malaise that was settling over the country. In time, these "troubles from within" would intertwine with the "troubles from without," exacerbating the growing mood of despair and paving the way for more radical solutions to the problems of the nineteenth century.

## Troubles from Without

Out of the north came the Russians. During the eighteenth century, Russian explorers and government officials followed their nation's destiny eastward, settling the great reaches of Siberia, pushing onto the islands of the Kuril archipelago, and fanning out along the coast of the North American continent in search of furs, trade, and adventure. As the Russian presence grew along the northern Pacific rim, officials in St. Petersburg in 1799 chartered the Russian American Company to administer those territories and exploit the resources of the region. By that time many Russians had begun to imagine that great profits would flow from opening trade with Japan, and Catherine the Great authorized Lieutenant Adam Laxman to lead a naval expedition to request the establishment of official commercial relations. In the Sixth Month of 1792, Laxman sailed into Nemuro Bay, but not until the autumn of 1793 did Matsudaira Sadanobu, chief senior councillor and shogunal regent, deign to respond. In a bluntly worded letter, Matsudaira claimed it was common practice for Japan to destroy or seize ships arriving from countries with which it did not enjoy friendly relations and to imprison their crews. However, since Laxman was "ignorant of Japanese laws," Matsudaira continued, he had decided to relent and permit the Russian to return home. Perhaps because he wished to avoid a violent confrontation, the senior councillor granted an additional concession: He authorized one Russian ship to enter Nagasaki Harbor at a later date, thus implying that further negotiations might be possible.

Preoccupied with events in revolutionary France, Russia did not exercise its permit until the autumn of 1804, when Nikolai Petrovich Rezanov, the managing director of the Russian American Company, sailed into Nagasaki Harbor to ask for the formal inauguration of trade. Again, the shogunate was intransigent. Officials kept Rezanov waiting for six months, confined to his ship and a claustrophobic onshore residence, and then advised him that the only foreigners permitted to step foot on Japanese soil were Chinese and Dutch traders and envoys invited from Korea and the Ryūkyū Islands. "This is a hereditary law for the protection of our country's frontiers," the communication asseverated. "How can our government change a hereditary law merely on account of your country?"[12] The note ended abruptly: "You must sail home quickly." Fuming in disgust, Rezanov did sail north to a Russian outpost on the Siberian coast, but then frustrated and disgruntled captains under his command launched a series of raids against Japanese settlements on Sakhalin and the southern Kuril Islands in 1806 and 1807. In the smoking ruins of one fishing village, they left words of warning, etched into a copper plate: "If the Japanese persist for long in denying the just demand for trade, the Russians will lay waste the northern part of Japan."

The Red Hairs threatened the same possibility from the south. In 1808 the British frigate *Phaeton* sailed boldly into Nagasaki Harbor in search of Dutch merchantmen, who were regarded as enemies after Holland had been forced into a wartime alliance with Britain's foe, Napoleonic France. Although they found no Dutch ships at anchor, sailors from the *Phaeton* abducted Dutch officials, and when the shogun's magistrate ordered the ship to depart immediately, its nineteen-year-old captain brazenly demanded food, water, and ship's stores. Convinced that the Englishman was maniacal enough to make good his threat to turn his fifty cannons against Japanese and Chinese vessels in the harbor, the local city magistrate provided supplies to the *Phaeton* and then committed suicide for having failed to protect Nagasaki.

The ease with which the *Phaeton* defied the shogun's magistrate and breached the port's defenses humiliated officials in Edo, and they became more troubled after hearing rumors that the British might press demands for trade upon the Japanese. Thanks to reports submitted by the Dutch, the shogunate was fully informed about how the British had gained control over most of northern India, taking the opium grown there and trading it at Canton for Chinese tea, silks, and porcelains. The Canton trade grew rapidly, with British sales of opium increasing fivefold between 1800 and 1832, and many traders shared the expansionist impulses of the British foreign secretary, who in 1834 wondered aloud "whether it may not be possible to establish commercial intercourse with Japan."[13]

Britain's startling victory over China in the Opium War, fought between 1839 and 1842 after Chinese officials attempted to suppress traffic in the narcotic, gave the Japanese even more reason to fret about the Red Hairs' intentions. The treaty ending that conflict ceded Hong Kong to Britain and established the treaty port system. Under the terms of the negotiations, five Chinese entrepôts were designated open cities, where British subjects could reside, trade, and enjoy the privilege of extraterritoriality—that is, the right to conduct themselves in accordance with British laws and be tried by British consular courts, not Chinese judges. Other countries quickly signed similar agreements with China, including in each a most-favored-nation clause, thus providing that all treaty powers receive new concessions won by any one of them. Dutch accounts about the outcome of the Opium War brought ominous news to Edo: The industrial progress of the West had created an insatiable craving for trade, and it now seemed only a matter of time before Britain or some other powerful nation used gunboat diplomacy to extend the treaty port system across East Asia.

Incensed by the Western incursion into Asia, many intellectuals wrote essays and memorialized the shogunate to urge that the foreigners be kept at arm's length. Some of the most passionate and influential arguments came from Aizawa Seishisai. Born in Mito domain, Aizawa became a leading member of the so-called Mito School, a group of scholars who in the early decades of the nineteenth century scoured Japan's philosophical and religious landscape in search of solutions to the emerging domestic and foreign crises. In a series of political tracts written in the 1820s, Aizawa outlined the foreign threat in cultural and religious terms. To his mind, Western power flowed from a spiritual wellhead, and he saw Christianity as a state cult that clever Western leaders adroitly manipulated in order to capture the allegiance of their own peoples and those whom they wished to colonize. "Now," Aizawa asserted, the European powers "endeavor to attack all nations in the world. The wicked doctrine of Jesus is an aid in this endeavor. Under the pretext of trade or whatever, they approach and become friendly with people in all areas, secretly probing to see which countries are strong and which weak. If a nation's defenses are weak, they seize it by force, but if there are no weaknesses to pounce on, they take it over by leading the people's minds astray with the wicked doctrine [of Christianity]."[14]

Japan was vulnerable, Aizawa continued, because of its own deep-seated cultural malaise. Living in cities, the samurai had grown soft and pampered; merchants cared only for luxury; commercial growth had caused inequities among the social estates; shogunal and domain authorities governed irresponsibly; everyone had lost his moral bearings, having been corrupted over the centuries by such sinister foreign creeds as "Buddhism, the ideas of perverse Confucians, petty scholasticism." The situation, he warned, was precarious: "Japan is in a state similar to that of a patient who has barely escaped death from a usually fatal disease. Since it lacks a strong, inner constitution, it is easily susceptible to influences from without."[15]

Aizawa had specific countermeasures in mind: Samurai should be returned to the land, political institutions reformed, coastal defenses reinforced, and foreigners repelled from Japanese soil. Most of all, however, the Japanese had to rediscover their own "national essence," their *kokutai*. As used by Aizawa, the term resonated with the ideas expressed by some scholars associated with the National Learning movement; his *kokutai* connoted a harmonious amalgam of government and religion that presumably had infused Japanese political life in the golden days of antiquity, before the introduction of all those debilitating foreign beliefs. With the blessings of native deities, Aizawa contended, Heavenly Sovereigns in the past had conducted rites of governance, provided the people with food and the material necessities of life, and bestowed ethical instruction upon them. In return, he wrote, "All people in the realm were of one heart and mind; they were so endeared of their rulers that separation was unbearable." To regain that unity and the strength that flowed from it, Aizawa believed, the shogunate had to revive the monarch's role as the leader of religious-based state rituals. In that way Japan could forge a synthesis of state and religion superior to those found in the West, the regime would win the loyalty of all Japanese, and the country would be able to resist the European threat. In the conclusion to his seminal *Shinron* ("New Theses"), completed in 1825, Aizawa wrote that "to elucidate the *kokutai*, to be informed on world affairs, to understand fully the barbarians' nature, to strengthen national defense, and to establish a long-range policy—these represent the best form of loyalty and filial devotion, the best method of recompensing Royal Ancestors and Heavenly Deities, and the best way for the shogunate and daimyo to rescue their peoples and dispense benevolent rule for eternity."

Shogunal authorities took seriously their responsibility to defend Japan from violent incursions. To some observers, a strong defense against Russian encroachment required Japan to extend its dominion over the land of the Ezo. One famous geographer and scholar of Dutch Learning summed up that view succinctly after surveying the northern islands at the very close of the eighteenth century: "We must establish a mutual frontier between Japan and other countries and create a fortress to withstand foreign enemies."[16] Leading officials in the shogunate needed little prompting; in the wake of the Laxman visit, Edo dispatched an expeditionary force of one thousand samurai to Ezochi, and by 1807 the shogunate had placed the vast northern territory under its direct jurisdiction, established administrative offices at the port town of Hakodate, and stationed armed garrisons along the coast, which it reinforced after Russian marauders terrorized villages on Sakhalin and the Kuril Islands.

So that Ezochi might appear to be an integral part of the Japanese homeland, officials sought to Japanize the Eastern Barbarians. According to one directive, "The reasons for bringing Ezochi under the rule of central authorities are that the island is undeveloped, and the barbarians have poor clothing, food, and housing and do not know the moral way. Officials sent there will enlighten and educate them, gradually bring them to adopt Japanese customs, and make them gratefully submit to us and not be won over by foreign countries."[17] Japanese intrusion into Ezochi did have a benevolent side—the Hakodate magistracy dispatched physicians into the hinterland to treat Ainu—but for the most part assimilation efforts were coercive in nature. To bring civilization to the northern frontier, shogunal officials banned native festivals, instructed the Ainu to worship Japanese *kami*, compelled them to adopt Japanese dress, urged them to abandon the "uncivilized" habit of eating meat, and told the men to shave their beards and cut their hair in the style of Japanese commoners. To encourage compliance, officials invited cooperative Ainu to ceremonial banquets and presented them with "assimilation medals."

To enhance its posture of strength, the shogunate also articulated a more rigid interpretation of national seclusion. The new hard-nosed policy began with Matsudaira Sadanobu's letter to Laxman in 1793 informing the Russian that Japan customarily destroyed ships flying the flags of countries not formally recognized by Japan. The senior councillor was not being historically accurate, however, since the original seclusion edicts issued in the 1630s had applied exclusively to Roman Catholic missionaries and Iberian traders. Moreover, Japan had almost never attacked foreign ships entering Japanese waters during the late seventeenth and eighteenth centuries but instead either turned them away diplomatically or else escorted them to Nagasaki and repatriated the crews to their home countries. Matsudaira's intention, clearly, was to reconfigure tradition in order to support his decision to extend the seclusion rules to another country and to justify the use of armed force.

The shogunate's response to Rezanov confirmed the new initiative, and in 1825, following an armed raid by a British foraging party against a small island south of Satsuma, officials in Edo issued the Order for the Repelling of Foreign Ships. That made the applicability of the exclusion edicts nearly universal by instructing the daimyo to fire on any unauthorized ship approaching the Japanese coast and to incarcerate all landing parties. Although the shogunate relaxed the ordinance in 1842, permitting foreign ships to be provisioned on condition that they depart immediately, it continued to repeat its determination to keep Japan's doors shut to the Western world. In 1844 King William II of Holland wrote to the shogun that "disasters now threaten the Japanese Empire."[18] Everywhere in Europe, the monarch explained, commerce and industry flourished, while the invention of steamships had shrunk the world. Countries wished to trade with one another, he cautioned, and any "nation preferring to remain in isolation at this time of increasing relationships could not avoid hostility with many others." In conclusion, William II offered to assist the Japanese in adjusting to the new global conditions, in exchange for expanded relations between the two countries. Politely but firmly, the shogun's advisers declined the king's overtures. "Ancestral law," they replied, forbade the establishment of treaty relations, and "since the ancestral law has been once fixed, posterity must obey."[19]

## America Precipitates a Crisis

The Americans would compel the shogunate to change its mind. Sailing from Nantucket, New Bedford, and other ports along the New England coast, American whalers began to appear in the waters off Japan in the 1820s, and a decade later more than two hundred ships operated in the northern Pacific. Those vessels used the Sandwich (Hawaiian) Islands as a base during their expeditions, which usually lasted a year or more, but the captains also wanted to be able to take on water and supplies at Japanese ports, which were closer to the great hunting grounds in the Bering and Okhotsk seas. During the 1840s growing resentment about the inconveniences stemming from the shogunate's isolation policy, as well as occasional ill-treatment of shipwrecked sailors cast up on Japan's shores, prompted some American politicians to propose the establishment of official relations with Japan.

The lure of trade added more pressure for a treaty. The acquisition of California and the Oregon coastline in the 1840s conjured up visions of expanded commerce with Asia. Already American businessmen conducted a substantial trade with Canton, but their ships sailed from East Coast ports and faced a long, arduous journey across the Atlantic and Indian oceans. The discovery of gold in 1849 ignited in California a remarkable economic boom, which business interests hoped to multiply through trade with China and Japan. At the same time, with the promise of a cross-continental railway in the offing, San Francisco beckoned as a shipping terminus that would permit American vessels to ply the shorter route across the Pacific. In that context, Japan loomed both as a potential trading partner and as an anchorage where ships bound for China could stop for supplies and where the new steamships could fill their hoppers with coal.

Many Americans hoped to do more than merely take profits from Asia; they also wished to confer the presumed advantages of their civilization upon peoples they saw as inhabiting a less fortunate part of the globe. The Industrial Revolution had brought unimaginable prosperity to the countries of western Europe and North America. Consequently, trade was morally good, argued the businessmen who petitioned Washington to open relations with Japan, because America could share all the wonders of the new industrial age with the underprivileged Japanese, secluded for so long on their narrow islands. Missionaries conceived of Asia in similar terms, asserting that the blessings of Christianity were a gift that the pious West ought to bestow upon the heathen East. In words that would have chilled Aizawa's soul, Samuel Wells Williams, a prominent missionary and one of the first Americans to claim proficiency in the Japanese language, wrote that opening Japan would reveal "God's purposes of making known the Gospel to all nations. I have a full conviction that the seclusion policy of the nations of Eastern Asia is not according to God's plan of mercy to these peoples, and their government must change them through fear or force, that the people may be free."[20]

Such thinking by businessmen and religious leaders was deeply rooted in American notions about its Manifest Destiny. In the early decades of the nineteenth century, that concept had justified the acquisition of new territories as the United States marched across the continent. Having reached the West Coast, many Americans in the 1840s developed a passion to leap out across the Pacific, although in ways that were as cultural and commercial as they were territorial. Such persons possessed energy and confidence in abundance, and while none of them had ever heard of Aizawa, they shared his assumption that America's prowess rested on the superiority of its political, economic, scientific, and religious institutions. The United States had advanced far beyond countries like Japan, they agreed, and they had absolutely no doubt that American culture should now be exported everywhere. "Commerce is the great agent in the civilization and christianization of the world," began an editorial in one California newspaper. "A *perfect* civilization cannot exist in the absence of the true principles of freedom. The freest government on earth is that of the United States—it therefore enjoys the highest civilization. Aside from the pecuniary advantages which will necessarily result from the prompt establishment of our commerce upon the Pacific, it is the only means by which we can fulfill our high destiny—the universal extension of the principles of American freedom. Commerce not only civilizes, christianizes, and enriches, but with the aid of the American principles of liberty, it extends the 'area of freedom.' "[21]

In 1852 the American president Millard Fillmore authorized the dispatch of a naval expedition to Japan and drafted a letter for delivery to its authorities that set forth America's objectives. Despite the fervor for America's civilizing mission in the world, Fillmore phrased his country's aims in modest, even innocent terms; his overarching hope, he began, was simply that "the United States and Japan should live in friendship and have commercial intercourse with each other."[22] Within that framework, the president continued, America had three specific requests to put to Japan. First, he wrote, "it would be extremely beneficial" for both nations if Japan would "change the ancient laws as to allow a free trade between the two countries." Second, he asked the Japanese to treat shipwrecked sailors "with kindness." Finally, with so many American ships plying the Pacific, he wished "that our steamships and other vessels be allowed to stop in Japan and supply themselves with coal, provisions, and water."

In command of the American mission was the proud, dogged, obdurate commodore Matthew C. Perry, a tested veteran of the Mexican War and the scion of one of America's most distinguished naval families. Old Bruin, as he was nicknamed, set forth from Newport, Rhode Island, with four of the navy's finest warships at his command. In his pocket he carried Fillmore's letter and a directive from the State Department that instructed him to be patient in his dealings with the Japanese and expressed the hope that all would go smoothly. But the mission statement also dealt with possible obstinacy on the part of the Japanese: "If, after having exhausted every argument and every means of persuasion, the commodore should fail to obtain from the government any relaxation of their system of exclusion, or even any assurance of humane treatment of our shipwrecked seamen, he will then change his tone, and inform them in the most unequivocal terms that they will be severely chastised."[23] Very clearly, the United States was willing to wage war to ensure compliance with its request for peace and friendship.

Perry arrived at the entrance to Edo Bay on July 8, 1853, the third day of the Sixth Month according to the Japanese calendar. Six days later, with a great show of pageantry, Old Bruin went ashore to deliver Fillmore's letter to an assemblage of the shogunate's representatives. Perry also presented the Japanese with two letters of his own in which he characterized the isolation policy as "unwise and impracticable."[24] Consequently, he hoped "that the Japanese government will see the necessity of averting unfriendly collision between the two nations, by responding favorably to the propositions of amity, which are now made in all sincerity." In any event, he concluded, he would depart Japan's waters forthwith, but he would return the next spring, "with a much larger force" if necessary, to learn the shogun's response to President Fillmore's requests.

## 1854—1860: *Concessions to Foreigners, a Hard Line at Home*

Perry's arrival posed an insolvable dilemma for the shogunate. The man in charge of managing the crisis was the pragmatic Abe Masahiro. A senior councillor since 1843, Abe had supervised the strengthening of Japan's coastal defenses and fully realized that preparations were still woefully inadequate. That left Japan with little choice, in his view, but to yield to America's demands. Yet he also knew that if the shogunate abandoned the seclusion policy, criticism could rain down upon its head from many quarters. Seeking to escape his predicament, Abe tried to build a consensus. He sent translations of the Fillmore and Perry letters to all daimyo and solicited their advice on whether Japan should sign a treaty or not, fight or seek peace. Their replies provided little guidance. A few of the lords favored opening the country, and a handful declared their willingness to risk conflict to preserve national isolation. Most, however, simply waffled, counseling the shogunate to deny the request for trade but admonishing it somehow to avoid hostilities.

True to his word, Perry sailed back into Edo Bay, on February 14, 1854, and Abe, still lacking a mandate, quickly entered into negotiations with the commodore, whose flotilla now numbered eight of the world's most lethal warships. As discussions proceeded, Perry presented the Japanese with gifts intended to demonstrate the wonders of modern industry, including a Morse telegraphic device and a quarter-size steam locomotive capable of speeding several men at a time, straddled awkwardly across a miniature passenger carriage, around 370 feet of track. The Japanese entertained Perry's crews with an exhibition of sumo; the Americans reciprocated with a minstrel show. Finally, on March 31, 1854, the two nations set pen to the Treaty of Peace and Amity between the United States and Japan. Signed in Kanagawa (later renamed Yokohama), the agreement began by promising perpetual peace. Then came the specifics: American ships would be permitted to call at the ports of Shimoda and Hakodate, where they could take on provisions; shipwrecked sailors would receive good treatment; Americans were free to travel within an eighteen-mile radius of the two ports; and an American consul would take up residence at Shimoda. Perry, sailing home, could take with him satisfaction for having won most of the concessions Fillmore desired, save the privilege of opening trade, and for ending Japan's seclusion policy.

In Edo, Abe could take comfort in having weathered the crisis and avoided war, but new storms clouded the horizon soon enough. By the end of 1856 Russia, France, and Britain had demanded, and received, treaties similar to the Kanagawa agreement. In August 1856 Townsend Harris arrived in Shimoda as American's first consul general. A blustery, hard-drinking New York merchant turned China trader, Harris had lobbied vigorously for a diplomatic posting in Asia after his business interests had collapsed in failure. Despite his personal misadventures, he was a strong proponent of international trade, and once in Shimoda, he immediately began to harangue Japanese officials to sign a commercial treaty, suggesting menacingly that it was better to settle matters with him than to wait for the gunboats to reappear.

The initial round of treaty signing and subsequent rumors that Edo would succumb to Harris's high-pressure tactics kindled a fierce debate about the merits of the shogunate's policies. At one end of the spectrum stood antiforeign daimyo such as Tokugawa Nariaki of Mito, the retired lord of that influential collateral domain. Replying to Abe's request for advice in 1853, the crusty elder statesman had thundered that war was a more honorable option than knuckling under to a foreigner's demands, and after Abe signed the Kanagawa Treaty (the common name for the agreement with the United States), Nariaki proposed that the Japanese negotiators commit suicide and that the pact be rewritten in terms more favorable to his country.

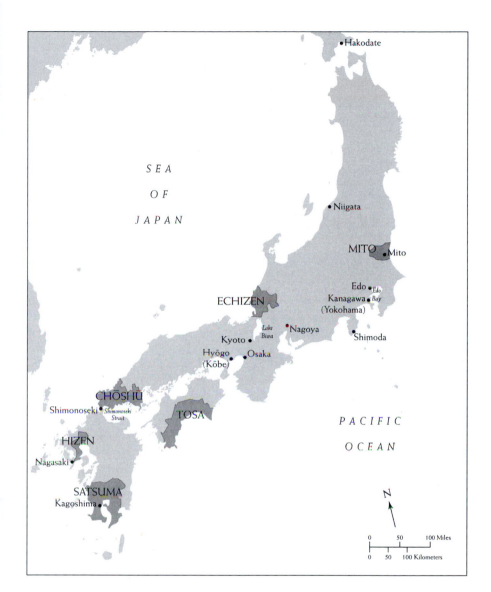

**MAP 4.1** *Japan in the 1860s*

Moreover, he remained totally unconvinced that trade would benefit Japan. "To exchange such worthless goods of theirs as woolen cloth or glass objects for such valuable goods of ours as gold, copper and iron," he wrote, "incurs a lot of disadvantages without even a little advantage."[25] At heart, Nariaki was a nationalist who believed that opening Japan placed in jeop-

ardy not just a culture and way of life but a territory and a nation as well
as an economic and political order.

Among intellectuals, none was more critical of the shogunate than
Yoshida Shōin. As a young low-ranking samurai in Chōshū domain Yoshida
had studied military science, and in the early 1850s he had journeyed to
Nagasaki and Edo to learn about his country and meet with other scholars.
Enormously curious and adventurous, Yoshida in 1854 attempted to stow
away aboard Perry's flagship so that he could go to America and study the
secrets of Western strength firsthand, only to be discovered and turned over
to Japanese authorities. Back in Chōshū, Yoshida was permitted to teach at
the local domain school, where he conveyed his ideas about national politics to several young men, including Itō Hirobumi and Yamagata Aritomo,
who later played key roles in the Meiji Restoration. Yoshida adamantly opposed the treaties because they violated fundamental tenets of the Japanese
polity, the *kokutai*, as expressed in the phrase *sonnō jōi* ("Revere the Heavenly
Sovereign, Expel the Barbarians"). Aizawa and other members of the Mito
School had explicated those terms earlier, taking *sonnō* to signify the gratitude due to the Heavenly Sovereign by the shogun and equating *jōi* with
the prohibition of Christianity. Yoshida gave the ideas a more radical interpretation. For him, *sonnō* meant that the monarch should participate directly in the political process by offering his views about the problems
confronting the nation and that all persons should obey the throne absolutely, while *jōi* necessitated rescinding the treaties and physically expelling foreigners from Japanese soil. Thus, Yoshida charged, Abe had acted
improperly on two counts: Not only had his treaties violated Japan's cultural and territorial integrity, but his decision to enter into agreements with
foreigners had usurped the prerogative of the Heavenly Sovereign. To rectify matters, Yoshida called for young men of pure intentions to step forth
and take direct action against corrupt officials.

Other Japanese desired to work out a more flexible solution to the crisis, and many intellectuals, writing in pamphlets and memorials submitted
to daimyo and the shogunate, lent their support to the notion of *kaikoku* ("to
open up the country to foreign intercourse"). One of the more influential
was Sakuma Shōzan, a samurai from central Japan who had studied with
several scholars of Dutch Learning and served his daimyo lord as an adviser
on military science. After the Opium War, Sakuma poignantly phrased the
question that preoccupied so many Japanese: How did China—a cultural
paragon and powerful giant that seemed impervious to conquest by
barbarians—ever lose in battle to a puny upstart like Britain? The reason,
Sakuma responded, derived from cultural conceit: China suffered because

its leaders had an inflated sense that it was superior to other civilizations and thus had denigrated the rise of Western science and mathematics. In a series of essays written in the 1850s, Sakuma popularized the slogan "Eastern Ethics, Western Science." Confucian-based morality remained a viable philosophy for the private sphere, Sakuma claimed, but it did not supply pragmatic answers for meeting the Western challenge. It was imperative, he believed, that Japan adopt the useful elements of Western technology and marry them to Eastern morality if it wished to stand up to the aggressive barbarians.

The daimyo of several large, important domains thought along similar lines. They shared the antiforeign and nationalistic sentiments of Tokugawa Nariaki, but they also believed that it was pointless to continue bullheadedly to refuse Western overtures for treaties and trade; stubbornness merely invited an attack upon the Japanese islands and the same humiliation that had befallen China. "One cannot suppose," Ii Naosuke wrote in 1853, when he was still the lord of Hikone domain, that "the world will be at peace and our empire safe if we enforce only the policy of national seclusion." It would be preferable, he continued, to open the country, amass wealth through trade, and then "prepare strong military armaments, enhancing our military prestige even in the eyes of the lands overseas."[26]

Hotta Masayoshi, who had replaced the ailing Abe as the shogunate's chief policy maker, counted himself in the "open country" camp and set about negotiating a commercial treaty with Harris. By February 1858 the two sides had reached tentative agreement about the fundamental points to be included in the pact. Sensitive to criticism that the shogunate had not been paying sufficient heed to the monarch's wishes, Hotta tried to outflank his opponents by asking for Kyoto's endorsement. It was a serious misstep. The court, somnolent since the early seventeenth century, was increasingly conscious of the role it might potentially play in resolving the crisis gripping the country, and Kyoto's predilections were decidedly antiforeign. Late in the Third Month, Heavenly Sovereign Kōmei informed Hotta that the draft was unacceptable because "to revolutionize the sound laws handed down from the time of Ieyasu would disturb the ideas of our people and make it impossible to preserve lasting tranquillity."[27] Uncertain about how to resolve his differences with Kyoto, the senior councillor resigned.

Hotta's replacement was the decisive Ii Naosuke, the sixth member of his family to serve as the shogun's chief policy adviser. No sooner had Ii settled into Edo than Townsend Harris arrived with news that China, having been thumped in battle a second time, had agreed to a new treaty with

Britain. Moreover, Harris hinted, the Red Hairs were about to dispatch their warships to Japan to compel the signing of a commercial agreement. Convinced that the threat was real and immediate, Ii signed the United States–Japan Treaty of Amity and Commerce on July 29, 1858. The Harris Treaty, as the agreement is commonly known, provided for the formal exchange of diplomatic representatives and scheduled the future opening of Edo, Kanagawa, Osaka, Hyōgo (Kōbe), Nagasaki, and Niigata as ports and cities where foreign merchants could establish residences and enjoy the privilege of extraterritoriality. In addition, the pact placed Japanese tariffs under international control and pegged import duties at levels that benefited foreign traders. In the following weeks Ii signed commercial treaties with the Netherlands, Great Britain, France, and Russia, acceding in each case to the inclusion of the most-favored-nation clause.

Ii anticipated resistance to his moves, especially since he did not seek royal sanction for the new round of treaties. Ruthlessly he struck before his opponents could organize themselves. In the summer of 1858 the shogunate forced into retirement, or placed under house arrest, Tokugawa Nariaki and other daimyo who had opposed the treaties. In Edo, Ii purged from office underlings who favored a conciliatory policy toward the opposition daimyo, and he ordered antiforeign court nobles to relinquish their positions. The shogunate arrested more than one hundred men in the service of the opposition lords and aristocrats and executed eight of them. That fate also awaited Yoshida Shōin who, living his ideal of direct action, schemed to assassinate a leading shogunal official. When the shogunate's police discovered the plot, they arrested Yoshida and carted him to Edo, where he was beheaded in the Tenth Month of 1859.

## 1860–1864: *The Union of Court and Camp*

Ii paid for his grim suppression of dissent on that snowy morning in the Third Month of 1860, when the young assassins from Mito and Satsuma domains honored Yoshida's injunction to take direct action against misguided officials. Rocked by the event, the shogunate abandoned its hard line and attempted to shore up support by adopting a more conciliatory attitude toward Kyoto and the great daimyo. Under the rubric of *kōbu gattai* ("Union of Court and Camp") officials arranged for the new shogun, Iemochi, to wed Princess Kazu, the sister of Heavenly Sovereign Kōmei. Moreover, Iemochi agreed to journey personally to Kyoto to consult with the court about affairs of state. His grandiose procession in the spring of

1863, made in the company of three thousand retainers, was the first shogun-al visit to Kyoto in more than two hundred years. Symbolically, the trip down the Tōkaidō Highway underscored what men such as Aizawa and Yoshida had been asserting: The shogunate could no longer dominate the court politically, as it had in the days of Ieyasu and Iemitsu, and no shogun could hope to rule effectively without borrowing publicly from the monarch's treasure house of cultural prestige and religious authority.

The new emphasis on conciliation also prompted Edo to hold out the olive branch to the great lords, pardoning those punished by Ii and even agreeing to appoint to advisory positions several outside lords and heads of collateral houses, who normally would have been excluded from holding any shogunal office. In general, the daimyo reacted favorably to the shogun-ate's initiatives, hoping that the calls for political unity would work to their advantage as well as the country's. Perhaps the most supportive were the "able daimyo," an unofficial designation given to lords who had carried out self-strengthening programs after Perry's arrival. Among the more acclaimed able daimyo was Shimazu Nariakira of Satsuma domain. An enthusiastic pro-ponent of Dutch Learning, Shimazu dispatched his retainers to study with foreign experts in Nagasaki and Edo and sponsored the translation of West-ern works on science and navigation for use in domain schools, believing, as he wrote in 1856, that "it is the urgent duty of all samurai to cooperate in learning of conditions in foreign lands so that we may adopt their good points to supplement our deficiencies, reinforce the military might of our nation and keep the barbarian nations under control."[28] Acting on those principles, Nariakira introduced Western-style military training for his ar-tillery units, formed new rifle companies, and founded a naval academy. Deeply impressed with Western technology, he himself took up photogra-phy and installed gas lighting within his castle compound. More ambitiously, he opened a shipyard in the harbor of the domain's castle town of Kagoshima to construct steamships, built a refinery where workers produced modern cannons and rifles, and established a Western-style factory to manufacture gunpowder, glass, ceramics, and agricultural implements.

Lords of other influential domains, such as Echizen, Hizen, and Tosa, undertook similar reform programs, although on a more modest scale. On the basis of their experiences, those daimyo believed it incumbent upon the shogunate to enact similar reforms on the national level so as to enhance Japan's strength and wealth in face of the foreign incursions. In 1858 Matsu-daira Shungaku of Echizen addressed a memorial to the shogunate that con-tained a list of typical suggestions: "The services of capable men must be enlisted from the entire country; peacetime extravagance must be cut down and the military system revised; the evil practices by which the daimyo have been impoverished must be discontinued; defense preparations must be made; the daily livelihood of the whole people must be fostered; and schools for the various arts and crafts must be established."[29] Matsudaira started on his agenda after accepting an invitation to serve as an adviser to the Edo regime; to spare the reforming daimyo unnecessary expenses and permit them to divert more funds into self-strengthening programs, Matsudaira in 1862 persuaded the shogunate to relax the alternate attendance requirement by permitting family hostages to leave the shogun's city and allowing most lords to spend just one hundred days every three years in Edo.

Standing adamantly opposed to the Union of Court and Camp, however, were several hundred *shishi*, self-styled "men of high purpose." The overwhelming majority of *shishi* came from lower- and middle-ranking warrior families in western Japan, and they tended to be young, barely in their teens or early twenties when Perry's squadron arrived at Edo's door. Dissatisfaction bound the *shishi* together; their families had experienced firsthand the economic deprivations wrought by stipend cuts and inflationary pressures, and many of the young men had tasted frustration when they found that their humble status blocked appointment to responsible positions in government, despite their education at domain schools and passionate commitment to improving local conditions. Perry's gunboat diplomacy and the signing of unequal treaties also drew the *shishi* together. As Western intimidation mounted during the 1850s, young samurai concerned with Japan's future gravitated to Kyoto and Edo. In those great metropolises, alive with the excitement of the day, the young men flocked to private academies and fencing schools, where they internalized the *sonnō jōi* rhetoric popularized by Aizawa Seishisai and Yoshida Shōin and dedicated themselves to the "high purpose" of direct action against Japan's foes.

Ii Naosuke's decision to sign commercial treaties with the Western powers and to crush his domestic opponents galvanized the *shishi*. An idealistic, romantic aura came to envelop the men of high purpose, chiefly because they swore absolute devotion to the Heavenly Sovereign, acted with a reckless bravery and disregard for their own personal safety, and indulged voraciously in sake, women, and midnight adventures. Bravado may have been the *shishi*'s stock-in-trade, but they were also political pragmatists and deadly serious about preserving Japan's cultural integrity. Committed to expelling the barbarian, *shishi* in Yokohama launched a campaign of terror against foreigners in 1859 and 1860, cutting down European merchants, Russian sailors, the Chinese servant of a Portuguese merchant, and a Dutch sea captain. In 1861 an extremist from Satsuma killed Henry Heusken, secretary and translator for Townsend Harris, and fellow *shishi* attacked the British legation in Edo, where they hacked two consular officials to death and seriously wounded another.

Perhaps the most consequential acts of antiforeignism occurred about nine months apart in 1862 and 1863. In the Eighth Month of 1862 four British civilians were enjoying a day's outing near Yokohama when their mounts strayed into the procession of Shimazu Hisamitsu, the de facto ruler of Satsuma following Nariakira's death in 1858, as he made his way from Edo to Kyoto with the intention of helping knit together the Union of Court and Camp. Infuriated at what they perceived as the foreigners' insolence, Shimazu's warrior escort drew their swords. In the flash of a moment, they wounded two of the foreigners and left a merchant, Charles Richardson, dead in the roadway. Early in the Fifth Month of the next year, young radicals in Chōshū domain turned their shore batteries against an American cargo ship traversing the Shimonoseki Strait on a voyage to Shanghai, and later the same month they fired on Dutch and French warships passing offshore.

Young *shishi* also lashed out against their domestic foes who had guided the purges of the late 1850s and crafted the policies that allegedly ignored the monarch's will and made Japan vulnerable to foreign incursions. Ii Naosuke had been the first to fall, and in the two years between the autumns of 1862 and 1864 *shishi* extremists, many from Chōshū, Satsuma, Tosa, and Hizen, carried out more than seventy assassinations. Detested police officials and their informants in Edo and Kyoto topped the hit list, but the advocates of *sonnō* and *jōi* also struck down Sakuma Shōzan, who had sermonized about the utility of Western technology, and even lopped off the heads from the wooden statues of three Ashikaga shoguns that stood at the entrance to a Kyoto temple. As bizarre as that last act might seem at first blush, it conveyed an obvious symbolic message. The activists desecrated the likenesses of Japan's medieval shoguns, who had a reputation as despotic rulers, just days prior to Iemochi's entry into Kyoto in 1863 and placed the severed heads near the approach to a major bridge that he was scheduled to cross. There they hung up posters impeaching the regime. "Today many people clearly surpass these traitors," one manifesto began. "If they do not immediately repent these ancient evils and offer their assistance to the court, then all the loyalists on earth will rise up together and punish them for their crimes."[30]

In 1863 *sonnō jōi* activists plotted a daring coup d'état, an assault on the royal palace intended to free the Heavenly Sovereign from shogunal forces occupying Kyoto and place him at the head of a loyalist army that would strike against foreigners and confiscate all Tokugawa landholdings in western Japan. Just as the putschists were about to act in the middle of the Eighth Month, however, guard units backing the shogun moved against the rebels, many of whom retreated to Chōshū domain, which had emerged as a sanctuary for those harboring antishogunal sentiments. A second *shishi* assault the next summer, supported by recently formed militia units from Chōshū as well as loyalists from a handful of other domains, ended in disaster. The rebels entered Kyoto at dawn on the nineteenth day of the Seventh Month 1864 but were routed by proshogunal forces massed around the palace compound. The Battle of Hamaguri Gate, as the incident became known, left many *shishi* dead, and fires set during the conflict destroyed nearly thirty thousand residences in Kyoto.

The *shishi* overplayed their hand in 1863 and 1864, inviting retaliation from both the shogunate and foreign powers. The leaders of Satsuma domain were first to feel the sting of an aroused foreign community when British ships avenged Richardson's death by bombarding the castle town of Kagoshima in the Seventh Month of 1863, setting fire to large portions of the city and destroying the Western-style industrial establishments constructed with so much hope by Shimazu Nariakira. In the fall of the following year a flotilla of seventeen Western ships blasted Chōshū's coastal defenses, landed troops to spike the cannons at Shimonoseki, and carried away a handsome ransom, paid by the domain to reacquire its leading port city. Just days before that debacle, on the twenty-third day of the Seventh Month 1864, shogunal supporters arranged to have Chōshū branded an "enemy of the Court" for having encouraged the activists who stormed the palace in Kyoto. The shogunate called on twenty-one domains to furnish samurai for a punitive expedition, and by the beginning of the Eleventh Month some 150,000 troops were poised on Chōshū's borders. Only after high-ranking conservative officials in Chōshū agreed to issue a formal apology, suppress *sonnō jōi* partisans, execute three members of the domain's inner ruling circle who had abetted the putsch, and expel activist courtiers who had fled Kyoto did the shogunate declare victory and disband its army.

The attacks upon the *shishi* and their refuge in Chōshū in 1864 splintered the movement, and individual loyalists scattered to their home domains. Although the *shishi* are sometimes dismissed as irrational extremists, the violence they wrought helped turn the course of Japanese history. The young radicals contributed to the politicization of the monarch and his courtiers, just as their robust sense of nationalism and glorification of the Heavenly Sovereign defined the tenor of permissible discourse in the 1860s. As the *shishi* gathered in Kyoto and other leading cities, older status and geographic divisions began to dissolve, leading to a new sense of unity and common purpose among warriors from different parts of Japan. Their assassinations, attacks on foreign ships, and attempted coups set shogun against daimyo, pitted court against camp, and made a shamble of the *kōbu gattai* policy. Of even more consequence, many men of high purpose who survived the battles of 1864 found a way to remain politically active within their home domains, where they helped forge a broader alliance of warriors and daimyo who were to topple the shogunate just four years later.

## 1864–1868: *The Final Showdown*

Animated by Chōshū's submission, leading officials within the shogunate, including Oguri Tadamasa, commissioner of finance from 1862, began to push for reforms that would strengthen the shogunate militarily, revitalize its authority over Kyoto, and open the possibility of abolishing daimyo domains unfriendly to the government in Edo. For assistance, the shogunate turned to the French minister Léon Roches, who arrived in the shogun's capital in 1864. Determined to establish ties with a regime that he believed would persevere as Japan's national government, Roches in 1865 agreed to help finance the construction of an ironworks at Yokohama and a modern shipyard at Yokosuka, south of Edo. By that time the shogunate had imported more than ten thousand rifles through Yokohama and was beginning to reorganize its samurai legions into cavalry, artillery, and infantry units, with the aim of developing a professional standing army equipped with modern weapons. Drawing confidence from its self-strengthening efforts, on the nineteenth day of the Fourth Month 1865 the shogunate announced its intention to organize a second punitive expedition against Chōshū after a civil war within that domain had brought many *sonnō jōi* activists to positions of local authority.

Edo's military buildup did not sit well with those new leaders in Chōshū or with their compatriots in Satsuma. In the former, Itō Hirobumi, Yamagata Aritomo, and other former *shishi* who assumed key positions following the domain's civil war had long since dismissed the shogunate as inept; in the latter, the events of 1864 and 1865 demoralized Shimazu Hisamitsu, a former advocate of the Union of Court and Camp, and he increasingly relied on the advice of Saigō Takamori, Ōkubo Toshimichi, and other middle- and lower-ranking samurai of a younger generation who had little tolerance left for the government in Edo. Such animosity was not diminished by the fact that all those leaders now considered *jōi* a dead letter. Itō and several colleagues had returned from a secret trip to England in 1863 impressed with the West's wealth and power, and the bombardment of Satsuma and Chōshū was proof to everyone of the foreigners' military superiority. Dismayed by the shogunate's aggressive disposition and sensing a showdown, Satsuma and Chōshū raced to increase their own "wealth and power." Each placed orders through Nagasaki traders for thousands of rifles and cannons, Chōshū contemplated opening a port to foreign traders, and Satsuma ordered machinery for a cotton-spinning factory and steam-powered sugar refinery from England.

Even as the shogunate and the domains of the southwest edged toward confrontation, economic problems associated with the inauguration of foreign trade racked the country, intensifying the distrust that many ordinary people felt toward Edo's policies and ultimately raising questions in the popular mind about shogunal legitimacy. Japan opened its ports at a moment when the total volume of world trade was expanding exponentially, and the West quickly developed a fondness for Japanese tea and raw silk thread. Overall, Japan's foreign trade exceeded even the most optimistic expectations as exports quadrupled and imports grew ninefold between 1860 and 1865. Burgeoning foreign demand brought prosperity to families that grew tea and raised silkworms, but it held negative consequences for many other sectors of the population. As the cost of raw silk thread soared, weavers in Kyoto and Kiryū faced unemployment when they had to boost prices for the finished cloth they sold to domestic customers. In some parts of the country, urban dwellers found themselves paying more for food as farmers converted paddy to the production of tea and mulberry trees, thus helping shove up the price of rice more than 700 percent between 1863 and 1867.

A currency crisis fueled the inflationary fires. During the latter part of the Tokugawa period the shogunate minted coins on the assumption that gold and silver would exchange at a rate of 1:5. Western coins, however, were based on a gold to silver ratio of 1:15. The discrepancy touched off a "gold rush" in the winter of 1859–1860 as foreigners brought silver into Japan and exchanged it for Japanese gold coins, which they then exported to reconvert into greater quantities of silver. The shogunate checked the drainage of gold by reminting old coins and issuing new ones to bring Japanese coinage ratios into line with world standards. Doing so, however, debased the currency and contributed to rapid inflation that drove up the price of all essentials, especially rice. Other woes added their weight to economic problems in the years after Perry's arrival. A catastrophic earthquake shook Edo in 1854, leaving perhaps 100,000 dead; Westerners brought a cholera epidemic into Japan's ports in 1861; and 1866 saw severe crop failures.

Initially, Japan's commoners exhibited a blend of naïve curiosity, nervous apprehension, and nationalistic outrage toward the foreigners arriving on their soil. In the year after Perry's arrival, peddlers in Edo sold more than a million copies of some five hundred different *kawaraban*, crude prints that cost little and disseminated news of the day in an entertaining fashion. Many of the broadsheets featured portraits of the commodore, illustrations of the miniature locomotive and other American gifts, accounts of negotiations with the foreigners, maps of distant nations, and stories about customs and lifestyles in Europe, Russia, America, and such fanciful places as a Country of Giants in South America and a Country of Women in northern Europe. Other *kawaraban* adopted a more malicious tone, portraying Perry as a Buddhist devil. According to the text of one broadsheet, Old Bruin's heart beat with hatred, and the evil commodore intended to destroy the samurai, ruin the businesses of merchants, and bring distress to the peasantry. Still other news sheets suggested ways to drive away the "foreign dogs," such as calling on native deities to "kill the barbarians using a beam of bright light as a weapon."[31]

As the economic stresses associated with the arrival of the West became more apparent in the 1860s, Japan's commoners began to redirect their criticisms toward the shogunate. Increasingly, *kawaraban* complained about the difficulty of eking out a living when inflation and unemployment were so epidemic, and a poster tacked up in Edo in 1865 condemned foreign trade for the suffering it caused and urged the removal of a barbarian-subduing shogun who had failed to carry out his duties. When poor harvests led to food shortages in 1866, commoners in Edo rioted for just the third time in that city's history, castigating authorities for failing to undertake relief measures and for permitting rice dealers to hoard grain. "Among the government officials are many bad people," began one poster. "Commissioner of Finance Oguri and his colleagues think it is fine that prices rise. Since we have no other way to save our lives, we are going to attack Oguri's office compound. Then we will kill his evil henchmen and save the people from disaster."[32] As things turned out, Oguri escaped the crisis unharmed, but the message had been delivered. "It is difficult to know when the lower classes will rise," wrote one high official, "but it appears that they become more discontented daily. This is really frightening."

Mass uprisings in the countryside in 1866, a larger number than during any other single year in the entire history of the Tokugawa shogunate, added to the social chaos. On the Musashi Plain northeast of Edo, at Shindatsu in Mutsu Province, and in more than one hundred other rural areas, tens of thousands of poor peasants, tenant farmers, and agricultural day laborers rose up that summer of 1866, voicing common grievances. "Looking carefully into the origins of this disturbance," wrote one observer in Shindatsu, "we see new taxes on raw silk and silkworm egg cards, thirty percent increases in interest rates, and extraordinary price increases, especially for rice and other cereals."[33] Enraged villagers marched on tax collection offices and the homes of wealthy landlords and moneylenders who had exploited the rural poor, and they demanded cheap rice, tax relief, and the return of pawned goods and mortgaged land. When refused, rioters burned tax records, pillaged storehouses, ransacked private homes, carried away bags of rice and casks of miso, smashed furniture and trampled on clothing, and even dug up the family graveyards of those whom they despised the most. Driven to violence by the hardships of the present, many demonstrators in the mid-1860s conceived of their actions as a step toward a better tomorrow. Across Japan rioters spoke of *yonaoshi* ("world renewal"). For most peasants, the term signified discontent with ruling elites and envisaged a rural community, freed from injustice, where farm families worked hard, helped one another, and enjoyed the well-being of abundant harvests.

Against the backdrop of mounting popular discontent, tensions between the Edo government and the powerful domains of western Japan came to a head in the summer of 1866, when Iemochi ordered several daimyo to supply him with troops for the proposed second expedition against Chōshū. In the eyes of its critics, the shogunate's attempt to punish such a respected domain as Chōshū was a reckless undertaking. For more than a decade, they charged, the government in Edo had failed to address adequately "troubles from within and without." It had bungled foreign policy, its domestic policies lacked credibility, and now it seemed preoccupied more with furthering its own "selfish" interests than with tending to important national concerns. As Shimazu Hisamitsu observed in a memorial to the court, the shogun's foreign policy had "incurred general criticism and alienated opinion everywhere."[34] On top of that, "merchants and the humblest classes have flouted the law," rioting even in cities administered directly by the shogunate. Such widespread popular unrest, Shimazu continued, threatened to divide the country and demonstrated Edo's incapacity to provide satisfactory leadership. To strike out against Chōshū in the midst of such turmoil, he asserted, risked having Japan "torn to pieces by a mounting tide of disputes" and created an environment where foreign powers might be tempted to expand their imperialistic privileges.

Iemochi established his personal campaign headquarters at Osaka Castle, but nothing went as he envisioned. Satsuma refused to contribute troops to the shogun's expeditionary force, thus honoring a secret agreement negotiated with Chōshū in the First Month of 1866 pledging mutual support should the shogunate attack either domain. Several other daimyo likewise ignored Iemochi's levies, and the riots in Edo and Osaka compelled him to assign some of his most dependable units to garrison duty in those cities. His difficulty in mustering his forces forecast the future to Saigō Takamori, who had helped arrange the alliance between Satsuma and Chōshū. The shogun's presence at the head of the expeditionary army, the Satsuma warrior wrote, "means only that he will go to greet his nemesis in person. This campaign will not enhance the shogunate's authority."[35] Saigō was right. Determined to defend their home soil, Chōshū's armies easily turned aside the shogunate's undermanned and poorly commanded battalions, which retreated to Edo after Iemochi died unexpectedly in the Seventh Month of 1866.

To the horror of the dissident domains, in the autumn of 1867 the new shogun announced yet another self-strengthening program that would revamp administrative practices, raise taxes, and use French loans and military advisers to restore Tokugawa military might. In the southwest, men began to formulate plans to overthrow a regime that seemed dangerously out of control and intent on wiping out dissenting daimyo. For Kido Takayoshi, a leading figure in Chōshū who had escaped death after the Battle of Hamaguri Gate by hiding out with his geisha mistress, it was as if "Ieyasu had been born again," and he wrote that Japan "will fall into the toils of the shogunate and France unless authority is quickly restored to the Court."[36] In Kyoto, antishogunal courtiers, such as the influential Iwakura Tomomi, openly encouraged rebellion. "In the heavens," Iwakura wrote in the summer of 1867, "there are not two suns. On earth there are not two monarchs. Surely no country can survive unless government edicts stem from a single source. Hence it is my desire that we should act vigorously to abolish the shogunate."

Many ordinary people shared those sentiments. In the early autumn of 1867 commoners near Nagoya said that amulets inscribed with the name of Ise Shrine fell from the heavens, an omen of a better future. During the next several weeks similar talismans rained down on residents of villages and towns along the Pacific seaboard from Hiroshima to Edo, and hundreds of thousands of people took to the streets in celebration. Male and female alike donned outlandish costumes, cross-dressed, tossed aside their cares and worries, stuffed themselves with food and drink, danced through the streets, made love in alleyways, and broke into restaurants and coerced the customers to join the carnivalesque debauchery. Drums and gongs, chimes and whistles could be heard everywhere, as could the revelers' singsong, defiant phrase, repeated endlessly as they danced away the autumn of 1867, "Ee ja nai ka, ee ja nai ka" ("Why not? It's okay! Ain't it grand? What the hell!").

On one level, the frenzied dances and rowdy, lewd behavior of the merrymakers symbolized despair about a fast-changing, unpredictable economy and a polity that had fallen into disarray. But the crowds that thronged the streets were doing more than airing their frustrations: Their songs and ditties lampooned the shogunate, ridiculed its policies, denied its legitimacy, and helped pave the way for its downfall. "From the west," went one parody, "Chōshū's butterflies come soaring in / While money gushes out through the port of Kōbe / Why not? It's okay! Ain't it grand? What the hell!"[37] In Fujisawa, a town on the Tōkaidō Highway just west of Yokohama, people filled the streets in the Eleventh Month of 1867, dancing, carousing, storming the houses of the wealthy to commandeer provisions, and sharing food, drink, and affections. At dusk on the final day of revelry, according to a picture scroll of the events, a silent procession left the town, black flags flying and coffin in hand. Inscribed upon a banner were the words "Mount Nikkō, Shrine of Tōshō Dai Gongen"; the good townsfolk of Fujisawa were holding a mock funeral for the Tokugawa shogunate.

The actual burial of the House of Tokugawa was not far off. As 1867 drew to an end, contingents of armed rebels from Satsuma and Chōshū moved toward Kyoto. On the morning of January 3, 1868, warriors from Satsuma stormed into the royal compound, where they were welcomed by Iwakura and other antishogunal courtiers. Later that day Kōmei's fifteen-year-old son, who had ascended the throne upon his father's death the previous year and who soon would become known to the world as Emperor Meiji, issued a proclamation that abolished the office of shogun; restored power to the Heavenly Sovereign; created new government offices to be staffed by court nobles, daimyo, and other "men of talent"; and promised a "renewal of all things" in order to end the distress of the people.

The loyalists faced some opposition, but Saigō Takamori molded volunteers from Satsuma, Chōshū, Tosa, Hizen, Echizen, and several other domains into an effective "royal army" that drove the shogun's battalions back toward Edo, which fell in the Fourth Month of 1868. Although the new government granted amnesty to the shogun and his supporters, scattered resistance continued into the autumn in the northeast, where some daimyo distrusted and feared the powerful new leaders who hailed from the opposite end of Japan, and the Boshin Civil War finally ended only when the remnants of the Tokugawa naval forces surrendered at Hakodate in the spring of 1869.

## Conceptualizing the Meiji ishin

Saigō, Itō, Kido, and the other men who brought down the Tokugawa polity usually are not regarded as the heroes of one of the world's great revolutions. They did not proclaim any stirring new values that would inspire all humankind, as the promise of *liberté*, *égalité*, and *fraternité* had in France the previous century, nor did they set out to advance the interests of an economically and socially marginalized class, as happened in Russia and China the next century. Other aspects of the seizure of power robbed 1868 of the high drama that surrounded other revolutionary moments: The men who attacked the shogunate cloaked their actions in tradition by calling for a restoration of rule by the Heavenly Sovereign, and their victory came relatively quickly, with comparatively little terror or sustained violence.

But the young men of 1868 intended to do far more than stage a coup d'état that would resurrect the inherited values of the past and save their home domains from extinction. In the early decades of the century Japan's "troubles from within" had raised serious questions about the ability of the traditional polity to respond to problems of samurai impoverishment and morale, adapt to the economic transformations set in motion by protoindustrialization and the commercialization of agriculture, cope with social chaos, answer criticism from intellectuals, and make room for the new political consciousness evident in acts of collective dissidence. The "troubles from without," which began in earnest with Perry's arrival, revealed the structural weaknesses and ideological bankruptcy of the shogunate, and the regime's capitulation to foreign demands earned it the animosity of "men of high purpose" and the loathing of the peasants and urban dwellers who suffered the consequences of opening the country to trade. The men who seized power in 1868 were nationalists who railed against Japan's semi-colonial status, and as suggested in the memorials of Matsudaira Shungaku and Shimazu Hisamitsu, they were Japanese who were sympathetic to the problems confronting their countrymen. Radicalized by the events of the 1850s and 1860s, filled with rage and resentment, they were profoundly dissatisfied with their world, and they wanted to change it.

Itō, Saigō, Iwakura, and the others possessed no specific blueprint for future change when they took over the helm of state in 1868, but they did have a general sense of the new directions they wished to travel. Discussions among the insurgents in 1867, as they gathered their strength to move against the shogun, pinpointed the need to create more flexible governing institutions that would enlist the abilities of men of talent, promote national unity under the aegis of the Heavenly Sovereign, and improve living conditions for everyone. The self-strengthening programs undertaken by some domains in southwestern Japan bespoke a dawning recognition that industrialization and foreign trade could enhance national strength and create domestic prosperity. The paralyzing economic and social chaos of the 1860s persuaded many radicals that only the most drastic action could usher in a new era of stability and well-being, leading them to abandon the philosophies of the past and experiment with new ideas about rearranging the social order and restructuring political ideologies. Fear and anger, aspiration and expectation, a disbelief that a once-proud country had come to such a sorry state—all commingled to convince the men of 1868 and the people of Japan that only innovative, radical changes could correct the disarray and save the future.

The men who marched into Kyoto in January 1868 employed an ancient symbol to justify the overthrow of the old order and to legitimate the revolutionary policies they contemplated. Among themselves, many radicals in the middle of the 1860s spoke cryptically of "stealing the jewel," implying that they had no intention of actually restoring direct rule to the Heavenly Sovereign. That was so, but the locution was not a cynicism. The feelings of loyalty that Itō, Saigō, and their compatriots expressed toward the throne were genuine. What the rebels desired was to return the monarch to his traditional role as the sovereign who conducted rituals of state and endorsed the actions of those who ruled in his name. Loyalism, in that sense, explained to the people of Japan why the insurgents had to dispose of the shogunate, which had turned Kyoto into a political backwater, and it sanctioned a future experiment that would revolutionize Japan's political, economic, and social institutions. Somewhat later the Japanese took from classical Chinese thought a seldom-used term, *ishin*, to describe the seizure of power and the new policies initiated after 1868. Translated into English as "restoration," the ideographs used to write *ishin* implied something very different: a renewal, a new beginning of all things, to be accomplished by harnessing together the energies of all segments of society. It was an appropriate adoption, for during the 1870s and 1880s new beginnings were to bring to Japan political, economic, and social changes as revolutionary as those experienced by any country in the world during the last three centuries.

# CHAPTER 5

# "New Beginnings"

On the fourteenth day of the Third Month 1868, Japan's teenage emperor (to use the translation of *tennō* that had become common parlance) summoned nearly four hundred officials to the Imperial Palace in Kyoto, where they were read a statement of national policy. Known as the Charter Oath, the document pledged the following:

1. Deliberative assemblies shall be widely convoked, and all matters of state shall be decided by public discussion;

2. All classes high and low shall unite in vigorously promoting the economy and welfare of the nation;

3. All civil and military officials, and the common people as well, shall be allowed to fulfill their aspirations, so that there may be no discontent among them;

4. Base customs of the past shall be abandoned, and all actions shall conform to the principles of international justice;

5. Knowledge shall be sought throughout the world, and thus shall be strengthened the foundation of the Imperial polity.[1]

Symbolic of the hopes expressed in the Charter Oath, on the eighth day of the Ninth Month 1868, imperial oracles proclaimed that the young emperor's reign would take the name Meiji, the era of "Enlightened Rule." Kido Takayoshi and the other young revolutionaries who drafted the Charter Oath on behalf of the emperor did so with urgent, pragmatic goals in mind. In the spring of 1868 the new government was more a dream than a reality. Imperial armies were still fighting their way to Edo, and civil war with the northern domains threatened to divide the country; the fledgling regime had no treasury and was spending money faster than it could take in revenues; and the Western powers had made it clear that they expected the new leadership to put a permanent end to antiforeignism and to provide political stability. Against that backdrop, the framers of the Charter Oath addressed their immediate problems. The first clause made an appeal for national unity by suggesting that the small clique of revolutionaries would not monopolize decision making but would include other influential persons and agencies in policy formulation. The next two articles expanded upon that overture by offering all people, regardless of their station in life, an opportunity to "fulfill their aspirations," while the final two assertions signaled to foreign observers that Japan would become a stable, responsible member of the international community.

During the 1870s the new Meiji regime overcame its opponents and imposed upon Japan a revolutionary settlement that secured for itself an incontrovertible hold over administrative, police, and taxing authority. As the men of 1868 gathered power and earned recognition as Japan's legitimate government, they articulated additional long-range goals. One frequently proclaimed aim was to safeguard Japan's national sovereignty and prevent further foreign encroachment—"to establish the independence of our country," as Chōshū's Yamagata Aritomo once put it, and "to preserve the nation's rights and advantages among the powers."[2] Perhaps the most oft-stated motive was the simply expressed, boldly unequivocal determination to become a great and respected country, equal to the most advanced nations on the face of the globe. Itō Hirobumi voiced that sentiment when he visited Sacramento, California, in 1872, promising the somewhat startled city fathers that he and his colleagues would "labor to place Japan on an equal basis, in the future, with those countries whose modern civilization is now our guide."[3]

Those overarching motives of national independence and future greatness inspired a host of complementary missions: to revise the unequal treaties and remove Japan from semicolonial status, to foster national unity, and to sweep away the problems of the past in order to build strength and wealth. That accumulation of goals imparted a fresh meaning to the promises expressed in the Charter Oath, and by the time the Meiji period turned three decades old, Japan's leaders had acted to create a constitutional polity and convoke a national assembly, to industrialize and inculcate capitalism, and to reorganize the country's social structure. In his memoirs, Itō took pride in those accomplishments, noting that Japan had fulfilled the Charter Oath by securing "for the country prosperity, strength, and culture, and the consequent recognized status of membership upon an equal footing in the family of the most powerful and civilized nations of the world."[4]

## The Revolutionary Settlement

One of the more pressing matters for the young men who had driven the Tokugawa shogunate from power was to create a centralized political structure that would permit them to exercise authority effectively throughout the entire nation. Accordingly, not long after announcing the Charter Oath, the loyalists arranged to promulgate the Seitaisho, sometimes referred to as the Constitution of 1868, which vested all authority in the Dajōkan, or Grand Council of State. First established as part of the reforms of the seventh and early eighth centuries that brought the Japanese state into existence, the Dajōkan served as the chief policy-making and administrative organ of Japan's early imperial state before waning in significance. As revived in 1868, the Dajōkan was headed by a grand minister of state, two vice-ministers, and several councillors who presided over various bureaus. With little delay, the revolutionaries from Satsuma and Chōshū, in league with their radical allies at court, moved to claim a monopoly over the important positions within the agency; during the late 1860s and 1870s such men as Iwakura Tomomi, Ōkubo Toshimichi, Kido Takayoshi, Itō Hirobumi, and Yamagata Aritomo were seldom far from the center of action. The ministers and councillors met frequently, reached collective decisions about all major state policies, and issued decrees and orders upon imperial ratification. The Dajōkan proved to be a very efficient form of revolutionary government; it wore the badge of tradition while permitting a small number of men to hoard power, argue out their decisions with dispatch, and then implement their policies through their own ministries. Perhaps for that reason, it remained the central executive organ of the new regime until the inauguration of a modern cabinet system in the middle of the 1880s.

The men at the revolutionary center also sought to extend their authority over the nearly 280 still-independent daimyo domains. Itō and Kido were among the first to suggest that replacing the old domains with a new system of modern prefectures controlled directly by the Dajōkan could achieve a permanent solution to the problem of political fragmentation. But they also realized the risks that accompanied such a drastic undertaking, so they moved sequentially and employed a mix of coercion and positive incentives to win their way. The new regime took its first step in the summer and autumn of 1868, when it dispatched liaison officials to all castle towns to discuss problems of local administration. Early the next year the leading figures within the emerging central government who hailed from Satsuma, Chōshū, Tosa, and Hizen persuaded those daimyo to surrender their documents of enfeoffment to the emperor. Many other lords followed suit, and on the seventeenth day of the Sixth Month 1869, the imperial government, which by then had moved to Edo and renamed the city Tokyo, announced that it would accept the return of such registers from all daimyo. In that stunning move, the new government deprived the daimyo of their traditional autonomy and substantially increased its ability to control administrative policy, although it permitted the lords to stay on as "imperial governors."

By 1871 Kido, Ōkubo, and their colleagues in the Dajōkan were prepared to proceed with the final abolition of the domains. As men who had looked with abhorrence upon a similar scheme by the shogun just years earlier, Kido and the others were keenly aware of the possibility of opposition, so they mustered ten thousand troops in Tokyo under the command of Saigō Takamori. That summer the emperor summoned dozens of the imperial governors to the new capital, and on the fourteenth day of the Seventh Month had read to them a short, simply worded edict that did away with the domains and created in their place 302 prefectures (soon reduced to 72 and later to 48) and three administrative cities, each under the jurisdiction of a new governor appointed by the Dajōkan. The news, according to one foreign observer, reverberated like a "thunderbolt," and the British minister to Japan marveled at how swiftly the new Japanese leaders were able to cen-

*Saigō Takamori*

tralize authority, an achievement "almost beyond the power of man," in his words, that in Europe would have required years of bloodshed.[5] Several reasons accounted for the success of the new state: Some former daimyo were plainly tired of trying to rule in such chaotic times, Saigō's army intimidated others, many were undoubtedly attracted by the generous stipends and titles of nobility that all deposed lords received, and a great number surely must have concluded that the centralization of authority was necessary if Japan was to survive as a unified country.

To underscore its determination to wipe away the "base customs" of the past so that all people could "fulfill their aspirations" and "unite in promoting the economy and welfare of the nation," the new Meiji government dismantled the old Confucian-based social order, as well as the privileges and restrictions that had defined the samurai, peasant, artisan, and merchant estates. In the summer of 1869, when the Tokyo government accepted the surrender of domain registers from the daimyo, it also formally reclassified the population as nobles, former samurai, and commoners. At the time some 427 families from among the ex-daimyo and old court aristocracy were named nobility, or *kazoku*. *Shizoku*, the designation for high-ranking ex-samurai, and *sotsu*, the new term for more ordinary warrior families, together composed about 6 percent of Japan's total population of 30 million. Farmers, merchants, and artisans were all lumped together as *heimin*, ordinary citizens, and made up almost 90 percent of the nation. Left out of the new classification were the outcasts and clerics, approximately 1.75 and 1.25 percent of the population respectively. Over the next several years the regime lifted restrictions that formerly had limited occupational and social mobility. In 1871, for instance, it designated outcasts as ordinary citizens and permitted all commoners to take surnames. At about the same time, it authorized the alienation of farmland, dissolved the Tokugawa system of guilds and protective associations, and recognized marriage and adoption between classes.

Vast segments of the population found status deregulation liberating, but the consequences of the policy initiative weighed heavily on some samurai. Not only did the ex-warriors lose their monopoly on surnames, but in 1876 the government also deprived them of the right to carry swords. Most serious of all, the new regime stripped them of their hereditary stipends. When it disestablished the old domains in 1871, the Tokyo government assumed the responsibility for paying samurai stipends, which immediately accounted for almost one-third of the central government's expenditures. Alarmed by the size of that obligation, Ōkubo and others pressed for the abolition of the subsidies. Not all the new leaders, however, were convinced of the wisdom of such a plan: Kido believed that it was morally wrong to

## MAP 5.1  Japan's Modern Prefectures

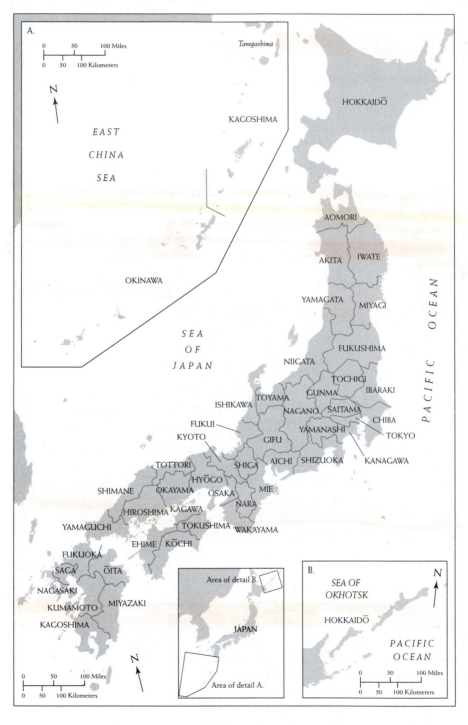

abandon those who had protected the country for so many centuries, and both he and Iwakura feared the possibility of a counterrevolution. In the end Ōkubo's fiscal arguments carried the day. Late in 1873 the Dajōkan offered to give fixed-term, interest-bearing government bonds to ex-samurai who surrendered their stipends, and three years later it made the exchange obligatory for all. In doing so, the government employed a math that gave itself significant budgetary relief: In the aggregate, annual interest payments on the bonds came to just half the amount paid as stipends, and inflation steadily reduced the cost of future bond redemptions.

The decision to withdraw stipends was facilitated by another extraordinary policy initiative, the formation of a conscript army, which removed the raison d'être for maintaining a military estate. Some elements within the Meiji leadership envisioned converting the former samurai into a professional army, but Yamagata Aritomo put forth a compelling set of arguments about the advantages of creating a conscript army made up of men drafted from all segments of society. Part of his reasoning grew out of his personal experiences. As a leading member of the *sonnō jōi* movement in Chōshū Yamagata in 1863 had helped organize the Kiheitai, a volunteer militia that included men from all social classes among its approximately four hundred members. The Kiheitai was bloodied in the Shimonoseki bombardment of 1864 and fought with distinction against the shogunate's expeditionary forces in 1866 and in the Boshin Civil War. That success predisposed Yamagata toward the idea of establishing a modern army based on universal conscription, and a visit to Europe in 1869 and 1870, where he witnessed firsthand the strength and modernity of the Prussian and French conscript armies, reinforced his inclinations. Perhaps even more important, European leaders tutored Yamagata about how conscription could mobilize the energies of the people behind the state and forge ties of loyalty between the government and its citizenry.

After his return to Japan, Yamagata won appointment as the vice-minister of military affairs and orchestrated the enactment of the Conscription Ordinance. Promulgated on January 10, 1873, the document echoed Yamagata's hopes: "By this innovation the rulers and the ruled will be put on the same basis, the rights of the people will be equal, and the way will be cleared for the unity of soldier and peasant."[6] Specifically, the new law provided that all males serve the colors for three years upon reaching twenty years of age and spend an additional four years in the reserves. Like the French legislation it took as a model, the ordinance excused family heads and heirs of farms and family businesses, and it made provision for purchasing an exemption. Since the army and navy also continued to accept samurai volun-

teers, the reality of a military force composed of universally conscripted ordinary citizens was not immediately realized. Still, the inauguration of conscription was a landmark measure: Socially it constituted another step in
disfranchising the samurai estate and creating a society based on equality
of opportunity, and militarily it vastly strengthened the regime's authority
by creating a force capable of providing internal security.

The fiscal burdens associated with the conduct of administration,
stipendiary payments, and military reform required a stable and predictable
revenue base. Levies upon the production of rice and other grains obviously
remained the most promising source of taxes, but Ōkubo Toshimichi, finance minister from the early 1870s, sought to introduce new principles of
taxation. In particular, he aimed to eliminate the annual fluctuations in revenue collections that had been such a problem for shogunal and domain
governments during the Tokugawa era by replacing agricultural levies submitted in kind with fixed cash payments and by calculating imposts according to the value of an individual's landholdings rather than the putative
crop yield of an entire village. Matsukata Masayoshi, an ex-samurai from
Satsuma who had served as a prefectural governor in Kyūshū before entering the Finance Ministry in Tokyo, favored land tax reform for another reason. In an important memorandum circulated among the members of the
Dajōkan, Matsukata pointed out that tax rates varied greatly by region and
that it was necessary to standardize collection procedures and to equalize
the tax burden in order to avoid the kind of social unrest that had been
prevalent in the closing decades of the Tokugawa period.

On July 28, 1873, the emperor issued the Land Tax Reform Law, emphasizing his desire that "the tax be levied impartially in order that the
burden may be shared equally among the people."[7] Accordingly, the government gave certificates of ownership to individuals who farmed specific
plots of land and assigned a monetary value to the holdings. The tax rate
then was set at 3 percent of the land's value, to be paid annually in cash by
the legal owner. The tax reform was pregnant with consequence. As designed, it replaced the complex and inequitable Tokugawa practices with a
more efficient system that stabilized government revenues and gave the
Meiji regime tax receipts roughly equivalent to the total land taxes collected
by the shogunate and all the daimyo domains. The victory, however, carried with itself an unintended but highly adverse consequence: While stan-
dardizing the tax rate brought welcomed reductions to some farm families,
it simultaneously increased the burdens shouldered by others. In some locales during the middle of the 1870s, smoldering resentments about taxes
turned violent, constituting part of a vehement opposition to the new regime

that was seeking to finalize its uncontested control over administrative, legislative, taxing, and military powers.

## Beating Back the Opposition

The Japanese stood at a historical crossroads in the early 1870s. The revolutionary settlement being imposed by the Meiji regime threatened to shatter the traditional political and social order and transfer control over the nation's destiny to the hands of the new government. At the same time, the promise of the Charter Oath to abandon the "base customs of the past" and to seek knowledge "throughout the world" suggested that other waves of historical change soon would break over the nation. For all Japanese, those events heralded a revolutionary moment when choices had to be made: People could resist the new regime's claims to power and oppose its slate of reforms, or they could agree to forsake the past, grant their support to the new leadership, and accept a fundamental restructuring of the conditions under which they lived and worked. By the end of the decade the overwhelming majority of ordinary Japanese had decided that it was in their interest to embrace the Meiji Dream of a brighter future. Before that consensus was achieved, however, some people—hesitant to place their fates in the hands of leaders whose names were still relatively unknown and apprehensive about the direction that reform was headed—opted to oppose the new regime by refusing to obey its laws, pay its taxes, or fight its battles. In a handful of regions, recalcitrant peasants objected violently to plans to dismiss local officials, revise the taxation system, and conscript an army. In Okayama, for instance, more than three thousand villagers marched on the castle town in 1871 to demand a tax reduction and the reinstatement of their lord, who had treated them well in the past, and in Yamagata Prefecture people joined mass demonstrations, submitted petitions, made trips to Tokyo, and physically attacked representatives of the Meiji government, all to protest the appointment of a new governor and his imposition of ancillary taxes. Rural violence against the new land tax peaked between 1873 and 1876, when Tokyo's determination to smooth out regional disparities in tax rates ended up increasing the real tax burden for some villagers. Other peasant households reserved their greatest scorn for the "blood tax." The government edict announcing compulsory military service used that infelicitous expression to mean that citizen soldiers should be prepared to make the ultimate sacrifice in defense of their country. Some farm families, however, took the words literally, and more than sixteen antidraft protests erupted in the spring and summer of 1873, when rumors abounded that men carrying large glass bottles were roaming the countryside and draining the lifeblood from potential conscripts. In the end the Meiji regime alternated the carrot and the stick to weather the contention in the countryside by explaining its motives more clearly, cutting the land tax by nearly 20 percent in 1877, and dispatching its police forces to quell protests where necessary.

More troublesome for the new Meiji government were large-scale acts of *shizoku* dissidence. The regime's plans to deprive the samurai estate of its traditional perquisites met with bitterness in many circles, but the catalyst that drove some warriors to participate in countercoups against the new regime was the Dajōkan's refusal to endorse a bizarre recommendation to invade Korea in 1873. On several occasions between 1869 and 1873 Japan requested Korea to recognize the Meiji government formally, but the Korean court turned aside such overtures, largely because the Hermit Kingdom did not wish to jeopardize its traditional tributary relations with China. Those ancient diplomatic protocols required Korea periodically to send emissaries to Beijing, where they acknowledged China's cultural and political suzerainty by kowtowing subserviently to the emperor of the Middle Kingdom. In return the Chinese government bestowed honorary titles on the Korean king, promised military protection, and permitted Korean merchants to conduct a limited but extremely profitable trade in tandem with the ritual exchange of Korean tribute for Chinese gifts. In light of that tradition, Korea was not abruptly about to restructure its relations with Japan in 1873; China might well take umbrage at any diminution of its role on the Asian mainland and fold its protective umbrella, leaving Korea to face the uncertainties of the 1870s on its own.

Saigō Takamori, whose prestige as one of the "Heroes of 1868" was unparalleled, interpreted the rebuffs as a grave insult to the Japanese emperor and his ministers of state, and in 1873 he led a splinter group within the Dajōkan that demanded a punitive expedition against Korea. Saigō's letters and other writings leave an image of a taciturn man with a propensity to view the world in simple, starkly absolute terms. A man of no uncertain convictions, he condemned the Korean court for lacking "virtue," just as he denounced his colleagues in Tokyo for being "morally corrupt" when they dared suggest that samurai ought to be stripped of their customary privileges and responsibilities. The warrior from Satsuma had risked his all to overthrow the Tokugawa regime in the 1860s, but never once had he imagined that the new Meiji regime would consider the samurai dross to be consigned to the slag pile of history. Turning the problem over in his mind, Saigō came to see an invasion of the Korean peninsula as an outlet for the ambitions and energies of frustrated warriors, as a way to discredit Ōkubo and other leaders who seemed bent on strangling the samurai estate, and as an opportunity to resuscitate a future role for the samurai within the Meiji settlement. Impulsive and dedicated to the cult of action, he even went so far as to propose that he personally journey to Korea to reopen discussions in the belief that he would be assassinated there and thus provide a convenient pretext for a Japanese military expedition.

For several key government leaders, Saigō's machinations lay far beyond the pale. In Tokyo, Ōkubo lobbied hard with members of the Dajōkan, arguing that Japan had to lay the foundations of national strength and wealth before it could allow itself to be caught up in foreign intrigues. From his sickbed Kido Takayoshi, whose poor health led to his untimely death just four years later, composed memorials that hammered at the same point. Japan's "wealth and strength were not developed," he argued, and the country "lacked civilization."[8] Given its woeful position, the nation's leaders had to assign priority to "conducting our finances with economy." Prudence dictated that the Japanese "give heed to our own affairs" and push ahead with the revolutionary settlement rather than risk the future by pursuing dangerous games overseas. The case was settled only in October 1873, when the young emperor endorsed the peace party's views following a decisive audience with Iwakura Tomomi.

The Korean affair drove a rift through the country's ruling alliance. Within days of the emperor's decision, Saigō and other members of the prowar faction resigned their government positions and returned to their hometowns. As a consequence, the ruling circle narrowed, with Iwakura, Ōkubo, Itō, Yamagata, Kido, and Matsukata emerging as the leading members of an oligarchy that for the rest of their lives would exert a decisive influence on the formulation of important policies. Together, during the 1870s and 1880s those men defined the agenda for national change, concentrating Japan's energies and resources on internal reforms designed to achieve the goals of prosperity and strength, equity with the West, and security from imperialistic predators. Before they could bring the Meiji settlement to completion and turn the next page on their program for future change, however, Ōkubo and his fellow oligarchs had to contend with countercoups launched by those who left Tokyo in anger in 1873.

The first to take up arms was Etō Shinpei, a key member of the Dajōkan who had steered the effort to reform Japan's legal system. When Ōkubo and his allies scotched the proposal to invade Korea, Etō resigned his post as justice minister and returned to his native Saga Prefecture, carved out of the former Hizen domain. A natural lightning rod for ex-samurai disgruntled with the Dajōkan's peace policy and its attempts to destroy the samurai class, Etō first campaigned for the inauguration of a national legislature to replace that governing body. As his effort came to naught, he gathered some three thousand dissident samurai around him and in February 1874 attacked banks and government offices. Ōkubo personally took charge of an expeditionary force and quickly quelled the Saga Rebellion. Etō himself managed to flee, but Ōkubo's troops tracked him down and returned him to Saga. Two months later the government executed Etō and publicly exposed his decapitated head on a pillory as a gruesome deterrent to other potential rebels.

Following a series of fervent but isolated *shizoku* uprisings in western Japan in 1876, which the Meiji government put down with dispatch, Saigō Takamori led the dissidents' most serious challenge to the new regime. Accompanied by several hundred members of the imperial guard and metropolitan police force who had resigned their commissions, Saigō departed the capital in 1873 for his native Kagoshima. At home in the former Satsuma domain, he lived on a stipend granted for past services to the throne, but he totally abandoned politics and happily took up the life of a gentleman farmer, working the land, hunting and fishing, and tramping the countryside with his beloved dogs. The rustic life, far removed from what he aphoristically saw as the corrupting politics of Tokyo, brought Saigō much joy, which he expressed poetically:

> **Since ancient times misfortune has been the usual price of worldly fame,**
>
> **Far better then to trudge home through the woods, carrying a spade upon my shoulder.**[9]

Whatever his desire for a bucolic retreat from political intrigues, Kagoshima Prefecture in the 1870s was filled with angry young samurai who felt betrayed by the Meiji government and looked upon Saigō as their hero and savior. Not entirely immune to their affections, Saigō in 1874 pledged a portion of his annual stipend to help underwrite a system of private academies in hope of bringing some discipline and moral training to the lives of those disconsolate young men. Additional funding for the schools came from prefectural officials who, as advocates of local autonomy, criticized the Dajōkan for continually centralizing decision-making authority in its own hands and for ignoring regional needs when setting policy. By 1876 the system of private academies, which enrolled several thousand students, consisted of infantry and artillery schools in the prefectural capital of Kagoshima and branch schools in each rural district, where scions of warriors gave some thought to the traditional Chinese classics but dedicated most of their time to classes on physical fitness and military tactics.

Before another year had passed, the students would involve a reluctant Saigō in an act of sedition. Late in 1876 a suspicious Tokyo government sent spies to Kagoshima to gather information about the private academies. Within weeks the students unmasked the outsiders and tortured one of them into confessing that the central authorities were planning to dissolve the academies and murder Saigō. Despite the fragile reliability of that coerced revelation, the students primed themselves for further action, and late in January 1877 they illegally carted off weapons and ammunition from government arsenals in Kagoshima after learning that officials in Tokyo were dispatching ships to transfer the ordnance to warehouses in Osaka.

At the time Saigō was off on a hunting trip, but he hurriedly returned to Kagoshima when he learned of the assaults on the arsenals. He was furious with the students for their impetuous action. Saigō was a man of immense physical proportions, a full head taller than the average Japanese with a girth to match, and his frequent fits of temper left few unimpressed. His eruptions typically were short-lived, however, and he soon forgave the students and reconciled himself to the inevitable. His old colleagues, even those like Ōkubo who hailed from Satsuma, would never pardon the attacks on the government's arsenals; Tokyo would judge the raids to be open acts of rebellion, and retaliation was certain. As the founding patron of the academy system in Kagoshima the aging veteran naturally held himself responsible for the fate of the students, who had muddled their way into a situation from which they could not hope to extract themselves. But even more seemed at stake. Saigō's long-standing frustrations with Tokyo's policies suggested that 1877 represented one final opportunity to defend a personal identity, a warrior ethos, and a traditional way of life that had come under unrelenting assault and was about to disappear. What other choice was there, Saigō concluded, but to unfurl the banners of rebellion? His only concern was to make it clear that he was not being disloyal to the emperor. The culprits, he wrote, were his former friends and colleagues, the "great criminals of the universe," who had deceived and misled the throne and therefore had to be deposed.

His mind now set, Saigō swiftly mobilized his forces, and the rebel army marched out of Kagoshima on the morning of February 15. Magically, a rare snowstorm blanketed the city, a reminder of another momentous day in Japanese history when men of pure and honorable intentions had cut down Ii Naosuke and began the overthrow of a corrupt regime. A week later, halfway up Kyūshū, Saigō's battalions met their first obstacle, the gov-

ernment's conscripts garrisoned at Kumamoto Castle. Saigō threw wave after wave of his warriors against the castle's four thousand defenders, but to
his surprise and chagrin, the vastly outnumbered conscripts of peasant and
merchant origin held their ground against the samurai attackers. As the siege
continued, the government rushed additional divisions to Kyūshū. With almost sixty thousand men under arms, Ōkubo in March ordered an all-out
counterattack that forced Saigō's armies, which at their peak numbered thirty
thousand men, to make a long and bloody retreat back to Kagoshima.

In September, Saigō and the few hundred men who remained by his side
dug into the low hills just to the north of the castle. On September 23 Yamagata Aritomo, the commanding field general of the imperial armies, addressed a letter to Saigō, imploring him to put down his arms. Employing
intimate language that old friends might use with one another, Yamagata expressed his "compassion" and "sympathetic understanding" for Saigō's actions.
Still, Yamagata went on, it was evident that "the Satsuma men cannot hope
to accomplish their purpose," and it was time to end this "sad situation" where
friends fought friends and kinsmen killed one another. Saigō read the missive
in silence and sent no reply. The next morning Yamagata attacked, and a bullet caught Saigō as he strode into battle, entering his right hip and ripping its
way through his pelvis and into the left femur, according to the official au-
topsy report. Such a traumatic battlefield wound presumably would have resulted in shock and almost immediate death, but a more romanticized legend
grew up around Saigō's demise. After being hit, according to the new heroic
account, Saigō composed himself, faced in the direction of the far-off Imperial Palace, and used his sword to commit ritual suicide. The conscript army
had prevailed; the Satsuma Rebellion was at an end.

Saigō's insurrection was the samurai's last hurrah. Their death rattle was
heard on a spring morning the following May, when a group of ex-samurai
accosted Ōkubo Toshimichi as he made his way to a meeting at the Imperial Palace. At a spot just a few moments walk from where Ii Naosuke had
met his fate eighteen years earlier, six assailants pulled Ōkubo from his carriage and stabbed him to death. At their trial the assassins accused Ōkubo
of promulgating laws arbitrarily and of prejudicing Japan's national honor
by mishandling foreign relations, charges that Ii had faced earlier. Whereas
1860 marked the beginning of revolt, however, 1877 and 1878 represented
a closure of the revolutionary moment. Those years witnessed the final assassination of a leading oligarch and the last serious attempt to overturn the
new government by force, events that left the Meiji leadership free to pursue its dreams for the future without any threat of sustained, violent resistance from reactionary diehards.

## Learning about the West

Even as the Meiji oligarchs asserted their claims to authority in the 1870s, hammering out the initial reforms that drew power into their hands and beating back their opponents, they began to search for ideas and prototypes that might guide their continuing efforts to achieve the Meiji Dream of national independence, treaty revision, equality with the West, and domestic tranquillity and prosperity. As they pondered the future, many Meiji leaders looked to the West for lessons about how to organize political institutions, create economic wealth, and foster social harmony. Other Japanese outside government were equally fascinated by the political vitality, military invincibility, and wondrous science and technology of Western nations. The intense interest in the West shared by the nation's leaders and some of its most influential private citizens begot an era of *bunmei kaika* ("Civilization and Enlightenment"). That new phrase rolled off the tongues of all in the 1870s as the Japanese contemplated ways to shrug off the "base practices of the past" and realize their hopes for a better, more secure life.

The turn to the West was facilitated by the rapid spread of Dutch Learning during the late eighteenth and early nineteenth centuries. After Perry's arrival, however, many Japanese were no longer content to learn about the West merely through books and surrendered themselves to a zeitgeist that one young man described as a "desire to speed to foreign shores and take up the great task of observing far-off lands."[10] The first wave of the curious went abroad in the 1860s. A few stole off furtively. Among them was Niijima Jō, who begged passage aboard an American merchantman in 1864 and later returned as Japan's first ordained Protestant minister. Others went as part of special delegations: In 1862 the shogunate sent several young samurai to study at the University of Leiden, the pioneering institution of Japanese studies in Europe, Itō Hirobumi and Inoue Kaoru were in a contingent that Chōshū domain secretly dispatched to England in 1863, and in 1866 the Tokugawa government named Nakamura Masanao to lead a group of students to London.

Most Japanese who journeyed to the West in the 1860s did so as members of shogunal diplomatic missions. The prominent finance commissioner Oguri Tadamasa and Fukuzawa Yukichi, a young samurai who had achieved proficiency in Dutch and English, were on the *Kanrin Maru* when that ship took Japan's first official embassy to the United States in 1860 for the purpose of ratifying the Treaty of Amity and Commerce. So intense was interest in that mission that Walt Whitman wrote his "A Broadway Pageant"

*Japan's first diplomatic mission to the United States, 1860*

to celebrate America's wonder at seeing Asians parade down the streets of New York:

> I too, arising, answering, descend to the pavements, merge with the crowd, and gaze with them.
> Superb-faced Manhattan!
> Comrade Americans!—to us, then at last, the Orient comes.
> To us, my city,
> Where our tall-topt marble and iron beauties range on opposite sides—to walk in the space between,
> To-day our Antipodes come.[11]

In all, the shogunate sent seven missions to the United States and Europe before its demise in 1868. Besides their diplomatic duties, the three hundred or so representatives who traveled to foreign shores investigated the institutions and cultures of the nations they visited, adding to Japan's fund of knowledge about the West and doing much to modify the popular image of Americans and Europeans as uncivilized barbarians.

The floodgates to Western knowledge opened wide in 1868. Within a decade several hundred Japanese were studying in the United States and Europe, and an even greater number of foreigners, many in the employ of the national and prefectural governments, lived in Japan, instructing the Japanese in the finer points of Western political administration, medical practices, legal philosophies, technological advances, and education systems. Increasingly, international expositions provided another avenue for learning about the wonders of the outside world. One of the last shogunal missions to Europe attended the Exposition Universelle held in Paris in 1867, as did a delegation from Satsuma domain. The Meiji government sent representatives to Vienna in 1873, Melbourne in 1875, Philadelphia in 1876, Paris in 1878, and Sydney in 1879 and 1880. In 1877 the new regime hosted its own First National Industrial Exposition in Tokyo. For that event, which opened on August 18, the government erected an art gallery and temporary Western-style buildings dedicated to farming, machinery, and natural products. In all, more than sixteen thousand exhibitors from Japan and abroad displayed almost 100,000 items, ranging from windmills to steam engines. The emperor and empress attended opening day festivities, and the exposition attracted an average of more than fifteen hundred spectators a day before closing on December 31.

## The Iwakura Mission

One of the more remarkable ventures in learning about Western cultures came in 1871, when Iwakura Tomomi led a delegation of government leaders on an extended journey to the United States and Europe. The mission's primary objective was to make goodwill visits to the heads of fifteen countries that maintained official diplomatic relations with Japan. The embassy also hoped to sound out foreign governments about the possibility of renegotiating the irksome unequal treaties that infringed on Japan's national sovereignty. The size and composition of the mission, however, suggested that its third task—to learn firsthand about the West and ferret out its secrets for success—might be its most significant. In all, forty-nine officials, including such important members of the inner circle as Itō Hirobumi, Ōkubo Toshimichi, and Kido Takayoshi, set sail from Yokohama on the twelfth day of the Eleventh Month 1871. They divided themselves into subgroups assigned to study the constitutions and political systems of the West; col-

*The Iwakura Mission departs for the United States*

lect economic information about trade, industry, banking, taxation, and currency; and investigate educational systems and philosophies. Accompanying the officials were fifty-eight students, among them five girls aged six to fifteen, who were slated to remain overseas for several years as students.

After landing in San Francisco, the embassy traveled to Washington, where meetings with President Ulysses S. Grant and Secretary of State Hamilton Fish drove home a sobering realization: The world's leading powers would not accede to treaty revision until Japan had proved its modernity by reforming its domestic laws and institutions so as to make them more similar to those found in the West. The delegation thereupon moved diplomatic discussions to the back burner and focused its energies on learning about the West. Breaking into their subgroups, Iwakura and his colleagues visited all manner of places: prisons and police offices, schools and museums, mints and chambers of commerce, shipyards and textile mills and sugar refineries. The pace was unrelenting, according to the mission's official diarist:

No sooner had our train arrived and we unloaded our baggage at the hotel than our tour began. During the daytime we rushed about from place to place, viewing machines that peeled and locomotives that roared. We stood amidst the acrid smell of steel with smoke billowing around us and became covered with soot and dirt. Returning to our hotel at dusk, we barely had time to brush off our dirty clothes before the hour of our banquet approached. At the banquet we had to maintain a dignified manner; if invited to the theater, we had to strain eyes and ears to follow what took place on stage, and all of this led to exhaustion. No sooner had we retired at night, than morning greeted us with an escort sent to guide us around a factory.[12]

The members of the Iwakura Mission may have been exhausted, but what they saw enthralled them. Originally the officials had scheduled seven months for their trip, but they extended their sojourn by a year, returning only in the autumn of 1873, when the debate over Korea demanded their attention. By that time the commissioners had visited nine cities in the United States and spent a full year in Europe, where they traveled from Liverpool to Rome, Marseilles and Paris to St. Petersburg and Stockholm.

Two questions came to the fore as the Iwakura Mission made its way across America and Europe. First, the commissioners wondered, How did the West arrive at its contemporary condition? To what, that is, could one attribute the wealth, power, and cultural achievements that seemed so evident everywhere in the United States and Europe? Second, how might the island nation of Japan, the "antipodes" of Whitman's poem, so geographically removed from the West, shape its own quest for modernity so that it too might enter the ranks of the world's advanced nations? No easy answers emerged, but certain postulates did suggest themselves. Foremost was the uncontested confirmation of the superiority of Western science and technology. Writing from America in January 1872, Kido confessed that previously he had not realized just how advanced the West really was. Japan's "present civilization," he concluded, "is not true civilization, our present enlightenment is not true enlightenment."[13] Moreover, members of the mission concluded, modernity was an inevitable consequence of the past; it was the accumulation of the West's particular historical experiences—the total sum of its cultural values, social organization, and educational practices as they evolved over time—that accounted for the present superior ranking of the United States and the countries of western Europe within the hierarchy of nations and for their ability to overwhelm the traditional cultures of Asia.

In addition, while "the West" was convenient shorthand, the commissioners came to realize that Euro-America was not an undifferentiated whole. Some nations had progressed farther than others, or as the mission's diarist put it, England "swaggers fearlessly in the world" and "Setting out from Paris, the farther east one goes, the shallower civilization gradually becomes."[14] Such distinctions were extremely important for the Japanese to comprehend since the nations of the West appeared to be engaged in a struggle among themselves for wealth and power. Put into the Social Darwinian context so popular in the middle of the nineteenth century, the nations that most successfully embraced modern technology, civilized institutions, and liberal values seemed destined to dominate the international environment; those who failed to do so faced colonization or even extinction.

The notion that the world was a dangerous place and that modernity was rooted deeply in the West's own distinctive past experiences came as troubling messages, but the journey to the United States and Europe yielded one extremely hopeful maxim as well. More than one member of the Iwakura Mission was astonished to learn that the West's technological and industrial brilliance had flowered only recently. "Most of the countries in Europe shine with the light of civilization and abound in wealth and power," wrote the mission's diarist. "Their trade is prosperous, their technology is superior, and they greatly enjoy the pleasures and comforts of life. When one observes such conditions, one is apt to think that these countries have always been like this, but such is not the case—the wealth and prosperity one sees now in Europe dates to an appreciable degree from the period after 1800. It has taken scarcely forty years to produce such conditions. Those who read this record should reflect upon the lesson to be drawn for Japan."[15]

That recency suggested, as the diarist implied, that Japan should be able to bridge the gap between itself and the advanced nations of the West if the country's leaders acted wisely and judiciously to acquire foreign industry, technology, and learning. Among those, political reform and industrialization seemed to claim the highest priorities. For Kido, parliamentary institutions constituted the "hallmarks" of a higher civilization, the most promising way to rationalize the political order and ensure unity of purpose between the rulers and the ruled. Ōkubo, in contrast, was more impressed with manufacturing. "Our recent travels," he wrote from London, "have taken us to many very interesting and famous places. There is nowhere we have not been. And everywhere we go, there is nothing growing in the ground, just coal and iron. Factories have increased to an unheard-of extent, so that black smoke rises to the sky from every point of the compass. This is a sufficient explanation of England's wealth and strength."[16]

## Intellectuals and Educators

Many individual Japanese in the private sphere were as determined as the Meiji leadership to study the outside world and bring the advantages of modernity to Japan. Niijima Jō, who sailed off to the United States in 1864, was graduated from Amherst College in 1870, becoming the first Japanese to receive a degree from a Western institution of higher learning. A Christian convert, Niijima continued his theological training at Andover Seminary and lent his services as a translator to the Iwakura Mission. After his return to Japan, he successfully called upon Kido and other Meiji leaders for permission to establish a Christian academy in Kyoto. Named Dōshisha, the school began operations in November 1875 with just eight students but quickly attracted large numbers of youths who subscribed to Niijima's view that Westernization, civilization, and Christianity formed an inseparable trinity necessary for future progress. "It is the spirit of liberty, the development of science, and the Christian morality that have given birth to European civilizations," was how Niijima once put it. "We cannot therefore believe that Japan can secure this civilization until education rests upon the same basis."[17]

Other intellectuals turned to translation as a way to disseminate the ideals of Civilization and Enlightenment. One after another during the 1870s the thoughts of Mill, Bentham, Spencer, Tocqueville, Guizot, and Rousseau concerning civil liberties, natural rights, utilitarianism, and rational positivism became available in Japanese translation. Perhaps the single most influential foreign book of the *bunmei kaika* era was Samuel Smiles's *Self-Help*, which reportedly sold more than one million copies, four times the number marketed in Britain and the United States. Freely rendered, and even totally rewritten in parts by Nakamura Masanao, who became familiar with Smiles's hortatory writings during his stay in London, the translated version of the best seller implicitly condemned the hierarchical status system of the Tokugawa era and encouraged Smiles's ethos of "achieving success and rising in the world." Throughout the volume Nakamura underscored his key point: Each individual had the duty to work hard and to cultivate his own talents in order to advance in the world and make Japan a stronger country. An entire generation of Meiji youths drew inspiration from Nakamura's rendition of Smiles's opening lines: "The proverb, 'Heaven helps those who help themselves' is a truism, empirically verifiable. In this adage lies the success or failure of everything in human affairs. In broader terms, when the majority of a nation's people 'help themselves,' that state is filled with vigor and is strong in spirit."[18]

The most prominent, indefatigable propagator of Western knowledge in the 1870s was Fukuzawa Yukichi. Born into an impoverished samurai family from Nakatsu domain in Kyūshū, Fukuzawa from his youth despised what he regarded as the "narrow stiffness" of the Tokugawa status order. To escape the bleak confines of his foreordained future, he went to Nagasaki in 1854 and then to Osaka to study the Dutch language and Western sciences. Four years later he traveled to Edo, only to discover to his dismay that English, not Dutch, was the common language of the international community. Undaunted, he turned his tireless enthusiasm to the study of English, and in 1860 he boarded the *Kanrin Maru* as a translator for the first Japanese embassy to the United States. Two years later he traveled with another shogunal mission to England, France, Holland, Portugal, and Russia, where he absorbed all he could of Western civilization.

Fukuzawa's observations led him to conclusions that paralleled those of other enlightenment figures. Japan was weak and backward, he decided, because its traditional culture did not promote the kind of scientific curiosity, self-reliant independence, and ethos of individual achievement that characterized Western peoples. To help inculcate in Japan the values he treasured in the West, Fukuzawa became an educator, publicist, and writer. In 1868

*Fukuzawa Yukichi*

he affixed the name Keiō Gijuku (Keiō Academy, Keiō University from 1910) to a school for Dutch Learning that he had started in Edo a decade earlier and made it into one of Japan's leading training centers for young men interested in Western scholarship. Six years later, in February 1874, Fukuzawa joined Nakamura as a charter member of the Meirokusha (Meiji Six Society), established to "promote Civilization and Enlightenment" through public lectures and its journal, *Meiroku zasshi*, which became an important vehicle for introducing new ideas about such diverse topics as ethics and religion, politics and the nature of government, international relations and foreign trade, and the position of women and the function of the family in society. Somewhat later Fukuzawa began to publish his own journal, and in 1882 he founded one of Japan's first newspapers.

Fukuzawa's voluminous and lucid writings, twenty-two volumes in a modern collected edition, summed up the entire thrust of enlightenment thinking about the negativity of the Japanese past and the shining beacon of Western culture. His *Gakumon no susume* ("An Encouragement of Learning," 1872–1876) contained a ringing indictment of Japan: "If we compare the knowledge of the Japanese and Westerners, in letters, in techniques, in commerce, or in industry, from the largest to the smallest matter, there is not one thing in which we excel. Outside of the most stupid person in the world, no one would say that our learning or business is on a par with those of the Western countries. Who would compare our carts with their locomotives, or our swords with their pistols? In Japan's present condition there is nothing in which we may take pride vis-à-vis the West. All that Japan has to be proud of is its scenery."[19]

To overcome their backwardness, according to Fukuzawa, the Japanese needed to replicate the cultural practices that heralded the progress of the West. He coined the term "Civilization and Enlightenment" in his widely read multivolume *Seiyō jijō* ("Conditions in the West," 1867–1870). "Examining history," Fukuzawa wrote, "we see that life has been dark and closed, and that it advances in the direction of civilization and enlightment."[20] In the same volumes the young pro-Westernizer provided his readers with information about those foreign institutions he hoped the Japanese would emulate, such as schools, hospitals, newspapers, libraries, museums, workhouses, and orphanages. But more than the physical manifestations of the West's greatness, Fukuzawa urged the Japanese to grasp the cultural essence of the West. "Schools, industries, armies and navies are the mere external form of civilization," he wrote in 1872. "They are not difficult to produce. All that is needed is the money to pay for them. Yet there remains something immaterial, something that cannot be seen or heard, bought or sold, lent or borrowed. It pervades the whole nation and its influence is so strong that without it none of the schools or the other external forms would be of the slightest use. This supremely important thing we must call the spirit of civilization."[21]

That observation about the "spirit of civilization" brought Fukuzawa to a final prescription: Japan needed a new kind of citizen who was unfettered by the restrictions of the past and open to new ways of thinking about self and society. "Heaven did not create men above men, nor set men below men," he wrote at the beginning of *Gakumon no susume*. No longer bound by the restrictions of the traditional status system, each individual was free to go as far as his own hard work, pluck, diligence, and perseverance would take him. For Fukuzawa, as for Nakamura and Smiles, achievement-oriented individualism was the true source of Civilization and Enlightenment, and only people of ambition and accomplishment could create a secure, strong, and prosperous nation.

## Fostering Civilization and Enlightenment

Convinced by what they had seen abroad and encouraged by the growing excitement for Civilization and Enlightenment at home, Kido, Ōkubo, and the other members of the Iwakura Mission returned to Japan in 1873 committed to building a "Prosperous Nation, Strong Military," as summed up in another popular phrase of the day, *fukoku kyōhei*. Still, they realized, one could not blithely launch a complex program of reform. A gradual approach was needed in order to sort out the relationships among political, economic, social, and cultural change. Also, since the West offered no single blueprint of modernity but, rather, delivered a collection of models for emulation and inspiration, one had to study the prototypes closely to see which were most appropriate for Japan. An imperial greeting presented by the mission to the president of the United States in March 1872 foreshadowed that consensus. "We expect and intend to reform and improve," the emperor of Japan wrote, "so as to stand upon a similar footing with the most enlightened nations. The civilization and institutions of Japan are so different from those of other countries, however, that we cannot expect to reach the desired end at once. It is our purpose to select from the various institutions prevailing among enlightened nations such as are the best suited to our present condition and adopt them, in gradual reforms and improvements of our policy and customs, so as to be upon equality with them."[22]

The agrarian discontent and turmoil stirred up by disgruntled samurai that confronted Iwakura and his confederates upon their return to Japan reaffirmed their conclusion that any ambitious program of political and economic change had to await the further consolidation of power and the closing of the revolutionary moment. In the meantime, the Meiji leaders could hope to foster Civilization and Enlightenment by promoting Western ways of thought and introducing examples of material culture. Even before the Iwakura Mission arrived back in Tokyo, for instance, the government decided to establish a modern school system. The Fundamental Code of Education, issued in the Eighth Month of 1872, divided the country into university, middle school, and elementary school districts and mandated four years of compulsory education for all boys and girls beginning from age six. The new school system deemphasized the Confucian morality found in the schools of the Tokugawa period, promoting instead a curriculum that stressed the practical arts and sciences, self-improvement, and the development of the individual. Consequently, students learned basic reading, writing, and arithmetic in the thousands of elementary schools that had opened by 1875, but they also studied translated Western materials on history, geography, and science.

More visible and tangible than the new educational ideas were the Western-inspired dress, food, and architecture encouraged by the Meiji government. The military outfitted its new conscript army in Western-style uniforms, and the emperor and his officials adopted foreign dress for public ceremonies. Before long, many ordinary Japanese in the country's urban centers began to show a preference for Western garments, although some devised curious combinations, such as wearing a kimono over trousers. Rolled black umbrellas, diamond rings, and gold watches became conspicuous as popular symbols of an enlightened and progressive attitude, and an urban, self-defined avant-garde considered it fashionable to eat beef, drink beer, and sip coffee.

Even the physical face of Japan's cities started to change as the new regime put up buildings intended to symbolize the vigor, determination, and optimism inherent in the search for Civilization and Enlightenment. In Osaka the Meiji government employed Thomas James Waters, an English engineer and architect, to design a national mint. Completed in 1871, the complex included a long, squat foundry block flanked by a director's residence and reception pavilion. Not all critics wrote favorably about the somewhat awkwardly apportioned portico at the center of the facade, seeing it as an embarrassed attempt at Greek Revival, but the mint certainly projected an image of substance, stability, and permanence—attributes that the new government wished to advertise as its own. In Matsumoto and dozens of other provincial cities around the country, the Meiji leaders constructed imposing new schools, typically two-story structures complete with elaborate porticos, ornate entranceways, and majestic cupolas. The architectonic message was obvious. "It was new, and built from the start as a school, with a second storey and windows all round, which made the rooms almost dazzlingly bright, a playground, imposing black gates, with the school's name inscribed on the posts, and a flagpole. It *looked* like a school," marveled one enthusiastic young pupil.[23]

For the people of Tokyo, the government rebuilt the Ginza, a neighborhood of humble artisan shops south of the great merchant center of Nihonbashi. After fire had consumed the area in 1872, the Meiji government commissioned Waters to compose an entire district of red brick. When the rebuilding was completed three years later, it contained nearly a thousand Westernized brick buildings and streets illuminated by gaslights. In time the Ginza became home to enterprises spawned by the impulse for Civilization and Enlightenment: Shiseidō, the first prominent manufacturer of Western cosmetics, began as a Ginza pharmacy just after the great fire, while young Hattori Kintarō set up his Seikō Watch Company in the heart of the Ginza in 1881 and erected a clock tower that, in various incarnations, remained the area's defining architectural symbol for nearly a century.

Not far from the Ginza, the government built for itself the Rokumeikan, the Hall of the Baying Stag, whose name derived from an ancient Chinese

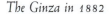

*The Ginza in 1882*

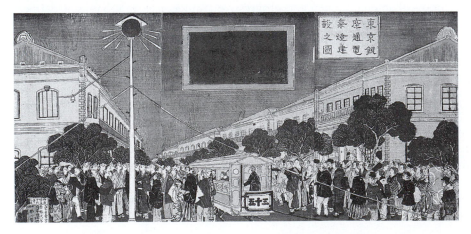

poem and signified a welcoming summons to a convivial gathering. The Rokumeikan, however, was anything but traditional. Conceived of by Inoue Kaoru, a ranking government official, the Hall of the Baying Stag was a two-story brick structure executed in an ornate Italianate style. With rooms for reading, dining, music, and billiards, the hall became the capital's elite social center, where wealthy and cosmopolitan Japanese could mix with influential foreign dignitaries. It also featured a spacious ballroom, and when Sunday evening waltzes became a fixture on social calendars, the term "Rokumeikan" turned into a synonym for the social elan and the faddish Westernization of the late 1870s and early 1880s.

"At the present time an immense number of European customs are pouring in upon us," wrote one influential government official in 1874; "it is as though a bottle has been overturned. Clothing, food and drink, houses, laws, government, customs, even all kinds of crafts and scholarly pursuits—there is nothing which we are not today taking from the West."[24] The winds of Westernization blew most tempestuously during the decade of the 1870s, that "revolutionary moment" when the people of the country had to decide whether to resist the fledgling regime or to support the young Meiji leadership. Not unnaturally, some individuals felt repulsed by the exaggerated passions for Civilization and Enlightenment. On one level, cartoonists and satirists expressed their alienation by caricaturing persons in Western dress or by coining popular ditties. "Thump one of those heads freshly barbered in Western style," went one jingle, "and it sounds back 'bunmei kaika.'" On a more serious note, fear of what unbridled Westernization implied for the future of the samurai estate contributed to the decision of Saigō Takamori and Etō Shinpei to leave government in 1873 and stand at the head of countercoups.

For many other Japanese, however, the idea of Civilization and Enlightenment seemed to hold out an optimistic promise that the future could be better, that the nation could prosper and individuals flourish. Even in a provincial city such as Kanazawa, far removed from Tokyo, where the impact of Westernization was felt first and most fully, the certainty of progress embedded in the slogan bunmei kaika cast up an encouraging alternative to the collective memory of all the "failed expectations" that had weighed people down before 1868. In that castle town, impoverished samurai in the first half of the nineteenth century had torn out their landscape gardens in order to grow fruits and vegetables to sell in the city's markets. In the 1870s members of those same samurai lineages assisted in opening new schools, helped found hospitals, and joined their merchant neighbors in developing new business enterprises whose products, ranging from ceramics to textiles, were displayed prominently at all those international expositions in Europe and Australia. Across Japan, the contrast between a past in which aggravations and miseries had been so manifold and a present in which opportunities to rectify those inherited problems seemed about to blossom encouraged people to overcome whatever doubts they might have had about the new Meiji regime and to accept, at least provisionally, its claims to act as the legitimate government of the country. Whether they would continue to do so depended on how successfully the Meiji leaders advanced the "new beginnings" set forth in the Charter Oath concerning representative government, the furtherance of economic prosperity, and the creation of a society of opportunity.

## CHAPTER 6

# Crafting a Constitutional Polity

or Itō Hirobumi, it was the defining, crowning moment in what his colleagues hailed as a lifetime of achievement. On the morning of February 11, 1889, Itō approached the emperor of Japan, whose throne rested atop a red-carpeted dais in the refurbished reception chamber of the imperial compound. Resplendent in formal Western-style dress, and in full view of a gallery filled to overflowing with Japan's peerage, ministers of state, prefectural governors, high-ranking military officials, and foreign diplomats, Itō offered up to the emperor a scroll inscribed with Japan's new constitution. Without either reading or examining the document, the emperor promptly handed it down to the prime minister, Kuroda Kiyotaka, who "received it with a deep reverence."[1] Turning, the emperor "nodded" and departed the hall to the strains of "Kimigayo," Japan's newly composed, although still unofficial, national anthem. Outside, bells rang and cannons roared. In a ceremony that had lasted just a few brief moments, Emperor Meiji had bestowed upon his subjects the Constitution of the Empire of Japan.

As the symbolism of the ceremony suggested, however, the monarch had little to do with the actual preparation of the new "fundamental law of the state"; its chief architect was Itō, who had spent the better part of a decade pondering and crafting its every phrase. Even so, Itō had not worked in calm isolation. During the years he and other Meiji leaders spent con-

*The promulgation of the constitution, 1889*

templating and drafting a constitution, a storm of controversy swirled around them as many of their countrymen sought to influence the shape of the new law of the land, whose promulgation, nearly everyone agreed, was essential if the Japanese were to travel the road of progress, as promised by the slogan "Civilization and Enlightenment," and if Japan were to prove to the West that it deserved respect and equal treatment within the community of modern nations.

## The Oligarchs Contemplate a Constitution and Representative Government

While Itō ultimately assumed the central role in drafting Japan's constitution, he was not the first among the new Meiji leaders to consider seriously such a document. That distinction fell to Kido Takayoshi, the native of Chōshū who had helped pen the Charter Oath, with its promise of deliberative assemblies, and who as a member of the Iwakura Mission had spent much of his time abroad examining Western political systems. What Kido learned in Europe convinced him of the practical utility of constitutionalism and representative government. Leaders in the United States and Europe had been unmistakably forthright: Kido and the other oligarchs could never expect to revise the unequal treaties until Japan acquired the idealized attributes of Western political culture, until, that is, Japan ceased being a country where men exercised power arbitrarily and, instead, in the eyes of the West became a nation governed in accordance with rational laws. Moreover, in Kido's view of things, the great vitality of Western political systems flowed from the popular support that the people of each country willingly gave to their government. If the new Meiji state would write a constitution and create a participatory role in government for responsible elements of the citizenry, he calculated, it too could harness the energies and enthusiasms of the population around itself. Similarly, he believed, a country without a working constitution could never hope to be unified internally and thus would always risk falling prey to foreign intervention. Persuaded of constitutionalism's numerous benefits, Kido upon his return to Japan oversaw the compilation of a slate of recommendations that he submitted to his colleagues in November 1873. In that document, he outlined a constitutional system in which the emperor served as the fountainhead of power, ministers of state exercised power in the monarch's name, and a bicameral assembly discharged legislative responsibilities.

Other Meiji leaders soon committed themselves to the constitutional initiative. Ōkubo Toshimichi, an especially influential member of the new ruling elite in the mid-1870s, agreed that a constitutional monarchy with a carefully limited and strictly defined distribution of powers would "establish harmony between the ruler and the people," and in February 1875 Kido, Ōkubo, and Itō hosted a meeting in Osaka to discuss constitutionalism. At that Osaka Conference, the young Meiji leadership decided to establish a Chamber of Elders to debate legislation and deliberate upon a constitution and to convene periodically an Assembly of Prefectural Governors to discuss local administration and tax laws. An imperial rescript issued that April announced those measures and also promised to adopt constitutional government "gradually," in due and deliberate course.

By 1880 the Chamber of Elders, composed chiefly of legal scholars and men named as nobles in 1869, had readied a set of proposals for the oligarchs to consider. In broad terms, its draft adhered to the general patterns of European constitutional monarchies. The emperor accordingly would be vested with supreme command over the army and navy, the authority to appoint ministers of state, and the right to declare war, make peace, and conclude treaties. Other powers were to be distributed more widely. Legislative responsibilities, the document suggested, should be "divided between the Emperor and Parliament," with the upper house having the right to impeach ministers and the lower house possessing the sole authority to approve annual budgets.

Certain of the chamber's recommendations, in particular its delegation of significant powers to the legislature, did not sit well with the majority of the Meiji oligarchs. As proponents of Civilization and Enlightenment men like Kido and Itō welcomed the advent of a constitution and representative government. However, as the emperor's letter to President Grant in 1872 made clear, the Meiji leaders planned to move cautiously and pragmatically. They had no wish to mimic blindly European examples but, rather, intended to "select" foreign institutions that were "best suited" to Japan's needs and then "adopt" those arrangements so that they both fitted the Japanese historical experience and contributed to the goals of future reform. Consequently, in the political debates of the late 1870s, the members of the inner circle favored retaining a prominent role for the imperial institution and drawing strict limits around the influence of any future legislative body. For them, the throne—the keystone of the Japanese state since its inception in the seventh century—could serve as an anchor of continuity in a sea of change, and they adamantly insisted that the emperor must remain as Japan's sovereign, as the primary source of all political authority and legitimacy.

Between 1880 and the spring of 1881, seven leading councillors elucidated those themes in individual commentaries on the chamber's proposals. Iwakura Tomomi, the oldest of the oligarchs, dismissed its ideas as too "un-Japanese," and he advocated strengthening the imperial prerogative by granting the throne the right to issue ordinances with the force of law and by freeing government from fiscal dependency on a parliament. Yamagata Aritomo, father of the new conscript army, agreed. He was willing to share responsibilities. "If we gradually establish a popular assembly and firmly establish a constitution," he wrote, "the things I have enumerated above—popular enmity towards the government, failure to follow government orders, and suspicion of the government, these three evils—will be cured in the future."[2] But within that context, he went on, there could be "no argument on the point that the constitution should lay down that the land should be forever governed by an Emperor of unbroken family lineage." Itō concurred that the monarch and the ministers appointed by the throne had to provide the center of gravity for any future political arrangements, and he urged circumspection and careful planning: "I say that we should not establish a parliament hastily. This does not mean that we, the ruling group, want to remain at the helm of state and occupy the highest posts as long as possible. Although it is very desirable to establish limited monarchy by convoking a parliament, we must not do anything that would seriously modify our national polity. We should first make the footings firm, then erect the foundation posts, and finally raise the house. This must be done in an orderly fashion."

## Opposing Paradigms, Contentious Debate

Inspired by rhetoric about Civilization and Enlightenment in the 1870s, many private individuals in Japan agreed with the Meiji leaders that representative institutions would open up a new and brighter future for Japan, but they embraced more liberal views about constitutionalism and wished to proceed at a faster pace than did Itō and his associates. In the autumn of 1873, Itagaki Taisuke was one of the disgruntled councillors within the Dajōkan who resigned their positions following the bitter dispute concerning policy toward Korea. Whereas Etō Shinpei and Saigō Takamori took up arms against their former comrades, however, Itagaki returned to his native Tosa and founded the Public Party of Patriots (Aikoku Kōtō). As its head Itagaki drafted a memorial, submitted to the government in January 1874, that criticized the "unbridled" and "despotic" authority of officials in Tokyo, hailed the principle of no taxation without representation, and demanded the immediate creation of a national assembly "chosen by the people" and endowed with substantial powers of governance.[3]

Since Itagaki found himself standing outside the corridors of power in 1874, many Japanese regarded his Tosa Memorial less as a resounding call to the principles of Western-style liberalism than as a self-serving political broadside that expressed his jealousy about how men from Satsuma and Chōshū, the so-called Satchō clique, attempted to keep their hands on the main levers of power. Whatever Itagaki's motives, however, his petition drew immediate support from numerous ex-samurai, who were extremely unhappy with the oligarchs' intentions to create a conscript army and abolish stipends. Willing and eager to explore the meaning of concepts such as freedom, democracy, and representative government, ex-samurai in many places quickly organized political associations that beat the drums for a national parliament and, at the same time, attempted to improve economic conditions for warrior families by sponsoring credit unions and offering advice about how to manage new business enterprises. In 1875 Itagaki and his Self-Help Society (Risshisha), founded a year earlier and named after Samuel

**FIGURE 6.1** *Political Associations, 1874–1889*

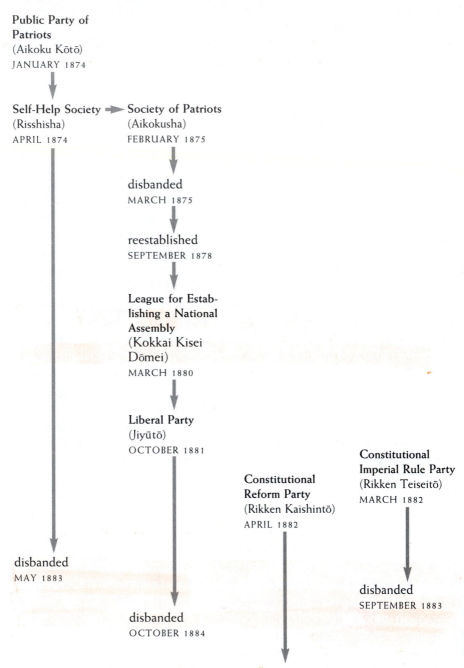

Public Party of
Patriots
(Aikoku Kōtō)
JANUARY 1874

Self-Help Society ➡ Society of Patriots
(Risshisha)          (Aikokusha)
APRIL 1874          FEBRUARY 1875

disbanded
MARCH 1875

reestablished
SEPTEMBER 1878

League for Estab-
lishing a National
Assembly
(Kokkai Kisei
Dōmei)
MARCH 1880

Liberal Party
(Jiyūtō)
OCTOBER 1881

Constitutional
Imperial Rule Party
(Rikken Teiseitō)
MARCH 1882

Constitutional
Reform Party
(Rikken Kaishintō)
APRIL 1882

disbanded
MAY 1883

disbanded
SEPTEMBER 1883

disbanded
OCTOBER 1884

Smiles's influential prescription for success, established the Society of Patriots (Aikokusha) in hopes of coordinating the efforts of the various organizations that had sprung up across the country.

In the middle of the 1870s intellectuals, urbanites, and villagers began to voice their own demands for "freedom and popular rights." As enthusiasm for a Popular Rights Movement swelled, growing numbers of ordinary Japanese joined political societies that sprang up in small towns and villages across the country. Incredibly, by the end of the decade perhaps one thousand such organizations were meeting on a regular basis, and they brought together merchants, artisans, laborers, and farmers to listen to popular orators and to discuss major issues of the day. All topics were open to debate, from current political events to economics, history, and the relationship between natural rights doctrine and the contemporary needs of women, a subject introduced by such female activists as Kishida Toshiko and Fukuda Hideko.

Many of the societies reserved a special place on their agenda for consideration of a new constitution and legislative assembly. As debates about the future political system unfolded, many leaders of the socially diverse Popular Rights Movement argued that the essential purpose of the Meiji Restoration was to promote the general welfare of the people, and they further claimed that liberal, broadly representative institutions were best designed to accomplish that goal. Moreover, members of the local political clubs spent considerable time examining the ideas presented in translations of such classical works of Western political thought as John Locke's *Second Treatise on Civil Government*, Jean Jacques Rousseau's *Social Contract*, and John Stuart Mill's *On Liberty* and *Considerations on Representative Government*. Given those intellectual wellsprings, it is not surprising that men and women in the Popular Rights Movement tended to see history as a struggle between authoritarian regimes and rising popular power and articulated notions of constitutionalism that relied heavily on Western doctrines of natural rights, which invested sovereignty in the people, not in the monarch. Drawing on such inspiration, the charter of the Sekiyōsha, a political society founded in the foothills of Fukushima Prefecture by Kōno Hironaka, the son of an ex-samurai family turned farmers, began: "We have come together because government is for the people, and inherent rights of life and personal freedom, which are higher than the mountains and deeper than the sea, will endure forever on this earth."[4]

Astoundingly, some of the local groups did not just talk about constitutions but sat down and collectively drafted their own. To date, historians have discovered approximately thirty such documents. While the specific clauses contained in the drafts vary considerably, taken as a whole, the people's constitutions envisaged a much more liberal and generous sharing of power than Itō and the other Meiji leaders had in mind. In typical fashion, the constitution formulated by the Learning and Debating Society of Itsukaichi, a small marketing town in the mountains northwest of Tokyo, guaranteed the people's rights to justice, freedom, and happiness. It also delegated extensive powers to a national assembly, including the authority to approve treaties and to veto any administrative or imperial action that impinged upon the freedoms granted to the citizenry.

Moreover, most of the new political associations advocated the promulgation of a constitution in much more rapid fashion than the due and deliberate course promised by the imperial rescript of 1875. As the Popular Rights Movement gained momentum in the late 1870s, Sakurai Shizuka, a farmer from Chiba, published a stinging criticism of the government's gradual approach to constitutionalism in a leading Tokyo newspaper, and he further called upon the ordinary men and women of Japan to join together in a petition movement designed to force the Meiji oligarchs to institute representative government. The response was overwhelming. When the Society of Patriots convened for its semiannual meeting in March 1880, thousands of representatives from twenty-four prefectures attended, bringing with them petitions bearing more than 100,000 signatures. Renaming themselves the League for Establishing a National Assembly (Kokkai Kisei Dōmei), the delegates vowed to set the torch to a grassroots campaign, and by the end of the year nearly a quarter of a million people had put their names to twelve different petitions and forty-two memorials demanding the immediate establishment of representative government.

The Meiji government attempted to ride out the growing storm by proposing timely concessions, tempered with repressive laws and ordinances. Kido invited Itagaki to the Osaka Conference in February 1875, for instance, in the hope that the promise of implementing representative government would lure the malcontent samurai from Tosa back into government service. Three years later the oligarchs responded to the growing popular clamor for representative government by establishing prefectural and city assemblies, to be convened for one month each year to deliberate upon bills submitted by the prefectural governor. On the other side of the equation, in June 1875 the regime issued the Press Ordinance, which authorized the police to suspend any newspaper that published material deemed threatening to the public order, and in April 1880 the Public Assembly Ordinance imposed stringent regulations that required police permission for all public assemblies, allowed discussion only of preapproved topics, and denied soldiers, police, teachers, and even students the right to attend political meetings.

The government's preemptory tactics, however, failed to contain the nationwide petition movement, and matters came to a head during the Crisis of 1881. Ōkuma Shigenobu, a former *shishi* from Hizen whose financial expertise had proved invaluable in helping the new regime solidify its power, precipitated the crisis when he broke ranks with his fellow councillors over the issue of constitutionalism. Ōkuma's comments on the proposals drafted by the Chamber of Elders echoed the demands of the more radical elements of the Popular Rights Movement by recommending that Japan adopt a British-style parliamentary system. In stark contrast with his fellow oligarchs, Ōkuma argued for a constitutional scheme that delegated primary political authority to a popularly elected national assembly and to cabinets organized by the majority party in the legislature. Moreover, he admonished his colleagues to move immediately and call elections for the following year.

Those suggestions alarmed the other councillors, who became even more agitated when Ōkuma opposed their plans to sell the assets of the Hokkaidō Colonization Office, established in 1869 to develop the economic potential of the northern island. When the Colonization Office failed to turn a profit after a decade of operations, its director, Kuroda Kiyotaka, proposed selling its assets to a consortium of businessmen led by an old crony from Satsuma, at a nominal cost to be paid with an interest-free loan from the government. Ōkuma exploded in outrage, as did members of the Popular Rights Movement, when terms of the sale leaked out. Caught in a maelstrom of criticism, in October 1881 Itō and his fellow councillors forced Ōkuma to resign from their ranks and sought to assuage public opinion by rescinding the sale and arranging for an imperial rescript declaring: "We shall summon representatives and open a national assembly in the 23rd year of Meiji [1890]."[5]

## Mr. Itō Writes a Constitution

The emperor's dramatic announcement on October 12, 1881, committed the oligarchs to action. In anticipation of the proclamation, Iwakura had spent that summer working out a set of constitutional guidelines that would permit the oligarchs to retain control over the impending experiment with representative government. His thoughts focused on Prussia, which, among the advanced Western nations, he reasoned, served as the most appropriate constitutional model. Like his own island country, Prussia was a newly created nation, fashioned from a varied collection of semiautonomous regions, and it had chosen to rely on a strong executive and bureaucracy for leadership because the social and economic foundations necessary for democratic, parliamentary rule were so transparently weak. Specifically, Iwakura's "general principles," which the Dajōkan formally adopted the day before the emperor issued his rescript, granted the throne the right to appoint all state ministers and senior officials, provided for a cabinet that would be independent from the parliament, and short-circuited parliamentary control over the government's fisc by stipulating that the budget of the previous year would remain in effect if the legislature did not approve a new one. Having agreed upon a constitutional outline, the oligarchs entrusted Itō with drafting the specific document, and in March 1882 he departed for Europe to consult with the West's foremost legal scholars.

The pledge for a constitution drove the regime's opponents toward new modes of political activism. Deprived of the very issue that had aroused so much public enthusiasm, many of the oligarchs' critics opted to jockey for better position within the forthcoming system by organizing themselves into political parties. Just days before the rescript, Itagaki had cast the League for Establishing a National Assembly into the Jiyūtō, or Liberal Party. With Itagaki as party president, and steered by a standing committee composed of men who favored doctrines of French liberalism, the Liberal Party adopted a platform that called for popular sovereignty, a vigorous parliament, and firm guarantees for individual rights and civil liberties. Other parties soon joined the fray. On March 14, 1882, the very day Itō departed for Europe, Ōkuma announced his intention to form the Constitutional Reform Party, or Rikken Kaishintō, whose members included many former students of Fukuzawa Yukichi, such as the vocal Popular Rights advocate Inukai Tsuyoshi. Billing itself as a moderate party that advocated a British-style parliamentary democracy led by a ceremonial monarch, the Constitutional Reform Party won support from students, urban intellectuals, and prominent financiers. Less than a week later Fukuchi Gen'ichirō, the chief editor of the influential newspaper *Tōkyō nichinichi shinbun*, and other leading journalists formed the Constitutional Imperial Rule Party (Rikken Teiseitō) to lend support to the government's cause.

Although most members of the Popular Rights Movement who found their way into the new political parties remained concerned chiefly with trying to influence the structure of the future parliamentary system, other activists, many associated with the Liberal Party, directed their energies toward mass protests, including some that took up issues far removed from constitutionalism. The so-called Fukushima Incident was the first of a dozen or so such large-scale demonstrations in the early 1880s that ended in violence. In the autumn of 1882 the Tokyo government appointed Mishima Michitsune, a former samurai from Satsuma domain, the governor of Fukushima Prefecture. Strong-willed, inflexible, and utterly loyal to his superiors, Mishima immediately began to suppress the Popular Rights Movement in Fukushima, granted official support to the progovernment Constitutional Imperial Rule Party, and announced his intention to double local taxes and conscript labor for road construction projects. Kōno Hironaka, founder of the Sekiyōsha in 1875 and head of the Fukushima branch of the Liberal Party, organized resistance to Governor Mishima's "despotic rule," and many farmers refused to pay taxes or join labor crews. Mishima, with the support of Tokyo, acted swiftly and resolutely. When a thousand or more protesters marched on a police station on November 28, 1882, he ordered a mass roundup of Liberal Party members and sympathizers, six of whom, including Kōno, were later found guilty of treason and sentenced to lengthy prison terms. In a futile act of revenge, radical members of the Liberal Party in neighboring Ibaraki Prefecture hatched a plot to assassinate Mishima and some of the oligarchs, and on September 23, 1884, they issued a revolutionary manifesto from their base on Mount Kaba. Police quickly moved in, and one rebel died in the fighting. The government hanged seven of the survivors and jailed the rest.

Other protests centered on economic issues, and the government brooked little patience with those either. In 1881 Finance Minister Matsukata Masayoshi enacted deflationary policies in order to combat an inflationary spurt in the economy. In the end Matsukata achieved his goal, but only at the expense of a severe rural depression that lasted nearly four years. Particularly hard hit were sericulturists and small-scale producers of cash crops, who relied on short-term debt and could not repay their outstanding loans with the reduced prices that they received for their crops. Across Japan, from Fukushima in the north to Fukuoka Prefecture in the south, organizations of hard-pressed farmers banded together in debtors' parties or poor people's parties to agitate for debt moratoriums and reduced interest rates. In Chichibu, a mountainous sericulture district in western Saitama Prefecture, rural protest turned violent. There local peasant leaders, many associated with the Liberal Party, called upon the prefectural government to lower taxes and negotiate debt relief with local creditors. When such pleas brought no response by the end of October 1884, farmers sacked the homes of unscrupulous moneylenders, stormed government offices to destroy debt records, and intimidated the rich into making donations for poor relief. The Tokyo government quickly rushed in troops seasoned at

Mount Kaba, and by November 10 they had restored order in Chichibu. Shortly, more than three thousand peasants found themselves under arrest, and in February 1885 the government hanged five of the leaders of the Chichibu Incident.

The swift, unequivocal retribution by the state shattered the Popular Rights Movement and immobilized the Liberal Party, which voted to dissolve itself in the fall of 1884. To make certain that the lid did not again come off the cauldron of protest, the government continued to hound individual radicals. In 1885, for instance, police arrested Fukuda Hideko and her lover Ōi Kentarō for plotting to overthrow the Korean monarchy and install a more liberal regime there in the wild, naïve hope that the example of a reform-minded government on the peninsula somehow would goad the Meiji regime to adopt more progressive policies at home. Two years later the oligarchy issued the Peace Preservation Law of 1887, which imposed stringent regulations on public meetings, speeches, and the press. The heart of the new measure, Article 4, authorized the chief of the Tokyo police to expel from the city any person living within an eight-mile radius of the Imperial Palace who was "judged to be scheming something detrimental to public tranquillity."[6] Within days of its issuance, Mishima Michitsune, newly appointed Tokyo police chief after his stint in Fukushima, arrested and banished from the capital more than 570 suspected activists, including several prominent figures in the Popular Rights Movement.

In Europe, Itō seems to have remained largely oblivious of the clamor in the Japanese countryside touched off by the Fukushima Incident. The objective of his foreign expedition, he wrote later, was "to make as thorough a study as possible of constitutional government, of their various provisions, as well as of theories and opinions actually entertained by influential persons."[7] In pursuit of such wisdom, Itō first went to Berlin, where he consulted with constitutional experts Rudolf von Gneist and Albert Mosse. From there Itō journeyed to Vienna to meet with Lorenz von Stein before traveling on to Paris and London, where his group heard Herbert Spencer lecture on the theory of representative government. Itō's conversations and tutoring sessions with the greatest names in Western constitutional theory apparently did not open up any new intellectual vistas for him but, rather, reconfirmed in his mind the sagacity of what he had long believed and what the Dajōkan had adopted as "general principles" in 1881—namely, Japan's quest for modernity and international respect would be served best by creating a Japanese version of what Itō called a "constitutional Rechtsstaat." By that, Itō reported upon his return to Tokyo in August 1883, he meant that sovereignty should be lodged with the monarch, governing authority would be most properly delegated to a cabinet of state ministers responsible only to the emperor and totally independent of the legislature, and a bicameral legislature with a popularly elected lower house should be entrusted with only truncated powers.

Now that the diverse and occasionally divergent thoughts of the oligarchs had coalesced into a consonant harmony about the sort of constitutional system they wanted, Itō in 1884 began to implement several structural reforms designed to prepare the way for a constitutional regime: naming a peerage to populate an upper house in the legislature, shaping a modern cabinet and bureaucracy, and putting the final touches to the reform of local government that had begun with the creation of prefectures in 1871. His timing was propitious. The petition campaign unleashed by Popular Rights activists in the late 1870s had forced the oligarchs to promise a constitution by 1890, but the government's repression of the movement in 1884 opened up a clear field for Itō to run. He would deliver a constitution within the time frame agreed upon—an imperial promise was, after all, a sacred vow, and the oligarchy intended to implement a constitutional monarchy in any event—but he was now free to undertake the necessary preparations in orderly, measured steps and to write a constitution unfettered by any need to compromise with an obstreperous opposition.

Itō's opening move was to establish a new system of peerage, instituted by the promulgation of an imperial ordinance on July 7, 1884. Modeled upon German practices, the Peerage Act did away with the social distinctions created in 1869 and conferred new noble status upon 508 family heads, sorted into the ranks of prince, marquis, count, viscount, and baron. Admitted to the nobility were members of the old court aristocracy—"highborn descendants of illustrious ancestors," in the emperor's phrase—and those rewarded for having rendered meritorious service to the new state, especially "civil and military officers who have signalised themselves by supporting me in the restoration of my rule."[8] Thus, Itō and Yamagata became counts while the heirs of Kido and Ōkubo were made marquis; Itagaki and Ōkuma, however, remained commoners. All ranks came with hereditary financial stipends, and incumbents were eligible for appointment to the upper house when the first national assembly was convened in 1890.

In December 1885 Itō reformed the executive branch of government, creating a modern cabinet system. In that month the Dajōkan passed out of existence, replaced by a cabinet composed of a prime minister and several additional ministers who presided over individual bureaucratic departments. It was the prime minister's responsibility to coordinate the formulation of governmental policies, sign all laws and ordinances, and oversee the activities of the other cabinet members, even though in theory they were directly accountable to the emperor, who officially appointed them to office. At the same time, new regulations detailed how particular ministries were to conduct their affairs and stipulated that they be staffed with "men of talent."

Itō encountered few hitches when introducing the new administrative organization and procedures, largely because the experiences of the early modern era had familiarized everyone with bureaucratic structures and routines. Although the transition went smoothly, the engineering met a mixed reception. Most Western observers were quick to praise Japan's new cabinet system for embodying the most respected contemporary conceptions of a modern bureaucracy, with offices defined by specific function and with all officeholders below the level of minister chosen on the basis of civil service examinations and professionally trained within their branches of service. Yet, as Itō's critics were quick to note, the new system also permitted the Satchō clique to reinforce its basis of power: Eight of the original ten cabinet ministers had grown up in those two former domains, and Itō himself, a Chōshū native, became Japan's first prime minister, serving from December 22, 1885, until April 30, 1888, when he passed the baton to Satsuma-born Kuroda Kiyotaka.

Concern with the system of prefectural government also found a place on Itō's agenda, largely because Yamagata Aritomo argued so convincingly that stable local government was a necessary prerequisite to the successful promulgation of a constitution since, like conscription, it fostered popular allegiance and promoted national unity. Given a free hand by Itō, Yamagata sought advice from Albert Mosse, invited from Germany to sit at Itō's side during the final drafting of the constitution. "If you ask why I had a European draft the law even though the spirit of self-government can be found in our own traditional practices," Yamagata wrote, "it was in order to be in step with the institutions extant among the great powers, and the German system was the most suitable."[9]

Given Yamagata's predilections, it is not surprising that deliberations with Mosse produced a set of ordinances, issued between 1888 and 1890, that replaced the old magistrate–city elder/village headman–*goningumi* linkage with a more comprehensively organized structure that held prefectural, town, and village governments more accountable to central authority. In the end the new system took on a Janus-faced appearance. On the one hand, the new laws nurtured popular loyalty by allowing the local citizenry to elect some of its own officials. On the other hand, in exchange for that modicum of involvement in the political process, Yamagata expected absolute obedience from below, and he made each administrative level sub-ject to the supervision of the next higher layer of officialdom. At the apex of the pyramid sat the Home Ministry with broad powers to design policy and delegate duties so that little room remained for the kind of community self-management that had characterized village and neighborhood life in the early modern era.

Final work on drafting the constitution began in 1885, first at Itō's Tokyo residence, then at his villa on Enoshima, a small inshore island south of the capital, chosen for its privacy and magnificent views of Mount Fuji. Itō gath-ered around him certain trusted colleagues, such as his longtime protégé Inoue Kowashi, and the Germans Mosse and Hermann Roesler, who had left the University of Rostock in 1878 to become an adviser to Japan's Min-istry of Foreign Affairs. For three years the group prepared, discussed, and revised countless drafts, patiently considering the nuances and implications of each proposed clause; only in the spring of 1888 was Itō prepared to un-veil his canvas. Upon Itō's advice, on April 30 the emperor established a Privy Council to scrutinize and ratify the draft, with the understanding that after the promulgation of the constitution the body would continue to func-tion as an advisory agency that could address future questions of constitu-tional interpretation and counsel the emperor about matters of state. The Privy Council consisted of a minimum of twelve men appointed for life by the emperor, and cabinet members were permitted to attend meetings. Itō viewed the Privy Council as such an important supracabinet agency that he resigned as prime minister to become its first president. With his preap-proval, the councillors offered a few amendments to his constitutional draft, for instance, giving the legislature the right to initiate as well as to discuss and vote on laws, and then put its seal of approval to its president's work. "Constitution Itō," as the newspapers dubbed him, was now ready to pre-sent the fruits of his labors to the emperor so that His Majesty might in turn bestow them upon the people of Japan.

## Civic Virtue and State Ideology

As the oligarchs moved toward constitutionalism, they sought to define a political orthodoxy and promote ideals of civic virtue that would convert the residents of the nearly three hundred scattered domains that had ex-isted before 1871 into *kokumin*, "national citizens" unquestioningly loyal to the new state and bonded together around a core of common political val-ues. Itō and his colleagues had reason for concern: The optimism of the *bun-*

*mei kaika* epoch had favorably disposed many Japanese toward the regime, but the oligarchs scarcely could hope to complete their slate of reforms if they were unable to establish the legitimacy of the new constitutional state. Consequently, all national leaders in the 1870s and 1880s lent a hand to the conscious enterprise of cobbling together a package of ideological values and civic ideals that would enable the ordinary Japanese to make coherent sense of the evolving political arrangements engineered by the young regime and to construe for themselves a meaningful place within the new Japan of the Meiji era.

Each oligarch seemed to have his own individual contribution to make to the construction of a suitable political ethos. Itō spoke wistfully of a "common folk" who were peaceful and docile, honest, industrious, happy to sacrifice their individual interests for the sake of their neighbors—"splendid material with which to build up a strong nation," as he put it.[10] Inoue Kowashi, for his part, preferred to stress loyalty and patriotism as the key ingredients of citizenship; without those virtues there could be no national unity, and little that was worthwhile would be accomplished. Yamagata Aritomo certainly shared Inoue's convictions, and he was also a bitter foe of private interest, represented in the political realm by the opposition's political associations, since they threatened to drown a collective, harmonious, and nonpartisan struggle for progress in a sea of divisiveness, disunity, and chaos.

As the oligarchs worked through their ideas, they concluded that the emperor should provide the nucleus for a political orthodoxy, just as he would constitute the heart of the new political system. But that message needed to be heralded with colorful banners and loud trumpets since, as Iwakura noted in the 1870s, the shogun had overshadowed the emperor during the Tokugawa era, with the consequence that "the imperial will is as yet unknown in the remote and distant parts" of the realm.[11] Thus, the young Meiji leadership sent the emperor off to visit the hinterlands of Japan so that "all the people of the nation will turn their eyes and see the greatness of the emperor's conduct."[12] In the two and a half centuries of Tokugawa rule Heavenly Sovereigns ventured outside their home city of Kyoto just three times; in the forty-five years of his enthronement, the Meiji emperor made 102 excursions, including the six Great Circuits of 1872, 1876, 1878, 1880, 1881, and 1885. Traveling by every conveyance available, the handsome young monarch covered thousands of miles, visited every major island, accepted the well-wishes of the farmers who came in from their fields to offer a humble bow, and lodged with local notables, usually entering their residences through a newly erected gate and taking his comfort upon an imperial privy especially installed for the occasion. Attending the emperor, not surprisingly, were men like Kido, Itō, Ōkubo, Kuroda, and Iwakura, all of whom spent some time on the road. The processionals, they agreed, were a grand scheme; the imperial presence informed "the people of the emperor's great virtue" and represented "the opportunity of displaying direct imperial rule in the flesh, thus dispelling misgivings" about proposals for a constitutional monarchy.[13]

As the emperor traversed his islands, many outside government began to voice opinions about political orthodoxy that echoed the values preached by the oligarchs. Fukuchi Gen'ichirō was among the journalists who lined up behind Itō and the other oligarchs. Although scandalized by what he called "the government's slipshod ways in the Hokkaidō land deal," the editor of the *Tōkyō nichinichi shinbun* agreed that constitutionalism was desirable and that the emperor ought to be the sovereign linchpin of the new system.[14] Sovereignty, Fukuchi reiterated in dozens of editorials in the early 1880s, had to be decided in accordance with each nation's historical circumstances. To underscore his point, he wrote about Japan's *kokutai*, adopting the emotion-laden term, usually rendered as "national essence" or "national polity," that had been at the center of anti-Tokugawa rhetoric in the 1850s and 1860s. Japan's *kokutai*, Fukuchi reminded his readers, rested on the principle that a divine line of emperors had reigned, and reigned wisely, since the dawn of Japanese history. As Japan entered the modern world, he continued, it was appropriate that the structures of governance

*Emperor Meiji, 1872*

change, but the essence of authority, the *kokutai*, must be maintained un-changed. "The gods," he wrote passionately, "decreed at the time of the first ascension to the throne that the affairs of state" should be entrusted to the emperor. Thus, even within a constitutional framework, it was necessary that "all government be carried out by imperial will." By adhering to the "fixed principle" of the *kokutai*, he argued, the government would ensure it-self of the allegiance of the citizenry as the emperor led everyone forward on a steady and peaceful evolution into modernity.

Certain intellectuals also attempted to articulate a political ethos that bound the new world of representative government within a framework of traditional virtues. Hozumi Yatsuka, still a student and only approaching the threshold of a long career as a constitutional scholar, contributed in 1882 a series of essays to Fukuchi's *Tōkyō nichinichi shinbun* that expressed his abhorrence of political parties since they placed the egocentric interests of private citizens above the needs of the state. In many instances, Hozumi wrote, "the liberty of the individual must be sacrificed for the sake of soci-ety as a whole," and the best defense against the tyranny of the masses, he asserted, was to place sovereignty with the emperor, who would then rule through a strong, independent bureaucracy that enjoyed secure tenure in office, public respect, and generous salaries.[15]

Even Confucianists, on the defensive throughout much of the era of Civilization and Enlightenment, elbowed their way into the dialogue about political ethos. By the beginning of the 1880s such men as Motoda Nagazane, tutor to the emperor, and Nishimura Shigeki, moralist and au-thor, had become alarmed by the oligarchs' enthusiasm for Western-style reform. In Nishimura's judgment, Itō was not doing nearly enough to pro-mote traditional morality, and his flirtation with Prussian ideas of constitu-tionalism were bound to fail because the oligarch was merely transplanting things Western into Japan in helter-skelter fashion. The irascible Motoda was characteristically blunt; Itō and his colleagues, he fumed, seemed de-termined to convert the "Japanese into painted replicas of Europeans and Americans."[16] The Confucianists' prescription was simple: Return to time-tested values. Morality, Nishimura wrote, was the foundation of everything, from one's personal life to the structure of government, and to be moral, he stressed, was to observe "the spirit of loyalty, filial piety, honor, duty, valor, and shame which had been the traditional foundation of our country since ancient times."[17] The point was obvious, Motoda concurred. Any new po-litical arrangement had to orbit tightly around the emperor since he was the model of virtue, the custodian of the ancestral precepts transmitted across the ages.

The remarkable synergism arising from the multiple concerns about establishing an appropriate political ethos was not lost on Itō as he pondered his constitution. Indeed, by the time he drew together his drafting committee in the middle of the 1880s, he had developed views about the emperor that diverged significantly from those being urged upon him by the European experts. Mosse and Roesler subscribed to the notion of social monarchy, in which an abstract state, embodied in the person of the monarch, stood above society and carried out reforms for the benefit of the citizenry. However, they went on, Europe's historical past bore the scars of those occasions when unrestrained royal prerogatives had distilled into personal absolutism. Thus law and legal institutions were necessary in the present day so that the throne would exercise its power in a manner that fostered the well-being of all social classes.

Itō agreed that reliance on law and restraints against the arbitrary exercise of power by strong monarchs were essential components of any modern constitutional system. He also concurred with his chief lieutenant, Inoue Kowashi, that while the emperor "governs the people, he does not personally administer the government," a function more appropriately entrusted to ministers of state.[18] Yet, as Itō later also reminisced, "the Crown was an institution far more deeply rooted in the national sentiment and in our history than in other countries. It was indeed the very essence of a once theocratic State."[19] As a consequence, he declared, it was evident "that the mere imitation of foreign models would not suffice, for there were historical peculiarities of our country which had to be taken into consideration." Specifically, he concluded, it was imperative that the constitution "take care to safeguard the future realness or vitality of these imperial prerogatives, and not let the institution degenerate into an ornamental crowning piece of the edifice." In the end Itō and Inoue framed a constitution that recalled a cardinal principle of the Japanese past: The emperor reigned but seldom ruled. The final document placed considerable powers in the hands of state ministers, but Itō and Inoue personally wrote the articles that dealt with the imperial house, adopting language to make it abundantly clear, as Itō put it, that "the first principle of our constitution is the respect for the sovereign rights of the emperor." Foreign models were useful, perhaps even essential, but Itō was determined that Japan's quest for political modernity proceed on its own terms and in a manner congruent with the most hallowed traditions of its past.

To convey better their sense of civil ethics to the population at large, the oligarchs promulgated two well-publicized rescripts. The first, the Imperial Rescript to Soldiers and Sailors, flowed chiefly from the pens of

Inoue Kowashi and Yamagata Aritomo, with some last-second stylistic flourishes added by the progovernment journalist Fukuchi Gen'ichirō. On January 4, 1882, the emperor presented the rescript personally to the army
minister at the palace, a ceremony intended to symbolize the throne's direct authority over the military. In its very first article, the document proclaimed "loyalty" to be the "essential duty" of the soldier and sailor and asked
rhetorically, "Who that is born in this land can be wanting in the spirit of
grateful service to it?"[20] The ideal of service to the throne, the rescript then
admonished, could be corrupted by the selfishness and divisiveness of party
politics. Thus, to be loyal meant to stand outside the fray of the political
arena: "Remember that, as the protection of the state and the maintenance
of its power depend upon the strength of its arms, the growth or decline of
this strength must affect the nation's destiny for good or evil; neither be led
astray, therefore, by popular opinions nor meddle in politics, but with single heart fulfill your essential duty of loyalty, and bear in mind that duty is
weightier than a mountain, while death is lighter than a feather."

The second rescript sought a wider audience, the entire youth of the
nation. In the autumn of 1890, just before the convocation of the first Imperial Diet, Prime Minister Yamagata instructed Inoue Kowashi and Motoda Nagazane to compose a document for dissemination to all schools
articulating the bedrock ethos that supported the new state, with its brand-
new constitution and system of participatory government. Encoding a political ideology within a statement outlining guiding principles for education,
the Imperial Rescript on Education opened with the declaration that Japan's
unique *kokutai*, "the fundamental character of Our Empire" in the official
English translation, sprang from the intimate bonds that from time immemorial had united Japan's benevolent rulers with their loyal subjects: "Our
Imperial Ancestors have founded Our Empire on a basis broad and everlasting, and have deeply and firmly planted virtue; Our subjects ever united
in loyalty and filial piety have from generation to generation illustrated the
beauty thereof."[21] From that construction flowed a variety of prescriptions
about the present: The Japanese were to be filial to parents, affectionate to
siblings, true to friends. Above all else, the rescript exhorted students to be
"good and faithful subjects," and it instructed them to "advance public good
and promote common interests; always respect the Constitution and observe the laws; [and] should emergency arise, offer yourselves courageously
to the State; and thus guard and maintain the prosperity of Our Imperial
Throne coeval with heaven and earth." Throughout the country, school
principals required their charges to memorize the text, and its solemn recitation, together with obeisance to a photograph of the emperor and the

singing of "Kimigayo," became an obligatory part of all important school ceremonies.

The symbolism of the imperial presence, "coeval with heaven and earth," proved enormously compelling, and the power of its message appealed to even the most ardent sympathizers with the Popular Rights Movement. Of course critics blasted the Satchō oligarchs as self-seeking, opportunistic, and corrupt, the very antithesis of what they preached, but during the 1880s nearly all the regime's foes came to accept the basic premises of imperial constitutionalism. The polemics held a high pitch, but none of the constitutional drafts proposed by the government's opponents during the latter half of the decade failed to place the emperor at the center of the political world. Similarly, people across a broad range of the political spectrum embraced the oligarchs' notions of acceptable political discourse and civic morality: obedience to emperor; loyalty to nation; the sanctity of rule by a disinterested, well-intentioned bureaucracy presided over by imperially appointed ministers; selfless service; denial of divisiveness inherent in interest group politics; and sublimation of private interest to the greater collective good of the nation. Such rhetoric did not yet constitute an official "state ideology"—that would be formulated more clearly in the 1890s and the opening decades of the twentieth century—but the notions of imperial orthodoxy, civic responsibility, and good citizenship were extremely useful to the oligarchs, for they served as political and moral bonds that defined a national citizenry, drawing the *kokumin* together and readying them to accept Mr. Itō's new constitution.

## The Constitution of the Empire of Japan

For Itō and his colleagues, the Constitution of the Empire of Japan announced Japan's modernity to the world, exemplified the nation's enlightened progress, and established new concepts of political authority, all delicately wrapped in the legacy of the past and legitimated by ancient values. Symbolism was important to Itō Hirobumi, and the promulgation of the constitution demonstrated the full measure of his creative ingenuity. The day chosen for its unveiling was February 11, a national holiday commemorating the mythological founding of the country in 660 B.C.E. by Jimmu, the legendary first emperor. Early that morning in 1889 the Meiji emperor, cloaked in ancient court garments, performed Shinto rituals before a special shrine erected deep inside the imperial compound. There he informed his ancestors of the new "fundamental law of the state." He was granting the constitution, he told them, out of "consideration of the progressive tendency of the course of human affairs and in parallel with the advance of civilization."[22] His goal, he explained, was "to give greater firmness to the stability of Our country and to promote the welfare of all the people within the boundaries of Our dominions," and his actions, he assured them, would guarantee "that the observance of Our laws shall continue to the remotest ages of time." That ceremony completed, the emperor changed into Western clothing and appeared in the European-style reception hall. There he received the constitution from Itō and handed it down to Prime Minister Kuroda, a sign to all that the constitution was being bestowed upon the nation by a gracious sovereign.

The document itself was clearly the repository of tradition and the embodiment of modernity. The first seventeen articles, grouped together under the heading "Chapter 1," concerned the emperor.[23] The very first article established that "The Empire of Japan shall be reigned over and governed by a line of Emperors unbroken for ages eternal," while the following clauses declared him "sacred and inviolable" with full and sole possession of "the rights of sovereignty." The remainder of Chapter 1 specified the monarch's duties. Of particular importance, it empowered the emperor to open, close, prorogue, and dissolve the Imperial Diet. In addition, according to Article 6, the emperor "gives sanction to laws, and orders them to be promulgated and executed." Article 8 extended that prerogative, authorizing the throne to issue "Imperial Ordinances in the place of law" when the Diet was not sitting, and other provisions designated the emperor the supreme commander of the armed forces and entitled him to declare war, make peace, and conclude treaties. However, the constitution also guarded against the arbitrary exercise of power by circumscribing imperial prerogatives; one clause, for instance, specified that "Imperial Ordinances are to be laid before the Imperial Diet at its next session" and further declared that no ordinance could "in any way alter any of the existing laws."

Chapter 2 took up "the rights and duties of subjects." The two chief duties were to pay taxes and to serve in the army and navy when called upon. The rights were more numerous: to have "the liberty of abode" and be free from unlawful entry or search; to be entitled to a trial by judge; and to enjoy the "inviolate" right of property, "freedom of religion," and "the liberty of speech, writing, publication, public meetings and associations." Most of those rights and privileges were not granted unconditionally but, rather, were qualified by such phrases as "within the limits of the law" and when "not antagonistic to their duties as subjects." Moreover, any right could be abrogated in times of national emergency. It was essential, Itō noted in his commentaries, "to make exceptional provisions to meet exceptional contingencies. For it must be remembered that the ultimate aim of a State is to maintain its existence." As a consequence, according to Itō, "in times of danger, the State will have to sacrifice without hesitation part of the law and of the rights of the subjects."[24]

The next several chapters established a bicameral legislature and outlined the duties of ministers of state and the Privy Council. Both ministers and councillors were to provide advice to the throne, and in another check on imperial power, no law, ordinance, or rescript could take effect unless countersigned by the appropriate minister. The newly enfranchised Imperial Diet consisted of a House of Peers, composed of nobles and imperial family members appointed by the emperor, and a House of Representatives, elected by the people. Either house could initiate bills and make representations to the cabinet, and all legislation required the consent of both bodies. The constitution also empowered the Diet to vote on an annual state budget. But several articles qualified that important right. Article 67 stipulated that "already fixed expenditures based . . . upon the powers appertaining to the Emperor . . . shall be neither rejected nor reduced by the Imperial Diet." That clause reflected the oligarchs' fear that a cantankerous, popularly elected Diet might someday jeopardize national security by trimming appropriations for the armed forces, which fell into the category of "fixed expenses . . . appertaining to the Emperor." Article 71 circumscribed the Diet's budgetary powers even further. It stipulated that whenever the legislature did not pass a budget, "the Government shall carry out the Budget of the preceding year."

Itō did not escape unbloodied from the fierce debates over constitutionalism that raged during the early Meiji era, but by mixing concessions with legal suppression and ideological suasion, he and his fellow oligarchs ultimately achieved their goals. The Constitution of the Empire of Japan reflected the ideas set forth in the "general principles" that Iwakura articulated at the beginning of the 1880s: It established mechanisms for sharing power with elected representatives of the nation's citizenry, but at the same time it drew boundaries around the exercise of legislative initiative, reserved sovereignty for the emperor, and delegated preponderant political authority to state ministers appointed by the throne.

The promulgation of the constitution also marked an important step toward fulfilling another ambition: acceptance into the comity of the world's advanced nations. Almost from the day they seized power, the Meiji oligarchs had been determined to build internal strength and foster national unity so that they could go forward with the task of creating a modern, powerful country, worthy of respect in the eyes of the West. Only through such a process, they believed, could Japan maintain its national independence, revise the humiliating unequal treaties, and, as Yamagata once put it, "preserve the nation's rights and advantages among the powers."[25] The constitution helped Japan earn the international respect that it desperately sought and to attain great power status. In his later years Itō expressed his satisfaction with the constitutional experiment. "Looking backwards over sixteen years of its operation," he wrote, "it is not without a certain degree of gratification that I feel the experiment has been, in spite of its many shortcomings, upon the whole a success."[26]

One might well forgive Itō the conceits of his accomplishments, but in fact, as the present unfolded into the future, politics under the Meiji constitution evolved in ways that he could scarcely have imagined. For all its deference to imperial prerogatives, the modernistic fundamental law of the land empowered new elites, including the prime minister and his cabinet, the Privy Council, the Diet, and the military and civilian bureaucracies, all of which would compete vigorously for a share of political influence in the years and decades ahead. The ebb and flow of that contest among multiple elites ultimately took Japan in directions totally unforeseen by Itō when he approached the red-carpeted dais that February morning in 1889 to present his constitution to the emperor of Japan.

# CHAPTER 7

# *Toward an Industrial Future*

t he immutable axiom "Prosperous Nation, Strong Military" echoed its way through the early Meiji period, defining the goals of large-scale economic development. By undertaking industrialization at the same time that they were scouting out a path toward constitutionalism, the Meiji oligarchs expected to see all manner of benefits billow forth from the smoke-stacks of economic progress. Wealth would earn Japan respect in the eyes of the West and provide a foundation of national strength so that the newly modernizing nation could escape the predatory threat of Western imperial-ism. Indicative of its priorities, the new government relied on the Ministry of Public Works and the Home Ministry, established in 1870 and 1873 respec-tively, to import technology from abroad and organize the manufacturing ef-fort at home. Soon enough, another slogan—"Increase Production, Promote Industry" (*shokusan kōgyō*)—crowded its way into the Meiji lexicon.

The determination to Increase Production, Promote Industry also of-fered a solution to forbidding domestic problems that threatened to abort the Meiji experiment. The countercoups led by Etō Shinpei and Saigō Takamori were lesson enough that the Meiji leadership needed to provide the old retainer class with employment opportunities and prospects for a brighter future. Moreover, the commercial treaties negotiated in 1858 and 1866 had imposed unfair tariff and exchange rates upon Japan. The unhappy result was a sudden spurt of imports and an extraordinary outflow of specie, which brought on severe inflation and endangered many forms of domestic handicraft production and processing. Fearful throughout the 1870s and 1880s about the consequences that might befall the regime should it be unable to win the allegiance of the common people of Japan, the oligarchs were determined to improve prospects for long-term political stability and earn acceptance for the new constitutional polity by overcoming the economic dislocations that accompanied the opening of the country and by creating the basis for future prosperity.

By the time the first Diet convened in 1890, the Japanese had surmounted most of the early economic problems, and the country was well on its way to joining the ranks of the world's industrial powers. As happened with constitutionalism, the oligarchy was to cast itself in a leading role, assuming credit for engineering the institutional changes that created a favorable environment for accelerating economic growth, but Japan's transition from a predominantly agrarian to a thriving manufacturing economy could never have taken place without the entrepreneurial inventiveness of untold scores of the nation's ordinary men and women.

That economic progress, however, did not come without a price tag. Clearly, prosperity flowed across Japan in the last half of the nineteenth century, and most people were better fed and housed at the end of the Meiji period than their ancestors had been in the 1860s. But not everyone received an equal share of the benefits that accompanied an expanding economy, and some lost their health and even their lives as they struggled both to get ahead and to help their country. Accordingly, just as certain men and women believed that the new parliamentary system placed them at a political disadvantage, so too did tens of thousands of individuals feel victimized by economic modernity, "sacrificed," as one critic noted, "on the altar of industrial progress."

## State Intervention and the Economic Infrastructure

Japan's economic prospects in the early Meiji period appeared dismal as superior Western products flooded the island country. Machine-made cotton cloth from abroad was stronger and cheaper than material woven at home on handlooms, kerosene outsold the more expensive and less efficient traditional lamp oils pressed from vegetable seeds, Chinese sugar somehow tasted sweeter than the domestic variety, and imported woolens quickly became prized for their warmth and reasonable price. As Table 7.1 shows, the

**TABLE 7.1** *Value of Japan's Exports and Imports, 1868–1895*
(in millions of yen at current prices)

| YEAR | EXPORTS | IMPORTS | TOTAL | BALANCE |
|------|---------|---------|-------|---------|
| 1868 | 22.988 | 19.350 | 42.338 | 3.638 |
| 1869 | 12.909 | 21.659 | 34.568 | (−8.750) |
| 1870 | 14.543 | 35.004 | 49.547 | (−20.461) |
| 1871 | 17.969 | 22.076 | 40.045 | (−4.107) |
| 1872 | 17.027 | 26.175 | 43.202 | (−9.148) |
| 1873 | 21.635 | 28.107 | 49.742 | (−6.472) |
| 1874 | 19.317 | 24.487 | 43.804 | (−5.170) |
| 1875 | 18.611 | 31.899 | 50.510 | (−13.288) |
| 1876 | 27.712 | 26.544 | 54.256 | 1.168 |
| 1877 | 23.349 | 29.979 | 53.328 | (−6.630) |
| 1878 | 25.988 | 37.722 | 63.710 | (−11.734) |
| 1879 | 28.176 | 38.015 | 66.191 | (−9.839) |
| 1880 | 28.395 | 42.246 | 70.641 | (−13.851) |
| 1881 | 31.059 | 35.767 | 66.826 | (−4.708) |
| 1882 | 37.722 | 33.354 | 71.076 | 4.368 |
| 1883 | 36.268 | 32.449 | 68.717 | 3.819 |
| 1884 | 33.871 | 33.617 | 67.488 | .254 |
| 1885 | 37.147 | 33.499 | 70.646 | 3.648 |
| 1886 | 48.876 | 37.364 | 86.240 | 11.512 |
| 1887 | 52.408 | 53.153 | 105.561 | (−.745) |
| 1888 | 65.706 | 65.455 | 131.161 | .251 |
| 1889 | 70.061 | 66.104 | 136.165 | 3.957 |
| 1890 | 56.604 | 81.729 | 138.333 | (−25.125) |
| 1891 | 79.527 | 62.927 | 142.454 | 16.600 |
| 1892 | 91.103 | 71.326 | 162.429 | 19.777 |
| 1893 | 89.713 | 88.257 | 177.970 | 1.456 |
| 1894 | 113.246 | 117.482 | 230.728 | (−4.236) |
| 1895 | 136.112 | 129.261 | 265.373 | 6.851 |

Adapted from Shinya Sugiyama, *Japan's Industrialization in the World Economy 1859–1899*
(London: Athlone Press, 1988), pp. 46–47.

value of Japan's exports trailed imports for twelve of the fourteen years between 1868 and 1881. The message was as clear as it was apocalyptic: Unless Japan could reconstruct its domestic economy, develop import substitutes, and balance its foreign trade accounts, one official predicted, the country "will fall into a condition wretched beyond description. Specie will become scarce, currency will continue to depreciate, prices will rise, and the strength of our nation will be swept away."[1]

Ōkubo Toshimichi, chief of the newly founded Home Ministry, worried about his country's future, and he articulated the belief that state intervention was necessary if Japan was to industrialize quickly, an idea that became an article of faith for many oligarchs in the early 1870s. "Generally speaking," Ōkubo wrote after visiting the cotton mills of Birmingham and the shipyards of Glasgow as a member of the Iwakura Mission, "a country's strength is dependent upon the prosperity of its people. The prosperity of the people in turn depends upon their productive capacity." The ordinary people of a nation, he continued, might through dint of extraordinary effort launch some manufacturing industries, but an examination of the conditions in Europe, he concluded, "reveals no instance when a country's productive power was increased without the patronage and the encouragement of the government and its officials."[2]

With many traditional handicrafts facing ruination and the ex-samurai up in arms, the oligarchs labored to complete communication and transportation facilities that would support industrialization. Commodore Perry had presented the Japanese with their first Morse telegraphic apparatus, and in 1869 the new Meiji government hired an English engineer to construct a telegraph line from Tokyo to Yokohama, with public service between the two cities beginning the next year. The Ministry of Public Works promoted rapid expansion of the system. By the time the first Diet convened in 1890, government work crews had strung nearly ten thousand miles of wire over the mountains, through the forests, and across the rivers of Japan, and more than two hundred telegraph offices provided virtually instantaneous communication among the country's major cities. That same year public telephone exchanges became operational in Tokyo and Yokohama. By the turn of the century nearly fifty cities boasted telephone exchanges, linked together by long-distance lines, and operators placed more than forty-five million calls for the growing number of subscribers.

The centerpiece of Japan's modernistic communication systems was the post office. Not long after they assumed power, the young Meiji leaders decided that Japan needed a government-operated postal service "to make communication in the land simple and easy."[3] Early in 1871 the government instructed officials in towns along the Tōkaidō Highway to open offices where people could deposit mail, and on the first day of the Third Month the first post left Tokyo for Osaka, where it arrived seventy-five hours later, precisely on schedule. The next year Maejima Hisoka, a protégé of Ōkuma Shigenobu's, was entrusted with developing the system, and he quickly extended service throughout the country. Dubbed "the father of the post," Maejima relied heavily on what he learned about the British postal service during a yearlong stay in that country, instituting in Japan a system of uniform rates, fees paid through the purchase of stamps, the sale of money orders, and provisions for carrying parcel post. By 1890 there were more than five thousand post offices in Japan, and they handled nearly 225 million pieces of mail and processed almost 75 million money orders.

Some of that mail was carried up and down the old highway system on the backs of couriers, in carts, and even aboard the newly invented rickshaw, but increasingly the government turned to the railroad. The young Meiji leaders contemplated the construction of railroads not just as an adjunct to their postal operations but also as vital to the overall development of industry and strategically necessary to Japan's defense needs. Aware, as well, of the enormous capital requirements of railroad construction, the government concluded that it, not private enterprise, would have to take the initiative. Consequently, late in 1869 the Japanese leadership formally decided that the first two routes would run between the Shinbashi section of Tokyo and Yokohama, the bustling new port that served the capital, and between Osaka and Kōbe, the leading commercial center and new entrepôt of western Japan respectively. To finance those projects, the Japanese floated bonds in the London market, and in the spring of 1870, with materials and technology procured in England, construction began on the artery from Tokyo to Yokohama.

The opening celebration for the Tokyo to Yokohama line in October 1872 was nearly as grandiose as the ceremonies arranged for the promulgation of the constitution seventeen years later. The appearance of the emperor himself underscored the significance that the new Meiji state attached to railroad construction and attested to the importance of the steam locomotive as the quintessential hallmark of progress and civilization. On the morning of October 14, Japan's leading government officials stood in rapt attention at Shinbashi Station as Emperor Meiji ascended a gaily decorated passenger carriage and then welcomed aboard a gathering of foreign dignitaries for the inaugural run to Yokohama, while warships in Tokyo Bay offered twenty-one-gun salutes. Two years later, with considerably less public ceremony, trains began to carry passengers and freight between Osaka and

Kōbe. In 1877 service was extended from Osaka to Kyoto; twelve years after that, in 1889, Japan celebrated the completion of the Tōkaidō trunk line, and people could whiz past the old post towns, completing their travel between the major cities of eastern and western Japan in less than a day.

The government added two more important girders to the infrastructure supporting modern economic development when it created a national currency and began to put together an integrated banking system. The New Currency Regulation of 1871 established the yen as Japan's unit of currency, replacing the confusing welter of coins and nearly sixteen hundred kinds of paper notes that circulated during the late Tokugawa period. A year later, in 1872, the National Bank Ordinance authorized the founding of so-called national banks to facilitate the accumulation of mercantile capital for industrialization and to promote the orderly development of the currency system. Following practices in the United States, the national banks could both accept deposits and issue their own yen-denominated bank notes, which from 1876 were not convertible into specie. By the end of the decade more than 150 national banks had opened their doors for business. The largest of the new financial institutions was the Fifteenth National Bank, established in the late 1870s by nearly 480 former daimyo and court nobles and capitalized at 17.8 million yen, or roughly 40 percent of the aggregate capital of all national banks.

Even as they were laying down the infrastructure for modern economic development, the Meiji leaders began to operate strategic and military enterprises directly. The new regime inherited some of those from the Tokugawa shogunate and the old domains. Such was the case with the Nagasaki Shipyards, which the shogunate had constructed in the late 1850s with Dutch assistance; the Yokosuka Shipyards, a similar Tokugawa venture, built in 1866 under the supervision of French naval engineers; and a shipbuilding facility established by Mito domain in 1853 at Ishikawajima, an island in Edo Bay. The young men who staffed the Public Works and Home ministries, which controlled the shipyards, were quick to grasp how technologies developed for the military might have other useful applications. Consequently, the shipyards not only constructed cargo vessels and warships for Japan's new navy but also contained machine tool and other factories whose output contributed to the civilian sector of the economy. Engineers at Yokosuka, for instance, manufactured some of Japan's first steel furnaces; its technicians planned the construction of lighthouses, government buildings, roads, and harbors; and its many satellite factories turned out steam engines, boilers, and other types of machinery used in mining and textile production.

The government also established model factories and managed certain civilian businesses in the hope of stimulating private enterprise. In those instances, the planners within the Home and Public Works ministries had several ancillary purposes in mind: to create employment opportunities and encourage commercial development in economically backward regions, to demonstrate the efficacy of modern technology, and to build up light industries whose products could compete with foreign goods, thus leading to import substitution and a righting of Japan's chronic trade deficits. Perhaps the most highly coordinated effort in that regard was the Hokkaidō Colonization Office, which promoted sake brewing, founded a sugar refinery, opened flour mills, and oversaw the construction of fish canneries as part of the Meiji government's efforts to settle and develop that northern island.

Ōkubo and his colleagues also invested heavily in government-operated textile mills in order to foster modern manufacturing practices in that key industry. Cotton spinning and silk reeling were well-developed home industries in the Tokugawa period that fell on hard times after Japan opened its ports to foreign trade. Cotton producers were hit almost immediately after 1858, as Japanese cloth, spun on handlooms, simply could not compete in price or quality with that churned out on the new machines that clamored away in so many British hamlets and Indian villages. Unable to set quotas or impose additional levies on imports because of the restrictions decreed by the unequal treaties, the Home Ministry encouraged mechanization in order to upgrade the quality of domestically produced cloth. Hoping to tempt local men of wealth to invest in the latest technology and open spinning mills, the ministry laid out significant amounts of its precious revenues to mechanize two cotton mills, one in Osaka and another in Kagoshima, which the Meiji regime had inherited from the daimyō of Satsuma domain.

In contrast with cotton, sericulture and silk reeling initially flourished after the Tokugawa regime signed the 1858 commercial treaties, as an outbreak of blight in Europe prompted traders to bid up the price of Japanese silkworm eggs and raw silk. Throughout the 1860s the wharves at Yokohama groaned under the weight of raw silk, and in 1868 silk accounted for approximately 40 percent of Japan's total exports and for nearly half of all the tax revenues that the new government derived from exports during its first year in power. From the very next year, however, French and Italian sericulture recovered, and demand for hand-reeled Japanese silk, criticized as coarse and lumpy, dropped precipitously. The solution, to one official at least, seemed apparent: "Japan's raw silk is of poor quality solely because the nation has no good machinery. It therefore behooves us to build European-style machines."[4]

Those machines were soon pounding away at the government's most famous model factory, the silk filature it established with great fanfare at Tomioka, in Gunma Prefecture. Officials in the Home Ministry spared no expense, for that project was to constitute the cornerstone of Japan's modern silk-reeling industry and reestablish silk exports as a source of the foreign capital that was crucial to the survival of the new regime. In short order the government erected modern brick buildings, brought in state-of-the-art equipment, and hired a French businessman with experience in the silk trade in Lyons and Yokohama to supervise the enterprise. In July 1872 operations began. Running the new steam-powered reeling machines were some four hundred young women, since an additional goal at Tomioka was to provide employment for daughters of ex-samurai, who, once trained, could fan out across the countryside and become instructors at other newly founded and privately owned filatures. In all, the young Meiji government laid out a considerable sum, nearly 200,000 yen, to build and equip Tomioka, and to many it seemed money well spent. The first silk reeled at the filature enjoyed brisk sales in Lyons and Milan, and even won second prize at the 1873 International Exposition in Vienna.

## The Matsukata Deflation and New Economic Directions

Unfortunately for the Meiji oligarchs, not all efforts to Increase Production, Promote Industry went smoothly. Despite the hoopla that surrounded their conception, for instance, few government-operated businesses lived up to expectations. The Hokkaidō Colonization Office struggled mightily, but accomplishments came slowly as few migrants wished to test the rigors of developing Western-style agriculture and business enterprises on Japan's northern frontier. Railroad development was also a disappointment. Nothing remotely matched the steam locomotive as an unmistakable sign of modernity and progress, yet some members of the Meiji inner circle opposed railroad expansion on the ground that the young government had better uses for its scarce financial resources. While still a member of government, Saigō Takamori voiced the most strenuous objections. "If in our envy of the greatness of foreign nations," the blunt Saigō argued, "we rush ahead without regard for the limitations of our own strength, we will end by exhausting ourselves without accomplishing anything. We must immediately dismiss the matter of constructing steam railways and concentrate on increasing our military power."[5] Ironically, military officials came fully to appreciate the strategic value of railroads as a means of rapidly deploying troops only after Japan's conscript army had traveled on rail to the ports of Yokohama and Kōbe when they sallied forth to quash Saigō's rebellion in 1877. Still, by 1880 Japan had laid less than one hundred miles of track.

To the chagrin of many oligarchs, the model textile factories, founded at such great expense, seldom engendered much enthusiasm among prospective entrepreneurs. Problems were legion at the Tomioka silk filature, where the sophisticated, steam-powered machinery imported from France proved far too expensive for private producers to contemplate buying and installing at their own factories. Moreover, managers at Tomioka were poorly informed about technical matters and ill prepared to run the factory. On occasion they even barred aspiring entrepreneurs from entering their plant, fearing that superiors in Tokyo would catch wind of their incompetence. Furthermore, the women employed at Tomioka with the expectation that they would train later generations of operatives at privately owned mills seldom stayed long enough to become skilled at their jobs. Finally, although the silk reeled at Tomioka initially earned a reputation for high quality, the filature itself seldom turned a profit, despite hefty state subsidies. In 1875 the deficit reached a massive 220,000 yen, more than the oligarchs had expended to build and equip the plant, and it had become a financial albatross draped around the government's neck.

Inflation added to the government's woes in the late 1870s. When more than one hundred new national banks opened for business between 1877 and 1879, their notes injected into Japan's financial markets a flood tide of currency not backed by reserves of hard metal. Moreover, since the government used specie to finance the importation of all military and industrial equipment and to pay the salaries of foreign advisers such as Waters and Mosse, Japan's gold and silver reserves fell by half between 1877 and 1880. The taproot of the problem, however, was deficit spending. Demands on the government fisc had been extremely heavy in the 1870s as the oligarchs simultaneously allocated funds to suppress internal revolts, commute samurai pensions, subsidize government-owned enterprises and model factories, invest in the infrastructure, and modernize the army and navy.

Few options presented themselves to the new regime as the oligarchs sought revenues to cover the deficits they rang up tackling the multiple problems that confronted them. Fear of arousing rural unrest made the Meiji leaders reluctant to boost land taxes, and Iwakura's famous epithet that he would rather sell Kyūshū and Shikoku to foreigners than borrow more money overseas reveals the fear held by most oligarchs that floating loans abroad would invite foreign control over domestic policy. With little other recourse, Ōkubo and Ōkuma Shigenobu, who served as finance minister within the

Dajōkan structure for much of the 1870s, pursued their goal of government-sponsored industrialization largely by printing reams of new money. As a result, the gold value of the new paper yen fell drastically, and domestic prices soared. As the decade wore on, speculation and hoarding added to the inflationary fires; in anticipation of even higher prices, farmers began to withhold crops from the market, and in Tokyo the cost of rice more than doubled between 1877 and 1880. In a chain reaction, inflation undermined the competitiveness of Japan's products on international markets, even while it substantively reduced the actual value of the revenues that the government derived from the fixed-value land tax. The inflationary crisis, together with the other economic problems that came to the fore at the end of the 1870s, seemed poised to overwhelm the successes of the decade and turn the vision of rapid industrialization into a chimera.

During the summer and early autumn of 1881 discussions among the oligarchs tended toward the conclusion that some program of financial retrenchment had become necessary. With Ōkuma in political disgrace because of his views on constitutionalism and with Ōkubo dead, cut down by discontented ex-samurai in 1878, financial policy making landed on the desk of Matsukata Masayoshi, the Satsuma-born architect of the land tax reforms initiated in 1873 and a vocal proponent of fiscal orthodoxy. Matsukata was not universally admired; in Ōkuma's frequently repeated put-down Matsukata was so mediocre that only his Satsuma credentials spared him from a lifetime as "an ordinary prefectural governor," a post he had held in Kyūshū in the early 1870s. But as finance minister from October 1881 Matsukata acted decisively to attack inflation, create a stable currency, and encourage laissez-faire capitalism so that the government could retire from the costly business of directly promoting industry. Between 1881 and 1885 he slashed administrative expenditures, increased indirect taxes, and placed many government enterprises on the sales block. Those actions produced a budget surplus, which he used to buy up notes previously issued by the national banks, thus soaking up the surfeit of paper currency. Looking toward a permanent solution to the currency problem, Matsukata devised a schedule for transforming the national banks into ordinary commercial banks, as shown in Table 7.5 below, and in 1882 chartered the Bank of Japan as a central bank with a monopoly over the issuance of paper currency.

Those actions cut two ways. In the short term, they threw the country into a severe economic downturn. Matsukata's decision to chop government spending and hike taxes took hold at the moment when the domestic price of rice was starting to slip downward in a natural market correction of the overspeculation of the late 1870s and, in an unfortunate pairing of woes, the world economy was entering a slump. The convergence of those events caused an abrupt decline in consumer demand and a free fall in the prices that farmers received for their silk, tea, rice, and other crops. Hardship and suffering stalked Japan's rural families between 1882 and 1885. Hard statistics are rare, but newspapers were filled to the margins with reports of rural distress, such as paupers near the city of Kanazawa who asked to be imprisoned rather than starve to death, and anecdotal evidence suggests that as many as one in ten rural families lost its land in those years because it could no longer afford to pay the land tax. Growing indebtedness was perhaps the most pernicious effect of the Matsukata deflation, and it gave rise to scores of peasant disturbances, ranging from the submission of group petitions and the formation of debtors' parties to acts of collective violence, such as the Fukushima and Chichibu incidents that drew Popular Rights activists to the side of the farmers.

From the longer-range perspective, however, Matsukata resurrected the Meiji economic dream. As dreadful as his policies were for a significant proportion of the farming population, his financial retrenchment whipped inflation, stabilized prices, balanced the budget, and righted tax revenues. His banking initiatives added to the government's growing stock of successes in creating an infrastructure that would support further development. Perhaps most significantly, the enactment of the Matsukata reform program reoriented the government's industrial policy, turning the emphasis away from direct state ownership of enterprises and toward an approach that favored the kind of laissez-faire orthodoxy popular in the industrially advanced nations of western Europe. In this regard Matsukata had been deeply influenced by the free enterprise thinking that he had learned from Léon Say and other French economists during a stay in Europe in 1878. Upon his return to Japan, Matsukata outlined his thoughts about the economic role of the state. "The Government should never attempt to compete with the people in pursuing industry or commerce," he wrote in an 1882 memorial, "for in such matters it can never hope to equal in shrewdness, foresight and enterprise men who are actuated by the immediate motives of self-interest. It is always best, therefore, for the Government not to take immediate concern in trade and business, but to leave those matters to be conducted and developed by individual efforts and enterprise."[6] Such thinking came to exemplify the government's approach to economic modernization for the next several decades. Matsukata and his colleagues were to rely chiefly on the private sector to lead Japan's quest for industrialization, providing assistance where they could to create a favorable institutional setting and to nurture an environment supportive of the growth of private enterprise.

## Private Entrepreneurs and the Growth of Light Industry

Even before Matsukata assumed the financial helm of state, the bootstrap efforts of ordinary men and women began to exert a significant impact on the growth of the Japanese economy. Budding entrepreneurs could be found scattered across the Japanese archipelago, in all the cities, towns, and villages where the collective memory of the problems of the late Tokugawa era—the recollection of failed reforms, unjustly high grain prices, and contentious disagreement about how best to promote commercial development— provided a compelling reason to pursue with vigor the new opportunities of the early Meiji period. Few of those prospective businesspeople ever earned a reputation that spread beyond the circumference of their own lo- cale, but in a world where little could be taken for certain, they scrambled to make a living and get ahead as best they could. In doing so, they brought a measure of prosperity to themselves and their neighbors, added to the ag- gregate value of the manufacturing sector of the economy, and provided significant amounts of semimanufactured and finished goods for export, as exemplified in Tables 7.2 and 7.3.

Some enterprising merchants succeeded by focusing their efforts on im- proving the quality and marketability of traditional products and handicrafts. In the old castle town of Kanazawa, to take one example, the abolition of do- mains in 1871 removed the traditional barriers to interregional trade and gave local producers of gold and silver leaf fresh opportunities to compete in na- tional and even international markets. In the early nineteenth century those craftsmen, who hammered out thin sheets of gold and silver foil used to dec- orate Buddhist household altars, porcelain, lacquerware, and folding screens, had petitioned local authorities for permission to open workshops to produce leaf. Since existing shogunal edicts restricted the manufacture of leaf to offi- cially licensed artisanal associations in Edo and Kyoto, however, negotiations dragged on with little result, and fewer than one hundred artisans in Kanazawa ever were engaged in the trade. After the Meiji regime dissolved old trade as- sociations and their monopolies, however, Kanazawa's leaf trade picked up im- mediately, with nearly fifteen hundred people engaged in the craft by the year 1880. What accounted for that dramatic expansion, besides the quality and cost competitiveness of the Kanawaza product, was freer access to markets. Most of the leaf fashioned in the 1870s and 1880s was sold in Kyoto and Nagoya for use on religious iconography, and after World War I Kanazawa's manufac- turers displaced Germany's to capture nearly 90 percent of the world market.

In Ninomiya, the intrepid female entrepreneur Tatsu'uma Kiyo extended her successes as household head during the late Tokugawa period and built

**TABLE 7.2** *Value of Manufacturing Production, 1874–1912*
(in millions of yen at constant 1934–1936 prices)

| YEAR | FOOD PRODUCTS | TEXTILES | LUMBER & WOOD PRODUCTS | CHEMICALS | STONE, CLAY & GLASS PRODUCTS | IRON & STEEL | NON-FERROUS METALS | MA-CHINERY | PRINTING & PUBLISHING | OTHER | TOTAL |
|---|---|---|---|---|---|---|---|---|---|---|---|
| 1874 | 422.801 | 59.991 | 44.243 | 72.492 | 16.829 | 2.128 | 4.586 | 4.300 | .855 | 57.497 | 685.722 |
| 1876 | 447.409 | 57.177 | 58.259 | 80.269 | 17.230 | 1.906 | 7.694 | 6.184 | 1.189 | 67.156 | 744.473 |
| 1878 | 469.619 | 84.922 | 55.514 | 89.755 | 17.079 | 3.440 | 9.912 | 10.106 | 1.657 | 75.985 | 817.989 |
| 1880 | 512.504 | 117.955 | 51.169 | 108.774 | 14.747 | 3.952 | 9.258 | 16.408 | 2.734 | 73.955 | 911.456 |
| 1882 | 544.286 | 103.966 | 50.816 | 96.917 | 12.350 | 3.260 | 9.664 | 16.819 | 2.936 | 75.157 | 916.171 |
| 1884 | 577.490 | 120.964 | 50.171 | 100.145 | 11.078 | 2.866 | 13.127 | 14.347 | 3.041 | 84.531 | 977.760 |
| 1886 | 551.573 | 163.733 | 58.579 | 107.410 | 14.867 | 4.372 | 14.389 | 14.541 | 3.966 | 104.592 | 1,038.022 |
| 1888 | 623.352 | 225.027 | 50.372 | 109.021 | 17.497 | 7.429 | 17.848 | 15.814 | 5.237 | 112.780 | 1,184.377 |
| 1890 | 668.917 | 300.419 | 48.360 | 111.969 | 18.087 | 5.281 | 21.763 | 17.653 | 6.766 | 130.111 | 1,329.326 |
| 1892 | 711.623 | 402.335 | 49.049 | 137.243 | 23.743 | 2.735 | 22.239 | 20.459 | 7.483 | 152.575 | 1,529.484 |
| 1894 | 810.746 | 468.878 | 59.610 | 154.611 | 25.182 | 5.930 | 21.007 | 28.953 | 7.802 | 155.914 | 1,734.633 |
| 1896 | 891.765 | 539.823 | 65.490 | 147.296 | 32.202 | 9.531 | 19.596 | 39.037 | 13.125 | 138.751 | 1,896.616 |
| 1898 | 1,018.760 | 569.962 | 82.045 | 158.394 | 28.974 | 8.319 | 18.990 | 52.815 | 17.972 | 147.489 | 2,103.720 |
| 1900 | 1,018.479 | 508.749 | 87.867 | 186.362 | 30.956 | 5.800 | 22.746 | 68.881 | 23.191 | 147.954 | 2,100.985 |
| 1902 | 937.327 | 515.433 | 88.788 | 203.385 | 36.491 | 7.645 | 24.609 | 70.952 | 29.161 | 179.623 | 2,093.414 |
| 1904 | 947.204 | 469.038 | 96.023 | 229.442 | 36.334 | 15.644 | 25.498 | 98.028 | 32.564 | 144.873 | 2,094.648 |
| 1906 | 1,047.632 | 611.852 | 91.237 | 230.450 | 49.722 | 21.498 | 27.093 | 127.654 | 45.377 | 194.452 | 2,446.967 |
| 1908 | 1,110.726 | 642.078 | 93.979 | 255.730 | 53.938 | 27.393 | 46.669 | 159.410 | 50.596 | 184.361 | 2,624.880 |
| 1910 | 1,150.251 | 804.394 | 97.621 | 270.933 | 70.588 | 44.902 | 53.664 | 196.826 | 59.445 | 210.891 | 2,959.515 |
| 1912 | 1,242.572 | 942.136 | 101.163 | 307.339 | 83.626 | 58.360 | 64.067 | 272.202 | 77.726 | 208.548 | 3,357.739 |

Adapted from Kazushi Ohkawa and Miyohei Shinohara, with Larry Meissner, eds., *Patterns of Japanese Economic Development: A Quantitive Appraisal* (New Haven: Yale University Press, 1979), pp. 302–4.

**TABLE 7.3** *Percentage Distribution of Exports and Imports, 1874–1911*
(percentage shares of total imports or exports calculated from ten-year
moving averages in current prices)

**EXPORTS**

| | PRIMARY PRODUCTS | MANUFACTURES | | | |
| | | | | OTHER LIGHT MANU- | HEAVY MANU- |
| PERIOD | TOTAL | TOTAL | TEXTILES | FACTURES | FACTURES |
|---|---|---|---|---|---|
| 1874–1883 | 42.5 | 57.5 | 42.4 | 6.9 | 8.2 |
| 1877–1886 | 39.5 | 60.5 | 43.0 | 7.8 | 9.7 |
| 1882–1891 | 33.0 | 67.0 | 45.6 | 9.0 | 12.4 |
| 1887–1896 | 26.3 | 73.7 | 48.9 | 11.3 | 13.5 |
| 1892–1901 | 21.0 | 79.0 | 52.6 | 13.2 | 13.2 |
| 1897–1906 | 16.6 | 83.4 | 53.6 | 15.9 | 13.9 |
| 1902–1911 | 14.1 | 85.9 | 53.8 | 17.2 | 14.9 |

**IMPORTS**

| | PRIMARY PRODUCTS | | | | MANUFACTURES | | | |
| | | CRUDE FOOD- | RAW MATERIALS | | | | OTHER LIGHT MANU- | HEAVY MANU- |
| PERIOD | TOTAL | STUFFS | FUELS | OTHER | TOTAL | TEXTILES | FACTURES | FACTURES |
|---|---|---|---|---|---|---|---|---|
| 1874–1883 | 8.8 | 0.7 | 5.0 | 3.1 | 91.2 | 54.0 | 17.8 | 19.4 |
| 1877–1886 | 10.3 | 0.8 | 6.1 | 3.4 | 89.7 | 49.6 | 18.7 | 21.4 |
| 1882–1891 | 18.7 | 5.0 | 6.4 | 7.3 | 81.3 | 37.4 | 17.4 | 26.5 |
| 1887–1896 | 28.2 | 7.1 | 5.0 | 16.1 | 71.8 | 28.2 | 14.6 | 29.0 |
| 1892–1901 | 36.4 | 9.9 | 4.4 | 22.1 | 63.6 | 16.8 | 14.2 | 32.6 |
| 1897–1906 | 43.1 | 13.8 | 4.7 | 24.6 | 56.9 | 11.8 | 12.3 | 32.8 |
| 1902–1911 | 45.2 | 12.5 | 4.0 | 28.7 | 54.8 | 9.6 | 10.8 | 34.4 |

Adapted from Kazushi Ohkawa and Miyohei Shinohara, with Larry Meissner, eds., *Patterns of Japanese Economic Development: A Quantitive Appraisal* (New Haven: Yale University Press, 1979), p. 135.

her family's Hakushika (White Stag) brewery into Meiji Japan's largest sake empire by increasing production and even founding her own shipping company in order to expand sales in western and northern Japan. With the profits, Tatsu'uma diversified, investing aggressively in Osaka real estate, founding a marine and fire insurance business, and branching into rice wholesaling, wood and coal sales, and the manufacture of wooden matches. Perhaps her most important bequest to her family's enterprise was a spirit of entrepreneurship, as the Hakushika brewery established in Golden, Colorado, in the 1980s became one of the first sake refineries in the United States.

Along with traditional commodities and handicrafts, many Japanese in the 1870s and 1880s tried to manufacture for themselves replicas of the intriguing new consumer goods being introduced from the West. Tokyo entrepreneurs founded the Seikō watch and Shiseidō cosmetic firms, while in Osaka several men simultaneously pioneered the manufacture of buttons in Japan. Traditional styles had not required such fasteners, but demand arose in the 1870s, as the military services and many ordinary Japanese adopted Western clothing for everyday wear. Since imported buttons were expensive, the Osaka producers experimented with using traditional files, whetstones, and knives to fabricate buttons from local supplies of oyster, abalone, and conch shells. Unable to import foreign machinery because of the prohibitive cost, they tinkered with existing technology, inventing a hand-turned gimlet to bore holes and concocting a plum blossom oil to clean and polish the button surfaces. Thanks to such technological adaptations, the number of petty manufacturers, who typically employed fifty or sixty workers, increased rapidly, and by 1896 Japan was able to export nearly 175,000 yen of shell buttons, about six times the value of imported buttons. In similar fashion, other persons of ingenuity and ambition founded domestic workshops and labor-intensive small-scale enterprises that turned out such new consumer products as eyeglasses, matches, tin boxes, toys, clocks, enameled ironware, cutlery, and bicycles, thus helping actualize Japan's transition from an agrarian to a manufacturing economy.

## Contributions from the Rural Sector

The quickening pace of industrialization during the Meiji era also drew sustenance from the rural sector of the economy, as farm families continued to engage in by-employments and cottage industries. Clearly evident was the legacy of Tokugawa period commercialization, for by the early Meiji years it was a rare village where peasant families did not supplement their incomes by producing and marketing some sort of handicraft, from footgear to sedge hats and straw rain jackets, yarn and cloth, candles and lighting oil, thong sandals and *tabi* socks, soy sauce and salt, and lumber and charcoal. In the Ina Valley in southern Nagano Prefecture, to extend into the early Meiji decades one example of the long-term effects of the protoindustrialization seen in the Tokugawa era, virtually every sort of rural craft production either held its own or expanded output as national demand for the villages' lacquerware and paper products held strong.

Among traditional rural-based manufactures, the most spectacular growth and organizational change occurred in the reeling of raw silk thread. The boom of the 1860s had alerted Japanese producers to the potentialities of the silk trade, and in the 1870s they rummaged about for ways to improve the competitiveness of their product. No less than government planners, those men were convinced that mechanization would produce silk that had a brighter sheen, greater strength, and vastly more commercial potential. The entrepreneurs-to-be found, however, little to inspire their efforts at the expensively equipped model filature in Tomioka; rather, they substituted wooden buildings for brick ones, used nature's good earth as floors, engaged local blacksmiths to devise wooden frames in place of costly imported iron machines, and employed village carpenters to construct water mills as substitutes for steam engines. Such technological adaptation was extraordinarily successful, as producers reduced their fixed capital cost to less than 10 percent of the amount the government expended per worker at the Tomioka plant. Additionally, the rural silk-reeling entrepreneurs enjoyed access to a plentiful supply of some of the world's best cocoons, raised by farm families living around the factories, and they were blessed with almost inexhaustible reserves of cheap labor, drawn from the women of the nearby villages. Even though most factories remained small, with the majority having fifty or fewer employees, aggregate output soared, and by century's end the production of raw silk amounted to approximately 7 to 10 percent of Japan's total manufacturing output and accounted for nearly one-third of its total commodity exports.

Besides producing a variety of consumer goods, people in rural Japan influenced the pace and direction of Japan's economic modernization in a variety of other ways. Some of their contributions were obvious, others more subtle and complex, but all were related to the Meiji agricultural spurt, an impressive leap in the output of rice and other crops, as demonstrated in Table 7.4. Statistics for the early Meiji years are not entirely reliable, but for the period as a whole it seems that productivity per unit of cultivated rice paddy increased approximately 1.7 percent annually. That extraordinary performance resulted neither from the reorganization of the agrarian economy nor from an expansion of cultivated area. Rather, the farm family remained the typical unit of production, as it had been in the Tokugawa period, and most families continued to maintain small holdings that they could till mostly with their own labor. What enabled those traditional families to produce more was the introduction of new ways of disseminating familiar knowledge. During the Tokugawa period individual farmers in scattered villages had experimented with innovative agricultural methods, but despite the best efforts of men like Ninomiya Sontoku, such knowledge spread relatively slowly. The strong commitment to growth and change that swept Japan in the early Meiji period, however, brought forth a system of paid itinerant agricultural lecturers, the formation of agricultural discussion groups, and the organization of seed exchange societies, all of which helped broadcast information about crop varieties, fertilizers, farming techniques, and animal husbandry more rapidly and widely than before so that farm families could make more productive use of existing land and labor.

The pace of innovation also accelerated in the early Meiji period as farmers expanded the stock of traditional knowledge. Some contributed by successfully breeding nearly a dozen new strains of rice that yielded substantially greater quantities of grain per plant. Perhaps the most famous of those was Shinriki (The Power of the Gods), developed by a farmer in Hyōgo Prefecture in 1877 and grown extensively throughout western Japan by 1890. The full productive potential of varieties such as Shinriki in turn depended upon the application of greater amounts of fertilizers than could be derived from the traditional, self-supplied sources of night soil and other nutrients, so Meiji farmers devised ways to use commercial fertilizers more effectively. Moreover, the new fertilizers required deeper plowing, a circumstance that prompted rural innovators to redesign plows and motivated farmers to buy and use more draft animals. Finally, experience taught farm families other new practices that improved yields, such as the use of a newly invented rotary weeding tool.

In contrast with the contributions made by myriad individuals in the private rural sector, officials within the Dajōkan played only a muted role in promoting the Meiji agricultural spurt. Indeed, in the 1870s the Meiji oligarchs stepped off on the wrong foot when they attempted to introduce Western-style cattle and sheep grazing, crops such as potatoes, corn, grapes, and olives, and machinery of little use on Japan's small family farms. Only after the establishment in 1881 of the Ministry of Agriculture and Commerce, which absorbed many of the economic planning responsibilities previously assigned to the Home and Public Works ministries, did the national government finally set up agricultural societies and experimental stations to promote the indigenous crops and techniques that were emerging from the trial and error experiments of Japan's farmers.

The consequences of the increased productivity of the early Meiji period were manifold, as the average growth rate in grain production sub-

**TABLE 7.4** *Agricultural Output, 1874–1912*
(in millions of yen at constant 1934–1936 prices)

| YEAR | FIELD CROPS | | | COCOONS | LIVESTOCK | TOTAL PRODUCTION | INDEX OF OUTPUT * |
| | RICE | OTHER CROPS | TOTAL | | | | |
|---|---|---|---|---|---|---|---|
| 1874 | 920 | 408 | 1,328 | 33 | 8 | 1,369 | |
| 1875 | 970 | 414 | 1,384 | 35 | 8 | 1,427 | |
| 1876 | 922 | 420 | 1,342 | 37 | 9 | 1,388 | |
| 1878 | 886 | 435 | 1,321 | 41 | 9 | 1,371 | |
| 1880 | 1,000 | 501 | 1,501 | 52 | 11 | 1,564 | 100.0 |
| 1882 | 975 | 514 | 1,489 | 59 | 12 | 1,560 | |
| 1884 | 889 | 537 | 1,426 | 51 | 18 | 1,495 | |
| 1885 | 1,023 | 548 | 1,571 | 48 | 21 | 1,640 | 110.6 |
| 1886 | 1,087 | 584 | 1,671 | 49 | 23 | 1,743 | |
| 1888 | 1,086 | 597 | 1,683 | 52 | 30 | 1,765 | |
| 1890 | 1,184 | 617 | 1,801 | 52 | 21 | 1,874 | 119.7 |
| 1892 | 1,138 | 619 | 1,757 | 66 | 25 | 1,848 | |
| 1894 | 1,150 | 675 | 1,825 | 80 | 31 | 1,936 | |
| 1895 | 1,098 | 682 | 1,780 | 99 | 33 | 1,912 | 122.5 |
| 1896 | 996 | 653 | 1,649 | 81 | 33 | 1,763 | |
| 1898 | 1,302 | 713 | 2,015 | 89 | 36 | 2,140 | |
| 1900 | 1,139 | 733 | 1,872 | 121 | 43 | 2,036 | 138.6 |
| 1902 | 1,015 | 692 | 1,707 | 113 | 44 | 1,864 | |
| 1904 | 1,413 | 746 | 2,159 | 124 | 56 | 2,339 | |
| 1905 | 1,019 | 754 | 1,773 | 120 | 48 | 1,941 | 152.1 |
| 1906 | 1,272 | 778 | 2,050 | 130 | 45 | 2,225 | |
| 1908 | 1,427 | 823 | 2,250 | 153 | 49 | 2,452 | |
| 1910 | 1,281 | 819 | 2,100 | 168 | 62 | 2,330 | 170.4 |
| 1912 | 1,380 | 892 | 2,272 | 190 | 66 | 2,528 | |

* Five-year averages.

Adapted from Kazushi Ohkawa and Miyohei Shinohara, with Larry Meissner, eds., *Patterns of Japanese Economic Development: A Quantitive Appraisal* (New Haven: Yale University Press, 1979), pp. 91 and 288–92.

stantially outpaced the population growth, which averaged about 1.1 percent per annum. Meiji farm families fed their country. Increased domestic productivity also had the happy result of keeping to a minimum the need to expend valuable specie importing foodstuffs; indeed, the rural sector generated significant amounts of export income, as seen in Table 7.8 below. Perhaps more significantly, farm families enjoyed higher incomes. Given the fragmentary nature of the statistical data for the early Meiji decades, caution is in order when one assesses the trajectory of rural incomes. Moreover, the Meiji experience certainly was uneven, and counterexamples of rural poverty and periods of hard times, such as the Matsukata deflation, were clearly visible in the late nineteenth century. But it is also evident that on average, the steady growth of agricultural output translated into higher disposable incomes. Many rural families used their extra cash to advance their standards of living, and domestic demand for new consumer products became a key factor stimulating the growth of light industry in the Meiji period. In addition, the state siphoned off rural income via the land tax, which it then used to help finance its government-operated factories and infrastructure projects. Finally, rural households voluntarily transferred portions of their incomes to the industrial sector. Some families, for instance, bought equipment so they could engage in silk reeling or some other form of by-employment, while others deposited their surplus cash in so-called quasi banks. The number of such institutions appeared in profusion in the 1880s, as shown in Table 7.5. Relatively small and medium-size merchants and landlords in prefectures that produced large surpluses of commercial crops established most of the quasi banks, and the institutions lent funds mainly to finance cottage industries that processed agricultural goods and to support the production and export of commercial crops, such as silk and tea.

## King Cotton and Japan's Industrial Pioneers

As light industries gathered momentum during the early Meiji period, cotton spinning and weaving emerged as Japan's leading source of manufacturing growth. At the time of the Meiji Restoration there was a single cotton mill in Japan; a decade later there were still just three such enterprises, all government-operated, with a total output of barely 1 million pounds of thread. By the end of the century, however, dozens of privately owned mills operated almost around the clock, production topped 250 million pounds, and cotton thread and cloth represented nearly 25 percent of the value of the country's total manufacturing output. The rapid expansion of the cot-

**TABLE 7.5** *Banks, 1873–1899*

| YEAR | NATIONAL BANKS | | | COMMERCIAL BANKS | | | QUASI BANKS | | |
|---|---|---|---|---|---|---|---|---|---|
| | NUMBER | TOTAL [a] CAPITAL | AVERAGE [b] CAPITAL | NUMBER | TOTAL CAPITAL | AVERAGE CAPITAL | NUMBER | TOTAL CAPITAL | AVERAGE CAPITAL |
| 1873 | 1 | 2,441 | 2,441 | 0 | 0 | 0 | c | c | c |
| 1874 | 4 | 3,432 | 858 | 0 | 0 | 0 | c | c | c |
| 1875 | 4 | 3,450 | 863 | 0 | 0 | 0 | c | c | c |
| 1876 | 5 | 2,350 | 470 | 1 | 2,000 | 2,000 | c | c | c |
| 1877 | 26 | 22,986 | 206 | 1 | 2,000 | 2,000 | c | c | c |
| 1878 | 95 | 33,596 | 168 | 1 | 2,000 | 2,000 | c | c | c |
| 1879 | 151 | 40,616 | 152 | 10 | 3,290 | 329 | c | c | c |
| 1880 | 151 | 43,041 | 168 | 39 | 6,280 | 161 | 120 | 1,211 | 10 |
| 1881 | 148 | 43,886 | 177 | 90 | 10,447 | 116 | 369 | 5,894 | 16 |
| 1883 | 141 | 44,386 | 190 | 207 | 20,487 | 99 | 573 | 12,071 | 21 |
| 1885 | 139 | 44,456 | 193 | 218 | 18,750 | 86 | 744 | 15,397 | 21 |
| 1887 | 136 | 45,839 | 208 | 221 | 18,896 | 86 | 741 | 15,112 | 20 |
| 1889 | 134 | 47,681 | 225 | 218 | 17,432 | 80 | 695 | 14,421 | 21 |
| 1891 | 134 | 48,701 | 232 | 252 | 19,796 | 79 | 678 | 13,827 | 20 |
| 1893 | 133 | 48,416 | 232 | 604 | 31,030 | 51 | — | — | — |
| 1895 | 133 | 48,951 | 236 | 792 | 49,967 | 63 | — | — | — |
| 1897 | 58 | 13,630 | 113 | 1,217 | 149,286 | 123 | — | — | — |
| 1899 | 0 | 0 | 0 | 1,561 | 209,973 | 135 | — | — | — |

*Notes:* [a] Capital in thousands of yen.

[b] Excludes the Fifteenth National Bank, capitalized at 17.8 million yen.

[c] Unknown.

Adapted from Hugh T. Patrick, "Japan 1868–1914," in Rondo Cameron, ed., *Banking in the Early Stages of Industrialization: A Study in Comparative Economic History* (New York: Oxford University Press, 1967), p. 248.

ton industry, as shown in Table 7.6, profoundly affected the structure of Japan's trade relations. In the 1870s the country exported raw materials and relied heavily on imports for manufactured goods, about half of which were textiles. Three decades later, as demonstrated in Table 7.3 above, the situation had reversed itself: At the beginning of the twentieth century Japan imported substantial amounts of raw materials and exported mostly manufactured goods, especially reeled silk and factory-produced cotton thread and cloth. Equally important, the policy of import substitution had succeeded as the quantity of imported textiles fell to an insubstantial level. Just as Japan's farmers fed the country, so its manufacturers and mill hands clothed it.

The men who spearheaded the growth of Japan's cotton textile industry earned reputations as hard-driving entrepreneurs, and none stood more famous than Shibusawa Eiichi. Possessed of great personal charm, unerring business acumen, and a certain roguish unscrupulousness, Shibusawa in 1864 walked off his family's prosperous farm northwest of Edo to become one of Meiji Japan's most celebrated businessmen. As a protégé of Ōkuma

**TABLE 7.6** *Production of Cotton Textiles, 1880–1900*

| | COTTON THREAD | | | | COTTON FABRICS | |
| | QUANTITY [a] | | VALUE [b] | | VALUE [b] | |
| YEAR | PRODUCED | EXPORTED | PRODUCED | EXPORTED | PRODUCED | EXPORTED |
|---|---|---|---|---|---|---|
| 1880 | .156 | 0.000 | — | 0.000 | — | — |
| 1882 | .360 | 0.000 | — | 0.000 | — | — |
| 1884 | .635 | 0.000 | — | 0.000 | — | — |
| 1886 | .747 | 0.000 | — | 0.000 | — | — |
| 1888 | 1.529 | 0.000 | 3.584 | 0.000 | 12.3 | 0.2 |
| 1890 | 5.032 | 0.001 | 8.982 | 0.002 | 13.6 | 0.2 |
| 1892 | 9.838 | 0.005 | 15.621 | 0.008 | 19.1 | 0.5 |
| 1894 | 14.305 | 0.566 | 25.810 | 0.956 | 27.2 | 1.9 |
| 1896 | 19.277 | 2.076 | 39.661 | 4.029 | 39.1 | 2.2 |
| 1898 | 30.936 | 11.013 | 56.286 | 20.117 | 48.7 | 2.6 |
| 1900 | 30.981 | 10.019 | 73.620 | 20.589 | 61.3 | 5.7 |

[a] In millions of *kan* (1 *kan* = 3.75 kilograms = 8.278 pounds).

[b] In millions of yen at current prices.

Adapted from Keijiro Otsuka, Gustav Ranis, and Gary Saxonhouse, *Comparative Technology Choice in Development: The Indian and Japanese Cotton Textile Industries* (New York: Macmillan Press, 1988) pp. 28–29 and 47.

*Shibusawa Eiichi*

Shigenobu's, Shibusawa served for a time in the Ministry of Finance, where he played a key role in planning for tax reform and a modern banking system. In 1873 he resigned his government position to assume the presidencies of the First National Bank and the Ōji Paper Company, the first joint-stock company in Japan. During the 1880s the energetic Shibusawa became involved in organizing nearly five hundred different enterprises in such diverse areas as manufacturing, insurance, and transportation. Among his more successful undertakings was the Osaka Spinning Mill, which he founded in 1882. Aware that the small scale of the government-operated cotton mills, which had just two thousand spindles each, doomed them to unprofitability, Shibusawa massaged his banking connections to secure a loan from his own First National Bank and then persuaded a group of socially and economically prominent friends to invest a total of 250,000 yen in his new joint-stock company. With funds in hand, he purchased ten thousand spindles from Platt Brothers of Manchester, the world's leading manufacturer of textile machinery, and installed them in a plant he modeled on a Lancashire mill. In the 1910s his Osaka Spinning Company merged with other mills to form the Tōyōbō Company, one of the world's leading textile manufacturers.

Tōyōbō and other Japanese textile firms achieved international competitiveness not just because entrepreneurs such as Shibusawa were adept at raising capital, but also because Japanese businesspeople made a series of important technological adaptations and innovations in the 1880s and 1890s. Japan relied on the West as the source of technological knowledge, as when Shibusawa replicated a Lancashire mill in Osaka and filled it with Platt Brothers machinery, a dependency that gave rise to the unflattering view that the Japanese could only borrow and imitate, not invent. But those who were quick to denigrate the Japanese as technological copycats missed a crucial point: The wholesale importation of proved, affordable technology suggested itself as the fastest way for Japan to catch up with the industrialized West at the end of the nineteenth century. Moreover, out of emulation came innovation; Japanese textile producers tinkered with the models they acquired from abroad, adapting them to conditions at home and putting their constituent elements together in novel ways that sometimes produced manufacturing processes more efficient than the foreign originals. Shibusawa, for instance, cut costs by importing raw cotton from China and by locating his first mill in Osaka, the traditional center of the cotton trade and a source of ample labor. Additionally, in 1886 Shibusawa installed electric lighting throughout his mills, becoming the first textile manufacturer in the world to do so, and he then added a second shift of workers so that he could operate his expensive imported machinery twenty-two hours a day.

Shibusawa was also one of the first producers in Japan to switch from mule spinning, the dominant British technology, to ring spinning. Mule spinning machines had the advantage of producing fine-quality yarn from ordinary-grade raw cotton, but they had to be manned by skilled, and therefore expensive, labor. The ring spindles, in contrast, were much faster, since they could spin and wind yarn simultaneously, but they required a higher grade of raw cotton. Japanese innovators who wished to use ring spindles overcame that particular disadvantage by devising formulas for mixing together a variety of cheaper grades of raw cotton, yet still producing a thread suitable for sale at home and in many markets overseas. The new mixed yarn tended to break easily while being spun, however, thus requiring additional workers to repair the thread. Another complication was that Shibusawa and other millowners wished to cut their capital costs by substituting wooden bobbins for the original metal fixtures on the ring machines, even though the wooden ones required frequent changing, which made ring spinning even more labor-intensive. But the textile pioneers had an answer for that too: They replaced their skilled expensive male employees, originally hired to operate the mule machines, with young female workers, who would accept relatively low wages to perform the comparatively simple tasks of mixing the cotton, changing the bobbins, and mending breaks in the blended thread.

Japan's early industrialists took great pride in building manufacturing enterprises that were as efficient and competitive as their Western counterparts, but Shibusawa and the others frequently deprecated their accomplishments as nothing more than unselfish and loyal service to the state. It was permissible to borrow the West's technology, but few self-made businessmen in the late Meiji period wanted anything to do with a foreign philosophy of economic individualism that glorified personal gain. His single ambition, Shibusawa commented in 1915, had been to "devote my whole life to the development of industry. Through industry I thought I could discharge my obligation to my country. My personal fame and my family's wealth have never entered into my thought from the very start of my career. My burning desire was to promote the application of the collective welfare of the country; the development of Japan's industry; the increase of the public wealth; and to elevate the status of merchants and businessmen so that they could be placed on an equal footing with those of Europe and America."[7]

To some extent, such a business ideology was patently self-serving, designed to parry questions about the accumulation of personal fortunes vast beyond the ken of most ordinary Japanese. Seen in a different light, however, a rhetoric that stressed the selflessness and patriotic virtue of businessmen was perhaps inevitable in the closing decades of the nineteenth century, when the state was doing so much to forge a creed of civic morality and when talk of "national essence" and "national citizens" filled the air. Certainly Shibusawa's oft-repeated assertions that he devoted his entire energies to promoting "the welfare of the public" and that "the slightest idea of fame and wealth did not enter my mind" were phrases that also tumbled from the lips of the men who built the early *zaibatsu*, the business conglomerates that introduced large-scale corporations, modern management practices, and heavy industry to Japan.

## Big Business, Heavy Industry, and the Zaibatsu

Mitsui, Mitsubishi, Sumitomo, and Yasuda stand apart in Japanese business history as the four great *zaibatsu*, the financial cliques that began to take shape during the Meiji period, although the term *zaibatsu* itself was not heard much until the 1910s. Each conglomerate consisted of a far-flung network of legally distinct companies and subsidiaries. Within each *zaibatsu*, individual firms engaged in their own specialized business activities but were linked together by personal and historical relationships, common ownership, collective goals set by a centralized advisory committee, interlocking boards of directors, and access to a shared pool of capital and technology. In contrast with the small-scale enterprises prevalent in light industry, each *zaibatsu* controlled its own financial institutions, which provided it a sound basis for long-range corporate planning and finance. The *zaibatsu* also benefited from government favors and patronage, which further helped the Big Four to pioneer and later dominate the so-called modern sector of the economy—that is, heavy industries such as mining, shipbuilding, and the manufacture of machinery, metals, and chemicals.

Strong leadership, another characteristic of the *zaibatsu*, enabled the House of Mitsui to weather the chaos of the restoration years and eventually become Japan's largest conglomerate. The man who began to move the Mitsui family away from its roots as merchandisers par excellence, symbolized by the success of the Echigoya chain of dry goods stores, was the shrewd, calculating Minomura Rizaemon. If we are to believe the colorful life history that Minomura constructed for himself, he was the son of a poor, masterless samurai in Shinano Province in 1821 and in his youth worked as a common laborer and peddler before becoming a moneylender in Edo. As luck would have it, his shop was but a short distance from the mansion and office compound of Oguri Tadamasa, the shogunate's chief commissioner of finance from 1863 until 1868. Impressed by Minomura's quick way with the abacus and his canny ability to profit from currency manipulations, Oguri recommended the young man to the head of Mitsui's operations in Edo, who employed Minomura as his chief clerk.

Minomura proved his worth to the merchant house in short order. As a bold advocate of revitalizing the military power of the Tokugawa regime and punishing dissident domains, Commissioner of Finance Oguri frequently imposed extraordinary levies on leading merchant houses to pay for his proposed military and financial reforms. When a series of such raids on its purse in 1866 threatened the survival of the Mitsui dry goods establishment, Minomura inveigled his former benefactor to reduce the shogunate's demands substantially. Gratitude, however, does not seem to have been part of Minomura's emotional repertoire. Just two years later, elevated to the Mitsui inner council, he anticipated the downfall of the shogunate and persuaded his firm to make generous loans to the imperial forces, which helped Saigō and his confederates to march on Edo and prevail in the Boshin Civil War. By the time those hostilities ended, Oguri was dead, the only Tokugawa official to be executed by the new Meiji government, and Minomura

Rizaemon had emerged as the most influential member of the Mitsui house council.

Minomura and the Mitsui family soon reaped a handsome reward for having placed their bet on the royalist side. Early in 1868 the new Meiji leadership entrusted the supervision of its tax receipts to the House of Mitsui. Preoccupied with beating back its opponents and extending its political control over the country, the regime gave the private business firm wide latitude in setting up procedures for collecting public tax revenues, with the result that until 1882, when Matsukata created the Bank of Japan, the House of Mitsui enjoyed interest-free use of tax receipts between the time of their payment and their eventual disbursement. That windfall prompted the house council to seek approval from the government to found its own bank, chartered in 1876 as Japan's first private commercial bank. Over the subsequent decades, as the Mitsui Bank opened branches in more than thirty major cities around the country, the house council took the deposits acquired from its banking customers, added them to the profits derived from the dry goods business, and filled a war chest to bankroll Mitsui's expansion into trading and mining.

Masuda Takashi successfully guided the firm in that new direction following Minomura's death in 1877. The son of a minor shogunal official, Masuda traveled to the West as part of the 1864 shogunal mission and later was befriended by the oligarch Inoue Kaoru, a Chōshū activist who had helped pull together the alliance of dissident domains that toppled the shogunate. Blessed with an insider's connections, Masuda won a lucrative commission to provision government forces during the Satsuma Rebellion and later obtained exclusive rights for the recently organized Mitsui Trading Company to market all coal from the government's rich Miike Mines on Kyūshū. When the oligarchs decided to sell the mining operations in 1888, Masuda bid aggressively to purchase them and then turned Miike coal into "Mitsui gold." Moving rapidly, Masuda acquired other mines, folded them into the newly incorporated Mitsui Mining Company, set up branch offices from Tianjin to Singapore, claimed Asia's markets as his own, and even drove his competitors from Australia.

Nakamigawa Hikojirō mapped out Mitsui's next phase of development, steering the firm into new industrial endeavors and initiating the reorganization of the various Mitsui enterprises into a full-fledged *zaibatsu*. Nakamigawa was a nephew of Fukuzawa Yukichi's and in 1869, at age fifteen, left his Kyūshū home to travel to Edo, where he enrolled in his uncle's Keiō Academy. After translating a number of works on economics, American politics, and world geography from English into Japanese, Nakamigawa journeyed to London in the mid-1870s. Upon his return to Japan, he found employment in the Ministry of Public Works, headed then by Inoue Kaoru, and followed his new mentor to the Ministry of Foreign Affairs in 1879. Nakamigawa quit government service in 1881, emerging the next year as the head editor of Fukuzawa's new daily newspaper, the *Jiji shinpō*, which the restless Nakamigawa left in 1887 to assume the presidency of a private railway company.

In the summer of 1891, having racked up accomplishments in education, government service, journalism, and private business, Nakamigawa, upon the recommendation of longtime Mitsui confidant Inoue, was tapped to become the director of the Mitsui Bank, whose careless lending practices at the end of the 1880s had jeopardized its future successes. Nakamigawa made his presence felt immediately. Alarmed by the state of the bank's accounts, he abruptly ended the custom of granting unsecured loans to government officials, a consideration the bank had extended in gratitude for the numerous favors the House of Mitsui received from the Meiji regime. Moreover, he seized the private residences of certain high officials when they neglected to repay their mortgages as scheduled, and he recalled a shaky loan from the influential Higashi Honganji temple in Kyoto, making the banker the bête noire of Buddhist faithful everywhere when the temple's head abbot had to launch a nationwide collection campaign.

Strengthened by his banking successes, Nakamigawa convinced fellow leaders within the Mitsui circle to begin investing in industrial enterprises. Foreseeing continued expansion in worldwide demand for textiles, he purchased several cotton-spinning companies, including the Kanegafuchi mill, which he built into one of the largest in Japan. Moreover, when the government announced a public auction of its Tomioka filature in the autumn of 1893, the Mitsui Bank snapped it up at a bargain basement price and, with additional investments to expand the scale of production, turned it into a profit-making venture. To those acquisitions, Nakamigawa added such firms as the Ōji Paper Company and the Shibaura Engineering Works, laying the foundation for Mitsui's emergence in the twentieth century as one of the world's most powerful industrial combines.

Just as he reformed the bank, so Nakamigawa became a staunch advocate of replacing the old Mitsui family council with what he saw as a more rational, modern form of business organization. Consequently, in 1893 he converted the bank, the Echigoya dry goods chain (later renamed the Mitsukoshi Department Stores), and the trading and mining operations into separate joint-stock companies and created an executive board to coordinate planning. Under the new structural arrangements, completed in 1909, members of the Mitsui family held all outstanding shares of every Mitsui firm; skilled career businessmen, recruited increasingly from Keiō and other leading universities, managed the enterprises; and a holding company decided general policy, plotted common strategies, and made important management decisions about matters that affected all the allied firms.

The other *zaibatsu* evolved in a manner similar to Mitsui's, although each developed its own distinctive corporate culture. Iwasaki Yatarō, remembered as a hard-bitten man of no little arrogance, founded Mitsubishi, which became Japan's second largest *zaibatsu*. The son of a farmer in Tosa domain, Iwasaki in his youth purchased the rank of a minor samurai and in 1867 joined the domain's trading operations in Nagasaki, where Tosa had opened facilities in order to acquire Western technology and weapons. Iwasaki soon made a minor reputation for himself by settling a rather large debt to foreigners that Tosa's traders had accumulated over the years. In gratitude, when the domains passed out of existence in 1871, the daimyo of Tosa bestowed upon Iwasaki eleven ships, a considerable sum of cash, and the right to assume control of the domain's camphor, tea, dried bonito, and lumber enterprises.

Iwasaki's good fortunes soared in 1874, when the Meiji oligarchs decided to sell thirteen steamships to him at a nominal price, since they believed that a well-equipped, privately owned marine shipping company, endowed with assistance from the government, would serve Japan's strategic needs as well as help correct its persistent balance of payment problems by reducing dependence on foreign carriers. In confirmation of the policy of private ownership–public support, the government in September 1875 transferred the balance of its modern steamships to Iwasaki and agreed to provide him with operating subsidies as well. Delighted, Iwasaki painted his soon-to-be-famous three-diamond logo on the ships and founded the Mitsubishi Steamship Company, headquartered in Tokyo. The vessels of the new company quickly dominated Japan's waters and, in accordance with instructions from the government, began service between Yokohama and Shanghai. Within a short time, to the shock of many, Iwasaki used his favorite tactic of deeply slashing prices to force the British Peninsular and Oriental Steam Navigation Company (P&O) from the Shanghai-Yokohama route. Later Iwasaki's fleet took the name NYK (Nippon Yūsen Kaisha) and inaugurated service to China, Korea, and Russia. By century's end NYK had expanded beyond its Asian base to become a world leader on routes that linked Japan's ports with those in Australia, the United States, and Europe. The Mitsubishi diamonds had become a symbol the world would remember.

As the profits rolled in, Iwasaki quickly launched new endeavors. In 1878 he established the Tokyo Maritime Insurance Company, and two years later he began a warehousing operation and a moneylending enterprise that functioned as a source of credit for Mitsubishi businesses and later evolved into the Mitsubishi Bank. The year after that, he added the government-owned Takashima Coal Mine, located on a small island south of Nagasaki, to his growing collection of companies, and in 1887 Mitsubishi purchased the Nagasaki Shipyards from the Meiji government on easy terms. That same year the growing conglomerate ventured into real estate speculation by acquiring, again at a favorable price, a large tract of government land in downtown Tokyo just to the east of the Imperial Palace, which the firm later developed into the affluent Marunouchi business district. In 1893, Iwasaki Yanosuke, who had succeeded his younger brother, established Mitsubishi Limited. Owned outright by the Iwasaki family, the new company imposed centralized control over the activities of the various Mitsubishi endeavors, which were incorporated as divisions of the limited partnership.

The enterprises of the Sumitomo and Yasuda *zaibatsu* clustered more tightly around a principal core business. The Sumitomo family constituted one of the great merchant houses of Osaka during the early modern era, building a fortune from the ore that it extracted from its Besshi Copper Mine and winning appointment as the official purveyor of copper to the shogunate. Production from the Besshi lode dipped considerably in the early nineteenth century, but the economic ebullience and promise of the Meiji era revitalized the Sumitomo family, which hired foreign engineers, introduced Western-style technology at the mine, and tripled output between 1868 and 1885. Its base in mining secure, the Sumitomo then branched out. By the end of the Meiji period its interests included banking, warehousing, and metal processing, and its general trading department exported copper, coal, tea, and raw silk, carried abroad on the vessels of the OSK shipping company, the Ōsaka Shōsen Kaisha, founded in 1882, when some fifty small firms came together under Sumitomo guidance.

The Yasuda *zaibatsu* concentrated on banking. Its founder, Yasuda Zenjirō, claimed that he earned his first money peddling flowers in his native Toyama before going to Edo in 1864, where he became a street corner money changer. Yasuda showed remarkable instincts for mastering the cutthroat techniques of exchange manipulations in the confusing years surrounding the restoration, amassing profits that he used to found his own bank in 1880. An unabashed skinflint—he packed his own lunch for the office and left home at the crack of dawn in order to get the early-morning discount on Tokyo's new streetcars—Yasuda died one of Japan's wealthiest individuals, the principal owner of nineteen banks, three insurance companies, three railways, and an electric company. Although his ruthless business practices brought him bountiful personal blessings, Yasuda, like Shibusawa Eiichi, framed his accomplishments in terms of national goals and service to his countrymen. In all apparent sincerity, Yasuda once declared that he had never formed a company without first ensuring that "the purpose of the enterprise be good and that it operate for the public benefit, contributing to the welfare of the people and the progress of society."[8]

Many new big businesses remained separate from the emergent *zaibatsu*. Those included the Tsukiji and Hyōgo shipyards founded by Kawasaki Shōzō, Suzuki Tōsaburō's sugar refining firm, and several important banks. Similarly in the 1880s and 1890s many private railway companies came into being as freestanding enterprises. The creation of privately owned railroads dates to Matsukata Masayoshi's appointment as finance minister. A forceful advocate of private enterprise, Matsukata dropped the government's program of state construction and management of the rails and inaugurated a policy of encouraging private railway development through subsidies and other forms of public assistance, just as he was doing with the shipping industry. The first beneficiaries of the shift in government strategy were a group of investors who founded the Nippon Railway in 1881 and received official approval to construct four trunk lines emanating outward from Tokyo. The oligarchs did more than just hand over a charter to the new enterprise, however. To ensure that Nippon Railway could raise enough capital and set a successful precedent for future ventures, the government guaranteed shareholders an annual return of 8 percent on capital, lent land to the company, waived taxes on company-owned real estate, and even surveyed and constructed the trunk line that ran north from Tokyo to Aomori.

When Nippon Railway's profits exceeded expectations in 1884, an investment mania swept Japan, and between 1885 and 1892 more than fifty groups applied to establish private rail companies. The government issued charters to fourteen of them, blessing ten with the same sorts of subsidies, profit guarantees, and tax breaks that underwrote Nippon Railway's rapid success. The results were dramatic. Measured in terms of total assets, in 1896 private railroad companies accounted for seven of Japan's ten largest joint-stock companies, by 1890 private railway firms controlled more miles of lines than did the government railway, and by the time government decided to nationalize the rails in 1907, in the aftermath of a war with Russia, the nearly five thousand miles of track laid down by private lines spanned all of Japan's major islands. Enticed by such amenities as interior electric lighting, dining cars, and onboard toilets, people took to the rails, with ridership climbing from 23 million in 1890 to 114 million a decade later. The popularity of travel by rail also gave rise to new industrial ventures: The first complete built-in-Japan steam locomotive rolled down the rails in 1912, the

**TABLE 7.7** *Meiji Railroads, 1872–1907*
(length of track in miles)

| YEAR | NATIONAL RAILROADS | PRIVATE RAILROADS | TOTAL MILEAGE | PERCENT PRIVATE |
|------|------|------|------|------|
| 1872 | 18 | 0 | 18 | 0 |
| 1876 | 65 | 0 | 65 | 0 |
| 1880 | 98 | 0 | 98 | 0 |
| 1884 | 182 | 81 | 263 | 31 |
| 1888 | 506 | 406 | 912 | 45 |
| 1892 | 551 | 1,320 | 1,871 | 71 |
| 1896 | 632 | 1,875 | 2,507 | 75 |
| 1900 | 950 | 2,905 | 3,855 | 75 |
| 1904 | 1,461 | 3,232 | 4,693 | 69 |
| 1907 | 4,453 | 446 | 4,899 | 9 |

Adapted from Steven J. Ericson, *The Sound of the Whistle: Railroads and the State in Meiji Japan* (Cambridge: Council on East Asian Studies, Harvard University, 1996), p. 9.

final year in the reign of Emperor Meiji, Japan's first official rail passenger forty years earlier.

## "Sacrificed on the Altar of Industrial Progress"

In 1877 Furukawa Ichibei purchased the Ashio Copper Mine, located in Tochigi Prefecture, just across a mountain pass from Tokugawa Ieyasu's mausoleum at Nikkō. The second son of Kyoto tofu dealers, Furukawa was the Meiji economic dream incarnate: He accumulated a tidy nest egg by exporting silk and then multiplied his fortune after establishing Japan's first mechanized silk filature in 1871. When he took over the Ashio operations, the mine was yielding a mere fraction of its earlier output, and he personally led miners into dangerous abandoned shafts, eventually discovering a massive new vein in 1884. Furukawa exploited the rich mother lode with the best technology he could buy, and by 1890 Ashio was producing nearly half of Japan's refined copper and had become the largest copper mine–refining complex in Asia. In 1899 readers of the influential monthly *Taiyō* voted Furukawa, the man of modest origins who had made good for himself and created wealth for Japan, one of the Twelve Great Men of Meiji, ranking him alongside Itō Hirobumi, Fukuzawa Yukichi, and Shibusawa Eiichi.

Not many of the eleven thousand workers at Ashio agreed with that assessment. In the 1880s they labored long, hot hours in hazardous conditions, hacking out by hand blasting holes for dynamite, hammering away at ore-laden rock with hammers and chisels, and pushing handcarts loaded with the ore and rock to the surface, where it was crushed and refined. Conditions improved somewhat after Furukawa built Japan's first hydroelectric plant in 1890; compressed air drills and electrified tramways facilitated work in the shafts, and centrifugal fans cooled and cleaned the air. Other dangers and tribulations remained, however. Even though they provided little supervision in the pits, mine officials demanded kickbacks from pay packets. Until the end of the century miners largely policed themselves through vigilante committees that dished out cruel punishments, often cutting off ears, noses, or limbs and, in extreme cases, even beating offenders to death. Hardened criminals, conscripted from Tochigi jails to offset labor shortages, heightened tensions in the pits. In 1881 five penal laborers overwhelmed their guard, escaped through a mine shaft, and fled into the surrounding mountains. Authorities captured four of the escapees but had to hire eighteen local "hunters" to track down and shoot the fifth.

Under such circumstances, it was not easy to recruit workers, and Furukawa had to rely on lodge bosses, independent agents who hired workers, arranged work assignments, distributed pay, and housed and fed their charges in private lodges. Still, miners worked and lived in bleak conditions. Lodge bosses were stern figures, and the accommodations, according to one journalist, "resemble long barracks assembled from rough wooden planks, with flimsy roofs weighted down by rows of stones of various sizes. They have neither ceiling nor floor; crude straw mats are laid on bare ground around open hearths. No ceiling, no tatami, no furniture; a constant accumulation of rubbish, filthy eating utensils, and bedding covered with soot and dirt. A person who sets eyes on all this abundance of filth for the first time is rendered quite speechless."[9]

Unpopular with his workers, Furukawa was a villain to people who lived along the Watarase River valley. The Ashio refinery discharged its effluents into the river, and as early as 1880 local residents were becoming accustomed to the sight of dead fish floating down the Watarase. By the late 1880s almost all marine life had disappeared from the valley, and nearly three thousand families that had made their livings fishing the river were plunged into destitution. Matters took an even more ominous turn the next decade. The expansion of mining operations caused an almost insatiable demand for timber to shore up mine shafts, provide the ties for the electric tramways, and produce the tons of charcoal needed for smelting and refining. Furukawa stripped the trees from hillsides around Ashio, and with little to stop the runoff of winter snows and spring rains, floodwaters covered the valley floor with a thick layer of silt in 1890. To villagers, it seemed as if the hand of death had passed over their fields. Vegetation shriveled up, new seedlings would not grow, silkworms fed on mulberry leaves picked from trees in the affected area died, and men and women working outdoors developed running sores on their feet and hands.

Tanaka Shōzō, a former member of the Popular Rights Movement and the stricken district's elected representative to the first House of Representatives, brought the pollution incidents to the attention of the nation. The self-educated son of a Tochigi farmer, Tanaka passionately believed that ordinary people "should not be sacrificed on the altar of industrial progress." Speaking on the floor of the Diet in December 1891, he pointed out that a law about to go into effect clearly stated that "when mining enterprises are injurious to the public interest, the Ministry of Agriculture and Commerce shall revoke the concession granted," and he concluded by asking what the government intended to do to relieve the suffering of the people in the Watarase Valley.[10] Two months later he rose again, this time to proclaim, "The government has abandoned the people whom it has a constitutional duty to protect. To destroy the people is to destroy the nation. Does the so-called 'government' realize what it is doing?"[11]

Officials in Tokyo answered early in 1892. "The public benefits that accrue to the country from the Ashio mine," one figure in the Ministry of Agriculture and Commerce wrote, "far outweigh any losses suffered in the affected areas."[12] Consequently, the report noted, the situation did not warrant closing the mine. Moreover, spokespersons explained later, the amount of pollution evident at Ashio was not even serious enough to be deemed "injurious to the public interest." That meant the government had no legal standing in the case, and relief measures were thus a private matter to be worked out between the mine's ownership and the people of the area. The government's policy of nonintervention led to the environmental disaster Tanaka feared: Before the 1890s were over, arsenic, chromium, sulfuric acid, magnesia, chlorine, aluminum oxide, and other pollutants had ruined at least one hundred square miles of farmland and inflicted serious economic losses on thousands of families. Although the scientific evidence never was beyond dispute, most observers also concurred that the pollutants contributed to higher than normal death rates and generally poor health in towns and villages along the entire length of the river.

As problems mounted, the people of the Watarase Valley organized an opposition movement. At first they wrote petitions asking for relief and the closure of the Ashio Copper Mine. Then, in 1897 eight hundred villagers joined a mass march on government offices in Tokyo to protest their victimization. Activists also met privately with government officials and eventually persuaded the minister of agriculture and commerce to make a personal inspection of the devastated villages. At the same time, Tanaka continued his attack on Furukawa in the Diet, newspapers carried pollution-related stories on their front pages, and a variety of prominent critics, including the socialist Kōtoku Shūsui and the journalist Tokutomi Sohō, began to call for government action.

Sensitive to the growing public outcry and distressed by what its officials saw on inspection tours of the Watarase Valley, the Ministry of Agriculture and Commerce in May 1897 ordered Ashio's management to build secure beds to store discarded slag, construct filtration ponds to clean pit water, and install limewater sprayers to neutralize the acidic smoke that poured from the mine's smokestacks. Directives set clear dates for compliance and warned that the mine would be closed if the deadlines were not met. His options foreclosed, Furukawa installed the expensive pollution controls, and by 1904 many villages downstream from Ashio had begun to report more normal harvests.

Although conditions improved, pollution did not disappear from the Watarase Valley. For one thing, there was no way to remove or neutralize the contaminants that already had accumulated on the riverbed. Moreover, copper mining was a very dirty business everywhere in the world at the end of the nineteenth century, and no existing technology was totally capable of purifying mining wastes or protecting the environment against ecological damage. Consequently, people living along the Watarase River continued to fall ill in disproportionate numbers for several generations. As Japan's first pollution incident receded from the nation's consciousness, some of those families simply lived with their problems. Others turned to the modern court system, and a government-mediated settlement between the Furukawa Mining Company and the pollution victims finally took place in 1974, one year after the copper had petered out and the mine closed.

## The Emergence of a Modern Economy

In the 1890s the sight of belching smokestacks and the familiar sound of the steam whistle screaming from trains crisscrossing the countryside carried the unmistakable message that Japan, an isolated, agrarian country a generation earlier, was headed down the tracks toward modern economic growth. By century's end irreversible structural changes were fully under way, as manufacturing became well established and premodern forms of production increasingly gave way to mechanized industry. Moreover, all sectors of the economy were growing faster than Japan's population, thus yielding a sustained increase in output per capita, another indicator of a modern economy. The fastest growth rate was in manufacturing, which annually claimed a greater share of gross domestic product relative to agriculture, as shown in Table 7.8. Considered with Tables 7.2 and 7.3, the data illustrate

**TABLE 7.8**  *Structural Changes in the Economy, 1868–1910*

A. CHANGING PROPORTIONS OF AGRICULTURE AND MANUFACTURING

| YEAR | GROSS DOMESTIC PRODUCT * | PROPORTION (%) PRODUCED IN: | |
| --- | --- | --- | --- |
| | | AGRICULTURE | MANUFACTURING |
| 1885 | 3,774 | 42.1 | 7.0 |
| 1890 | 4,639 | 39.8 | 7.9 |
| 1895 | 5,375 | 37.0 | 8.9 |
| 1900 | 5,966 | 34.7 | 11.2 |
| 1905 | 6,214 | 31.6 | 12.6 |
| 1910 | 7,424 | 30.9 | 15.6 |

\* In millions of yen at constant 1934–1936 prices.

B. EXPORTS BY COMMODITY
   (annual averages in millions of yen at current prices)

| | FOOD-STUFFS | RAW MATERIALS | SEMI-MANUFAC-TURED GOODS | FINISHED GOODS | OTHERS | TOTAL |
| --- | --- | --- | --- | --- | --- | --- |
| | % | % | % | % | % | % |
| 1868–1870 | 4 (31) | 4 (25) | 6 (41) | 0 (1) | 0 (2) | 14 (100) |
| 1871–1875 | 7 (39) | 3 (18) | 7 (37) | 1 (3) | 1 (4) | 19 (100) |
| 1876–1880 | 10 (38) | 3 (12) | 11 (41) | 1 (5) | 1 (4) | 27 (100) |
| 1881–1885 | 11 (31) | 4 (12) | 16 (46) | 3 (8) | 1 (3) | 35 (100) |
| 1886–1890 | 16 (26) | 7 (12) | 26 (45) | 8 (13) | 2 (4) | 59 (100) |
| 1891–1895 | 19 (19) | 10 (10) | 46 (46) | 24 (23) | 4 (4) | 102 (100) |
| 1896–1900 | 22 (13) | 20 (12) | 81 (47) | 45 (26) | 5 (3) | 173 (100) |
| 1901–1905 | 35 (12) | 27 (9) | 133 (46) | 85 (30) | 8 (3) | 288 (100) |
| 1906–1910 | 47 (11) | 39 (9) | 197 (47) | 132 (31) | 6 (2) | 421 (100) |

Adapted from Penelope Francks, *Japanese Economic Development: Theory and Practice* (London: Routledge, 1992), p. 39, and Shinya Sugiyama, *Japan's Industrialization in the World Economy 1859–1899* (London: Athlone Press, 1988), pp. 224–25.

two other features of Japan's emerging economic modernity: the initial rise of technologically advanced heavy industries and a shifting pattern of export trade as textiles and other manufactured goods displaced an earlier export mix dominated by agricultural and raw materials.

It is easier to describe Japan's quest for economic modernity than to explain why the country's successes came with such apparent rapidity, compared with the experiences of many other nations. Clearly, the Tokugawa legacy had a significant impact on the direction of events during the Meiji period. The growth of handicrafts, protoindustrialization, and the development of cash crops in the eighteenth and early nineteenth centuries provided a storehouse of knowledge, skills, and organizational experience that were useful for expanding commercial agriculture and rural-based manufactures after the restoration. Similarly, the appearance of banking services in the Tokugawa era offered valuable precedents for Meiji entrepreneurs. Old-fashioned in comparison to the modern financial institutions that emerged in the 1880s and 1890s, the traditional money changers and merchant houses of the late Tokugawa period had a sophisticated understanding of commercial transactions and were thoroughly familiar with the collection and reinvestment of deposits, the use of letters of credit and bill discounts, and the employment of cash advances and other credit devices to fund cottage industry, practices that provided a set of guides for the men who opened commercial and quasi banks in the Meiji years. It is also possible to suggest generally that traditional values of discipline, diligence, sacrifice, frugality, loyalty to family, and fidelity to community stood the entire citizenry in good stead as Japan advanced into the Meiji years.

The Tokugawa heritage provided a fertile seedbed hospitable to commercial growth, but government officials and private businesspeople in the Meiji era carried out other necessary tasks: importing the seedlings of industrial capitalism from the West, transplanting modern production techniques into Japanese soil, and tending to the flowering of modern economic growth. Not every rotation of the government's spade turned up something of use, as the model factories bear witness. But certain contributions of the Meiji government were essential to the ongoing struggle to Increase Production, Promote Industry. The effort to build an infrastructure stands out in that regard. So too does the oligarchs' decision to foster such key enterprises as shipping and railroads by granting them profit guarantees and operating subsidies. The matter of policy formulation is more complicated. The Tokugawa shoguns had seen some advantage to commercial development as long as they could closely regulate it and keep it from upsetting the political status quo. The Meiji leadership, in contrast, saw economic growth as a means of solving the financial problems that had accumulated in the latter part of the Tokugawa period and as a way to preserve Japan's autonomy against a potentially dangerous West. Consequently, while different Meiji oligarchs sometimes favored contrary industrial strategies, as when Ōkubo and Matsukata squared off concerning the virtues of laissez-faire capitalism, the leaders were united in agreeing that modern economic growth had to be adopted as a national goal.

The consensus on a national objective helped galvanize the entrepreneurial energies of individual men and women across Japan, who in any case were driven by their own visions of a more bountiful economic future. A surprising number of those pioneers who pursued economic modernity lived in relative autonomy, managing their button factories and gold leaf workshops and silk filatures; others, such as Tatsu'uma Kiyo, built more substantial enterprises; a very few, like Iwasaki and Yasuda, carved out international reputations as heads of business empires. But no matter where their place in the rich and complicated mosaic of Meiji economic history, those men and women marshaled their capital, gathered together resources, acquired technology and fiddled with it to make it fit their circumstances, and fashioned products that they sold to their neighbors at home and to unknown customers overseas. Some government policies, especially Matsukata's deflationary program of the early 1880s, which created the stability that made sustained growth possible, smoothed the way for those businesspersons, but in the end the individual initiative of Japan's entrepreneurs breathed life into the Meiji economic dream.

There was also a providential, almost serendipitous quality to Japan's economic accomplishments. In some ways, the country was fortunate that the West had started down the path of industrialization a few decades before Perry's arrival, for as a late developer, the newly opened island nation could learn from the experiences of Euro-Americans and make use of their technological innovations. At the same time, the West was not so far ahead in the 1870s and 1880s that the Japanese despaired of catching up; indeed, the gap between East and West was narrow enough that it inspired determination to bridge it. It was to Japan's benefit, as well, that it began its economic journey when new marketing networks were emerging on an international scale. A revolution in transportation and communication was transforming the world into a global marketplace in the second half of the nineteenth century, and to their delight, the Japanese discovered that they already grew and could soon manufacture a variety of goods that people overseas wanted, from tea and raw silk to gold leaf and buttons and cotton textiles.

*Planting rice seedlings*

The trend lines of growth arched upward in the early Meiji decades, and Japan was to build on its initial achievements to become one of the world's leading economic powers at the beginning of the twentieth century. But while the overall development of the nation seemed to be proceeding at a good pace, many ordinary people were to learn, much to their chagrin, that they had to bear the burden of progress. The educated readers of one of Japan's most respected magazines voted Furukawa one of the Twelve Great Men of Meiji, and his Ashio Copper Mine contributed to the country's economic modernization. But the sort of progress represented by that enterprise extracted a staggering cost from a mass of unsung workers, who toiled in conditions that wrecked their health and shortened their lives, and from ordinary families who had to drink poisoned water and eat food grown on polluted land. Japan's quest for wealth and power cast up numerous heroes and a great many victims who paid dearly for national greatness.

Controversy and contention filled the Meiji years. Itō Hirobumi and the other oligarchs clashed with opponents in the Popular Rights Movement about what kind of constitution and system of representative government best suited the nation. So too did Furukawa and Tanaka advance fundamentally different conceptions about Japan's economic development: The capitalist extraordinaire accepted the proposition that his country needed to industrialize as rapidly as possible, with ecological and human costs demoted to secondary status, while Japan's pioneer environmentalist believed that the principal goal of economic modernization was to contribute to the well-being of the people. In similar fashion, as the nineteenth century drew to a close, men and women across the land offered competing ideas about how the family, education, religion, and conditions in the workplace might be transformed in order to bring about their particular vision of the Meiji Dream.

# CHAPTER 8

# Living the Meiji Dream

n the summer of 1885 female factory hands at the Amamiya Silk Reeling Company in Kōfu temporarily walked off the job to protest the capricious conduct of male supervisors who showed favoritism toward "the fair of face" and treated plain-looking women harshly. A year later, on June 12, 1886, nearly one hundred factory girls again marched out of the Amamiya filature. This time the strikers sought refuge in a local temple, where they discussed their grievances and plotted strategy. The women were angry that the mill's owner intended to reduce wages while adding thirty minutes to the workday. Nor were they pleased with a long list of fines that ownership threatened to impose on workers who did not comply with the new regulations or with a rule that once hired, a woman would not be allowed to take a job at a different mill for one year.

Factory hours at Kōfu's mills already were long enough, according to the protesters. In the summer of 1886, operations began at 4:30 A.M., and after a one-hour break from 12:30 to 1:30, it was back to the machines for a numbing second shift that ran until 7:30 P.M. Moreover, most of the mill hands came from the ranks of Kōfu's urban poor or from farming villages around the city, and some women walked as much as an hour each way between home and factory, setting out as dawn reddened the sky and returning as the stars began to shine. Even those who lived closer, however, were scared by the commute. Bands of thugs loitered around the town and its outskirts, and lengthening the working day meant increasing the danger of being mugged or raped or even kidnapped and sold into prostitution.

The number of strikers at Amamiya quickly doubled to include virtually the entire work force. With no way to keep the filature open, the owner's mediators agreed to meet with the strikers' representatives. At first, management suggested that it would preserve the 4:30 A.M. to 7:30 P.M. workday if the women would accept a thirty-minute lunch period and the elimination of most toilet breaks. The workers balked at that idea, and after long hours of negotiation the owner of the Amamiya mill dropped plans to lengthen working hours, eliminated new regulations that would have imposed heavy fines on women who arrived at work late (or left early) by even a few minutes, and promised to consider "other ways to improve conditions."[1] Having settled most of the grievances to their satisfaction, the strikers returned to work on June 16 and left the question of wages for another day.

The confrontation between labor and management in Kōfu received just momentary coverage from the nation's press before receding to the hazy fringes of Meiji history. Such fleeting attention was a disservice to the young women at the Amamiya filature since their walkout in 1886 constituted the first organized industrial strike in Japanese history. Their actions represented, as well, a significant attempt by a marginalized group to find its own voice and articulate its hopes for the Meiji experiment in economic modernization. Like the miners who sweated in the pits at Ashio, the women at Amamiya toiled long hours for low wages, and their resistance to lengthening the workday was a way of bargaining to sell their labor for the best price possible. In addition to improving their material circumstances, the women were fighting a determined battle to assert some degree of control over the terms of their employment by demanding a say on work rules and by insisting that ownership consider "other ways to improve conditions" on the shop floor.

Perhaps the events at Amamiya lingered in the limelight only briefly because so many other issues competed for the public's attention. As the nineteenth century drew to a close, the Meiji government engaged in social engineering that promised to exert a significant impact on how various segments of the population experienced the Meiji Dream. Even as it scheduled its initiatives for political and economic reform, the regime drew up an agenda for social change that would legally define relationships between husbands and wives, promote a system of education that subordinated the aspirations of the individual to the needs of the state, and privilege certain religions over others. Like the contest for the workplace—and just as with the battles over constitutionalism and the debates between Furukawa Ichibei and Tanaka Shōzō about whether economic modernity should enrich the state or benefit ordinary people—the attempt of government to intervene in the home, decide how children were to be educated, and steer people down certain religious paths left some Japanese content, some angry, some baffled, and some still struggling to find a voice.

## Factory Workers

If the industrialization of the Meiji period created capitalists and company managers, it also brought forth a new class of factory workers, many of whom experienced conditions not far removed from the harsh realities at Ashio and Amamiya. To be certain, even at the end of the nineteenth century, factory laborers remained a relatively small proportion of Japan's total work force as nearly two-thirds of all gainfully employed persons still made a living in agriculture. Nevertheless, the number of factory workers rose dramatically, from a few thousand in the 1870s to nearly 300,000 in 1892 to somewhat more than 400,000 in the late 1890s. As Japan faced the new century, the neoteric proletariat developed its own nascent working-class mentality, challenged management's conceptions about the nature of employer-worker relations, and added a new way of life to Japan's already complex social milieu.

The female textile worker represented the prototypical factory hand during Japan's initial stages of industrialization. At the turn of the century nearly 60 percent of all industrial workers found employment in silk filatures and cotton mills, and well over 80 percent of them were women, as indicated in Table 8.1. At the beginning of the Meiji period the owners of the new silk filatures that used water and steam power in the reeling process hired local women, preferably those who had experience working the looms in the factorylike establishments founded by weaver-entrepreneurs in the years before the restoration. As the number of mechanized filatures grew dramatically in the 1880s and 1890s, however, recruiters moved farther afield, into economically depressed rural areas where unmarried teenage girls from poor tenant families were willing to leave home to work in the new factories. Similarly, cotton-spinning mills, which usually were located on the outskirts of cities in central Japan, at first hired operatives from among the local urban dwellers, but as competition for labor heated up, agents fanned out into the surrounding prefectures, searching for girls who would agree to bid good-bye to family and friends and work away from home.

Generally, recruiters were independent brokers who received a commission from the mill or filature for each young woman they delivered to the factory. The agents promised the prospective workers salubrious work and living environments: They would spend their days in airy, clean mills, live in spacious dormitories, eat an abundance of delicious food, enjoy pleasurable days off, and receive generous wages that would improve standards of living for their families. In exchange for such agreeable terms of employment, the girls and their fathers signed contracts guaranteeing that the

**TABLE 8.1**  *Number of Female Textile Workers, 1886–1909*

| YEAR | SILK FILATURES | TOTAL WORKERS | FEMALE WORKERS | (%) | COTTON MILLS | TOTAL WORKERS | FEMALE WORKERS | (%) |
|---|---|---|---|---|---|---|---|---|
| 1886 | 411 | 26,800 | na | | 87 | 8,400 | na | |
| 1891 | 562 | 44,100 | na | | 60 | 26,400 | na | |
| 1899 | 2,117 | 115,000 | 107,000 | (93) | 1,370 | 114,000 | 93,000 | (82) |
| 1909 | 2,945 | 184,000 | 174,000 | (95) | 4,256 | 211,000 | 177,000 | (84) |

Adapted from William Johnston, *The Modern Epidemic: A History of Tuberculosis in Japan* (Cambridge: Council on East Asian Studies, Harvard University, 1995), pp. 75 and 77.

girls would work for a specified period, usually three or five years. To cinch the agreement, brokers usually offered the family earnest money, an immediate cash advance that sometimes amounted to one-third or even one-half of the daughter's total expected earnings for the contract period. The remainder, the recruiter promised, would be paid in annual or semiannual installments that the girl could spend on her days off or carry back to her family when she returned home for the extended New Year's vacation, which ran from late December into January.

Whatever her hopes, the average girl seldom had as much money in her pocket as she anticipated. Once on the job, she received almost nothing, perhaps an occasional pittance for pocket money on holidays or other special occasions. Moreover, the girls had to pay interest on the earnest money, recompense the company for their room and board, and fork over "punishment fees" whenever they turned out thread that the foreman judged deficient in fineness, strength, or luster. Many firms also posted company rules and deducted from wages fines for tardiness, smoking in unauthorized areas, feigning illness and not reporting to work, defacing attendance sheets, lying, and even complaining or inciting others to complain. In the end most girls seem to have earned twenty-five to thirty yen a year, in an era when the annual cash expenditures of a tenant family averaged approximately fifty-nine yen. But some unfortunates who were hit with multiple fines and punishment fees found that they worked all year for nothing. In some particularly ruthless mills it was not uncommon for one-quarter of the girls to end the year owing the companies money.

Moreover, the young women quickly discovered that working conditions in the mills and filatures were very different from the rosy picture painted by the recruiters. Most workers had only a couple of days off each

*Young workers in a textile mill that has been tidied up for the photo session*

month. Moreover, twelve-hour shifts were the rule in the cotton mills, where Shibusawa and other owners liked to use two crews to run their expensive machinery around the clock. Circumstances were just as tough in silk filatures, where, according to one report compiled by the Ministry of Agriculture and Commerce, "work usually starts at daybreak and ends at night. In some places work ends at sunset during the long days of summer, but in other seasons it lasts until 8 or 10 o'clock in the evening with lamp light. This means that working hours in silk filatures are from 13 or 14 to as high as 17 or 18 hours a day"[2]

Not only were working hours long, but they also were filled with discomfort and peril. The work floor was crowded, noisy, and hot; temperatures often reached one hundred degrees in the summer, and girls collapsed on the shop floor. In the ill-ventilated factories, fine silk floss and cotton fluff filled the air, got into eyes, mouths, and ears, and blocked pores on the women's skin. The male foremen were as nasty as army drill sergeants, often beating slower than average workers with bamboo sticks. In their haste to work faster, girls got their hands and feet tangled up in the machinery; by century's end the loss of a finger or toe was so common that many company doctors stopped noting such accidents on injury reports. There were other dangers as well. Some supervisors were sexual predators who used intimidation to get their way with the vulnerable and brutally raped others. Also, with so much flammable material lying about, fire was never more than a careless moment away. One conflagration at the Osaka Spinning Company in 1892 destroyed machinery inside the mill, razed thirty-four private residences beyond factory grounds, and killed ninety-five (mostly female) workers.

Many factory dormitories were prisonlike structures, surrounded by eight-foot fences topped with broken glass and sharpened bamboo spears to keep the girls from running away. Inside, living conditions were dreadful. Quarters were cramped; for living and sleeping space, each worker had to make do with less than one standard tatami mat of approximately six feet by three feet. Some companies made the girls share bedding, provided only one bath for every forty or fifty workers, and did not set out disinfectant to clean the toilets. The typical dorm at century's end served a basic diet of grains, tofu, beans, dried sardines, and seaweed dishes such as *hijiki*. Girls from especially poor families thought that they ate better than at home; others complained that the food was poorly prepared and dished out in an unappetizing manner. In either case, servings often were insubstantial, scarcely enough, according to one government report, to support the nutritional needs of a growing young person.

The combination of wretched working conditions, unsanitary living arrangements, inadequate diet, and tension born of overwork and sexual harassment left the women in a state of constant fatigue. After a tour of some mills in 1898 the Christian convert and educator Iwamoto Yoshiharu wrote, "I saw the factories. I saw the factory girls' dormitories. And I saw the factory girls who worked the night shift completely exhausted, stark naked, overcome by sleep, with no other luxury than lying with their eyes shut."[3] Not surprisingly, many women tried to escape by scaling the formidable dormitory fences or slipping away during rare holidays outside factory gates. Since police often cooperated with management to hunt down escapees, it seems remarkable that some 20 percent of the female workers at the Osaka Spinning Mill and 40 percent at the Mie Spinning Company left work in 1898, and at both plants only 25 percent of the young women served the entire contract period during the late 1890s.

Among those who stayed, high incidences of such diseases as bronchitis, pneumonia, and trachoma-induced blindness were common. Floss-filled air and high levels of carbon dioxide caused lung damage, and perhaps one in every four or five mill girls eventually suffered pulmonary tuberculosis.

In all, the death rate for mill girls stood at more than double the national average for sixteen- to twenty-year-old females. Company doctors had no effective treatment for serious illness, such as tuberculosis, and the owners of the mills and filatures usually sent sick workers home to die. "Soon after I went to work in the Yamaichi Filature in Nagano Prefecture," one woman recalled about her experiences at the turn of the century, "my younger sister Aki came to work there, too." After about two years Aki fell terminally ill. "She had come to the factory determined to earn one hundred yen a year and make our mother happy," the older sister remembered. "I can never forget her sad eyes as she left the factory wan and pale. It would be impossible, I felt, for a person as sick as she was to travel more than one hundred kilometers across a rugged mountain pass. But they would not let her stay in the factory. There was no money to send her to the hospital. There was nothing for her to do but go home."[4]

Out of the hardships of the 1880s and 1890s emerged the beginnings of new working-class attitudes. When reflecting on their circumstances, many female textile workers mixed low self-esteem with a determined pride about the contributions they made to the success of the company. Not surprisingly, some girls saw themselves as helpless victims. "Factory work is prison work," went one song popular among silk reelers. "All it lacks is iron chains."[5] Other workers joined in songs that expressed a bitter awareness about exploitation: "To kill a factory girl / You don't need a knife; / You just strangle her / With the weight and fineness of the thread." At the same time, many young women self-consciously identified themselves as kōjo, "factory girls" who existed on a plane separate from owners and management. Moreover, they knew that their low wages translated into enormous profits for Shibusawa and other entrepreneurs: "Don't sneer at us / Calling us "Factory girls, factory girls"! / Factory girls are / Treasure chests for the company."

Defiance too was part of the mentality of working-class girls. Sometimes they expressed their rebellious attitude by making heroines out of women, such as Iwataru Kikusa, who resisted oppressive males. One evening while walking outside the factory grounds, Iwataru fought off a man who had raped and murdered other silk workers by squeezing her attacker's testicles so hard that he let go of his stranglehold. Soon girls in nearby filatures were singing:

Don't scornfully say,
"Factory girl, factory girl."
Iwataru Kikusa is
A real factory girl.

Iwataru Kikusa is a shining
Model of a factory girl.
Let's wrench the balls
Of the hateful men!

Mr. Overseer, Mr. Supervisor,
You'd better watch out!
There is the example
Of Iwataru Kikusa.

Who dares to say that
Factory girls are weak?
Factory girls are the
Only ones who create wealth.

At other times the girls boldly hurled their anger at the owners. "Silk thread manufacturers," one woman wrote in the late 1880s, "treat us abominably. They think we are like slaves, like dirt. We think the silk-thread bosses are vipers, are our bitter enemies."[6] In 1886 the girl workers at Amamiya translated that kind of rage into direct action by launching Japan's first industrial strike. That event at Amamiya inspired operatives at other textile factories to take action. In 1889 young women at the Tenma Cotton Spinning Company in Osaka went out on strike to get higher wages; three years later nearly 150 textile workers in Kōfu walked off the job to protest wages, working conditions, and "unfair treatment"; and in 1898 women at the Tomioka filature struck for better food, a longer New Year's holiday, and better pay. Across Japan, working women at the end of the nineteenth century demonstrated a rising consciousness of themselves as *kōjo*, factory girls who could hope to improve their lives by banding together to confront owners and managers.

Men constituted less than 50 percent of the total number of factory hands in the 1880s and 1890s, but they enjoyed a particular prominence because they had expertise that was in high demand and were concentrated in "modern" factories that specialized in metalworking, shipbuilding, and the manufacture of machine tools, munitions, and chemicals. In general, owners of the new shipyards, arsenals, and machine shops preferred to hire traditional artisans, such as carpenters, coopers, and smiths, who quickly could master new technology and become boilermakers, lathe operators, machinists, and so forth. Like the female textile workers, men in heavy industry spent their days on shop floors that were dirty, dark, and dangerous. Unlike the women, however, the male employees generally did not have to fear physical punishments or sexual abuse, and as skilled workers they earned wages significantly higher than those paid to factory girls, as noted in Table 8.2.

**TABLE 8.2**  *Average Daily Wages for Selected Occupations, by Gender, 1892*

| OCCUPATION | GENDER | AVERAGE DAILY WAGE IN YEN |
|---|---|---|
| Skilled worker, Tokyo Munitions Factory | male | 0.52 (1885) |
| Skilled worker, Yokosuka Shipyards | male | 0.31 (1885) |
| Carpenter | male | 0.27 |
| Metalworker | male | 0.25 |
| Day laborer | male | 0.18 |
| Operative, cotton mill | male | 0.17 |
| Seasonal agricultural wageworker | male | 0.16 |
| Operative, silk filature | female | 0.13 |
| Seasonal agricultural wageworker | female | 0.09 |
| Operative, cotton mill | female | 0.09 |
| Weaver | female | 0.08 |

Adapted from E. Patricia Tsurumi, *Factory Girls: Women in the Thread Mills of Meiji Japan* (Princeton: Princeton University Press, 1990), p. 105, and Hiroshi Hazama, "Historical Changes in the Life Styles of Industrial Workers," in Hugh Patrick, with Larry Meissner, ed., *Japanese Industrialization and Its Social Consequences* (Berkeley: University of California Press, 1976), p. 25.

Men in heavy industry also enjoyed considerable autonomy from managerial discipline. Workers tended to cluster around more skilled masters, or labor bosses, known as *oyakata*. The *oyakata* often bid on specific jobs and then recruited (or supervised the hiring of) a crew of journeymen and apprentices whom the master trained and paid from a fixed fee he received from the factory owners. Thus, at the Yokosuka Shipyards in the early 1890s, each plant had a factory manager, an office staff that handled the paperwork concerning contracts, inventories, and so forth, and several foremen, each of whom oversaw a number of *oyakata*. Upper management, however, understood little about the actual production process and thus seldom leaned very hard on the *oyakata*, who "ruled as cock of the walk" in the words of Yokoyama Gennosuke, the first serious observer of the new working classes.[7] Moreover, since the *oyakata* bore final responsibility for completing each project in a timely manner and his profit depended on maintaining a margin between his expenses and the advance payment he received from management, he jealously guarded his prerogative to supervise workers and to determine the schedule and pace of work on the shop floor.

Male industrial workers tended to change jobs frequently. In contrast with textile manufacturing, where there seemed to be a bottomless pool of girls who could fill jobs that required little training, even apprentices and journeymen in heavy industry rested secure in the knowledge that they possessed new and still-esoteric job skills. Consequently, in the words of one report, experienced male workers "lightly move to other factories on the promise of the slightest pay increase."[8] In addition to better pay, men who hopped from factory to factory equipped themselves with a range of new talents that in turn permitted them to demand better wages when they moved on to yet another new city and signed on with another new *oyakata*.

Mobile, proudly independent, confident in their newly learned skills, men in heavy industry developed an attitude toward management that contrasted with that of the textile girls. While militant female workers in the mills saw the owners as "vipers" and "bitter enemies" and struck over specific issues such as wages and working hours, skilled male workers tended to phrase their concerns in terms of respect and status, calling on owners to exhibit benevolence and to look out for the well-being of the worker in exchange for greater diligence and loyalty. Thus, men who walked off the job at the end of the century typically lobbied owners for "humane treatment." When machinists at the Nippon Railway Company initiated a job action in 1899, for instance, they pressed management for improved standing within the enterprise. Specifically, they negotiated for new job titles that connoted greater respect, treatment equal to that accorded workers of higher rank, and the same kinds of semiannual pay raises and bonuses granted to white-collar officials and technicians.

Polite society did not look kindly upon the new working classes. Accounts in newspapers frequently equated factory girls with prostitutes, another category of female worker who sold her time and body cheaply, only to end up abused, diseased, and discarded after just a few years on the job. The same newspaper reporters usually dumped industrial laborers into a broad class of working poor that included traditional craftspeople, unskilled day laborers, rickshaw pullers, and ragpickers. Skilled workers earned more than other members of "lower-class society," to use the contemporary phrase, but for all their pride and fierce sense of dignity, workers lived in sad parts of most towns, in decrepit shanties with leaky roofs and rotting walls. Moreover, according to the calculations of Yokoyama Gennosuke, even a relatively well-paid machinist who in 1898 worked twenty-six days a month and took home thirteen yen for his efforts had a tough time making ends meet. After deducting outlays for rent, basic foods such as rice and vegetables, fuel and lighting, and a yen or so for drinking money, the worker's family of four had less than one yen left to spend for clothing, the barber, and using the public bath. In all, Yokoyama estimated, nearly two-thirds of Tokyo's machinists lived in poverty, and he described a grim life of visits to loan sharks, drinking and gambling, domestic violence, and neglect of children.

Journalists were more kindly disposed toward what they called the middle propertied classes and upstream society. The former consisted of traditional retailers who owned their own streetfront shops as well as an emerging class of teachers, professionals, and factory managers and foremen. As used by social critics, the term "middle propertied classes" signaled respect for families that worked hard and lived stable, comfortable lives. Plutocrats and *narikin* populated the ranks of upstream society. A *narikin* is a minor pawn in the chesslike game of *shōgi* that suddenly can turn into a powerful piece, and journalists deployed the term to describe such entrepreneurs as the button manufacturers of Osaka and the founders of the Seikō watch and Shiseidō cosmetic firms in Tokyo. Like its French equivalent, "nouveau riche," the expression could carry slightly pejorative overtones, but most journalists also admired the venturesomeness and stubborn determination to succeed displayed by the *narikin*. They showed even more open awe for the plutocrats, the great captains of industry like Furukawa, Shibusawa, and the heads of the Iwasaki, Mitsui, and Sumitomo families, whose great mansions and grand lifestyles seemed to entitle them naturally to the adulation of the masses.

## Husbands and Wives

If the new hierarchy of social classes experienced the Meiji economic dream in different ways, all Japanese found their family lives in flux at century's end. With the country being buffeted by every variety of political and economic change, the government turned its attention to drafting a new civil code to cover family relationships, property rights, contracts, commercial transactions, and so forth. Most legal scholars favored such an effort, recognizing that codification was necessary in light of the enormous changes taking place within Japan, but officials within the government also were responding to stern statements from Western nations that Japan must adopt a body of civil law acceptable to them before moving forward with treaty revision. In 1890, after considerable deliberation, the Meiji regime promulgated a legal code, modeled on French precedents, and announced that the new legislation would take effect on January 1, 1893.

Almost immediately a sharp controversy broke out as jurists trained in English and German law attacked the new code for adhering too closely to its French archetype. Nonplussed by the hostility that flared up within the Japanese legal community, the Diet postponed the scheduled implementation of the civil laws and convened a new council to reconsider matters. Itō Hirobumi chaired the review committee, but clearly its most influential member was Hozumi Nobushige, a distinguished professor of law at Tokyo University. As matters turned out, Hozumi and his allies had few objections to the parts of the code dealing with property rights, contracts, and commercial law. Rather, they riveted their attention on the sections "Family" and "Household Succession," whose French-inspired provisions, in the stinging phrase of Hozumi Yatsuka, noted constitutional scholar and Nobushige's younger brother, threatened "the final destruction of loyalty and filial piety."[9]

Hozumi Nobushige was a traditionalist who agreed with his brother that "the family system gradually weakened" during the closing decades of the nineteenth century, and he likewise was alarmed that "the individual began to take the place of the family as the unit of society."[10] He confidently offered a solution to the problem: Give the household precedence over the individual by creating a legal foundation for the old ie system. In addition, he especially admired the tradition of strong patriarchal authority and the practice of primogeniture that prevailed among samurai households in the early modern era. Consequently, the revised Civil Code, which became law on July 16, 1898, made the household a corporate entity, mandated that the position of household head pass to the eldest son except in extraordinary circumstances, and vested enormous powers in the modern father; he alone chose the family's place of residence, managed all household property and business affairs, determined the disposition of family assets, and had the authority to approve or disallow the marriages of his children, up to the age of twenty-five for daughters and thirty for sons.

As part of their attempt to carry out what many called the samuraiization of the family, the authors of the Meiji Civil Code subordinated women to the male head of household. In their overall effect, the new laws treated a "wife" as a useful but replaceable module within the recontextualized ie structure and virtually reduced married women to the status of legal incompetents. The primary obligation of a wife, as outlined in the Civil Code of 1898, was to provide the ie with a male heir and the household with additional labor. Once wed, a woman could not testify in courts of law, bring a legal action without her husband's permission, transact business without his consent, or initiate a divorce except in cases of desertion or extreme cruelty (and a wife's adultery, but not her husband's, was ground for both divorce and criminal prosecution). When a marriage did falter, the woman was to leave the house, and the children stayed with the *ie*. Symbolic of the change that made the patriarchal and patrilineal family of warrior tradition into the nation's norm, urban commoners in the late Meiji period began to use the old samurai term *oku-san* ("the lady in the rear of the house") as the new word for a modern wife.

Without denying that women should seek fulfillment within the household structure, some officials and ideologues envisaged a slightly different role for adult women, as encapsulated in the expression *ryōsai kenbo* ("good wife, wise mother"). Nakamura Masanao, the translator of Samuel Smiles's *Self-Help* and later the head of the Women's Normal School (now Ochanomizu Women's University), coined the term *ryōsai kenbo* to describe a model for women that folded the latest in Western thinking into what, for him, were familiar but still-worthy Japanese notions about womanhood. According to Nakamura, a good wife and wise mother would remain in the private sphere, but she would be accorded a respected role within the household as the moral foundation of the family, the person responsible for properly raising and educating the children, and a loyal "better half" who would support her husband as he advanced in his career in the public sphere.

Hatoyama Haruko emerged as one of the more outspoken proponents of *ryōsai kenbo* ideology at the end of the nineteenth century. An 1881 graduate of the Women's Normal School and later a prominent educator there, Hatoyama hoped that becoming good wives and wise mothers would enable women to improve their status so that they would be something more than cogs in the male-dominated family system. Like Nakamura, Hatoyama exhorted her students to be efficient household managers and caring mothers, and she urged women to turn the home into a sanctuary, a safe haven where the husband could relax and renew himself to meet the challenges of his career. Drawing on a view of domesticity that was familiar in the West at the end of the nineteenth century, Hatoyama also believed that wives should be intelligent enough, and well enough educated, to be true helpmates to their husbands.

The advocates of *ryōsai kenbo* directed their rhetoric chiefly at the women of well-to-do families. For many, Itō Umeko, spouse of the prominent government leader, stood as a paragon of the new wife. In the 1880s she learned English so that she could stand at her husband's side and converse with foreigners, and she even presided over so-called "improvement circles" where elite Tokyo women gathered to study European fashions, learned to appreciate Western foods, and mastered the new social etiquette they would need when they accompanied their husbands to official receptions and the balls held at the Rokumeikan. In contrast, most ideologues took a more relaxed attitude toward spouses of tradesmen and farmers; they could live as "good wives" in the old sense, toiling in the fields and working in the shops to produce income that would help their families survive. The class implications of *ryōsai kenbo* were not lost on such women. The son of a family that ran a cosmetics shop in Kyoto recalled that his mother was very careful to use the fashionable word *oku-san* only with the wives of *narikin* and such professionals as policemen, teachers, and government officials. Nor did he miss the cynical smile that sometimes played across her face when she did business with the new *oku-san*; "what made them different from most women like my mother," he observed, "was that they did not work."[11]

Another neologism, *hōmu*, vied for attention. As used in fin-de-siècle Japan, the concept of home shared considerable common ground with *ryōsai kenbo*, but its backers preferred to emphasize the importance of romantic affection between husband and wife. Iwamoto Yoshiharu, who helped popularize the expression after cofounding *Jogaku zasshi* ("The Magazine of Women's Learning"), criticized the *ie* for fostering oppression and held up the *hōmu* as a new and different ideal for the family, a place where mutual love and a spirit of happy cooperation united all members of the family. To be certain, the woman in the new home still raised the children and did the housework, but she also stood equal to her husband. In contrast with the traditional marriage, in which the newlywed woman entered the household of her husband and became an apprentice to her mother-in-law, in the new *hōmu* way of thinking, the bride instantly became the mistress of her own family, a soulmate as well as helpmate to her husband.

Hozumi Nobushige and many ranking government officials intended the 1898 Civil Code to stand absolute as the final statement about the family and gender roles, but it did not. Rather, the effort to implement social legislation at the end of the nineteenth century generated a vigorous discussion about domesticity that was to flower as Japan moved forward into the new century. Although *ryōsai kenbo* ideology exerted a powerful influence over future generations, fresh voices joined the debate about the state's role in determining family and gender relations. Increasingly, Japanese women themselves entered the contest to define femininity as graduates from women's secondary schools, founded at the end of the century to train the good wives and wise mothers, proceeded to raise significant questions about what constituted an ideal family and what role women should play, in both society and the household.

## Children and Schools

On September 2, 1871, just four days after the Dajōkan abolished daimyo domains and created prefectures, the new government established a Ministry of Education and assigned it the responsibility of designing a nationwide system of compulsory education. The Meiji leaders acted out of a mix of motives. Some, like Itō Hirobumi, argued that Japan could not achieve Civilization and Enlightenment without an educated citizenry. Others, such as Iwakura Tomomi and Ōkubo Toshimichi, believed that merit-based public education was necessary to train capable national leaders for the future. Moreover, universal education, in their minds, would give all Japanese the skills necessary to enhance their economic prospects, thus helping build a strong nation. In the words of Kido Takayoshi, "The strength and prosperity of a country lie in the strength and prosperity of the people. If ordinary people are held back by ignorance and poverty," he wrote in 1869, "the beautiful phrase 'imperial restoration' has no meaning and the effort of keeping up with the leading countries of the world must fail."[12]

The Meiji government moved expeditiously to formulate its plans, and on September 4, 1872, the Dajōkan promulgated an Education Order that divided Japan into 53,760 primary and 256 middle school districts, called for the establishment of eight universities, and mandated four years of compulsory education for every child. The preamble to the proclamation enunciated the twin, complementary purposes of education. On one hand, the document emphasized that individuals should see schooling as a means of advancing and improving their lots in life. On the other hand, the government also intended that the new system produce moral and patriotic citizens who would study practical arts and sciences in order to benefit society and build a strong, modern nation.

Ministry of Education officials worked energetically to get the new system up and running in the early 1870s. As a result of their efforts, by the middle of the decade several hundred thousand youngsters were attending elementary and middle school. The Tokugawa legacy clearly worked in the ministry's favor. Thus, while the Meiji government constructed many new schools and began to train teachers, it certified most of the old *terakoya* and private academies as elementary schools in the fall of 1872 and converted former domain schools into middle schools. In addition to inheriting an abundance of experienced teachers and existing classrooms, the new regime found that publishers were accustomed to merchandising textbooks, and the fact that generations of samurai and commoner families had recognized schooling as part of their daily routine inclined many to accept the new educational directives.

Despite a promising start, devilish problems nagged the ministry. Officials were disappointed in enrollment patterns. As late as 1880 only 60 percent of school-age boys and 20 percent of girls attended elementary school, a level only modestly higher than a generation earlier. Moreover, samurai offspring and city children were more likely to complete the four years of compulsory education than were village kids, and elementary school attendance rates tended to lag behind the national average in prefectures on the periphery of the country. Equally troublesome in the view of government officials were the enormous disparities that characterized the educational experience. Depending on the school they attended, students studied different materials. The Ministry of Education disseminated new translations of Western works on history, science, and philosophy, none more influential than Smiles's *Self-Help* and the almost word-by-word rendering into Japanese of *The Elements of Moral Science*, a philosophical treatise on values and morals written by Francis Wayland for his students at Brown University. Many of those who attended Japan's new schools, however, had to make do with tattered copybooks and texts formerly used in *terakoya*, such as *Shōbai ōrai* ("A Guide to Commerce"), and some youngsters still painfully waded through ponderous Confucian classics.

The ministry also had to contend with scathing criticism from Confucian traditionalists during the 1870s. Motoda Nagazane, the imperial tutor who later blasted Itō's ideas on constitutionalism as a misguided effort to convert the "Japanese into painted replicas of Europeans and Americans," had little truck with Western texts on morals and ethics or with the notion that education should be formulated to serve the needs of the individual. In his 1879 "Great Principles of Education" Motoda blamed Western books such as *The Elements of Moral Science* for destroying traditional ethics and broadcasting irresponsible theories that were bound to produce ineffectual government officials and recreant citizens. Disaster awaited Japan, Motoda concluded, unless the Ministry of Education quickly realized that "the essence of education—to pursue the way of man by mastering knowledge and skills, righteousness, loyalty and filial piety—lies in the great principles explained in our ancestral precepts and native classics" and that "people will cultivate sincerity and practice good conduct if ethical teachings are based on Confucius."[13]

By the early 1880s many oligarchs were growing increasingly sympathetic to the concerns voiced by Motoda and other conservatives. The political turmoil of the late 1870s and early 1880s, together with the effort to draft and promulgate a constitution, naturally made the Meiji leaders yearn for ways to cultivate a dutiful citizenry that would support the government. Yamagata Aritomo, who worried so much about national unity, even asserted that Japan needed to pay full attention to "military preparation and education" if it wanted to ensure itself a bright and secure future. "Unless the people love their country as their parents and are willing to safeguard it with their lives," he wrote, "the country cannot exist even for a day." Moreover, Yamagata continued, "only education can cultivate and preserve the notion of patriotism in the people," and the best way to inculcate patriotism is to teach "the national language, history, and other subjects" to each schoolchild.[14]

The culminating expression of such sentiments came in the Imperial Rescript on Education, issued just before the convocation of the first Imperial Diet in the fall of 1890 as part of the ongoing effort to rally public support behind the new constitution and the political system it enshrined. Written in a pious tone, the document asserted that the fundamental purpose of education was to inculcate traditional values and encourage the people of Japan to be unquestionably loyal to emperor and nation. "Be filial to your parents [and] affectionate to your brothers and sisters," the document exhorted, and, it continued, "bear yourselves in modesty and moderation; extend your benevolence to all; pursue learning and cultivate arts, and thereby develop intellectual facilities and moral powers." Finally, it instructed Japan's youth to "always respect the Constitution and observe the laws; should emergency arise, offer yourselves courageously to the State; and thus guard and maintain the prosperity of Our Imperial Throne coeval with heaven and earth."[15] Mori Arinori, the first person to serve as minister of education after the cabinet system was instituted in 1885, put it more succinctly: "The principle of education shall hereafter be to cultivate persons who will be the faithful subjects required by the Empire."[16]

Guided by such rhetoric, the Ministry of Education during the 1880s engineered a number of mid-course adjustments intended to make schooling more responsive to national goals. During his stint as minister of education from 1885 to 1889, Mori reorganized the school system to sort out students more efficiently according to ability and to place them on tracks that led to appropriate future careers. Left in place were the primary schools, whose mission was "to provide such training as will enable the young to understand their duties as Japanese subjects, to conduct themselves in an ethical fashion, and to secure their own individual well-being."[17] Graduates from primary school with the time and inclination for further study advanced to middle school, where for five years they studied ethics and learned skills to prepare them for careers as low-level managers, plant foremen, and so forth. More promising graduates of middle schools who passed an arduous examination could win admission to one of the newly created two-year (later three-year) higher schools. "Those who study in the higher school," Mori explained, "will enter society's upper crust. The higher schools should cultivate men worthy of directing the thoughts of the masses: be they bureaucrats, then those of the highest echelon; be they businessmen, then those for the top management; be they scholars, then true experts in the various arts and sciences."[18]

Under Mori's stewardship, the Ministry of Education also began to make good the earlier intention to establish a set of national universities to educate the most elite level of scholars, bureaucrats, and business leaders. Beginning with Tokyo University in 1877, the government eventually founded so-called imperial universities in Kyoto (1897), Tōhoku (1907), Kyūshū (1910), Hokkaidō (1919), Osaka (1931), and Nagoya (1939). In complementary fashion, the Normal School Ordinance of 1886 established a set of colleges that specialized in training primary and secondary school teachers. Specifically, each prefecture was to found one normal school to educate elementary school teachers, and one higher normal school located in Tokyo prepared its graduates for careers at the secondary level.

During the 1880s the Ministry of Education also took steps to ensure itself greater control over the curriculum taught in the nation's public

*Female university students, 1907*

schools. In 1886 it decreed that elementary school students receive instruction in arithmetic, reading and writing, composition, and physical education (it added science, geography, and Japanese history in 1907). Acting on Mori's injunction that primary school graduates "understand their duties as Japanese subjects" and "conduct themselves in an ethical fashion," ministry bureaucrats increasingly centered the school day on ethics courses that celebrated patriotic sentiments and a traditionally oriented civic morality. By the end of the 1880s *Self-Help* and *The Elements of Moral Science* had disappeared from the classroom, replaced by ethics primers authored by Japanese scholars and published by the ministry itself. For the most part, those new texts stressed the importance of benevolence, sincerity, honest intentions, the determination to succeed, filial piety, friendship, frugality, modesty, and decorum.

The introduction of Japanese ethics texts was part of a broader transformation that eventually saw government officials gain the authority to determine what materials would be used in every classroom. As early as 1881 the Ministry of Education issued a list of texts it considered acceptable, and the 1886 Elementary School Law required ministry approval for any book included in a public school syllabus. Finally, in 1903, the ministry stipulated that all elementary schools had to adopt identical texts, which it itself compiled and distributed. Consequently, boys and girls in every town and village not only studied Japanese values and mores but also learned exactly the same stories about the paragons of Japan's past: the public-spirited Ninomiya Sontoku; the compassionate Tokugawa Ieyasu honoring the spirits of deceased comrades-in-arms; a woman from a wealthy family who stoically bore the deprivations of her married life; an industrious soy sauce vendor who, after becoming well-to-do, went to great trouble to locate and reward a person who had assisted him when he was poor.

The system put in place during the 1880s bequeathed a mixed legacy to future Japanese. In some large measure Mori Arinori and officials within the Ministry of Education fulfilled their ambitions. By the end of the Meiji era elementary school attendance for both boys and girls was approaching 100 percent, as people realized that education was a ladder one could climb to better jobs and more comfortable lifestyles. Moreover, most observers concurred that the ethics-based curriculum was one factor that gave rise to a patriotic citizenry. Similarly, many credited the education system with producing literate young people who had the requisite skills demanded by the new emerging industrial society (especially after a track leading from primary school to technical and vocational middle schools was added in 1899), and few would disagree that the higher schools and universities turned out an elite of rigorously trained professional bureaucrats, erudite scholars, and sharp-witted businessmen.

Others, however, were troubled by the new directions in education policy. Some critics took exception with the core principles of the new system. Those opponents came from a variety of backgrounds and occupied the full length of the political spectrum, but all shared the conviction that education ought to nurture individual interests and abilities rather than subject schoolchildren to a standardized curriculum. They further agreed that it was not the job of teachers to spoon-feed prescribed thoughts and ideas to their pupils. Instead, they argued, true educators encouraged students to participate actively in the learning process so that they would become independent-thinking and well-rounded adults.

Ueki Emori, a leading figure in the Popular Rights Movement, laid out his thoughts in an essay entitled "On Popular Education." Like many other members of the political left in the late 1870s and 1880s, Ueki accepted the doctrine that human rights were naturally endowed, and he believed that the most desirable future political order would rest on the concept of popular sovereignty. In his view, it naturally followed that a liberal education that enhanced the talents of each individual was necessary if the Japanese were to enjoy their natural rights and become enlightened participants in the governing process. Thus, he wrote, the fundamental purpose of education should be to "encourage and nourish the development of man's naturally given abilities in as wide a sense as possible." More bluntly, he concluded, "Freedom is more precious than order," and "a life without wisdom is more like death than life."[19]

The philosopher and historian Miyake Setsurei brought a different perspective to bear. An opponent of unrestrained Westernization, he called for the development of a cultural nationalism that recognized the Japanese as the autonomous bearers of a distinctive national essence. Miyake, however, was no hidebound traditionalist; to the contrary, he possessed a global vision that drew attention to the interrelationships between the "cells"—the individual person and the national unit—that coalesced into an organic, universal human experience. In all living entities, he explained, each cell fulfilled a particular role in promoting the overall well-being of the organism of which it was a part. Thus, each individual and nation had something to contribute to the advancement of world culture, which Miyake characterized as the realization of the universal human ideals of truth, goodness, and beauty. "To devote oneself to one's country is to devote oneself to the world," he wrote, and to "exalt the special characteristics of one's people is to nurture the human race."[20] Since the betterment of world culture depended on the free and full development of the capacities of each person and nation, Miyake continued, Japanese education should not follow the rigid mold cast by the Ministry of Education but instead should concentrate on promoting the individual talents and abilities of each and every student.

Other critics raised questions about the gender inequities built into the educational structure. From their inception primary schools had been co-educational, but the middle and higher school tracks created in the mid-1880s admitted only males. Dissatisfied, women began to show up at the doors of private schools, many run by Christian missionaries. By 1889 some twenty private secondary schools, together with eight public institutions opened by the government, enrolled a total of more than three thousand young women who wished to receive more than an elementary education. A decade later the Ministry of Education responded to the growing demand for a woman's track by formulating a plan to establish a girls' high school in each prefecture. Seen as the equivalent of the boys' middle school, the new secondary institutions provided four to six years of study to young women who had completed primary school.

Once open, the new girls' high schools presented a sequence of courses designed to train the students to be model wives and mothers. In particular, staunch supporters of *ryōsai kenbo* within the Ministry of Education insisted that texts elaborate on a woman's obligations to her family, and the curriculum featured courses on "domestic science," later renamed "household management science." Under either rubric, instruction focused on such topics as personal health, child care, home nursing, cooking, dressmaking, and deportment. In addition, the content of courses in other disciplines was presented as knowledge that a woman should acquire so that she could manage a household competently. Consequently, students at girls' high schools studied biology as a basis for maintaining healthy homes and solved math problems that improved their ability to oversee family expenditures on food and clothing.

Many women who saw themselves as future homemakers expressed satisfaction with the education they received at the new secondary schools. Other women were of a different mind. Among them was Yajima Kajiko, the daughter of a samurai family in Kyūshū who left her abusive alcoholic husband, moved to Tokyo, and between 1889 and 1914 headed Joshi Gakuin, a renowned Christian women's school. Yajima and her allies raised fundamental questions about the orientation the Ministry of Education had imparted to women's education. Why shouldn't women be educated to have careers outside the home as well as within it? Why not prepare women to be economically independent, if they so wished, and, the critics continued, rather than implement different curricula, why not give women the same education as men so that both genders might play similar roles in society? While such interrogatives centered on women, in essence they brought to the fore the same central quandary raised by Ueki and Miyake: Was education to be a process that served the aspirations and needs of the individual, or was it to be a social obligation, training designed to benefit the state and create the sort of society government officials envisioned? Such questions could not be settled at the end of the Meiji period, but they did define a set of issues that Japanese would have to address as they pursued their quest for modernity in the impending new century.

## Clerics and Converts

As part of its attempt to inculcate loyalty to the emperor and thus draw a mantle of legitimacy around itself, the new Meiji government embarked on a policy to place Shinto at the center of the nation's religious life. Before 1868 Shinto shrines and Buddhist temples coexisted side by side, most persons placed their faith in both *kami* and Buddhist divinities, and the boundaries between the two forms of worship were vague enough that people viewed some *kami* and Buddhist deities as manifestations of one another. Moreover, Shinto had a bifurcated nature. On one level, in Kyoto the Heavenly Sovereign conducted prescribed rituals that reaffirmed his divine ancestry and gave symbolic meaning to the shogunate's claim to rule in his name. Although most ordinary Japanese knew something about the sacerdotal role of the Heavenly Sovereign, if for no other reason than the emergence of Kyoto and Ise Shrine as popular travel destinations, they did not participate in such lofty ceremonials. Rather, for most men and women Shinto simply meant worshiping local *kami* during festivals at village and neighborhood shrines. In the decades at the end of the nineteenth century the Meiji government set out to change that by elevating Shinto over Buddhism and by drawing all Japanese into religious practices that made clear the importance of the emperor and Shinto divinities to the nation's religious and political well-being.

In 1868 there were approximately seventy-five thousand shrines in Japan, and the young Meiji leaders soon took the initial step toward creating so-called State Shinto when they arranged those centers of worship into a single national hierarchy, thus creating Shinto's first comprehensive organizational structure. At the apex of the new pyramid sat Ise Shrine, dedicated to Amaterasu, the progenitor deity of the imperial family and protective goddess of the entire nation. Next came other imperial and national shrines, and then five descending categories of civic shrines. The imperial and national shrines received generous financial support from the central government, and their priests enjoyed the status of national civil servants, while prefectural and local governments supplied some funding to many lower-level civic shrines. At the same time, the government ordered each household to affiliate with a shrine, thus making shrine membership universal and obligatory for the first time in Japanese history.

During the Meiji period the government also promoted the visibility of Shinto by refurbishing Ise and other high-ranking centers of worship and by constructing twenty-seven new shrines dedicated to persons who had served the throne over the course of time. The most prominent of the new Special Shrines, as they were called, was Yasukuni Shrine. Built in Tokyo in the summer of 1869 to venerate the souls of those who had fallen in the campaigns to reestablish imperial rule, Yasukuni eventually became the final resting place for all Japan's future war dead. The particular honor associated with being enshrined at Yasukuni was that the rites of interment signified an apotheosis, a symbolic transformation of the soldier's soul into a national deity. Ceremonies were held at the shrine each spring and autumn to honor those who made the ultimate sacrifice for the nation, and Emperor Meiji personally attended on several occasions.

The government also established a new ritual calendar centered on the nation and emperor. During the early modern period most shrines conducted their festivals in accordance with local preferences and with scarce thought to coordinating their activities with other parishes. Meiji leaders dramatically altered the character of ritual life when they introduced a series of celebrations that were to be led by the emperor and observed at shrines nationwide. The sequence began on January 1, when the emperor in Tokyo and Shinto parishioners across the country venerated the deities of the four directions to welcome the New Year; proceeded through such events as the commemoration of Jimmu's conquest and the founding of the Yamato dynasty, on February 11; and concluded in the fall with two ceremonies: the Kannamesai, when the emperor bowed in the direction of Ise Shrine and offered the firstfruits of the harvest to Amaterasu while his representatives there presented newly harvested rice to the Sun Goddess, and the Niinamesai, when the emperor entered a special hall inside his palace compound to partake of the bounties of the harvest in communion with the deities. By the 1880s those rites were being observed simultaneously at the Imperial Palace, Ise Shrine, and the imperial and national shrines, and increasingly, government officials expected the civic shrines to celebrate them as well.

The new religions founded by charismatic teachers in the early nine-teenth century drew fire at the beginning of the Meiji period. In the decades after their founding, Tenri, Kurozumi, and other millennial sects attracted tens of thousands of followers through faith healing and the promise of a better life here on earth, and by the 1880s several had grown into vigorous nationwide organizations. Although the new religions incorporated Shinto beliefs into their eclectic liturgies, many mainstream Shinto clerics turned against them as old-time parishioners increasingly gave their devotion and contributions to the new denominations. The Meiji government also viewed the new religions with suspicion because of their propensity to blame the existing political order for life's problems, as well as their proved ability to bond people together across traditional boundaries of gender, class, and region.

As the Meiji regime implemented its program of State Shinto, the new religions began to fear for their survival and cast about for ways to avoid persecution. Some deliberately strengthened their Shinto identity by reaf-firming the prominence of Amaterasu in the pantheon of deities, incorpo-rating more Shinto prayers into their acts of worship, and stressing the importance of traditional values, such as sincerity (makoto). Simultaneously, sect leaders carefully wove state ideology into their teachings. Just as the priesthood in State Shinto was doing, thousands of Tenri and Kurozumi evangelists began to praise the restoration of imperial rule, and as they moved about the country, they explained to believers that government poli-cies such as conscription, taxation, compulsory education, and the imple-mentation of a civil code were sacred goals that fulfilled the divine wishes of the kami. As the new religions tailored themselves to fit the state's con-ception of what a religion ought to be, the Meiji government reciprocated by recognizing Tenri, Kurozumi, and eleven other independent sects as con-stituting Sect Shinto. In practice the thirteen sects remained separate from the hierarchy of shrines that made up State Shinto, but they could claim to be legitimate religions whose creeds represented a variant strain of ortho-dox Shinto.

As part of elevating Shinto, the Meiji government tipped the religious scales against Buddhism. On the twenty-eighth day of the Third Month 1868, the government ended a millennium of religious syncretism when it ordered the separation of Buddhism from Shinto, specifically the removal of all objects of Buddhist worship from Shinto shrines and the dissociation of Shinto and Buddhist divinities. Over the next three years the new regime confiscated sustenance lands that the shogunate and individual daimyo had assigned to particular temples and issued proclamations encouraging monks and nuns to grow their hair, eat meat, return to lay life, and marry. The effects were dramatic. By the end of 1871 the eighty or so monks who performed services for the Tōshō Dai Gongen, Ieyasu's deified spirit, had left Nikkō, taking with them much of the Buddhist regalia. In all, by 1876 approximately 20 percent of Japan's eighty-seven thousand Buddhist temples had closed their halls of worship, and more than fifty-six thousand monks and five thousand nuns had returned to lay life.

Shinto zealots—in particular clerics who felt inferior to Buddhist priests in complexes that contained both temples and shrines—interpreted the separation edict of 1868 as condoning violent attacks on Buddhism. One highly charged act of aggression took place that spring, when some forty Shinto priests associated with Hie Shrine, located at the base of Mount Hiei and subordinate to the Temple Enryakuji, armed themselves with spears, stormed the venerable Enryakuji, and burned hundreds of statues and sutras. Nationwide, the wave of violence passed by 1871, but not before Shinto fanatics destroyed, stole, or auctioned off hundreds of thousands Buddhist sutras, paintings, statues, temple bells, and other ritual objects.

Proponents of State Shinto also had to contend with a revival of Christianity during the Meiji period. Catholic priests visited Edo and Yokohama as soon as those cities were officially opened to foreign residents in 1859 and were happy to learn that communities of "hidden Christians" still existed in remote southern Kyūshū. About half of those, some thirty thousand people in all, eventually decided to return to the reintroduced church. Representatives of three Protestant churches also arrived in Japan in 1859, and evangelists from several denominations followed soon thereafter. The Meiji regime lifted the old prohibitions on Christianity in February 1873, and the missionaries began to search for converts.

The proselytizers faced an uphill battle in the contest to win religious hearts. Most government officials maintained a cool attitude toward foreign creeds, as reflected in the 1889 constitution, which provided that Japanese could enjoy religious freedom only "within limits not prejudicial to peace and order, and not antagonistic to their duties as subjects." The Shinto faithful brandished such slogans as "Destroy Heresy, Manifest Orthodoxy" to attack Christianity, and many Buddhists took anti-Christian stances, believing somehow that it was necessary to refute Christianity in order to revive Buddhism. "Christian truth is biased and incomplete," wrote one prominent Buddhist in the 1880s. "Compared to the Buddhist truth, it is like the tip end of a hair or a shadowy echo. Ah, how clear is Buddhist truth, how obscure that of Christianity, similar to the dimming of the stars before the moon's brilliance. How can I even discuss the two religions on the same day?"[21]

*Buddhist fanatics attack Christians*

Such widespread opposition was hard to overcome, and by the end of the century somewhat less than 1 percent of all Japanese professed to be Christians, including approximately 100,000 Catholics and some 30,000 members of the Russian Orthodox Church.

In the end the government's campaign to promote State and Sect Shinto had mixed results. At first, many ordinary men and women did not immediately celebrate the new rituals of State Shinto. Villagers in particular continued to be attuned to the old ways, giving a lukewarm reception to events on the new ritual calendar while continuing to turn out en masse for traditional local festivals. Similarly, even as late as the 1880s police in some major provincial cities had to walk the streets reminding citizens to fly the national flag on the new holidays that were celebrated as part of the religious calendar, such as February 3, Emperor Meiji's birthday.

Moreover, Buddhism ultimately survived the attack on it. Despite the disorder of the early 1870s, ordinary households continued to affiliate with temples, where they held family funerals, cared for grave sites, and depended on priests to perform ancestral memorial services. Christianity also persevered into the new century, in part because its adherents were far more visible than their small numbers might suggest. Missionary efforts to found orphanages, hospitals, and leprosariums attracted to the faith Japanese reformers who were concerned about prostitution, poverty, and other social problems and who found hope in Christianity's messages about charity and doing good unto others. In addition, various churches opened women's secondary schools in the 1870s and 1880s, when the government was reluctant to do so, and many prominent Japanese educators, including Iwamoto Yoshiharu, Yajima Kajiko, and Nakamura Masanao, were converts to Christianity. Christians also established some of Japan's leading private colleges, including the Meiji School for Women, where Iwamoto served as headmaster for a while, and Dōshisha, which was founded by the convert Niijima Jō in Kyoto in 1875 and later became Japan's first coeducational university.

Nonetheless, the privileging of Shinto and the reorientation of shrine life toward a national focus profoundly changed the nature of Japanese religiosity. As the nineteenth century approached its conclusion, more Japanese than ever before were aware of the nuances of Shinto doctrine, and gradually, as civic shrines joined the imperial and national institutions in celebrating the new ritual calendar, the liturgy of all shrines across the nation pulsated according to a single plan. Moreover, by enlisting the priesthood as supporters of the Meiji leadership, proponents of State Shinto successfully grafted government ideology onto Shinto theology. The labeling of the new religions as legitimate varieties of Shinto also had an impact on the religious life of countless Japanese. Enormously popular, the denominations categorized as Sect Shinto took the new amalgam of state ideology and religious belief to all areas of the country and to all levels of society. More than anything else, events in the initial decades of the Meiji period relegated Buddhism and Christianity to the rear pews and set the stage for an expansion of relations between organized religion and the state in the first half of the twentieth century by opening up the possibility that religious doctrine and state ideology could work in tandem to persuade ordinary men and women to obey government directives and policy.

## Peering Ahead

In August 1899 staff writer Kikuchi Yūhō began to publish his *Ono ga tsumi* ("My Sin") in the newspaper *Ōsaka mainichi*. By the time Kikuchi concluded his serialized novel the following summer, he had defined a new genre of popular fiction, the *katei shōsetsu*. In the 1890s Japanese increasingly used *katei*, which combined the ideographs for "house" and "garden," as the native equivalent for *hōmu*, and the new *katei shōsetsu* were "household novels," or perhaps less literally "domestic romances," that featured a female protagonist, a plot that explored the complications of building a satisfying marriage, and a happy ending. Popular among the new middle and upstream classes, the domestic romances aired for public discussion issues about the family, education, and religion that concerned so many Japanese as one century was about to end and another begin.

An imbroglio-per-episode plot kept Kikuchi's readers enthralled. "My Sin" opened with the seduction of the heroine, Tamaki, a naïve provincial maiden who had arrived in Tokyo to attend a girls' high school. After she became pregnant, her lover, a medical student who happened to be a Christian convert, abandoned her, and her father journeyed to Tokyo to help his daughter. When a baby boy was born, Tamaki's father sent it away, telling his daughter it had died. Later Tamaki married a Kyoto aristocrat, Takahiro, whose first marriage had ended in failure after his wife's infidelity, and the couple eventually had a son. During a seaside vacation, an older boy—her child of sin, Tamaki discovered—befriended her son by Takahiro, but both boys perished in a drowning accident. Believing the tragedy to be her punishment for having kept her youthful *affaire d'amour* a secret from her husband, Tamaki confided in Takahiro. Emotionally shattered, he insisted that they separate; he embarked on foreign travels, and she enlisted as a Red Cross nurse. Several years later Tamaki rushed to Takahiro's side when she learned that he had been stricken with typhoid fever. As she nursed him back to health, Takahiro revealed that over the years he had come to appreciate Tamaki's essential goodness and realized that her sin was one of innocence. The novel ended with Tamaki pregnant, the reunited couple happily awaiting the birth of their second child.

"My Sin" offered the readers of the *Ōsaka mainichi* an intriguing, contrasting mix of perspectives on the issues of the day. Tamaki's father represented the views of *ryōsai kenbo* ideologues; his ambition was to give his daughter an education that would make her a good wife and wise mother. Tamaki's cruel deception at the hands of the heartless medical student, however, played on the fears of parents and implied that they rethink plans to expose their daughters to the dangers of student life. Yet in the end Tamaki's career as a nurse suggested that women needed an education in order to support themselves if necessary, and her mastery of a career skill made her reunion with Takahiro possible.

"My Sin" also brought Christianity under scrutiny. Kikuchi did not identify Tamaki's school, suggesting only that it was the kind of missionary enterprise conservative rhetoric attacked for encouraging romantic illusions that unleashed carnal desires and turned young women into easy prey for licentious males. He further hinted at the sinister underpinnings of both Christianity and Western romance by making the medical student a Christian convert and describing Tamaki as "a poor lamb finally falling into the clutches of a wolf."[22] Yet Kikuchi admired *Jogaku zasshi*, the forum for early Japanese feminists and Christian intellectuals and educators. Thus he also cleverly cast the "wolf" as a young man gone astray, a rogue believer who violated noble Christian teachings that celebrated the sacredness of romantic love and prohibited "illicit intercourse." By the time the serial ended, "My Sin" had placed Christian values above the provisions of the new Civil Code. It was better, Takahiro told readers, to accept Christ's admonition to forgive social transgressions than to ostracize fallen women. "For the first time," he explained, "I understand that society should be governed not only by morality but also by love; if morality does not originate in love there is no way that human life can be governed harmoniously."

Discussion about romantic love naturally led Kikuchi to broach questions about spousal relationships. Tamaki's father and aunt personified the more or less official view that a woman's primary obligation was to serve her family. Tamaki's father conceived of her education in those terms, and her aunt observed, "In a woman's eyes there is nothing beyond the household. While there may be some who enjoy it when their husbands have brilliant careers in society, a woman, by her nature, is not like that. If she can create a happy household, that alone is satisfying." The behavior of Tamaki and Takahiro suggested that an alternative relationship might be more gratifying. Ultimately the couple ignored the advice of meddling in-laws and based their marriage on equity and romantic love. Moreover, they reconciled only after Tamaki had had a successful, if brief, career in the public sphere, and their second child was a symbol of wedded bliss, not the core of a functionally designed family unit.

At the end of the nineteenth century the Meiji government and its supporters were energetically enacting legal codes, crafting school systems, and manipulating religions in hopes of molding personal behavior around sanctioned norms. In the view of government leaders, such social engineering complemented their political and economic reforms and helped fulfill the Meiji Dream of a strong, prosperous, and modern Japan. As demonstrated by the characters in novels like "My Sin," however, most Japanese were not prepared to permit the government free license to determine the circumstances of their own daily lives. Rather, they realized what was at stake, struggled to rearticulate the government's objectives in light of their own diverse backgrounds, and constructed their own sets of expectations about the future. In that regard the 1890s merely brought to the fore issues that would need to be addressed in the opening decades of the twentieth century.

Largely absent from the pages of romance novels were miners, factory girls, and male blue-collar workers. Still struggling to be heard, still dismissed by their social betters, early in the new century the working classes too were to raise questions about the Meiji Dream, asking in particular why certain political, economic, and social programs were necessary and who was to benefit from them. As they demanded a greater voice in deciding the country's future directions, workers not only drew further attention to conditions in Japan's factories but added another perspective to the multitude of contending opinions about what made an ideal marriage and family, how education ought to be structured, and what beliefs ought to be held dear.

# Japan in the New Century

# Chronology

## PART III  JAPAN IN THE NEW CENTURY

**1855**

◻ *February 7 (Twelfth Month, twenty-first day of the previous lunar year)* The Tokugawa shogunate signs the Russo-Japanese Treaty of Amity

**1871**

◻ *Eighth Month, twenty-eighth day* The government prohibits use of the derogatory names *eta* and *hinin* and decrees that outcasts enjoy the same rights and duties as other imperial subjects

◻ *Eleventh Month* Angry Taiwanese murder shipwrecked sailors from the Ryūkyū Islands

**1872**

◻ The Land Regulation Ordinance allows the Hokkaidō Colonization Office to appropriate Ainu lands and redistribute them to Japanese settlers

**1873**

◻ *May 26* Villagers in Okayama Prefecture attack *burakumin* communities, killing and injuring twenty-nine persons and destroying three hundred homes

**1874**

◻ *May 22* Japanese expeditionary force lands on Taiwan

**1875**

◻ *May 7* Japan and Russia sign the Treaty of St. Petersburg giving Russia rights of sovereignty over Sakhalin, Japan over the Kuril Islands

**1876**

◻ *January* Japan dispatches three warships into Korean waters

◻ *February 26* Japan and Korea sign the Treaty of Kanghwa

◻ *May 9* Ueno Park is opened to the public

**1879**

◻ *April 4* The Ryūkyū Islands are incorporated into Japan proper as Okinawa Prefecture

**1884**

◻ *December 4–7* With Japanese assistance, Kim Ok-kyun attempts the Kapsin Coup

**1885**

◻ *March 16* Fukuzawa Yukichi publishes his influential essay "Datsu-A ron" ("The Argument for Abandoning Asia")

◻ *April 18* Japan and China sign the Tianjin Convention

**1887**

◻ *February* Tokutomi Sohō publishes the first issue of *Kokumin no tomo* ("The Nation's Friend")

**1889**

◻ *February 11* Emperor Meiji promulgates the Constitution of the Empire of Japan

◻ *February 12* Prime Minister Kuroda Kiyotaka pledges his support for transcendental cabinets

**1890**

◻ *July 1* The first general elections are held

◻ *November 25* The Diet convenes for the first time

◻ *November 29* The Constitution of the Empire of Japan goes into effect and the emperor officially opens the First Diet

◻ *December 6* Prime Minister Yamagata informs the Diet that Japan's foreign policy will be shaped around the concept of a line of sovereignty and a line of advantage

**1892**

◻ *February 3* Deguchi Nao founds the Ōmoto sect

**1894**

◻ *March 28* Kim Ok-kyun is assassinated in Shanghai

◻ *April and May* Tonghak rebels take control of Korea's southern provinces and approach Seoul

◻ *June 1* The Tokyo government learns that the Korean court has requested help from China to suppress the Tonghak rebellion

◻ *June 2* The Japanese cabinet decides to dispatch an expeditionary force to Korea

◻ *July 16* The Anglo-Japanese Commercial Treaty promises an eventual end to unequal treaties

◻ *August 1* Japan formally declares war on China

**1895**

◻ *April 17* Japan and China sign the Treaty of Shimonoseki

◻ *April 23* Russia, in concert with France and Germany, advises Japan to return the Liaodong Peninsula to China

◻ *May 5* Japan retrocedes the Liaodong Peninsula to China

◻ *October 8* Queen Min is murdered

**1896**

◻ *October 21* China grants Russia permission to construct the Chinese Eastern Railway from Vladivostok across Manchuria to Lake Baikal

**1898**

◻ *March 27* China gives Russia a leasehold on the Liaodong Peninsula

◻ *June 22* Ōkuma Shigenobu and Itagaki Taisuke merge the Rikken Jiyūtō and Shinpotō to form the Kenseitō political party

◻ *June 30* Ōkuma becomes the first leader of a political party to be appointed prime minister

**1900**

◻ *March 10* The government promulgates the Public Order and Police Law

◻ *July 6* The cabinet decides to contribute troops to an international contingent to suppress the Boxer Rebellion in China

◻ *September 15* Itō founds the Seiyūkai

◻ *December 5* Yoshioka Yayoi establishes Japan's first medical college for women

**1901**

◻ *April 28* Abe Isoo helps found the Socialist Democratic Party (Minshutō), which dissolves itself on May 20

◻ *September 7* The Boxer Protocol gives Japan the right to station troops in the Peking-Tianjin region

**1902**

◻ *January 30* Japan signs the Anglo-Japanese Alliance

◻ *March 1* The Tōa Dōbunkai (East Asian Common Culture Society) is founded

◻ The Kasumigaseki district of Tokyo becomes renown for modern buildings that house major government offices

**1903**

🕮 *June 1* Hibiya Park is opened to the public

🕮 *October 1* The Electric Palace, Japan's first permanent movie theater, opens in the Asakusa district of Tokyo

**1904**

🕮 *February 4* An imperial conference endorses a cabinet decision to go to war against Russia

🕮 *February 8* The Japanese Navy attacks Russian ships near Port Arthur

🕮 *February 10* Japan declares war on Russia

**1905**

🕮 *January 1* Japanese forces take Port Arthur

🕮 *May 27–28* The Japanese Navy defeats the Russian fleet in the Battle of Tsushima

🕮 *September 5* Japanese and Russian representatives sign the Treaty of Portsmouth; antitreaty riots erupt at Hibiya Park and other places around Japan

🕮 *November 17* The Korean-Japanese Convention makes Korea a Japanese protectorate

**1906**

🕮 *March* Itō Hirobumi arrives in Seoul as Japan's resident general

🕮 *August 1* The Japanese government creates the Kwantung Army to protect its new possessions in Manchuria

🕮 *November 26* The Japanese government forms the South Manchuria Railway Company

**1907**

🕮 *June* A Korean delegation appears at the Second Hague Conference on World Peace

🕮 *July 19* In Korea, Resident General Itō forces the abdication of Emperor Kojong as Japan assumes control over Korea's domestic affairs

🕮 *July 24* Korea signs an agreement ceding comprehensive administrative control over domestic matters to the Japanese Resident General

🕮 *August 1* Resident General Itō disbands the Korean army

**1908**

🕮 *January* Hani Motoko and her husband publish the first edition of *Fujin no tomo* ("Woman's Friend"), which had appeared from 1903 under the title *Katei no tomo* ("Friend of the Home")

🕮 *August 27* The Japanese government charters the Oriental Development Company

**1909**

🕮 *October 26* A Korean patriot assassinates Itō Hirobumi in Harbin

**1910**

🕮 *August 29* The treaty of annexation, signed between Japan and Korea on August 22, takes effect

**1911**

🕮 *January 24 and 25* Kanno Suga and Kōtoku Shūsui are hanged for their participation in the High Treason Affair

🕮 *September 1* Hiratsuka Raichō begins to publish the magazine "Bluestocking"

🕮 *September 22* Matsui Sumako stars in Ibsen's *A Doll's House*

🕮 *October* The new Shirokiya department store opens at Nihonbashi in Tokyo

**1912**

🕮 *July 30* Emperor Meiji dies, and the Taishō era begins

🕮 *August 1* Labor leaders found the Yūaikai

🕮 *September 13* Funeral ceremonies are held in Tokyo to commemorate the death of Emperor Meiji; General Nogi and his wife Shizuko commit suicide

## 1913

February 7 Katsura Tarō announces his intention to found a new political party to be named the Dōshikai

December 23 Katō Takaaki is named party president in the inaugural convention of the Dōshikai

## 1914

July 28 World War I commences

August 23 Japan declares war on Germany

October 1 The new Mitsukoshi department store opens at Nihonbashi in Tokyo

October Japanese forces occupy the Caroline, Marshall, and Mariana islands

November 7 Germany surrenders its leasehold in Shandong Province to Japan

December 20 Tokyo Central Station opens

Matsui Sumako's "Katusha's Song" becomes Japan's first hit recording

## 1915

January 18 Japan presents the Twenty-one Demands to China

May 25 China agrees to the first four subsets of the Twenty-one Demands

## 1918

July 23 A protest by women in Toyama Prefecture marks the beginning of a summer of rice riots

September 29 Hara Takashi is named prime minister and heads Japan's first party cabinet

December 7 Students at the University of Tokyo found the Shinjinkai

## 1919

January 5 Matsui Sumako commits suicide

March 1 The Samil (March First) Independence Movement begins in Korea

August 12 Admiral Saitō Makoto is appointed governor-general of Korea and launches an era of "cultural rule"

November 24 Activists in Osaka found the Federation of Women's Organizations of Western Japan

December 22 Business leaders and officials from the Home Ministry found the Harmonization Society

## 1920

March 15 A sudden decline in prices for rice and raw silk signals the beginning of the postwar recession

March 28 Hiratsuka Raichō, Ichikawa Fusae, and others found the New Woman's Association

November 15 Japan becomes a charter member of the League of Nations

December 17 The League of Nations gives Japan a mandate to administer the Caroline, Mariana, and Marshall islands

## 1921

April 4 Itō Noe, Yamakawa Kikue, and other socialist women found the Red Wave Society

April 15 Hani Motoko and her husband establish the college Jiyū Gakuen

June 29 Workers at the Kawasaki and Mitsubishi shipyards in Kōbe begin a fifty-day strike

November 12 The Washington Conferences opens

November 20 The South Seas Development Company begins operations

November Korean students in Japan organize the revolutionary Black Wave Society

December 13 Japan signs the Four-Power Treaty

December Moderate leaders of the Korean immigrant community found the Sōaikai

**1922**
▢ *February 6* Japan signs the Washington Naval Treaty and Nine-Power Treaty on the final day of the Washington Conference
▢ *March 3* Burakumin activists found the Suiheisha (Levelers' Society)
▢ *April 20* The Diet amends the Public Order and Police Law of 1900 to remove prohibitions against women joining political associations
▢ *July 15* Intellectuals and political radicals establish the Japan Communist Party
▢ *December 2–17* Japan withdraws its troops from Shandong Province

**1923**
▢ *February 20* The Marunouchi Building opens
▢ *September 1* The Great Kantō Earthquake devastates the Tokyo-Yokohama area
▢ Minobe Tatsukichi explicates the organ theory of government in his *Kenpō satsuyō* ("Outline of the Constitution")

**1924**
▢ *March* The Japan Communist Party dissolves itself
▢ *June 11* Katō Takaaki, head of the Kenseikai, is appointed as prime minister, inaugurating an era of party government
▢ *December 1* The Tenancy Conciliation Law takes effect
▢ *December 13* Ichikawa Fusae and other activists found the Women's Suffrage League

**1925**
▢ *March 29* The Diet passes a universal manhood suffrage bill

▢ *April 22* The Peace Preservation Law takes effect

**1926**
▢ *March 5* The inaugural meeting of the Labor-Farmer Party (Rōdō Nōmintō) is held in Osaka
▢ *August 6* Existing radio stations in Tokyo, Osaka, and Nagoya are merged into NHK
▢ *December 4* The Japan Communist Party formally reestablishes itself
▢ *December 5* Abe Isoo helps found the Socialist People's Party (Shakai Minshūtō)
▢ *December 9* The Japan Labor-Farmer Party (Nihon Rōnōtō) is founded
▢ *December 25* Emperor Taishō dies
▢ *December 28* The Shōwa period begins

**1927**
▢ *April 22* The government announces a three-week banking moratorium
▢ *May 28* The Tanaka cabinet dispatches troops to protect Japanese residents at Qingdao
▢ *September 16* A strike begins at the Noda Soy Sauce Company

**1928**
▢ *March 15* Police carry out mass arrests of communists and other political activists
▢ *April 19* A settlement is reached in the strike at the Noda Soy Sauce Company; the Tanaka cabinet dispatches troops to protect Japanese residents at Jinan
▢ *May 3* Fighting breaks out between Japanese and Chinese troops in Jinan

# CHAPTER 9

# The Acquisition of Empire

*t*okyo sweltered in the lingering heat of late summer as thousands of men made their way to Tokyo's Hibiya Park, an oasis of greenery next to the Imperial Palace. Joining them, according to drawings in magazines, was a sprinkling of women, despite the fact that the Public Order and Police Law of 1900 prohibited females and minors from participating in political assemblies. Humid and uncomfortable as that afternoon was, those ordinary citizens of Japan were gathering to hear speeches on the same day, September 5, 1905, that Japan's representatives were scheduled to initial the Treaty of Portsmouth, formally ending a war with Russia. The conflict had been bitter, but Japan had scored several victories on land and at sea, and the peace agreement, brokered in an old New England town by the American president Theodore Roosevelt, recognized Japan's achievements by giving that nation Russian territory and railroad concessions in northern Asia.

The prime minister and his cabinet lauded the victory over Russia as a great moment in the history of modern Japan. For the men who had committed their country to the uncertainty of war, the triumph over a Western power represented the consummation of the Meiji Dream, a grand achievement that simultaneously confirmed the success of Japan's modernization efforts, certified the nation's release from semicolonial status, marked acceptance into the comity of great powers, and offered the prospect of a more secure future. The outside world endorsed that assessment. Editorials in the *New York Times* suggested that the victory assured Japan's future "peace and safety" and opened up "boundless opportunities of industrial growth and national development."[1]

Surprisingly, the thirty thousand or so craftsmen, shop clerks, and factory workers who came to Hibiya Park on September 5 intended not to praise the treaty but to protest it. To their way of thinking, the government had not extracted nearly enough concessions from Russia; rather, "clumsy" and "weak-willed" negotiators had settled for a "shameful" peace. As firecrackers exploded, balloons floated into the air, and brass bands banged out patriotic songs, speaker after speaker urged the cabinet and emperor to "reject the humiliating treaty" and order the army to resume "the brave fight to crush the enemy."[2] As the rally drew to a close, some flag-waving participants began marching toward the Imperial Palace. When the police attempted to block their way, tensions mounted, tempers flared, and fights broke out. The people had only clubs and stones to use against police swords, but they enjoyed an advantage of numbers, and soon they ran wild, sacking police stations and setting fire to government buildings. The authorities declared martial law the following day, and by the time a heavy rain extinguished the violence on September 7, some 350 buildings had been destroyed, five hundred police and at least an equal number of protesters had suffered wounds, and seventeen demonstrators lay dead.

Violence delivers messages that are at once bold and subtle. Among other things, the rioters at Hibiya were affirming their place in the national polity. They were proud that their individual sacrifices and accomplishments, on the farm and in the workplace, in the classroom and on the battlefield, had contributed to the nation's collective achievements in the decades since the restoration. They had earned the right to their opinions, and as *kokumin*, citizens of the nation, they had come to Hibiya Park to express their disagreements with official policy. But beyond the rancor of the moment, a commonality of interests bridged the gap between the demonstrators and the government. The men and women at Hibiya were patriots, and like the nation's leaders, they were absolutely unwilling to accept anything less than equal status as one of the leading powers on the face of the globe. Fiery nationalism and an unyielding determination to secure respect and honor from the international community bound together citizen and government at the beginning of the new century.

The eruption of national self-pride and the confluence of powerful emotions around common goals and objectives evident at Hibiya Park in September 1905 contained within itself another important message, the beginnings of an answer to a question of historical import. Before 1868 Japan had been a secluded country, with limited foreign relations; only once in its entire recorded history of more than a thousand years had it attacked one of its neighbors, during Hideyoshi's megalomania in the late sixteenth century. How was it, then, that as Japan pursued its quest for modernity, its leaders and citizens alike would insist on the advantages of an aggressive foreign policy, fight wars with China and Russia, and acquire an empire?

## Redefining Borders and Relationships

In the 1870s, a generation before the crowds shouted their approval of Japan's wartime victories, the Meiji leaders labored to restructure the country's traditional relationships with its neighbors in Asia. The West no longer would tolerate Japan's customary practice of restricting contacts with foreign nations, and in the view of men like Itō Hirobumi and Yamagata Aritomo, theirs was a small and relatively powerless country that had to comply with Western diplomatic norms. Those new criteria required nations to clarify their borders so that they could be drawn precisely on maps, sign formal treaties with other sovereign members of the international community, and exchange diplomatic representatives to manage relationships and solve unforeseen problems that might arise in the future.

Accordingly, in the 1870s the Meiji oligarchs set about the twin tasks of fixing Japan's territorial limits and adjusting relations with its nearest neighbors in a way that conformed to Western expectations.

The Meiji government especially wanted to establish a clear boundary somewhere to the north of Hokkaidō, a name it used officially from 1869. The oligarchs shared the assumption that Japan needed that major island for both economic and strategic reasons. In particular, the Russian advance across the northern Pacific and the memory of the incidents sparked by the Laxman and Rezanov expeditions played on the minds of the young Meiji leaders, who hoped to stymie Russia's ambitions in the north by keeping its soldiers and traders as far from the heart of Japan as possible. To the oligarchs' relief, the Russo-Japanese Treaty of Amity, signed early in 1855, had recognized Japanese sovereignty over Hokkaidō and the offshore islands in the Kuril chain as far north as Etorofu, although it left open the status of Sakhalin.

After the restoration the new regime buttressed Japanese claims to Hokkaidō by chartering the Hokkaidō Colonization Office, encouraging migration to the north, and stepping up efforts to assimilate the Ainu. Created in 1869 to develop the commercial potential of the former Ezochi, the Hokkaidō Colonization Office recorded only modest accomplishments — promoting sake brewing and the fishing industry—before being abolished in 1882. Perhaps its most lasting achievement was the establishment of Sap-

**MAP 9.1** *The Northern Islands*

poro Agricultural College, which later became one of Japan's seven imperial universities and was renamed Hokkaidō University in 1949. Founded in 1876 and based on the U.S. land-grant model, Sapporo Agricultural College employed several foreign teachers, one of whom, William Smith Clark, gained immortality for himself by offering his students the still oft-repeated advice "Boys, be ambitious."

The primary mission of Sapporo Agricultural College was to facilitate the agrarian development of Hokkaidō. In the 1870s the new Meiji regime needed both to help ex-samurai acquire the means to support themselves and to populate the northern frontier with families from the home islands, so that the outside world would recognize Hokkaidō as being an indivisible part of Japan. Encouraging former warriors to migrate to Hokkaidō and become farmers offered a solution to both problems. By 1889 some two thousand samurai families had taken advantage of a plan that permitted them to use government loans to buy wasteland in Hokkaidō at half its market value. Meanwhile, nearly eight thousand former warriors settled in military colonies. Each militia family received land that previously had not been cultivated, a house, utensils, farm equipment, and a three-year supply of food after agreeing to till the soil and help defend Hokkaidō in case of invasion. Immigration rose more substantially in the 1890s, after the government announced it would provide all newcomers, regardless of social background, with homesteads they could cultivate rent- and tax-free for ten years, after which they received title to the land.

As part of its northern policy, the Meiji government undertook to deny the ethnicity of the Ainu and complete their assimilation into Japanese society. Replicating the shogunate's earlier initiatives, in the 1870s the new regime ordered the Ainu to stop wearing earrings and tattooing themselves and pressured them to adopt Japanese clothing and hairstyles. In the Meiji years, however, assimilation programs went far beyond appearance to eradicate an entire way of life. Mindful of the counsel offered by such foreign advisers as Horace Capron, the former U.S. commissioner of agriculture who had helped devise the plans that overpowered native resistance to the conquest of the American West, the Meiji regime compelled the Ainu to worship at Shinto shrines and assume Japanese names; to save time and trouble in that regard, census officials sometimes gave whole communities the same surname. In school, Ainu children were taught the Japanese language and read texts that stressed the blessings that came to those who revered the emperor and served the nation loyally.

Most of all, authorities intended to convert the Ainu from hunters and gatherers—"a barbarous and fierce savage people who were not quite human," according to some—into civilized agriculturists.[3] The Meiji government, however, did not permit the Ainu to farm the lands they previously had hunted and fished. The Land Regulation Ordinance of 1872 pictured Hokkaidō as a vast wilderness and drew a distinction between using land and owning it. "The mountains, forests, rivers and streams where the natives fished, hunted, and gathered wood," one clause read, "shall be partitioned and converted to private or collective ownership." Thus, the woodlands and hills that had supported the Ainu way of life became the so-called wastelands given to Japanese immigrants as homesteads and farms. As settlers moved into the Ainu homeland, authorities relocated native communities to less desirable areas, handed out a few tools and seeds, and told the displaced families to learn how to farm. The policy culminated in the 1899 enactment of the Former Natives Protection Law, which stipulated that Ainu families wishing to engage in agriculture receive two to five hectares of farmland. Soon, however, most lost their plots to Japanese neighbors, often through devious means, and ended up working in fisheries and living in city slums. Such policies damaged Ainu culture beyond repair, and by the end of the Meiji era Hokkaidō was undisputedly Japanese; in 1908, the 18,000 Ainu living in Hokkaidō constituted only 1.25 percent of the island's total population of 1.45 million.

The oligarchs were less certain about how to establish a presence on Sakhalin and the northern Kuril Islands, where Japanese families lived interspersed with Russians and native islanders. There seemed to be little compelling reason to extend Japanese sovereignty to those sparsely settled bays and inlets, an action that would raise complicated questions of administration and defense since, in the new vocabulary of Western-style diplomacy, people living there would become "citizens" entitled to the protection of the state. Still, the Meiji oligarchs hesitated to draw the national borders too close to the shores of Hokkaidō, lest they appear timid of Russia and thus create an unflattering image that might tarnish the new regime's prestige. With those concerns in mind, the Meiji government in 1875 sent representatives to Russia to negotiate a settlement to the northern question. Discussions proceeded smoothly, and on May 7 the two sides concluded the Treaty of St. Petersburg, by which the Japanese received title to the entire Kuril archipelago in exchange for abandoning claims to Sakhalin.

To the west, the Meiji government incorporated Tsushima into Nagasaki Prefecture to buttress its assertion that Japan's border with Korea ran between the former island domain of the Sō family of daimyo and the peninsula. Adjusting other aspects of the relationship with Korea, however, proved troublesome. Traditionally, Korea considered itself a vassal kingdom within the Chinese tributary system. Despite the exclusive nature of that patron-client relationship, the Chinese suzerains permitted the peninsular country to send diplomatic embassies to Edo during the Tokugawa period and to conduct limited trade with Japan through the auspices of the Sō daimyo. Following their assumption of power in 1868, the new Meiji leaders requested the Korean court to recognize the "restoration of imperial rule." Frustrated by Korea's continuing rebuffs, some members of the Japanese inner circle, notably Saigō Takamori, proposed in 1873 that Japan send a punitive expedition to Korea. Saigō's outburst touched off a fierce debate among the oligarchs, but in the end cooler heads, such as Itō and Ōkubo

Toshimichi, prevailed by advancing the argument that a Korean expedition would invite Western countermoves against a still-vulnerable Japan.

Itō and Ōkubo tabled their reservations just three years later, when the Meiji leaders tapped fellow oligarch Kuroda Kiyotaka, who had been serving as the director of the Hokkaidō Colonization Office, to reopen negotiations with Korea. Stealing a page from Commodore Perry's primer on diplomacy, in January 1876 Kuroda sent a flotilla of modern warships into Korean waters. When Korea's traditional mentor failed to respond to Japan's bold maneuver, the Korean monarchy felt it had little choice but to accede to Japanese demands. The Treaty of Kanghwa, signed on February 26, 1876, stipulated that "Korea, an independent sovereignty, and Japan, her compeer, in furtherance of their mutual desire for lasting peace and friendship, do hereby settle and conclude the forms and conditions of their intercourse upon terms of equality and mutual regard."[4] Despite such noble sentiments, the subsequent "articles of eternal peace and amity" were decidedly in Japan's favor inasmuch as they opened three Korean ports to Japanese trade and authorized Japan to establish consulates in those ports so that resident Japanese could enjoy the privilege of extraterritoriality. Ironically, less than two decades after the Euro-American powers had used gunboat diplomacy to reduce Japan to semicolonial status, Japan forced its nearest neighbor to accept a Western-style unequal treaty that severely compromised its sovereignty.

Setting Japan's southern borders and recasting relations with the Ryūkyū Islands also involved China. Like Korea, the Ryūkyū Islands at the beginning of the Tokugawa era existed both as a self-contained kingdom and as a Chinese tributary state. To complicate matters further, samurai from Satsuma domain in 1609 took the Ryūkyūan king hostage and two years later compelled him to sign an agreement, kept secret from the Chinese, that acknowledged Satsuma's overlordship and authorized trade between the islands and the daimyo domain. In the autumn of 1871, when Japan's new government abolished the old domains, it decided to claim nominal sovereignty over the Ryūkyū chain by placing the islands under the administrative oversight of Kagoshima Prefecture, which encompassed the territory of the former Satsuma domain.

The young regime confirmed its resolve to extend Japan's official domination southward when some fifty fishermen from the Ryūkyū Islands were massacred after being shipwrecked on Taiwan, officially part of China's Fujian Province. Within Japan, public opinion called for the Meiji government to avenge the harm done to "Japanese citizens," the Ryūkyūan fishermen, by "punishing" the "uncivilized" people of Taiwan. A military campaign against Taiwan seemed an attractive policy option, and after talks with Chinese officials ended inconclusively, the Japanese government dispatched a punitive expeditionary force early in 1874. Japanese troops landed in Taiwan on May 22 and quickly overcame local resistance. In postexpedition negotiations, the Chinese court recognized the "justice" of Japan's actions, and the following year the Meiji government ordered Ryūkyūan leaders to discontinue the tributary relationship with China. Finally, in 1879, the Japanese government forced the last Ryūkyūan king to abdicate and formally incorporated the islands into Japan proper as Okinawa Prefecture.

During the 1870s the Japanese government maneuvered forcefully to promote the country's diplomatic interests. The oligarchs' actions, however, did not add up to a premeditated plan for continental expansion. Rather, in the first decade of its existence the new Meiji government had the more limited objectives of clarifying the nation's borders and reorganizing its relations with its closest neighbors to correspond with Western practices. By the end of the decade the oligarchs had achieved those goals: Japanese sovereignty extended over Hokkaidō, the Kuril archipelago, Tsushima, and the Okinawan islands; public opinion applauded the government for negotiating a treaty with Russia that demonstrated Japan's resolve to stand up to a Western nation; and most people hailed the Treaty of Kanghwa as evidence that Japan had advanced far enough that it could begin to enjoy some of the same prerogatives that the powerful Western states considered their due.

## An Emerging Imperialist Mentalité

Japanese attitudes toward their neighbors changed dramatically in the 1880s as a new and more virulent strain of Western imperialism threatened to overwhelm East Asia. During the late nineteenth century the powerful nations of the West that had so fascinated the Iwakura Mission—Britain, France, Germany, Italy, and the United States—achieved new levels of political centralization and commercial development. One outgrowth of the American Civil War and a series of military confrontations in Europe was an awareness of how the production of national wealth enhanced the ability of any one country to maintain domestic political cohesion and to protect itself against hostile neighbors. Consequently, to promote national strength and prosperity, governments in western Europe and North America in the late nineteenth century championed industrialization, created nationwide transportation and marketing networks, encouraged cooperation between labor and capital, and protected domestic industry and agriculture against foreign competition.

The impulse to build powerful national economies brought with it new geopolitical attitudes. Increasingly, the so-called Great Powers that were going through the process of political centralization and economic modernization felt the need to possess colonial empires that could contribute to the metropolitan nations' development. Since the inception of the Industrial Revolution in the eighteenth century, Euro-American traders, bankers, and industrialists had sought to maximize their personal profits by exploiting sales to overseas markets and by buying up cheap raw materials and foodstuffs to ship home. Governments, none more so than Britain's, routinely supported their merchant chiefs by asserting "special rights" in far corners of the globe. In the closing decades of the nineteenth century, however, imperialistic conquest became a more overtly defined state policy, and many nations began to place the full weight of their bureaucratic and military resources behind efforts to acquire colonies, protectorates, and spheres of influence so as to augment the wealth, power, and prestige of the mother countries.

The belief that any successful modern power must boast an empire touched off a fierce rivalry for overseas possessions. The European states quickly gobbled up Africa: In 1881 France claimed Tunis as a protectorate, the next year Great Britain occupied Egypt, and in 1883 Germany began to make its influence felt in the southwest corner of the continent. The United States moved into the Pacific, overthrowing the Hawaiian monarchy in 1893 and then competing with Germany and Great Britain for influence in the Samoan, Gilbert, and Marshall island groups. In Asia the Sino-French War of 1884–1885 brought Vietnam into the French colonial empire, just as Britain was folding Burma into its own. Everyone clamored for concessions in China: By the 1880s the list of Western nations with special rights and privileges in China included not just Great Britain, France, Russia, and the United States but also Portugal, Denmark, Holland, Spain, Belgium, and Italy. By the time the passion for empire building peaked in the first decade of the twentieth century, most of Africa, the Middle East, Asia, and the Pacific had fallen victim to Western imperialism, and across that broad swath of the globe only seven countries still existed as fully independent, sovereign nations.

The aggressive Western penetration of Asia persuaded many Japanese that their nation had to rethink its relationship with its neighbors in Asia and the belligerent powers of the West. Within the halls of power, the person most responsible for formulating Japanese foreign policy was Yamagata

Aritomo, the veteran oligarch who had overseen the creation of the Japanese conscript army, designed the system of local government when he served
as home minister in the 1880s, and accepted the position of prime minister
late in December 1889. Yamagata was a cautious pragmatist, preoccupied
with Japan's security. He saw the world in the bleak terms of realpolitik,
and Korea in particular drew his dour attention. In his perception, Japan's
neighbor was a weak and backward nation, possible future prey for the
predatory British or the ambitious Russians, who were about to build the
Trans-Siberian Railway across northern Asia to Vladivostok. The completion of that transportation link, Yamagata concluded, posed a long-term
threat to Japan's vital interests since it would position the czar's armies to
move on Manchuria or even Beijing. Moreover, he knew, Russia hungered
to have a year-round port as the terminus for its new railroad, and since
Vladivostok iced over during the winter, Russia's generals would be tempted
to secure access to Korea's more temperate harbors.

If either Britain or Russia secured even a toehold on the Korean peninsula, Yamagata feared, Japan's independence ultimately would be placed in
jeopardy. Accordingly, in an address to Japan's First Diet on December 6,
1890, Prime Minister Yamagata outlined his foreign policy objectives. The
primary goal of his administration, he said, must be to "preserve our independence and enhance our national position."[5] To that end, he went on,
Japan must be prepared to defend both a "line of sovereignty" and a "line
of advantage." The former was contiguous with the newly settled national
borders, while the latter defined a surrounding buffer zone whose neutrality was essential to Japan's security needs. As Japan approached the new
century, Yamagata averred, its line of sovereignty hugged Tsushima's shore-
line, and the line of advantage ran through Korea. "If we wish to maintain
the nation's independence among the powers of the world at the present
time," the prime minister ended, "it is not enough to guard only the line of
sovereignty, we must also defend the line of advantage." That said, he introduced a budget providing for the rapid expansion of Japan's land and
naval forces.

Outside government, the educator and journalist Fukuzawa Yukichi also
anguished over events in Asia. In the 1860s and 1870s Fukuzawa had encouraged the all-out importation of Western ideas and institutions in the
belief that the world was a benign place where nations "teach and learn from
each other, pray for each other's welfare, and associate with each other in
accordance with the laws of nature and man."[6] In the early 1880s, however,
he grew more cynical as he fretted about the approach of Western imperialism and pondered the lessons of Social Darwinism. Previously, Fukuzawa

confessed, he had believed that the benevolent and impartial application of international law governed relations among nations. In reality, he now realized, the world operated according to the law of the jungle, *jakuniku kyōshoku*. All countries struggled for power and wealth, and the mighty devoured the weak. The United States and the advanced nations of Europe, he warned, were far stronger than such countries as China and Korea, and the encroachment of the West threatened Asia with the same sort of humiliation and material destruction being visited upon Africa and the Middle East.

That course of events, Fukuzawa cautioned, endangered Japan directly. He passionately believed that his nation was different from its neighbors. Alone among the countries of Asia, he claimed with pride, Japan had begun to modernize, to reshape itself in the image of the West, and thus had proved itself ready to stride the path of progress arm in arm with other civilized nations. Unfortunately, he went on, the West did not, could not recognize that fact. Euro-Americans, he lamented, wore racial blinders and did not distinguish one Asian country from another. In their perception, China and Korea were despotic, half civilized, and obstinately bound to the scorned customs of the past, and they would assume that Japan was too. How, he shook his head, could Japan avoid being crushed by the Western juggernaut?

Fukuzawa proposed two answers to his own question. First, he declared, Japan must build up its military strength, and it must stand ready to use it. "When others use violence," he wrote, "we must be violent too." Second, he argued, Japan needed to encourage its Asian neighbors to reform themselves so that they could withstand the Western onslaught. If they refused, he reasoned, Japan should compel them to do so. He reminded his countrymen of a parable: A man who lives in a stone house is not safe from fire if his neighbor lives in a wooden one. The person with the more secure abode should try to persuade his neighbor to rebuild, of course, but if "a crisis should be at hand, he is justified in arbitrarily invading his neighbor's land— not because he covets his neighbor's land or hates his neighbor, but simply to protect his own house from fire."

Fukuzawa restated his argument in an influential essay he published in March 1885 in his newspaper, the *Jiji shinpō*. He chose as his title "Datsu-A ron" ("The Argument for Abandoning Asia") and began by repeating the familiar contrasts between a progressive Japan and a backward China and Korea. Given the West's proclivities, Fukuzawa intoned, Japan must not associate too closely with either Asian neighbor; to do so would merely undermine its own reputation. Japan, he concluded, should be prepared to act ruthlessly to protect itself. "We cannot wait for neighboring countries to become enlightened and unite to make Asia strong," he wrote. "We must rather break out of formation and join the civilized countries of the West on the path of progress. We should not give any special treatment to China and Korea but should treat them in the same way as do the Western nations."

Other influential writers during the late 1880s and early 1890s proclaimed the advantages of imperialism more openly. In his first book, published in 1886, Tokutomi Sohō accepted the idea, articulated by Herbert Spencer and other Western intellectuals, that all advanced industrial societies were by nature peaceful and nonaggressive. It did not take Tokutomi long, however, to change his mind completely. Japan had chalked up some remarkable accomplishments in politics, education, and commerce, he observed in 1893, but it still could not persuade the West to revise the damnable unequal treaties—"our shame, our dishonor," as he characterized them—that the island nation had endured for more than thirty years. Like Fukuzawa, he placed the blame on racist attitudes. Japan was the "most progressive, developed, civilized, and powerful nation in the Orient," he wrote, but it seemed, he added remorsefully, that his country would never escape "the scorn of the white people."[7] Imperial expansion, Tokutomi continued, presented Japan's last good chance to earn the respect of the Great Powers, ensure its security and survival as a nation, and even bring civilization to other countries in East Asia.

Government leaders and opinion makers also were sensitive to the notion that the acquisition of greater economic advantages in Korea could serve Japan's security needs. Certainly, the swelling volume of trade following the signing of the Treaty of Kanghwa augured well for future prospects: Between 1877 and 1893 the value of Japanese commodities shipped to the peninsula increased fourfold, and in return Japanese traders purchased about 90 percent of all Korean exports of rice and soybeans. In June 1894 Matsukata Masayoshi, whose policies as finance minister a decade earlier had prepared a secure base for Japan's modern economic growth, contemplated ways to develop the Korean economy to Japan's advantage. Specifically, he wrote his fellow oligarchs, Japan should "make" Korea open new ports and "secure rights to mine coal, lay telegraph lines, and build a railroad line between Pusan and Seoul," concessions, he claimed, that would "truly be to the advantage of both countries."[8] That same summer the popular press also clamored for new economic privileges in Korea. Spiritedly, *Kokumin no tomo* ("The Nation's Friend"), which quickly became Japan's most widely read political journal after its founding by Tokutomi in 1887, repeated most of Matsukata's wish list and demanded the end to existing restrictions on Japanese business activities in Korea.

The Japanese who pondered the fate of their nation as Western imperialism spread across Asia were not malicious individuals. They did not harbor any particular animosity toward fellow Asians, and no person in a position of authority concocted or endorsed any concrete plan calling for the acquisition of territory overseas or the economic domination of Asia. Collectively, however, men like Yamagata, Matsukata, Fukuzawa, and Tokutomi were developing a *mentalité* that countenanced imperialistic behavior. By the early 1890s they and many of their countrymen, from the political right and left, both inside and outside government, had reached the same conclusion: The world was a dangerous place, Western imperialism and racist attitudes posed grave threats to Japanese independence, and their country was justified in contemplating action outside its national borders in order to preserve its national integrity. Seizing upon the rhetoric of expansionism that filled the air, they helped forge an emerging consensus that Japan must be assertive, must even victimize others, if it wished to avoid being victimized itself.

## War with China

Japan acquired the beginnings of a colonial empire after vanquishing China in the war of 1894–1895, a conflict spawned in the vortex of Korea. As was the case with most other peoples of Asia in the late nineteenth century, Koreans found themselves divided about how best to deal with the challenge of the West. By the early 1880s the court was dominated by a conservative faction determined to preserve a Confucian-based society, enforce an exclusionist foreign policy, and continue Korea's reliance on China for advice and protection. Rising in opposition was a group of young self-styled progressives, led by Kim Ok-kyun, who admired Japan's response to the West and believed it essential that Korea undertake reforms similar to those being pursued by the Meiji oligarchy.

Japanese consular officials in Seoul cultivated ties with the progressives, hoping to assist the installation of a reformist regime that would strengthen Korea and thus enable the kingdom to resist domination by outside powers that might also be hostile to Japan. In Tokyo, Fukuzawa and other prominent pro-Westernizers befriended Kim when he traveled to Tokyo in search of information about modernizing strategies in 1881 and 1882, two years before Fukuzawa published his "Datsu-A ron." Encouraged by such support, Kim organized a coup attempt against the Korean monarchy. Using weapons smuggled to him from Japan and openly assisted by guard units posted to Japan's legation in Seoul, Kim and his followers stormed the royal palace on December 4, 1884. The rebels seized King Kojong, murdered several of his ministers, and declared the formation of a new "independent, pro-Japanese" government. Korean conservatives, however, immediately appealed to Chinese garrison forces for help, and after three days of fighting they restored order to the capital. With the collapse of the so-called Kapsin Coup, Kim fled to Japan, while angry Koreans took their revenge by killing forty Japanese and burning the legation to the ground.

The oligarchs called on Itō Hirobumi to calm the troubled waters. Even though he was in the midst of preparing for the advent of constitutional government, Itō immediately journeyed to China to confer with Li Hongzhang, who was responsible for managing China's relations with Korea. The Japanese envoy understood that most foreign observers considered his country to be on the wrong side of the moral fence, and the ever-cautious Itō had no desire to roil up further trouble that might bring Japan into conflict with any of the Great Powers or lead to a full-scale showdown with a China that everyone believed was stronger than Japan. Li meanwhile had his own problems to contend with, notably skirmishes with France along the Vietnamese border and Britain's advance into Burma. With neither side in a position to be overly stubborn, Itō and Li soon reached an agreement. The Tianjin Convention, concluded on April 18, 1885, stipulated that neither Japan nor China would station troops in Korea or move forces onto the peninsula without giving prior written notification. At home the Tokyo government ordered a crackdown on activists, arresting Fukuda Hideko and Ōi Kentarō in October 1885 for conspiring to instigate a new coup, and forced Kim to take up exile in Shanghai.

The Tianjin Convention did not bring about lasting stability. From Japan's perspective, Korea's domestic politics remained impossibly chaotic, and a modest reform program launched by the monarchy in the wake of the Kapsin Coup seemed to be producing only disappointing results. At the same time, Yamagata's determination to carve a line of advantage around the Japanese islands, Fukuzawa's call for his country to deal with Korea "in the same way as do the Western nations," and the growing export trade combined to ensure that Japan would remain sensitive to conditions on the peninsula. Among those concerns, Japan's strategic interests continued to hold special prominence. In 1885 Major Klemens Meckel arrived from Germany to teach at the Army War College and advise the general staff, and he coined a metaphor that became indelibly ingrained in the military and popular mind. Korea, Meckel lectured, was "a dagger pointed at the heart of Japan" and thus had to remain outside the control of a third power, especially Russia. Increasingly in the late 1880s, "measures to guarantee the independence of Korea," as Yamagata phrased it, became the uncontested axiom for Japan's strategic planners.

Matters came to a head early in 1894. That March alleged agents of the Korean government murdered Kim in Shanghai. Chinese authorities returned the corpse to Seoul, but the Japanese press and Kim's many sympathizers in Japan protested vehemently when the Korean authorities dismembered the body as a warning to other would-be reformers. That same spring the Japanese government looked on with growing alarm as leaders of the Tonghak, a new religion that had become extremely popular in Korea's southern provinces, rallied peasants and marched on Seoul, threatening to overthrow the regime unless it undertook reforms to improve the lot of Korea's poor. In Tokyo apprehension deepened further when King Kojong asked China for military assistance to quell the domestic unrest. As some three thousand Chinese troops were disembarking near Seoul in June, Japan's policy makers convened to decide on a response.

Action was at the top everyone's agenda. In the view of Japan's leaders, China clearly had violated the Tianjin Convention by dispatching forces without informing Tokyo, and the prospect of a weak Korea once again allied closely with a disintegrating China resurrected the specter of Russian or British intervention in affairs on the peninsula. As discussions unfolded, the Japanese consul to Seoul proposed that Japan negotiate "a treaty under which Korea accepts Japanese protection, then intervene in Korea's domestic and foreign affairs so as to achieve progress and reform, leading to wealth and strength; for thereby we will on the one hand make Korea into a strong bulwark for Japan, while on the other we extend our influence and increase the rights enjoyed by our merchants."[9] Japan's leaders soon coalesced around that set of goals, and in the late spring of 1894 they dispatched an expeditionary force to Korea. Following a series of skirmishes with Chinese forces, Tokyo officially declared war on China on August 1, 1894.

Few foreign observers expected the island nation to prevail over the continental giant. The arms buildup initiated by Yamagata in 1890 had prepared Japan well, however, and Japanese forces overwhelmed the Chinese defenders at P'yŏngyang on September 16, won a decisive naval battle the following day against Chinese warships near the mouth of the Yalu River, seized Port Arthur on November 21, and on February 12, 1895, destroyed the Chinese fleet at Weihaiwei, where the disgraced Chinese admirals committed suicide. An exhilarated Yamagata lobbied to extend the campaign deeper into China proper, but Itō, who had stepped back into the position of prime minister, worried about the cost of the war effort and felt uncertain about Western reactions should Japanese forces penetrate too far into central and southern China. Bet-

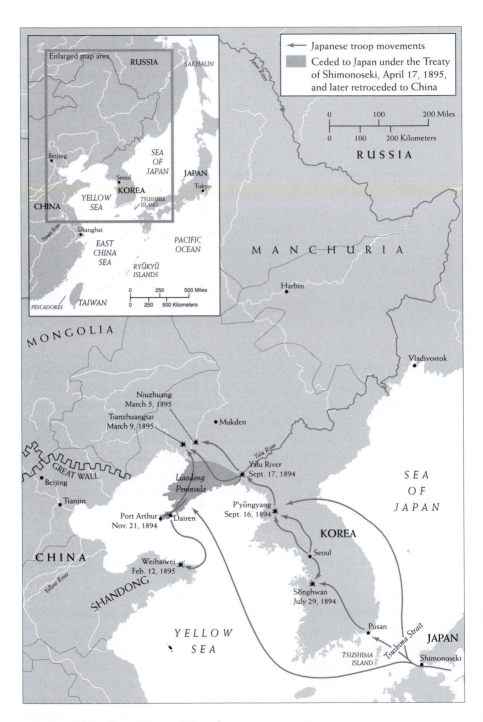

**MAP 9.2** *The Sino-Japanese War of 1894–1895*

ter, Itō insisted, that Japan negotiate an end to hostilities, so once again he and Li Hongzhang sat down to resolve the differences between their two countries.

Ten years earlier Itō had traveled to China; in 1895 Li had to journey to Japan, a clear sign that the Japanese oligarch held the better cards. To further his odds, Itō informed Li that English, which Itō had spoken for decades, would be the official language of the conference and for any agreements signed at Shimonoseki. As Li scrambled to find translators, Itō slapped a harsh slate of demands onto the table: affirmation of "the full and complete independence and autonomy of Korea"; cession of the Manchurian province of Liaoning as well as Taiwan and the nearby Pescadores islands; payment of a war indemnity amounting to nearly 500 million yen; the opening of four new treaty ports; and the granting of commercial privileges that included the right to navigate the upper reaches of the Yangzi River and to import machinery and operate manufacturing establishments in Chinese treaty ports. Li bargained as skillfully as he could, given the circumstances, but made little progress until a Japanese fanatic shot and wounded him just below the left eye. Shamed in front of the world, Itō agreed to reduce the indemnity by one-third and to confine Japanese territorial claims in Manchuria to the Liaodong Peninsula. The oligarch stuck to the rest of his demands, however, and the Treaty of Shimonoseki, signed on April 17, 1895, made Japan the world's first non-Western imperial power.

The 1890s were an especially proud moment for many Japanese since their country also achieved the long-sought goal of treaty revision with Western powers. In the spring of 1894 Great Britain, which had been particularly stubborn in refusing to yield treaty rights, decided to cultivate Japanese goodwill as a way to inhibit Russian ambitions in northern Asia. The Anglo-Japanese Commercial Treaty of 1894, signed in London on July 16 of that year, abolished the segregated, enclavelike British settlements within Japanese cities and provided for the abolition of extraterritoriality in five years. By 1897 the other treaty powers, impressed with Japan's new military prowess, had entered into similar agreements that also recognized Japan's tariff autonomy and provided for the complete equalization of all relations by 1911.

The events of the 1890s—the victory over China, the generous settlement agreed upon at Shimonoseki, and the casting aside of the unequal treaties—stirred up a swelling wave of patriotic feeling in Japan. Newspapers filled their pages with heroic accounts from the front and built readership by carrying serialized novels about the war, and one large daily even sponsored a prize competition for war songs that aroused chauvinistic emotions. Fukuzawa Yukichi, meanwhile, urged his countrymen to devote each

*"Heroic" Japanese soldiers engage Chinese forces*

word, each action to promoting a Japanese victory, and he characterized the conflict as "a religious war" fought "between a country that is trying to develop civilization and a country that inhibits the progress of civilization."[10] For Tokutomi Sohō, the triumph over China gave Japan the international respect denied to it in the past. The West, he crowed, now realized that "civilization is not a monopoly of the white man" and that the Japanese too had "a character suitable for great achievements in the world."

Other expressions of national pride denigrated the Chinese. An ethnocentrism born of geographic remoteness and a cultural self-consciousness that took shape during the period of self-isolation long had colored Japanese thoughts about outsiders. At the end of the nineteenth century such feelings of cultural distinctiveness merged with a growing sense of nationalism to change older views of China, long the object of emulation for most Japanese. The new sentiments, derisive and condescending in flavor, spiced the writings of men like Fukuzawa, but nowhere were they more strikingly evident than in wood-block prints of the war. Commonly, printmakers portrayed Li as a comical incompetent and dressed his advisers in garish greens and screaming reds as they sat around, mouths agape, wondering what to do. Battlefield scenes placed the tall, handsome Japanese soldiers in heroic poses, looking distinctly European with carefully trimmed hair and elegant mustaches. The Chinese, by contrast, wore pigtails and had jutting cheekbones, broad noses, and slanting eyes. Hacks and well-known artists alike produced such prints, which enjoyed enormous popularity. Years later the famous novelist Tanizaki Jun'ichirō recalled, "I would go almost every day and stand before the Shimizuya, a print shop with a large stock of triptychs depicting the war. There was not one I didn't want, boy that I was, and I was horribly envious of my uncle who would buy all the new editions as fast as they appeared."[11]

## Triumphing over Russia

The agony of the Triple Intervention soon deprived the Japanese of their thrill of victory. At the end of the nineteenth century the powerful nations of Europe were preparing to carve the Chinese "melon" into discrete spheres of imperialistic influence, leaseholds where they could set up military bases and develop railroad and mining concessions, and the czar's government was resolved to reserve for itself a generous slice in the north of China. Consequently, on April 23, 1895, just days after the signing of the Treaty of Shimonoseki, St. Petersburg "advised" Tokyo to return the Liaodong Peninsula to China. France and Germany, the czar's representatives explained, concurred with that "friendly counsel." The Japanese government sought American and British intervention, only to be told that it would be futile, and dangerous, to resist Russia. On May 5, after meeting with his cabinet, Prime Minister Itō swallowed hard and announced that Japan would restore Liaodong to Chinese control.

News of the retreat devastated the Japanese public. Tokutomi Sohō, who had set off to see the Liaodong Peninsula for himself, arrived just after negotiators reached agreement at Shimonoseki. "It was late April," he wrote in his diary, "and spring had just arrived. The great willows were budding; the flowers of North China were at the height of their fragrance. Fields stretched out before the eye; a spring breeze was blowing. As I traveled about and realized that this was our new territory, I felt a truly great thrill and satisfaction." Just days later he was "vexed beyond tears" when he learned of the Triple Intervention. "Disdaining to remain for another moment on land that had been retroceded to another power," he scooped up a handful of pebbles from the beach at Port Arthur as a "souvenir" of his pain and humiliation and "returned home on the first ship" he could find.

The anguish that Tokutomi and other patriotic Japanese felt deepened in the months after the Triple Intervention as Russia began to meddle in Korea's domestic matters. The Japanese diplomatic corps in Seoul became especially nervous when Russian advisers ingratiated themselves with Queen Min, who had emerged as a rallying point for anti-Japanese sentiment. The leading Japanese official in Seoul made matters worse in October 1895, when he instructed a motley crew of legation guards and civilian adventurers to take the queen into custody and install pro-Japanese reformers at court. Carried away by the intrigue, in the early-morning hours of October 8 the Japanese contingent, accompanied by Korean "trainees," broke into the palace, stabbed Queen Min to death, and then dragged her corpse into the garden, where they doused it with kerosene and lit a match. Fearing for his life, King Kojong invited Russian to station a contingent of Russian marines in Seoul, and in February 1896 he sought protection in the Russian legation. Later that year the Korean government granted Russia mining and timber rights on the northern part of the peninsula.

The international community was quick to express its outrage at the hideous murder of Queen Min. Tokyo, which had not given its approval to any plot, at first disavowed Japanese involvement. When American eyewitnesses put the lie to that denial, the Japanese government recanted and punished some of the miscreants. Whatever its embarrassment over the gruesome misadventure, however, Japan's leaders came away from the affair with the painful realization that victory over China had not guaranteed respect for Japan's line of advantage on the continent. That message hit home hard in subsequent months as Russia took for itself the privileges and territory in Manchuria that the Triple Intervention had denied the Japanese. In 1896 St. Petersburg demanded from Beijing the right to construct the Chinese Eastern Railway from a point near Lake Baikal westward across Manchuria to Vladivostok, thereby shortening considerably the journey from Moscow to the maritime provinces. Two years later the Russians bullied the Chinese into giving them a twenty-five-year leasehold on the Liaodong Peninsula and permission to build a spur linking the great naval base at Port Arthur to the new Chinese Eastern Railway at Harbin.

By the time Russia entrenched itself in Manchuria, on the shoulder of Korea, the government and the people of Japan were standing united in the belief that the "shame of Liaodong" and the growing Russian presence in northern Asia required a firm response. More than ever, Tokyo was determined to win full recognition for its special interests in Korea and to preserve the peninsula's independence from Western powers. To that end, Japan clearly needed additional military strength and an even more iron-willed foreign policy. Consequently, the cabinet and the Diet cooperated to boost military budgets, from 24 million yen before the Sino-Japanese War to 73 million in 1896 and 110 million the following year, appropriations that made it possible nearly to double the size of the army and to acquire enough warships from European builders to make the Japanese fleet the largest in Asian waters.

Concurrently, the Tokyo government initiated a diplomatic offensive designed to win Japan allies and the respect of other powers. In 1900 it contributed nearly one-half of the forty thousand troops that made up an eight-nation expeditionary force dispatched to Beijing to put down the Boxer Rebellion, an antiforeign uprising by nationalistic Chinese who that June laid siege to the British legation and killed German and Japanese diplomatic officials in the Chinese capital. In recognition of its efforts, Japan was invited to attend the peace conference. That was the first time that it had participated in such an international gathering as a full-fledged member, and the Boxer Protocol, signed on September 7, 1901, gave Japan the right to station troops in the Beijing-Tianjin region to protect its diplomatic personnel. The following year Japan entered a military agreement with Great Britain. In the Anglo-Japanese Alliance of 1902, the two nations recognized each other's privileges in China, affirmed Japan's special interests in Korea, and provided for joint action if Russia, in concert with a fourth power, attacked either one.

Even as it went about buttressing its military and diplomatic positions, Japan sat down with Russia to try to hammer out a modus vivendi for northern Asia. The discussions were tense and difficult, made more so by Russia's refusal to withdraw a large army of some fifty thousand troops it had rushed into Manchuria to protect Russian railroad workers and their families during the Boxer Rebellion. At one point the Japanese pinned their hopes on a proposal suggested by Itō to "exchange Manchuria for Korea." That is, in the finest imperialist practices of the day, Tokyo would recognize St. Petersburg's paramount interests in Manchuria if Russia would honor Japan's claims to a special position in Korea and guarantee the preservation of Korea's independence. The czar's representatives showed little enthusiasm for initialing such a deal, however, and the talks wandered into a blind alley.

As the negotiations bogged down, war fever built in Japan. Most Japanese shared Tokutomi's shock and humiliation over the Triple Intervention and believed that treaty revision and the 1902 alliance with Great Britain affirmed Japan's status as a major power worthy of more respect than the Russians were willing to grant. The belligerent popular press trumpeted the same themes over and over, shrilly declaring that the nation must chastise the Russian bear and take decisive measures to secure its position in Korea. Intellectuals added their voice to the clamor for the country to use force to make the czar fold his hand. In June 1903 seven professors from Tokyo Imperial University wrote to the prime minister. Their statement, quoted at length in the newspaper *Tōkyō nichinichi shinbun*, urged immediate war and asserted that only "a fundamental solution" to the Manchurian problem could secure Japan's position in Korea.

Despite the increasingly tense popular mood, the cabinet moved cautiously, debating at length the options available to it and considering carefully every proposal that it thought might move negotiations forward. In the end, however, there seemed no way to break the deadlock, and late in January 1904 the prime minister and his cabinet resolved to go to war, a decision reaffirmed on February 4 in a meeting held in the presence of the emperor. Japan's leaders were not unanimously optimistic about their country's prospects. They agreed, however, on three points: Japan would remain vulnerable as long as Russia retained its influence in Manchuria, the czar was not likely to make concessions at the bargaining table anytime soon, and a war, even if it eventually ended in a draw, would enhance Japan's prestige and standing among the Great Powers. Having made up its mind, the government moved quickly: On February 6, 1904, Japan severed diplomatic relations with Russia; two days later the Japanese Navy attacked Russian ships at Port Arthur, and on February 10 the emperor officially declared war during a visit to Yasukuni Shrine, burial place for Japan's war dead.

General Nogi Maresuke, a hero of the earlier Sino-Japanese War, led the Third Army onto the Liaodong Peninsula in February and March, occupied Dairen, and in August 1904 laid siege to Port Arthur, which fell on New Year's Day 1905. A second infantry corps advanced up the Korean peninsula and linked up with the Third Army to take the city of Mukden in March 1905. As feared, the fighting was extremely brutal. The long, bitter siege of Port Arthur involved slaughter that foreshadowed the carnage of the First World War. General Nogi lost 15,000 men in the assault of Hill 174 alone, and another 10,000 taking Hill 203; in all, more than 56,000 Japanese died before their flag flew over Port Arthur. Two months later, at Mukden, some 320,000 Russians held out for ten days against 250,000 Japanese soldiers, one-quarter of whom fell dead or wounded in the bloody street fighting. By the spring of 1905 the Japanese Army was wobbling: More than 100,000 enlisted men were dead, few experienced officers remained in the field, munitions were scarce, and despite some impressive victories, no one on the general staff suggested that the army any longer possessed the ability to deliver the coup de grace to the Russians, who could field twice as many divisions as could the Japanese.

At sea, Admiral Tōgō Heihachirō won a great victory in the spring of 1905 that brought Russia to the negotiating table. The previous October forty-five ships of Russia's Baltic Fleet briskly sailed from the Gulf of Finland with orders to blast the Japanese out of Port Arthur. Denied entry to the Suez Canal by Britain, the fleet had to make an arduous journey around Africa and across the Indian Ocean. With neutral ports closed to them, Russian sailors

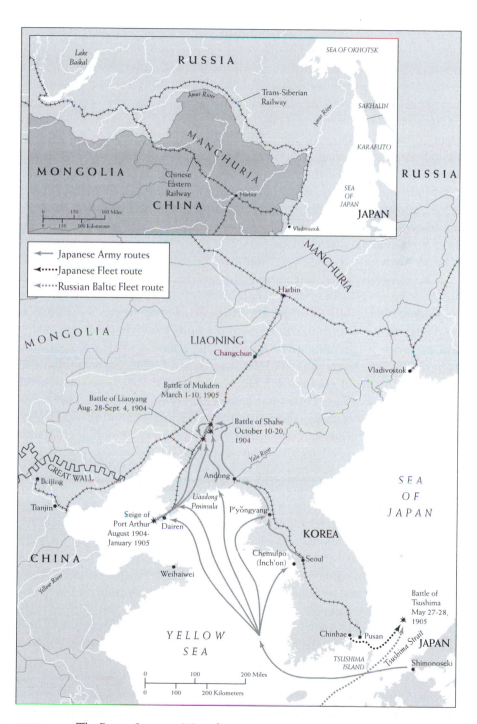

**MAP 9.3** *The Russo-Japanese War of 1904–1905*

sometimes had to fight their away ashore to seize supplies of coal, food, and water; at other times, low on morale, they passed monotonous hours on deck inciting fights among captured monkeys and dogs. Waiting patiently for their approach into Japanese waters was Admiral Tōgō's flotilla of newly commissioned battleships, swift cruisers, and darting torpedo boats—the pride of Japan's recent military buildup. Unsuspecting, the Russians entered Tsushima Strait in parallel columns on May 27, and Admiral Tōgō "crossed the T," sailing in front of their formation so as to bring the maximum firepower of Japanese cannons to bear. By the evening of the following day the Japanese Navy had annihilated the Russian fleet, sinking thirty-four ships and severely damaging eight others, while losing just three torpedo boats. The Russo-Japanese War had reached a stalemate. The emperor's armies could not hope to push the czar's battalions out of Manchuria, and Russia had no way of dislodging General Nogi from the cities and territories he had overrun.

The Japanese asked Theodore Roosevelt to mediate a settlement, and the American president convened a peace conference at Portsmouth, New Hampshire. After difficult negotiations, Japan and Russia on September 5, 1905, signed the Treaty of Portsmouth, an agreement that seemed to signify a victory for Japanese. The second clause stipulated that Russia must recognize Japan's "preponderant" interests in Korea and not oppose any measures that Japan might undertake there. Additional provisions granted Japan the Russian leasehold over the Liaodong Peninsula (which the Japanese referred to as the Kwantung Territory), the czar's railroad and mining rights in southern Manchuria, and sovereignty over the southern half of Sakhalin, to which the Japanese gave the name Karafuto. Those were generous provisions, and in the eyes of most of the world, Japan's victories at land and sea indisputably heralded its arrival as a major power.

Many ordinary Japanese viewed matters from a somewhat different perspective. They had bidden farewell to their sons at country railroad stations, contributed life savings to the nation's war chest, carried lanterns in victory celebrations, rolled bandages, and folded good-luck origami for troops at the front. Conceived in the back rooms of government, the conflict began as a coldly calculated ploy designed to improve Japan's position on the chessboard of international politics, but it became the people's war, infused with their ardor and emotional commitment. Moreover, most Japanese did not know the full story of the army's sacrifices in Manchuria. Rather, having feasted on euphoric reports about Admiral Tōgō's stunning victory at Tsushima Strait and newspaper story after sensational newspaper story about the magnificent triumphs at Port Arthur and Mukden, the average Japanese citizen had unbounded, even fantastic expectations: that Japan might lay claim to most of Russian Siberia or at least its entire Pacific coast. When its representatives to the peace conference did not acquire all Sakhalin and failed to bring home even an indemnity to offset war costs, which amounted to a staggering 1.7 billion yen, the public felt betrayed, and they erupted in riots at Hibiya and dozens of other places around Japan. The victory over Russia was Japan's first truly national war; the popular demonstrations expressed pride in the country's accomplishments and affirmed that the citizens of the country, no less so than the oligarchs, would insist that it secure for itself a position of prominence in the world.

## Colonizing Korea

When Yamagata informed the Diet in 1890 of his determination to defend Japan's line of advantage, he believed that the nation's security needs would be satisfied if Korea reformed itself and the imperialist powers jointly guaranteed the kingdom's neutrality. Following the war with China and the humiliating Triple Intervention, many policy makers adopted the more extreme view that Japan itself must be strong enough to ensure that no other nation unduly influenced affairs on the peninsula. When the collapse of negotiations with Russia dimmed the possibilities of working out a permanent solution to the "Korean problem," some took their thinking one step further: Japan needed to exert direct political dominion over Korea. Thus, not long after hostilities with Russia erupted, in a meeting convened on May 31, 1904, the cabinet decided that Japan must assume responsibility for Korea's internal stability and national security.

In the fall of 1905, Itō Hirobumi traveled to Seoul as a special envoy to implement that policy. In November he negotiated the Korean-Japanese Convention of 1905, a forced agreement that turned the peninsular country into a Japanese protectorate by providing for the establishment of the Office of the Resident General vested with the authority to dictate Korea's foreign relations and use Japanese troops to enforce domestic law and order. The following March Itō returned as the resident general, and in July 1907 he engineered the abdication of Kojong, who by then was calling himself an emperor and his country an empire in a vain attempt to bolster Korea's international prestige. Over the next few days Itō hammered out a new compact that gave comprehensive control over domestic matters to the Office of the Resident General and then disbanded the Korean Army on August 1, 1907. Endowed with considerable civil and military prerogatives, Resident General Itō and his several thousand Japanese advisers began to

*Itō Hirobumi and the Korean crown prince, 1907*

reform Korea's currency and tax structure and modernize its telegraph, telephone, and postal services.

When it convened in May 1904, the Japanese cabinet reflected on the economic as well as political and strategic advantages that would accrue from Japanese mastery over Korea. Several ministers pictured a trading strategy that would have Japanese firms import Korean foodstuffs and raw materials while selling to Koreans cotton cloth, ceramics, watches, perfume, buttons, eyeglasses, matches, kerosene lamps, and all the other products of Japan's burgeoning light industries. With those ends in mind, the Office of the Resident General extended Japanese fishing grounds into Korean coastal waters and negotiated timber concessions and mining rights that it could assign to "reliable men of capital." Similarly, the Japanese government provided generous construction subsidies and guaranteed bond issues, just as it had done domestically, to complete construction of a railroad linking Seoul with the southern port of Pusan. The new line had obvious military importance, but it also exerted a significant developmental impact since it ran through the most populous sections of Korea, opened up new markets, and brought down the cost of transporting goods.

Responding to such initiatives, more than 125,000 Japanese had taken up residence in Korea by 1908, as indicated in Table 9.1. A few were priests and teachers, and some came to seek work in the construction trades, ply their skills as artisans, or take jobs as porters and coolies with the army's quartermaster corps. Still others set up small manufacturing enterprises that produced leather goods, ceramics, and so forth, while footloose peddlers roamed the Korean countryside, selling goods at a circuit of periodic markets held on regular days in village or town centers. In Korea's cities many migrants opened restaurants, tearooms, and houses of prostitution that catered to the expatriate community and the bureaucrats who served in the Office of the Resident General.

Japanese farmers also migrated to Korea. Tokyo tried to help matters along by chartering the Oriental Development Company in August 1908. Funded partially by the government, the company offered discount train and boat fares to Korea, arranged for homestead sites (often on land confiscated from the fallen Korean court), and extended low-interest, long-term loans to get the settlers started with their new lives. One intention was to provide new opportunities for people from the poorer regions of the Japanese countryside. Another was to boast agricultural production on the peninsula. That, according to planners, would have two benefits: Larger quantities of relatively cheap Korean rice, soybeans, and other agricultural products would flow into Japan's urban centers, to the advantage of those consumers, and the increased incomes of the rural population in Korea would serve to stimulate demand for Japanese manufactured goods. The Oriental Development Company got off to a slow start, however, sending just 116 families to Korea in 1910, its first year of operation. Those settlers joined some four thousand other Japanese farmers who had made their way to the peninsula without official help and who by then owned about 3 percent of Korea's arable land.

Japanese big businesses were reluctant to establish a presence in Korea. Many industrialists worried about political instability on the peninsula, bemoaned the absence of a more fully developed infrastructure, and thought that the Chinese market offered better long-term prospects. Nevertheless, there was a steady expansion in the volume of goods exported to Korea after 1895, and entrepreneurs like Shibusawa Eiichi soon warmed to the idea of investing in Korea. In 1906 that indefatigable deal maker brokered an arrangement by which three major Osaka cotton firms (including Shibusawa's Osaka Spinning Mill) organized an export cartel, the San'ei Cotton Textiles Association, to market their products in Korea, using the Mitsui Trading Company as their sales agency and operating with discounted for-

**TABLE 9.1**  *Japanese Residents in Korea, 1908*

| OCCUPATION | NUMBER | PERCENT |
|---|---|---|
| Commerce | 47,398 | 37.6 |
| Miscellaneous | 16,815 | 13.3 |
| Officials | 15,584 | 12.4 |
| Laborers | 15,237 | 12.1 |
| Manufacturing | 11,763 | 9.3 |
| Agriculture | 4,889 | 3.9 |
| Unemployed | 4,424 | 3.5 |
| Prostitutes, entertainers | 4,253 | 3.4 |
| Fishing | 2,956 | 2.3 |
| Physicians, midwives | 1,166 | 0.9 |
| Teachers | 918 | 0.7 |
| Journalists | 379 | 0.3 |
| Priests | 278 | 0.2 |
| Legal experts | 108 | 0.1 |
| Total | 126,168 | 100.0 |

Adapted from Hilary Conroy, *The Japanese Seizure of Korea: 1868–1910: A Study of Realism and Idealism in International Relations* (Philadelphia: University of Pennsylvania Press, 1960), p. 469.

eign exchange provided by Shibusawa's Dai-Ichi Bank. The venture was successful, and Japanese cotton manufacturers went on to dominate the Korean textile market and contribute to the rapidly accelerating pace of commercial exchange, as set forth in Table 9.2.

Although some Koreans welcomed the Japanese modernization projects, others fiercely resisted what they saw as the illegitimate takeover of their government and economy. Western imperialism usually pitted a modernizing nation-state against diverse tribal groups or ethnically heterogeneous peoples who had neither the common will nor sufficient resources to rebuff their conquerors. Japan, however, had locked horns with an entirely different foe. Korea had been a unified country for almost exactly as long as its island neighbor, and the Koreans believed themselves to share an ethnicity, culture, language, and set of religious practices that predated by a thousand years or more political consolidation in the seventh century. They remembered Hideyoshi and the murder of Queen Min, and as past merged with

TABLE 9.2  *Japanese Trade with Korea, 1876–1910*

| YEAR | EXPORTS VALUE (¥1,000) | EXPORTS PERCENTAGE OF TOTAL EXPORTS | IMPORTS VALUE (¥1,000) | IMPORTS PERCENTAGE OF TOTAL IMPORTS |
|------|------|------|------|------|
| 1876 | 20 | 0.1 | 13 | 0.1 |
| 1878 | 245 | 0.9 | 205 | 0.6 |
| 1880 | 974 | 3.4 | 1,256 | 3.3 |
| 1882 | 1,587 | 4.1 | 1,202 | 3.9 |
| 1884 | 213 | 0.6 | 276 | 0.9 |
| 1886 | 829 | 1.7 | 563 | 1.8 |
| 1888 | 707 | 1.1 | 1,042 | 1.6 |
| 1890 | 1,251 | 2.2 | 4,364 | 5.3 |
| 1892 | 1,411 | 1.5 | 3,046 | 4.3 |
| 1894 | 2,365 | 2.1 | 2,183 | 1.9 |
| 1896 | 3,368 | 2.9 | 5,119 | 3.0 |
| 1898 | 5,844 | 3.6 | 4,796 | 1.8 |
| 1900 | 9,953 | 5.0 | 8,806 | 3.4 |
| 1902 | 10,554 | 4.1 | 7,958 | 2.9 |
| 1904 | 20,390 | 6.4 | 6,401 | 1.7 |
| 1906 | 25,210 | 5.9 | 8,206 | 2.0 |
| 1908 | 30,273 | 8.0 | 13,718 | 3.1 |
| 1910 | 31,450 | 6.7 | 16,902 | 3.6 |

Adapted from Peter Duus, *The Abacus and the Sword: The Japanese Penetration of Korea, 1895–1910* (Berkeley: University of California Press, 1995), p. 263.

present, they found reason to disdain the Japanese among them. "In the comparative nakedness of the women, in the noise and violence of the shop-keepers, in the litter they leave on the streets," wrote one Westerner of the Japanese he saw in Korea in the early twentieth century, "there is nothing to suggest the delicate culture of Japan."[12] Proud and obdurate, Koreans were not about to give up their country meekly to such *pieds noirs*, the "scum of the Japanese nation" according to the Western observer.

Opposition took different forms. Some Koreans, such as the several high officials who committed suicide when their country became a protectorate, simply refused to cooperate with the Japanese occupation forces. In June

1907 Emperor Kojong unsuccessfully appealed to the international community, sending a secret delegation to the Second Hague Conference on World Peace to plead for a declaration supporting Korea's independence. That same summer violence broke out on a massive scale after Itō dissolved the Korean Army and disaffected ex-soldiers began to attack the garrison forces, assault Japanese residents in Korea, and take revenge against countrymen who collaborated with the foreign regime. Itō in turn called out the Japanese Army, but Korean guerrillas, "righteous armies," as they called themselves, carried on the struggle from provincial redoubts. The fighting was ruthless, and by 1910 some eighteen thousand Koreans and another seven thousand Japanese had perished.

In the midst of that turbulence, on October 26, 1909, a young Korean patriot gunned down Itō Hirobumi, who had just relinquished the Office of the Resident General and was on an inspection tour of Manchuria, as he stepped from his train at the railway station in Harbin. In Tokyo the incident revived talk of annexation, a move that Itō himself had opposed, somehow harboring the illusion that he could marshal widespread Korean support and goodwill for Japanese modernization efforts. His assassination, however, made it clear to Japanese policy makers that "Korean officials and people," in the wry words of the foreign minister, "have not yet been brought into a satisfactory relationship to us."[13] Determined now to seize Korea outright, the Japanese drew up a treaty of annexation. Signed on August 22, 1910, and enacted just seven days later, the covenant renamed Korea Chōsen, made it into a colony of Japan, and placed total authority over civil and military matters in the Government-General of Korea, headed by a Japanese imperial appointee. Given the tense relationship between the home country and its latest possession, the emperor appointed an army man, Terauchi Masatake, to be the first governor-general, a post the ironfisted general held until he assumed the office of prime minister of Japan in October 1916.

## Japanese Imperialism

Fear and apprehension of the West made a fertile seedbed for the growth of Japanese imperialism. As young samurai Itō, Yamagata, and many other Meiji leaders watched the West reduce their country to semicolonial status, and as oligarchs they had to contend with a new round of Western intrusion into Asia that threatened to overwhelm Japan and put to ruin their modernizing efforts. Acutely aware of their country's weakness vis-à-vis the

**MAP 9.4** *The Japanese Empire in 1910*

Great Powers, Japan's government reacted defensively and justified its acquisition of empire as a countermeasure designed to preserve its national independence in a volatile and potentially lethal international environment. Frightened that it would become "meat" for the West's banquet, in the blunt words of one prominent political figure, Japan instead invited itself to be "a guest at the table."[14]

That desperate sense of vulnerability was the primary reason Japanese policy makers riveted their attention on Korea, the infamous dagger they needed to keep out of the hands of opportunistic Western powers. Similarly, the demands embedded in the Treaty of Shimonoseki that China surrender Taiwan and the Liaodong Peninsula to a large degree reflected the navy's wish to have a base to guard the southern approaches to Japan and the army's desire to expand the line of advantage to protect Korea's northern flank. The economic dimensions of Japan's expansionism in the nineteenth century were subordinate to geopolitical concerns. Specifically, the government hoped to capture economic privileges and develop commercial interests in Korea in order to buttress Japan's political and strategic position. In that regard, Japan's flag went before trade, and strategic anxieties drove its leaders to the decisions to wage war against China and Russia.

The events of 1894 and 1904, however, represented something more than a reflexlike response taken by a small nation to protect itself against an imminent threat to its existence by a larger predator. Rather, Japan's government deliberately, consciously, and knowingly chose the course of imperialism, and its expansion had an aggressive as well as a defensive cast to it. By the late 1880s its leaders were fully aware of the multiple benefits— prestige, strategic advantage, material wealth—realized by nations that projected their power abroad and claimed markets and raw materials overseas. Consequently, while Yamagata, Itō, Matsukata, and the other oligarchs did not possess a fixed ideology or master plan for expansion, they did have great ambitions for their country and did not fear to leap into the fray when opportunities presented themselves. Japan hungered to enter the circle of leading nations, and in an era when imperialism and international standing went hand in hand, there was little to inhibit its leaders from emulating the actions of the Great Powers.

Nor did Japanese negotiators sit modestly at the bargaining table. To the contrary, they expanded the definition of imperialism at Shimonoseki when they secured the right to open factories and other manufacturing establishments in China. For some time Britain had pressed hard for such a concession, and its realization, combined with the existing rights to conduct trade, exposed China to unprecedented economic exploitation. Moreover, with the exception of the Triple Intervention, when discretion presented itself as the wisest course, Japan acted assertively to preserve the bounty of war. In the late 1890s it deployed some sixty thousand troops to overcome an uprising of Taiwanese who resisted colonization, and the following decade its occupation army brutally suppressed Korean insurgents. For Japan's government, the new century and the quest for modernity included unequivocal commitments to constitutional and parliamentary government, industrialization and capitalism, and a strong and imperialistic foreign policy.

The Japanese public supported aggressive action overseas and the acquisition of empire. Men like Fukuzawa and Tokutomi helped mold the consensus behind expansionism, and ordinary Japanese rejoiced in the battles won against China, lining up to buy prints of the action. A few socialists and pacifists expressed dismay at the outbreak of hostilities with Russia, but most Japanese passionately supported their nation and favored adding Taiwan and Sakhalin to their growing empire. Such popular support made it easier for the government to opt for war and later to annex Korea, and it meant that all Japanese could derive collective satisfaction from fulfilling long-sought ambitions: security, equity, and first-class status among the leading powers of the world. For many the dawn of the new century held considerable promise.

# CHAPTER 10

# New Awakenings, New Modernities

"On the night of the Imperial Funeral," Natsume Sōseki wrote in one of his most famous novels, "I sat in my study and listened to the booming of the cannon. To me, it sounded like the last lament for the passing of an age."[1] Emperor Meiji died on July 30, 1912, and with the approach of his elaborate state obsequies, scheduled for September 13, many Japanese slipped into a pensive, almost melancholy retrospection about what his long reign had meant for the country. With the same sense of sad regret that Sōseki captured in his prose, everyone seemed to understand that an era, a grand epoch, when Japan took the first steps from tradition to modernity, was fading into history. In countless special editions, newspaper editors mourned His Majesty's final illness and in the next column tallied his accomplishments: a united people, constitutional government, industrialization, and national security—what everyone was revering as *Meiji no hokori*, the "Pride of Meiji."

On the morning of the state funeral, General Nogi Maresuke dressed in full military uniform and visited the Imperial Palace to pay his final respects to the emperor. The popular hero of the Russo-Japanese War returned home late in the afternoon and shared a simple meal with his wife, Shizuko. Just after sundown, as the booming of the cannon signaled the passage of the emperor's hearse through the palace gates, Nogi and his wife seated themselves in front of a portrait of the emperor. Beside him on the tatami Nogi placed his last will and testament. "I can no longer serve my lord," it read. "Feeling extremely distressed by his death, I have resolved to end my life."[2] The general then took his sword and disemboweled himself, while Shizuko plunged a dagger into her heart.

The couple's act of *junshi*—the venerated, yet seldom practiced and long since outlawed samurai custom of following one's master to death—stunned the nation. To most Japanese, the suicides cruelly violated their sense of modernity. "I had almost forgotten," wrote Sōseki, "that there was such a word as *junshi*." That one of the most illustrious symbols of an age should choose to die in such a quixotic, now unimaginable manner suggested another thought: Not only had the Meiji era passed, but it already had become an anachronism. As people moved beyond the grief of the moment in the late summer and early fall of 1912, they realized that the Pride of Meiji, the great first steps in nation building, had been completed earlier, in the 1890s. It was time to put aside nostalgia for the past and explore the promise of the new century.

On the afternoon of Emperor Meiji's death in 1912, his son assumed the throne as the Taishō emperor, only to live in a world of shadows until he succumbed to the effects of mental illness in 1926. Although the Taishō reign was short and clouded by the emperor's infirmities, the concept of a Taishō era has come to express a more optimistic mood and buoyant spirit that pervaded Japan from the conclusion of the Russo-Japanese War of 1904–1905 until the Great Depression at the end of the 1920s. During those two and a half decades, many Japanese felt they were living in qualitatively new times and awoke to the possibility of crafting fresh political and social conventions that built upon the Pride of Meiji.

Ultimately the quest for new modernities took many directions, but Nitobe Inazō pointed toward one widely preferred destination when he urged his fellow Japanese to become cosmopolitan "world citizens." A convert to Quakerism who had studied in the United States and Germany, married an American, and published several famous books interpreting Japanese society, Nitobe implored his countrymen to abandon a stubborn fondness for the particularistic ethics of the past. Instead, he argued, the Japanese had to visualize themselves as possessing attitudes, values, and behaviors that were the common property of all peoples who made up the emerging democratic and capitalist world order. Japan, in short, should become part of a global community, a "province of the world," to use another Taishō phrase, where even persons like Henrik Ibsen and Leo Tolstoy were "no longer foreigners."[3]

## Party Politicians Challenge the Oligarchs

The Constitution of the Empire of Japan, promulgated on February 11, 1889, created a tripartite division of power and responsibility. As drafted by Itō Hirobumi, that fundamental law of the land placed the emperor at the apex of the governing structure by identifying him as the locus of sovereignty and granting him the authority to appoint ministers of state, declare war, and conclude treaties. Although Itō and his fellow oligarchs intended the emperor to serve as head of state, they wished to delegate the actual management of political affairs to the premier and cabinet. In Itō's vision, the ministers would be wise and prudent men dedicated to acting in the enlightened interest of the nation as a whole when deliberating upon the major decisions that determined the country's fate. At the same time, the framers of the constitution felt the need to allow some degree of citizen involvement in order to harness the loyalties and energies of the people behind the state. To that end, the constitution provided for a popularly elected House of Representatives endowed with powers to introduce legislation and participate in the budgeting process.

Even with the new constitution in place, the Meiji oligarchs labored mightily to coordinate the formulation of national policy during the 1890s. As men who had risked all to topple the Tokugawa shogunate and struggled to found the modern Japanese state, it was natural that Itō and his colleagues would try to remain at the center of the nation's political life. In furtherance of that objective, they invented a particular extraconstitutional practice that permitted them to monopolize the premiership and dictate the composition of the cabinet. After promulgating the constitution, the emperor began to designate certain experienced leaders as *genrō*, "elder statesmen" who could advise him about political matters, including the appointment of state ministers. The first two Meiji leaders named elder statesmen were Itō and Kuroda Kiyotaka, in 1889, and Matsukata Masayoshi and Yamagata Aritomo headed a small group of other prominent individuals who received the honor soon thereafter. Informal advisers to the throne, the *genrō* simply nominated one another to lead the nation; in the decade following the promulgation of the constitution in February 1889, Itō, Kuroda, Matsukata, and Yamagata essentially took turns serving as prime minister. In addition, the oligarchs and their supporters claimed many important cabinet posts: Matsukata acted as Yamagata's finance minister, Yamagata as Kuroda's home minister, Kuroda as Itō's communications minister, and so forth.

Many Japanese, however, expected the convocation of the First Diet in November 1890 to mark the dawn of a new era in Japanese politics. Out-

**TABLE 10.1**  *Japanese Prime Ministers, 1885–1901*

| PRIME MINISTER | CABINET NUMBER | CABINET TERM |
|---|---|---|
| Itō Hirobumi | First | December 22, 1885–April 30, 1888 |
| Kuroda Kiyotaka | | April 30, 1888–December 24, 1889 |
| Yamagata Aritomo | First | December 24, 1889–May 6, 1891 |
| Matsukata Masayoshi | First | May 6, 1891–August 8, 1892 |
| Itō Hirobumi | Second | August 8, 1892–September 18, 1896 |
| Matsukata Masayoshi | Second | September 18, 1896–January 12, 1898 |
| Itō Hirobumi | Third | January 12, 1898–June 30, 1898 |
| Ōkuma Shigenobu | First | June 30, 1898–November 8, 1898 |
| Yamagata Aritomo | Second | November 8, 1898–October 19, 1900 |
| Itō Hirobumi | Fourth | October 19, 1900–June 2, 1901 |

spoken journalists voiced disappointment that the concentration of power in the hands of a self-appointed cabinet merely perpetuated rule by the same handful of familiar insiders. The reading public concurred; in the 1899 poll conducted by the magazine *Taiyō* to identify popular and respected national figures, no oligarch came anywhere close to matching the number of votes garnered by Fukuchi Gen'ichirō ("journalist"), Shibusawa Eiichi ("business-man"), or Fukuzawa Yukichi ("educator"). Within the political arena itself, tested veterans of the Popular Rights Movement took to task the cabinets of the 1890s for lacking an ideological commitment to liberal democratic principles. Anointing themselves "champions of the people," such men as Itagaki Taisuke and Ōkuma Shigenobu, who earlier had opposed what they called clique government, formed political parties to contend for seats in the Diet. Persistently and patiently, party politicians assaulted the corridors of power; eventually they wrestled the reins of government from the hands of the oligarchs and their protégés and during the Taishō period inaugurated an era of party government when the heads of major political parties routinely served as prime minister and named their own cabinets.

The battle for control of the nation's political destiny began in earnest on July 1, 1890, when Japanese voters went to the polls for the first time to elect 300 men to serve in the House of Representatives. The results heartened supporters of the "popular parties," for politicians associated with Ōkuma's Kaishintō and Itagaki's Rikken Jiyūtō, founded officially the following March, together captured a majority of 171 seats. Once the Diet

*Convocation of the First Diet in 1890*

convened, it did not take the party politicians long to locate the levers of power. Time after time during the 1890s feisty Diet members took the floor to lob oratorical bombs at the ministers and denounce the government's domestic policies. In the first Diet sessions Tanaka Shōzō condemned officials for tolerating an environmental disaster at Ashio, while other party politicians blasted a succession of prime ministers for "failing" to accomplish treaty revision, perhaps the most emotional issue of the early 1890s, and paraded such slogans as "Relief for the People" while castigating oligarchic cabinets for proposing tax increases.

The representatives' most puissant weapon was their constitutional right to sit in judgment on the government's annual budgets. Sensing that they had discovered the prime minister's vulnerable Achilles' heel, party politicians quickly drew their knives: In the very first Diet, representatives called

**FIGURE 10.1** *Mainstream Political Parties, 1890–1932*

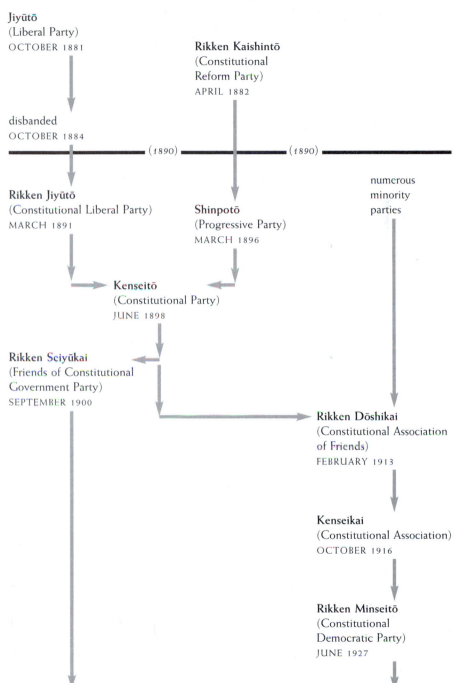

for an 11 percent reduction in the budget submitted by the cabinet, and they made similar demands in nearly every subsequent Diet session. According to the constitution, whenever the Diet disapproved a proposed budget, a cabinet could carry over the previous year's level of appropriations. No prime minister, however, wished to exercise that option in a decade when international tensions were mounting and national security demanded annual increases on expenditures for armaments. Consequently, almost every year the oligarchic prime ministers had to swallow some budget cuts and strike deals on legislative proposals in order to preserve the core of their appropriations requests.

The bitter parliamentary struggles of the early 1890s fed the antiparty biases of many *genrō*, who condemned "partisan" politicians for "blindly" advancing their own "narrow, self-serving agendas" and for behaving in "divisive ways" that made it "impossible" for the prime minister and his cabinet to rule effectively. Not satisfied just with returning verbal tit for tat, some oligarchs sought out more sophisticated means to limit party influence. As early as February 12, 1889, the afternoon after the emperor personally handed him the constitution, Prime Minister Kuroda pledged his support for "transcendental" cabinets that would exclude party members from office. Since the government was a servant of the sovereign emperor, not of the people, Kuroda explained, it was imperative to appoint men of national stature as state ministers so that cabinets could "always steadfastly transcend and stand apart from the political parties, and thus follow the path of righteousness."[4]

Despite Kuroda's tough rhetorical stance, the oligarchs eventually had to rethink their attitudes toward political parties. For one thing, in election after election voters returned a majority of party members to the lower house. Philosophical concerns also carried some weight. Despite their deep antipathy for party politicians, ultimately the *genrō* did not wish to derail the experiment with constitutional, parliamentary government. To do so would make waste of the long and frequently painful effort to create a modern political system, cause irreparable harm to Japan's international reputation, and probably doom its attempts to complete revision of the unequal treaties. Itō, for one, warned that even "one mistake in the progress and direction" of establishing a parliamentary system would earn the censure of those Westerners who already "question the suitability of constitutional government for the Orient."[5]

During the war years 1894–1895, patriotism provided for an unusual interlude of cooperation and harmony between the entrenched oligarchs and obstreperous party politicians. As divided as the Japanese might be over domestic issues, everyone felt the need to pull together during a period of national danger, and the Diet promptly passed war budgets in full and other-wise supported the cabinet. The experience of working together for the common good apparently made compromise seem a more acceptable pos-sibility to many *genrō* and party politicians. From the oligarchs' perspective, an entente promised to garner greater legislative support for their programs and improve the likelihood that the constitutional experiment would suc-ceed. For party politicians, conciliation offered the chance to step into cab-inet positions and exert greater influence over policy making and budget deliberations.

The initial steps in the rapprochement came in 1896. In April, Itō aban-doned the principle of transcendentalism and named Itagaki Taisuke, the Rikken Jiyūtō's president, to be his home minister; that fall, Matsukata tapped as his foreign minister Ōkuma Shigenobu, president of the Shinpotō polit-ical party. Two years after that, in 1898, Itagaki and Ōkuma merged their organizations into the Kenseitō, the Constitutional Party. Certain that the new entity would win a decisive majority in the House of Representatives in the forthcoming election, the *genrō* decided to nominate Ōkuma as prime minister. Although his cabinet, formed at the end of June 1898, soon fell victim to internal bickering over the distribution of ministerial posts and did not conduct a single Diet session, Ōkuma is remembered as the first leader of a political party to be named prime minister.

## Mainstream Parties, the Political Crowd, and Party Cabinets

The rise of the Kenseitō reaffirmed a notion that Itō had been espousing for some time: Oligarchic prime ministers routinely should include party politicians in their cabinets. The parties after all had succeeded in en-trenching themselves in the Diet, Itō reasoned, and the Meiji constitution also had entrusted the civil bureaucracy and military services with impor-tant functions: The cabinet relied on bureaucrats to help write and imple-ment legislation, and the army and the navy protected the country. According to Itō's calculations, a multiplicity of political elites deserved to participate in the policy-making process, and a prime minister could gov-ern successfully only if he built a broad basis of support by forming so-called national unity cabinets that included a mix of party members, civil bureau-crats, and military officials.

Moreover, Itō emphatically believed that the time had arrived for him to form his own political party. In addition to having a supportive and well-organized cabinet, to be truly effectual a prime minister needed to earn the goodwill of the House of Representatives. Ideally, a progovernment party sympathetic to the oligarchs could control the House, assure that the Diet answered to national rather than partisan interests, and provide responsible politicians to serve in a national unity cabinet. Amid much fanfare, in September 1900 Itō announced that 111 members of the Kenseitō were joining him to found the Rikken Seiyūkai. Throwing in with the new party were another 41 individuals, mostly from bureaucratic backgrounds.

The Seiyūkai, to use the party's shortened and common name, soon claimed a place for itself on the national political stage. Itō continued as party president until 1903, when he left to promote Japan's interests in Korea and meet his fate at the train station in Harbin. Replacing the venerable oligarch as new head of the Seiyūkai was Itō's faithful protégé, the court noble Saionji Kinmochi, who earlier had served successively in his mentor's cabinets as minister of foreign affairs, education, and finance. Saionji's chief lieutenant in party affairs was Hara Takashi, a former journalist and member of the Ministry of Foreign Affairs. A man frequently chastised for pairing razor-sharp political instincts with a rusty sense of ethics, the hard-driving Hara dedicated his very being to increasing the Seiyūkai's influence. To win voters to the new party, he dipped deep into the pork barrel, promising schools, roads and bridges, harbor improvements, and railroad lines to districts that elected Seiyūkai candidates. Under his direction, the party also cultivated the goodwill of prefectural governors. Those officials oversaw the disbursement of prefectural tax revenues, a rich source of local economic largess, and supervised the prefectural police, who could be mobilized to harass opposition candidates even while burying allegations, often accurate, that Seiyūkai campaign workers stuffed ballot boxes or falsified election returns. Hara also cuddled up to big business, whose contributions helped cover the legitimate costs of electioneering as well as the practice of paying off election brokers, men who bought and sold blocs of votes in local precincts. Those tactics invited considerable public criticism, but they were effective: From 1908 to 1915 the Seiyūkai held an absolute majority of seats in the lower house.

Yamagata, who never would soften his rocklike contempt for politicians, organized a counterattack against the Seiyūkai. When Itō announced the formation of his new party in 1900, Yamagata mobilized a network of sympathetic allies in the armed services, civil bureaucracy, and House of Peers to support the appointment of his own protégé, Katsura Tarō, as prime minister. Nine years younger than Yamagata, Katsura had been born in the same hometown in Chōshū domain. While still in his teens, Katsura fought valiantly

**TABLE 10.2** *Japanese Prime Ministers, 1901–1918*

| PRIME MINISTER | CABINET NUMBER | CABINET TERM |
|---|---|---|
| Katsura Tarō | First | June 2, 1901–January 7, 1906 |
| Saionji Kinmochi | First | January 7, 1906–July 14, 1908 |
| Katsura Tarō | Second | July 14, 1908–August 30, 1911 |
| Saionji Kinmochi | Second | August 30, 1911–December 21, 1912 |
| Katsura Tarō | Third | December 21, 1912–February 20, 1913 |
| Yamamoto Gonnohyōe | First | February 20, 1913–April 16, 1914 |
| Ōkuma Shigenobu | Second | April 16, 1914–October 9, 1916 |
| Terauchi Masatake | | October 9, 1916–September 29, 1918 |

against the Tokugawa shogunate, and he rose to the rank of general in the modern army fathered by Yamagata. After commanding a division in the Sino-Japanese War, Katsura became the army minister in Yamagata's second cabinet. As prime minister from 1901 to 1906 Katsura successfully guided Japan through the war with Russia.

Despite his stature and considerable accomplishments, Katsura eventually had to compromise with the growing strength of the Seiyūkai, a process that led him to found Japan's second major political party. In return for Seiyūkai support during the Russo-Japanese War, Katsura acquiesced in the appointment of Saionji as his successor, and the two alternated as prime minister until 1913. In the end, however, Katsura grew intolerant of having to share power with Saionji, and after being appointed to head his third cabinet, the ex-general announced early in February 1913 that he would form his own political party. Almost immediately many adherents of several minority parties, themselves frustrated at the success of the rival Seiyūkai, flocked to his banner. Although Katsura gave up the premiership on February 20, 1913, and died of cancer a few months thereafter, his party, the Rikken Dōshikai (renamed the Kenseikai in 1916 and the Rikken Minseitō in 1927), survived and flourished.

The emergence of two strong mainstream parties paved the way for the realization of party government in Japan. More immediately, the rice riots of 1918 provided the catalyst that sparked the shift to party cabinets. Between 1914 and 1919 wartime inflation relentlessly drove up the retail prices of most consumer goods while the earnings of many lower- and even middle-income households inched upward only modestly. When rice prices exploded in 1918, leaping by 60 percent in some cities in July alone, irate consumers took matters into their own hands. The unrest began on July 23, when women in a small fishing hamlet in Toyama Prefecture mounted a protest against the cost of local rice; spread like wildfire to Osaka, Kōbe, Nagoya, and other industrial centers in western Japan; and engulfed nearly five hundred towns and villages before dying out in mid-September. Everywhere, it seemed, angry citizens were listening to speeches, joining nonviolent sit-ins and marches, forcing rice dealers to sell their stocks at a discounted "fair price," and clashing with police and the army in full-scale street battles. In all, the summer of 1918 constituted the largest mass demonstration in modern Japanese history, as a million or more people took to the streets.

Although the scale of protest in 1918 was unprecedented, the political crowd long had been a part of Japanese history. In the early modern period, peasants and urban commoners wrote petitions, assembled in front of office compounds of daimyo officials, and occasionally rioted to protest unreasonable rice prices and government polices that affected them adversely. The constitution of 1889 changed Japan's political culture by providing for popular participation in the legislative process. Nevertheless, the election laws enfranchised only males aged twenty-five and over who paid fifteen yen or more in direct national taxes. Accordingly, only 450,000 men, approximately 1.1 percent of the total population, could vote in 1890, and while the tax requirement was reduced to ten yen in 1902, just 1.5 million men, or 2.5 percent of the population, were eligible to vote in the parliamentary elections held in 1917. As a consequence, people without the vote participated in numerous contentious actions during the Meiji and Taishō periods, marching from Ashio to Tokyo in 1897 and gathering at Hibiya Park in 1905, in order both to criticize government policies and to demand a greater political voice in deciding the future of their region and nation.

The crowds fought similar parallel campaigns in the summer of 1918. On one front, hard-pressed consumers demanded that local officials and the cabinet of Prime Minister Terauchi Masatake mandate cheaper rice prices, release government reserves from warehouses, import more from the colonies—do whatever was necessary to reduce the price of grain and other basic commodities. In complementary fashion, the demonstrators called for new leadership and expanded rights for themselves. "We are citizens," shouted one demonstrator in Nagoya, and after laying the blame for the summer of discontent on the "worthlessness of the present cabinet," he concluded that "the present government must be brought down."[6] Echoed another Nagoyan: "The soaring price of rice is a crime perpetrated by the Terauchi cabinet. It is a matter of utmost urgency that we act as soon as possible to topple this government that has violated the will of the people." Such injunctions were rooted in an age-old notion—the fundamental concern of government should be the welfare of the people—and further implied that popular opinion must infuse the decision-making process. "How about universal suffrage?" asked one newspaper that covered events. "This, too, is something the people's hearts desire. To put the matter simply, the recent unrest springs from 'the unequal distribution of power and wealth.' A 'fair distribution' is what the public really longs for."

The protesters provoked a mixed reaction from the cabinet. As was the case at Chichibu in 1884 and Hibiya in 1905, an oligarchic government did not flinch from taking drastic action. To supplement local police, Prime Minister Terauchi, a former general and a protégé of Yamagata Aritomo's, called out the army and navy in the summer of 1918, mobilizing nearly 100,000 troops to suppress disturbances in 120 localities in twenty-six different prefectures. Often the mere presence of armed infantry persuaded rioters to stay behind their street barricades, but when the soldiers and marines felt threatened, they sometimes turned their rifles and machine guns against protesters who had only stones, clubs, and bamboo spears for weapons. No troops were killed in the skirmishes, but by the time the riots ended in September, 30 civilians were dead and scores more had been wounded. Across Japan, police herded dissidents into jail, and courts swiftly delivered assembly-line justice. In Tokyo one judge settled fifty cases in a single afternoon, and everywhere magistrates had concluded most proceedings by year's end. In all, more than 5,000 individuals were found guilty of various crimes and given stiff sentences. Most went to jail, some for life, and even relatively minor offenses, such as accepting rice that demonstrators had forced merchants to sell at a discount, merited a heavy fine or imprisonment, depending on the predilections of the judge.

On the other side of the ledger, officials acceded to many of the demands issued by the people in the street. In mid-August the central government announced that the Taishō emperor, deeply concerned about the welfare of his subjects, had personally donated three million yen to establish a national relief fund; the cabinet added ten million yen to that; and by the end of the month contributions of one million yen each from the Mitsubishi and Mitsui *zaibatsu* had brought the fund's total to fifteen million yen. In addition, the government stepped up imports of inexpensive rice from Korea and Taiwan, funded a plan to increase cultivated acreage in Japan, financed the construction of additional granaries to hold food reserves, and enacted new laws regulating commodity trading so as to reduce the possibility of inflationary price bubbles.

The protesters' most momentous achievement came on September 29, 1918, when Hara Takashi, president of the Seiyūkai, succeeded Terauchi Masatake as prime minister. In handing the reins of government to the president of an established political party, the emperor and his advisers merely intended to quiet demonstrators who had voiced their derision for an oligarchic cabinet. For most observers, however, Hara's appointment had a larger meaning: It marked the advent of party government since his cabinet was the first to be headed by an elected member of the majority party in the lower house, have the majority of ministerial posts filled by party members, and govern when the Diet was in session. Situated in a broader historical context, some commentators noted, the shift from national unity to party cabinets was not just the consequence of the rioting in 1918 but, rather, represented the culmination of a long struggle for party government begun by participants in the Popular Rights Movement and carried to completion by the political crowd.

## Taishō Democracy and Liberalism

When he visited Japan in 1915, Thorstein Veblen reminded everyone of a theme dear to his heart: The introduction of science and industry in Europe and America had given rise there to analogous cultural values and parallel political arrangements, especially in countries like Britain and the United States. Moreover, Veblen claimed to see an "intellectual similarity" and "psychological equivalence" between Japanese and Westerners.[7] Consequently, he predicted, as Japan became more modern, its citizens would turn their backs on the "Spirit of Old Japan" and embrace the "ideals, ethical values, and principles" that pervaded the advanced nations of the globe. In turn, the foundation of comparable values would support a superstructure of political institutions similar to those found in Europe and North America. Visiting Japan four years later, John Dewey was even more effusive. "Liberalism," he wrote for the *New Republic*, "is in the air."[8] Democracy had been putting down roots for some time, Dewey explained to his American readers, and it would become established permanently when Japan routinely made cabinets responsible "to the Parliament instead of to the Emperor." Dewey had no doubt that such would happen. Hara's appointment signaled that "Japan will move steadily towards democracy," he concluded, and "the change will come without a bloody and catastrophic upheaval."

Dewey misjudged the significance of violence and protest in Japanese history, but events in the 1920s made him and Veblen seem perspicacious.

Between 1922 and 1924 the emperor and his advisers retreated to the practice of naming national unity cabinets, summoning two admirals who had won distinction in the Russo-Japanese War and a former president of the Privy Council to head administrations that consisted chiefly of career bureaucrats and aristocrats serving in the House of Peers. The reversion to nonparty cabinets angered many Japanese, however, and they mounted a nationwide protest movement "to protect constitutional government." When the Kenseikai and Seiyūkai captured nearly all the Diet seats in elections held in the spring of 1924, the *genrō* saw little choice but to acquiesce to the appointment of Katō Takaaki, head of the majority Kenseikai, as prime minister. Thereupon, it became the accepted practice for the emperor to

**TABLE 10.3** *Japanese Prime Ministers, 1918–1932*

| PRIME MINISTER | PARTY AFFILIATION | CABINET NUMBER | CABINET TERM |
|---|---|---|---|
| Hara Takashi | S | | September 29, 1918–November 13, 1921 |
| Takahashi Korekiyo | S | | November 13, 1921–June 12, 1922 |
| Katō Tomosaburō | | | June 12, 1922–September 2, 1923 |
| Yamamoto Gonnohyōe | | Second | September 2, 1923–January 7, 1924 |
| Kiyoura Keigo | | | January 7, 1924–June 11, 1924 |
| Katō Takaaki | K | First | June 11, 1924–August 2, 1925 |
| Katō Takaaki | K | Second | August 2, 1925–January 30, 1926 |
| Wakatsuki Reijirō | K | First | January 30, 1926–April 20, 1927 |
| Tanaka Giichi | S | | April 20, 1927–July 2, 1929 |
| Hamaguchi Osachi | M | | July 2, 1929–April 14, 1931 |
| Wakatsuki Reijirō | M | Second | April 14, 1931–December 13, 1931 |
| Inukai Tsuyoshi | S | | December 13, 1931–May 16, 1932 |

S denotes Seiyūkai affiliation.
K denotes Kenseikai affiliation.
M denotes Minseitō affiliation.

tap the head of the leading party or majority coalition in the House of Representatives to serve as prime minister and name a cabinet. Between 1924 and 1932 six different men served as prime minister. Each was the president of the Seiyūkai or the Kenseikai–Minseitō, and party members generally held the most important ministerial portfolios.

Although some critics dismissed Katō as a political dilettante who merely had the good fortune to marry the eldest daughter of the founder of the Mitsubishi financial empire, his admirers applauded him as a zealous, hardworking advocate for party government. However one chose to view the former diplomat, it is clear that when he called his first cabinet meeting to order in June 1924, Katō was presiding over another notable moment in Japanese political history: the routinization of party government. Between the convocation of the First Diet in 1890 and the mid-1920s, power slipped away from the oligarchs and their protégés and into the grasp of party politicians. A number of transition points marked that evolutionary process: the compromises between the oligarchs and parties in the latter half of the 1890s; the establishment of the Seiyūkai in 1900 and the Dōshikai in 1913; the appointment of a dyed-in-the-wool politician, Hara Takashi, to head a party cabinet following the rice riots of 1918; and finally the understanding, expressed in Katō's appointment, that political parties as a matter of course could expect to name one of their own as prime minister, to occupy most cabinet seats, and to exert a preponderant role in the formulation of national policy. In the minds of nearly everyone, an era of party government had arrived, and people spoke openly about the flowering of "Taishō democracy."

No constitutional amendments had to be enacted or new political institutions created for that transition to take place. Rather, the pliable nature of the Meiji constitution itself tolerated shifts in the center of political gravity and allowed for a variety of relationships to exist among governing elites. For that reason, party politicians could exploit differences among the *genrō* and their lieutenants, with the ironic consequence that Itō Hirobumi and Katsura Tarō, two men with distinctly ambivalent feelings about politicians, founded Japan's two major parties. Despite those elitist origins, true politicians with new ways of thinking eventually moved into the presidencies of those two parties. In contrast with Kuroda Kiyotaka, the *genrō* who saw the cabinet as the servant of the throne, party leaders such as Katō Takaaki believed that ministers should be answerable to the people and rightfully ought to be chosen from the elected representatives in the lower house of the Diet.

Most liberal commentators in Japan welcomed the arrival of party government. Persons who identified themselves as being on the political left were an intellectually diverse lot and often differed among themselves on specific issues. In general, however, they upheld the dignity of the individual, prized freedom of expression, advocated the equality of the sexes, and welcomed greater popular participation in politics and in the creation of cultural norms. As a group they did not wish to repudiate the Meiji constitution, but in the 1910s and 1920s most did favor modification of political institutions and practices so as to permit the liberal vision of modernity to prevail.

Perhaps the most formidable advocate of liberalism and parliamentary democracy in Japan during the Taishō years was Yoshino Sakuzō, a university professor and tireless contributor to leading journals of the day. Yoshino shared an intellectual bloodline with those who earlier had argued that the ultimate purpose of the Meiji Restoration was to advance the well-being of the people. Since government existed to promote the welfare of the general populace, Yoshino reasoned, the people themselves ought to be the primary judges of whether government was functioning in a responsible manner. His faith in what he called *minpon shugi* ("democracy based upon the people") led him to cast an uneasy eye on the Seiyūkai and Kenseikai since he considered the leaders of those parties "narrow-minded" elitists who did not pay sufficient heed to the conscience of the people.[9] Nevertheless, in his estimation, popular elections and cabinets held accountable to the Diet constituted the mechanisms that permitted ordinary people to shape their own political destinies. Yoshino's ideas also reconciled the appearance of democratic, parliamentary practices with a constitution that lodged sovereignty in a semidivine emperor, thus making it possible for Japanese to honor their own imperial tradition while participating in an "inevitable world trend," the emergence of a circle of advanced nations bound together by the "spirit of democracy."

The Taishō period also witnessed the formulation of an organ theory of government that legitimated the emergence of party cabinets in Japan. The most influential proponent of that line of constitutional interpretation was Minobe Tatsukichi, a professor at Tokyo University. In his *Kenpō satsuyō* ("Outline of the Constitution," 1923), Minobe argued that the state was a legal person composed of separate institutions, or organs: the emperor, cabinet, Diet, bureaucracy, and so forth. While stressing that each organ had to function properly to keep the Japanese body politic healthy, Minobe attributed especially vital roles to the emperor, as "the bearer in his person of the state's sovereignty," and to the Diet, because it "expressed the highest will of the state."[10] The emperor and Diet, however, were separate from each other. Consequently, the Diet did not depend upon the emperor for its power but existed as "an organ representative of the people," an interpretative nuance that sanctioned cabinets composed of elected representatives. The constitution had not specifically provided for such a development, Minobe conceded. Nevertheless, he suggested favorably, the events of the new century had made party government the "customary practice" in Japan, just as it was in Britain.

The political agenda advanced by the Kenseikai–Minseitō party further sharpened the perception that Japan was awakening to the dawning of liberalism. In comparison to the Seiyūkai, which during the Taishō period earned a reputation for combining a conservative social orientation with a tough-nosed stance on foreign policy issues and generous funding for the military, the Kenseikai–Minseitō leaders tended to keep close watch over the purse strings, favored government intervention to help solve social problems, and advocated cooperating with the Great Powers to police the international scene. The contrast between the two parties reached a peak in the 1920s when the Katō and Wakatsuki cabinets cut military budgets, presided over the implementation of universal manhood suffrage, and drafted legislation designed to guarantee a minimal level of social security. Not all bills found their way into law, but Kenseikai–Minseitō proposals to set minimum wage levels, strengthen factory laws that protected women and children, provide unemployment insurance, expand a health insurance program for workers, boost pensions for retired civil servants and military personnel, and weave a safety net for the aged, disabled, and mothers with dependent children encouraged favorable comparisons with the democratic states of the West and lent credence to Dewey's observation that liberalism was filling the air.

## Cooperative Imperialism

Japan completed its acquisition of empire during World War I and then collaborated with the Euro-American powers to preserve its place in the ranks of leading imperialist nations. When hostilities broke out in Europe in the summer of 1914, Japan honored its commitments under the terms of the Anglo-Japanese Alliance and entered the conflict on the Allied side. On August 17 Japan's foreign minister sent an ultimatum to Berlin announcing his county's intentions and, in a subtle purgation of long-repressed bitterness, inserted into the text some of the exact phrases and language that the Germans had employed when they joined the Triple Intervention against Japan

**MAP 10.1** *The Japanese Empire in 1922*

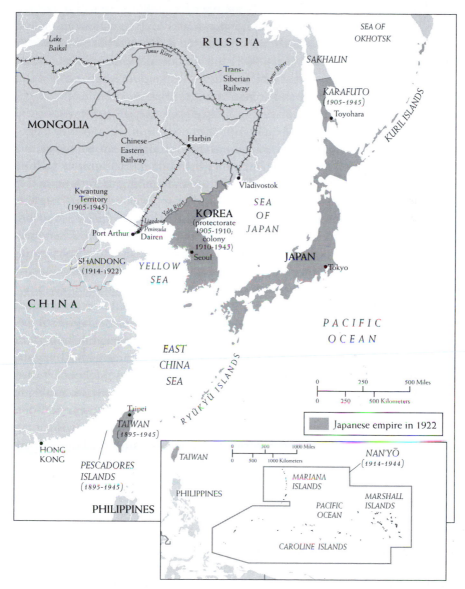

in 1895. The emperor officially proclaimed his nation's entry into World War I on August 23, 1914, and by November Japanese forces had seized the German leasehold in China's strategic Shandong Province, which jutted into the Yellow Sea south of Manchuria, and moved against German holdings in the Caroline, Mariana, and Marshall island groups in Micronesia.

The Japanese government also expressed its lingering imperialistic impulses in the infamous Twenty-one Demands, presented to Chinese authorities on January 18, 1915. The proposals were sorted into five clusters, and in the eyes of the Japanese cabinet, the first four merely ratified or extended existing privileges by confirming Japan's inheritance of Germany's rights in Shandong, disallowing further cessions of the Chinese coast to a third power, and extending until the end of the century Japan's leasehold in Manchuria, won in the Russo-Japanese War and due to expire in 1923. The fifth set, which the Japanese government delicately labeled "desires" rather than "demands," moved in a radically different direction. Those articles called on China to employ Japanese political, financial, and military advisers, a measure that would have turned the country into a virtual Japanese protectorate. An outraged Chinese public responded by boycotting Japanese goods, and even Japan's new American ally condemned its actions. Japanese negotiators diplomatically dropped the objectionable "desires" but pressured the Chinese government into accepting the remaining demands in a series of notes and treaties signed on May 25, 1915, which China was to remember as a day of national humiliation.

In Europe the numbing, unprecedented carnage and destruction of World War I came to an end in November 1918, and the following spring leaders of the major powers gathered in Paris to sign peace agreements and formulate plans to ensure a more stable world. Many analysts attributed the primary cause of "the war to end all wars" to the unbridled, near-maniacal rivalry for overseas possessions as well as to the proliferation of bilateral treaties, often concluded in secret, that had divided nations into opposing camps whose competing interests, in retrospect, seemed to make armed conflict almost inevitable. To promote future stability, American and British peacemakers argued, countries had to restrain their imperialistic instincts and enter into multinational agreements designed to preserve a balance among everyone's interests. The most articulate advocate for the new world order was the American president Woodrow Wilson, who called for the creation of a League of Nations as a capstone organization that would represent all nations equally and see to it that none fell victim to another's aggression.

In Asia the focus of Wilsonian internationalism was China, the hotbed of imperialistic ambitions, and in the autumn of 1921 the United States invited interested powers to Washington to plan a new order for the Pacific region. Japan's plenipotentiary to the Washington Conference was Shidehara Kijūrō, a career diplomat who had arrived in Washington in 1919 as Japan's ambassador and later returned home to serve as minister of foreign affairs from 1924 to 1927 and 1929 to 1931 in a succession of Kenseikai–Minseitō cabinets. Shidehara was committed to keeping the empire intact. At the same time, he firmly believed that Japan's future hinged on its ability to fulfill its economic potential as an industrial power and become a prosperous trading nation. In his vision, peace and stability in northern Asia, and particularly in China, offered the best opportunity for Japanese businesses to exploit the economic privileges his country had acquired when it signed treaties at Shimonoseki and Portsmouth.

Discussions in Washington reaffirmed other judgments that Shidehara had been formulating. To his way of thinking, Japan could not afford to isolate itself from the advanced nations of the world, especially Great Britain and the United States. Two decades earlier, the Triple Intervention had taught Japan a difficult lesson about what happened to countries that had no friends. In that context, contributing troops to the international expeditionary force that put down the Boxer Rebellion in 1900 and signing the Anglo-Japanese Alliance of 1902 constituted promising first steps toward building bridges to the West, and now the Washington Conference presented an opportunity for Japan to enter into a fuller collaborative relationship with the Euro-American powers. Furthermore, Shidehara accepted the proposition that the elimination of imperialistic competition for territory and exclusive spheres of influence, as envisaged by Wilson, would create a favorable environment for Japanese economic expansion. Consequently, Shidehara and his supporters within policy-making circles agreed that Japan had to move away from high-handed, expansionistic policies, as represented by the Twenty-one Demands, and cooperate with Wilson's efforts to preserve peace and the status quo in China and the entire Pacific region. That goal also meant that Japan should observe the principle of nonintervention in China's domestic affairs and join the League of Nations, which first convened in November 1920.

The Washington Conference produced a series of pacts and covenants that embodied Wilson's hopes for a new diplomacy. On December 13, 1921, representatives from Japan, the United States, Great Britain, and France put their signatures to the Four-Power Treaty. That agreement provided for collective resolution of future problems in East Asia by terminating the bilateral Anglo-Japanese Alliance of 1902 and enjoining all signatories to respect one another's territorial possessions and to consult jointly whenever disagreements arose. The conference concluded on February 6, 1922, with the signing of the Washington Naval Treaty and the Nine-Power Treaty. The former (also known as the Five-Power Treaty since Italy joined with the signatories to the Four-Power Treaty) sought to strike a military balance of power in the Pacific. Among its more important provisions, the pact established a ratio of 5:5:3 for capital ships, such as aircraft carriers and battleships, in the American, British, and Japanese navies respectively and further specified that the United States and Great Britain would maintain no fortifications west of Hawaii or east of Singapore. The accord in effect gave the Japanese Navy parity in East Asian waters with fleets that the Anglo-American powers could station on the perimeter of the Pacific. Finally, the Nine-Power Treaty (which added China, Belgium, the Netherlands, and Portugal to the group that agreed to the Washington Naval Treaty) reaffirmed the principles of America's Open Door policy, first espoused in 1899 and 1900, by calling on all the powers to "respect the sovereignty, the independence and the territorial and administrative integrity of China"; to refrain from undertaking further expansion at China's expense; and to maintain "the principle of equal opportunity for the commerce and industry of all nations."[11]

From Shidehara's perspective, the orientation agreed upon during the Washington Conference carried significant benefits for his nation. In terms of prestige, Japan's inclusion within the inner circle at Paris and Washington reaffirmed its status as one of the foremost world powers. Commercially, Japanese business was in a better position to expand its presence in the growing Chinese market and pursue the development of the leasehold in southern Manchuria. Politically, Japan not only retained its existing colonial possessions but even added the sanction of multinational treaties for the rights it had obtained at Shimonoseki and Portsmouth. In addition, it received from the League of Nations a mandate to administer the former German-held islands in the Pacific, which it referred to as the Nan'yō, or South Sea territories. To show its good earnest for those arrangements, Japan withdrew its forces from Shandong Province.

## Managing the Empire

Even while assuming a prominent role in the comity of imperialist nations, Japanese had to look inward and decide how they wished to manage their empire. One of the first colonial administrators to take up that task was Gotō Shinpei, an official in the Home Ministry who was appointed the governor of Taiwan in 1898. A dedicated student of colonial theory, Gotō as-

*Nitobe Inazō*

sembled an impressive library of contemporary works that analyzed how European imperialists ran their overseas protectorates. Additionally, he gathered around him a brain trust of young, cosmopolitan advisers that included Nitobe Inazō, who had witnessed firsthand the colonization of Hokkaidō during his student days at Sapporo Agricultural College and who later served as the undersecretary-general of the League of Nations.

For Gotō and his subordinates, colonialism was a global phenomenon that conferred upon each metropolitan country a reciprocal set of prerogatives and obligations. Thus, Japan, like other imperial powers, was entitled to pursue its own self-interests in its overseas territories. Balancing that sense of privilege, however, was the responsibility to undertake the civilizing task of "lifting up" dependent peoples, a moral trust expressed in French as *mission civilisatrice*, in Portuguese as *política da atração*, and more crudely in English as the "white man's burden." To that equation, Gotō and his associates added two additional propositions: Industrial and commercial development was crucial to both aspects of Japan's colonial mission, and the policies that breathed life into the Meiji economic dream could be utilized abroad to benefit both the indigenous peoples and the home islands. Nitobe brushed an eloquent veneer over those various strains of thought when he wrote: "The highest and ultimate purpose of colonialism is the development of the human race. If we neglect humanitarianism then our great mission will have little success."[12]

In Taiwan, Gotō committed himself to implementing his notion of a modern, enlightened colonial administration. As soon as he settled into office, he launched a coordinated effort to promote agriculture and stimulate commercial activities. Inspired by Meiji practices, the governor's staff disseminated modern farming technology, financed transportation and communication facilities, and enticed Japanese firms to invest in Taiwan by offering them such incentives as monopsony rights, low taxes, and guaranteed dividends. Such efforts boosted rice output significantly, laid the foundation for a profitable sugar industry, and doubled Taiwan's gross domestic output during the Taishō period. Simultaneously, Gotō's regime set about "lifting up" the native population. Taking a cue from colonial practices elsewhere, the governor drew up a lengthy agenda that included making elementary education more accessible; constructing hospitals, improving sanitary conditions, and sponsoring public health programs; and rebuilding Taipei into a stately European-style capital city of parks, fountains, and broad, tree-lined boulevards.

In the South Sea islands Japanese officials in the 1920s likewise focused their efforts on developmental projects when they took up the League of Nations' mandate to "promote to the utmost the material and moral well-being and social progress" of the indigenous population. As did their counterparts in Taiwan, white-uniformed colonial bureaucrats, working in cool bougainvillaea-covered cottages, zealously collected statistics and drew up plans to construct roads and harbors, open schools, and improve health and sanitation. Back in Tokyo, government officials and leading public figures encouraged emigration to the islands. Besides creating fresh opportunities for the settlers to improve their lot in life, authorities wanted the migrants to establish agricultural colonies that would send food supplies back to the mother country and simultaneously carry out the "moral imperative" of introducing modernity to the islands.

Many Japanese answered the call to move to the South Seas; by 1939 the seventy-seven thousand Japanese colonizers far outnumbered the fifty thousand indigenous residents. A few of the new arrivals fished the local waters; some became agriculturists, mainly cultivating coffee and fruit; and still others opened small general stores, purveying beneath sun-baked tin roofs a variety of Japanese goods that altered native tastes and lifestyles. Perhaps the largest contingent of emigrants eked out livings as tenant farmers and field hands for the South Seas Development Company. Formed in 1921 by a Japanese entrepreneur, the enterprise received tax subsidies, rent-free use of land, and a virtual monopoly on sugar refining from the colonial administration. So privileged, the South Seas Development Company diversified into a range of other endeavors, from phosphate mining to coconut production, and became the dominant commercial power in Micronesia.

Japanese flocked to Karafuto on the northern perimeter of the empire, and by 1926 they made up more than 90 percent of the colony's population of some 207,000. To most of the immigrants, Karafuto seemed an integral part of the home islands, the Taishō analogue to Hokkaidō of a generation earlier, which had had a similar frontier atmosphere and challenging climate. A civilian governor dispatched from Tokyo administered the colony from his residence in the newly remodeled city of Toyohara. His other chief responsibility was to coordinate efforts by Mitsui, Mitsubishi, and the Kuhara Mining Company to develop the economic potential of the colony, especially its fisheries and vast reserves of timber, coal, and oil. The lack of adequate transportation facilities handicapped the exploitation of those natural resources, but by 1925 Karafuto was supplying the home islands with more than 10 percent of their oil.

A large number of Japanese moved to Manchuria during the Taishō period. The Treaty of Portsmouth gave Japan the right to occupy the Kwantung Territory on the southern tip of the Liaodong Peninsula. In addition, Japan received authorization to operate the portion of the Russian-built Chinese Eastern Railway line that ran from Port Arthur to Changchun, which it renamed the South Manchuria Railway, and to exercise jurisdictional and administrative authority in a vaguely defined zone adjacent to the railroad tracks. To carry out those multiple responsibilities, the Japanese government on August 1, 1906, created the Kwantung Army and four months later established the South Manchuria Railway Company. A part of the Imperial Army, the former consisted of military units dispatched from Japan proper to defend the country's new rights in Manchuria. The latter was a more complex organization that functioned both as a commercial company and as an agency of the Japanese government. Funded with private and government capital, the SMR had a board of directors appointed by the cabinet in Tokyo and returned dividends to its private shareholders from the profits gained through managing the railroad line and developing the region's economic resources. At the same time, it took responsibility for municipal governance, public works, health, and education in more than one hundred cities and towns in the leased zone.

Committed to making the South Manchuria Railway Company a great colonizing force in southern Manchuria, the Japanese cabinet transferred Gotō Shinpei from Taiwan to be its first president. He pursued his new duties with typical vigor. By the end of the Taishō years the SMR had upgraded service so that express trains made the 450-mile run from Port Arthur

*The Central Plaza in Dairen, 1935*

to Changchun at an average speed of 35 miles an hour, added a spur linking Mukden with Korea, built hotels near stations along the line, encouraged soybean production for export to the world market, opened major coal
mines and ironworks, constructed electric power plants, underwrote the
start-up costs of petroleum refineries, dredged harbors, and made Dairen
into one of the Pacific's leading ports, all while investing in schools, parks,
libraries, and hospitals. The results impressed Japan's citizenry as total net
revenue generated by SMR operations jumped from two million yen in
1907–1908 to fifteen million in 1917–1918 and then thirty-four million in
1926–1927.

Economic development on such a scale made the Kwantung Territory the
most industrialized region on continental Asia. Moreover, since the Japanese who resided in the railway zone benefited most from the SMR projects,
a swelling tide of migrants from the home islands moved into the area, pushing the Japanese population of southern Manchuria from 25,000 in 1907 to
220,000 in 1930. A fraction of them were the same sort of scam artist and
failed carpetbagger that had aroused such disgust in Seoul, and a relative
handful, perhaps a thousand families or so, were honest farmers in search

of a better life. Most, however, came to work in the far-flung operations of the South Manchuria Railway Company.

In Korea, the tenacious General Terauchi Masatake and his successors as governor-general in the 1910s acted resolutely to quell dissent and build a foundation for stable colonial rule. Immediately after annexation, Japanese authorities banned all political associations, replaced private newspapers with a single government publication, and removed Korean history texts and biographies of illustrious Koreans from libraries and schools. To enforce its laws, the Government-General replaced Korean police with Japanese military gendarmes and authorized them to conduct "administrative trials" that were not subject to higher judicial review. In 1916 alone, the military police pronounced nearly eighty thousand such summary judgments, and with a mere thirty exceptions, the gendarmerie meted out fines, jail terms, and corporal punishments, such as whipping with bamboo canes, to the Korean miscreants.

Throughout the 1910s officials within the Government-General sought to fulfill the cabinet's mandate to develop the peninsula as an outlet for goods manufactured in the home islands and as a source of cheap agricultural imports, especially after the rice riots of 1918. To make certain that indigenous businessmen did not develop industries that could compete with Japanese firms shipping goods to Korea, the Government-General late in 1910 promulgated the so-called Company Law which stipulated that all new enterprises had to be officially licensed. In subsequent years Korean entrepreneurs-to-be grew increasingly frustrated when they discovered that such authorizations were extremely difficult to obtain; between 1910 and 1918 the Government-General issued only 105 licenses, 93 of which went to Japanese-owned companies. In rural areas, life for Korean families took a decided turn for the worse after a land survey, completed in 1918, overturned nearly forty thousand undocumented claims to landownership. The Oriental Development Company and other Japanese-owned agricultural cooperatives snapped up much of the newly available land and became rapacious landlords, despised by the dispossessed Korean families, who suddenly led a very precarious existence as tenants paying rent on land that formerly had been theirs to farm.

Korean grievances against Japanese political and economic policies mounted during the 1910s, and the sudden death of the former emperor Kojong early in 1919 sparked a popular movement against colonial rule. On March 1 students in Seoul gathered at Pagoda Park to read a declaration of independence, and elsewhere in the city posters went up alleging that the Japanese had poisoned the ex-sovereign and demanding that the principle

*Koreans hanged for supporting the Samil Independence Movement*

of national self-determination, which Wilson was advocating so vigorously, be applied to Korea. In the following days similar nonviolent demonstrations erupted across the country, and in April a group led by Syngman Rhee, who was to serve as the president of the Republic of Korea from 1948 to 1960, formed a government-in-exile in Shanghai. Within Korea itself, the Samil (March First) Independence Movement, as it was called, continued for months and united well over a million Korean men and women from all walks of life in nationalistic protest against Japanese colonialism.

The Japanese government eventually decided to ameliorate its policies, but not before its gendarmerie brutally suppressed the insurgency. Showing little mercy or tolerance, the police beat and raped suspected dissidents in hundreds of Korean towns and villages, even locking protesters inside a church and burning it to the ground in one especially notorious incident. By summer's end more than fifty thousand Koreans had been incarcerated, and seven thousand others were dead. The violence of 1919 profoundly shocked many Japanese. Few wished to admit, even to themselves, that their brand of colonial rule was so harsh as to provoke widespread discontent. Furthermore, as the newest and only non-Western member of the imperialist circle some feared that the massive uprising in Korea might imperil Japan's standing with the Great Powers. "The uprising in Korea," the liberal Yoshino Sakuzō wrote, "is a great stain upon the history of the Taishō period, which we must exert every effort to wipe away. Unless we do so successfully it will not only reflect upon the honor of the most advanced country in East Asia, but will have a serious impact on our national destiny."[13]

Prime Minister Hara Takashi tried to put the best face on matters by telling the world that Japan would tutor Koreans so that they eventually could enjoy expanded civil liberties and exercise more political autonomy. "The desire of most Koreans is not for independence," he explained to one American journalist, "but to be treated as equals of the Japanese. I intend to see to it that the Koreans have such equal opportunities in education, industry, and government."[14] To calm the waters further, Hara sent a new governor-general to Seoul. Arriving in August 1919, Admiral Saitō Makoto carried with him instructions to implement an era of *bunka seiji* ("cultural rule") by replacing the detested gendarmerie system with an exclusively civilian police force, wiping the Company Law off the books, and relaxing regulations on publishing and political activities.

As Saitō defused tensions in Korea, other Japanese visited the West to explain Japan's goals as a colonial power. On a cross-country tour of the United States, Nitobe Inazō began his stock speech with the reflection that Japan was among a select handful of nations that had "wisely adapted their national self-consciousness to the law of organic growth" and become "colonial Powers," while Korea fell into the ranks of countries that, "like the Foolish Virgins of the parable, were not ready to act at this call of the century" and thus "were bereft of their independence."[15] Still, Nitobe continued, although in condescending language that did more to indict Japan's colonial policy than to explicate its objectives, "I count myself among the best and truest friends of Koreans. I like them. I think they are a capable people, who can be trained to a large measure of self-government, for which the present is a period of tutelage." Already, he claimed, Japanese colonial administrators had chalked up numerous successes: "Mining, fishery, and manufacturing have advanced. The bald mountains have been covered with young trees. Trade has increased by leaps and bounds." Japan's new "cultural rule" promised even more progress in the future. "Study what we are doing in Korea," Nitobe lectured his audience, for "Japan is a steward on whom devolves the gigantic task of uplifting the Far East."

The world gave spokespersons like Nitobe a mixed review. Within the colonial empire itself, critics scornfully brushed aside the rhetoric of benevolent paternalism and instead asserted that Japan more usually acted in its own blatant self-interest. As happened in Korea, they claimed, colonial economies everywhere remained subordinate to the needs of the home islands. Industrialization programs, whether undertaken by the SMR or the

South Seas Development Company or the mining and timber companies on Karafuto, brought more benefit to Japanese entrepreneurs than to the native populations. Outside of Karafuto, colonial overlords maintained tight control over internal affairs, denied a political voice to the people they ruled, and funded only second-rate educational facilities. From Manchuria to the South Seas, colonized men and women thought of imperialists like Nitobe as naïfs blinded by an inflated sense of moral superiority. For those who lived under colonial rule, life had revealed a harsh new maxim: No matter how loudly planners and theoreticians talked about humane policies, in reality self-important officials, callous policemen, and greedy merchants determined what daily life was really like.

Many Western observers took a more benign view of the colonial policies implemented by a fellow member of the imperialist club. Euro-American visitors lauded Taiwan's "amazing progress" under Japanese stewardship, remarked upon the "zeal" demonstrated by colonial administrators as they pursued their "desire to improve the social and moral condition of the natives" in Micronesia, and wrote glowingly about Japan's "benevolent assimilation" of Korea, which was bringing modernity to the peninsula after "corrupt and weak monarchs" had "plundered, oppressed, and degraded" their own people for centuries.[16] Even though the violence directed against civilians during the Samil Independence Movement appalled them, many American missionaries in Korea applauded Hara's new policies and agreed with the prime minister's assessment of the situation. "The most intelligent and far-seeing" Koreans, wrote the resident bishop of the Methodist Episcopal Church in May 1920, "are persuaded that there is no hope of speedy independence, and that they must settle down for a long period to build up the Korean people, in physical conditions, in knowledge, in morality, and in the ability to handle government concerns."[17]

In the early 1920s it was easy for Westerners to sympathize with Japan. Japanese colonial administrations resembled their Euro-American counterparts in temperament and purpose, and when Nitobe talked about the "gigantic task of uplifting" indigenous populations, he merely was preaching to the choir. Moreover, if the Japanese had acted like a stern parent in Korea, the British, French, and Americans too had disciplined their fair share of Irish troublemakers and other colonial malcontents. Thus, whatever bumps Japanese colonial officials encountered along the way, by the end of the Taishō years it appeared to many foreign observers that Japan had brought law and order to the territories it controlled, crafted promising development plans for Manchuria and Karafuto, initiated responsible reform in Korea and Taiwan, and addressed its mandated obligations in the South Pacific.

## The Urban Middle Class

The new awakenings and sense of change that pervaded the opening decades of the early twentieth century stimulated many Japanese to think afresh notions of self, family, and society. The victories over China and Russia, cooperative diplomacy and a growing affinity with the West, the advent of parliamentary democracy, continued industrial growth, the establishment of universal education, the appearance of new forms of mass media, and an infinity of other factors flowed together in the 1910s and 1920s in ways that encouraged many to question received values and envision new lifestyles. The willingness to experiment socially first manifested itself in Japan's major urban centers, where an emerging middle class, an outgrowth of the earlier middle propertied classes, challenged the status quo and refashioned social norms to meet the demands and expectations they held for the new century.

Most newspapers and official statistical compilations included in the middle class government officials, doctors, teachers, policemen, military officers, bankers, corporate managers, and even certain skilled blue-collar factory workers who made their living in large cities, such as Tokyo, Osaka, and Nagoya. On the whole, such men were well educated and reasonably well remunerated. So too were the women who moved into the middle-class workplace throughout the 1910s and 1920s as teachers, telephone operators, typists, office workers, department store clerks, bus conductors, midwives, nurses, and even doctors after Japan's first medical college for women, founded by Yoshioka Yayoi in 1900, finally received full accreditation midway through the Taishō period.

*Female bus conductor*

The proportion of working women and the overall size of the urban middle class were small, but growing. In 1922 approximately 3.5 million of Japan's 27 million women worked, slightly more than a quarter of them in occupations identified with the middle class. The trend lines arched upward, however. By 1926 there were 57,000 female nurses, compared with 13,000 in 1911, and the number of female white-collar workers in government offices doubled between 1920 and 1930. In all, the percentage of Tokyo's work force with middle-class occupations rose from slightly more than 5 percent in 1908 to 21.5 percent in 1920, when an estimated 8.5 percent of Japan's total population of 56 million persons fell into the middle class. That rate of increase and the prominence of the new occupations imbued middle-class urbanites with the feeling that they were setting the cultural tone for the entire nation.

New workplaces were as much a part of Japan's modernity as the concept of a middle class itself. In Tokyo most of the middle class worked

*The emperor and empress passing new government buildings at Kasumigaseki*

downtown, in the Ginza, Kasumigaseki, and Marunouchi districts. The Ginza retained its reputation, forged initially in the Meiji period, as a retailing and banking center. Nearby the Kasumigaseki area achieved public prominence around the turn of the century, when the government put up imposing brick structures to house the Supreme Court, Metropolitan Police Department, and most national ministries. During the 1920s many leading corporations and businesses began to locate their headquarters at Marunouchi, a block of land just to the west of the Ginza that had become home to Mitsubishi enterprises in 1890. Two architectural triumphs symbolized the florescence of the Marunouchi area: the completion in 1914 of the ornate Tokyo Central Station, whose towers and adjoining galleries were done "in the French style" after the mayor of Tokyo instructed the architect to design something that would startle the world, and the construction in 1923 of Japan's largest office complex, the Marunouchi Building.

Middle-class men and women worked for a variety of reasons. For many, money was an important consideration. Most men supported themselves if single, and more often than not they were their families' chief breadwinner when married. Similarly, about 13 percent of the female respondents to a survey taken in Tokyo in 1922 were single, divorced, or widowed, and a significant proportion of them supported dependent children and parents. In that same survey a majority of married middle-class working women indicated that their incomes went directly into the household budgets, either to make ends meet or to enable the families to indulge in some luxuries. Economic necessity, however, was not the sole motivation. Many men and women, whether married or not, presumably drew personal satisfaction from pursuing careers. Others cherished the possibility of leading single lives, and employment made that option possible. "I am making no preparations for marriage," wrote one female telephone operator to a survey question, "and I want to learn an occupation that will make me self-reliant."[18]

New kinds of magazines spread information about alternative possibilities for individual behavior and family life. The most widely read of the new domestic monthlies was *Fujin no tomo* ("Woman's Friend"), which achieved a circulation of nearly three million copies by the end of the Taishō era. Its founder and editor, Hani (née Matsuoka) Motoko, drew upon transmuted forms of *ryōsai kenbo* and *hōmu* to formulate a message that sought to reconcile tradition with a new vision of social modernity. In particular, writers in the journal urged women to develop their own talents and abilities, reach their potentials as individual human beings, and dare to pursue careers in teaching, medicine, and other professions. At the same time, *Fujin no tomo* celebrated marriage and family, depicting in issue after issue the fulfillment that came from being both a loving mother and devoted home-maker. The vision created in the magazine was that of a Taishō supermom, an idealized woman able to reconcile the freedom of female self-awareness with the burdens of traditional obligations and careful to balance the demands of a career with a personal life.

Motoko lived out the vision promoted in her magazine. Born in 1873 to a former samurai family that raised horses in Aomori Prefecture, the precocious young woman marched with the first graduating class of the Tokyo First Higher Girls' School in 1891. A convert to Christianity, Motoko continued her studies at the Meiji School for Women (where Iwamoto Yoshiharu, premier spokesperson for the *hōmu*, was headmaster), fell in love with a young man from Kyoto, returned to northern Japan to teach at a public elementary school and then a Catholic girls' school, and in 1895 resigned to wed her suitor from Kyoto. The marriage was an unmitigated disaster. "As an educated women from the northeast," Motoko wrote in her autobiography, she could not abide life in the "intolerably vulgar" imperial capital, and after her husband "took to drinking," she retreated to Tokyo "to find a more meaningful way of life."[19] For a brief time she worked as a maid in the household of the pioneering woman physician Yoshioka Yayoi. There Motoko met many career-oriented women, and in 1897 she secured a position as a copy editor at Tokyo's largest newspaper, the *Hōchi shinbun*. Talented, she became Japan's first woman newspaper reporter when she started to research and write her own pieces about matters close to the daily life of the readership, such as child care and religion in the life of ordinary people.

In 1901, Motoko married fellow journalist Hani Yoshikazu, seven years her junior and future partner in her journalistic and educational ventures. The couple had two daughters and in 1903 launched *Katei no tomo* ("Friend of the Home"), which they renamed *Fujin no tomo* in 1908. Motoko saw the publication as a way to question "attachment to outmoded values," awaken "new visions," and encourage the "genuinely free development of the individual." In the following years, articles commented on such issues as the emotional lives and employment problems of women, discussed the importance of consumer unions and women's suffrage, and provided practical, if somewhat didactic, advice about household budgets, health issues, and children's education. With the magazine an unqualified success, the couple in 1921 founded a college, the Jiyū Gakuen, which opened the following year in a building designed by Frank Lloyd Wright. The *jiyū* ("freedom") in the school's name signaled Motoko's belief that women should be "free" to think for themselves, to shoulder life's responsibilities, and to believe in Christ. Her accomplishments made her a role model for many women, but in her autobiography she carefully reminded her admirers that homemaking and career were mutually enriching. "Our home has been the center of our work," she wrote about herself and her husband, "and our work has been an extension of our home life: the two are completely merged without demarcations of any kind. I am truly grateful for this ideal union that is the very essence of both our work and marriage. Together, we have found our place in life."

Articles in magazines like *Fujin no tomo* as well as in major urban newspapers never tired of trotting out the word "cultured" when discussing the new urban middle class. In innumerable accounts the typical family was seen living on the outskirts of the city or in an adjoining suburb, where it owned a *bunka jūtaku*, a two-story "cultured house" that included four or more rooms, complete with such up-to-date appointments as a floored kitchen and a Western-style sitting room. Husband, wife, and children also constituted a "cultured family," a nuclear unit that happily enjoyed an increasingly cosmopolitan "cultured life." The home was an important setting for that idealized family life, and its most important artifacts, the piano and the radio, became the focal points of family togetherness.

The first radio stations began operations in Tokyo, Osaka, and Nagoya in 1925, and the following year the government merged those three independent companies into a national monopoly, NHK (Nihon Hōsō Kyōkai; Japan Broadcasting Corporation), which remained the country's sole broadcaster for more than two decades. Between 1926 and 1932 the number of radio receivers rose from approximately 350,000 to 1.4 million. During that time radio remained essentially an urban medium; in 1932 nearly 25 percent of all metropolitan households owned receivers compared to less than 5 percent in rural counties. In their cultured home, the middle-class family could gather in the sitting room to enjoy Western classical music as well as "radio novels" and domestic comedies written by major playwrights especially for the new medium.

The middle-class family apparently found satisfaction in discovering the pleasures and rhythms of the modern city together as well. On Sundays and holidays, according to novels, newspaper accounts, and representations in wood-block prints, mom, dad, and the kids traveled into the city center on public transportation (in Tokyo horse-drawn trolleys gave way in 1903 to electric ones that soon carried more than 100,000 passengers a day, and taxicabs moved about the city from the first year of the Taishō period). Within the city the family sought out some of the same seasonal pleasures that had brought pleasure to Tokyoites for generations, delighting in a springtime stroll along the embankments of the Sumida River to view cherry blossoms or stopping by shrines on autumn festival days to buy amulets and special foods from street vendors.

Increasingly the Taishō family headed for the new public parks that dotted the city. The first public park opened in 1878 on the northern edge of the city, and by the time the Taishō family walked through its gates, Ueno Park included zoological gardens, several art and science museums, and the country's first zoo. A more heralded symbol of Taishō, however, was the centrally located Hibiya Park, which opened in 1903 on the site of a former military parade ground. At Hibiya, where demonstrators gathered to protest the Treaty of Portsmouth, middle-class families could admire some of the oldest trees in the city and glimpse a portion of the former escarpment and moat of Edo Castle. For most, however, the real attractions were the park's Western-style accoutrements: lawns and seasonal flower beds; a sports area dedicated to the new craze for bicycling; a monumental fountain featuring a magnificent water-spewing crane; a modern bandstand, capped with a great cupola, where orchestras performed on Sun-

*A middle-class family at Hibiya Park*

days and national holidays; and a restaurant serving foreign-inspired re-
freshments.

Visits to modern department stores also excited the Taishō family. From
Hibiya Park, it was just a short walk across the Ginza to the great Mitsukoshi and Shirokiya emporiums, which stood face-to-face at the opposite
ends of the bridge at Nihonbashi, the former heart of merchant Edo. If the
location was traditional, the stores were unabashedly modern and innovative. In 1911 the Shirokiya (forerunner to today's Tōkyū chain) made a bid
for customers by putting up a delightfully eclectic four-story building, equip-
ping it with the country's first elevator, and staffing it with female clerks
identically attired in Western-style clothing. Three years later the Mitsukoshi company (the registered name of the former Mitsui dry goods store
from 1904) countered by erecting a five-story Renaissance structure. Said
to be the largest building east of Suez, the new Mitsukoshi featured central
heating, Japan's first escalator, banks of elevators, and row after row of glass
display cases. At the department stores, middle-class families could purchase
the latest products: Morinaga-brand milk chocolate and caramels (on sale
from 1913), Mitsuwa soap (1916), Pilot fountain pens (1918), Calpis, a milk-
based soft drink (1920), and Pine sewing machines (1924). The new department stores, however, appealed to the middle class by purveying culture
and entertainment as well as merchandise. Their game rooms, exhibition
halls, roof gardens, and Western-style restaurants made a trip to the Mitsukoshi or Shirokiya an anticipated event for all members of the family.

## Adventurous Youth

While downtown, the middle-class families frequently bumped into *moga*
and *mobo*, the cultural icons for students and other young, unmarried adults
in Japan's major urban centers who were bent on staking out a new identity for themselves. The words, part of an intriguing lexicon of slang original to the late Taishō era, were shortened forms for *modan gaaru* and *modan
boi*, "modern girl" and "modern boy" respectively. In the mid-1920s those
youths were not difficult to spot, even in a crowd. The *moga* favored short
hair, clipped to leave the ears and nape of the neck exposed, shockingly
short and boldly patterned skirts, and high-heeled shoes and sheer stock-
ings designed to show off her legs; one popular song, meanwhile, envisioned
a *mobo* decked out in a blue shirt, green tie, bell-bottoms, bowler hat, and
*roido* (Lloyd) eyeglasses, the kind of horn-rimmed spectacles popularized by
Harold Lloyd. The coiffure of choice for young men was "all-back," with
the hair slicked straight back from the forehead and not parted.

*A mobo chats up a cafe waitress*

Tokyo's *moga* and *mobo* made "hanging out on the Ginza" into an art form. For that pastime, they coined another new idiom, *Ginbura*, a contraction of Ginza and *burabura*, meaning to wander around aimlessly and take pleasure in the chance encounters that came one's way. While in the Ginza area young people could drop in at beer halls and cabarets, visit jazz clubs, try the newest steps at dance halls, and catch plays at theaters that presented original works by Japanese playwrights and translated dramas by such Westerners as Henrik Ibsen and Maurice Maeterlinck. Another familiar haunt was Asakusa, famous for monstrously popular movie theaters, such as the Electric Palace (Denkikan), which opened in 1903 as Japan's first permanent cinema, and for "Asakusa opera," an expression that encompassed all sorts of musical productions from genuine Western grand opera, such as *Rigoletto* and *The Magic Flute*, done with Japanese casts, to chorus line revues and locally produced farces.

Out of the demimonde of the Ginza and Asakusa gushed movies, plays, and larger than life personalities that captured the imagination of Japan's youth and helped spread an awareness of the new urban culture to all regions of Japan. The first truly national star of the new century was Matsui Sumako. Born in the countryside in 1886, she arrived in Tokyo in 1902, worked as a seamstress, fled two unhappy marriages, and in 1905 joined a drama society, where she discovered her true passion, acting. In 1911 Matsui's portrayal of Nora in Ibsen's *A Doll's House* provoked intense discussion in magazines and the popular press for its suggestion that neither marriage nor man's authority within the home ought to be considered sacrosanct. Two years later the beautiful young actress appeared in Hermann Suder-

*The Taishō look*

*Matsui Sumako*

mann's *Die Heimat*, which in Japan opened under the title *Magda*, the name of the lead character. In France and Italy the greatest actresses of the day, Sarah Bernhardt and Eleonora Duse, made the play an enormous hit, and in Japan Matsui created another sensation by starring in a role that idolized a young woman who defied her father's dictates and became an opera singer.

Creative and energetic, Matsui almost single-handedly created an entirely new market for the music recording industry. In 1914 she toured the country in Leo Tolstoy's *Resurrection* and released a phonographic recording of "Katusha's Song," which sold twenty thousand copies and ignited a boom for popular music. Over the next decade an outpouring of new tunes caught the buoyant spirit of that portion of Japan's youth that seemed more interested in the pleasures of today than the responsibilities of tomorrow. "Tokyo March" (*Tōkyō kōshin-kyoku*), composed in 1929 for use in a motion picture with the same name and distributed free to bars and cafés throughout the capital, teemed with new foreign-based neologisms such as *jazu* (jazz), *rikyūru* (liqueur), and *dansā* (a taxi dancer):

Dancing to jazz, staying up until all hours, drinking liqueur.
At daybreak, the dancers shed their tears . . .
During rush hour I picked up a rose,
And in that rose I found memories of my sweetheart.[20]

Other stanzas of the hit song glorified the youth culture of the capital by evoking the allure of the Marunouchi, Asakusa, and Ginza districts, and one began "Shall we take in a movie? / Shall we have a cup of tea? / Better yet, shall we steal away on the Odakyū instead?"[21] The last reference was to the Odakyū Electric Railway Company, which ran express trains to towns south of Tokyo, where sunny beaches and wooded hills provided a retreat for romantic couples who wished to escape the prying eyes of family and friends.

The Japanese began to make "movies" in 1899, just two years after importing the first Edison Vitascope and Cinématographic Lumière, and by the middle of the Taishō period more than a dozen companies were churning out well over one hundred films a year. Many of those—especially samurai epics and productions that poked fun at the tribulations of white-collar workers, such as 1924's smash hit *Nichiyōbi* ("Sunday")—drew middle-class couples to theaters. Targeting younger audiences were "erotic comedies," such as "The Woman Who Touched the Legs" (*Ashi ni sawatta onna*) and "An Electrician and His Wife" (*Denkō to sono tsuma*). That last production starred Kurishima Sumiko, who was nearly as popular in the 1920s as Matsui Sumako had been in the 1910s; when one of Kurishima's films opened in 1924, fans purchased more than four thousand copies of her photograph in a single day.

As was the case with the advocates of the new middle-class family, the appearance of rebellious youth foretold a reordering of traditional gender relationships. But if Hani Motoko and other professional women hoped to achieve a new equivalency with their spouses within the context of a mutually satisfying family life, the modern girl flaunted an open sexuality to demonstrate that she would not be enslaved by the chains of conventional morality. The short hairstyle was intended to be openly erotic. The *moga* also was fond of suggestive flirting, risqué double entendres, and promiscuous come-ons, at least according to articles in magazines such as *Fujin kōron* ("Women's Review"), founded in 1916 as a forum on women's issues, and *Kingu* ("King," 1925), which featured sections on current events, offbeat social trends, entertainment, fashion, sports, humor, and the arts.

Behavior may well have accorded with image. In Tokyo the police periodically swept through Hibiya Park on warm summer evenings to roust out young couples who crept into the park after middle-class families returned to their homes, and the male editor of *Fujin kōron* took it as a matter of course when one young woman whom he interviewed sent him a note reading, "I am lonely sleeping by myself today. Please come visit."[22] The whole nation marveled at the twists and turns in the life of Matsui Sumako. Always passionate and sometimes emotionally mercurial, the actress carried on a flamboyant, public love affair with her married director and mentor, who deserted his wife and children to move in with her. After he died unexpectedly of influenza, the actress caused the entire country to gasp on January 5, 1919, when she hanged herself backstage after she starred in the opening performance of *Carmen*.

---

Hani Motoko and Matsui Sumako were cosmopolitan women, fully conversant with the behavioral norms, social constructs, and intellectual trends that were becoming the common property of persons in all modernizing nations. Between them, they represented the enormous vitality and explosive energy that characterized the Taishō epoch, as Japanese from all walks of life set out to explore the new political, professional, and social possibilities that were opening before them. Fundamentally, however, the two women stood at polar extremes. Hani spoke for middle-class women who sought fulfillment within the context of family, home, and profession, and their values and modes of behavior made the *moga* crowd appear hedonistic and self-indulgent. Matsui, by contrast, was a shining cultural heroine for young women who considered or wished themselves to be fully emancipated individuals and whose lifestyle sneered at what they saw as the warmed-over traditionalism of the bourgeois matron.

That Hani and Matsui each created a following for herself in the same decade says something significant about the very serious tensions and differences of opinion that accompanied the new awakenings and the quest for new modernities during the Taishō era. To many Japanese, liberal democracy, cooperation with the West, paternalistic colonialism, and participation in a cultural milieu where Ibsen and Tolstoy were "no longer strangers" represented the mainstream course of development, the road to progress that would enable them to become world citizens as well as Japanese. Not all their countrymen agreed with that prescription, however. Just as the supposed contentment of a middle-class life failed to strike a chord with women such as Matsui, so too did other Japanese come in time to harbor doubts about the purported virtues of democracy, capitalism, and collaboration with the Western powers. As the 1910s and 1920s unfolded, those Japanese whose aspirations remained unsatisfied rose in protest, and strife and contention became part of the verve and dynamism that infused the Taishō era.

# CHAPTER 11

# The Tumultuous Twenties

A s one of Japan's foremost economists, Kawakami Hajime rejoiced in the benefits that industrialization promised to bring his countrymen at the beginning of the new century. Economic development already had made Japan more secure and powerful, he believed, and the products that poured from its factories and workshops augured a general improvement in standards of living. Providing all citizens, rich and poor, with an opportunity to possess the material goods that made life comfortable was a matter of considerable importance to Kawakami, for he was a humanist who embraced the imperative of absolute unselfishness. In 1905, when still in his mid-twenties, Kawakami separated from his wife and child to enter a Buddhist cult, the Garden of Selflessness. While absorbed in meditation, he fell into a deep mystical trance, "directly confronted death," and awoke more resolved than ever to eliminate all personal desires and to serve the public good by teaching. More than once, explained Kawakami, completely unfazed by the mixing of religious traditions, the anchor of his moral code was Christ's Sermon on the Mount: "Give to him that asketh thee, and from him that would borrow of thee, turn not thou away" (Matthew 5:42).

In the years following his appointment to the economics faculty at Kyoto University in 1908, Kawakami began to question his early enthusiasm for industrialization. Everywhere around him he saw hardship and maldistribution of wealth. At first, he attributed this coexistence of the pitiful worker and the affluent middle class to the relative immaturity of Japan's economic modernity, but a visit to Europe from 1913 to 1915 convinced him that poverty haunted even the most advanced industrial societies. Gaps between rich and poor always would exist, he explained in his best-selling

*Binbō monogatari* ("Tales of Poverty," 1917), because industrialization took the ethic of self-interest as its anchor and capitalism made exploitation into a virtue.

In search of a way to advance Japan's economic development and simultaneously eliminate poverty, Kawakami took up the study of socialism. Gradually he gravitated toward Marxist theory, and ultimately he found in the dictum that each individual should produce according to his abilities and receive according to his needs an idea that resonated with the humanism he had discovered earlier in Christ's Sermon on the Mount. For Kawakami, Marxism became an irresistible alternative to capitalism because it promised both rapid industrialization and the equitable distribution of wealth. In 1928, taking to heart his students' criticism that the truthfulness of any theory lies in its human praxis, the mild-mannered professor resigned his post at Kyoto University and began to speak before labor groups and to campaign for leftist candidates to the Diet.

Kawakami's route from scholar to political activist was his own to travel, but his journey symbolized an intellectual transition that many Japanese made during the Taishō period. Just as Hani Motoko and Matsui Sumako challenged traditional concepts of women and family, so others raised questions about the efficacy of industrial capitalism, the prudence of cooperative diplomacy, and the ability of parliamentary democracy to craft solutions to the problems that confronted the nation and its citizens. During the 1920s a chorus of acrimonious voices rose in tumultuous debate about the political, economic, and social future of Japan.

## The Contrasting Sides of the Modern Economy

Despite the agony of higher rice prices for urban consumers, World War I brought good economic times to many businesses. The retreat of British traders from their export markets in India and China created opportunities for alert Japanese firms to increase sales of textiles and other consumer goods in those areas, and at home domestically produced commodities replaced the Western imports that were vanishing from Japanese store shelves. Moreover, fledgling enterprises that had begun to appear in the heavy industry sector at the beginning of the century—companies such as Kōbe Steel (incorporated in 1905), Mitsui Mining (1911), Sumitomo Electric Industries (1911), and the government-owned Yawata Iron and Steel Works (1901)—profited immensely from Allied orders for munitions, machine tools, chemicals, cement, and iron and steel. With the merchant fleets of the belligerent

powers pressed into wartime service, Japanese shippers gained new customers, and domestic shipyards expanded output to fill new orders. In all,
Japan's real gross national product jumped by 40 percent between 1914 and
1918, an average annual rate of nearly 9 percent; profits soared, often top-
ping 50 percent of paid-up capital for leading companies; and the 1919–1920
edition of the *Japan Year Book* noted that the number of *narikin* "millionaires"
had increased by 115 percent between 1915 and 1919.

Propelled by the momentum of the World War I boom, Japan in the
1920s passed several major milestones in its long-term transition from an
economy based primarily on agriculture and light industry to one in which
heavy industry and urban factory production represented the most significant forms of economic activity. During the 1920s, as shown in Table 11.1,
manufacturing's proportion of the gross domestic product approached and
then surpassed that of the agricultural sector. At the same time, the recently
founded heavy industries came to account for an ever-greater share of manufacturing output. In the early 1890s, on the eve of the war with China,
Japan still was a massive importer of manufactured goods and relied heavily on exports of primary products, as depicted in Table 11.2. By the end
of World War I, however, that situation largely had reversed itself: Manufactured goods accounted for 90 percent of all exports, imports of primary
products exceeded manufactures, and to many observers the structure of the
Japanese economy seemed to be taking on the pattern that typified the advanced industrialized countries of the West.

Despite impressive aggregate growth, severe growing pains accompanied Japan's emergence as a full-fledged industrial power during the Taishō
period. One especially troublesome problem was the roller-coaster nature
of the country's economic performance. Although net domestic product
grew during the Taishō years, increasing by 60 percent between 1910 and
1920 and by another 30 percent during the 1920s, Japan suffered agonizing slumps after the Sino-Japanese and Russo-Japanese wars, and the turbulence continued throughout the 1920s, as indicated in Figure 11.1. Japan's
accelerating pace of industrialization and the growth of trade during World
War I made the island nation more vulnerable than ever to fluctuations in
the world economy, and a particularly severe recession followed on the heels
of the wartime boom as export demand for war-related capital goods dried
up and Western traders reclaimed their markets in southern Asia. Then, just
as businesses were making a tolerable recovery from the postwar downturn,
the Great Kantō Earthquake rocked Tokyo and surrounding cities on September 1, 1923. The tremors began as people were preparing the noon meal,
and the devastating quake and subsequent firestorms left more than 100,000

**TABLE 11.1** *Structural Changes in the Economy, 1885–1930*

A. CHANGING PROPORTIONS OF AGRICULTURE AND MANUFACTURING

| YEAR | GROSS DOMESTIC PRODUCT * | PROPORTION (%) PRODUCED IN: | |
| | | MANUFACTURING | AGRICULTURE |
|---|---|---|---|
| 1885 | 3,774 | 7.0 | 42.1 |
| 1895 | 5,375 | 8.9 | 37.0 |
| 1905 | 6,214 | 12.6 | 31.6 |
| 1912 | 8,121 | 15.7 | 30.0 |
| 1914 | 7,993 | 18.3 | 33.9 |
| 1916 | 10,134 | 19.4 | 29.1 |
| 1918 | 10,588 | 20.5 | 26.2 |
| 1920 | 10,937 | 18.6 | 27.3 |
| 1922 | 12,122 | 19.6 | 22.8 |
| 1924 | 12,475 | 18.9 | 22.2 |
| 1926 | 13,111 | 20.1 | 21.3 |
| 1928 | 14,401 | 21.2 | 20.4 |
| 1930 | 13,756 | 25.6 | 22.8 |

* In millions of yen at constant 1934–1936 prices.

Derived from Kazushi Ohkawa and Miyohei Shinohara, with Larry Meissner, eds., *Patterns of Japanese Economic Development: A Quantitative Appraisal* (New Haven: Yale University Press, 1979), pp. 278–79.

B. PERCENTAGE SHARES OF MANUFACTURING OUTPUT

| | 1877 | 1900 | 1920 | 1938 |
|---|---|---|---|---|
| All manufacturing * | 100.0 | 100.0 | 100.0 | 100.0 |
| Heavy industries | 13.6 | 13.3 | 30.4 | 51.4 |
| Metals | 1.4 | 1.4 | 7.8 | 14.4 |
| Machinery | 1.1 | 2.9 | 13.7 | 20.4 |
| Chemicals | 11.1 | 9.0 | 8.9 | 16.6 |
| Light industries | 68.6 | 72.7 | 58.4 | 38.1 |
| Textiles | 10.1 | 25.5 | 27.8 | 23.6 |
| Foods | 58.5 | 47.2 | 30.6 | 14.5 |
| Other | 17.8 | 14.0 | 11.2 | 10.5 |
| Ceramics | 2.1 | 1.5 | 2.2 | 2.6 |
| Wood products | 6.6 | 4.1 | 2.3 | 2.6 |
| Miscellaneous | 9.1 | 8.4 | 6.7 | 5.3 |

* Figures are based on seven-year moving averages (five-year averages for 1938).

Adapted from Ryōshin Minami, *The Economic Development of Japan: A Quantitative Study*, tr. Ralph Thompson, Kumie Fujimori, and Minami, with assistance from David Merriman (New York: St. Martin's Press, 1994, 2d ed.), p. 100.

**TABLE 11.2** *Distribution of Imports and Exports, 1880s–1920s*
(percentage shares of total imports or exports calculated from
ten-year moving averages in current prices)

| | IMPORTS | | EXPORTS | | | |
|---|---|---|---|---|---|---|
| PERIOD | PRIMARY PRODUCTS | MANU-FACTURES | PRIMARY PRODUCTS | TOTAL MANU-FACTURES | LIGHT MANU-FACTURES | HEAVY MANU-FACTURES |
| 1877–1886 | 10.3 | 89.7 | 39.5 | 60.5 | 50.8 | 9.7 |
| 1882–1891 | 18.7 | 81.3 | 33.0 | 67.0 | 54.6 | 12.4 |
| 1892–1901 | 36.4 | 63.6 | 21.0 | 79.0 | 65.8 | 13.2 |
| 1902–1911 | 45.2 | 54.8 | 14.1 | 85.9 | 71.0 | 14.9 |
| 1912–1921 | 52.6 | 47.4 | 9.0 | 91.0 | 71.7 | 19.3 |
| 1922–1931 | 56.6 | 43.4 | 6.8 | 93.2 | 80.3 | 12.9 |
| 1927–1936 | 61.0 | 39.0 | 6.7 | 93.3 | 73.6 | 19.7 |

Derived from Kazushi Ohkawa and Miyohei Shinohara, with Larry Meissner, eds., *Patterns of Japanese Economic Development: A Quantitative Appraisal* (New Haven: Yale University Press, 1979), p. 135.

dead, destroyed more than 60 percent of all homes in Tokyo, and leveled nearly every factory and workshop between Tokyo and Yokohama, Japan's most intensely developed industrial zone. To stimulate reconstruction of the nation's industrial base, the Japanese government provided new sources of credit to banks, which then extended loans to businesses wishing to rebuild. Economic growth rates began to climb once again, but in the spring of 1927 rumors spread that banks holding the loans were in danger of collapse. In April panicky depositors began to withdraw their savings, and the government declared a three-week banking moratorium as dozens of lending institutions shuttered their doors. Over the following year the financial sector got its balance sheets back in order, only to see the Japanese economy engulfed in the worldwide depression that followed the 1929 crash of the U.S. stock market.

Other problems surfaced as the manufacturing sector of the Japanese economy split into distinct halves during the Taishō era. The top tier of the dual structure, as economists termed it, consisted chiefly of profitable heavy industries, companies that were members of leading *zaibatsu* conglomerates, and certain large textile firms, such as Kanebō, the mammoth company that started operations in 1887 under the name Kanegafuchi Bōseki, became part of the Mitsui *zaibatsu* in 1889, and later moved into cosmetics and pharma-

**FIGURE 11.1** *Economic Growth, 1890–1930*

A. Growth Rate of Net Domestic Product per Decade (Percent)

| | | | |
|---|---|---|---|
| 1890–1900 | 67.6 | 1910–1920 | 61.5 |
| 1900–1910 | 42.7 | 1920–1930 | 33.4 |

Based on midpoint five-year averages.

Adapted from Hugh T. Patrick, "The Economic Muddle of the 1920s, " in James W. Morley, ed., *Dilemmas of Growth in Prewar Japan* (Princeton: Princeton University Press, 1971), p. 214.

B. Yearly Growth Rates

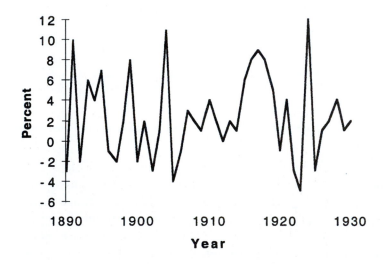

Adapted from *Japan: An Illustrated Encyclopedia*, vol. 1 (Tokyo: Kodansha, 1993), p. 305.

ceuticals. Making up the bottom half of the bifurcated dual structure were small- and medium-scale workshops that produced textiles and other consumer goods, which they could market on a cost-competitive basis, as well as small subcontractors that supplied parts to larger firms.

One particular feature of Japan's economic modernization was that small and medium-size businesses continued to shape its industrial profile in significant ways. As late as 1929, firms with four or fewer employees produced some 20 percent of all manufactures, and those with five to ninety-nine employees turned out an additional 40 percent. Moreover, during the 1920s most job growth occurred in such establishments. Statistically, there was an 11 percent increase in the labor force in the 1920s, but employment in firms with more than five hundred workers fell by ninety thousand (16 percent of the 1920 base). Thus, throughout most of the Taishō period, a surprisingly large proportion of Japan's manufacturing output took place in relatively small, labor-intensive workshops or factories that typically had more in common with the light industries prevalent in the Meiji era than with the bastions of modern heavy industry whose smokestacks seemed to dominate the Taishō landscape.

Life often was difficult for owners and workers in small enterprises in the lower half of the dual structure. Those firms usually were undercapitalized, and their plants poorly equipped, so that wage cuts, layoffs, and bank-

*A Tokyo slum in the late 1920s*

ruptcies were commonplace whenever the economy hit one of its periodic downdrafts. Moreover, productivity and profit margins remained low throughout the 1920s. To make matters worse, since several candidates applied for each available job, employers felt no need to raise wages. Much to their dismay, most men and women who labored in middle- and small-scale firms in the postwar era actually experienced a decline in real wages as adjusted for changes in the cost of living, and wage differentials separating workers in the upper and lower sectors of the dual economy widened considerably, as seen in Table 11.3.

Ailments in the rural sector also hobbled the Taishō economy. Between the 1890s and the end of the Taishō years, material conditions improved substantially in the countryside. Rising standards of living did not always bring economic stability to Japan's villagers, however, for farming remained a highly vulnerable undertaking in which a poor harvest or sudden decline in crop prices could be disastrous. Consequently, while many Japanese farmers shared in the World War I boom, profiting handsomely from better prices for rice and silk cocoons, cultured by nearly two of every five farm families, the postwar decade was filled with peril. Income derived from rice sales plunged precipitously after 1918, as the government stepped up imports of cheap grain from Korea and Taiwan, and prices for cocoons slipped by 30 percent between 1925 and 1929 and by another third by 1931. Bountiful harvests worldwide during the 1920s meant that Japanese farmers did not receive much for other crops either. As prices at the farm gate dropped sharply and then hovered at depressed levels for several years, the 1920s

**TABLE 11.3** *Wage Differentials by Firm Size, 1909–1933*

| WORKERS PER ESTABLISHMENT | 1909 | 1914 | WORKERS PER ESTABLISHMENT | 1932–1933 |
|---|---|---|---|---|
| 5–9 | 84.5 | 79.0 | 5–10 | 61.2 |
| 10–29 | 90.0 | 83.6 | 10–50 | 74.0 |
| 30–49 | 95.1 | 88.0 | | |
| 50–99 | 99.0 | 92.5 | 50–100 | 81.1 |
| 100–499 | 101.4 | 93.6 | 100–500 | 89.2 |
| 500–999 | 100.0 | 100.0 | 500+ | 100.0 |

Derived from Yasukichi Yasuba, "The Evolution of Dualistic Wage Structure," in Hugh T. Patrick, with the assistance of Larry Meissner, ed., *Japanese Industrialization and Its Social Consequences* (Berkeley: University of California Press, 1976), p. 258.

turned into one long recession in the countryside. To add to the psycho-logical distress of hard times, a noticeable gap began to separate rural and urban incomes, and many villagers also felt that they did not receive the same educational and cultural opportunities available to city dwellers. Per-ceiving themselves to be increasingly disadvantaged, farm families and their spokespeople started to voice a discontent that was to become a potent and emotive issue in the politics of the interwar period.

## Restive Tenants

Farm families who rented a portion or all of their land bore the brunt of the agrarian recession of the 1920s. After the turn of the century there was a gradual rise in the proportion of cultivators who owned some land and rented additional paddy, so that by 1917 some 41 percent of all farm families were such owner-tenants, while another 28 percent were tenants who possessed no fields of their own, and only 31 percent of Japan's farmers owned all their land, which they either tilled themselves or rented out to others. Not only did owner-tenant and tenant families everywhere pay high rents—typically still set at one-half of the harvest, the rate that had prevailed in the early Meiji period—but cultivators in central and western Japan felt im-mediately the negative effects of downturns in market prices since they de-rived a significant portion of their annual income from the sale of such commercial crops as rice, barley, wheat, tobacco, and cocoons. At the same time that falling crop prices brought economic adversity to owner-tenant and tenant families, the postwar recession reduced opportunities to offset lost income by having one or more family members take factory jobs.

Fueling the discontent of the 1920s was the fact that farm families were more worldly than in the past. Seasonal and temporary factory jobs in nearby cities had spread knowledge about other lifestyles and demonstrated that there was nothing sacrosanct about the traditional norms that called for ten-ant families to be deferential to landowning elites. Similarly, conscription in the military had increased the self-confidence of young men from tenant backgrounds who advanced in rank and led others, including landlords' sons, into battle. For all villagers, the experience of attending schools stimulated an interest in such topics as the social justice of democracy and capitalism, while the availability of magazines and newspapers brought home the intellectual impact of the Russian Revolution and encouraged discussion about socialism, the value of labor, and the common plight of peasants everywhere.

Reduced incomes in the 1920s raised the specter of true hardship for poorer tenant families that lived close to the economic margins. Few owner-tenants, in contrast, were disastrously worse off than before the war, but their new cosmopolitanism and the prosperity of the late 1910s had imbued them with greater expectations about what life might offer and made them unwilling to accept declining standards of living. Everywhere, but especially in the regions of Japan where commercialized agriculture was commonly practiced, owner-tenants and tenants banded together in tenant unions to bargain collectively with landlords. Altercations between tenants and landowners had occurred sporadically in the late Meiji period, but the number of such confrontations multiplied dramatically during the decade of the 1920s, when authorities tabulated more than eighteen thousand disputes, as shown in Table 11.4.

Rent reduction was the self-proclaimed goal of nearly three-quarters of all protestations initiated by tenant families during the 1920s, and the discontent hurled the majority of their complaints at absentee landlords. Traditionally, resident landlords had involved themselves directly in the political and social lives of their tenants by mediating petty quarrels, arranging marriages, hosting holiday feasts, and paying for local festivals. Moreover, landlords typically had spread out a safety net for less fortunate fellow villagers, providing jobs repairing tools and cleaning storage facilities during the agricultural off-season and forgiving a portion of rents during especially tough

**TABLE 11.4** *Tenant Disputes, 1920–1929*

| YEAR | NUMBER OF DISPUTES | NUMBER OF TENANTS INVOLVED | TENANT UNION MEMBERSHIP |
|------|--------------------|-----------------------------|--------------------------|
| 1920 | 408 | 34,605 | — |
| 1921 | 1,680 | 145,898 | — |
| 1922 | 1,578 | 125,750 | — |
| 1923 | 1,917 | 134,503 | 163,931 |
| 1924 | 1,532 | 110,920 | 232,125 |
| 1925 | 2,206 | 134,646 | 307,106 |
| 1926 | 2,751 | 151,061 | 346,693 |
| 1927 | 2,052 | 91,336 | 365,332 |
| 1928 | 1,866 | 75,136 | 330,406 |
| 1929 | 2,434 | 81,998 | 315,771 |

Adapted from Richard J. Smethurst, *Agricultural Development and Tenancy Disputes in Japan, 1870–1940* (Princeton: Princeton University Press, 1986), pp. 321 and 347.

years. By the Taishō period, however, a large number of landlords, nearly 50 percent in some economically advanced regions, had abandoned their native villages for nearby cities, where supported by their rents, they pursued new occupations or simply enjoyed the pleasures of urban life. Such absenteeism ruptured the traditional bonds of intimacy and mutual obligations that held villages together and exposed the urban-dwelling landlords to criticism.

Tenant protest in the Taishō period achieved mixed results. In the overwhelming majority of cases, as seen in Table 11.5, complainants either prevailed or wrangled concessions from the landlords. Viewed from that perspective, the protests achieved the immediate goals that the tenants set for themselves. In the long run, however, the practice of tenancy continued, raising doubts about the consequences of urbanization and capitalism and creating a sense of crisis that ultimately invited the intervention of the state into village life.

## Contentious Workers

At the beginning of the new century, Japan's urban work force also expressed a hearty determination to overcome what many decried as unfair and miserable conditions of employment. Women in textile mills struggled under notoriously difficult circumstances, and male shop hands in the emerging factory industries fared little better. The migratory labor practices of the nineteenth century had bequeathed to shop hands a reputation as social reprobates with a nasty thirst for drinking, gambling, and domestic quarreling. That assessment plunged some men into a morass of self-doubt. "The world is a strange place," groaned one young worker in 1913. "When I am dirty with sweat and oil I feel that even my heart is soiled, and I wonder if we workers are not different animals from human beings."[1]

Evolving employment practices in heavy industry compounded feelings of low self-esteem. By World War I many major corporations were requiring laborers to don drab company smocks or provide their own makeshift clothing, which stood out against the Western suits favored by managerial employees and clerk-technicians, the other primary work groups. In addition, whereas most modern companies in the upper tier of the dual structure paid clerks by the month and managers by the year, they doled out daily wages to workers and did not provide factory hands with the fringe benefits—company housing, profit-sharing bonuses, and health care schemes—that middle-class managers and clerk-technicians were beginning to expect as part of their compensation packages.

**TABLE 11.5**  *Tenant Demands and Dispute Resolution, 1920–1929*

| YEAR | NUMBER OF DISPUTES | TENANT DEMANDS | | DISPUTE RESOLUTION | | | |
| | | RENT REDUCTION | OTHER | COMPROMISE | TENANT VICTORY | TENANT DEFEAT | NOT SETTLED/ OTHER * |
|---|---|---|---|---|---|---|---|
| 1920 | 408 | — | — | 255 62.5% | 53 13.0% | 5 1.2% | 95 23.3% |
| 1921 | 1,680 | — | — | 1,340 79.8 | 109 6.5 | 14 0.8 | 217 12.9 |
| 1922 | 1,578 | — | — | 815 51.6 | 86 5.4 | — | 677 42.9 |
| 1923 | 1,917 | 1,831 95.5% | 86 4.5% | 1,451 75.5 | 89 4.6 | 32 1.7 | 345 18.0 |
| 1924 | 1,532 | 1,402 91.5 | 130 8.5 | 1,148 74.9 | 75 4.9 | 32 2.0 | 277 18.1 |
| 1925 | 2,206 | 1,919 87.0 | 287 13.0 | 1,625 73.7 | 93 4.2 | 13 0.6 | 475 21.5 |
| 1926 | 2,751 | 2,283 83.0 | 468 17.0 | 2,025 73.6 | 101 3.7 | 20 0.7 | 605 22.0 |
| 1927 | 2,052 | 1,459 71.1 | 593 28.9 | 1,371 66.8 | 56 2.7 | 9 0.4 | 616 30.0 |
| 1928 | 1,866 | 1,191 63.8 | 675 36.2 | 1,261 67.6 | 60 3.2 | 29 1.6 | 516 27.7 |
| 1929 | 2,434 | 1,490 61.2 | 944 38.8 | 1,615 66.4 | 127 5.2 | 63 2.6 | 627 25.8 |

* Includes resolutions that required the tenant to return the holding to the landlord (cited infrequently) and cases that for some reason lapsed before a settlement was reached

Derived from Ann Waswo, *Japanese Landlords: The Decline of a Rural Elite* (Berkeley: University of California Press, 1977), pp. 99 and 108.

*A woman leads a strike at the Fuji Spinning Mill, 1925*

Even as unkind images about the working class dominated public perceptions, workers and those sympathetic to their plight formed associations to improve the social standing of laborers and negotiate more favorable treatment in the workplace. In that spirit, the Yūaikai (Friendship Association), which emerged as the main voice for male factory workers after its founding in August 1912, aimed to provide mutual aid to its membership, improve the character, skills, and status of factory hands, and cultivate more harmonious relations between labor and management. By 1918, thirty thousand men had joined, and many submitted letters to its twice-monthly newsletter exhorting fellow workers to lead more frugal, sober, and stable lives. At the core of the Yūaikai philosophy were the interlinked notions that workers must be diligent and show respect for owners, who in return bore the obligation to treat their employees benevolently. "We workers are powerless souls born and raised under pitiful circumstances," one article in the Yūaikai's official publication concluded. "We crave powerful protectors with warm human feelings. We beg you to show hearts of parents. If you do, we too will show you hearts of children by working hard for you."[2]

**TABLE 11.6** *Labor Unions, 1919–1931*

| YEAR | NUMBER OF UNIONS | UNION MEMBERSHIP | PERCENT OF INDUSTRIAL WORK FORCE IN UNIONS |
|------|------------------|------------------|--------------------------------------------|
| 1919 | 187 | — | — |
| 1920 | 273 | — | — |
| 1921 | 300 | 103,412 | — |
| 1922 | 389 | 137,381 | — |
| 1923 | 432 | 125,551 | — |
| 1924 | 469 | 228,278 | 5.3 |
| 1925 | 457 | 254,262 | 5.6 |
| 1926 | 488 | 284,739 | 6.1 |
| 1927 | 505 | 309,493 | 6.5 |
| 1928 | 501 | 308,900 | 6.3 |
| 1929 | 630 | 330,985 | 6.8 |
| 1930 | 712 | 354,312 | 7.5 |
| 1931 | 818 | 368,975 | 7.9 |

Adapted from *Kadokawa Nihon-shi jiten* (Tokyo: Kadokawa Shoten, 1976, 2d ed.), p. 1288.

By the middle of the Taishō period many workers and leaders in the emerging labor movement had breathed more specific meaning into the concept of benevolence by calling on owners to pay higher wages, improve the working environment, and extend to blue-collar workers the kinds of non-wage benefits enjoyed by managerial employees. When companies failed to satisfy supplications for more humane treatment, laborers abandoned the comfortable rhetoric that evoked traditional familial ethics and instead turned to the rougher tactics of direct action. Some simply laid down their tools and walked away, as disillusioned workers had done in the Meiji era. As late as 1918 barely 50 percent of the women employed in the textile industry stayed with a single firm for as long as one year, and at one of Kanebō's leading spinning mills nearly two-thirds of the female operatives left employment without permission each year between 1905 and 1915. In heavy industry male workers routinely deserted one employer for another in search of better pay or an opportunity to enhance their skills, and annual turnover rates of 75 percent were not uncommon in the 1910s.

Increasing numbers of restive workers also began to enroll in unions during the 1920s. At the turn of the century Article 17 of the Public Order and

Police Act of 1900 had made it illegal for anyone to use "violence, threats, public defamation, agitation, or solicitation" to encourage others to join a union or engage in a work stoppage.[3] Although the ordinance did not explicitly ban unions or strikes per se, it did mean factory workers generally had to voice their hopes and aspirations through moderate fraternal associations, such as the Yūaikai. In 1919, however, the Hara cabinet decided to reinterpret the law in a more lenient manner that permitted "peaceful" unions and strikes, and the number of unions mushroomed immediately, as seen in Table 11.6. As unions organized the rank and file, they also began to speak more self-confidently and aggressively about entitlements and workers' rights in place of the traditional rhetoric of benevolence. Even the Yūaikai changed its name, settling on Sōdōmei (more formally, Nihon Rōdō Sōdōmei, the Japan Federation of Labor) in 1921, and adopted a more confrontational attitude as it began to campaign for the recognition of workers' right to engage in collective bargaining, the introduction of a minimum wage, and the prohibition of child labor.

The new belligerency led to a growing number of strikes, as seen in Table 11.7. Workers at all levels of the industrial hierarchy engaged in work stop-

*The strike at the Noda Soy Sauce Company, 1928*

**TABLE 11.7**  *Strikes and Other Work Stoppages, 1897–1931*

| YEAR | NUMBER OF DISPUTES | NUMBER OF PARTICIPANTS | YEAR | NUMBER OF DISPUTES | NUMBER OF PARTICIPANTS |
|------|------|------|------|------|------|
| 1897 | 32 | 3,517 | 1915 | 64 | 7,852 |
| 1898 | 43 | 6,293 | 1916 | 108 | 8,413 |
| 1899 | 15 | 4,284 | 1917 | 398 | 57,309 |
| 1900 | 11 | 2,316 | 1918 | 417 | 66,457 |
| 1901 | 18 | 1,948 | 1919 | 497 | 63,137 |
| 1902 | 8 | 1,849 | 1920 | 282 | 36,371 |
| 1903 | 9 | 1,359 | 1921 | 246 | 58,225 |
| 1904 | 6 | 897 | 1922 | 250 | 41,503 |
| 1905 | 19 | 5,013 | 1923 | 270 | 36,295 |
| 1906 | 13 | 2,037 | 1924 | 333 | 54,526 |
| 1907 | 57 | 9,855 | 1925 | 293 | 40,742 |
| 1908 | 13 | 822 | 1926 | 495 | 67,234 |
| 1909 | 11 | 310 | 1927 | 383 | 46,672 |
| 1910 | 10 | 2,937 | 1928 | 397 | 46,252 |
| 1911 | 22 | 2,100 | 1929 | 576 | 77,444 |
| 1912 | 49 | 5,736 | 1930 | 906 | 81,329 |
| 1913 | 47 | 5,242 | 1931 | 998 | 64,536 |
| 1914 | 50 | 7,904 | | | |

Adapted from *Kadokawa Nihon-shi jiten* (Tokyo: Kadokawa Shoten, 1976, 2d ed.), p. 1288.

pages. In March 1921, for instance, women at the Tokyo Muslin Company walked off the job to underscore their demands for better pay, an eight-hour day, the elimination of night work, and better food in the dormitories. That same summer, in what became the largest strike in the Taishō era, nearly thirty thousand skilled workers at the Kawasaki and Mitsubishi shipyards in Kōbe laid down their tools to force management to consider seriously their entreaty for higher wages and improved working conditions. The longest strike occurred in 1927 and 1928 at the modestly sized Noda Soy Sauce Company, located in Chiba Prefecture and maker of the popular Kikkōman brand.

The Noda strike demonstrated how bitter labor disputes could become by the middle of the 1920s and how difficult it could be to reconcile differences between management and workers, as the average work stoppage lengthened to approximately thirty days, up from a norm of eleven days in

1919. The Noda dispute began on September 16, 1927, when some two thousand workers called on ownership to boost pay and officially to recognize their union, a local affiliate of the Sōdōmei. Management dug in its heels. Although Noda's owners had submitted to a series of demands for shorter hours and improved housing after workers established the local union in December 1921, they now were determined to purge their factories of any trace of disruptive union influence. In reaction to the union demands, management officially fired all striking workers in the fall of 1927 and hired temporary employees. Matters thereupon turned nasty: The discharged workers attacked the scabs, blinding one by throwing acid in his face; the police roughed up men on a picket line; and the strikers retaliated by threatening plant managers, who barricaded their homes and sent their families to live with distant relatives. Finally, the two sides decided to sit down with a panel of mediators, led by the venerable Shibusawa Eiichi. On April 19, 1928, Noda's ownership agreed to permit about one-third of the discharged workers to return to their jobs and to pay severance bonuses to the remainder, but it prevailed in its insistence that the local union disband.

On balance, factory workers who were willing to switch jobs, organize unions, and go out on strike won considerable concessions from management in the late 1910s and 1920s. By some estimates, more than half the labor disputes in the 1920s ended with management yielding to all or a significant portion of the employees' demands, just as the owners at Noda had done. In particular, factory workers in heavy industry seem to have been especially successful in winning wage increases during the World War I boom and in preserving them in the subsequent recession. Moreover, by the Taishō period a few textile mills and many large-scale enterprises in the upper half of the dual structure had extended a considerable number of nonwage benefits to skilled blue-collar workers.

The turn toward paternalism constituted a direct, self-conscious response by ownership to the threat of a militant labor movement and represented an attempt to persuade workers that they did not need to join labor unions in order to better their circumstances. Kanebō pioneered the implementation of paternalistic practices in the textile industry. As company officials came to realize that Japan was not blessed with an endless supply of young girls willing to risk serious injury and even death from tuberculosis to complete five-year work contracts, they implemented programs intended to promote the image of the firm as a surrogate family. To facilitate communication between management and labor, Kanebō set out suggestion boxes into which workers could deposit complaints or comments about how to improve conditions in the mills, sponsored an in-house magazine, and distributed a newsletter to the girls' home villages. For unmarried mill hands, it upgraded dormitory facilities and the food served in its dining halls; for married employees living in company housing, it subsidized consumer cooperatives, day nurseries, and kindergartens. For its entire work force, Kanebō established recreational facilities and offered evening courses on sewing, social etiquette, the tea ceremony, flower arranging, calligraphy, and music.

In similar fashion, large enterprises in the heavy industry sector started to accord new benefits to valued but scarce and hard-to-retain blue-collar workers during the Taishō period. Just three months after the Yūaikai founded a local at the Shibaura Engineering Works in 1915, for instance, management organized a mutual aid society for workers funded by payroll deductions and company contributions, opened an infirmary, announced that anyone crippled on the job would receive a year's pay, and established a retirement plan. Several shipyards and steel mills introduced similar benefits during the World War I boom as a means of combating severe shortages of technical personnel and of deterring experienced blue-collar workers from moving to other companies. Other large enterprises soon followed suit, and by the end of the 1920s common inducements included the promise of permanent employment, annual wage increases based on seniority, seasonal bonuses and retirement allowances tied to length of service, health care, in-company training programs, and a variety of cultural amenities, such as libraries, game rooms, and athletic fields.

As managers brought such benefits on-line, they utilized the workers' earlier language about benevolence to create an image of the company as family, a supposedly close-knit, contented entity whose members respected and cared for one another. As Gotō Shinpei explained when he donned the hat of minister of communications in Katsura's second cabinet, "workers should help and encourage one another as though they were members of one family. A family should follow the orders of the family head and, in doing what he expects of them, always act for the honor and benefit of the family. I attempt to foster among my employees the idea of self-sacrificing devotion to their work. I also preach the principle of loving trust."[4] To give concrete expression to such rhetoric, many employers in heavy industry created factory councils. Advisory in nature, they typically brought together equal numbers of managers and factory hands elected by fellow workers to discuss such topics as productivity, wages, and company welfare facilities.

The initiatives undertaken by Kanebō, Shibaura Engineering Works, and other firms established an idealized model that later became referred to as the Japanese Employment System. Although the introduction of paternalistic practices during the Taishō period constituted a key turning point in the long-term evolution of labor-management practices, Japan did not become a work-ers' paradise. Significantly, only a relatively small proportion of the country's blue-collar factory hands, and scarcely any unskilled laborers, benefited from the new programs. Most small businesses tucked away on the bottom rungs of the dual structure lacked the financial wherewithal to replicate the non-wage enhancements offered to workers in major corporations. Moreover, even large firms in the heavy industry sector seldom provided a complete menu of new benefits to their employees, and Kanebō was more the exception than the rule among textile companies that employed mostly women. Addition-ally, workers often were unable to take advantage of educational and recre-ational programs; after working all day, few girls at Kanebō had the energy or inclination to master the tea ceremony, flower arranging, or other polite accomplishments in favor with young ladies of the middle class.

In contrast with the rather gaunt advantages enjoyed by workers, em-ployers reaped healthy gains from the new system, even in its infancy. In the first place, by the late 1920s labor turnover in heavy industry had dropped dramatically to the range of 15 to 20 percent a year, far below the level of the previous decade, even though some textile firms, including Kanebō, found it more difficult than they wished to retain employees. Moreover, a more sta-ble work force translated into greater profits for owners since they could re-duce budgets for recruitment and training. Firms additionally offset the expense of retaining their well-compensated permanent employees by carry-ing on their payrolls a substantial number of less skilled and temporary em-ployees who did not receive extensive benefits and who could be laid off or fired at the first downward tick of the business cycle. Just as significantly, the new practices dampened the enthusiasm of workers to unionize. Permanent employees who received significant nonwage benefits and whose elected rep-resentatives had a voice in factory councils were inclined to negotiate directly with management to resolve disagreements. Concurrently, many owners steadfastly refused to recognize unions as legitimate bargaining partners, just as the owners of the Noda Soy Sauce Company had done. Consequently, in 1931 only 8 percent of the nonagricultural work force belonged to a union, and even that proportion shrank steadily during the 1930s.

## Widening the Margins of Political Debate

The majority of workers who participated in the labor movement during the Taishō period accepted the system of industrial capitalism that was evolving in Japan and, like tenant families, mobilized themselves to acquire what the 1918 newspaper editorial concerning the rice riots called a fair distribution of economic benefits. In contrast, during the 1910s and 1920s other Japanese totally lost faith in capitalism, agreeing with Kawakami Hajime that it ruthlessly exploited the underprivileged and perverted the Meiji Dream, which, to their minds, had envisaged more comfortable and prosperous lives for everyone. Believing that wealth and power are intertwined, dissidents on the more radical end of the political spectrum trumpeted the virtues of alternative systems, such as socialism and communism, and some formed leftist political parties for the purpose of advancing the circumstances of their countrymen.

Socialist thought in Japan was almost as old as capitalist ideology itself. As early as the 1890s persons such as Abe Isoo, author and university professor, espoused the belief that close government supervision over the production and distribution of goods would best serve the interests of the ordinary people of Japan. In the spring of 1901 Abe and like-minded individuals founded the Socialist Democratic Party (Shakai Minshutō), Japan's first but very short-lived socialist party, whose platform enunciated a range of noneconomic issues that inspired moderate leftists at the beginning of the new century: pacifism and the reduction of armaments, the abolition of the House of Peers, and the establishment of universal suffrage.

Other leftists advocated more radical change. Kōtoku Shūsui and Kanno Suga were among Japan's first prominent anarcho-syndicalists. A cofounder of the Socialist Democratic Party in 1901, Kōtoku at first advocated using constitutional means to replace "the government of the politicians, of the stock manipulators, of the militarists, of the aristocrats by a government of the people." The initial step in the process, he continued, should be "to allot political power to the whole body of the populace," and he proposed ultimately "to abolish the private ownership of land and capital and to restore the fruits of production to the hands of the producers."[5] After conferring with American radicals in San Francisco in 1905 and 1906, however, Kōtoku returned to Japan persuaded that only direct action, a massive general strike by workers, could topple the government and place economic and political power fully in the hands of the working classes.

Kanno, a fledgling journalist who was winning a reputation as a hardnosed critic of the government, encouraged Kōtoku to sedition after she began living with him in 1909. A self-declared "radical thinker, even among anarchists," she once declared that "it is necessary to arouse the people by instigating riots, undertaking revolutionary action, and engaging in assassinations."[6] Soon she identified Emperor Meiji as "the root of all the crimes being committed, a person who must be killed," and in 1910 she and Kōtoku participated in the High Treason Incident, a bungled attempt to assassinate the monarch. Having been captured by the police and convicted behind closed courtroom doors, Kanno, Kōtoku, and ten coconspirators were executed in January 1911. Just days before she was garroted, Kanno wrote in her prison notebook: "Snow has settled on top of the pine trees and the dead branches of the cypress trees. The world has been covered in silver during the night. Let it snow, let it snow! A foot, two feet. Pile it up high. Envelop this sinful city of Tokyo in snow, like a city buried in ashes. Level the entire landscape."

The High Treason Incident brought on what some described as the "winter years" for the Japanese radical left, but Ōsugi Sakae soon rekindled the anarchists' spirit, elaborating his philosophy in several journals that he edited. In his view, society consisted of just two classes, the conquerors and the conquered, and virtually all institutions, from government to organized religion, served as instruments of human subjugation. "Society progressed," Ōsugi wrote, and consequently, "the methods of subjugation also developed." He then named "the methods of violence and deception: Government! Law! Religion! Education! Morality! The Army! Police! Courts! Parliaments! Science! Philosophy! Art! All other social institutions!"[7]

An advocate of self-liberating action, Ōsugi passionately rejected any suggestion of seeking reform through the Diet and instead urged workers to initiate walkouts and other contentious demonstrations that he believed would lead to the abolition of the state and the destruction of capitalism. His anarchism fed his predilection for defying social conventions as well. In 1916 he abandoned his wife and jilted another lover, the well-known journalist Kamichika Ichiko, to move in with Itō Noe, a noted feminist and

*Ōsugi Sakae (center) and Itō Noe*

fellow anarchist. The Ōsugi–Itō liaison became headline news that November, when the enraged Kamichika stabbed Ōsugi while he and Itō were vacationing at a seaside resort.

Diet approval of the Universal Manhood Suffrage Act in March 1925 created a new opportunity for members of the political left to pursue their goals within the framework of parliamentary politics. Sponsored by Prime Minister Katō Takaaki and his colleagues in the Kenseikai, the measure eliminated tax qualifications for voting and extended the franchise to nearly all males over the age of twenty-five. To some extent, Katō was acting on the conviction that broader participation in the political process represented an "inevitable world trend," in the popular phrase of the day, that Japan had to join if it wished to keep pace with other advanced powers. The Kenseikai, however, also was responding to demands from the people for a greater political voice. For several years, Yoshino Sakuzō and other contributors to liberal journals had been calling for a more democratic Japan, and labor organizations had begun to stage demonstrations in major cities to promote the cause of universal manhood suffrage. That agitation from below, combined with the rice riots, the growing militancy of the tenant and labor movements, and the anarchists' calls for violent revolution, persuaded even reluctant legislators to endorse the suffrage bill as a means to head off further mass discontent.

No sooner had the ink dried on the new law than a plethora of "proletarian parties" sprang up to press for the interests of workers and tenants. Especially prominent among the new parties were the Labor-Farmer Party (Rōdō Nōmintō), founded in March 1926 by labor leaders and sympathetic figures from the political left such as Abe Isoo, and the Japan Labor-Farmer Party (Nihon Rōnōtō), formed that December. Both were relatively moderate organizations that promised to use democratic, parliamentary means to improve living standards for the working and farming classes. According to the founding statement of the Labor-Farmer Party, its members intended to "displace the established political parties," the Seiyūkai and Kenseikai, "which represent only the interests of the privileged classes," and to "use legal means" to remedy "unfair land and production systems" and "bring about the political, economic, and social emancipation of the proletarian class."[8] Despite such ambitions, just two candidates backed by the Labor-Farmer Party and one from the Japan Labor-Farmer Party won Diet seats in the February 1928 elections, the first held after the enactment of universal manhood suffrage.

Somewhat more successful was the Socialist People's Party (Shakai Minshūtō), founded in December 1926 and initially headed by Abe. Its founding document repudiated laissez-faire capitalism, which it condemned as being incompatible with the economic, social, and political well-being of ordinary people. "The capitalist system of production and distribution," it stated, "impedes a sound livelihood for the people," and the party further pledged to use "rational means" to build "a political and economic system centering upon the working class."[9] Specifically, the four successful candidates fielded by the Socialist People's Party in the February 1928 elections brought to the Diet a platform that called for nationalizing basic industries, enacting land reform that would redistribute fields to tenant families, initiating welfare legislation favorable to workers and tenants, abolishing restrictions on civil liberties, and extending the franchise to women.

Farther to the left was the Japan Communist Party, founded in secret on July 15, 1922, by a small coterie of journalists and political activists inspired by the success of the Russian Revolution. Outlawed by the government and bedeviled with factional disputes, the JCP dissolved itself two years later, only to reemerge as an underground party in December 1926. The JCP engaged largely in propagandistic and educational activities and enjoyed only a muted influence. Still, it did manage to draw into its circle such prominent persons as Kawakami Hajime, who formally joined in 1932, as well as other intellectuals and students who moved toward Marxism because it gave them a systematic methodology for analyzing how all nations might undergo the transition from feudalism to capitalism and from capitalism to socialism.

## "The Day the Mountains Move Has Come"

Feminists and students joined the great debates of the Taishō era. The crescendo of voices added a passionate concern for social justice to the ongoing struggle for political and economic fairness being waged on many fronts, and the hopes they articulated for the future frequently clashed with the notions of modernity being put forth by the middle class and government officials. Many of the new firebrands acted individually, sizable numbers allied themselves with the emerging proletarian parties, and millions of others joined new organizations founded to press for the interests of their particular groups. The burgeoning popular involvement in mass social movements added to the pluralistic atmosphere of the times and helped fuel the growing excitement and turmoil of the 1920s.

After watching Matsui Sumako's riveting performance in *A Doll's House* in the autumn of 1911, one critic referred to Nora as a fictional character that would stimulate real-life "new women" in Japan to redefine their roles in the home and society. A vigorous debate about the ideal qualities that the New Woman ought to represent took place on the pages of the *Seitō* ("Bluestocking"), a journal begun in September 1911 by Hiratsuka Raichō, who chose for its title a name linked closely in the public mind with militant international feminism. To draw her readers' attention to the forlorn condition of women in the twentieth century, Hiratsuka greeted readers to the inaugural issue with a stirring poetic allusion to Japan's most important progenitor deity, the Sun Goddess Amaterasu:

> In the beginning, woman was the sun.
>   An authentic person.
> Today, she is the moon.
>   Living through others.
>   Reflecting the brilliance of others.
> And now, "Bluestocking," a journal created for the first time with the
>   brains and hands of today's Japanese women, raises its voice.[10]

Hiratsuka put her finger directly on the pulse of women across the country, who flooded the "Bluestocking" office with thousands of letters containing both well-wishes and pleas for advice about everyday problems they confronted as women.

One of the voices featured in the magazine belonged to the famous poet Yosano Akiko, who graced the first issue with a verse that was to inspire generations of women, both in Japan and internationally:

---

*Yosano Akiko in a hat she purchased in Paris*

The day the mountains move has come.

I speak, but no one believes me.

For a time the mountains have been asleep,

But long ago they all danced with fire.

It doesn't matter if you believe this,

My friends, as long as you believe:

All the sleeping women

Are now awake and moving.[11]

A prolific contributor to the "Bluestocking" and other leading literary magazines, Yosano rejected a world based on male privilege and refused to confine herself to a life whose perimeters were circumscribed by the notion of good wife, wise mother. Rather, she asserted that autonomy from outside control was crucial to the conception of the New Woman. Married to a poet whose reputation did not match her own and mother to eleven children, Yosano suggested that women had many roles—daughter, wife, mother, friend to others, citizen to the nation, human being to the world— and must be free to find personal fulfillment in all those various realms. Each woman, she believed, had the ability to satisfy the obligations of her many different lives, but only if she enjoyed economic independence, equal education and employment opportunities, and fair and impartial treatment under the law.

In contrast with Yosano's uncompromising emphasis on individualism, other feminists preferred to carry on a collective struggle for greater equality, and throughout the Taishō period, local women's associations took root in every prefecture. They espoused a variety of feminist issues, ranging from expanded political rights for women to the disestablishment of legalized prostitution and passage of legislation to prevent men with venereal diseases from marrying—all intended to advance the welfare of women and promote equal rights for both sexes. By 1927 the largest women's association in the country was the three-million-strong Federation of Women's Organizations of Western Japan, founded in Osaka in 1919.

During the 1920s some women focused their efforts on the right to vote, a quest they considered necessary if women were ever to gain full equality with men, improve access to higher education, and enhance the position of mothers within the family. In March 1920 Hiratsuka Raichō joined Ichikawa Fusae, a former newspaper reporter from Nagoya who had helped establish a women's section in the Yūaikai, to found the New Woman's Association. Just two years later that group scored a significant victory when it persuaded the Diet to overturn provisions of the Public Order and Police Act of 1900 that prohibited women from joining political associations. The New Woman's Association dissolved itself not long thereafter, and in December 1924 Ichikawa organized the Women's Suffrage League to continue the campaign for the franchise. The league was rewarded for its efforts in 1931, when a Minseitō cabinet agreed to sponsor legislation permitting women to vote in local elections and, with the consent of their husbands, to hold local office. The House of Peers rejected the bill, but both the government and feminists anticipated that women's suffrage soon would become reality.

Not all women believed that democracy and capitalism offered solutions to their problems, and they advocated instead a socialist revolution to liberate both men and women from irrational economic and social systems created by self-interested elites. Yamakawa Kikue was of a such a mind. A century after her great-great-grandmother had walked away from her samurai "husband" and young son to return to her natal merchant household in Mito domain, Yamakawa wrote with burning passion about the need for a revolution that would benefit women of all economic classes. In her estimation, proposals for suffrage, individual rights, and expanded educational opportunities primarily helped only middle-class, "bourgeois," women, whereas her heart went out to the struggling worker. In one magazine article she recalled her encounter with a group of young women while out walking one cold morning. The workers, shabbily dressed and hurriedly snatching a meager bite to eat as they made their way toward a dirty, noisy workshop, seemed to Yamakawa to be "a cross between human, machine, and animal." She then related the emotions that had run through her when she visited a factory earlier: "I wanted to apologize to these women. I wanted to prostrate myself before them. I wanted to do this because I was tormented by the guilty feeling that I—we—are the ones who have corrupted them, who have cheated them, who have trampled on them. So, I wanted to apologize to them, to tell them that I was their friend. I looked down upon them, as they knelt, barefoot, in the unheated hall. I have never forgotten those feelings of guilt and distress."[12]

Only a thorough housecleaning, Yamakawa said, could allow Japan to rebuild a better society. To that end she urged women to dedicate their energies to a "general proletarian class movement." She poured her thoughts into a manifesto she wrote for the Red Wave Society, an association dedicated to realizing the socialist dream. "For centuries," she began, "women and workers have endured together a history of oppression." Ours, she went on, "is a society which has driven many of our sisters into prostitution, and for the sake of its own aggressive ambitions has taken away our beloved fathers, lovers, children and brothers." Because of that, she concluded, the Red Wave Society "declares all-out war on this cruel, shameless society. Women who wish to be liberated, join the Red Wave Society. Socialism offers the only way to save humankind from the oppressions and abuses of capitalism. Sisters, who love justice and humanity, join the socialist movement!"[13]

Even as the debate about the New Woman unfolded into new and ever more radical directions, male undergraduates at Tokyo University in December 1918 established the Shinjinkai, or the New Man Society, to discuss the problems of social reform and political democracy. In concordance with similar groups formed on more than fifty other campuses, Shinjinkai members idealized "the masses" as the repository of all that was good in Japanese society and harangued the established parties and government for not doing more to assist the average farmer and laborer. "As we face the dawn," asked the students in the first issue of the Shinjinkai's magazine, who "should take charge of the reform of Japan today? How about the privileged classes who now occupy the positions of national leadership? How about the educated classes, the bureaucrats, the military, the party politicians, the capitalists, the university professors?" Decidedly not, the students answered. "Their record clearly shows too much wickedness, vulgarity, and lack of principle to win the confidence of the masses. We have already given up hope in the ruling class." Thus, the Shinjinkai organizers ended, "the drive for reform must come from youth itself, youth whose conscience is pure, intellect keen, spirit afire. The blood of youth is untainted, the standpoint of youth is impartial, the ideals of youth are lofty. Has not the day come for the youth to rise up as one?"[14]

The notion that "the ruling class" could not deliver political and economic justice to Japan's ordinary people propelled members of the student movement into a variety of activities. Some translated the works of Western socialists and helped organize public lectures and speaking tours dedicated to progressive causes. During the 1920s numerous activists within the Shinjinkai became prominent labor organizers, even taking a hand in leading the Yūaikai in more militant directions, while others involved themselves with the tenant union movement. As radical causes became a more powerful magnet by the middle of the decade, many Shinjinkai members came to consider themselves Marxists and joined the underground Japan Communist Party, preaching revolutionary solutions to the economic and social ills of the Taishō era.

## The Voices of Minorities

Japan's ethnic minorities and the adherents of maverick religions also called for greater social and economic equality during the 1920s. Oppressed by daimyo lords and shogunal governors in the Tokugawa period, the Ainu continued to suffer various forms of discrimination in the modern era. Although the Meiji government conferred citizenship upon Ainu, it drew attention to their cultural differences from mainstream Japanese by officially categorizing them as a "former indigenous people" and undertaking an assimilation campaign that accomplished little except to deprive them of their traditional lands and segregate them in self-contained villages and urban ghettos. As Japan flexed its colonial muscles in the late nineteenth and early twentieth centuries, new notions about racial identity and the superiority of the Japanese, so evident in perceptions of Koreans and Taiwanese, also colored conceptions of the Ainu. Increasingly many Japanese began to see the Ainu not as an ethnic minority with distinctive cultural habits but as a separate and inferior race. In 1912, Nitobe Inazō, who then held the chair of Colonial Policy at Tokyo University, articulated that view when he wrote that the Ainu, "a race akin to the Lapps," had "not yet emerged from the Stone Age" and "possessed no art beyond a primitive form of horticulture."[15] In similar fashion, other intellectuals and government officials stigmatized Ainu as "hairy" antediluvian savages, a "dying race" incapable of adapting successfully to the challenges of modern civilization.

Undereducated, crippled by poverty, and isolated in scattered hamlets and urban enclaves, the Ainu possessed few means to combat such attitudes or oppose government policies. As a result, in the Taishō period several prominent Ainu spokespeople sought final assimilation into mainstream society, and in 1930 they formed the Ainu Society, an organization that operated under the supervision of the Social Section of the Hokkaidō prefectural government, to lobby for welfare measures and more equitable treatment as citizens of the Japanese state. Other members of the minority community, in what might be seen as passive resistance to acculturation and the disintegration of Ainu traditions, began to preserve folktales and epic stories of the past. In 1915 one anthropologist took down the fictional account of a "long-forgotten" Ainu attack on the ancient imperial capital of Kyoto and the abduction of aristocratic maidens, and just before she died in 1922 at the age of nineteen, Chiri Yukie compiled for publication a set of oral tales that included the now-famous "Song of the Owl God," the story of a boy, "once rich but now poor," whose noble bearing is recognized by the Owl God, who sees through the lad's ragged clothing and restores him to his rightful place above "those who used to be poor but are now rich."[16]

Japan's outcast community also mounted a campaign against discrimination during the Taishō period. Forty years earlier, in 1871, the Meiji government had abolished the derogatory epithets *eta* and *hinin* and decreed that "henceforth the people belonging to these estates shall be treated in the same manner both in occupation and social standing as the common people."[17] The emancipation edict cut two ways, however. Although theoretically lifting restrictions on residence and marriage, it also eliminated official monopolies on butchering and the production of leather goods, thus undermining the ability of many *burakumin*, as the outcasts preferred to call themselves, to earn a livelihood.

The social standing of the nation's 800,000 *burakumin*, somewhat less than 2 percent of the country's total population, did not improve either. Fearing that contamination and pollution would spread into their own communities, many "common people" protested the government's edict and even attacked minority settlements, killing and injuring twenty-nine *burakumin* and destroying three hundred homes in one notorious incident in May 1873. Throughout the Meiji era few *burakumin* could find employment in factories unless they hid their identity from employers, teachers relegated minority children to the back of the classroom and arranged play groups so that outcast students would not come into physical contact with their classmates, public baths and barbers refused to serve them, and as late as 1902 a district court judge in Hiroshima upheld the right of a non-*burakumin* wife to divorce her minority husband on the ground that he was from an "inferior racial group."

At the beginning of the new century members of the minority community began to organize self-improvement societies with the purpose of urging fellow *burakumin* to educate themselves better and to adopt middle-class customs and mores so that they could integrate with mainstream society. When those efforts to assimilate bore little fruit, impatient *burakumin* adopted more militant tactics. Persuaded that mainstream society would forever deny them an opportunity to fulfill their dreams and aspirations, young activists in 1922 met in Kyoto to organize the Suiheisha (Levelers' Society). Pledging themselves to "achieve total liberation by our own efforts," members of the Suiheisha's two hundred local branches launched a "denunciation campaign," calling for public apologies from anyone who discriminated against *burakumin*.[18] Such tactics did produce some results: In Osaka several landlords began to rent to minorities, and in Hiroshima public baths opened their doors to all customers.

The Suiheisha's modest triumphs, however, failed to satisfy many within the minority community, who came to believe that only the revolutionary emancipation of the working class as a whole would bring them freedom. In 1921 Sano Manabu, an active member of the Shinjinkai who was to join the Japan Communist Party the following year, published an influential essay in the magazine *Kaihō* ("Emancipation") advocating a general socialist revolution and urging *burakumin* to unite with other workers, fellow victims of capitalistic exploitation. That plea and growing disillusionment with the Suiheisha's inability to win quicker results had an impact, as shown by the increasing numbers of *burakumin* who allied themselves with the labor and tenant organizations and entered the proletarian parties.

Also living on the political and economic margins of society were Korean immigrants to Japan. Legally the annexation converted Korean citizens into Japanese subjects, and starting with the World War I boom, thousands moved to the Japanese islands in search of better education and employment opportunities. During the 1920s a widening stream of poor young men from villages in southern Korea set off to Japan to search for work after massive land acquisitions by the Oriental Development Company and other Japanese-owned agricultural corporations had driven their families into tenancy. Many Koreans who spent time in Japan found reason to return eventually to the peninsula, but enough stayed that the number of Koreans resident in Japan rose from approximately 1,000 at the time of annexation to nearly 300,000 by the end of the 1920s, as shown in Table 11.8.

Except for a few thousand students and a small cohort of restaurateurs and shopkeepers, most Korean immigrants in the 1920s took jobs as coal miners, construction workers, and unskilled factory laborers on the bottom rungs of the dual economy. Poorly compensated to begin with, many Koreans found themselves condemned to grinding poverty when their pay packets turned out to be considerably more slender than those received by Japanese coworkers doing the same jobs. To make matters worse, the immigrant laborers had to tolerate charges that they "stole" jobs from ordinary Japanese and undercut wage levels by agreeing to work for less pay. Koreans in Japan found themselves the victims of social discrimination as well. Newspapers stereotyped them as shiftless and prone to commit crimes, and few landlords in middle-class neighborhoods deigned to rent lodgings to them. "In customs," noted one government study, "Koreans are basically different from Japanese, and, because their everyday lives are extremely unclean and disorganized, it is only natural that they are rejected by people living nearby. Koreans are generally narrow-minded, extremely suspicious and jealous, and are apt to misunderstand things. Moreover, there is a ten-

**TABLE 11.8** *Koreans Resident in Japan,*
*1909–1930*

| YEAR | KOREANS RESIDENT IN JAPAN |
|------|---------------------------|
| 1909 | 790 |
| 1915 | 3,989 |
| 1920 | 30,175 |
| 1925 | 133,710 |
| 1930 | 298,091 |

Adapted from George De Vos and Changsoo Lee, "The Colonial Experience,
1910–1945," in Lee and De Vos, eds., *Koreans*
*in Japan: Ethnic Conflict and Accommodation*
(Berkeley: University of California Press,
1981), p. 37.

dency among Japanese people to treat them as members of an inferior
race."[19]

In the face of unrelenting hostility and discrimination, Koreans settled
into ghettos near the industrial zones around Tokyo, Yokohama, Nagoya,
Kōbe, and Fukuoka. The largest Korean community was in Osaka, where
by 1930 immigrants made up nearly 10 percent of that city's population and
lived in conditions similar to those of the *burakumin* outcasts. The residents
of the urban enclaves responded in a variety of ways to their harsh circumstances. Some vented their rage by committing crimes against Japanese, not an unnatural reaction by discouraged immigrants who almost
everywhere tend to consider any member of the oppressive majority group
fair game. Other segments of the Korean community turned to more politically oriented alternatives. With the help of Ōsugi Sakae, for instance, Korean students in November 1921 formed the Black Wave Society to promote
a political revolution that would bring into being a new society based on the
equality of classes, genders, and nationality groups. Similarly, Koreans began to form labor organizations, some of which adopted radical agendas.
The founders of the Osaka Confederation of Korean Laborers pledged "to
secure victory in the class struggle" and "to overthrow the capitalist system."[20]

More moderate Korean leaders feared that political confrontation and labor organizing merely invited antagonism from Japanese authorities, and in
December 1921 they founded the Sōaikai (Mutual Affection Society) to im-

prove the image of the immigrant community and promote Korean-Japanese friendship. As a conciliatory organization that accepted colonialism as an inescapable reality, the Sōaikai condemned radical activity as self-defeating. With branches in Tokyo and other major cities, it functioned as a mutual aid society that assisted Korean laborers in finding work, helped negotiate settlements to workshop disputes, provided food and shelter to the unemployed, and subsidized medical care. The immigrant community warmly supported the society, and its membership rolls included nearly 100,000 names by the end of the Taishō period.

A fast-growing wave of new religious sects provided refuge for some of Japan's discontent. By 1924 government officials had classified ninety-eight groups as "newly arising religions," a category that grew fourfold by the end of the decade, when adherents of the new denominations numbered several million. Like the generation of new religions founded during the late Tokugawa period, the mass religious movements of the twentieth century boasted charismatic leaders, appealed to the economically and socially disadvantaged, promised to help people overcome the hardships of this life, and held out hope for the coming of a utopia on earth.

The most prominent new religion was the Ōmoto sect, founded by Deguchi Nao, an elderly, widowed rural woman with no formal education. Like the founders of many other millenarian religions, Nao led a life of endless hardship, which she described as existing in "a cauldron burning in the fires of hell."[21] In 1892, when she was sixty-five years old, she fell into a trance and claimed that a puissant spirit had possessed her body, thus empowering her to heal the afflictions of others and offer cogent advice about any manner of problem, from mundane marital difficulties to existential crises. Ōmoto's phenomenal growth began in 1898, when Nao met the young Ueda Kisaburō. An effective and creative interpreter of Nao's religious message, Ueda eventually married her daughter and, under the name Deguchi Onisaburō, became the sect's leader. Blessed with a compelling and forceful personality, Onisaburō frequently dressed in the brightly colored kimono of a female shaman to announce his divine powers and occasionally viewed the sect's public parades while mounted on a white horse, a pose conventionally reserved for the emperor when he reviewed the imperial troops. From the denomination's great pilgrimage center just outside Kyoto, he denounced the rift that had grown up between Japan's rich and poor, freely condemned capitalists and landlords for bringing misery to ordinary men and women, and constructed an elaborate eschatology that prophesied an end to all evil and the redistribution of wealth and property. His message resonated with working women, unskilled factory laborers, shopkeepers, and peddlers—those most in need of a new sense of community and spirituality to help them overcome the anomie of industrialization and city life—and by the end of the Taishō years somewhere between 400,000, in the government's calculation, and three million people, according to the sect's tabulations, had become Ōmoto converts.

## "Shepherds of the People"

Feisty tenants and disgruntled labor, intrepid feminists and radical students, seething minorities and outcasts, *moga* and *mobo*, anarchists and Communists: To many within the governing establishment it appeared that the country was coming apart at the seams. In the 1920s the disruptive consequences of modernization—the competing attraction of new visions, the dislocations inherent in industrialization, the tensions associated with new modes of living, and the stresses that accompanied imperialism—were imploding on one another. The tumult of the twenties alarmed many bureaucrats and members of the mainstream parties, who sought ways to restrain the more extreme forms of radicalism that seemed at times to threaten the very existence of the state.

On occasion some officials resorted to violence to suppress supposed enemies and discipline uppity minorities. "Doom was writ red and large on the eastern sky," according to one eyewitness, after the Great Kantō Earthquake struck at noon on September 1, 1923, creating "a red desert here and there a crematory" and filling rivers and canals with tens of thousands of "the floating dead."[22] In the ensuing chaos, rumors began to circulate that Koreans were poisoning wells, and police fueled the growing sense of panic by authorizing a radio broadcast warning that Koreans were "burning houses, killing people, and stealing money" and instructing people to "use all necessary measures" to protect themselves and their property.[23] Although the rumors were groundless, army reservists and civilian vigilantes began to roam the streets of Tokyo and other cities, hunting down and massacring several thousand Koreans before the violence subsided. In subsequent days the police ordered the mass arrest of Japanese socialists and other political activists and murdered a dozen of them in their jail cells. Among the victims were the anarchists Ōsugi Sakae and Itō Noe, strangled to death by a police captain.

More than violence, however, the government relied on legal measures to rein in radical activity in the 1920s. At the same time that it approved universal manhood suffrage, the Diet passed the Peace Preservation Law of 1925. Drafted by bureaucrats within the Ministry of Justice, the measure

*The Great Kantō Earthquake*

stipulated that anyone "who organizes a group for the purpose of changing the national polity (*kokutai*) or of denying the private property system, or anyone who knowingly participates in such group" could be jailed for ten years, or even executed after the law was amended three years later.[24] On March 15, 1928, the police evoked the law when they rounded up more than sixteen hundred suspected Communists and radical students. In the wake of the March 15 Incident, the government banned the Labor-Farmer Party for enlisting subversives, and university presidents forced the Shinjinkai to dissolve.

In contrast with those authorities who employed coercion to maintain social and political order, other members of the ruling circle preferred to count on persuasion to gentle dissidence and integrate the awakening interest groups into the established political community. Thus, the "shepherds of the people," as one Home Ministry bureaucrat referred to himself and his colleagues, crafted policies designed to herd the citizenry away from radical ideologies, solve Japan's "social problems," and overcome the divisiveness that was an inherent part of rapid modernization.[25] In quest of such goals, those officials sometimes reached out to existing organizations. Not infrequently leaders of those interest groups cooperated with state authorities in controlling the activities of the rank-and-file membership, usually because collaborating with the state offered the associations an opportunity to advance their own agendas.

In 1919, just as the labor and tenant unions began to display the potential for disruption, the government attempted to allay radical sentiments within the outcast community by hosting conferences at which minority leaders, Diet members, and bureaucrats could discuss the plight of *burakumin*. Shortly thereafter the Home Ministry began to make additional moneys available for public works projects in areas with significant outcast populations. In the case of the Korean immigrant community, the government funneled money to the moderate Sōaikai, which used the funds to support its welfare work and in turn expand its membership. In exchange, Sōaikai leaders maintained close links with the police, reporting on crime and union activities. After the Great Kantō Earthquake, the Sōaikai even organized Koreans to help clean up Tokyo in the hope of mitigating the intense hostility between the immigrants and their Japanese neighbors.

To dampen tensions between management and labor, some "shepherds" within the Home Ministry lobbied major businesses to improve workers' compensation and expand paternalistic benefits. In 1919 the government also established the Harmonization Society, a semigovernmental organization headed by business leaders and officials from the Home Ministry, to promote cooperation and equanimity between labor and management. The society's founding document declared that "harmonization" involved respect for the rights of others, a willingness to compromise for the sake of society, and the promotion of industrial development through mutual cooperation. Specifically, the organization arbitrated labor disputes when so requested, conducted research on labor problems, and made policy recommendations to the government. When the society proved less capable of resolving disagreements than had been hoped, the government created a special Labor Affairs Section within the Home Ministry and assigned trained conciliation officers to prefectural police departments. In 1926 such governmental and private arbitration efforts settled 40 percent of all work stoppages.

The rural countryside provided a fertile environment for the growth of new linkages between the people and government agencies. In the opening decades of the new century, farm families began to fear the mercurial ups and downs of the rural economy and the looming consequences of full-scale industrialization. Yokoi Tokiyoshi, a professor of agricultural science at Tokyo University, gave voice to their antiurban, anti-industrial inclinations when he argued that modern economic growth inexorably created a gap between wealthy cities and impoverished villages. Although farmers were the only "class with integrity," he wrote, the unfortunate among them "suffer agonizing distress under the oppression of the rich. Wealthy capitalists use every means to make the poor suffer, and city people violate the interests of the villagers."[26]

Some villagers were equally distressed by the appearance of adventurous youth and New Women and the continuing intrusion of Western culture, with its unrelenting emphasis on individualism, commercialism, and hedonistic self-gratification. "I occasionally meet a woman who cuts her hair very short and makes up her face with rouge, lipstick, and an eyebrow pencil," wrote one farmer in 1928. "But when I scrutinize her clothes, I find them not matching her hair style and make up. She seems to be satisfied with herself only because she can catch the attention of others. I find her modern, but my feeling toward her is that of contempt."[27]

Farm families crowded the ramparts at the beginning of the twentieth century to protect themselves against modernity's onslaught. One tactic they pursued was to shore up economic conditions in the rural countryside. Many rural communities between 1900 and 1914 formed agricultural cooperatives to help arrange the sale of crops, purchase tools and seeds at favorable prices, and introduce new technology. Another strategic initiative involved strengthening the village's psychological defenses. Across the countryside Hōtoku (Repaying Virtue) Societies, inspired by the teachings of the Tokugawa period agronomist Ninomiya Sontoku, valorized a rural ethos built around such bedrock values as family solidarity, social obligation, group consensus, mutual assistance, hard work, and frugality.

Many bureaucrats sympathized with the notion that Japan's future development, its very ability to maintain its newly won status as a world-class imperial and economic power, depended upon a stable, prosperous countryside. They also listened carefully to Yokoi's admonition that "It is ultimately the responsibility of the nation-state to help the weak" and to his contention that only the government had the ability to orchestrate policies that would permit "commerce, industry, and agriculture to all advance together."[28] Consequently, officials within the Home Ministry expedited the expansion of agricultural cooperatives and encouraged the formation of Hōtoku Societies by drawing them together into a national organization under the ministry's jurisdiction. Later, when the postwar recession engulfed the countryside, the government enacted the Tenancy Conciliation Law of 1924, which established machinery for mediating disputes between landlords and tenants, and two years later promulgated the Regulations for the

Establishment of Owner-Cultivators, which provided low-interest loans to help tenant families acquire land of their own.

## Whither Japan?

At the Washington Conference in 1921 and 1922, Shidehara Kijūrō endorsed the Wilsonian orthodoxy of free trade, economic growth through peaceful competition, and a cessation to aggressive empire building. He also agreed that the world's most powerful nations should cooperate to maintain international stability, chiefly by entering into multilateral pacts such as the Nine-Power Treaty, and that they must refrain from violating further the territorial and administrative integrity of China if they wished to see Asia at peace. From June 1924 to April 1927 he had the opportunity to implement those policies as the foreign minister in the Kenseikai cabinets led by Katō Takaaki and Wakatsuki Reijirō. At no time, however, did Shidehara's ideas go uncontested, and at the end of the decade an emerging diplomatic crisis in China threw the future direction of Japanese foreign policy into doubt.

Among Shidehara's critics were Japan's anti-imperialists, many of whom identified themselves as liberals or as members of the political left. Most socialists objected to imperialism on philosophical grounds; for them the expansion of colonial empires was part of capitalism's march against working classes everywhere. Others criticized empire building on a more pragmatic basis. The colonies contributed very little to Japan's economy, some liberals argued, and the maintenance of empire merely earned the nation the wrath of its Asian neighbors. Still other Japanese expressed a moral despair about the misery that their country was visiting on others. In the late 1920s Yanaihara Tadao, a distinguished economist who occupied the chair of Colonial Policy at Tokyo University that Nitobe once held, passionately decried the economic insecurity, spiritual desperation, and political hopelessness that had overwhelmed Korea after annexation. Why, he asked, did not Japan's policy makers simply understand that Koreans wanted to control their own destiny? "Go to Korea and look!" he wrote. "Every pebble by the roadside cries out for freedom."[29]

Shidehara's counsel to cooperate with the West received a tepid reception as well from pan-Asianists, who stressed Japan's Asian roots and drew unflattering contrasts between the East and the West. Okakura Kakuzō, founder of one of Japan's most distinguished fine arts universities and later curator of the Asian collection at the Boston Museum of Fine Arts, sounded that theme in his *Ideals of the East*, published at the beginning of the century:

"Asia is One. The Himalayas divide, only to accentuate, two mighty civilizations. But not even the snowy barriers can interrupt for one moment that broad expanse of love for the Ultimate and Universal, which is the common thought-inheritance of every Asiatic race, enabling them to produce all the great religions of the world, and distinguishing them from those maritime peoples of the Mediterranean and the Baltic, who love to dwell on the Particular, and to search out the means, not the end, of life."[30]

In the Taishō period, many pan-Asianists interpreted such sentiments to mean that Japan could enjoy a secure and prosperous future only if it honored its Asian past and maintained close political, economic, and cultural ties with its neighbors, especially China. Determined to promote mutual understanding, some pan-Asianists founded organizations such as the Tōa Dōbunkai (East Asian Common Culture Society), which maintained a school in Shanghai where Japanese could study Chinese language and culture and a preparatory school in Tokyo for Chinese students wishing to matriculate at Japanese universities.

Distrust of the West ran especially high among the pan-Asianists who were members of Japan's delegation to the Paris Peace Conference. Memories of the Triple Intervention and other past racial slights by the West haunted those skeptics, who awaited the arrival of Wilson's new world order with considerable trepidation. In particular, they were afraid that the West intended to use the League of Nations to perpetuate the ascendancy of the white race. "Our real fear," wrote Prince Konoe Fumimaro, a member of the House of Peers and emissary to the conference, whose father had founded the Tōa Dōbunkai, "is that the League of Nations might let the powerful nations dominate the weak nations economically, and condemn the latecoming nations to remain forever subordinate to the advanced nations."[31]

Apprehension about Western prejudice against Asians became so intense at Paris that Japanese plenipotentiaries drafted a clause on racial equality to insert into the League's covenant. The proposal was a blandly worded declaration that member nations would not discriminate against one another on the basis of race or nationality and would try "as much as possible to grant de jure equality" to foreign subjects living in their territory. Some observers thought the Japanese hypocritical for championing the cause of nondiscrimination, given their country's own troubled history with Korea, but large segments of the Japanese public took racial equality as a litmus test of the West's sincerity. After all, as one newspaper editorial noted, the League could succeed in promoting international cooperation and peaceful economic competition only if nations treated one another fairly. No Western nation at Paris endorsed the proposal, however, and the disappointed

Japanese delegation had to satisfy itself merely with making a speech about racial equality to include in the official record of the conference.

Shidehara's most formidable opponents were other Japanese who, like the pan-Asianists, believed that Japan's future lay in Asia but who dismissed cooperation in favor of more assertive promotion of Japan's rights and interests on the continent. Perhaps the most outspoken proponent of a proactive foreign policy was Tanaka Giichi. A career military officer who rose to the rank of general under the mentorship of Yamagata Aritomo, Tanaka in 1925 accepted an invitation to become the president of the Seiyūkai. Two years later, in April 1927, he assumed the premiership and served concurrently as his own foreign minister. A staunch conservative, Tanaka abhorred the rise of political radicalism in Japan, and his cabinet approved the March 15, 1928, roundup of Communists and other leftists. In foreign policy, Tanaka and his allies within the Seiyūkai argued that Japan was an Asian nation with regional security needs that often ran counter to those of Western powers such as Britain and the United States.

Events in northeastern China preoccupied Tanaka. By the end of the Taishō period, Japanese nationals constituted the paramount foreign presence in China, outnumbering all Westerners put together, and the overwhelming majority of the fifty thousand diplomats, company managers, shopkeepers, and construction workers who made up the Japanese community in China settled in coastal cities between Shanghai and Beijing. Moreover, China had become far more important economically to Japan than any of its formal colonies. China supplied the island nation with growing amounts of cereals, raw cotton, agricultural fertilizers, and minerals. Moreover, the enormous, almost uncountable Chinese population beckoned as a lucrative market for Japanese manufactures, and Japanese banks, trading firms, and factories happily opened their doors for business in the treaty ports of China. The most numerous of the China-based Japanese companies were cotton-spinning firms, and the number of spindles in operation, shown in Table 11.9, provides a significant index of how China had become so much more important economically to Japan than to its Euro-American competitors.

North of Beijing, Japan claimed to possess "special rights and interests" in Manchuria. The assertion of privilege rested, first of all, upon provisions in the internationally sanctioned Treaty of Portsmouth and on the contention that Chinese sovereignty no longer extended north of the Great Wall. Moreover, the prodigious efforts of the South Manchuria Railway Company had turned the Kwantung Territory into a vital economic zone that drew tens of thousands of Japanese settlers in search of fame and for-

**TABLE 11.9**   *Ownership of Cotton Spindles in China, 1895–1930*

|        | TOTAL NUMBER OF SPINDLES | CHINESE-OWNED | JAPANESE-OWNED | WESTERN-OWNED |
|--------|-------------------------:|--------------:|---------------:|--------------:|
| 1895   | 180,984                  | 180,984       | 0              | 0             |
| 1900   | 539,895                  | 379,347       | 0              | 160,548       |
| 1905   | 582,673                  | 398,213       | 23,912         | 160,548       |
| 1910   | 755,917                  | 540,073       | 55,296         | 160,548       |
| 1915   | 1,031,297                | 619,391       | 169,952        | 245,954       |
| 1920   | 2,832,920                | 1,774,974     | 801,662        | 256,284       |
| 1925   | 3,572,440                | 2,034,816     | 1,332,304      | 205,320       |
| 1930   | 4,497,902                | 2,499,394     | 1,821,280      | 177,228       |

Adapted from Kang Chao, *The Development of Cotton Textile Production in China* (Cambridge: East Asian Research Center, Harvard University, 1977), pp. 301–4.

tune. From a different perspective, those concerned with military security saw Manchuria as an indispensable buffer—a new "line of advantage," to resurrect Yamagata's term—that protected Korea and ultimately the homeland itself from the Russian bear. Finally, memories of bloody sacrifices in the Russo-Japanese War and the great victories won by General Nogi and Admiral Tōgō created a romantic aura around Manchuria that absorbed the psychological emotions of ordinary Japanese. "Here in far-off Manchuria," began one popular song, "Hundreds of leagues from the homeland / Our comrades lie beneath the rocky plain / Lit by the red setting sun."[32]

The thick overlaying of economic and strategic interests, Tanaka believed, made Japan's relationship with northern Asia quantitatively different from that of the Western powers, none of which had as much at stake in the region as did his island nation. In the long run, the greatest potential threat to Japan's position, Tanaka thought, could come from a China reunited under a strong central government that might try to restrain Japanese businesses and reclaim jurisdiction over Manchuria. After the Revolution of 1911 toppled the last imperial dynasty, fighting among rival warlords threw China into chaos. By the mid-1920s, one of those contenders for power, Chiang Kai-shek, had established a sphere of authority in southern China, and in 1926 his armies launched the so-called Northern Expedition, an attempt to extend the ascendancy of Chiang's political apparatus, the Guomindang (Nationalist Party), into the provinces around Beijing.

Infused with a growing sense of nationalism, Chinese citizens increasingly organized boycotts against foreign goods and mounted antiforeign demonstrations in major cities during the 1920s. As tensions mounted, hostile crowds increasingly targeted resident Japanese as the embodiment of foreign aggression, and in March 1927, just before Tanaka became prime minister, several Japanese businessmen were killed during riots in Nanjing. Once in office, Tanaka adopted a policy of mobilizing Japanese troops to protect local Japanese businesses and residents. On May 28, 1927, as Guomindang troops moved into Shandong Province, the Tanaka cabinet announced its decision to dispatch two thousand troops from Dairen to Qingdao, "an emergency measure," according to the Ministry of Foreign Affairs, that was "forced upon the Japanese Government in self defense and in order to insure the safety of Japanese residents."[33] The following April, Tanaka sent five thousand troops from bases in Japan for the same purpose. In May 1928 those units clashed with Chiang Kai-shek's forces in Jinan, the bloody skirmishes left hundreds of Chinese soldiers and civilians dead, and reports about appalling atrocities, including the castration and blinding of prisoners, aroused bitter anti-Japanese feelings in China's urban centers.

The Jinan Incident was an ominous close to a decade that had opened with the promise of international cooperation and nonintervention in China's domestic affairs. The contrasting policies promoted by Shidehara and Tanaka involved a fundamental difference of opinion about how Japan ought to confront the future in a world where the island nation still felt vulnerable to depredation by Western racists, despite its having gained recognition as a leading military power. Joining the debates over foreign policy were anti-imperialists and pan-Asianists, who suggested still other ways for Japan to interact with its neighbors and find a secure niche for itself. An even greater mix of voices asked sharp questions about the domestic future. The new century had opened up fresh possibilities in Japan's quest for modernity. By the end of the Taishō period, however, there was precious little agreement about how to overcome the challenges of industrialization, share the fruits of economic development equitably, redress the grievances of the underprivileged, answer the demands of feminists and youth, reconcile urban and rural society, and structure a political system that could both make room for a variety of contentious viewpoints and still win acceptance with broad segments of the population. As matters turned out, just as the debates about Japan's future directions moved toward a climax in the late 1920s, the Great Depression and a flare-up of hostilities in Manchuria were to rock the nation and move it in unexpected directions.

# PART IV

# Japan at War

# Chronology

## PART IV JAPAN AT WAR

**1929**
- *October 24* The New York stock market crashes, heralding the onset of the Great Depression

**1930**
- *January 21* London Naval Conference opens
- *Summer* Cherry Blossom Society is formed

**1931**
- *March* Members of the Cherry Blossom Society plan a coup
- *September 18* Elements of the Kwantung Army blow up a railway line near Mukden, starting the Manchurian Incident
- *September 19* The Kwantung Army seizes Mukden and Changchun; Prime Minister Wakatsuki announces a policy of nonexpansion of hostilities
- *September 21* Units of Japan's Korean Army enter Manchuria to support the Kwantung Army
- *September 21–25* Crowds jam a public park in Osaka to cheer newsreel footage of the fighting in Manchuria
- *September 22–23* Kwantung Army captures Jilin
- *September 24* The Wakatsuki cabinet puts its seal of approval on the seizure of Jilin
- *October 17* Members of the Cherry Blossom Society are arrested for plotting a coup
- *November 20* The Kwantung Army enters Qiqihar
- *December 11* The Wakatsuki cabinet resigns
- *December 13* Inukai forms his cabinet, and the new Finance Minister Takahashi Korekiyo takes Japan off the gold standard
- *December 31* The Kwantung Army occupies southwestern Manchuria

**1932**
- *January 7* Secretary of State Henry Stimson proclaims the "non-recognition doctrine"
- *January 28* The Shanghai Incident begins
- *February 5* The Kwantung Army enters Harbin
- *February 9* A member of the Blood Brotherhood guns down a former finance minister
- *February 29* The Lytton Commission arrives in Japan
- *March 1* Manchukuo is established as an independent country
- *March 5* Members of the Blood Brotherhood assassinate the managing director of Mitsui enterprises
- *May 15* Young naval officers assassinate Prime Minister Inukai

*September 15* The Japan-Manchukuo Protocol extends diplomatic recognition to Manchukuo

*October 2* The Lytton Commission releases its report condemning Japanese actions in Manchuria

**1933**

*January 12* Police arrest Kawakami Hajime

*January 28* The Kwantung Army enters Rehe

*February 20* Kobayashi Takiji dies from tortures after being arrested for "thought crimes"

*February 24* The League of Nations accepts the Lytton Commission's report

*March 27* An imperial edict makes official Japan's withdrawal from the League of Nations

*May 6* Fighting breaks out south of the Great Wall

*May 31* The Tanggu Truce provides for the demilitarization of the eastern portion of Hebei Province between the Great Wall and Peking-Tianjin

*June 7* Sano Manabu renounces his belief in communism and endorses Japan's actions in Manchuria

**1934**

*March 28* The government promulgates the Petroleum Industry Law

**1935**

*February 18* Members of the House of Peers launch an attack on Minobe Tatsukichi's organ theory of government

*April 9* The Home Ministry bans three books by Minobe

*June 10* The He-Umezu Agreement provides for the withdrawal of Guomindang troops from Hebei Province

*June 27* The Doihara-Qin Agreement provides for the withdrawal of Guomindang military and political personnel from Chahar

*August 12* Lieutenant Colonel Aizawa Saburō assassinates General Nagata Tetsuzan

*September 18* Minobe Tatsukichi resigns from the House of Peers

*December 8* Police destroy the main temple and headquarters of the Ōmoto sect

**1936**

*January 1* The Dōmei News Agency begins operations

*February 26* The First Division begins the Two Twenty-six Incident

*May 29* The Diet passes the Automobile Manufacturing Industry Law (implemented on July 11)

*July 3* Lieutenant Colonel Aizawa faces the firing squad

*July 5* Leading figures in the Two Twenty-six Incident are convicted, and executions begin on July 12

*December 12* Chiang Kai-shek agrees to join a united front against Japanese agression

**1937**

*March 30* The Ministry of Education publishes *Kokutai no hongi* ("Cardinal Principles of the National Polity")

*June 4* Konoe becomes prime minister

*July 7* Fighting breaks out at the Marco Polo Bridge

*August 8* The conflict spreads to Shanghai

*August 14* Chiang Kai-shek orders a general mobilization

*September 28* Suffrage and feminist organizations form the League of Japanese Women's Organizations

*October 5* Roosevelt speaks out against an "epidemic" of "international lawlessness"

*October 25* Cabinet Planning Board is created and entrusted with comprehensive economic planning

*November 11* Guomindang forces begin to retreat from Shanghai

*December 1* Yanaihara Tadao resigns from Tokyo University

*December 13* Japanese troops march into Nanjing and pillage the city and surrounding towns and villages

*December 14* The Provisional Government of the Republic of China is inaugurated in Beijing

*December 27* Nissan transfers its corporate headquarters to Manchukuo and takes the name Manchurian Heavy Industries Corporation

**1938**

*January 11* The government announces the formation of the Ministry of Health and Welfare

*April 1* The Diet passes the National General Mobilization Law, which takes effect on May 5

*April 10* The Electric Power Industry Act takes effect

*July 1* The American government announces a "moral embargo" of aircraft and parts to Japan

*July 30* The Industrial Patriotic Federation is created

*October 21* Japanese forces occupy Canton

*October 27* Japanese armies take Hankou

*November 3* Konoe announces that the ultimate purpose of the war in China is to establish a "New Order in East Asia"

**1939**

*February 10* Japan occupies Hainan Island

*March 31* Japanese forces occupy the Spratly Islands

*April 5* The Film Law takes effect

*April 8* The Religious Organizations Law extends government control over religious groups

*July 8* The government promulgates the National Service Draft ordinance

*July 26* Washington notifies Japan it intends to abrogate the 1911 Treaty of Commerce and Navigation

*October 20* The Price Control Order and the Temporary Wage Measures Order freeze all prices, wages, salaries, rents, and freight rates

**1940**

*March 30* In Nanjing, Wang Jingwei forms the Reorganized National Government of the Republic of China

*July 23* Konoe calls for a New Order Movement

*July 26* The cabinet approves the "Outline of Basic National Principles," a blueprint for the New Order Movement

*August 1* Foreign Minister Matsuoka Yōsuke announces Japan's desire to create a Greater East Asia Coprosperity Sphere

*August 6* The United States prohibits the sale of aviation gasoline and lubricating oil to Japan

*August 15* Political parties dissolve themselves in anticipation of the formation of the Imperial Rule Assistance Association

*August 30* The French government agrees to permit Japanese forces to enter northern French Indochina

*September 11* The Home Ministry forms neighborhood associations throughout the country

*September 23–29* Japan completes the occupation of the northern provinces of French Indochina

▢ *September 27* Italy, Germany, and Japan sign the Tripartite Pact

▢ *October 12* The Imperial Rule Assistance Association is established

▢ *October 16* The United States embargoes the sale of scrap iron to Japan

▢ *October 31* The government bans jazz performances and closes Tokyo's dance halls

▢ *November 23* The Industrial Patriotic Federation is reorganized as Sanpō, or the Greater Japan Industrial Patriotic Association

▢ *December 7* The cabinet endorses the voluntary establishment of control associations

### 1941

▢ *January 16* The army organizes the Greater Japan Young Adults' Corps

▢ *April 13* Japan and the Soviet Union sign a nonaggression pact

▢ *April 16* Hull enunciates his "four principles"

▢ *July 22–28* Japan occupies southern French Indochina

▢ *July 25* Roosevelt freezes all Japanese assets in the United States

▢ *July 26* The United States beefs up its air power in the Philippines

▢ *August 14* Roosevelt and Churchill sign the Atlantic Charter

▢ *September 6* An imperial conference sanctions the decision to initiate hostilities if diplomacy does not succeed by mid-October

▢ *October 2* Hull informs the Japanese ambassador that a summit meeting between Roosevelt and Konoe is not possible

▢ *October 8* The emperor appoints Tōjō Hideki as prime minister and instructs him to make another attempt at negotiations

▢ *November 1–2* In a marathon seventeen-hour liaison conference,

Japan's leaders decide to make a final peace offer and set midnight, November 30, as the deadline for peace talks to succeed

▢ *November 7* Nomura presents Proposal A to Hull

▢ *November 15* Hull rejects Proposal A

▢ *November 26* Hull rejects Proposal B, and in Japan a liaison conference decides on war

▢ *December 1* The decision to commence hostilities is confirmed at an imperial conference

▢ *December 7* Japan attacks Pearl Harbor (December 8 in Japan)

▢ *December 12* The government announces that the conflict in China and the Pacific shall be called the Greater East Asia War

▢ *December 25* Japanese forces occupy Hong Kong

### 1942

▢ *January 2* Japanese troops enter Manila

▢ *February 2* The government forms the Greater Japan Women's Society

▢ *February 15* Japanese troops capture Singapore

▢ *March 5* Japanese forces occupy Batavia

▢ *March 8* Japanese troops enter Rangoon

▢ *April 30* Elections for the lower house of the Diet are held

▢ *May 20* Most Diet members join the newly formed Imperial Rule Assistance Political Association

▢ *May 26* Formation of the Japanese Literature Patriotic Association

▢ *June 4–6* Americans sink four Japanese carriers at the Battle of Midway

▢ *June 9* Tōjō reforms the IRAA, bringing all patriotic mass organizations under its umbrella

▢ *August 7* American forces land at Guadalcanal

☐ *December 31* Japanese decide to abandon Guadalcanal

**1943**

☐ *January* Tanizaki begins the serial publication of "The Makioka Sisters" in *Chūō kōron* ("The Central Review") although criticism by the military leads to suspension after two episodes

☐ *April 18* Americans shoot down Admiral Yamamoto's plane

☐ *May 12–July 29* American forces recapture Attu and Kiska

☐ *September 23* The cabinet announces that women may replace men in seventeen industrial sectors

☐ *November 1* Tōjō creates the Munitions Ministry

☐ *November 11* Americans land at Tarawa

**1944**

☐ *February 10* Labor registration laws are expanded to include all males aged twelve to fifty-nine and all unmarried females from twelve to thirty-nine

☐ *June 15–July 7* Americans take Saipan

☐ *June 30* The cabinet decides to evacuate school children from cities

☐ *July 18* Tōjō resigns as prime minister

☐ *July* The government suspends publication of *Chūō kōron* and *Kaizō* ("Reconstruction")

☐ *October 20* The Battle of Leyte Gulf begins

☐ *October 25* The first kamikaze pilots take to the skies

**1945**

☐ *February 14* Konoe presents a memorial to the emperor urging him to bring an early conclusion to the war

☐ *February 19* Americans come ashore at Iwo Jima

☐ *March 9–10* Firebombing of Tokyo leaves more than 100,000 dead

☐ *March 17* Iwo Jima falls

☐ *March* Manila falls

☐ *April 1* American troops invade Okinawa

☐ *June 21* American forces secure Okinawa

☐ *July 26* The Potsdam Declaration calls upon Japan to surrender unconditionally

☐ *August 6* The United States uses an atomic bomb to destroy Hiroshima

☐ *August 8* The Soviet Union launches attacks on Manchuria, south Sakhalin, the Kuril Islands, and Korea

☐ *August 9* The United States uses a second atomic bomb to destroy Nagasaki

☐ *August 15* The emperor announces Japan's surrender on national radio

# CHAPTER 12

# "A Period of National Emergency"

aptain Kawamoto Suemori laid the forty-two yellow packages of blasting powder with care. Shortly after 10:00 P.M. on September 18, 1931, he detonated them, displacing a portion of the tracks of the South Manchuria Railway Line as it passed the northern outskirts of Mukden. Kawamoto and his coconspirators intended to derail the Dairen Express, due just minutes later, and blame the act on the local Chinese warlord, Zhang Xueliang. Incredibly, when the train reached the damaged section of track, it swayed only slightly and passed on safely. Unruffled, Kawamoto relayed a prearranged message to his home base: "Engaged in action with Chinese forces who set off explosion along railroad."[1] Ostensibly in response to that "unprovoked aggression," units of Japan's Kwantung Army immediately attacked the barracks of Zhang's soldiers in Mukden and Changchun. Within forty-eight hours, Japanese troops occupied the two cities, and Doihara Kenji, a colonel in the Kwantung Army, named himself to head an emergency committee to govern Mukden, effectively detaching that provincial capital from Chinese control.

The fighting in Manchuria erupted while Japan was mired in depression. The New York stock market crashed in October 1929, and Tokyo soon felt the shock waves. Between 1929 and 1931 Japan's exports fell in half, its GNP declined by 18 percent, and investments in plants and equipment dropped by one-third. In urban centers, more than a million men and women joined the unemployment rolls as large businesses curtailed opera-

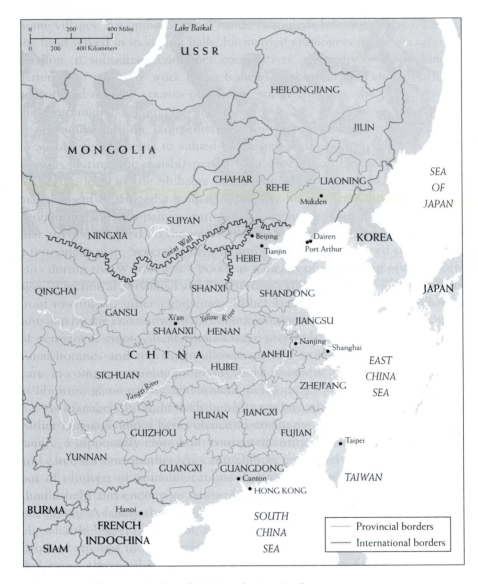

**MAP 12.1**  *China on the Eve of the Manchurian Incident*

tions, medium-size firms collapsed in bankruptcy, and owners of some small factories withheld pay for work done and even absconded with the money left in the cash drawer. With wages low and jobs hard to find, many younger workers returned to their ancestral villages to wait out the depression, only to find their relatives were faring no better. As demand for silk fell precipitously in 1930, farm families that raised cocoons earned only half their 1929 incomes. Rice prices declined so sharply that in some regions farmers received less for their crop than the cost of growing it, and overall rural incomes plunged from an index of one hundred in 1926 to just thirty-three in 1931. Life grew even harsher when crop failures punished northern Japan in 1931 and again in 1934. Food became so scarce that travelers reported seeing farm families stripping the winter bark from trees to expose eatable grubs, and thousands of starving families sold their daughters to urban brothels. Even the dead were affected: In some regions villagers used every excuse to avoid attending their neighbors' funerals, and those who did go left an IOU rather than the customary monetary offering, explaining that "when the economy gets better I will certainly bring the money."[2]

The Manchurian Incident and the Great Depression—the twin crises that racked Japan at the beginning of the 1930s—raised new doubts about the efficacy of capitalism and the ability of party cabinets to address the myriad political, economic, and social problems that confronted the nation. Clearly, everyone acknowledged, Japan had entered "a period of national emergency," and many pushed forward with new answers to the question of whither Japan.

## The Manchurian Incident

The leading architect of the Manchurian Incident was Ishiwara Kanji. A graduate of the Japanese Military Academy, class of '09, the young second lieutenant completed a tour of duty in Korea before entering the Army Staff College, where he finished second in his class in 1918 and stepped onto the fast track for promotion to higher rank. He subsequently served a year in China, accepted a posting to Germany for three years of research and language study, and in 1925 returned to Japan, a major assigned to lecture about the history of warfare at the Army Staff College.

A quixotic and unconventional thinker, Ishiwara painted an apocalyptic view of the future in his lectures. The lesson to be learned was simple, he explained: Warfare had become more violent and more encompassing than ever before. The invention of deadly poison gases, the invincible tank, and now the airplane with its awesome potential to project power over great distances meant that any future war would draw into its vortex of horror everyone in society—civilians as well as soldiers, innocent women and children as well as armed men. Using a term popular in German military circles, der totale Krieg, Ishiwara warned that another conflict, should it come, would be Total War: Destruction would be beyond comprehension, and a nation could hope to weather such a holocaust only if it were able to mobilize all its material, human, and spiritual resources.

It would be folly, he also cautioned, to imagine that World War I was "the war to end all wars." As a convert to the Nichiren faith, a contentious and sometimes militant Buddhist denomination founded in the thirteenth century, Ishiwara accepted the sect's fundamental tenet: Ultimately a "titanic world conflict, unprecedented in human history," would scour the globe and prepare the way for a reign of universal and eternal peace. His own interpretation of the scriptures suggested that this catastrophic showdown would take place within his own lifetime, and his sense of the strategic situation in the late 1920s led him to conclude that two new world powers, representatives of very different historical and religious traditions, would stand in the center of the conflagration. On one side of the Pacific Ocean, Ishiwara told his audience, the United States had moved to the forefront of Western societies, and on the opposite side of that ocean Japan was emerging as the undisputed leader of Asian civilization. Ultimately, inevitably, sooner rather than later, he prophesied, these two standard-bearers for mutually hostile ideological systems would meet not just in a Total War but in a Final War, and only one would survive to preside over the new era of world peace. Japan, he concluded, must begin preparations immediately for this impending Armageddon. That imperative meant that Japan must dominate East Asia, and in Manchuria it had to build up a powerful industrial base that would provide the resources and industrial might necessary to win the coming war of annihilation with the United States.

In October 1928 Ishiwara arranged to have himself assigned to the Kwantung Army. From the day he stepped ashore at Port Arthur he endlessly sermonized about Japan's need to control the region. He quickly formed friendships with other young officers who wished to expand Japan's "special rights and interests" in the Manchurian provinces in order to create a strategic buffer zone against the expansion of Soviet power and acquire vast, rich land areas that Japan's underprivileged might settle. The officers' clique reached a consensus among themselves: They could make an invaluable contribution to Japan's historic mission in the world if they tossed out the warlord Zhang Xueliang and claimed dominion over the territories north of the Great Wall. "The results of the army's occupation of Manchuria and Mongolia," Ishiwara wrote in April 1931, "will be important not only for the future of war, but will affect the course of the Japanese empire for one hundred years."[3]

By the spring of 1931 Ishiwara had become convinced that an opportune moment was at hand for the Kwantung Army to take unilateral action

to occupy Manchuria militarily. At home critics were denouncing the Minseitō cabinet for failing to overcome the problems wrought by the worldwide economic crisis. Meanwhile, voices from the right charged that the
prime minister had put the country's future at risk when he agreed to extend limits on naval armaments during the London Naval Conference, held
the previous year. Internationally, Ishiwara reasoned, no nation stood prepared to intervene against decisive Japanese action in Manchuria: The capitalist nations of the West remained mired in depression; the Soviet Union
was struggling to complete its Five-Year Plan; and Chiang Kai-shek, his
Northern Expedition having ended with only partial success, had refocused
his efforts on securing unchallenged sway over southern China, where he
formally established the Nationalist government on October 10, 1928. All
that was necessary, Ishiwara concluded in the spring of 1931, was a convenient pretext that would legitimate the takeover of Manchuria by the Kwantung Army.

The eruption of violence in Manchuria during the midnight hours of
September 18–19 shocked the civilian government in Tokyo. An alarmed
prime minister, Wakatsuki Reijirō, called his cabinet into emergency session
at 10:30 A.M. on September 19. Foreign Minister Shidehara Kijūrō voiced
suspicions that in reality the Kwantung Army, not Chinese troops, had
sparked the incident; sensitive to the gravity of the situation, he demanded
assurances from Army Minister Minami Jirō that "events would not be permitted to expand beyond the present point."[4] Wakatsuki, who also was
uneasy about military adventurism and shared Shidehara's belief that cooperation with the Western powers and nonintervention in Chinese affairs
served Japan's interests best, pressed Minami to "instruct the commanding
officer of the Kwantung Army not to enlarge the theater of conflict."

Minami and several other generals at central headquarters were not unsympathetic to the young officers in the Kwantung Army, nor did they dismiss out of hand the notion that Japan ought to promote its influence and
power in Manchuria. Still, the military high command had other considerations: Some generals were apprehensive about the possibility of Soviet intervention should Japan upset the status quo in northern China; others
expressed a reluctance to violate the tacit agreement, sealed in the wake of
Japan's intervention in the Boxer Rebellion three decades earlier, that the
military would not commit troops overseas without first soliciting the approval of the cabinet and obtaining an imperial instruction; and still others
feared the displeasure of the elder statesmen and the Diet should the military play too much the renegade. Consequently, when Wakatsuki emerged
from the cabinet meeting shortly after noon on September 19 to announce

his policy of nonexpansion of hostilities to the waiting press, Minami returned to headquarters and telegraphed orders to the commanding general of the Kwantung Army, enjoining him to maintain present positions and to refrain from engaging in further hostile acts.

Such interdictions from Japan's civil and military leaders did little to deter the young officers in the Kwantung Army. Ishiwara and those around him had complete confidence in the sanctity of their mission, and they justified their actions by announcing that they were exercising the "prerogative of field command," the time-honored right of local commanders to undertake operations in emergency situations without waiting for direct orders from central military headquarters. Thus, just days after the attacks on Mukden and Changchun, Ishiwara dispatched agents to Jilin with instructions to instigate disturbances that would make it appear as if the lives and property of the nine hundred Japanese residing in that provincial capital were in jeopardy. Seizing upon subsequent minor incidents as a pretext, Ishiwara and his accomplices on September 21 urged their commanding general to rush troops to the supposedly beleaguered city. After he refused, citing the instructions from Army Minister Minami, the young officers badgered him throughout the night, until finally at dawn the exhausted older officer relented and gave the command to dispatch forces. The conspirators then acted with dazzling speed; the Second Division took Jilin without firing a shot and proclaimed the independence of the surrounding province.

That second fait accompli complicated matters for Wakatsuki and the army general staff in Tokyo. Neither was pleased with the Kwantung Army (or with Japanese field units in Korea that crossed the Yalu River to support the Kwantung Army), yet senior generals hesitated to discipline field-grade officers, and Wakatsuki discovered that great portions of the Japanese public applauded the Kwantung Army for its bold actions. Beginning on the evening of September 21, excited crowds jammed an Osaka public park for several nights running to cheer footage of the fighting that one news chain flew in from Mukden. Moreover, mass media accepted uncritically the claim that the Chinese had initiated the conflict; the lead editorial in the September 20 edition of the daily *Asahi shinbun* reported that the clash at Mukden was a simple "response to the blasting of the South Manchuria Railway by Chinese troops." China, the editorial intoned, "must bear the entire responsibility for the incident. In the face of this clear violation of our vital rights and interests in Manchuria and Mongolia, the stern reality is that Japan must defend its rights even at great sacrifice."[5]

Such outbursts of popular patriotism made it difficult for Wakatsuki to repudiate the actions of the Kwantung Army, and on September 24 the

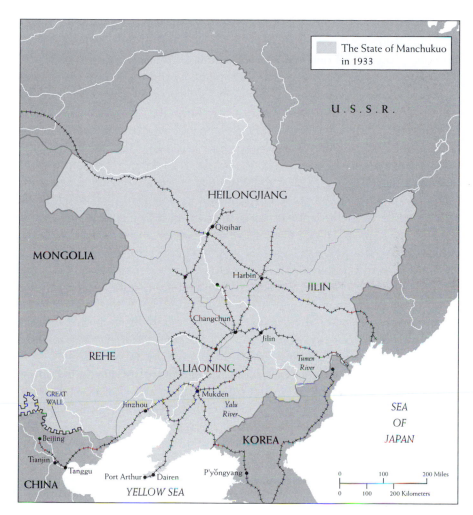

The State of Manchukuo
in 1933

U . S . S . R .

HEILONGJIANG

Qiqihar

MONGOLIA

Harbin

JILIN

Changchun

Jilin

REHE

Tumen
River

LIAONING

GREAT
WALL

Mukden

Jinzhou

Yalu
River

SEA

OF

JAPAN

Beijing

KOREA

Tianjin

Tanggu

Port Arthur    Dairen

P'yŏngyang

CHINA

YELLOW SEA

0          100          200 Miles

0      100      200 Kilometers

**MAP 12.2** *Manchuria and Northern Asia*

prime minister reconvened his cabinet and granted approval to the seizure
of Jilin. Subsequently, the Ministry of Foreign Affairs drafted a communiqué
setting forth the government's official position. The intent of Japan's actions, the Wakatsuki government explained to the world, was merely to protect the "rights and interests legitimately enjoyed" by its citizens resident in
Manchuria. Japan, the message continued, harbored "no territorial designs,"
and the government stood "prepared to cooperate with the Chinese Gov-

ernment in order to prevent the present incident from developing into a disastrous situation between the two countries and to work out such constructive plans as will once and for all eradicate causes for future friction."[6]

"Constructive plans" were not easily come by, however, and the pattern of independent, local action in Manchuria followed by begrudging acquiescence from Tokyo repeated itself often during the autumn of 1931. Determined to expand the perimeter of Japanese control, Ishiwara on the morning of October 8 donned flying togs to lead five aircraft in a surprise bombing attack on Jinzhou, to the southwest of Mukden. That unprovoked raid on a defenseless city shocked the outside world, but once again the high command in Tokyo voiced its approval ex post facto, balanced by yet another cable to the Kwantung Army instructing it to abandon any notion about expanding hostilities further. Yet, just weeks later, Ishiwara discovered another pretense for action: Chinese military forces had destroyed railway bridges near Qiqihar and then fired on Japanese repair crews. This time the general staff in Tokyo cabled the Kwantung Army authorization to dispatch a contingent to guard the bridges, a message that Ishiwara interpreted more broadly to justify the occupation of Qiqihar. By autumn's end the Kwantung Army controlled the capitals of the three Manchurian provinces of Jilin, Liaoning, and Heilongjiang.

As the Kwantung Army expanded its sphere of control, the daring young conspirators formulated a fresh scheme that envisioned converting Manchuria into a new, independent state that, in an oft-repeated phrase, would be "a paradise for all the races of the region." To a large extent the brainchild of Colonel Doihara, the plans called for a republic governed by prominent Chinese. It was clearly understood, however, that those men would be pliable figureheads who answered to the Kwantung Army, which would assume responsibility for defense, foreign relations, transportation, and communications. Doihara hoped to add a dash of legitimacy to this arrangement by having Puyi, a Manchu and the last emperor of China, serve as the chief executive of the new entity.

Although civilian leaders in Tokyo initially resisted the creation of a new nation, a frustrated Wakatsuki resigned in December 1931, and the conspirators in Manchuria pressed forward with their plans. Wakatsuki's successor as prime minister, Inukai Tsuyoshi, was the president of the Seiyūkai and a politician of considerable standing. Identified throughout his long career as a champion of parliamentary democracy, Inukai had helped Ōkuma Shigenobu form the Constitutional Reform Party fifty years earlier, in 1882, and then served eighteen consecutive terms in the House of Representatives after winning a seat in the first general election of 1890. When Inukai formed

*Japanese forces enter Harbin*

his cabinet in 1931, the elderly statesman hoped to negotiate a peaceful settlement to the Manchurian Incident, but frail of health and well into his seventies, he constantly trailed one step behind events. Moreover, a new army minister, the energetic and hard-nosed ultranationalist Araki Sadao, openly threw his support behind the efforts of the young field officers to create a new, independent state under Japanese control. Quickly, by the end of December, the Kwantung Army occupied most of southwestern Manchuria, in February 1932 Japanese troops overran Harbin, and on March 1 the republic of Manchukuo came into formal existence with Puyi as regent.

## The Revolutionary Right and Terrorism at Home

If the 1920s seemed to belong to the voices of the political left, the radical right made itself heard in the early 1930s. Like their cousins on the left, the students, rural activists, and military officers who made up the revolutionary right claimed that the selfish machinations of a few privileged groups, especially party politicians and the leaders of big business, had brought on

Japan's woes. But whereas the anarchists, leaders of the proletarian parties, and the student vanguard of the Shinjinkai imagined an egalitarian utopia of workers and farmers, the extreme right wing called for a Shōwa Restoration, employing the name of the new era that had begun with the ascension of the Shōwa emperor in 1926. Although most radicals on the right had only vaguely conceived notions of what such a Restoration might accomplish specifically, nearly all agreed that it was necessary for them, as it had been for the *shishi*, the "men of high purpose" of the 1860s, to push aside a corrupt and incompetent regime that had proved itself incapable of solving the nation's problems. As the old forms of governance collapsed, new leaders would emerge, just as they had in the Meiji period, to carry out the imperial will and construct a stronger, more prosperous Japan.

The founding document of the Cherry Blossom Society, organized late in the summer of 1930 by Lieutenant Colonel Hashimoto Kingorō, articulated the main concerns of the right wing and the aiming point for a Shōwa Restoration:

As we observe recent social trends, top leaders engage in immoral conduct, political parties are corrupt, capitalists and aristocrats have no understanding of the masses, farming villages are devastated, unemployment and depression are serious. Furthermore, when we examine our external relations, the rulers neglect the long-term interests of the nation, strive only to win the pleasure of foreign powers and possess no enthusiasm for external expansion. The positive enterprising spirit that marked the period following the Meiji Restoration has completely faded away. The people are with us in craving the appearance of a vigorous and clean government that is truly based upon the masses, and is genuinely centered around the Emperor. Although we, as military men, certainly should not participate directly in government, our devotion to serve the country, at times and as the occasion demands, could reveal itself and work for the correction of rulers and expansion of national power.[7]

Beyond a concern with the devastating social and economic consequences of the Great Depression, the hundred or so civilians and young officers who joined the Cherry Blossom Society shared Ishiwara Kanji's disdain for the "weak-kneed" China policy pursued by Minseitō cabinets. But while Ishiwara assuaged his discontent by engaging in direct action on the continent, Hashimoto and his coconspirators plotted a revolution at home. They set March 20, 1931, as the date for a coup. The plans were almost theatrically elaborate: Society members would lead a march of ten thousand persons on the Diet, "death-defying squads" would bomb the offices of the major political parties and the official residence of the prime minister, and leading generals would demand the resignation of the cabinet and the appointment of General Ugaki Kazushige, a well-known critic of party government, as the next prime minister of Japan. Unfortunately for the rebels-to-be, Ugaki refused to be a party to the conspiracy. A failed insurrection, the general feared, would tarnish the reputation of the army, and more important, he held to what, in most military circles, still constituted an unshakable article of faith: The military ought not meddle unconstitutionally in domestic politics. When Ugaki discovered what was afoot, he quickly acted to suppress the plot.

Several months later, in the autumn of 1931, the daring actions of the Kwantung Army revived the spirits of the members of the Cherry Blossom Society, who hatched a second coup plot. Plans were even more grandiose than in the spring, calling for an air bombardment to wipe out the cabinet in a single blow. In the simplistic, naïve dreams of the conspirators, General Araki then would step forward as prime minister and the society's leaders would assume major portfolios in his cabinet. Again, senior generals derailed plans for a Shōwa Restoration. Araki summoned the ringleaders to a geisha house–restaurant on the evening of October 16 and reprimanded them severely; the next day military police took Hashimoto and several of his colleagues into protective custody and later ordered the dissolution of the Cherry Blossom Society.

Assassinations carried out by the Blood Brotherhood, a radical civilian organization that attracted a mix of idealistic students and peasant youths to its ranks, added to the crisis atmosphere of the early 1930s. Moved to action by the tragedy of the Great Depression, the members of the Blood Brotherhood made "One Member, One Death" their slogan and vowed to rid Japan of the political and business leaders they regarded as enriching themselves unfairly at the expense of farmers and poor workers. Early in 1932 the brotherhood compiled a hit list of twenty-two prominent individuals, including ex-Prime Minister Wakatsuki, the elder statesman Saionji Kinmochi, and the head of the Mitsubishi family. On February 9 one member of the brotherhood shot and killed a former finance minister whose policies, the twenty-three-year-old assassin charged, had brought misery and starvation to Japan's farmers. The following month other members of the brotherhood gunned down the managing director of Mitsui enterprises as he stood outside corporate headquarters in the heart of downtown Tokyo.

The culmination of the political terror came on the Sunday afternoon of May 15, 1932, when a group of young naval officers stormed into Inukai's official residence and shot the prime minister to death. Other targeted political leaders escaped their assassins that day, but the capital looked on horrified as members of the cabal hurled hand grenades at central police offices, the Bank of Japan, the headquarters of the Seiyūkai, and several electric power stations. A manifesto issued by the participants in the May 15 Incident revealed the depth of emotional anger experienced by the rebels who were calling for a Shōwa Restoration: "Look straight at the present state of your fatherland, Japan! Where, we dare ask, can you find the genuine manifestation of the godliness of the Imperial Country of Japan? Political parties are blind in their pursuit of power and egoistic gains. Large enterprises are firmly in collusion with politicians as they suck the sweat and blood of the common people. Bureaucrats and police are busy defending the corrupt politico-industrial complex. Diplomacy is weak-kneed. Education is rotten to the core. Now is the time to carry out drastic, revolutionary change. Rise, and take action now!"[8]

The Manchurian Incident and the violence from the right in 1931 and 1932 marked a Copernican turn in Japan's foreign relations and domestic politics. On the continent the conception of the new state, carved from Chinese territory and dominated by a wing of the Japanese military, soured Sino-Japanese relations beyond redemption; began the isolation of Japan from an infuriated West, which viewed Japanese actions as naked aggression; and propelled the island nation along a path that would lead it to even more dangerous foreign confrontations. At home the assassinations and attempted coups exposed the fragile structure of Japanese politics, contributed to a snowballing loss of confidence in party politicians, and encouraged ideologues who romanticized the country's imperial past and sought to forge a new national polity.

## Going It Alone

Ishiwara Kanji and the army general staff may have believed that Japan was pursuing its legitimate destiny in northern Asia, but few people outside the island nation agreed with that view. Most Chinese were outraged. On the diplomatic front, Chiang Kai-shek's Nationalist government petitioned the League of Nations for help on September 20, 1931, as the Kwantung Army prepared to move on Jilin. In Japan several hundred Chinese students packed their bags and returned home, and expressions of anti-Japanese sentiment erupted across China: On October 5 thousands joined a mass demonstration to mark a day of mourning in Canton, on December 10 an estimated ten thousand students paraded through the streets of that city, and in Shanghai boycotts against Japanese goods became so unruly that the Municipal Council imposed a state of emergency on January 28, 1932.

Many Western nations added their criticisms of Japan's behavior, none more so than the United States. On January 7, 1932, Secretary of State Henry Stimson proclaimed that the United States would not acknowledge the legitimacy of Japan's military conquests since that nation had violated existing treaties and had made a mockery of accepted norms of international conduct. To put bite into the "nonrecognition doctrine," President Herbert Hoover moved elements of America's Pacific Fleet from the West Coast to Pearl Harbor. Western nations became further incensed after the Japanese Navy landed marines in Shanghai to protect Japanese businesses and residents in that city. Soon fighting broke out with the Guomindang Nineteenth Route Army, entrenched in a poor residential section of the city, and on January 29, 1932, Japanese planes bombed the neighborhood, killing a number of innocent civilians. Subsequently, the Japanese moved additional regiments into Shanghai, and the fighting left more than twenty thousand persons dead, wounded, or missing before the two sides finally agreed to a cease-fire in May. The outside world, horrified by the assault upon the civilian population, looked upon the Chinese as heroes, bravely and tenaciously defending themselves against a brutal enemy.

As world opinion hardened against what was seen as Japanese aggression, the League of Nations stirred itself to action. In November 1931 it appointed a commission chaired by British statesman Lord Lytton to conduct a thorough on-the-spot investigation of the situation. Lytton and his colleagues arrived in Japan on February 29, 1932, just days after the Blood Brotherhood had gunned down the former finance minister of the Wakatsuki cabinet and only hours before the creation of Manchukuo. By October 1932 the commission had finished its inquiries and had compiled a report that, while phrased with British tact and restraint, clearly rejected Japan's claim that military intervention in Manchuria was a proper and necessary act of self-defense. "Without a declaration of war," the Lytton Report concluded, "a large area of what was indisputably Chinese territory has been forcibly seized and occupied by the armed forces of Japan, and has, in consequence of this operation, been separated from and declared independent of China."[9]

The showdown between a resolute League of Nations and an unrepentant Japan took place in February 1933, when the international body met to consider the Lytton Report. Japan's delegate to the session was Matsuoka Yōsuke. Born in an obscure port town in western Japan in 1880, Matsuoka had left Japan at age thirteen, together with his cousin, and settled in Portland, Oregon. Adopted by an American family, he worked his way through public schools on the West Coast and earned a law degree from the Uni-

*Matsuoka Yōsuke addresses members of the League of Nations in Geneva, 1932*

versity of Oregon before returning to Japan to begin a career of public ser-
vice. As a member of the Ministry of Foreign Affairs for seventeen years,
Matsuoka held diplomatic postings in China, Russia, and the United States.
A man of driving ambition, Matsuoka in 1921 joined the South Manchuria
Railway Company, first as director and later as vice-chairman, and then in
1930 won election to the House of Representatives on the Seiyūkai ticket.
In the spring of 1932 the government sent him to China to negotiate a settlement to the Shanghai Incident, and later that year he became Japan's chief
delegate to the League of Nations.

A forceful orator in both English and Japanese, Matsuoka delivered an
impassioned defense of Japan's actions in Manchuria when he took the
podium in Geneva on February 24, 1933. China, he stated, lacked a legitimate government that could maintain law and order; it was weak and "backward," a country "in an appalling condition of disintegration and distress,"
where "tens of millions of people have lost their lives as a result of internecine
warfare, tyranny, banditry, famine and flood." Japan, in contrast, was "a great
civilizing nation" that "has been and always will be the mainstay of peace,
order and progress in the Far East." In a region that was hopelessly disor-

ganized, Matsuoka argued, Japan had made Manchuria into an island of stability and prosperity. In the spirit of good world citizenship, his nation also hoped to befriend China. "Our present effort to assist Manchukuo to her feet," he concluded, "will lead some day, I am confident, to the realization of Japan's desire and duty to help China. I earnestly beg you to deal with us on our terms and give us your confidence."[10] In the end, however, Matsuoka's eloquence was not persuasive enough, and the League accepted the Lytton Report, censoring Japan by the vote of forty-two to one (Japan), with one abstention (Siam). Silence dogging his footsteps, Matsuoka marched the Japanese delegation out of the assembly hall.

On March 27, 1933, after "many sleepless nights," the emperor issued an edict announcing Japan's formal withdrawal from the League of Nations, and the government set about systematically abrogating the numerous international agreements it had signed at the Washington Conference at the beginning of the previous decade. Exactly one month after the emperor's pronouncement, Matsuoka returned to Japan, after stopping in Portland to erect a marker and plant a tree at the grave of "my American mother." As his ship approached the dock at Yokohama, newspaper planes buzzed overhead, thousands of flag-waving citizens jammed the pier to catch a glimpse of their new hero, and NHK provided live radio coverage, all stirring testimony to the widespread public support of Japan's decision to go it alone.

## Defending Manchukuo, Expanding Hostilities

Among the inner circle of Japan's leaders, isolation from the international community reinforced the growing belief that the country's survival depended upon the creation of a secure hegemony in Asia, and the government moved to strengthen ties with the satellite state of Manchukuo. In September 1932 the two nations signed the Japan-Manchukuo Protocol, which extended formal diplomatic recognition to the new nation and made Japan responsible for its internal security and defense, and on March 1, 1934, Puyi discarded the title of regent and with great pomp and circumstance ascended the Altar of Heaven as the emperor of Manchukuo. The imperial dragon robes cloaked the new monarch with few real powers, however, for the commander of the Kwantung Army served concurrently as the Japanese ambassador to Manchukuo and ruled from behind the scenes. Under the watchful eye of that military figure, who possessed the right to make all personnel appointments to the Manchukuo government, a Board of General Affairs met every Wednesday to decide all state laws and policies, which a People's Congress then rubber-stamped. Japanese domination of the new state was clear: The director of the board was always Japanese, as were most leading figures within the state bureaucracy.

Although the Kwantung Army moved deftly to secure its grasp on the governing apparatus of Manchukuo, defending the new nation proved to be exceptionally frustrating. In strategic terms, the senior military leaders in Tokyo continued to view the Soviet Union as Japan's primary enemy, and Army Minister Araki repeatedly trumpeted the necessity for a preemptive strike against the Soviets, stridently lecturing the nation about what he called the impending Crisis of 1936, when he thought the danger of war would be greatest. Alarmed by such rhetoric as well as the presence of a new and hostile nation on its very borders, the Soviet Union between the outbreak of the Manchurian Incident and the end of 1935 responded by nearly doubling the number of its divisions stationed in the Asian theater, from eight to fourteen, and by increasing the number of combat aircraft from approximately 200 to 940.

Increasingly vociferous expressions of Chinese nationalism also troubled the leaders of Japan and Manchukuo. Marauding armed bands constantly ambushed Kwantung Army patrols and raided Japanese outposts north of the Great Wall. In the eyes of the Chinese, the guerrillas were mounting an honorable resistance against foreign aggression. The Japanese press, on the contrary, wrote about "bandits" and brutal, raping desperadoes. In actuality, the gangs were composed chiefly of dispossessed peasants and former followers of Zhang Xueliang, who had moved his main forces westward into Rehe Province. In all, the guerrilla bands enlisted perhaps 350,000 men in the spring of 1932, and many Japanese soldiers garrisoned in the remote towns of Manchuria and camped along railway lines often felt surrounded by a sea of hostile Chinese. Mao Zedong's Communist followers compounded problems for Japan's Kwantung Army. In October 1935 the Communists reached the end of their long march, settled in Yan'an in northern Shaanxi Province, and began to organize anti-Japanese campaigns.

In the face of the Soviet buildup and stiffening Chinese resistance, central military headquarters and the civilian government in Tokyo authorized a rapid expansion of the Kwantung Army, as seen in Table 12.1. With orders to mount "bandit-suppressing campaigns" and create demilitarized buffer zones around Manchukuo, the army in January 1933 marched into Rehe, where fighting began in earnest just as the League of Nations was about to consider the Lytton Report. The thrust into Rehe did little to promote Japan's cause with the international body, but by the middle of March its troops had reached the Great Wall, effectively bringing the entire province under the dominion of the Manchukuo government.

**TABLE 12.1**   *Buildup of the Kwantung Army, 1930–1939*

| YEAR | MANPOWER | INFANTRY DIVISIONS | AIRCRAFT | TANKS |
|------|----------|--------------------|----------|-------|
| 1930 | 10,000 | | | |
| 1931 | 64,900 | | | |
| 1932 | 94,100 | 4 | 100 | 50 |
| 1933 | 114,100 | 3 | 130 | 100 |
| 1934 | 144,100 | 3 | 130 | 120 |
| 1935 | 164,100 | 3 | 220 | 150 |
| 1936 | 194,100 | 3 | 230 | 150 |
| 1937 | 200,000 | 5 | 250 | 150 |
| 1938 | 220,000 | 7 | 340 | 170 |
| 1939 | 270,000 | 9 | 560 | 200 |

Adapted from Alvin D. Coox, *Nomonhan: Japan against Russia, 1939*, vol. 1 (Stanford: Stanford University Press, 1985), p. 84.

Soon, however, the Kwantung Army discovered that there was no end to the need for new buffer zones. The ultimate, frightful logic of Yamagata's original defense theory was that each new imperialistic acquisition and military confrontation required moving the line of advantage farther outward. Consequently, while Rehe guarded Manchukuo's western border, the Kwantung Army subsequently felt compelled to clear bandits and Chinese warlord armies from the southern side of the Great Wall in order to provide additional security for its client state. In the spring of 1933 the Japanese-trained and -led Manchurian Army crossed into Hebei Province and contrived a series of military and psychological maneuvers—bribing local warlords, transmitting fake radio commands to Chinese generals, and flying warplanes low over Beijing to terrify the civilian population—that drove the Chinese defenders south, toward Tianjin and the ocean beyond. Demoralized, the Chinese sued for peace, and on May 31, 1933, negotiations began in the coastal town of Tanggu. With a battleship and a squadron of their destroyers looming offshore, the Japanese imposed a humiliating treaty upon the Chinese. The Tanggu Truce established a demilitarized zone stretching from the Great Wall to the Beijing–Tianjin axis, ceded to the Japanese Army control of strategic mountain passes guarding the eastern approaches to Beijing, and stipulated that the Chinese exercise "strict control over anti-Japanese activities, which are the basic cause of Sino-Japanese conflict."[11]

Although Japanese forces had acquired a valuable foothold in China proper, inside the Great Wall, they still did not enjoy the security they desperately sought. In the fall of 1934 Chinese troops detained and physically abused Japanese patrols near Tianjin, and local officials tallied some fifty anti-Japanese incidents between January and May 1935. Concurrently Doihara Kenji lived up to his nickname, the Lawrence of Manchuria, by launching the so-called North China Autonomy Movement, an elaborate scheme to detach five northern provinces from Chiang Kai-shek's dominion and create "autonomous" pro-Japanese, pro-Manchukuo administrations under the nominal control of compliant Chinese. "Bandit suppression" and Doihara's intrigues led to two additional agreements with the Chinese that extended Japanese influence in northern China. The first, signed on June 10, 1935, between General Umezu Yoshijirō of the Kwantung Army and General He Yingqin, Chiang Kai-shek's military representative in northern China, banished the Guomindang Party and the Nationalist army from Hebei Province. The second, signed two weeks later by Doihara and General Qin Dechun, dictated similar terms for Chahar Province in Mongolia.

## The Demise of Party Government

The influence of political parties and party politicians declined rapidly following the assassination of Prime Minister Inukai in May 1932. Under ordinary circumstances, the premiership would have passed to the president of the Seiyūkai, which held a majority of the seats in the Diet. Those were not normal times, however, in the minds of the *jūshin* ("senior statesmen"), as the public called the assemblage of court officials and former premiers who had inherited from the *genrō* the task of nominating premiers for imperial confirmation. The lingering effects of the Great Depression, the Manchurian Incident, and outbursts of political terrorism led the senior statesmen to conclude that party cabinets could neither exert effective control over foreign policy nor contain the chaotic domestic situation, let alone lead Japan out of its economic troubles. The only way to surmount the crises of the early thirties, they agreed, was to return to national unity cabinets, which gave greater representation to capable individuals outside the political parties. The senior statesmen were not by temperament antiparty— after all, their spokesperson, Saionji Kinmochi, had championed the cause of party governments for nearly three decades—but they did perceive a need to appoint as prime minister a person of incontestable prestige, free from partisan ties, who could constrain political insubordination, rein in military adventurers, and construct a foreign policy that would preserve international peace.

When a grim-faced Saionji motored to the palace to report that decision to the emperor, the monarch concurred with the reasoning of the senior statesmen and set out his own thoughts about the sort of individual who might head a national unity cabinet. The new prime minister, according to the emperor, should be "a man of strong personality and character" who would respect the constitution and restore "military discipline."[12] For that task, Saionji and his fellow senior statesmen settled on Saitō Makoto, a retired admiral who had earned a reputation for personal courage and sober judgment as navy minister from 1906 to 1914 and as the governor-general who had introduced "cultural rule" to Korea following the uprising of 1919.

While the parties rode the seesaw of power downward, military and civilian bureaucrats rose to positions of paramount influence in national affairs. The distribution of cabinet portfolios constituted one important measure of that transition. During the era of party government, between 1924 and 1932, there had been seven cabinets, each headed by a prime minister selected from one of the two major political parties. In those cabinets the average number of members with party affiliations was 8.7, out of the 12 ministers who normally made up each cabinet. In the eight cabinets formed between 1932 and 1940, in contrast, no party politician served as prime minister and the average number of ministers drawn from the civil and military bureaucracies was 9.9 (of 13 portfolios). Moreover, party politicians found themselves increasingly isolated from the inner circle of policy makers. None, for instance, held an office that entitled him to join meetings of

---

**TABLE 12.2**  *Japanese Prime Ministers, 1929–1937*

| PRIME MINISTER | PARTY AFFILIATION | CABINET NUMBER | CABINET TERM |
|---|---|---|---|
| Hamaguchi Osachi | M | | July 2, 1929–April 14, 1931 |
| Wakatsuki Reijirō | M | Second | April 14, 1931–December 13, 1931 |
| Inukai Tsuyoshi | S | | December 13, 1931–May 16, 1932 |
| Saitō Makoto | | | May 16, 1932–July 8, 1934 |
| Okada Keisuke | | | July 8, 1934–March 9, 1936 |
| Hirota Kōki | | | March 9, 1936–February 2, 1937 |

M denotes Minseitō affiliation.
S denotes Seiyūkai affiliation.

the five ministers conferences. Convened by Prime Minister Saitō beginning in 1933, those convocations brought together the foreign, finance, army, and navy ministers and the premier to establish policy guidelines concerning diplomatic, fiscal, and national defense matters. In similar fashion, military and civilian bureaucrats dominated new supra-agencies, such as the Cabinet Research Bureau, that were created to cut across existing jurisdictions and better coordinate planning among various ministries.

Those agencies and bureaus became the strongholds of the "renovationist" or "new" bureaucrats, as newspaper and journal articles dubbed them. Despite the appellation "new," not all renovationist bureaucrats were recent graduates of the nation's leading public universities; a considerable number, in fact, were veteran "shepherds of the people" who had experimented with finding solutions to economic and social problems in the Taishō period. Whatever their tenure of service, however, the renovationists of the mid-1930s shared suspicions about capitalism, sympathized with the plight of the rural poor, assumed that party politicians lacked the moral fortitude and intellectual expertise to pilot Japan through its "period of national emergency," and stood committed to making bureaucracy the central element in the formation and execution of national policy.

The renovationist bureaucrats took as their most immediate priority the need to build up Japan's economy and war-making capacity. For most of them, such goals could be accomplished best by imposing greater state control over the economy, and two of their earliest achievements were the Petroleum Industry and Automobile Manufacturing Industry laws. The former, implemented in the summer of 1934, empowered the government to regulate the importing and refining of petroleum and also authorized officials to fix prices and stockpile petroleum products to use in a military emergency. An ambitious young bureaucrat named Kishi Nobusuke drafted the Automobile Manufacturing Industry Law to stimulate the growth of an industry that was of crucial importance to the economy in general and to Japan's military preparedness in particular. The enabling legislation, passed by the Diet in May 1936, required vehicle manufacturers to be licensed by the government (only two, Toyota and Nissan, received licenses in 1936), and it extended to them special government financing, tax breaks, and protection from import competition.

Although the political initiative was passing to other elites originally empowered by the Meiji constitution, political parties did not disappear entirely from the scene. As shown in Table 12.3, the Seiyūkai and Minseitō continued to dominate the Diet during the 1930s, and party politicians within that body played a vigorous, if diminished, role in the nation's pol-

TABLE 12.3   *Party Representation in the Diet, 1928–1936*

| ELECTION | SEIYŪKAI | MINSEITŌ | OTHER |
|---|---|---|---|
| 1928 | 217 | 216 | 33 |
| 1930 | 174 | 273 | 19 |
| 1932 | 301 | 146 | 19 |
| 1936 | 174 | 205 | 87 |

Adapted from Gordon Mark Berger, *Parties out of Power in Japan, 1931–1941* (Princeton: Princeton University Press, 1977), p. 66.

itics as they passed legislation, voted on budgets, debated the pros and cons of national policy, and exercised their right to interpellate members of the cabinet and the military and civilian bureaucracies. On occasion Diet members used their position to launch stinging criticisms of military and government policies, as when representatives from both parties denounced the 1934 budget for generously funding military requests while being tightfisted with appropriations to relieve rural distress.

Contention between Diet members and cabinet officials was not especially common, however, for the mainstream parties generally adopted agendas that were not too distant from the policies espoused by Prime Minister Saitō and his successor, Okada Keisuke, another ex-admiral. One reason was that Minseitō and Seiyūkai leaders did not relish a showdown over the future role of political parties at a time when the military was enjoying enormous public popularity. But just as important, many party rank and file enthusiastically agreed that Japan ought to pursue a more "positive" foreign policy as it sought its destiny in northern Asia. One manifestation of such patriotism among lawmakers was the passage of a Diet resolution on June 14, 1932, urging the cabinet to extend formal diplomatic recognition to Manchukuo immediately, despite the premier's preference to wait until the Lytton Commission completed its deliberations. Even more to the point, not once during the 1930s did the parties in the Diet refuse to approve the government's annual budgets, which rapidly increased military expenditures from 462 million yen in 1931 to 953 million yen in 1934 and then to 1.089 billion yen in 1936. The parties accepted the new politics and power alignments of the 1930s, and their actions invite comparisons with the 1920s, when party governments reduced the size of Japan's military establishment and when the Minseitō roundly denounced Tanaka Giichi's interventions in China.

## Reining in Political Discourse

Although newspaper and radio accounts of the cheering crowds that greeted Matsuoka at Yokohama created an image of a country united behind its government, many men and women took umbrage at aggression overseas and observed that gains on the battlefield were not yielding any solutions to the economic crisis at home. Articles oppugning the actions of the Kwantung Army filled the pages of liberal journals in 1931 and 1932. Writing in the April 1932 issue of the *Kaizō* ("Reconstruction"), Yanaihara Tadao, the specialist on colonial policy who taught at Tokyo University, denounced Japan's military actions in Manchuria as self-defeating and foretold their ultimate inability to withstand the increasingly robust vitality of Chinese nationalism. Farther to the left, the socialist Yamakawa Kikue contributed an essay to the November 1931 edition of the major woman's publication *Fujin kōron* ("Women's Review"), questioning whether mothers ought to bear more children if their offspring merely were going to end up as fodder for a militarist government. Even regional newspapers sounded a critical note. The *Kamishina jihō*, produced by village youth in Nagano Prefecture, put these questions to its readers in April 1932: "Manchuria is now in Japan's possession, but has your life changed? Has it become any easier? Have you been able to pay back any of the capital you borrowed? Have your sisters been able to make one kimono, or your brothers go to a café to listen to jazz? I know the answer: it is a resounding 'No!'"[13]

However earnest they may have been, dissidents found it increasingly difficult to speak out effectively. For one thing, displays of popular patriotism, such as the reception given to Matsuoka upon his return, discouraged the expression of antiwar sentiments. Moreover, many prominent liberals publicly accepted the new domestic policies and foreign policy initiatives of the early 1930s, further robbing nonconformist views of their legitimacy. Even Yoshino Sakuzō, one of Japan's best-known supporters of democracy, seemed ready to throw in the towel. Many Japanese, he wrote in 1932, viewed the accomplishments of the Kwantung Army as a welcomed contrast with years of "ineffectual negotiations" by party cabinets. In addition, they, even he, had grown resigned to the fact that party government in Japan "is an unholy alliance between unprincipled party leaders and equally unprincipled leaders of big business," with the consequence that official policies catered to "the interests of big business, while the little man, and particularly the farmer, is progressively impoverished." It was enough to make one despair, especially when one looked at the assault on democracy taking place in Europe. "There is a feeling among the Japanese," Yoshino concluded, "that if democracy is not quite good enough for those who invented it, then Japan, who has always slightly distrusted it, has no particular reason for keeping it going."[14]

Even more shocking to many was Yosano Akiko's newfound praise for militarism. Famous during the Taishō era for her feminist critiques, Yosano had first stepped into the public spotlight when she published several antiwar poems during the Russo-Japanese conflict of 1904 and 1905. The most prominent of those was a plea to her younger brother:

> Do not offer your life.
> The Emperor himself does not go to battle.
> The Imperial Heart is deep;
> How could he ever wish
> That men shed their blood,
> That men die like beasts,
> That men's glory be in death?[15]

In 1932, however, Yosano's "Citizens of Japan, A Morning Song" urged Japanese soldiers to endure "sufferings a hundredfold" and used the familiar metaphor about falling cherry blossoms, scattered by the wind at the peak of their beauty, to glorify the death of a soldier whose "scattered" body was "purer than a flower."[16]

General-audience magazines also valorized overseas expansion and encouraged people to unite behind the war effort. Publications such as *Shufu no tomo* ("Housewife's Friend") and *Fujin kurabu* ("Women's Club") carried tales of battlefield heroics, poignant stories of war widows, and helpful hints about how to economize on food and clothing during the national emergency. Photographs of troops in combat, Red Cross nurses, and volunteers preparing relief packages aroused patriotic feelings in a more direct, emotional manner. Other magazines carried similar stories, and after 1933 it was difficult to find on corner newsstands an alternative to the official view that Japan was acting in self-defense to protect its legitimate rights and interests in northern Asia.

Japanists further circumscribed the permissible limits of political discourse. From the middle of the Meiji period, some conservatives had begun to advocate *Nihon shugi*, or Japanism, as an alternative to rapid Westernization. In particular, they wished to preserve traditional values and what they saw as Japan's unique national polity, or *kokutai*. For many conservatives in the Meiji era, the concept of the *kokutai* revolved around two principles: A

divine line of emperors had ruled from time immemorial, and intimate familylike ties united the benevolent sovereign with his loyal subjects. The 1890
Imperial Rescript on Education defined that vision of the *kokutai* by declaring, "Our Imperial Ancestors have founded Our Empire on a basis broad
and everlasting," and by calling upon the emperor's "faithful subjects" to "offer yourselves courageously to the State; and thus guard and maintain the
prosperity of Our Imperial Throne coeval with heaven and earth."[17]

In the 1930s conservative Japanists viewed themselves as the defenders
of those ideals. As Japan entered its period of national emergency, they also
became virulently patriotic, openly contemptuous of the liberal, capitalistic
ideologies of the West, and harshly intolerant of anyone who failed to support the imperial family-nation in its time of need. Even Nitobe Inazō, the
quintessential apologist of Japanese colonialism, drew fire from Japanists in
February 1932, when he suggested at a press conference that two forces,
Communism and militarism, menaced the world. Of the two, Nitobe went
on, he feared that in the long run "militarism might do the more harm."[18]
The Imperial Military Reservists' Association, with three million members
nationwide, immediately rose up to condemn this as an attack on Japan's
military establishment and put out a stream of pamphlets accusing Nitobe
of being "disloyal," "unpatriotic," and "traitorous." So abusive did the threats
become that the normally unflappable Nitobe decided to appear before the
leaders of the association to offer a mea culpa; his statements, he explained,
had been "misconstrued."

The most spectacular attempt by rightists to silence someone who failed
to conform to their emperor-centered ideology involved the constitutional
scholar Minobe Tatsukichi. Minobe's theory that the emperor was only one
"organ" within the larger state and that other organs—the Diet, bureaucracy,
cabinet, and so forth—were constitutionally entitled to exercise specific
governing prerogatives had gained widespread acceptance during the Taishō
period, providing a legitimating philosophy for the emergence of multiple
governing elites and party cabinets. In the 1930s, however, Japanists sin-
gled out Minobe for intense criticism. Battle was joined in 1934 when right-
wing organizations, including the Imperial Military Reservists' Association,
published accusatory books and pamphlets charging that Minobe's thoughts
amounted to lèse majesté. "The emperor-organ theory is contrary to the
essence of our unparalleled national polity and blasphemes the sacredness of
the throne," claimed one tract. "It is absolutely incompatible with our traditional way of thinking. We warn all Japanese to bring about a greater respect
for our constitution, to clarify the concept of our national polity, to exalt the
Japanese spirit and to strive for all these goals loyally and sincerely."[19]

The Diet took up the issue on February 18, 1935, when members of the House of Peers, to which Minobe had received appointment three years earlier, impeached his ideas, and on March 26 it unanimously voted to condemn the organ theory. "The government," its resolution read, "should take decisive action against speech and theories inconsistent with the noble and peerless national polity of Japan."[20] The same month a member of the lower house filed formal charges of lèse majesté in the Tokyo District Court, citing the organ theory as being subversive to the *kokutai*, and on April 9 the Home Ministry banned three of Minobe's books. Disgraced, Minobe on September 18 resigned from the House of Peers.

The role of the Diet and Home Ministry in censuring Minobe brings to light another aspect of the new politics of the 1930s: Many government officials were willing to use the state's coercive powers to limit dissent and enforce a patriotic conformity upon Japan during its national emergency. Ironically, the more extremist wing of the political right itself fell victim to that pressure. The governing circles had little tolerance for rebels of any persuasion who advocated the violent overthrow of state authority, and in 1935 the police arrested 147 rightists suspected of seditious behavior. As might be expected, however, suppression was directed more aggressively against individuals and groups on the political left, as Table 12.4 shows. The police dragnet hauled in famous self-proclaimed Communists, such as Sano Manabu and Kawakami Hajime, as well as men and women merely suspected of harboring subversive ideas, including several elementary school teachers in Nagano Prefecture, accused of propagating anti-imperial thoughts in 1933.

**TABLE 12.4** *Arrests of Leftists, 1928–1941*

| YEAR | ARRESTS | INDICTMENTS | YEAR | ARRESTS | INDICTMENTS |
|------|---------|-------------|------|---------|-------------|
| 1928 | 3,426 | 525 | 1935 | 1,718 | 113 |
| 1929 | 4,942 | 339 | 1936 | 1,207 | 97 |
| 1930 | 6,124 | 461 | 1937 | 1,292 | 210 |
| 1931 | 10,422 | 307 | 1938 | 789 | 237 |
| 1932 | 13,938 | 646 | 1939 | 389 | 163 |
| 1933 | 14,622 | 1,285 | 1940 | 713 | 128 |
| 1934 | 3,994 | 496 | 1941 | 849 | 205 |

Adapted from Elise K. Tipton, *The Japanese Police State: The Tokkō in Interwar Japan* (Honolulu: University of Hawaii Press, 1990), pp. 156–57.

The police and public prosecutors who conducted the crackdown incarcerated Communists and some leftists in the hope of inducing a *tenkō*. The term means a "change of direction," but in the 1930s it more specifically denoted a public repudiation of one's former ideological beliefs. As one leading prosecutor explained, no single leftist was ever entirely "hopeless": "Since they are all Japanese, sooner or later they would all come around to realizing that their ideas were wrong" and return to the fold of loyal and obedient citizens.[21] To achieve that goal, police grilled detainees in endless interrogations, used self-criticism and other psychological subtleties to instill a sense of guilt about not supporting the family-nation, and, when all else failed, turned to corporal punishment.

The first great apostasy was that of Sano Manabu, a high official of the Japan Communist Party when arrested in 1929. Officials charged him with a "thought crime" since he led an organization that advocated the overthrow of the *kokutai*, and the court sentenced him to life in prison. In June 1933 Sano stunned the leftist community by declaring his change of faith. In a long memorandum written in his prison cell, he denounced the JCP as "a negative force, moving fast in the wrong direction," praised the emperor for "playing a central role in the movement to build a unified Japan," and endorsed Japan's actions in Manchuria, writing that "the expansion of the Japanese nation into a country which is remarkably backward in culture compared to Japan is in accord with the principle of historical progress."[22] Authorities publicized Sano's statement, and within a month more than five hundred other party members, nearly one-third of the Communists confined in Japan's jails, followed suit. Pleased with the results, police by the end of the decade had charged more than two thousand others with "thought crimes," most of whom eventually wrote out *tenkō* statements.

Not all who were arrested yielded to police tactics. Kobayashi Takiji, a noted author of proletarian literature, met death clinging to his beliefs. The political left celebrated Kobayashi's "Kani kōsen" ("The Factory Ship," 1929), a vivid account of the Imperial Navy's brutal suppression of a shipboard strike against harsh working conditions in the fishing industry, as a ringing exposé of the collusion between capitalists and military to exploit workers. Arrested on the morning of February 20, 1933, Kobayashi died in his jail cell before the day was over. Police claimed that simple heart failure was the cause of death, but others who examined the corpse found broken fingers, traces of hot tongs on the forehead, and numerous other gruesome injuries, including more than a dozen holes in one thigh apparently made by nails or a drill. Kawakami Hajime, arrested on January 12, 1933, did not have to endure torture, but four years in prison broke his health. He never did renounce his commitment to his Marxist ideology, but as a condition of his release in June 1937, he tacitly acknowledged the new limits on political discourse by agreeing to retire from political activism.

## Economic Revival and the Business Community

Ironically, for all the venomous rhetoric directed against party politicians in the early 1930s, it was Takahashi Korekiyo, one of the oldest and most esteemed members of Japan's inner circle of political elites, who engineered the country's climb out of the depths of depression. Born the illegitimate son of an obscure artist and teenage maid in Edo in the year that Commodore Perry opened Japan, Takahashi entered life in the most humble circumstances. As a youngster, however, he had the good fortune to be adopted by a samurai family from Sendai, and the daimyo lord of that domain sent the precocious Takahashi to study in America from 1867 to 1869. Upon his return to Japan, Takahashi obtained a position in the new Meiji government, and he rose through the ranks of the finance bureaucracy until 1892, when he joined the Bank of Japan. In 1913 he threw in his lot with the Seiyūkai and served as finance minister in 1913 and 1914, a portfolio he also held under Hara Takashi from 1918 until 1921, when he succeeded Hara as prime minister. After his own cabinet fell, Takahashi won election to the Diet, became the first head of the Ministry of Commerce and Industry when that agency was created in 1925, and once again, for a few brief weeks in the spring of 1927, resumed the duties of finance minister.

Inukai brought the veteran Takahashi into his cabinet in December 1931 to craft policies that would overcome the deleterious effects of the Great Depression. A Keynesian before Keynes himself articulated the theory of effective demand, Takahashi intuitively understood that the only way for a country to come out of a depression was to spend its way out, and as finance minister between 1931 and February 1936 he pursued a program of deficit spending with single-minded determination. Central government expenditures had declined from 1.74 billion yen in 1929 to 1.48 billion yen in 1931; Takahashi reversed that course by jacking up expenditures in 1932 by 32 percent, to 1.95 billion yen, and then by another 15 percent to 2.25 billion yen in 1933, with three-quarters of the increase in central government disbursements coming from bonds and other forms of deficit financing.

A considerable proportion of those new expenditures consisted of outlays for public works projects designed to resuscitate the shattered agrarian sector of Japan's economy. Between 1932 and 1934 the government ex-

**TABLE 12.5**   *Military Expenditures, 1928–1936*

| | | MILITARY EXPENDITURES AS A % OF: | |
|---|---|---|---|
| YEAR | MILITARY EXPENDITURES (MILLIONS OF YEN) | CENTRAL GOVERNMENT EXPENDITURES | NET DOMESTIC PRODUCT |
| 1928 | 519 | 29.4 | 3.6 |
| 1929 | 497 | 29.5 | 3.5 |
| 1930 | 444 | 41.7 | 3.6 |
| 1931 | 462 | 34.9 | 4.1 |
| 1932 | 705 | 39.1 | 5.5 |
| 1933 | 886 | 46.0 | 6.1 |
| 1934 | 953 | 48.3 | 6.3 |
| 1935 | 1,043 | 50.7 | 6.3 |
| 1936 | 1,089 | 52.0 | 5.9 |

Adapted from Hugh T. Patrick, "The Economic Muddle of the 1920s," in James W. Morley, ed., *Dilemmas of Growth in Prewar Japan* (Princeton: Princeton University Press, 1971), pp. 250–51.

tended some 800 million yen in low-interest loans to rural villages and spent a similar amount on undertakings intended to provide off-season work for impoverished villagers. The government further stoked the nation's economic furnace by more than doubling the budget for military expenditures between 1931 and 1936, as shown in Table 12.5.

To help matters further, on the very day he took office in December 1931 Takahashi cut Japan loose from the gold standard. Within a year the value of the yen relative to the dollar plummeted from the old fixed rate of $48.87 to just $28.12 per 100 yen, a devaluation of more than 40 percent. The consequent decline in the prices of Japanese goods in overseas markets fueled an export surge of cotton yarn, woven goods, ceramics, toys, iron, and steel that imparted additional momentum to Japan's economic resurgence and helped make it the first nation to recover industrially from the worldwide depression, as shown in Table 12.6. With the chemical and machinery industries also profiting enormously from military spending, Japan's net domestic product soared upward by more than 70 percent during the 1930s, the best decade to date in the nation's modern history.

The leading conglomerates—Mitsui, Mitsubishi, Sumitomo, and Yasuda—retained their dominant position in the economy in the early 1930s. The zaibatsu entered the Depression in relatively sound shape, with substantial reserves of cash, and they survived the economic cataclysm with relative ease. As Table 12.7 indicates, in just seven years between 1930 and 1937, the Big Four increased the amount of paid-up capital in their various enterprises by nearly 60 percent. Much to the benefit of their balance sheets, the conglomerates directed a considerable portion of that new investment into the fast-growing chemical and heavy industry sectors of the economy.

For all their apparent success, however, the zaibatsu discovered that they could not carry on with business as usual in the 1930s. The virulent, unrelenting attack from the radical right was merely the most exaggerated expression of a widespread, popular cynicism that portrayed the conglomerates as beasts of profit that preyed upon worker and consumer alike. The business giants scarcely helped their image by engaging in an orgy of dollar buying in the autumn of 1931. Sensing that the government eventually would devalue the yen, the zaibatsu snapped up dollars, which they used to repurchase yen after Finance Minister Takahashi abandoned the gold standard on December 13 and let Japan's currency sink to its market level. The zaibatsu reaped immense profits—Mitsui alone made perhaps fifty million dollars in currency speculation—and the Japanese public was furious.

As criticism of business conglomerates mounted and then turned violent after the Blood Brotherhood assassinated the managing director of Mitsui enterprises in March 1932, the zaibatsu adopted a more conciliatory posture. When Ikeda Seihin became the senior executive of Mitsui in September 1933, he launched a campaign that commentators likened unto a "business tenkō." For one thing, he dumped company officials who had done

**TABLE 12.6**  *Manufacturing and Mining Indices, 1930–1935*

| YEAR | JAPAN | UNITED STATES | ENGLAND | GERMANY | FRANCE |
|------|-------|---------------|---------|---------|--------|
| 1929 | 100.0 | 100.0 | 100.0 | 100.0 | 100.0 |
| 1930 | 94.8  | 80.7  | 92.3  | 85.9  | 99.1  |
| 1931 | 91.6  | 68.1  | 83.8  | 67.6  | 86.2  |
| 1932 | 97.8  | 53.8  | 83.5  | 53.3  | 71.6  |
| 1933 | 113.2 | 63.9  | 88.2  | 60.7  | 80.7  |
| 1934 | 128.7 | 66.4  | 98.8  | 79.8  | 75.2  |
| 1935 | 141.8 | 75.6  | 105.6 | 94.0  | 72.5  |

Adapted from Chalmers Johnson, *MITI and the Japanese Miracle: The Growth of Industrial Policy, 1925–1975* (Stanford: Stanford University Press, 1982), p. 121.

**TABLE 12.7** Zaibatsu *Investment by Industry Sector, 1930 and 1937*
(paid-up capital in millions of yen; data are for 1930/1937)

| | MITSUI | MITSUBISHI | SUMITOMO | YASUDA | TOTAL OF THE BIG FOUR | NISSAN | NITCHITSU |
|---|---|---|---|---|---|---|---|
| Heavy industry | 188/269 | 170/230 | 58/137 | —/3 | 416/639 | 66/269 | —/15 |
| Chemicals | 28/82 | —/65 | 2/42 | —/3 | 30/192 | —/100 | 39/108 |
| Textiles | 88/155 | 34/41 | —/— | 13/15 | 135/211 | —/— | 6/— |
| Ceramics | 22/38 | 7/18 | 3/— | —/— | 32/56 | —/— | —/— |
| Foodstuffs | 61/62 | 78/126 | —/— | —/— | 139/188 | —/70 | —/— |
| Other manufacturing | 124/206 | 11/10 | —/— | 10/24 | 145/240 | —/6 | —/— |
| Electricity and gas | 22/65 | 13/55 | —/19 | 24/52 | 59/191 | —/6 | —/64 |
| Transportation | —/23 | 87/103 | 63/63 | —/13 | 150/202 | —/7 | —/2 |
| Trade and commerce | 133/180 | 20/39 | —/15 | 6/11 | 159/245 | —/2 | —/3 |
| Finance | 70/71 | 108/143 | 59/61 | 126/141 | 363/416 | —/1 | —/— |
| TOTALS | 736/1,151 | 528/830 | 185/337 | 179/262 | 1,628/2,580 | 66/461 | 45/177 |

Adapted from Nakamura Takafusa and Odaka Kōnosuke, eds., *Nijū kōzō* (Tokyo: Iwanami Shoten, 1989), p. 123.

the most to incur the wrath of the Japanese public and military. Ousted immediately was the president of the Mitsui Trading Company, whose eye for a quick profit tempted him into selling salt to Zhang Xueliang during the early fighting in Manchuria and barbed wire to the Chinese Nineteenth Route Army during the Shanghai Incident of 1932. Moreover, Ikeda announced that rather than remain identified with callous moneymaking schemes, Mitsui would make its corporate name synonymous with giving. By the end of 1936 the firm had donated three million yen to the unemployed, provided thirty million yen to endow a charitable foundation known as the Mitsui Requital of Kindness Society, and pledged an additional sixty million yen to various worthy causes. The giants Sumitomo and Mitsubishi also anted up donations for the unemployed, and they followed another Ikeda initiative as well, issuing public stock in many of their subsidiaries as a way of dampening criticism that they were closed, family-run enterprises.

The established conglomerates shared another challenge in the 1930s, the emergence of such powerful rivals as Nissan, Nitchitsu (Japan Nitrogenous Fertilizer Company), and Nakajima Aircraft. Commonly called the new zaibatsu, the enterprises differed from the traditional combines in important ways. Few, for instance, were exclusively family-based, and most originated in manufacturing industries, whereas the old zaibatsu had first organized strong bases in mining or in such services as banking and shipping. The new zaibatsu also were more willing to cooperate with the military and renovationist bureaucrats than were the more cautious older conglomerates. Nitchitsu, for instance, built hydroelectric generating plants in northern Korea under the guidance of the Japanese occupation authorities in the 1920s. A decade later it had become one of the strongest corporations in Japan, thanks largely to earnings from the production of ammonium sulfate, gunpowder, and methanol, all of which were extremely competitive because they were produced with cheap electric power in Korea.

The highest-flying new zaibatsu was Nissan, organized by Aikawa (Ayukawa) Yoshisuke in 1928, after he took over his brother-in-law's mining company. Under Aikawa's direction, Nissan by the mid-1930s had expanded into a multisubsidiary empire that encompassed some seventy-seven companies, including such leading manufacturers as Nissan Motor Company, Nissan Chemical Industries, Hitachi Ltd., and Osaka Shipyard. By 1937 Nissan had become larger and more powerful than either Sumitomo or Yasuda, and it thrived thanks to the close ties that Aikawa cultivated with the military and renovationist bureaucrats during the military buildup of the early 1930s.

That new alliance emerged in full view in Manchukuo, where the Kwantung Army was pushing for rapid industrial development so that the satellite state could better serve as Japan's "economic lifeline," another term popularized by Matsuoka Yōsuke. To help matters along, the Board of General Affairs created new banking institutions and announced a policy of encouraging capital investment from the home islands. Those initiatives bore some fruit. Although the old *zaibatsu* firms remained suspicious of the military's known bias toward them, they joined with other companies to invest a staggering 1.25 billion yen in Manchukuo, and by the end of 1936 the new client state had become Japan's leading source of coal, pig iron, and soybeans.

Such success did not satisfy planning officers in the Kwantung Army. The volume of exports to Japan remained very low, compared with the inflows of capital, and one foreign observer ventured that the satellite state might well "become a definite liability rather than a lifeline" for the home islands.[23] In hope of pumping renewed life into the faltering industrialization campaign, officials in Manchukuo drew up a Five-Year Plan. The new blueprint called for replacing the practices of laissez-faire capitalism with a "controlled economy" in which government authorities would extend a shepherd's hand to manage important economic activities, and the Kwantung Army convinced the Ministry of Commerce and Industry to dispatch to Manchukuo one of its brightest young stars, Kishi Nobusuke, to oversee its implementation. Kishi, who had just authored the Automobile Manufacturing Industry Law and had close ties with Nissan, immediately invited Aikawa to move his high-technology firms to the continent. Aikawa jumped at the opportunity, and late in 1937 he transferred his corporate headquarters to Manchukuo and rechristened Nissan the Manchurian Heavy Industries Corporation. The arrangement called for Aikawa's conglomerate to be half owned by the Manchurian government and subject to its dictates. In return, state authorities guaranteed him net profits of 6 percent and a minimum return of 7.5 percent on the new corporation's bonds. Moreover, with the government's blessings, the new conglomerate swallowed most of the South Manchuria Railway Company and emerged as the leading industrial force in northern Asia.

## The Two Twenty-six Incident

The climactic eruption of the early 1930s burst forth in the early morning of February 26, 1936, when twenty-one junior officers of the crack First Division led nearly fourteen hundred soldiers out of their barracks in a bold attempt to overthrow the government. As snow fell throughout the morn-

*The Two Twenty-six Incident*

ing, blanketing the capital, assassination squads shot to death Finance Minister Takahashi, ex-Premier Saitō Makoto, and the inspector general of military education. Prime Minister Okada escaped death by a wisp of fate; the young officers who broke into his residence murdered his brother-in-law by mistake. Okada's wife hid the premier in a closet, then helped smuggle him out, dressed as a woman, after undertakers left the house with "my husband's body." Despite that fiasco, by noon soldiers of the First Division had seized the center of Tokyo, securing a perimeter that enclosed the Diet building, army headquarters, and the heights overlooking the Imperial Palace. Buoyed by the success of their initial attacks, the leaders of the coup d'état attempt demanded the installation of a new cabinet headed by a general sympathetic to their mission.

Like the leaders of the fruitless coups earlier in the 1930s, the instigators of the Two Twenty-six Incident claimed no personal ambitions for themselves but, in the words of one participant, "wished only to awaken the people and bring about a Shōwa Restoration."[24] Their particular vision of a Shōwa Restoration drew deeply from well-thumbed copies of *Nihon kaizō hōan taikō* ("An Outline Plan for the Reconstruction of Japan," 1923) by Kita Ikki, a nationalist ideologue of long standing. In his polemic, Kita called for a military coup d'état, suspension of the constitution, and three years of martial law, during which an army-led government would oust parties from power, nationalize key industries, break up large concentrations of land in order to benefit impoverished tenant farmers, and "remove the barriers which have separated the people from the emperor."[25] That accomplished, he concluded, Japan would be in a position to fulfill its noble mission as a civilizing force in the rest of Asia.

Kita nurtured close connections with the militants of the First Division, and his advice to act while there was still time to save the nation was one reason that the young men chose to attempt their coup in February 1936. Other concerns also shaped their decision. The young officers had experienced nearly four years of national unity cabinets under Saitō and Okada, and neither of those two ex-admirals, the radicals believed, had pursued Japan's interests in northern Asia with sufficient vigor. The revolutionaries reserved even more loathing for Finance Minister Takahashi, whose program of economic recovery had benefited the conglomerates, they conceded, but had not, to their minds, done enough to help Japan's farmers and small businessmen. Yet another factor was the emergence of two rival factions within the army. One clique, led by General Araki Sadao, proudly called itself the Imperial Way Faction. Its many adherents were almost mystically devoted to the emperor, and they were attracted by Araki's burning insistence that Japan could ensure its national defense only by relying on traditional martial values, spiritual training, and the personal virtue and courage of men in uniform. Members of the so-called Control Faction, which revolved around Generals Minami Jirō, Ugaki Kazushige, and Nagata Tetsuzan, held very different beliefs. Pragmatic and coolly rational, those men stressed mechanization of the army and economic planning, and they preferred to substitute firepower and modern technology for esoteric appeals to the "fighting spirit" of traditional Japanese warriors.

The sensational trial of Lieutenant Colonel Aizawa Saburō brought the bubbling pot of contention to a boil. Loyal to the Imperial Way Faction, Aizawa on August 12, 1935, assassinated General Nagata, an outspoken advocate of modernizing the army. The trial, which began on January 28, 1936, produced one of the more melodramatic moments of a decade that had already seen its share of histrionics. The lieutenant colonel magically transformed the defendant's box into his own public pulpit, mesmerizing the nation with a passionate articulation of the themes that flashed across the years of crisis: The emperor was surrounded by "corrupt advisers," the Minobe theory enabled the parties and plutocrats to misuse imperial prerogatives, and even within the military establishment a small "cabal" threatened national security. "I marked out Nagata," Aizawa testified, "because he, together with the senior statesmen and financiers and members of the old army clique like General Minami and General Ugaki, was responsible for the corruption of the army. He was the headquarters of all evil."[26] Projecting himself as a simple soldier who sought only to reform the army and nation, Aizawa won the admiration of people throughout Japan. Thousands sent him letters of encouragement; others mailed to him the severed tip of a finger, the grisly, traditional symbol of support.

The theatrics of the Aizawa trial stirred the junior officers of the First Division to action, and the falling snow of February 26 brought to their minds another wintry morning in 1860, when idealistic, dedicated young samurai moved the country closer to revolutionary upheaval by hacking to death Ii Naosuke, the chief policy maker of the shogunate, at the Field of Cherry Trees Gate, which stood within sight of the bivouac staked out by the modern rebels in the heart of Tokyo. But in 1936 the hopes of the "men of determination" of the First Division melted with the snow. The general staff of the navy was aghast at the possibility of a coup and angry that two members from its ranks had been targets of the assassins. On February 26 and 27, forty ships of the First Fleet broke off scheduled maneuvers, wheeled into Tokyo Bay, and aimed their cannons at rebel positions. So serious was the emergency that the Shōwa emperor, tutored from his youth in the need to preserve the monarchy and the Meiji constitutional system, ordered the army to squash the mutiny. "I deeply regret that they have murdered my most loyal and trusted ministers," he told one aide. "They are trying to pull a silk rope around my neck. What they did violated both the constitution and the rescripts of the Meiji emperor. I shall never forgive them, no matter what their motives are."[27]

The day after the emperor issued his instructions, the army general staff moved ten battalions into Tokyo and surrounded the rebels' positions with tanks and artillery. The mutineers bowed to reality, and by noon on February 29 the rebellion was over. The army pardoned nearly all the noncommissioned officers and ordinary soldiers but visited swift and unmerciful justice upon the junior officers who led the putsch: It tried them in camera and sentenced thirteen to death. The rebels' ideological mentor, Kita Ikki, also went before a firing squad, even though he had not participated in the actual coup attempt.

In many ways the Two Twenty-six Incident sobered the nation; after 1936 there were no more violent challenges to state authority in Japan. Collectively, the civilian right wing turned its back on political terrorism and self-glorifying acts of martyrdom, and inside the military, adherents to the

Imperial Way Faction found themselves placed on the reserve list or else transferred to meaningless assignments as less ideological, more cautious generals associated with the Control Faction came to the fore. Within the corridors of civilian government in 1936, the senior statesmen turned the cabinet over to a respected career bureaucrat, Hirota Kōki. As foreign minister from September 1933 until 1936 Hirota had enunciated a stern policy toward China, pressing Chiang Kai-shek to recognize Manchukuo. After assuming the premiership, Hirota still embraced the tenet that the continued existence of its client state was the fundamental axiom of Japanese foreign policy, but he also held out a conciliatory olive branch, proclaiming in his public speeches and pronouncements the belief that it was best to use diplomatic means to resolve Japan's differences with China and to restore stability to East Asia.

Even the ordinary citizens of Japan seemed to pause for a refreshing breath of normality in 1936, if we are to judge by the diary of Yamaji Yaeko, an unmarried daughter of an innkeeper in a small town in Kyūshū. The seventeen-year-old, whose higher school diploma made her reasonably well educated by the standards of the day, wrote of the "pity" she felt for Lieutenant Colonel Aizawa when he was marched before the firing squad on July 3, just nine days before the first batch of Two Twenty-six rebels was executed. After that, however, national events did not intrude into Yaeko's world; her days in the summer and autumn of 1936 were filled with occasional visits to the local cinema, surreptitious peeks at the "expert" stunts the boys at the neighborhood bicycle shop performed on their unicycles, and the joys of the turning seasons. "It will not be long before we see the golden harvest in the paddy fields," she wrote.[28] But in the summer of 1937 the outbreak of new hostilities in China was to shatter the tranquillity of her world, and as Japan slipped into the morass of a wider war with its Asian neighbor, the nation turned to the military for greater guidance, calls for economic planning and greater state control over business gained a fresh relevancy, and the emperor-centered ideas of the right wing found a new formulation as the orthodox ideology for the Japanese state.

# CHAPTER 13

# In Pursuit of a New Order

n 1930 movies still offered a respite to those who wished to forget for an evening the rigors of the Depression. Films depicting the sad and happy crosscurrents of urban life continued to captivate audiences, and Ozu Yasujirō emerged as the master of that idiom with his "Life of an Office Worker" (*Kaishin seikatsu*) and his 1932 classic "I Was Born, but . . ." (*Umareta wa mita keredo*), a comedy with serious overtones about two young boys adjusting to a new neighborhood, a new school, and new playmates in Tokyo. "Nonsense films" provided a more pure form of escapism. Typifying that genre were such erotic farces as "A Chronicle of the Newlyweds" (*Shinkon ki*) by another exciting young director, Naruse Mikio, and "Uproar over the Aphrodisiac Dumpling" (*Iroke dango sōdōki*), which had characters cavorting across the screen and stumbling into humorous predicaments and romantic misadventures with little regard for plot or characterization.

In the summer of 1937 Japan's adventurism in northern Asia escalated into all-out war with China, and soon the island nation sent off nearly one million young men to do battle. As Japan gathered itself for the extraordinary effort required to fight a full-fledged war on the continent, the government issued calls for a New Order that would place political authority in the hands of technocrats and men of integrity, organize the economic resources of the nation more efficiently, integrate the colonies into an autarkic zone capable of supplying the means of victory, and harness the psychological and moral energies of the people behind the war effort.

In pursuit of that last goal, the Film Law of 1939 called for the "healthy development of the film industry."[1] Translated, that spelled the demise of sexually frivolous movies and those dealing with complex social issues. In their place, as one Home Ministry directive stipulated, production companies were to turn out films that "elevate national consciousness, establish public morality, correct the understanding of Japan's domestic and international situation, and contribute to the advancement of public welfare in other ways." Like it or not, the 400 million paying customers who went to the movies each year at the end of the 1930s faced a diet of grim, realistic portrayals of battle such as "Five Scouts" (*Gonin no sekkōhei*, 1938) and "Mud and Soldiers" (*Tsuchi to heitai*, 1939). Ironically, the government's attempt to enforce conformity of thought and build support for the war effort did not help settle the conflict with China but in the end merely hardened attitudes toward other supposed enemies, with the tragic consequence that in 1941 Japan initiated a war with the United States.

## Sliding into War

Neither the army general staff nor the country's newly appointed prime minister, Konoe Fumimaro, was particularly apprehensive when details of the latest incident in China reached Tokyo. The confrontation seemed to be just another minor foulup that could be straightened out quickly and routinely. On the night of July 7, 1937, a company of Japanese soldiers, one of several international units stationed near Beijing under the provisions of the Boxer Protocol, was conducting ordinary field maneuvers near the graceful Marco Polo Bridge, some ten miles west of China's old imperial capital. The soldiers added realism to the training exercise by firing blank cartridges from their machine guns, as was regular practice, but that night, much to their surprise, they were answered by incoming live rounds, presumably from Chinese troops. After a roll call revealed one Japanese soldier to be missing, the company commander asked permission to search a nearby town, and when the Chinese balked at the request, the Japanese tried to enter the settlement forcibly. Following that second skirmish, each side rushed a battalion of men to the scene, even though the errant soldier had found his way back to his unit unharmed.

When central military headquarters in Tokyo received a situation report on the morning of July 8, the army chief of staff decided to downplay events and cabled instructions to the local Japanese commander to work out a settlement with his Chinese counterpart, a familiar method of resolving minor incidents in northern China. The chief of staff's action met with approval from several officers on the general staff who believed Japan must avoid petty military engagements in China that might broaden into a pro-

*The Marco Polo Bridge, near Beijing*

tracted war. Remarkably, one of the most articulate of the so-called noninterventionists was Ishiwara Kanji, the impulsive, cocksure mastermind behind the Manchurian Incident. Having been transferred in 1935 to the
general staff's Operations Division in Tokyo, Ishiwara agreed with colleagues who saw the Soviet Union as Japan's most immediate strategic problem in northern Asia, even while he continued to predict the eventual onset
of a Final War with the United States. Such threats compelled Japan to em-
bark on a long-term industrial and military buildup, Ishiwara asserted, and
that had justified the creation of Manchukuo since the new country could
contribute to Japan's attempt to achieve autarky, or economic self-sufficiency. But at this juncture, in the mid-1930s, Japan needed to maintain a
state of peace to buy time to develop its full economic and military capabilities. Looked at in such light, further military involvement in China, Ishiwara reasoned, simply invited "the same sort of disaster which overtook
Napoleon in Spain—a slow sinking into the deepest sort of bog."[2] Japan
must be on guard, the noninterventionists admonished, not to underesti-

mate the growing strength of Chinese nationalism and the tenacity with which Chiang Kai-shek's army would fight if backed into a corner; the continent was a quagmire that would suck in Japanese manpower and resources, leaving the nation vulnerable.

At three o'clock on the afternoon of July 8, just hours after the army chief of staff ordered a local settlement, Prime Minister Konoe called his cabinet together to review events. Konoe was still inexperienced as prime minister, but his pedigree and his preparation for the post were impeccable. Born in 1891 into one of Japan's most distinguished aristocratic houses and a graduate of Kyoto University, he had been groomed for public service by the venerable Saionji Kinmochi, who included the young prince in the Japanese delegation to the Paris Peace Conference in 1919. As Konoe matured, he followed in his father's political footsteps by serving as an energetic leader in the House of Peers, whose president he became in 1933. Saionji and the senior statesmen first asked Konoe to assume the duties of premier in the aftermath of the Two Twenty-six Incident, chiefly because the charismatic prince commanded respect from a broad spectrum of Japan's political elites and possessed a reputation for holding constitutional government in high esteem. Konoe declined Saionji's overtures in 1936 but agreed in June 1937 to a second solicitation from his longtime mentor.

Konoe entered office committed to finding a diplomatic resolution to the nagging "China problem," an aspiration he shared with ex-Premier Hirota Kōki, who returned to government as his foreign minister. Consequently, in the cabinet meeting of July 8, Konoe welcomed the army's

**TABLE 13.1** *Japanese Prime Ministers, 1936–1944*

| PRIME MINISTER | CABINET NUMBER | CABINET TERM |
|---|---|---|
| Hirota Kōki | | March 9, 1936–February 2, 1937 |
| Hayashi Senjūrō | | February 2, 1937–June 4, 1937 |
| Konoe Fumimaro | First | June 4, 1937–January 5, 1939 |
| Hiranuma Kiichirō | | January 5, 1939–August 30, 1939 |
| Abe Nobuyuki | | August 30, 1939–January 16, 1940 |
| Yonai Mitsumasa | | January 16, 1940–July 22, 1940 |
| Konoe Fumimaro | Second | July 22, 1940–July 18, 1941 |
| Konoe Fumimaro | Third | July 18, 1941–October 18, 1941 |
| Tōjō Hideki | | October 18, 1941–July 22, 1944 |

recommendation that the government downplay the affair at the Marco Polo Bridge, and he attached his support to the principles of "nonexpansion" and "local settlement." To the cabinet's relief, by July 11 the Chinese and Japanese commanders on the scene had appeared to work out a modus vivendi: The Chinese would apologize, punish the officers responsible for the incident, and pledge to suppress Communist guerrillas in the region.

Much to Tokyo's disappointment, however, Chiang Kai-shek refused to endorse the negotiations. The generalissimo previously had acquiesced to any number of local settlements with the Japanese military, but in the summer of 1937 he drew a line in the sands of northern China. He could risk such a bold action because his Guomindang political organization was in better military and economic shape than it had been a decade earlier. His words carried additional weight because he stood as head of the new Nationalist regime, established in Nanjing in 1928 and known familiarly as the Guomindang government since that party dominated affairs of state. More belligerent anti-Japanese attitudes among his countrymen, few of whom were willing to countenance further violations of their nation's sovereignty such as had been embedded in the He-Umezu and Doihara-Qin agreements, strengthened the old warlord's mettle. Additional pressure came from Mao's Communists, who were earning increased respect and popular support for their demand that Chiang end China's civil war and join them in a "united front" against Japanese aggression. If Chiang were to realize his ambition to have the Guomindang fully accepted by everyone as the legitimate government for all China, he would have to seize the mantle of Chinese nationalism by abandoning his two-pronged policy of appeasing Japan and husbanding his resources for "eradication campaigns" against his Communist opponents. Zhang Xueliang, who had established a new base for himself in Xi'an after being driven out of Rehe, made that point clear in December 1936, when Chiang journeyed to Zhang's headquarters to chastise his longtime ally for falling under the influence of the Communists. To Chiang's surprise, Zhang placed him under arrest and refused to release the Guomindang leader until he agreed to the united front strategy.

On the morning after the skirmish at the Marco Polo Bridge, the Communists issued an appeal for all Chinese to resist "the new Japanese invasion," and within days Chiang demonstrated his commitment to the "spirit of Xi'an" by directing the military commander in Beijing to reject the terms offered by the Japanese. Concurrently, the generalissimo began to move four of his best divisions north into Hebei Province, an open violation of the He-Umezu Agreement and Tanggu Truce. Ten days after the initial incident, on July 17, Chiang stood on the porch of his summer home and delivered a memorable public address in which he declared that no peaceful settlement was possible if Japan continued to infringe upon Chinese sovereignty. "If we allow one more inch of our territory to be lost," the generalissimo concluded, "we shall be guilty of an unpardonable crime against our race."[3] By adopting a confrontational strategy, Chiang magnified the significance of the Marco Polo Bridge Incident, inflating it into an issue that demanded settlement by national governments, not by local commanders in the field.

The Japanese did not shy away from escalation. Konoe, still hopeful of a peaceful settlement but absolutely unwilling to allow Japan to appear weak-willed, matched Chiang's rhetoric of July 17 with his own saber-rattling press conference and radio address in which he called on the generalissimo "to apologize" for "illegal, anti-Japanese actions." Leading generals, such as Tōjō Hideki and Koiso Kuniaki, stepped forward to argue for a strike against Chiang. They agreed with colleagues who considered the Soviet Union the greatest threat to Japanese security, but they also held the Guomindang armies in contempt and believed that a swift, bold attack would bring Chiang to his knees in quick order, leaving the army free to concentrate on the Soviets. In the expectation that a resolute show of force would compel Chiang to back down, the Konoe cabinet on July 27 formally put its seal of approval to a request from the army to send three divisions to China. The next afternoon bitter fighting again broke out near Marco Polo Bridge, and by early August Japan's China Garrison Army had occupied Beijing.

Almost immediately, like lightning splitting the Chinese landscape, hostilities jumped south to Shanghai. In early August Chiang moved nearly 100,000 troops into demilitarized zones established during the 1932 Shanghai Incident. The situation was tense: The Japanese military had only 2,500 marines in the area, and civilian Japanese resident in Shanghai knew that almost 200 fellow expatriates had been killed eleven days earlier when fighting engulfed a provincial city near Beijing. As a result, when Chinese security personnel attacked two Japanese marines in Shanghai on August 9, the ranking Japanese admiral asked Tokyo to send reinforcements promptly. On the morning of August 14, the cabinet approved the dispatch of additional divisions to the continent, and the patrician Konoe issued a statement claiming that China had assumed an "arrogant and insulting" attitude toward Japan and that his country had no option but to "resort to resolute action" to "chastise" the "atrocious" Chinese. That afternoon Guomindang bombers answered Konoe by flying over the foreign settlement in Shanghai and bombing Japanese naval installations. Hours later Chiang ordered a general mobilization and announced that "China is duty bound to defend herself and her national existence."[4] Unexpectedly, in a chain of events unplanned by either side, the skirmish at the Marco Polo Bridge had blown up into a full-fledged war, and although neither China nor Japan ever officially declared that a state of belligerency existed, fighting continued for eight years and one day.

## Stalemated in China

Ishiwara Kanji's warnings to the contrary, most Japanese strategic planners envisioned a fairly easy victory against an enemy whom they held in contempt. By quickly seizing important cities and rail lines—"points" and "lines," in military nomenclature—they intended to force Chiang to sue for an early peace. But to its surprised consternation, the Japanese Imperial Army found that it had misjudged seriously the determination of the Guomindang, which threw nearly 500,000 troops into the defense of Shanghai. Tied down for nearly three months in savage hand-to-hand combat in the streets of the city, the Japanese prevailed only after landing troops at an undefended bay thirty miles south of the city and outflanking the Chinese. With more than 600,000 men now committed to the China theater, Japanese soldiers raced west to engage Chiang in his capital city of Nanjing. Japanese troops pillaged the city on December 13, 1937, but Chiang already had slipped away to Hankou, some six hundred miles upriver on the Yangzi, and he steadfastly ignored all Japanese overtures to negotiate a diplomatic settlement.

Early in 1938 Konoe announced that he would no longer recognize Chiang's Nationalist regime as China's government, and Japan's generals, still in search of an elusive knockout punch, decided to broaden the war by sending eight additional divisions to the continent. In May, Japanese armies broke through a line of more than one hundred Guomindang divisions deployed around Xuzhou and took the ancient city north of Nanjing, whose possession for centuries had served as a litmus test of dynastic legitimacy for China's emperors. Chiang still did not contemplate surrender. Redoubling their efforts, Japanese troops captured Canton on October 21, and on October 27, following five months of bitter combat that left perhaps as many as 200,000 Chinese and Japanese corpses on the battlefield, Japan's legions staggered into Hankou, only to discover that Chiang already had dismantled its factories, schools, and hospitals and shipped them westward to Chongqing, the new Guomindang capital located deep in the vastness of southwestern China, beyond even the famed Yangzi gorges.

At the end of 1938 the frustrated Japanese found themselves stalemated. Even though it had nearly 850,000 men under arms in China, the Imperial

**MAP 13.1** *The War in China, 1937–1939*

Army in the south never would be able to push its way to Chongqing, and in the north Mao's Communists hounded the Japanese soldiers' every step, ambushed careless patrols, and even mauled larger units in mass battles. As the bitter war of attrition ground on, casualties mounted—by 1941 nearly 300,000 Japanese and reportedly 1 million Chinese lay dead—and still there was no foreseeable end to the fighting. Japan, just as Ishiwara had predicted, was bogged down in a Chinese quagmire. The emperor's armies controlled nearly all of China's major cities, but they could neither defeat the Guomindang armies nor annihilate the Communist partisans; Konoe had given up trying to discover a formula that would entice Chiang to the negotiating table; and national honor would not permit the Japanese to retreat. China had become Japan's Napoleonic nightmare, the war that would not end.

The Japanese news media paid solemn homage to the bravery of the nation's soldiers and patriotically heralded each new victory, but a tight net of government censorship kept hidden from the public another side of the war in China, the atrocities visited upon innocent civilians. Even in the best of circumstances in the 1930s many Japanese soldiers felt superior to other Asians, who seemed so "backward" for having failed to modernize as rapidly as Japan. Such a perception, when spiced by the tension of fighting on hostile foreign soil and hardened into shape by a military code of conduct that made scarce mention of the rights due an enemy population, left Japanese soldiers capable of committing shocking crimes against ordinary Chinese. The most infamous atrocity was the Rape of Nanjing, a storm of arson, brutality, rape, and wanton murder of unarmed civilians that raged unabated for several weeks after the Japanese occupied the city in December 1937. The full extent of the suffering experienced by the residents of Nanjing and surrounding towns and villages can never be known. Foreign observers at the time estimated the number of dead at around 40,000, later histories revised that figure upward to 200,000, and the memorial to the massacre in today's Nanjing speaks of tens of thousands of rapes and a total of 300,000 dead.

Nanjing was not unique. Throughout China, Japanese soldiers plundered Chinese property, shot farm animals for food, and raped women of all ages. In the north, where constant attacks from Communist partisans made it seem as if every single villager were an enemy guerrilla, Japanese routinely tortured and abused peasants by smearing them with benzene and setting them afire, by bayoneting pregnant women, and by forcing children to walk into suspected minefields. On the outskirts of Harbin the Japanese Army stationed its nefarious Unit 731. Camouflaged by the innocuous cover name of Epidemic Prevention and Potable Water Supply Unit, the bacteri-

*Chinese peasants defend their grain against Japanese*

ological warfare research group conducted experiments on living human beings, injecting them with bubonic and pneumonic plague, typhoid, syphilis, and other communicable diseases in order to develop more lethal strains and more efficient means of transmitting them. "If we didn't have a feeling of racial superiority, we couldn't have done it," confided one unit member, as he admitted dissecting terrified still-conscious subjects to extract plague bacteria from internal organs.[5] By the time the war ended, several thousand Chinese had perished in that research program, although no Japanese government has ever officially acknowledged its existence.

As Japan's weary soldiers slugged their way through the endless immensity of China, the nation's leadership sought to define and legitimate a war that had begun as an attempt to "chastise" Chiang Kai-shek. When China appealed to the League of Nations in September 1937, Foreign Minister Hirota spoke in terms of self-defense. Japan, he explained, was only trying to get the Guomindang to cease its anti-Japanese activities. The tireless phrasemaker Matsuoka Yōsuke, who in the autumn of 1937 sat on a cabinet advisory council composed of leading public figures, tried to cast China's political leaders as villains who menaced not just Japan but all Asia.

"The drunken orgy of China's own war lords" and "red communism," he wrote, had coalesced into a "festering sore deep down within the bosom of Eastern Asia" that now threatened "all Asian races with sure and inescapable death." Japan had "taken up her scalpel," he concluded, to perform the "heroic surgery" that the times required.[6]

Prime Minister Konoe, a dedicated pan-Asianist from his youth, articulated a more noble vision of Japan as the rightful leader of a new Asian order. From the time he had journeyed to Paris as a young man, Konoe had been an outspoken foe of the Washington treaty system, which he criticized as a crude attempt by the West to freeze the international status quo in order to ensure that the white race continued to dominate the world. The West, in his reckoning, theoretically might accord Japan the status of a first-rate power, but in fact, the island nation remained an economic have-not in a world presided over by imperialistic Western haves. Arms limitations, established by the Washington Conference and reaffirmed at London in 1930, merely served to keep Japan subservient to the great Western powers, especially the United States and Great Britain. National salvation, according to Konoe, depended on Japan's achieving economic self-sufficiency and overturning a malicious, racially biased system of international relations that relegated Asian nations to second-class citizenship in world affairs.

On November 3, 1938, Konoe's government celebrated the fall of Canton and Hankou with the formal announcement of a New Order in East Asia, and that evening the prime minister addressed the nation on radio. "What Japan seeks," he solemnly proclaimed, "is the establishment of a new order that will insure the permanent stability of East Asia. In this lies the ultimate purpose of our present military campaign."[7] The foundation of the New Order would be a "tripartite relationship of mutual aid and coordination between Japan, Manchukuo, and China." Unfortunately, Konoe lamented, Chiang Kai-shek was nothing but a Western puppet, a cat's-paw that curried favor with the Western powers simply to perpetuate his own corrupt rule, with the tragic consequence that the Chinese people were exposed to the dangers of Communism and Western imperialism. Ordinary Chinese citizens had nothing to fear from the Japanese, Konoe promised. On the contrary, he sympathized with the "ardent national aspirations" of the great Chinese masses who simply wished to liberate themselves from the ravages of Chiang's rule, and he looked forward to Chiang's defeat so that a new China could ally with Japan and Manchukuo in order "to perfect the joint defense against Communism, and to create a new culture and realize a close economic cohesion throughout East Asia." It was a carefully honed, masterful speech by a resourceful politician. At once Konoe justified Japan's military actions as transcending its own national interests, and he constructed a coherent vision of a moral, principled, and selfless nation whose sacrifices would free the Chinese people from the twin yokes of Guomindang suppression and Western imperialism, thus creating "a new structure of peace based on true justice."

## The New Political Order

Although Konoe's rhetoric inspired his countrymen, the prime minister was less able to translate his vision for a New Order in East Asia into an actual military or diplomatic settlement that would end the war in China on terms favorable to Japan, and in January 1939 the frustrated prince resigned from office. A year and a half later Konoe agreed to a second stint as premier,

*Prime Minister Konoe Fumimaro (far left) meets in his home with Foreign Minister Matsuoka Yōsuke, Navy Minister Yoshida Zengo, and Army Minister Tōjō Hideki in July 1940*

primarily because he hoped to initiate a New Order Movement, a set of drastic changes in national policy that would provide solutions to Japan's long-standing domestic and foreign crises. In a radio address entitled "Receiving the Imperial Mandate" and delivered on July 23, 1940, the day after he formed his second cabinet, Konoe declared that the old world order was collapsing, washing Asia's shores with waves of change. To cope with a radically different world, he told the nation, Japan had to rejuvenate itself by rebuilding its domestic political and economic structures. Three days later his cabinet approved the "Outline of Basic National Principles," a blueprint for the New Order Movement.

To a very large extent, the intellectual fathers of the New Order Movement were the members of a brain trust organized by Konoe in 1933, a year after the assassination of Prime Minister Inukai, for the purpose of reevaluating Japan's constitutional politics. By the time Konoe named his first cabinet in June 1937, the advisers were known formally as the Shōwa Research Association and included more than one hundred prominent intellectuals, scholars, journalists, politicians, businesspeople, and civil servants who, divided into a dozen or more committees, busily supplied the prime minister with innovative approaches to nearly the entire scope of Japan's domestic and foreign policies. Rōyama Masamichi, an activist scholar from Tokyo University, contributed perhaps as much as any individual to the task force that concentrated on political issues. Desperately concerned that Konoe have a united nation behind him as the prime minister sought to forge a New Order in East Asia, Rōyama was fascinated by the ability of charismatic leaders in Europe to manipulate the powerful emotionalism of fascist ideology to win the allegiance of the citizenry, and he desired that Japan "achieve internal unity similar to the Nazis."[8] Declaring that liberal democracy was outmoded in the rapidly changing world of the 1930s, Rōyama argued that Japan ought to impose fascism "from above" by creating a new "national organization," based on what he admiringly called "totalitarian principles," that would supersede older organs of government and decide national policies.

In August 1940 Konoe appointed thirty-seven individuals representing various sectors of Japanese society to a special Preparation Committee for the New Order. Drawing heavily upon the writings of Rōyama and proposals drafted by the Shōwa Research Association, the committee recommended creating a new organization to be known as the Imperial Rule Assistance Association. The IRAA, as envisioned by the committee, would be a popularly based yet quasi-government political party headed by the prime minister. Concurrently, cooperative councils composed of persons with similar occupations or cultural interests would be established at the municipal, county, and prefecture levels in order to "guarantee direct contact with the people," and the new structure would be capped by a national-level council that eventually would displace the Diet as the body that debated and ratified national policies. The result, committee members hoped, would be the creation of a durable mass-based political association that could "assist" the prime minister and his cabinet in implementing government programs.

Convinced that the distribution of political power sanctioned by the Meiji constitution no longer served Japan's needs, Konoe threw his political weight behind the proposal. The autonomy of the military services and the diffusion of power among several elite groups, he concluded, encouraged administrative turmoil and chaotic political infighting between the civil and military branches of government that might prove fatal as Japan tried to navigate its way through the extraordinary international crisis of the late 1930s. The political leverage afforded by heading a mass political association, Konoe hoped, would strengthen his hand in dealing with the Diet, military, and professional bureaucracy, thus producing more coordinated policies that would receive unqualified support from the citizenry, mobilized through the IRAA.

The proposal received a mixed reaction. At first, enthusiastic support came from a curious combination of army generals, who anticipated being able to manipulate the association to enlist popular support behind the war effort in China, and party politicians, who desperately hoped that a new mass party would permit them to reclaim political influence from the bureaucracy and military. Indeed, the country's chief political parties voluntarily dissolved themselves on August 15, 1940, even before the IRAA came into being. Despite such dramatic displays of support, however, a host of other organizations and individuals were decidedly less enamored of Konoe's brainchild, and in the end the IRAA came to represent a historical road not taken. Conservatives such as Hiranuma Kiichirō, who served as prime minister for eight months in 1939, objected that the proposed totalitarian IRAA was nothing but a "new shogunate" that would usurp the power of the emperor's government, and Japanists declared that the national polity, the hallowed *kokutai*, already united the emperor with subjects who naturally fulfilled their sacred obligation to "assist imperial rule." On a more mundane plane, senior officials within the Home Ministry feared the loss of bureaucratic turf and complained that the proposed network of occupationally based units would interfere with local administration at a particularly crucial time in the nation's history.

A natural compromiser who had little stomach for hand-to-hand political combat, Konoe quickly gave in to his critics (later in his life the prince called himself a "well-meaning child of fate," destined to fail at all to which he set his mind). When the IRAA came into being on October 12, 1940, local branches were established not in accordance with vocation or cultural groups but, rather, as appendages of existing administrative units, and they were placed under the jurisdiction of local officials, just as the career bureaucrats in the Home Ministry wished. During the autumn of 1940 the ministry gained virtually full authority over the IRAA, and in late December Konoe made another bow in the direction of his opponents by appointing Hiranuma home minister, thus setting the IRAA under the bureaucratic thumb of one of its staunchest opponents. Nor did the association ever threaten the prerogatives of the Diet, which continued to meet and at one point expressed its distrust of the new organization by refusing to appropriate funds for it.

"Fascism has come to Japan," lamented Yoshino Sakuzō in 1932.[9] What that venerable liberal feared was that putschists and "antidemocratic" movements would produce "fascism from below" in Japan. His comments serve as a reminder that Japan had historical commonalties with Germany and Italy: All three countries began to develop capitalist economies at a relatively late date; in each, democracy enjoyed only a brief and uneasy ascendancy as it fought to put down roots even while those countries struggled to overcome severe economic crises; and all three feared that the British or Americans would stymie their aspirations for empire, so necessary for economic self-sufficiency. In that sense, Yoshino had good reason to believe that Japanese fascists might find a path to power, repudiate parliamentary rule, and introduce economic principles of national socialism, just as their European counterparts posed to do.

Yet, in the end, Japan never did experience an epoch of fascism. There were Japanese who considered themselves fascists, just as there were individuals such as Rōyama Masamichi who were attracted by fascist ideology. For all that, and despite the obvious historical significance of rightist groups in Japan, fascists accomplished no major reforms and fascism as a movement chalked up no permanent successes. The collapse of the Two Twenty-six Incident foreclosed the possibility of fascism from below, and the stillbirth of the IRAA demonstrated how nearly impossible it was to impose fascism from above.

Japan's historical trajectory, its quest for modernity, remained distinctively its own. Unlike in Germany and Italy, the right wing in Japan never coalesced into a movement capable of overthrowing the established ruling elites, no single revolutionary party or mass organization seized the day, and no charismatic leader stood at the head of state. Throughout the 1930s the Meiji constitution remained viable, and the same institutional structures and elite groups that had governed the country from 1890 continued to preside over affairs of state. Still, Japan in the late 1930s was different from Japan in the late Meiji and Taishō periods. As was clear to all, the overwhelming sense of internal discord and external threat that emerged in the late 1920s and early 1930s severely shook the nation's earlier confidence in parliamentary government and economic liberalism. Moreover, the demise of political parties, the more muted role played by the Diet, and the expanded influence of the military and civil bureaucracies within the cabinet during the 1930s gave rise to a style of governance that was more assertive, authoritarian, and militaristic than before. If fascism is inadequate as a label to describe the transformations of the 1930s, perhaps it is appropriate to subscribe to a term fashionable within Japan at that time and to see the evolution of a "national defense state," in which the political culture and economy were reorganized to permit Japan to overcome the economic crisis of the 1930s and mobilize itself for an ever-expanding war.

## The New Economic Order

The inclination to view Total War, autarky, and the creation of a national defense state as an inseparable trinity can be traced to the writings of Ugaki Kazushige and Koiso Kuniaki in the latter half of the 1910s. Keen observers of the European conflict, those two young colonels concurred with Ishiwara Kanji that in modern warfare there could be no neutrals, conflict would be prolonged and require massive resources, and any belligerent that was not economically self-reliant was doomed. To prepare his country for the new and revolutionary manner of resolving conflict among nations, Koiso published a booklet outlining a two-pronged program: to develop Japan's colonies as a "resource base," a mission that Ishiwara and the Kwantung Army took up in 1931, and to centralize government control over the domestic economy so that the armed services could respond immediately and effectively should war threaten.

In the 1930s the renovationist bureaucrats and some academic economists also began to expound the virtues of a managed economy. For them the gyrations of the 1920s and the crowning thorns of the Great Depression demonstrated the bankruptcy of laissez-faire economics, and they sought a more effective way to cope with the stresses and dislocations of modernity. As Japan slid deeper into the China quagmire, the advocates for a planned economy lent increasing support to the contention that a resource-rich empire and direct state management of the economy were prerequisites for national survival. Writing in 1934, the economist Arisawa Hiromi argued, "In modern war, victory or defeat is determined not just by fighting strength on the battlefield but, rather, is decided mainly by the strength of the weapons industries. The state must utilize every economic instrument and devote all materials to the fight for survival."[10] Three years later, as Japan girded itself for full-scale war, he added: "The state has to exercise its power and directly assume leadership over economic activities. In a semiwar situation, an economy led by the state has to be coercive."

Prince Konoe elevated self-sufficiency and economic planning to explicit national goals during his first term as prime minister. Even as he was committing Japanese troops to the war in China during the autumn of 1937, the new premier reshaped the former Cabinet Research Bureau into a cabinet-level agency dubbed the Cabinet Planning Board (CPB), with the intention that it formulate and coordinate economic strategy. Dominated by renovationist bureaucrats and the army's strategic planners, the CPB quickly established a social welfare ministry and nationalized the electrical power industry. Each measure blended civilian with military concerns. Brought into being on January 11, 1938, the Ministry of Health and Welfare assumed administration of all medical care and social welfare programs and sought to improve the health of the nation's youth, particularly important to the military since a surprising number of recruits were failing their physical examinations. The Electric Power Industry Act, passed by the Diet and implemented on April 10, 1938, consolidated the electric power industry into nine companies placed under the supervision of the Ministry of Communications. That measure too was designed to serve popular needs by providing cheap electrical power to Japan's economically depressed regions, while ensuring that munitions factories received ample amounts of power for their needs.

Konoe had even more breathtaking schemes in mind. In preparation for the opening of the Seventy-third Imperial Diet, scheduled for December 26, 1937, the CPB drafted a national mobilization bill. Staggering in its scope and intentions, the measure authorized the government to deploy "human and material resources in such a way as to enable the State to give full scope to the efficient use of its strength for the realization of the purposes of national defense in time of war."[11] Specifically, the fifty-article law endowed government agencies responsible to the cabinet with powers to ration labor among industries on the basis of production needs, organize all industries into cartels that would implement government planning goals, and seize factories and land for wartime production purposes.

Opposition welled up immediately. Many Diet members, while loyally supporting the war against Chiang and the Guomindang, were not willing to risk such a grand experiment with the country's industrial structure during a period of international tension, and big business was astonished by the attack on private ownership and other core principles of laissez-faire capitalism. Even Konoe's mentor, Prince Saionji, declared that "the bill ignores the constitution," a charge echoed by many leading conservatives.[12] Ever the realist, Konoe swallowed a number of compromises in order to secure Diet approval, personally guaranteeing that the government would not invoke the more controversial provisions until the China Incident had run its course and further agreeing to allow a fifty-member screening committee to oversee any application of the legislation. Mollified, the Diet passed the National General Mobilization Law on April 1, 1938.

When Konoe formed his second cabinet in the summer of 1940, he resumed his attempts to advance government control over the economy. In the same speech of July 23 in which he outlined plans for a New Political Order, the prince spoke of a New Economic Order and the need to construct a national defense state if Japan were to move forward in China. In its latest evolution the prince's thinking went beyond even the implications of the mobilization law to imagine a more fundamental restructuring of the economy that would irrevocably turn it away from its capitalistic orientation. As was the case with the New Political Order, Konoe drew intellectual inspiration from the Shōwa Research Association, especially from the position papers of Ryū Shintarō, a popular economic pundit for the *Asahi* newspaper who enlisted in Konoe's brain trust in 1939.

Impressed by German success in raising industrial production and reducing unemployment, Ryū advocated using Nazi precedents to reform Japan's capitalistic system. In particular, he urged the government to set maximum limits for dividends and oversee the reinvestment of excess profits. On an even more controversial level, he recommended leaving ownership of major industries in private hands but transferring management to government employees, what he called the separation of capital and management. His plan, which the CPB largely adopted as its own, called for firms in each industrial sector to be organized into cartellike control associations that would implement government instructions concerning the allocation of resources and set production quotas for each member firm. Moreover, a government-supervised Supreme Economic Council would have jurisdiction over the control associations, thus assuring the bureaucracy a dominant role in coordinating economic policy.

Konoe's proposals again ran into fierce opposition. Business leaders viciously denounced the New Economic Order as a "red plot" hatched by secret Communists, hidden away in the CPB, who wished "to destroy our economic world and make our country into Russia."[13] The Japan Economic Federation, which included most of the nation's largest firms, charged that government bureaucrats were notorious bunglers and solemnly warned that government control over profits inevitably would cause a "contraction of business, a decrease in production, and a drastic drop in tax revenues." It was a carefully orchestrated attack, and on December 7, 1940, Konoe backed down when his cabinet endorsed a Plan for a New Economic System that was considerably less comprehensive than that which the renovationists had envisioned. The prime minister could only "encourage" the formation of control associations, no industry or company was nationalized, the traditional managerial class stayed in place, profits were allowed, and no national coordinating agency was created.

Konoe was bloodied in his battle to create a New Economic Order, but he was far from losing the war. Between the spring of 1938, when the National General Mobilization Law took effect, and the autumn of 1941, when he resigned as premier for the final time, the cabinet and renovationist bureaucrats unleashed a blizzard of more than one hundred laws and decrees that inserted the voice of the state into a myriad of economic activities. At times the prime minister sought Diet approval for his actions, but whenever that body proved recalcitrant, Konoe and his allies arranged for an imperial decree or activated one of the clauses of the National General Mobilization Law, despite his solemn promise not to do so during the China conflict. As Japanese forces drove toward Canton and Hankou in the fall of 1938, for instance, the newly proclaimed Machine Tool Manufacturing and Aircraft Manufacturing laws provided government subsidies to those strategically important enterprises, even while imposing a greater degree of state supervision over them. In November of the same year the army successfully pressed for the implementation of profit ceilings on major corporations; on October 20, 1939, the Price Control Order and Temporary Wage Measures Order placed caps on wages, retail prices, and rents; and in 1940 the government began to ration rice, sugar, and matches.

Nearly each turn of the calendar's pages in the late 1930s, it seemed, disclosed some new economic control measure. In several important ways the decade witnessed profound, even revolutionary alterations in the relationship between private capital and the state bureaucracy. Civilian renovationist bureaucrats and military planners forged a powerful new coalition that enabled them to dominate supracabinet agencies and to produce a broad set of proposals that moved the government from the kind of facilitative action favored a decade earlier by the shepherds of the people to more intrusive activities advocated by those who wanted to create a fully managed economy. In the years following the incident at Mukden, the government invented a whole new repertoire of techniques for intervention—central planning, wage and price controls, and the rationing of industrial raw materials and consumer goods—that fostered the growth of a national defense state and compelled Japan's major corporations to accept new ways of doing business. Despite the expansion of bureaucratic controls, however, when Konoe finally relinquished the premiership in the autumn of 1941, a decade after the outbreak of fighting in Manchuria, the Japanese did not labor under a totalitarian economic system any more than they lived under a fascist political regime. The proponents of state planning had not gotten their way entirely: *Zaibatsu* still roamed the economic terrain, and company managers had fought valiantly to preserve the concepts of private property and private ownership of business. As with politics and society, the economy remained partly free, partly controlled.

## Reordering the Empire

Konoe's call for a new order at home and in Asia centered on the desire to break Japan's dependence on an international capitalist system dominated by British and American interests. During the 1930s the world divided itself into protectionist dollar and sterling zones, and in response, many of Japan's economic planners called for the creation of a yen zone to reverse a trend that saw their country become increasingly reliant upon the Anglo-American powers and their colonies for resources, markets, capital, and technology. The spreading conflict in northern Asia added urgency to such arguments, and after the establishment of Manchukuo Japan attempted to integrate the economies of its colonies and dependencies more closely with that of the home islands to create an autarkic economic bloc. In some places the effort went fairly smoothly. By 1939 some 99.9 percent of the exports from Karafuto went to Japan, as did 93.2 percent of the exports from the Nan'yō dependencies and 86 percent of those from Taiwan. In Manchukuo, the Five-Year Plan implemented in 1937 was achieving only mixed results, but by 1940 that satellite was supplying Japan with significant amounts of coal, pig iron, steel ingots, gold, chemical fertilizers, and other essential commodities.

Japanese planners and military personnel had a more difficult time in occupied China. As the Imperial Army pushed and shoved its way inland in 1937 and 1938, it sought to construct a "suitable" regime that would at once win the loyalty of the Chinese people yet be subservient to Japan. In northern China the Japanese Army set up peace preservation committees, boards of prominent Chinese who sanctioned occupation policies, and on December 14, 1937, it rolled them into the Provisional Government of the Republic of China. Inaugurated in Beijing, the collaborationist regime was headed by Wang Kemin, a banker who previously had served as Zhang Xueliang's financial adviser.

Several months later, in March 1938, the Japanese created a second puppet regime, the Reform Government of the Republic of China, headquartered in Nanjing and entrusted with administering the central and southern provinces of occupied China under the careful scrutiny of Japanese "advisers." On March 30, 1940, occupation authorities dissolved the Provisional and Reform governments and transferred their functions to the Reorganized National Government of the Republic of China, led by Wang Jingwei. Educated at Hōsei University in Japan and a longtime rival of Chiang for control of the Guomindang, Wang perceived of Japan and China as natural allies, and he advocated a negotiated settlement with Japan despite all the bloodshed and atrocities of the late 1930s. Although vilified by many of his countrymen for what they regarded as treasonable collaboration, the naïve but patriotic Wang believed that by cooperating with the Japanese, he might be able to modulate the grimmer aspects of the occupation and preserve at least a façade of Chinese sovereignty within the occupied territories.

Determined to add occupied China to the yen bloc, Japanese occupiers set about exploiting its resources. In some cases, the Japanese military simply expropriated what it wanted, seizing Chinese companies it considered strategically significant and placing them under the management of Japanese firms or military units. Late in 1938 the Konoe government authorized the formation of the North China Development Corporation and the Central China Development Corporation. Capitalized with contributions from both private and government sources, the new organizations achieved a measure of success developing iron and coal mines, steelworks, hydroelectric projects, and harbor facilities in northern China and rebuilding railway lines destroyed in heavy fighting along the Yangzi River valley. As a result, the amount of coal produced in northern China and Mongolia increased from 10.7 million to 22.8 million tons between 1937 and 1941, while mines in those two regions and central China yielded 1 million tons of iron ore in 1939 and 5 million tons in 1942, the year of peak production.

Of Japan's possessions, Korea represented the sternest challenge to economic planners. During the 1920s so-called cultural rule produced a more tranquil peninsula, but the arrival of the tough-minded General Ugaki

Kazushige as the governor-general in July 1931 and the outbreak of the Manchurian Incident that autumn signaled a policy shift as Japan moved to build up the Korean economy for the benefit of the yen zone. With alacrity and a considerable degree of success, the Japanese occupation government expanded hydroelectric capacity, doubled the length of railroad tracks, built thirty-one thousand miles of auto roads, and fostered the growth of new manufacturing industries, as shown in Table 13.2. Some of Japan's traditional conglomerates invested in those projects, but more prominent were new *zaibatsu* such as Nitchitsu, which spearheaded the development of the chemical industry and constructed 90 percent of the peninsula's electric generating facilities, including a great dam across the Yalu River that rivaled in size the Hoover and Grand Coulee dams in the United States.

Governor-General Ugaki also began a policy of forced assimilation, which his successor, General Minami Jirō, fully implemented between August 1936 and May 1942. Concerned with harnessing the energies of the Korean population behind the industrialization program, and preoccupied as well with fostering docility among a people who in the past frequently had used violence to express opposition to the occupation, Ugaki and Minami intended to extinguish a separate Korean cultural identity and to inculcate Japanese values among Koreans, as was suggested in the new slogan "Korea and the Homeland, Together as One." Central to the new campaign were the establishment of "patriotic groups" to promote support for the war,

**TABLE 13.2**  *Manufacturing Output by Industry in Korea, 1930–1939*

|  | 1930 | 1936 | 1939 |
|---|---|---|---|
| Manufacturing | 39.5 | 52.1 | 77.0 |
| Textiles | 12.8 | 12.7 | 13.0 |
| Chemicals | 9.4 | 22.9 | 34.0 |
| Metals | 5.8 | 4.0 | 9.0 |
| Ceramics | 3.2 | 2.7 | 3.0 |
| Gas and electricity | 2.4 | 5.6 | 2.0 |
| Machine tools | 1.3 | 1.0 | 4.0 |
| Other | 4.6 | 3.2 | 12.0 |
| Agriculture | 57.8 | 45.2 | 22.0 |
| Forestry | 2.7 | 2.7 | 1.0 |
| Total | 100.0% | 100.0% | 100.0% |

Adapted from Carter J. Eckert et al., *Korea Old and New: A History* (Seoul: Ilchokak for the Korea Institute, Harvard University, 1990), p. 310.

the requirement that Koreans worship at Shinto shrines and recite an oath of loyalty to the emperor, a new elementary school curriculum that expanded coverage of Japanese language, history, and ethics, and a 1938 ordinance that permitted Koreans to become "special volunteers" in the Imperial Army.

The results of the industrialization and assimilation programs delighted Governor-General Minami. According to an announcement prepared by his office in 1941:

The benevolence of our Imperial Family has reached throughout Korea and bestowed upon the Korean people a peaceful life. Why is it that the government of Korea has prospered so in only thirty years? It is because each succeeding governor general devoted himself wholeheartedly to the task of disseminating the spirit of equality. Agriculture and mining have made notable progress, and manufacturing industries have developed remarkably. Business and commerce prosper and the volume of trade is expanding each year. Education has been improving and as culture has progressed, the customs and dress of the Korean people have become less and less different from those in Japan itself. A special military system has been established and as a result many Korean volunteers are now fulfilling their obligation to help defend the Empire.[14]

While the general congratulated himself for bringing the emperor's benevolence to the peninsula, most Koreans complained bitterly about Japanese hubris. Certainly, investments in the industrial infrastructure made during the 1930s proved advantageous to Korea's long-range prospects for economic development, but just as surely, Japanese policies shortchanged Koreans in the short run. Most Korean companies could not compete with Japanese firms, many of which enjoyed tax exemptions and official guarantees against losses. Even the Kyŏngsŏng Spinning and Weaving Company, the first large-scale Korean-owned industrial enterprise, depended on Japanese corporate associates for raw materials, technical advice, and marketing. Nor did many ordinary Koreans derive benefit from a machine tools industry that concentrated on manufacturing war-related goods or from a chemical industry that mainly supplied the Imperial Army with munitions and ordnance.

Moreover, while many Koreans found employment in the new Japanese factories, most held only menial jobs, serving under Japanese foremen and craftsmen in an ethnically demarcated workplace. Even when a Korean worked at the same job as a Japanese in the same plant, he received only one-third to one-half of the pay of his Japanese counterpart. Indeed, living conditions remained very harsh in the colony. Poverty was commonplace, few people had electricity, the infant mortality rate reached 50 percent in some regions, the colonial government spent nearly forty times as much money on a per student basis educating the children of Japanese residents in Korea as it did on native Koreans, and banks charged higher interest on loans to Koreans than to Japanese. What the Koreans detested most, however, were Japanese attempts to eradicate their proud cultural tradition, and nothing was more hated than the order promulgated in 1939 that "graciously allowed" all Koreans to abandon their birth names and adopt Japanese-style surnames and given names. That cruel act added a nearly unbearable dimension of psychological trauma to an already brutal system of colonial rule and illustrated the sophistry behind Japan's self-proclaimed mission to bring modern values and industrial development to the peninsula.

## Living through the Thirties

Movies were not the only expressions of popular culture to change during the 1930s. At the beginning of the decade "My Blue Heaven" and "Sing Me a Song of Araby," released by Japan Victor and sung in Japanese as *Watakushi no aozora* and *Arabia no uta*, became smash hits, even as a fresh wave of enthusiasm for Western music carried jazz into the dance halls of Japan's most provincial towns and cities. As the China crisis deepened, however, patriotic and war-related songs increasingly dominated the nation's airwaves. Meiji classics enjoyed a revival; "Defending or attacking, we put our trust in the black steel floating fortress" began the ponderous "March of the Warships" (*Gunkan māchi*) written in 1897.[15] Even more popular were martial lyrics set in a popular mode: "The Bivouac Song" (*Roei no uta*), written for a newspaper competition in 1937 and infused with a melancholy preoccupation with death, sold 600,000 pressings in just six months. In confirmation of the new seriousness, the government banned jazz performances and closed Tokyo's dance halls on Halloween Night 1940. The disappearance of those establishments marked just one way that the changing cityscape mirrored the forbidding austerity of the decade. In Tokyo the 1936 Diet Building (built largely with Korean labor) and the 1938 Dai-Ichi Life Insurance Building loomed as examples of the leadening effect produced by a fusion of reinforced concrete and Bauhaus-style architecture that also was in vogue in Berlin.

To a considerable extent, the cultural sterility of the late 1930s flowed from government efforts to unify civilian support behind the war effort and create a national defense state, impulses that were equally obvious in the

*A Tokyo dance hall, closed by government order on October 31, 1940*

field of education. The campaign to cleanse the nation of "dangerous thoughts" continued unabated even after Professor Minobe Tatsukichi left the Diet in disgrace. In 1937 Yanaihara Tadao bowed to official pressure and resigned his chair of Colonial Policy at Tokyo University rather than moderate his criticism of Japanese behavior in China. The following year the Justice Ministry indicted several other liberal professors at Tokyo University for "disseminating dangerous ideas," after they denounced the Two Twenty-six Incident and decried the "totalitarian politics" of the late 1930s.

Besides hushing its critics, the government sought to inculcate good citizenship among schoolchildren by introducing a new textbook, *Kokutai no hongi* ("Cardinal Principles of the National Polity"), published by the Ministry of Education on March 30, 1937, as an official statement of the government's concept of the *kokutai*. The purpose of the text, according to its own conclusion, was to overcome social unrest and "develop a new Japan by virtue of the Way of the Empire which stands firm throughout the ages at home and abroad, and thereby more than ever to guard and maintain the prosperity of the Imperial Throne which is coeval with heaven and earth."[16] Following a historical overview that paid special honor to the divine origins of the imperial line, a series of overtly nationalistic essays explored the virtues of Japan's "special and unique" customs, culture, religion, morality, and way of life. Throughout the volume, the prose sang the praises of the national achievements of the past, credited those accomplishments to the wisdom of the imperial house, and called upon the Japanese of the 1930s to prepare themselves to make any sacrifice necessary to preserve the integrity of the emperor and nation.

Along with mastering new texts, students had to undergo more physical training and participate in martial sports such as judo and kendo, which replaced baseball in the physical education curriculum. Even nonschool hours filled up with new obligations: After Konoe declared Japan's intention to forge a New Order in East Asia, students had to devote their spare time to community service projects, such as cleaning parks and picking up leaves, routine jobs that more and more often went undone as Japan's economy shifted to a wartime footing. Moreover, from 1939 youths between the ages of twelve and nineteen who had not elected to stay in school after completing the six years of compulsory education had to enroll in special youth schools, whose night classes included military training for boys, home economics for girls, and a generous serving of Japanese history and ethics for all.

The government extended its managerial hand to the news industry as well. The ministries of Foreign Affairs and Communications jointly authorized the formation of a new wire service, the Dōmei News Agency, brought into service on New Year's Day 1936, and granted it the privilege of distributing all international and most national news to Japan's newspapers and radio stations. Dōmei's bylaws also permitted the two ministries to approve the hiring of its top executives and take over its operations whenever doing so promoted "the public interest." As the crisis of the 1930s deepened, the government subjected newspapers to further restrictions. In July 1937 authorities instructed editors to shun antiwar and antimilitary stories and to avoid portraying Japan as warlike or aggressive. A year later the government proscribed articles that hinted at differences of opinion within official circles, intimated that the public might not be united behind the war effort, exaggerated problems faced by families of draftees, introduced gaudy new fashions, or flattered the lascivious urban demimonde of bars, cafés, and dance halls.

The government also paid increasing attention to what was carried over the nation's airwaves, and with good reason: During the 1930s radio became the principal news and entertainment medium in the country. Shortly after the Marco Polo Bridge Incident in 1937, the Communications Ministry expanded the influence of NHK when it adopted the Nazi slogan of "One House, One Radio" and even installed receivers free of charge in markets, shrines, and other public places in poor rural villages. By 1941 the number of radios had increased from 2.9 million to 6.6 million (fourth in the world behind the United States, Germany, and Great Britain), and not many Japanese lived beyond earshot of NHK announcers.

Officials fully appreciated the influence they might wield over public opinion by controlling radio broadcasting. Since NHK operated under the jurisdiction of the Communications Ministry, the formation of the Dōmei News Agency gave bureaucrats final authority over the scheduling and content of news programming. Not surprisingly, every single news report aired on February 26, 1936, consisted of official state announcements read verbatim, and two-thirds of the 1,844 news items broadcast in July 1937 concerned the outbreak of hostilities in China and came to NHK either from Dōmei or straight from government offices. By the end of the decade even entertainment programs had taken on a didactic tone as NHK began to feature daily "situation dramas" and longer twice-weekly "culture plays" that addressed the wartime crisis.

The growing sense of national emergency prompted many groups that earlier had assumed an oppositional stance toward the state to reassess their goals and tactics. One expression of that tendency came in the early 1930s, when thousands of workers joined so-called Japanist unions whose leadership hoped to improve working conditions by disavowing violent confrontations and demonstrating their loyalty to nation and emperor. Kamino Shin'ichi, originally a foreman at the Ishikawajima shipyards, organized one of the more influential Japanist unions. In concert with other members of the conservative right, he and his followers ridiculed the political parties as being corrupt, condemned liberalism and democracy as the failed ideologies of a decadent West, and sought to build a new industrial order, premised on the "unity of emperor and subject," in which laborers and capitalists would be "of one mind and spirit, fused in an inseparable solidarity."[17] As a consequence, they hoped, labor and management would set aside their differences and cooperate to raise production and improve conditions for factory workers. In contrast with older mainstream unions, whose membership numbers did not keep pace with the expanding work force, Japanist unions won considerable support among metal casters and shipbuilders in the Tokyo-Yokohama industrial belt, steelworkers in Kyūshū, and transport workers in the Osaka–Kōbe region.

Bureaucrats within the Home Ministry also envisaged an era of "industrial peace," when both labor and management would cooperate in fulfilling the "public goals" of the state rather than dissipate their energies in "private struggles" against each other. Such officials, who had exceedingly low thresholds for social disorder, believed that harmony would reign only if they intervened to suppress violent union militancy, while at the same time providing workers with job security and decent wages so that they would have the incentive to put their shoulders behind national objectives. Thus, in July 1938 the government authorized the formation of the semi-official Industrial Patriotic Federation. With officials from the Home Ministry featured prominently on its board of directors, the federation encouraged labor unions to dissolve themselves voluntarily in favor of factory-level "discussion councils" composed of representatives from labor and management that would serve as forums for the resolution of disputes and grievances. By the end of 1939 the federation embraced some nineteen thousand councils, covering nearly three million workers, and in July 1940 the remaining unions dissolved themselves into similar industrial patriotic associations.

Ichikawa Fusae and many other feminists also reevaluated their options as the atmosphere of the 1930s turned decidedly illiberal. The decline of the political parties deprived Ichikawa's Women's Suffrage League of its most influential supporters within elite governing circles, forcing its members to abandon the quest for the vote. Convinced that controversial campaigns for expanded political rights would not fare well, Ichikawa changed tack and attempted to advance the position of women in Japanese society by advocating welfare measures for mothers and children. Two months after the Marco Polo Bridge Incident, seven suffragist and feminist organizations responded to official calls for "A United Front" by forming the League of Japanese Women's Organizations, whose purpose was "to cope with the situation created by the national crisis and prepare for the reconstruction work necessary at the conclusion of the Incident."[18] In February 1938 Ichikawa and ten other prominent women demonstrated their new cooperative attitude when they joined nineteen other national figures in calling upon all Japanese women to worship the Sun Goddess at Ise Shrine, revere the imperial family, budget family expenses frugally, be good neighbors, dress simply, and abstain from alcohol.

The government also mixed intimidation with positive incentives to prod the Suiheisha to undergo an "organizational *tenkō*." In 1931 that association of outcast groups publicly expressed its opposition to the outbreak of hostilities in Manchuria and proclaimed solidarity with Chinese workers and peasants, and two years later it decried Japan's drift toward political fascism. The Home Ministry responded quickly: In 1933 police arrested more than one hundred of the organization's leading members, and between 1935 and 1937 it played to the Suiheisha's self-interest by tripling the amount of funds budgeted for solving the social problems of Japan's outcast families. In response, the group tempered its rhetoric and fell into step with the government's call for national unity. In that spirit, the *burakumin* organization agreed to "conform to the essence of the *kokutai* and contribute to national prosperity by the perfection of conciliation among the people," and at its fifteenth national convention, held in November 1938, it pledged its total support for the war.[19]

No group experienced more severe suppression than the new religions as Home Ministry bureaucrats embarked upon a crusade "to eradicate evil cults" for the crime of propagating lèse majesté. As manifested in such works as *Kokutai no hongi*, the government in the 1930s fostered the growth of an official orthodoxy centered upon a sacrosanct emperor who stood both as the head of state and as the benevolent father of the family of Japanese citizens. Although not overtly antiemperor, many of the new religions espoused doctrines that threatened the centrality of the imperial figure; prosecutors, for instance, condemned the Ōmoto sect for revering deities other than the Sun Goddess. The most dramatic moment in the government's campaign against "quack religions" came on December 8, 1935, when hundreds of police stormed Ōmoto headquarters, smashed the main shrine building, dynamited an auxiliary hall, decapitated religious statues, and arrested nearly a thousand sect members. Four years later the Diet passed the Religious Organizations Law empowering the government to disband any religious organization whose teachings did not conform with "The Imperial Way," and officials promptly suppressed other unorthodox religions.

An aversion for social disorder and a desire to "unify the will of the people" around national goals prompted bureaucratic officials in the 1930s to suppress or to co-opt the support of organizations that opposed government policies. Some of the associations, notably the Ōmoto sect, preferred to break rather than to bend, but most tempered their demands, shifted to less contentious goals, or even dissolved themselves. Although government pressure was perhaps the single most important factor behind the transformations, it was not the sole reason that so many individuals and organizations chose to alter their political and social agendas. In some instances, feminist and labor groups saw in cooperation and moderation a fresh opportunity to advance particular programs that were important to them. Nationalism was a powerful motivating force behind Japan's quest for modernity as well, and many Japanese in the 1930s believed it was natural to place the needs and demands of nation and emperor ahead of their own private interests. The result was a very different way of life as a preference for conformity and obedience pushed aside the political pluralism and social diversity of the Taishō years. Ultimately the new emphasis on loyalty and unquestioning service to the state nurtured an almost blind nationalism that led the Japanese deeper into the China quagmire and finally into a tragic war with the United States and its allies.

## Japan Moves South and Confronts America

When Konoe Fumimaro assumed the premiership for a second time in July 1940, he faced once again the challenge that had so vexed his first administration, the "unprecedented, great ordeal" of the China Incident. His search for a fresh solution to that unending agony, the prince suggested, would take Japanese armies beyond China and into the countries of Southeast Asia. In the same radio address on July 23, 1940, in which he called for the formation of a New Political Order, Konoe stressed that if Japan wished "to stand at the forefront of change" in a radically evolving world, it must deepen its bonds of collaboration with Manchukuo and China and even contemplate "expansion into the regions of the South Pacific." In a press conference held on August 1, Konoe's new foreign minister, the flamboyant Matsuoka Yōsuke, coined the term that forever would characterize the new formulation: Japan, he said, bore a noble responsibility to establish a "Greater East Asia Coprosperity Sphere," a zone that centered on Japan, Manchukuo, and China and "naturally" included both French Indochina and the Netherlands East Indies.

Konoe and Matsuoka added to the allure of a geographically extended coprosperity sphere by wrapping it in imperial shrouds. Any move south, they averred, would be accomplished "peacefully" and in accordance, as Konoe so carefully phrased it in his radio address, "with the lofty spirit of *hakkō ichiu.*" It was another skillful rhetorical flourish by the veteran wordsmith. As every Japanese schoolchild who had read *Kokutai no hongi* knew by heart, *hakkō ichiu* meant "eight cords, one roof" and first appeared in the eighth-century chronicle *Nihon shoki* to describe how the legendary first emperor Jimmu extended his dominion over the other clans of the early Japanese islands, which subsequently enjoyed unparalleled prosperity and security thanks to his imperial benevolence. Superimposed upon Asia in 1940, the resuscitated ideal pictured a quasi family of nations led by Japan and its patriarch–emperor; the "Imperial Way," Matsuoka intoned, would permit "every nation and every race" to find "its proper place in the world."

The temptation to look south was driven by more than just the sublime ideal of drawing the eight cords of the world under the protective shelter of one roof, however. According to Konoe, the Nationalist government in Chongqing clung to survival only because the United States and Great Britain exploited Western colonial possessions in Southeast Asia and supplied war matériel to Chiang Kai-shek. The prime minister surely knew better. In the late 1930s only negligible amounts of military supplies reached Chongqing along the Burma Road and through the few ports still open in southern China; indeed, in 1939 more aid actually came from the northwest, from the Soviet Union, and it averaged a mere 25,000 tons a month, the equivalent of just two cargo ships. Nevertheless, for a Japanese military establishment that had failed embarrassingly to "chastise" Chiang, it was difficult to resist making the West its scapegoat. In the autumn of 1938, even before Konoe hatched the idea of a coprosperity sphere, Army Vice-Minister Tōjō Hideki took the podium before an appreciative audience of military reservists and delivered a fire and brimstone speech that received national press coverage. The Japanese Army could bring the China Incident to a quick and honorable conclusion, Tōjō declared, were it not for the hostile meddling of London and Washington. Cut the supply lines from Southeast Asia to Chongqing, he explained, and Chiang's regime would collapse like a deflated balloon.

However much the Guomindang may or may not have depended upon Western nations for aid, an undeniable economic reality lurked behind the new wisdom that the Anglo-American powers now constituted the most ominous threat to Japan's security: Japan could use the resources of the West's colonies in the Pacific and Southeast Asia to its own great benefit. To the regret of many Japanese economic planners, in the late 1930s Japan still depended upon the United States for nearly one-third of its imports, from cotton to scrap iron and oil, and matters seemed to be growing worse. Between 1929 and 1932 Japan purchased from the United States 36 percent, or 163,500 metric tons, of its scrap iron, used to manufacture steel for munitions and ships; by 1938 American sources were supplying 74 percent of Japan's scrap (1,006,700 metric tons). Similarly, in 1938 Japan received more than 60 percent of its imported machine tools and nearly all sophisticated alloys such as vanadium and molybdenum from the United States. Traditionally self-sufficient in copper, Japan in 1939 extracted 90,000 tons of that metal from its mines, but industry was gobbling up so much for detonators and shell casings that the nation that year had to import 105,000 tons of copper, 93 percent from the United States. The situation for oil, the most critical of all commodities in the estimation of military planners, was extremely desperate. Japan relied on America for almost 80 percent of its fuel, and for special distillates, dependence stood at more than 90 percent. In the eyes of economic and military strategists, by the summer of 1940 Western colonies in Southeast Asia had come to represent a treasure trove of raw materials whose possession would allow Japan to vault into the ranks of the economic haves, to recall Konoe's phrase, and thus to free itself from dependence upon an increasingly hostile West.

Japanese views about a hardening Pacific rivalry with the United States did not go unrequited. The perceptions of ordinary Americans had a hard moral edge to them. If many Japanese had come to imagine themselves as the liberators of China and Southeast Asia from white imperialism, an overwhelming majority of Americans saw them as dangerous and self-deluded oppressors. More than any other factor, heartrending pictures and graphic accounts of the atrocities at Nanjing and elsewhere elicited a passionate anger from most Americans. In public opinion surveys of the late 1930s three-quarters of those polled consistently expressed sympathy with China, and far more were willing to have the United States make a decisive stand on the Sino-Japanese conflict than on any European issue.

Nor did President Franklin D. Roosevelt and the American government have any compassion to spare for Japanese pretensions in Asia. FDR regarded Japan's intrusion into China and its appetite for the resources of Southeast Asia as unequivocal threats to the most basic tenet of his foreign policy: that each nation should enjoy the rights of political self-determination and of unfettered, equal trade with the rest of the world. More practically, the president's advisers also argued that the United States needed to preserve its own access to the raw materials of Southeast Asia. "The Netherlands East Indies," Secretary of State Cordell Hull announced publicly, "produce considerable portions of the world's supplies of essential commodities such as rubber, tin, quinine, and copra. Many countries, including the United States, depend substantially upon these commodities."[20] The American consul general in Batavia, capital of the Netherlands East Indies, sounded a sharper alarm. American "industries are dependent to a remarkable degree on raw materials originating in Malaysia," he wrote in one memorandum, and losing those supplies "would throw our whole industrial and economic organization into chaos."

As the images of the Pacific's two greatest powers congealed into a bitter mold of mutual contempt and distrust, Konoe's cabinet and the military high command consummated the fateful decision to move south. On August 1, 1940, Foreign Minister Matsuoka presented the French ambassador with a demand that the government of French Indochina grant Japanese forces free passage for operations against China and permit them to use airfields to launch strikes against supply lines into China. "If the French authorities do not accept our requests," Matsuoka cautioned the ambassador, whose country had just surrendered to Germany, "we may be obliged to violate your neutrality."[21] On August 30 the French acceded to Tokyo's terms, with the proviso that Japan restrict its operations to the provinces along the Chinese border, and by the end of September the Japanese had completed their occupation of northern French Indochina.

Elated, an energized Foreign Minister Matsuoka launched what he enjoyed calling his blitzkrieg diplomacy. On September 27, 1940, he met in Berlin with representatives from Germany and Italy to sign the Tripartite Pact, binding the signatories to military and economic cooperation if any one of them was attacked by some other power. Matsuoka hoped the agreement would deter any belligerent American reaction to Japan's intrusion into French Indochina, and he strengthened his hand on December 21 by concluding the Thai-Japanese Alliance, in which the two countries pledged to develop "close and inseparable relations" and to assist each other in case of attack by a third party. Matsuoka next traveled to Moscow and on April 13, 1941, concluded the USSR–Japan Neutrality Pact. With Japan's northern flank secure, Japanese officials in July 1941 prevailed on the French to permit the Japanese Army to occupy southern French Indochina.

The American government answered each Japanese move. As the situation in China worsened after 1937, Secretary of State Hull became the primary proponent of waging an economic cold war against Japan. In his view, Japan's reliance on the American market for strategic goods made the smaller nation particularly vulnerable to economic sanctions, and the systematic application of ever-greater amounts of pressure would at some point, he believed, bring the Japanese to their senses. The secretary of state realized that he had to be careful about his calibrations. He did not wish to push Japan into a shooting war with the United States, but he did mean to convince that country's leaders about the folly of playing a high-stakes game in which the United States could continually up the economic ante. At some point, Hull hoped, moderates would return to power in Tokyo, Japan would fold its hand, and peace would be possible.

The sanctions began on October 5, 1937, when a visibly anguished President Roosevelt (who by then was privately referring to Germany and Japan as "bandit nations") delivered his famous quarantine speech in Chicago. Speaking out against an "epidemic" of "terror and international lawlessness," the president, while not mentioning Japan by name, hinted darkly that the United States had an interest in joining other nations to op-

**MAP 13.2** *East Asia in the Spring of* 1941

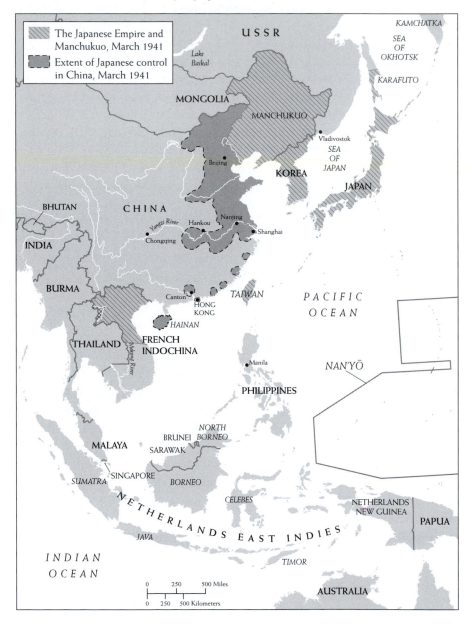

pose countries guilty of "creating a state of international anarchy and in-
stability." The next July, after more than a thousand Cantonese perished
during three days of ferocious aerial attacks, President Roosevelt asked
American manufacturers and exporters to impose a "moral embargo" on the
shipment of aircraft to countries that bombed civilian populations. When
Japan occupied Hainan Island in February 1939 and then annexed the
Spratly Islands, roughly halfway between French Indochina and British
North Borneo, Roosevelt imposed a formal embargo of aircraft and parts to
Japan and transferred elements of the U.S. fleet from their Atlantic bases to
the Pacific coast. On July 26, 1939, Washington followed that up by announcing its intention to abrogate the 1911 Treaty of Commerce and Navigation, which regulated trade with Japan, thus making it possible for
Roosevelt to extend his embargo to include aluminum, molybdenum, nickel,
and tungsten. The next summer, as Japan prepared to move into northern
French Indochina, the president and the secretary of state proscribed the sale
of aviation gasoline and lubricating oil, and when Matsuoka signed the Tripartite Pact in September 1940, Washington added scrap iron to the growing list of prohibited items.

The American policy of progressive economic pressure was to be tested
to the limits in 1941. In April, just days after Japan signed the nonaggression pact with the Soviet Union, Hull handed the Japanese ambassador in
Washington a list of preconditions for restoring normal economic relations
between Japan and the United States. Known as Hull's four principles, they
included respect for the territorial integrity of other nations, noninterfer-
ence in the internal affairs of other countries, the maintenance of equal commercial opportunity for all, and no alteration to the status quo except
through peaceful means. After Japan sent its armies into southern French
Indochina in July 1941, thus demonstrating its unwillingness to accept Hull's
conditions, FDR signed an executive order freezing all Japanese assets in
the United States, a measure that officials used to justify placing a total embargo on all oil exports to Japan. By the beginning of August, Great Britain,
the Netherlands, New Zealand, and the Philippines had done likewise.

So that no one would misinterpret America's determination to preserve
its interests in Asia, Roosevelt on July 26, 1941, named Douglas MacArthur
the commander of Filipino-American forces and dispatched several squadrons of modern fighters and long-range bombers to America's Pacific colony.
Two weeks later Roosevelt and Churchill met on an American battleship
off Newfoundland and cemented a strategic alliance by agreeing to the Atlantic Charter, signed on August 14. That set of eight principles reaffirmed
Wilsonian internationalism by enunciating a belief in the benefits that de-

rive from open and free trade and by calling for the disarmament of "nations which threaten, or may threaten, aggression outside of their frontiers." Moreover, the document stressed, the United States and Great Britain held as sacrosanct "the right of all peoples to choose the form of government under which they will live; and they wish to see Sovereign rights and self-government restored to those who have been forcibly deprived of them."[22]

## The Autumn of '41

The twin shocks of the total oil embargo and the Atlantic Charter produced within the Japanese cabinet and supreme military command anger and, ultimately, a deep, irrepressible fatalism about the inevitability of war with the United States. Throughout August 1941 Konoe convened a series of liaison conferences, meetings that brought together Japan's key leaders—generally the premier, foreign and finance ministers, the ministers of the army and navy, and the chiefs of the general staffs—to discuss strategic and diplomatic options. Everyone railed against the Anglo-American powers. The Atlantic Charter, some charged, was tantamount to a declaration of war, for it obliged nations to accept the Anglo-American vision of a world order or face military retaliation. The twin predatory powers, others stormed, wanted to push Japan out of China. But if Japan retreated, the consequences would snowball: Northern China would fall into the hands of Communists; Manchukuo and Korea would be endangered; Japan would be isolated and reduced to third-rank status. All the horrendous sacrifices of blood and treasure that the Japanese had endured since 1931 would be rendered meaningless.

The debates called attention to the economic predicament that Japan faced. The army general staff bemoaned the encirclement by the ABCD powers (the Americans, British, Chinese, and Dutch). Japan, it claimed, was being strangled to death; war was necessary in order to grasp the resources of Southeast Asia, or soon Japan would not have the wherewithal to defend itself. The navy concurred. Land operations in China, it noted with chagrin, had so depleted strategic reserves of oil that existing stockpiles would permit the fleet to remain at sea for less than twenty months, and should hostilities erupt, Japan could not expect to undertake any offensive operations after January 1942. For Navy Chief of Staff Nagano Osami, the choices were simple: Japan could sit by and do nothing, which would mean the painful, drawn-out agony of eventual surrender to Anglo-American demands, or the military could act now, while there was a 70 or 80 percent chance of victory. Prime Minister Konoe agreed that Japan desperately needed to acquire the resources of Southeast Asia, but the prince, ever ready to embrace all sides of every issue, fretted about the consequences should Japan start a war that it might not be able to win.

By the beginning of autumn Japan's leaders had arrived at a consensus, and early in September Konoe and other participants in the liaison conferences traveled to the east wing of the palace for an imperial conference. During the Russo-Japanese War the government had used imperial conferences, which brought together top civil and military officials in the presence of the emperor, as an opportunity for the prime minister to explain policy recommendations and receive the monarch's seal of approval. As Japan slid further into war with China, Konoe resumed the practice in 1938 so that his policies would glisten with the unassailable luster of legitimacy that only imperial sanction could provide. The imperial conference of September 6, 1941, was formal and somber. Despite the bleakness of the situation, Konoe said, his government wished to make one final attempt to negotiate a settlement with the United States. He would renew his invitation, originally extended weeks earlier, to meet personally with Roosevelt anywhere in the Pacific to convey to the American president "reasonable" peace terms. Japan, for its part, would express a willingness to withdraw from French Indochina and would agree not to expand its military operations outside the China theater. In return for those concessions, Konoe would insist that the United States and Great Britain "neither interfere with nor obstruct the settlement of the China Incident by our Empire," "refrain from actions that may threaten the defense of our Empire in the Far East," and "restore commercial relations with our Empire and supply those goods from their territories in the Southwest Pacific that our Empire urgently needs to sustain herself."[23]

Should Roosevelt remain intransigent and negotiations prove fruitless, the prime minister continued unemotionally, Japan would go to war: "In the event that there is no prospect of our demands being met by the first ten days of October through the diplomatic negotiations mentioned above, we will immediately decide to commence hostilities against the United States, Britain, and the Netherlands." After listening to a full discussion about the proposed course of action, the emperor signaled his wish that the nation's leaders give give diplomacy more time to work by reading a poem composed by his grandfather, Emperor Meiji:

Across the four seas,
   All are brothers.

In such a world,
   Why do the waves rage, the winds roar?[24]

With war against the ABCD powers now an imminent possibility, the army finalized its plans for ground assaults on the Philippines, Malaya, and Burma, while the brilliant, imaginative naval commander Yamamoto Isoroku put the finishing touches on his Pearl Harbor strategy. A realist, Yamamoto feared the military potential of the United States, but he was willing to gamble that a quick strike against the enemy fleet in Hawaii would cripple the U.S. Navy and earn Japan a temporary tactical respite, which it could use to fortify a defense perimeter running from the Kuril Islands to the Marshalls and Bismarcks in the central Pacific, then on to the Netherlands East Indies, Malaya, and Burma. With the rich resource zones of Southeast Asia and the Pacific islands in its possession, Japan could hunker down, wage a defensive war of attrition, and eventually negotiate an armistice with America, which, in Yamamoto's estimation, did not have the fortitude to fight a two-front war by itself if Germany completed its conquest of Europe, as was widely expected.

Whatever hopes Konoe may have harbored for his peace initiative in the autumn of 1941, America's leaders were scarcely impressed. For Hull and Roosevelt, a commitment from Japan to withdraw from all China had emerged as the sine qua non of American policy, and on several occasions throughout the tense, critical month of September, the secretary of state made it abundantly clear to the Japanese ambassador, Nomura Kichisaburō, that the United States simply would not abandon that position. Nor did Hull put any faith in a summit between Konoe and Roosevelt. In a meeting with Nomura on October 2, the secretary reiterated his four principles and in his blunt, straightforward manner told the ambassador that there simply was no point to arranging a summit unless the Japanese first agreed to abandon China entirely. Discouraged and fully aware that a withdrawal from China was utterly unacceptable to the Japanese Army, Nomura cabled Tokyo that negotiations had reached a "deadlock."

As Konoe's bid for a peaceful settlement faltered, the nerves of Japan's leaders stretched adrenaline-tight, and action, immediate action, seemed to offer the only possible release from the nearly unbearable tension of waiting for the inevitable first shots of war. In mid-September Army Minister Tōjō Hideki told Konoe that sometimes nations had to take risks even though they might not be able to calculate their chances for success. At a liaison conference on October 4, following Hull's rejection of a possible summit, Navy Chief of Staff Nagano declared, "There is no longer time for discussion. We want quick action." Shocked by the harsh language of that meeting, Konoe threatened to resign and then, pleading "illness," retreated to his seaside villa. Still not willing to make the final decision for war, he returned to Tokyo and summoned key ministers to his home on Sunday, October 12, his fiftieth birthday. Discussions circled the old familiar points: Withdrawal from China was unacceptable; American demands were unreasonable and would compel Japan to throw away years of sacrifice; Hull and Roosevelt were vindictive, uncompromising, and wished to see Japan reduced to a third-rank power, prostrate at their feet. The supreme command, Army Minister Tōjō reminded everyone, was bound by the decisions of the September 6 imperial conference: It was time to strike; to delay would merely give America time to build up strength. Four days later a despondent Konoe, who had brought his nation to the brink of war, informed the palace that he intended to resign.

On the advice of the senior statesmen, the emperor named General Tōjō Japan's next prime minister. Tōjō consistently had backed an assertive policy toward China and communism, and he had earned his nickname, the Razor, for aggressive leadership during a stint with the Kwantung Army, when his "Tōjō Corps" raced boldly across hundreds of miles of Mongolian steppes at the beginning of the China Incident. The Shōwa emperor turned to the general in October 1941 because the monarch agreed with those who wished to "wipe the slate clean" and make yet one more attempt to negotiate a settlement with the United States, and Tōjō's credentials indicated that the blunt, no-nonsense Razor could keep hard-liners within the military under control while Japan tried diplomacy once again.

Tōjō took seriously the imperial mandate to search for a peaceful resolution to the crisis, and at the end of October Japan's leaders nearly talked the issues to death in a seemingly endless series of liaison conferences. Frustration was evident everywhere. "The navy is consuming 400 tons of oil an hour," Nagano warned on October 23. "The situation is urgent. We want it decided one way or the other quickly." Seconded the army chief of staff: "Hurry up and go." Finally, in a seventeen-hour marathon session that began at 9:00 A.M. on November 1 and lasted into the following morning, Tōjō hammered out a new consensus. Japan would present two sets of terms to the United States. Under Proposal A, Japan would withdraw from French Indochina and from most of China, except for Hainan Island and certain territories in the north, which Japan could garrison for twenty-five years; in addition, Japan would agree to the principle of free trade in Asia if the United States enforced a similar doctrine throughout the world. If Proposal A was not acceptable, Japan's ambassador would tender Proposal B, a reworking of terms Konoe outlined on September 6, with the added proviso that the United States supply Japan with one million gallons of aviation fuel annually.

The meeting ended on a sullen tone. No one knew for certain how Roosevelt and Hull would react to the proposals. The majority of participants in the meeting of November 1–2 were pessimistic, however, and they insisted that if no favorable response were forthcoming from the United States by midnight on November 30, hostilities would commence at the earliest possible moment. Still, the new prime minister had not given up on peace. After discussing the liaison conference's deliberations with the emperor on the afternoon of November 2, Tōjō returned to his office and told an aide: "I swear to the gods, with these proposals I hope to reach an accommodation with the United States, whatever it takes."[25]

In Washington, Hull dismissed Proposal A out of hand, and on November 26 he passed a note to Ambassador Nomura that brought diplomacy to an end. Single-minded and resolute from his youth, Hull had learned the need to be stubbornly true to one's principles when he rode his horse across the hills of Tennessee as a circuit judge at the end of the nineteenth century. As secretary of state in the 1930s he condemned Japanese aggression in China, despised its blatant disregard of international treaties, and hoped that economic pressures would make peace possible. Sanctions, however, did not cow Japan's leaders; rather, they only became more determined than ever to carve out their own autarkic sphere, to the detriment of the United States. Japan's move into Southeast Asia, an area that was strategically and economically vital to the United States, made a shambles of Hull's policy, and finally, the secretary of state, physically and emotionally exhausted, decided to "kick the whole thing over"—to wash his hands of diplomacy and leave America's future to the army and navy. Hull's note to Nomura rejected Proposal B and reiterated the same tired, unworkable demands: Japan must withdraw from Indochina and all China, recognize Chiang Kai-shek's government, and renounce all extraterritorial rights on the continent.

It was already November 27 when Hull's message reached Tōjō, and his cabinet regarded it as an insult and as an ultimatum. Very clearly the United States and Japan could agree on virtually nothing. Washington would not condone Tokyo's vision of a New Order in East Asia, and Japan would not abide an American presence in the region that it deemed as imperialistic and as hostile to its security and economic survival. That afternoon a liaison conference agreed upon war, and on December 1 an imperial conference ratified the decision.

Tōjō opened the imperial conference by stating that his government had "exhausted every means at its disposal" to reach a diplomatic settlement, but that Hull and Roosevelt had "not conceded an inch." Since the "Empire's demands cannot possibly be achieved through diplomatic means," Tōjō concluded, war had become "inevitable."[26] Near the end of the meeting, Hara Yoshimichi, president of the Privy Council and a longtime confidant of the emperor's, summarized the views held by many of Japan's leaders:

In negotiating with the United States, our Empire hoped to maintain peace by making one concession after another. But to our surprise, the American position from beginning to end was to say what Chiang Kai-shek wanted her to say. The United States is being utterly conceited, obstinate, and disrespectful. It is regrettable indeed. We simply cannot tolerate such an attitude.

If we were to give in, we would give up in one stroke not only our gains in the Sino-Japanese and Russo-Japanese wars, but also the benefits of the Manchurian Incident. This we cannot do. We are loath to compel our people to suffer even greater hardships, on top of what they have endured during the four years since the China Incident. But it is clear that the existence of our country is being threatened, that the great achievements of the Emperor Meiji would all come to naught, and that there is nothing else we can do. Therefore, I believe that if negotiations with the United States are hopeless, then the commencement of war is inevitable.[27]

Even as Hara spoke, the Japanese fleet already was at sea, steaming toward Hawaii with orders to strike Pearl Harbor at dawn, December 7, local time; December 8 on Japan's side of the international dateline.

# CHAPTER 14

# *The Greater East Asia War*

It was still before dawn on Monday, December 8, 1941, when Prime Minister Tōjō's aide brought him awake. The Imperial Navy headquarters had just received the coded signal "Tora! Tora! Tora!" from the task force: The attack on Pearl Harbor was under way; success seemed to be at hand. As other messages trickled in throughout the morning, the dimensions of Japan's triumph began to emerge: The final tally credited Japanese pilots with sinking or damaging eight enemy battleships and a dozen other vessels, destroying nearly two hundred American planes, and inflicting almost four thousand casualties on U.S. servicemen, all at the cost of just twenty-nine Japanese aircraft and sixty-four men killed in action. In Tokyo, Tōjō "rejoiced" and gave "thanks to the gods" for this "miraculous success," this "auspicious beginning." The emperor received a detailed briefing at seven-ten, and the monarch shared Tōjō's joy. "Throughout the day," an aide recorded in his diary, "the emperor wore his naval uniform and seemed to be in a splendid mood."[1]

The Japanese public first learned that a momentous day was in the offing at 7:00 A.M., when NHK broadcast a cryptic bulletin that the Imperial Army had "entered into a state of belligerency with British and American forces in the western Pacific." Throughout the morning stirring patriotic songs filled the airwaves, and on city street corners newspaper vendors jingled bells to call attention to special editions. At noon NHK announcers read to a waiting nation the contents of the emperor's Imperial Rescript officially declaring war on the United States and Great Britain, and Tōjō delivered a brief address. Japan's aim, the emperor and prime minister emphasized, was to bring peace and stability to East Asia. Enveloping their rhetoric in moral rectitude, they criticized China for failing to understand

Japan's true intentions and denounced American and British attempts to extend imperialist domination over all Asia. The emperor's message stressed that the "trend of affairs," if left unchecked, ultimately would "endanger the very existence of our nation." Japan, he concluded, possessed "no other recourse" but to take up arms and "crush every obstacle in its path."

In the beginning Japan's military machine appeared invincible. On the first morning of the new war, only hours after Pearl Harbor, Japanese aviators caught General MacArthur's aircraft on the ground in the Philippines and destroyed most of them. Two days later Japanese bombers off the Malay Peninsula sank the new British battleship *Prince of Wales* and the heavy cruiser *Repulse*. With clockwork precision Japanese troops occupied Hong Kong on December 25, marched into Manila on January 2, 1942, and just a few weeks later accepted the surrender of all American and Filipino forces ("I shall return," General MacArthur vowed as he slipped away toward Australia). Imperial Army units swept down the Malay Peninsula and captured Singapore—Britain's jewel, the "impregnable fortress"—on the same afternoon, February 15, that paratroopers dropped from the sky and seized control of Sumatra's oil fields. Expeditionary forces, unstoppable, occupied Batavia on March 5, entered Rangoon three days later, and by late spring occupied the Solomon and Gilbert archipelagoes, even Wake Island in the central Pacific. The Japanese flag flew over one-quarter of the globe, and walking in his garden, the emperor observed that the fruits of victory had come so quickly there scarcely had been time to savor them all.

Nor would there ever be. Even as Japanese ships raced across the Pacific, America gathered its strength. By the end of 1942 the Imperial Navy and Army had begun to feel the effects of the U.S. counterattack, and within three short years Japan was to suffer an awesome defeat, its Greater East Asia Co-prosperity Sphere a shattered memory. In the months before Pearl Harbor, Japan's leaders warned about the country's fate should it fail to stand up against a "conceited, obstinate, and disrespectful" foe. But the American victory in the summer of '45 left Japan prostrate, and the repercussions of that vanquishing proved to be more consequential for the ordinary people of Japan than any of the dreadful warnings raised in liaison conferences during the fall of '41.

## War, Politics, and Economic Mobilization

With the nation irrevocably committed to Total War with the Western superpowers, Prime Minister Tōjō moved to strengthen his prerogatives as prime minister and orchestrate a coordinated program of national mobilization. When Tōjō became prime minister in 1941, he continued to serve as army minister, appointed himself home minister (a post he held until February 17, 1942), claimed various other portfolios for short periods, and headed the Munitions Ministry, created in November 1943 to give better direction to economic planning. By the middle of the war Tōjō had claimed an unprecedented combination of responsibilities and become the most powerful prime minister in Japanese history.

No matter how much authority he gathered within his arms, however, Tōjō never was able to tame completely the behavior of Japan's other political elites. Perhaps more than any other factor, the doctrine of independent supreme command frustrated his efforts to impose unitary control over the military. A cardinal principle of Japanese governance since the early Meiji period, the term alluded to the relative autonomy of the military, whose four leading officials, the army and navy ministers and the chiefs of staff, reported directly, and separately, to the emperor rather than to the prime minister. As a result, the prime minister never functioned as a true commander in chief, even after Pearl Harbor. Since Tōjō lacked the authority to interfere with operational decisions, the navy often went its own way in the Pacific and neglected to coordinate its plans with the army. Indeed, when the Imperial Navy suffered its first setback at Midway in June 1942, losing several aircraft carriers, the naval chief of staff did not even inform the prime minister about the debacle until a month after the sea battle.

Tōjō's army background gave him greater leverage over that service, but even there his authority was fragile. His colleagues in uniform, especially those senior to him, expected him to consult with them, and some held opposing ideas about how war aims ought to be pursued. In 1942 the general staff requested 620,000 tons of matériel for troops on Guadalcanal, a requisition that Tōjō wished to divert to another theater of operations. When the prime minister refused to release the supplies, a leading member of the general staff stormed into his office, called him a "stupid fool," and insisted that he reverse the decision. Later that year Ishiwara Kanji, who regarded Tōjō as a complete simpleton for having committed Japan to a disastrous war that it inevitably would lose because it could not compete with America in material terms, walked into the prime minister's office and challenged him either to resign or to shoot himself. Tōjō wielded authority within the military establishment, but he did not dominate it.

The civil bureaucracy also continued to exercise significant governing prerogatives during the war years, and some agencies crucial to mass mobilization even enhanced their spheres of authority. Just as with prewar administrations, government remained a federation of ministries and agencies, each of which jealously guarded its own privileges and competed with the others for funding, resources, and power. Moreover, leading bureaucrats were strong-willed individuals, and Tōjō could not dictate to them. In February 1944 Tōjō called in several leading judges, appointees of the Ministry of Justice, and enjoined them to impose stiffer sentences on those convicted of seditious acts. The judges simply turned aside Tōjō's injunctions. One stated flatly that the prime minister's instructions violated constitutional provisions for judicial autonomy, and another called on him to step down from office.

Even politicians in the Diet weathered various encroachments by Tōjō to remain a distinct part of the wartime political landscape. Unlike the German Reichstag, the Japanese Diet met regularly throughout the war, convening each year on December 26 for its annual three-month session, and the institution retained its traditional prerogatives to pass legislation, approve budgets, and summon Tōjō and his ministers for interpellations about the war and public policy. Fortunately for the prime minister, Diet members were genuine patriots, whose passionate speeches censuring the pernicious Anglo-American enemies echoed through the ornate halls of the chamber. Moreover, following the elections of 1942, most legislators joined the Imperial Rule Assistance Political Association (IRAPA), part of the IRAA, as a way of demonstrating their loyalty to the state. Under IRAPA direction, the wartime Diet approved all major bills that the cabinet introduced and put its seal of approval to each of the prime minister's annual budgets.

On the surface, Tōjō appeared to enjoy harmonious relations with a Diet that usually did little more than rubber-stamp his initiatives, and the war years certainly represented a nadir of parliamentary influence in Japanese political life. Yet beneath the façade of unity and docility, discontent with Tōjō always lurked close to the surface. Some prewar liberals refused to join the IRAPA, and many Diet members delivered unfavorable critiques of specific policies (authorities struck nearly one hundred items from the official record of the Eighty-fourth regular session, which lasted from December 1943 until March 1944). Frustrated by niggling parliamentary opposition and plagued by contentious foes within the civil and military bureaucracies, Tōjō never did become a Nazi-style dictator. He exercised his prerogatives as prime minister as fully as he could, but in the end he probably wielded less authority than Roosevelt and Churchill brandished within their governing circles.

Whatever political differences existed between Tōjō and the other governing elites, they shared the aspiration to place Japan's economy on a full wartime footing by asserting greater authority over the private sector. Increasingly, the government turned to forming the cartellike control associations envisaged in the Plan for a New Economic System endorsed by the Konoe cabinet in December 1940. The Iron and Steel Control Association became the first such new organization, in the spring of 1941, and when he became prime minister in October, Tōjō quickly moved to establish control associations for several business categories, including coal, cement, machinery, precision instruments, motor vehicles, foreign trade, and shipbuilding.

Under the new arrangements, a designated government ministry oversaw each association. Ownership and profits of individual firms remained in private hands, but each control association became responsible for meeting production targets set by the supervising ministry. For that purpose, each association named its own director, usually the chairman of one of the member companies (a Mitsui director managed the Coal Control Association; the chief executive officer of Mitsubishi led the Army Aviation Industry Control Association), and maintained a planning and research board to coordinate the activities of member companies. The staff for the Iron and Steel Control Association had three hundred full-time employees who collected information from individual companies, allocated raw materials among constituent members, regulated internal competition by setting individual production quotas, and generally ensured that all companies operated in a manner consistent with national goals.

In some instances the control associations achieved their objectives. The Iron and Steel Control Association hit 90 percent of its targets in 1941 and 1942, despite shortages of raw materials due to the United States embargo on the sale of scrap iron and the growing unpredictability of ocean shipping as hostilities spread across the Pacific. Nevertheless, Tōjō never was totally satisfied. To his mind, some control associations, especially those headed by prominent directors of powerful *zaibatsu*, acted too autonomously. He also complained that the bitter competition for resources among ministries and associations detracted from the war effort; one government official estimated that such rivalry cut aircraft production by half during the war.

Frustrated, in November 1943 Tōjō established the Munitions Ministry to assert more centralized control over enterprises engaged in military production. But the reorganization was to no avail, even though the new agency brought together the functions of the Cabinet Planning Board and the Ministry of Commerce and Industry and had Tōjō as its first head. Kishi Nobusuke—renovationist bureaucrat, old Manchukuo hand, and Tōjō's chief economic adviser—complained about simple bureaucratic inertia. "It often takes two or three months for the Munitions Ministry to reach a decision on an important matter," he observed. "Then the decision must be discussed at a meeting of the cabinet, which in turn issues an order to be executed at various government and industrial levels. Thus it may take half a year before the decision goes into effect. Even a wise decision is sometimes worthless by the time it is executed, for the situation by then has changed."[2]

Tōjō and his cabinet faced the additional challenge of organizing labor and efficiently channeling it into war-related industries. Government brought wages under its purview in 1939, and with the expansion of hostilities after Pearl Harbor, authorities increased compensation and allowances in certain industrial sectors as a way of attracting labor to strategically important areas. But the military's enormous requirements—the services drafted 2.4 million men by the end of 1941, 7.2 million by August 1945—soon made more coercive methods necessary, and authorities turned to conscripting labor for factory work. The National Mobilization Law of 1938 and the National Service Draft Ordinance promulgated on July 8, 1939, authorized the government to register all males aged sixteen to forty and unmarried females between sixteen and twenty-five. As military induction absorbed more and more personnel, the government began to call up males for labor service, and by war's end nearly 1.6 million young men had received the familiar set of white orders, nearly as unnerving as the red-colored military draft notices, summoning them to duty in Japan's factories.

Initially the Japanese government was reluctant to draft women to work in industry, preferring that they stay at home, where they could be dutiful

**TABLE 14.1** *Conscripted Labor,*
*1939—1945*

| YEAR | NUMBER |
| --- | --- |
| 1939 | 850 |
| 1940 | 52,692 |
| 1941 | 258,192 |
| 1942 | 311,649 |
| 1943 | 699,728 |
| 1944 | 229,448 |
| 1945 | 47,771 |
| Total | 1,600,330 |

Adapted from Jerome B. Cohen, *Japan's Economy in War and Reconstruction* (Minneapolis: University of Minnesota Press, 1949), p. 318.

wives and produce future citizens to help manage the Greater East Asia Co-prosperity Sphere. In a 1942 Diet speech Tōjō referred to Japanese women as the "warm fountainhead" that provided sustenance to other household members, and Tōjō Katsuko helped promote her husband's new fertility campaign by cheerfully proclaiming from her home in a fashionable section of Tokyo that "having babies is fun."[3] Mounting labor shortages prompted the government to reconsider its attitude toward conscripting women in the autumn of 1943, when the cabinet decided that women could replace men on a voluntary basis in seventeen industrial sectors. The next January Tōjō declared women could work in other essential industries, and a month later the government expanded the national labor registration to include women aged twelve to thirty-nine (and males twelve to fifty-nine). In the end the state never did draft women, but patriotism, good citizenship, and often in-

*Women university students volunteering for factory work*

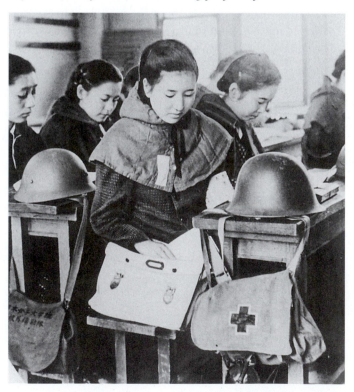

tense pressure from family and neighbors drove many young women into the factory. By the time Japan's armies captured Singapore in February 1942, 42 percent of Japan's work force was female (compared with 36 percent in 1930), and by October 1944 more women than ever before were toiling in strategic industries. Women constituted 60 percent of all employees in the electrical communications and pharmaceutical industries, 40 percent in ordnance plants, and 30 percent in aircraft production.

As labor shortages mounted during the war, the government turned to still other sources of manpower. From 1944 it began to draft students from middle school; eventually more than three million boys were called to work in war-related factories, and by August 1945 nearly one-fifth of all industrial workers were under twenty years of age. The Japanese government even impressed prisoners of war and foreign laborers. In 1945 perhaps fifty thousand POWs and another thirty thousand Chinese contract laborers toiled in Japan. The dirty and dangerous coal industry had a particularly voracious appetite for foreign workers. Few Japanese wanted to fill the shoes of miners conscripted into the military, and the Coal Control Association justified a special plea for a delegation of foreign laborers by noting that accidents and long working hours had resulted in "a poor feeling" by Japanese "toward working underground."

Each year during the war the Tokyo government also instructed the governor-general of Korea to dispatch a quota of workers to Japan. Some came voluntarily. Most, however, were shanghaied off farms and city streets by agents of the Japanese occupation gendarmerie, ferried to ports in western Japan, and packed into boarded-up trains for shipment to mines and factories. Between 1941 and 1945 as many as 600,000 to 1 million Koreans were brought to Japan. The greatest proportion of those men ended up in the mines (in 1945 fully half of all miners in Hokkaidō were from Korea), but Korean workers could be found in every sector of the Japanese economy, from shipbuilding to munitions and agriculture. Their presence helped change the complexion of the Japanese work force. In 1941 practically all workers in key sectors of the industrialized economy were adult Japanese males; by 1944 roughly half were Koreans, students, and women.

Despite all the complications presented by the control associations, rivalries among ministries, and problems of labor recruitment, the collective efforts of state agencies did manage to expand government control over the economy and fit a tighter harness around the nation's human and material resources. By some measures, the economy responded credibly to the demands placed on it. Despite shortages of raw materials and production bottlenecks during even the early stages of the war against America, citizens remained fed and clothed, the Japanese war machine purred along through-

**TABLE 14.2**  *Wartime Production Indices, 1937–1945*

|  | 1937 | 1938 | 1939 | 1940 | 1941 | 1942 | 1943 | 1944 | 1945 |
|---|---|---|---|---|---|---|---|---|---|
| Agriculture | 100 | 98 | 105 | 99 | 95 | 100 | 96 | 76 | 59 |
| Rice | 100 | 99 | 104 | 92 | 83 | 101 | 95 | 88 | 59 |
| Mining | 100 | 106 | 112 | 120 | 120 | 118 | 119 | 108 | 51 |
| Coal | 100 | 108 | 113 | 125 | 125 | 121 | 127 | 120 | 74 |
| Manufacturing | 100 | 103 | 114 | 119 | 123 | 120 | 121 | 124 | 53 |
| Steel | 100 | 115 | 123 | 128 | 132 | 140 | 156 | 146 | 52 |
| Machinery | 100 | 110 | 135 | 163 | 188 | 195 | 214 | 252 | 107 |
| Chemicals | 100 | 114 | 122 | 120 | 120 | 100 | 87 | 80 | 33 |
| Textiles | 100 | 83 | 83 | 75 | 60 | 48 | 31 | 17 | 6 |
| Foods | 100 | 101 | 104 | 90 | 78 | 69 | 58 | 47 | 32 |

Adapted from Nakamura Takafusa, "Depression, Recovery, and War, 1920–1945," in John W. Hall et al., gen. eds., *The Cambridge History of Japan*, vol. 6: Peter Duus, ed., *The Twentieth Century* (Cambridge: Cambridge University Press, 1988), p. 489.

out 1942, and as late as 1944 many key production indices stood above 1937 levels, as shown in Table 14.2.

## Marshaling the Home Front

In the weeks and months after Pearl Harbor the government forged a rhetoric of war in order to mold an enduring popular consensus behind the national effort and justify its actions to the peoples of Asia. Not surprisingly, the enunciation of Japan's war aims drew on the vocabulary established by the earlier Konoe cabinets: Japan was fighting not just for itself but for all Asia; the West was "immoral"—plutocratic, racist, culturally imperialistic, possessed of an "inordinate ambition," as the emperor's rescript declaring war put it, "to dominate the East." Japan's mission, articulated in a policy statement approved by the cabinet just hours after the attack on Pearl Harbor, was to wage a "sacred war" against the West, liberate the colonial peoples of Asia, and enable "all nations and all peoples to be at peace." To make certain that everyone understood its intentions, the Japanese government on December 12, 1941, announced a new name for the conflict in China and the Pacific, the Greater East Asia War.

To ensure that its people learned the lines of proper discourse, officials stepped up their oversight of the mass media. Fortunately for government censors, most reporters were patriotic, and they willingly cooperated to put war news in the best possible light and ferret out domestic stories that suited the 1942 cabinet directive to make all news and every radio program "conform to state purposes." Years later one correspondent with a national daily, the *Asahi shinbun*, remembered that fellow staffers were more "jingoistic" and "militaristic" than the men he had led as a first lieutenant on the China front, and a staff member of the competing *Yomiuri shinbun* recalled how he spent days on end visiting families of war dead, hoping to find particularly poignant stories about mourning mothers and the valiant deeds of idealistic young soldiers.

Still, zealous state authorities expressed displeasure at some stories: accounts that suggested popular discontent with economic controls, reproofs of state policy, and almost anything that hinted at pessimism. Annoyed officials had several sanctions at their disposal, from censoring specific reports to suspending offensive publications and furloughing recalcitrant reporters and announcers. The Japan Publishing Association, the control agency for magazine and book publishers, denied the monthly *Chūō kōron* ("The Central Review") paper stock with which to print its July 1943 issue because the journal carried the first two episodes of Tanizaki Jun'ichirō's serialized novel "The Makioka Sisters" (*Sasameyuki*). As a youth Tanizaki had admired woodblock prints of the Sino-Japanese War of 1894–1895, and in the 1920s he had emerged as one of Japan's master storytellers, taking the corrupting influence of Westernization and modernization as one of his main themes. In the crucible of the Greater East Asia War, however, government watchdogs deemed his now-classic "Makioka Sisters" to be "irrelevant" and "negative" because its "sentimental" plot about "bourgeois family life" did nothing to advance the war effort. A year later the control association compelled both the *Chūō kōron* and *Kaizō* ("Reconstruction"), the "peerless twin stars" among Japan's periodicals, to dissolve themselves "voluntarily" after police beat confessions out of suspected "Communist" staffers, raping one woman and killing two male employees of *Chūō kōron* in the process. That example of state-sponsored brutality was not unique. When a reporter for the daily *Mainichi shinbun* in early 1944 belittled Tōjō's military strategy as "unscientific," the Razor ordered its editors suspended, personally arranged to have the unfortunate journalist drafted into the army, and tapped his outfit for immediate frontline duty.

To build broad-based popular support, several government agencies created mass organizations that eventually enrolled nearly every single Japanese behind the war effort. On November 23, 1940, a day now celebrated as Labor Thanksgiving Day, the government reorganized the Industrial Patriotic Federation as the Greater Japan Industrial Patriotic Association. Under the tutelage of the Home Ministry, the new Sanpō (a popular appellation made by shortening the official name, Dai Nihon <u>Sangyō Hō</u>kokukai) endeavored to make certain that workers fully understood the need to meet production targets and were willing to bear the sacrifices necessary to do so, a problem that grew in proportion to the number of conscripts in the work force. To that end, Sanpō representatives distributed government propaganda to every shop hand and organized lectures, rallies, and panel discussions to explain Japan's wartime objectives. To win the workers' cooperation and make for a more harmonious workplace, Sanpō enterprise units involved themselves in many aspects of workers' lives, creating what were called comprehensive enterprise communities. Thus, in addition to dispensing extra rations of sake and rice to diligent workers, Sanpō ran consumers' cooperatives, sponsored savings programs, administered health insurance schemes, and set up centers where workers might seek advice about family and legal problems. In response to such incentives, membership in Sanpō soared, from approximately 3.5 million workers in 1940 to 6.4 million by war's end.

Following the Sanpō example, the cabinet urged the creation of patriotic associations for nearly every occupational and professional group in the country. Farmers joined the Greater Japan Agriculture Patriotic Association, writers the Japanese Literature Patriotic Association, and so forth. Prominent among the new organizations was the Greater Japan Women's Society, formed on February 2, 1942, when authorities merged the League of Japanese Women's Organizations with other women's groups founded in prewar years to promote such diverse goals as suffrage, consumer rights, and birth control. Single women over twenty years of age and all married women had to join the new mass organization, and by 1943 the GJWS had nearly nineteen million members who, in the words of its director, constituted "one great army organized to fight a Total War, an army in the form of the women of Greater Japan."[4] More specifically, GJWS members arranged sendoffs for departing soldiers, vowed to put away their gold jewelry and forgo extravagant wedding ceremonies, washed clothes at army hospitals, taught one another the nutritional value of foods, and once each month dutifully fixed their children a "Rising Sun box lunch," a simple dish of plain white rice flavored with a red pickled plum placed in the center to resemble the Japanese flag.

The army, for its part, pushed to have existing youth groups across Japan amalgamated into a single Greater Japan Young Adults' Corps. Created on January 16, 1941, membership soon numbered fourteen million male youths aged ten to twenty-five. At first the youngsters continued the same voluntary activities as before, cleaning parks, repairing country roads, and fixing up schools. Under the supervision of military personnel, the youth also found time to watch movies together and participate in weekend athletic contests, recreational activities that tightened the bonds between young people and the state officials. After Pearl Harbor the government increasingly mobilized the Young Adults' Corps to drum up support for the war by staging rallies, organizing parades, and spurring neighbors to patriotic efforts.

The Home Ministry was uneasy that the new mass associations might dilute its authority over the country's citizens. Skilled bureaucratic infighters, ministry officials had won control over the IRAA in March 1940, and in the spring of 1942 they persuaded the cabinet to affiliate most of the patriotic associations with the IRAA, and the Young Adults' Corps followed suit in the fall of 1943. By that time the Home Ministry had folded its nearly 1.3 million neighborhood associations into the IRAA as well. Authorized by a government edict dated September 11, 1940, each association (a dozen or so households on average) was supposed "to promote the people's moral training and spiritual unity" and "to assist in implementing all national policies." After the beginning of the Greater East Asia War, the ministry made the neighborhood groups responsible for allocating ration coupons for food and clothing, circulating government directives, selling war bonds, organizing local civil defense, collectively listening to special NHK broadcasts that articulated the nation's war aims, monitoring members' attitudes toward the war, and countless other duties designed to muster community spirit and hold the social fabric of the nation together.

By the middle of the war the Home Ministry had become the face of governing authority for most Japanese, nearly all of whom belonged to one or more IRAA patriotic associations. Whatever successes the IRAA enjoyed in mobilizing the nation and creating an ethos of total dedication to national unity, however, it never played a role analogous to the Nazi party organization in Germany. The IRAA did not become a mass party, nor did it assume policy-making functions. Moreover, the Home Ministry masters always had to share authority with the nation's other elites, especially Tōjō and the army and navy. Throughout the Greater East Asia War, the hydra-headed political system sanctioned by the Meiji constitution remained intact. Even so, Japan's wartime leaders did fashion a national defense state that made governmental authority more pervasive than ever before, and they succeeded in rallying the people around the war effort on a scale rarely observed anywhere.

## Ruling the Greater East Asia Coprosperity Sphere

The linked visions of a New Order and a Greater East Asia Coprosperity Sphere were solely Japanese inventions, fabricated by strategists who sought ideological underpinnings for their opposition to a perceived Anglo-American threat to Japanese national security. But the conceptions were more than empty conceits; they captured the idealism of many Japanese. "What kinds of treatments have the yellow and black races received from the white race?" asked one student in November 1941. "What has the white race done to the Native American Indians? What is going on with the 400 million people in India? What is happening to the 500 million people in our neighbor nation of China? How about the ignorant but innocent Indonesians?" Japan's mission, he went on, was a "moral" one, "based on the ideal of harmony among all races." Each nation, he concluded, must "have its own place of peaceful living, fulfill its obligations, and develop together. This is what we expect of the New Order for East Asia; together we will build Asia for the Asian people."[5]

The prospect of a revitalized Asia also resonated powerfully with people in the region who actually lived under Western domination. Indeed, nationalist leaders in many Southeast Asian countries hailed the arrival of Japanese armies as a means for lifting the yoke of Western imperialism. Within hours of the attack on Pearl Harbor, for instance, the government of Thailand granted Japan permission to use bases on Thai soil to invade British-held Burma and the Malay Peninsula, and a month later Thailand declared war on the United States and Great Britain. In Burma, Aung San, a prominent critic of British imperialism, organized the Burma Independence Army to fight alongside the Japanese as they marched on Rangoon in 1942, while Ba Maw, another radical nationalist, escaped from a British prison to become head of state within the Japanese occupation administration. Farther to the south and east, in the Netherlands East Indies, prominent anticolonialists Sukarno and Mohammad Hatta emerged from exile and Dutch prison to serve as advisers to the Japanese military occupationaires.

Japan's government played on the hopes of Asian nationalists. It granted independent status to Burma and the Philippines in 1943, and in November that year Tōjō invited representatives from Manchukuo, Thailand, the Philippines, Burma, and the Reform Government of China to attend the Greater East Asia Conference in Tokyo. At the conclusion of the convocation Ba Maw rose to thank the Japanese for helping Asians recapture a sense of common brotherhood and destiny, and the meeting issued a communiqué declaring that an autarkic coprosperity sphere offered the only certain route to "universal understanding, peace, and stability." Sometimes lost among florid pronouncements about Asian brotherhood is that fact that the Greater East Asia War did spell an end to Western colonialism across a vast swath of Asia that encompassed Burma and French Indochina, ran through the Malay Peninsula, and extended outward to the Philippines, the Netherlands East Indies, and New Guinea.

Although Western colonialists may have disappeared from most of Asia, many nationalist leaders, even those who initially had greeted the Japanese warmly, later learned to their chagrin something that the Koreans and Chinese already knew from harsh experience: Japanese colonialists could be as exploitative and brutal as their Western counterparts. The Tokyo government relied upon the military to administer occupied territories, and policy guidelines formulated by a liaison conference in November 1941, as Japan girded for war with the United States, instructed the occupationaires to control local economies strictly "in order to facilitate our acquisition of essential war materials." A year later one cabinet member put it more bluntly: "There are no restrictions on us. These are enemy possessions. We can take them, do anything we want."[6]

Violated earlier by the West, the nations and territories of the Greater East Asia Coprosperity Sphere now gave up to the Japanese military their energy sources, strategic materials, and war-related industrial production. Oil from the Netherlands East Indies was the great prize, and by 1943 the occupation government had tightened its grip over those islands so completely that Tōjō boastfully announced a permanent end to Japan's petroleum shortages. Military quartermasters and private traders acquired chromium, copper, iron ore, and manganese from the Philippines; lead, cobalt, and tungsten from Burma; rubber and tin from Thailand and French Indochina; bauxite from Malaya. Korea continued to send significant amounts of light metals and ferroalloys, and mines in northern China and Manchukuo yielded essential coal. During the war two-thirds of all energy consumed by the Japanese was derived from coal, about 20 percent of which was imported in 1943. Japanese citizens also depended on the empire for crucial foodstuffs, especially rice, as illustrated in Table 14.3.

Commercial exchanges with Japan usually ended up working to the detriment of local economies. The Japanese government set import and export prices and fixed currency exchange rates that favored the yen. Occupation authorities in the newly conquered territories gave little or no heed to fostering manufacturing industries that would benefit indigenous peoples, and acquisition policies were carried out only with the needs of Japan in mind. In Indochina the army arbitrarily commandeered rice harvests; when it required more raw materials for uniforms, it compelled some peasants to

**TABLE 14.3**  *Rice Imports and Domestic Production, 1937–1945*
(in thousand metric tons)

| | | IMPORTS | | | | | |
|---|---|---|---|---|---|---|---|
| CROP YEAR * | KOREA | TAIWAN | NETHER-LANDS EAST INDIES | THAILAND | BURMA | TOTAL IMPORTS | DOMESTIC PRODUC-TION |
| 1937 | 1123 | 809 | 1932 | 0 | 48 | 1,980 | 9,928 |
| 1938 | 1692 | 829 | 2521 | 0 | 25 | 2,546 | 9,862 |
| 1939 | 948 | 660 | 1608 | 0 | 26 | 1,634 | 10,324 |
| 1940 | 66 | 464 | 530 | 461 | 313 | 1,860 | 9,107 |
| 1941 | 551 | 328 | 879 | 677 | 461 | 2,517 | 8,245 |
| 1942 | 873 | 284 | 1157 | 741 | 628 | 2,581 | 9,999 |
| 1943 | 0 | 302 | 302 | 688 | 164 | 1,183 | 9,422 |
| 1944 | 583 | 217 | 800 | 39 | 35 | 874 | 8,784 |
| 1945 | 227 | 41 | 268 | 0 | 0 | 268 | 6,445 |

* Crop year ends October 31.

Adapted from Jerome B. Cohen, *Japan's Economy in War and Reconstruction* (Minneapolis: University of Minnesota Press, 1949), pp. 368–69.

rip up their rice paddies and plant jute. In the end even early sympathizers like Ba Maw became disillusioned; there was, he later lamented, "only one goal and interest, the Japanese interest; only one destiny for the East Asian counties, to become so many Manchukuos or Koreas tied forever to Japan."[7] Such became the warped reality of coprosperity.

Economic exploitation was only one section in a broader mosaic of colonial governance that assumed Japanese superiority and treated native populations with contempt. Fully versed in the imperial mythohistory that conceived of the Japanese as the world's "leading race," military governors reserved the best hotels and recreational facilities for the exclusive use of the occupation armies. Most military governors also enacted "Japanization" programs that required local peoples to bow to all Japanese in uniform, to observe Japanese holidays (April 29, the birthday of the emperor, became a Coprosperity Sphere celebration), and to mark the passage of years with the official Japanese calendar, so that 1942 became the year 2602, as counted from the legendary founding of the imperial state in 660 B.C.E.

More cruel were acts of physical brutality. Experience on the China front had taught Japan's invading troops to resent "liberated villagers" who always seemed to be plotting against them, and the soldiers of the Imperial Army carried with them to Southeast Asia and the islands of the Pacific suspicious attitudes, a belief in their own racial superiority, and a tendency toward inhumane behavior. Across Asia and the Pacific, Japanese soldiers became notorious for slapping, beating, and verbally berating non-Japanese upon the slightest provocation. Organized, institutionalized violence defined another aspect of occupation policy. In the Netherlands East Indies, Japanese occupationaires arrested known nationalists on trumped-up charges, rounded up peasants and shipped them to other areas as laborers, and executed Indonesians caught listening to Allied broadcasts on shortwave radio. After the capture of Singapore, Japanese authorities summarily arrested more than seventy thousand overseas Chinese suspected of subversive activities, thousands of whom, according to eyewitnesses, were tied together, loaded onto boats, taken to the middle of the harbor, and pushed overboard. On the Malay Peninsula the occupation army closed schools and converted the buildings into army barracks, allotted the indigenous population only one-half the rice ration distributed to Japanese, and beheaded Malays caught pilfering from military warehouses.

Women suffered horribly. The systematic denigration of women was most intense where so many problems began, in Korea. Working under instructions from the Imperial Army, recruiters signed up young women supposedly to work in overseas textile plants but instead sent them to primitive army brothels throughout Asia. Joining them were other Korean women, many still in their early teens, who were forcibly dragged off city streets and village lanes to serve as "comfort women" for Japanese soldiers and colonial administrators. Chinese, Filipino, Malaysian, and Dutch women captured in Singapore likewise were coerced into service. In all, as many as 100,000 to 250,000 women ended up in the brothels of the Imperial Army. There unknown tens of thousands died from disease and malnutrition, while terrified Japanese soldiers shot and bayoneted countless others in the closing days of the war.

In Asia the carnage wrought by war and abusive occupation policies was beyond imagination. In addition to the comfort women, as many as 70,000 Korean males died as manual laborers in Japan or as "volunteers" in the Imperial Army. The Filipino government counted 125,000 combined civilian and combat-related deaths, the Indian government estimated its war casualties at 180,000 in fighting on the Burma front, and the French claimed that 1 in 20 Vietnamese perished, chiefly as a consequence of Japanese agricultural policies that contributed significantly to the great famine of 1945. A United Nations report estimated that 3 million on Java and an additional

1 million Indonesians on the offshore islands were killed by the Japanese or died from hunger, disease, and lack of medical care. Probably one-half of the estimated 300,000 to 1 million Indonesians conscripted by the Japanese as forced laborers perished, and one official account claimed that of the 130,000 Europeans interned in the Netherlands East Indies, 30,000, including nearly 7,000 women and children, died in prison. The agony was greatest in China. The official figure for Chinese soldiers killed between 1937 and 1945 was set at 1.3 million, but to that must be added an incalculable number of civilian deaths, perhaps another 9 to 12 million. Such numbers defy precise calculation and can only hint at the savage brutality visited upon Asia's war-wasted innocents. Such became the grotesque reality of pan-Asian brotherhood.

## The Tide of Battle Turns

Stirred by the early successes that exceeded their most optimistic projections, Japan's military commanders in the spring of 1942 contemplated new operations that would push out Admiral Yamamoto's original defensive perimeter. Planners mapped out campaigns in China and eastern India, scheduled an invasion of the Aleutian Islands, and even proposed to attack Australia and to occupy the Hawaiian Islands. A few of the new ventures bore fruit—Japanese forces took Attu and Kiska in the Aleutians in June— but the Japanese soon discovered that they had spread themselves too thin. On April 18, 1942, the American carrier *Hornet* crept within six hundred miles of the Japanese coast, and Lieutenant Colonel James H. Doolittle led sixteen B-25 bombers on a strike against Tokyo, Nagoya, Osaka, and Kōbe. Although Doolittle's raiders caused more embarrassment than actual damage to the Japanese, two months later, at the beginning of June, a savage attack by an undetected U.S. task force cost Admiral Yamamoto four irreplaceable aircraft carriers as he steamed toward Midway Island, a base he coveted for operations against Hawaii. Later in the summer of 1942 American marines came ashore at Guadalcanal, and on New Year's Eve, after several months of tough jungle fighting, the Japanese decided to withdraw their forces. More quickly than they could have dreamed possible, the Imperial Army and Navy found themselves thrown onto the defensive; more horribly than they could ever have imagined, the brutality of war was to come home to the Japanese people.

By early 1943 it was clear that Japan's pre-Pearl Harbor assumptions had gone astray: Great Britain did not fall to Germany, and Americans proved neither as weak-willed nor as prone to negotiate as hoped. More significantly, American industry was not hamstrung by its capitalist ethic, and it responded with surprising agility to the challenge of fighting a world war. Between 1940 and 1942 the U.S. gross national product grew by more than one-third, and government expenditures for armaments soared from 17 to 30.5 percent of the expanding GNP. Although the Japanese economy performed tolerably during the initial years of the war, the island empire was locked in a one-sided battle with an economic Goliath whose productive capacity far outstripped its own. Ishiwara Kanji's prediction about the China quagmire had been on the mark, and he was correct as well about America's ability to outproduce Japan. Even in 1942, the first full year of war in the Pacific, American war-related manufacturing surpassed that of Japan, and by 1945 U.S. armaments factories were churning out ten times as many weapons. In numerical strength that the Japanese could not possibly hope to meet, the Americans dispatched to the Pacific theater fleets of aircraft, squadrons of carriers and battleships, packs of submarines.

During 1943 MacArthur attacked along the Solomon-Bismarck archipelagoes and the New Guinea coast while Admiral Chester Nimitz used the gathering American strength to secure the central Pacific, hopping from island to island, bypassing heavily fortified Japanese defense points to strike more vulnerable bases, and bringing American air power ever closer to the vital sea-lanes that linked Japan's home islands with Southeast Asia. The Imperial Japanese Army and Navy did not fare well in 1943: The army lost more than ten thousand men in the retreat from Guadalcanal, American pilots ambushed Yamamoto's airplane on April 18 in the Solomons and killed the fleet commander, in May, Japan lost the Aleutians to a U.S. counterattack, and in November, Tarawa, Japan's most important stronghold in the central Pacific, fell. "The real war," Tōjō told the Diet on December 27, "starts now."

Japanese defenses collapsed inward upon themselves as the American counteroffensive shifted into high gear in 1944. In the early summer Japanese air power suffered a stunning setback when the navy lost 405 of 430 planes in a failed attempt to defend Saipan. That fiasco cost Tōjō his professional life. Within Japan's inner circles, criticism of his performance as prime minister and war leader had been mounting for some time. Late in 1943 ex-Premier Okada Keisuke sounded a clear warning in a message to the palace urging Tōjō's ouster. Embarrassingly enough for the prime minister, anti-Tōjō sentiment erupted during a reception held at his official residence on March 25, 1944, when the Speaker of the House loudly called on him to "accept responsibility" for Japan's declining military fortunes and

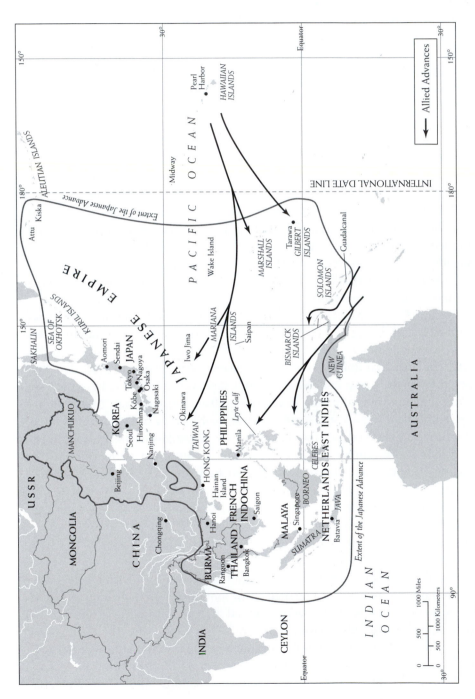

**MAP 14.1** *The Greater East Asia War*

**TABLE 14.4** *Japanese Prime Ministers, 1941–1945*

| PRIME MINISTER | CABINET NUMBER | CABINET TERM |
|---|---|---|
| Konoe Fumimaro | Third | July 18, 1941–October 18, 1941 |
| Tōjō Hideki | | October 18, 1941–July 22, 1944 |
| Koiso Kuniaki | | July 22, 1944–April 7, 1945 |
| Suzuki Kantarō | | April 7, 1945–August 17, 1945 |

"to resign"; applause, noted some in their diaries, spontaneously broke out across the room. On July 17, just ten days after the fall of Saipan, the senior statesmen met and refused to extend a vote of confidence to the Razor. The following day Tōjō resigned as prime minister and stepped down from government service.

Upon the recommendation of the senior statesmen, the emperor appointed General Koiso Kuniaki to replace Tōjō. But that old warhorse, who had served as governor-general of Korea from 1942, enjoyed no more success than Tōjō. "Hell," the naval chief of staff predicted after the fall of Saipan, "is about to descend upon us," and that autumn Nimitz and MacArthur converged on the Philippines. In the Battle of Leyte Gulf in October, Japanese naval captains, outgunned and outmaneuvered, lost six carriers. Its fleet in tatters, the once-proud Imperial Navy ceased to be a significant factor in the battle for the Pacific. Making good his vow to return, MacArthur brought his troops ashore and secured Manila early in 1945. The American victory in the Philippines virtually cut off Japan from Southeast Asia and turned the southwest Pacific into a strategic backwater. Now the Americans drove straight for Japan, taking Iwo Jima in March and invading Okinawa on the first day of April 1945.

The loss of the Philippines portended ruinous consequences for the Japanese economy. After the Battle of Leyte Gulf the spigot closed almost entirely on the rich flow of resources from the colonies and occupied territories. In 1942 tankers brought 40 percent of Southeast Asia's oil to Japanese ports; in 1944 that figure fell to 5 percent, and in 1945, to none at all. In 1941 Japan imported 5.1 million tons of iron ore, in 1944, just 1.7 million, and in the first quarter of 1945 only 144,000 tons reached Japanese factories. Denied vital resources, manufacturing output tumbled. Table 14.2 plots the dramatic drop-off in the steel, machinery, and chemical sectors during the last year of the war, and the consequent decline in armaments production, shown in Table 14.5, numbed military planners. Such figures translated into insurmountable

**TABLE 14.5** *Armaments Production, 1941–1945*

| YEAR | AIRCRAFT | | COMBAT VEHICLES | | SHIPS | | | |
| | FIGHTERS | BOMBERS | TANKS | ARMORED TRACTORS | BATTLESHIPS | CARRIERS | CRUISERS | DESTROYERS |
| --- | --- | --- | --- | --- | --- | --- | --- | --- |
| 1941 | 1,080 | 1,461 | 1,024 | 919 | 1 | 5 | 1 | 9 |
| 1942 | 2,935 | 2,433 | 1,165 | 1,489 | 1 | 6 | 2 | 9 |
| 1943 | 7,147 | 4,189 | 776 | 870 | 0 | 3 | 2 | 15 |
| 1944 | 13,811 | 5,100 | 342 | 741 | 0 | 4 | 1 | 31 |
| 1945 | 5,474 | 1,934 | 94 | 196 | 0 | 0 | 0 | 6 |

Adapted from Jerome B. Cohen, *Japan's Economy in War and Reconstruction* (Minneapolis: University of Minnesota Press, 1949), pp. 211, 237, and 262.

disadvantages on the battlefield. During the war air power became the decisive weapon of destruction. In January 1943 Japan could put 3,200 combat-ready aircraft into the skies against 3,537 for the United States; in January 1945 the comparable figures were 4,100 against 21,908.

Sent reeling by the American offensive, its resources depleted, the Japanese military turned to tactics of desperation, sacrificing its soldiers, sailors, and aviators by the tens of thousands in a heroic but ultimately tragic attempt to slow the enemy's advance and, perhaps, even to extract such a terrible human cost that he would come to the negotiating table. Beginning with Attu in 1943, Japanese defenders refused to surrender, opting instead to fight to the last man. The Japanese Field Service Code forbade soldiers to "suffer the disgrace of becoming a prisoner," and in any case, many expected to be killed if they did surrender themselves to Americans. Such a fear was not unfounded. On Tarawa the marine battle cry was "Take no prisoners!" and Charles Lindbergh, a civilian observer with American forces based in New Guinea, noted in his diary on June 26, 1944, that of several thousand Japanese soldiers captured, only a couple of hundred survived, the rest having met with "an accident." Beyond the natural instinct to serve one's country and to avoid death in captivity, Japan's military leadership relied on tactics that demanded sacrifice. In the central Pacific army commanders ceded the beaches to the Americans and marshaled their forces in mountain and jungle redoubts. Dug into caves and underground emplacements, Japanese soldiers fought to the death. The human toll was high, on both sides. At Attu the Japanese body count totaled 2,600, with just 28 prisoners; at Tarawa, 4,600 defenders died, 100 surrendered. More than 300,000 Japanese perished in operations in the Philippines in 1944 and 1945, and on Okinawa virtually the entire Japanese garrison of 110,000 troops went to their deaths while nearly 50,000 Americans (from an invading force of 172,000) were killed or wounded.

In the autumn of 1944 the appearance of the kamikaze pilot sanctified suicide as a national strategy. In October that year Vice Admiral Ōnishi Takijirō, a ranking official in the Munitions Ministry, arrived in the Philippines to coordinate preparations for the American assault. Acutely aware of Japan's hopeless inferiority in the production of aircraft, Ōnishi asked pilots under his command to volunteer to crash-dive their bomb-laden Zero fighters into American battleships, and on October 25 twenty-four pilots took off on the first suicide mission. They enjoyed incredible success, sinking one U.S. escort carrier and damaging several others. Heartened by the results, Ōnishi hastily recruited several more squadrons, and the army air force followed suit. Officials designated the new units as the Divine Wind Special Attack Corps, a reference to storms stirred up by Japan's deities to

*Female students wave farewell to kamikaze pilots*

drive off invading Mongol armadas in 1274 and 1281, although *kamikaze*, a colloquial reading of the ideographs for "divine wind," became the preferred appellation among Americans.

With the navy crippled and air power dwindling, the Japanese turned to the Special Attack Corps as their principal means of self-defense in the final year of the war. For a military that suffered from absurd material shortages, the suicide squadrons represented a miracle-to-come, an opportunity to mobilize Japan's final remaining resource, the fighting spirit of its youth, in a bold attempt to deliver a stunning blow to the opponent. The bravery of those who volunteered for the Special Attack Corps shone with undeniable brilliance, but their sacrifice did almost nothing to slow the American advance. By the conclusion of hostilities, almost five thousand young men had died in suicide missions, yet in total they had put only a few ships out of commission. Ironically, their most dramatic success came on the very first day of operations, and a real typhoon off the coast of the Philippines in December 1944 did more damage to the U.S. fleet than even the most fierce Divine Wind attack.

By 1945 the young martyrs sensed that their impending deaths would not alter substantially the outcome of the war. Disillusioned, a few plunged to their deaths shouting curses against their unit commanders and the coun-

try's political leaders into their radios. Most, however, sent home final poems and letters that expressed a poignant, elemental belief in family, emperor, and nation, values that sustained many of their countrymen as well
during the final dark year of the war. Just before setting off on his last flight,
one young airman wrote his father: "The Japanese way of life is indeed beautiful, and I am proud of it, as I am of Japanese history and mythology which
reflect the purity of our ancestors and their belief in the past. That way of
life is the product of all the best things which our ancestors have handed
down to us. And the living embodiment of all wonderful things out of our
past is the Imperial Family which, too, is the crystallization of the splendor
and beauty of Japan and its people. It is an honor to be able to give my life
in defense of these beautiful and lofty things."[8]

Wrote another young man: "We shall serve the nation gladly in its present painful struggle. We shall plunge into enemy ships cherishing the conviction that Japan has been and will be a place where only lovely homes,
brave women, and beautiful friendships are allowed to exist."

## Life under Siege

The nobility of youthful sacrifice did nothing to spare the Japanese populace from the ferocity of direct American attack. In June 1944 B-29 Super
Fortresses began to fly high-level "precision bombing" attacks against selected industrial targets, such as the Yawata steel mills in Kyūshū and the
Nakajima aircraft factory on the western outskirts of Tokyo. But faulty
bomb-aiming radar and other mechanical difficulties plagued the fliers (eight
raids on the sprawling Nakajima complex resulted in only slight damage),
so early in 1945 Major General Curtis E. LeMay, head of the Twentieth
Bomber Command, decided to shift tactics; he would load the Super
Fortresses with incendiaries, fly them low, and burn Japan's cities. Such attacks offered several promising advantages to the man who had coordinated
American bombing attacks against Dresden and other German cities. Much
of Japan's small industry was sprinkled throughout residential districts, where
highly flammable and tightly packed buildings presented the maximum potential for incendiary destruction. But more than that, in a war in which brutality against noncombatants had already become commonplace, LeMay and
his planning staff sought to rain death and destruction upon ordinary Japanese in order to break their morale and shatter their faith in their leaders.

LeMay became totally dedicated to the new strategy after the night of
March 9–10 when 334 B-29s, each carrying nearly six tons of oil, phos-

phorus, jellied gasoline, and napalm, took off from bases in the Mariana Islands and converged on the Asakusa district of northeastern Tokyo, the most densely populated quarter of the city. The damage was catastrophic. The heat from the four million pounds of incendiaries was so intense that canals and rivers bubbled, steel beams melted, and 80,000 to 100,000 people died, "scorched and boiled and baked to death" as the cigar-chomping LeMay put it in his memoir.[9] Within the sixteen-square-mile area that had been Asakusa, virtually nothing was left standing. In a single night one-fifth of Tokyo's industrial establishments disappeared, and incredibly, one million people were rendered homeless.

The B-29s returned to their bases, refueled, and took off again. In the next ten days they brought the killing and horror of war home to the men and women of Osaka, Kōbe, and Nagoya. The Japanese could do nothing to stop the attacks. They lacked effective radar, had only antiquated anti-aircraft batteries, and by the spring of 1945 could put up just two squadrons of night fighters. Throughout the long summer of '45 the Super Fortresses kept coming back, their bomb bays stuffed with more and more incendiaries. On May 26 five hundred bombers dropped four thousand tons of flammables on residential sections in northwestern Tokyo, and on June 10 a great airborne armada of two thousand bombers and fighters clobbered cities from Kyūshū to northern Honshū. By August B-29 attacks had turned sixty-six Japanese cities into combat zones; saturation bombing destroyed 40 percent of Osaka and Nagoya, 50 percent of Tokyo and Kōbe, 90 percent of Aomori, all of Sendai. The B-29s knocked out half of Japan's communications, scorched 40 percent of its industrial zones, made it nearly impossible

*Bombed-out Osaka*

for trains and coastal shipping to operate. Almost 25 percent of the nation's housing stock burned to the ground, nearly 250,000 Japanese died, and 300,000 more were maimed and injured.

Those who survived faced myriad hardships. Everything was in short supply in the summer of '45. In 1941 consumer goods accounted for 40 percent of GNP; in 1945, just 17 percent. What was available cost more. Workers' wages rose during the war, but commodity prices shot up even more steeply so that when adjusted for inflation, real wages in 1945 were one-third less than in 1939. Clothing was rationed, but textiles were in such short supply that most women dressed in drab *monpe*, a simple pantaloon-style outfit usually worn by farm women in the northeast, and men made do with threadbare suits from prewar years. Firewood became so expensive that even a weekly bath was a luxury, and some teachers burned their personal libraries just to warm themselves.

Food became scarce. Cold weather caused a poor harvest in 1944, just as the American air and naval blockade cut off supplies from the withering limbs of the empire. By the spring of 1945 there was just not enough food to go around, and desperate housewives increasingly turned to the black market. Urban dwellers crowded into trains bound for the countryside, only to discover that sweet potatoes, the new but seldom enjoyed staple of the Japanese diet, cost twenty times the legal price, soybeans thirty times, and rice seventy times. Despite the expense, Tokyo families had to rely on the black market for nearly 10 percent of their rice, 40 percent of their fish, and 70 percent of their vegetables.

Loneliness and separated families added another measure of misery to the war experience. As early as the fall of 1943 the cabinet urged anyone not needed in war plants—mothers with infant children, the old, and the infirm—to leave the major cities, although few chose to do so. After the bombings began in 1944, the government ordered 350,000 third to sixth graders evacuated from a dozen cities, and another 100,000 young people followed the next spring. Put up in vacant inns and country temples, the often depressed and homesick children struggled to keep up with their lessons and joined volunteer brigades to help out on nearby farms.

While the countryside was bursting with people, the cities of Japan took on a deserted look. More than 3 million left Tokyo in the weeks after March 9–10, and 6 million more poured out of the nation's other urban centers. In all, Tokyo's population during the war fell from 6.8 to 2.8 million; Osaka from 3.4 to 1.1 million; Kōbe from 967,000 to 379,000. Their families gone, those who remained behind found little with which to break the tension, or relieve the tedium, of living under siege. The dance halls and bars of the amusement quarters had long since shuttered their doors, their geisha and other female entertainers cajoled into factory work. Perhaps only a few residents of Tokyo rued the passing of ballet (at least after such productions as "Decisive Aerial Warfare Suite" became standard fare), but many felt dismay when the May sumo tournament was shortened to a week and moved outdoors after LeMay's B-29s damaged the regular arena and killed the high-ranking wrestlers Toyoshima and Matsuuragata. The few places left for refreshment in the summer of '45 were "people's bars," government-operated establishments that opened once a week and sold cheap beer and flasks of sake fortified with methyl alcohol, mockingly called bombs for the way the rice wine exploded in the mouth and scorched the throat.

By the summer of '45 many Japanese had become thoroughly disillusioned with the Greater East Asia War. There never was any organized antiwar movement in Japan and very few acts of illegal resistance beyond those committed by a small number of staunch Communists and socialists who mostly ended up in jail. More commonly, those who held misgivings about the war took haven in the contempt of silence, switched professions, or carried on with their work as if there were no war. The distinguished economist Kawakami Hajime secluded himself in his Kyoto home during the war, Tanizaki quietly finished "The Makioka Sisters" in anticipation of future publication, and the constitutional scholar Minobe Tatsukichi, whose works on constitutional theory had been discredited in 1935, persevered to publish his "Basic Theory of Economic Criminal Law" in 1944.

As the war wore on, ordinary Japanese resorted to graffiti and anonymous letters to express their contempt for a holy war gone disastrously wrong. People scribbled "Kill the Emperor" and phrases such as "Overthrow the Government" and "End the War" on lampposts and factory walls across the country. One Kyoto journalist reported that of the nearly two hundred letters a day his newspaper received in the closing months of the war, most denounced "officials and the military for their alleged failure to share the people's hardships." Others simply voiced their growing despair to neighbors. "What is so holy about a war that wastes goods and tens of thousands of our countrymen's lives in cruel strife," asked one parent whose child was killed in Singapore. "Can there be anyone at all who really wants to be a soldier?"[10] In all, the police bureau of the Home Ministry tabulated 406 incidents of serious antiwar dissent for the twelve months ending March 1944 and 607 for the subsequent year.

Factory workers posed a special problem for the state as production targets fell victim to shoddy work and chronic absenteeism. Even before the bombings started in 1944, worker attendance was a stubborn trouble spot, but declining morale, difficulties in commuting, and the need to spend time foraging for food in the countryside pushed absenteeism to alarming levels in 1945, as illustrated in Table 14.6. Workers who did show up were less diligent (as desperate as Japan was for planes, the military rejected as defective 10 percent of all aircraft produced in 1944), and they were increasingly prone to engage in work stoppages, generally over complaints about low wages and poor treatment by management. In 1941, officials recorded 159 strikes and slowdowns, but they tabulated 695 such disputes in 1943 and 550 for the first eleven months of 1944; quite clearly, Sanpō's goal of creating a harmonious enterprise community remained an elusive ideal.

In response to these fissures on the home front, the government urged people to work harder, to sacrifice even more. To a remarkable degree, most Japanese were willing to carry on with the battle, in spite of the bombings, shortages, separation from loved ones, and growing pessimism. Fear of the police and state coercion were important reasons for that, but so too was a sensitivity to the peer pressure exerted through neighborhood associations and the patriotic organizations of the IRAA; as one housewife noted in January 1945, no one wished to be the first accused of quitting. Ultimately most Japanese were loyal citizens who, impelled by an elemental love of homeland, simply did not wish to abandon their country in time of crisis.

**TABLE 14.6** *Absenteeism at Selected Tōshiba Factories, 1937–1945*

| YEAR | TSURUMI ENGINEERING WORKS | KOMUKAI WORKS | ŌMIYACHŌ WORKS | YANAGIMACHI WORKS |
|------|---------------------------|---------------|----------------|-------------------|
| 1937 | 5.8 | — | — | 7.6 |
| 1938 | 7.5 | — | — | 8.0 |
| 1939 | 9.1 | 8.0 | — | 7.7 |
| 1940 | 14.8 | 8.2 | 7.9 | 8.5 |
| 1941 | 15.1 | 9.3 | 8.5 | 8.2 |
| 1942 | 17.2 | 9.2 | 9.2 | 11.3 |
| 1943 | 22.3 | 15.2 | 9.4 | 18.8 |
| 1944 | 21.1 | 22.7 | 52.0 | 25.5 |
| 1945 | 51.0 | 66.4 | 57.8 | 31.6 |

Data are for all male and female employees (except Tsurumi: males only) for June each year (except Yanagimachi: December).

Adapted from Andrew Gordon, *The Evolution of Labor Relations in Japan: Heavy Industry, 1853–1955* (Cambridge: Council on East Asian Studies, Harvard University, 1985), pp. 316–17.

Gamely they endured one final mobilization. On June 13, 1945, the government dissolved the IRAA so that all civilian men aged fifteen to sixty and all women seventeen to forty could join units of the People's Patriotic Volunteer Corps, which were being formed in their neighborhoods and at their places of employment. Placed under army command, those civilian units trained together, drilled with crude bamboo staves, and dug pillboxes for themselves along the coast to prepare for the American invasion expected that autumn. All Japanese, according to the chilling calculus of the new official slogan, were now to come together as the Ichioku Tokkō, the "One Hundred Million Strong Special Attack Corps."

## Surrender

The American invasion of Okinawa brought foreign troops onto Japanese soil, and the senior statesmen recognized that it was time to seek an end to hostilities. The army, however, refused to be a party to any such consensus. The previous year a surprisingly effective ground campaign against Chiang Kai-shek's forces had brought several additional provinces under Japanese control and reinforced the army's sense of dignity and resolve. By the time the Americans came ashore on Okinawa, events in the China theater were no longer crucial to the outcome of the Greater East Asia War, but the army still had 5.5 million men in uniform, and it preferred to fight to the bitter end than to agree to any surrender that might, from its viewpoint, threaten Japan's future integrity or jeopardize the continued existence of the imperial institution. Confronted with the army's intransigence, the senior statesmen in late April 1945 advised the emperor to accept the resignation of Prime Minister Koiso and appoint Suzuki Kantarō to head a peace cabinet. The retired admiral enjoyed the confidence of the emperor— Suzuki's wife, Taka, had been the monarch's wet nurse, while Suzuki himself had served as grand chamberlain from 1929 until 1936—and the senior statesmen hoped that Suzuki could use his prestige to bring the army to heel.

The advocates of a negotiated settlement had been seeking out one another for a considerable time. Even as Japan's military ranked up victories in 1942, Yoshida Shigeru and several important members of the inner circle of bureaucratic and business elites covertly discussed the possibility of initiating a peace dialogue with the United States. As a former ambassador to Great Britain in the 1930s Yoshida had regarded cooperation with those two powers as essential for Japanese security, and like other members of the Anglo-American clique within the prewar Foreign Ministry, he was staunchly anti-Communist. His fears ran in two directions. On the one hand, the longer the war continued, he believed, the more likely it became that Tōjō's organizational controls and centralized economic planning would end up turning Japan into a Communist-style state. On the other hand, Yoshida was not seduced by Japan's early successes in the Greater East Asia War. He predicted ultimate defeat, and he worried that in the subsequent chaos a revolutionary movement might arise within the nation and destroy its traditional polity. Thus, he calculated, Japan ought to negotiate a gentlemanly settlement with the Americans, who, he believed, would grant generous peace terms.

Yoshida drew around himself a circle of like-minded individuals, dubbed the "YOHANSEN," an acronym for "Yoshida Anti-War," by the police who monitored their activities. Associated with the clandestine YOHANSEN were such luminaries as the former prime minister Wakatsuki Reijirō, the retired managing director of the Mitsui *zaibatsu* Ikeda Seihin, and even the moody and unpredictable Konoe Fumimaro. Originally, Konoe had conceived of his New Order in East Asia as a bulwark against both Communism and Western imperialism, but in the middle years of the war he modulated his critique of the United States. Increasingly, in the teeter-totter of his mind, the three-time prime minister became obsessed with a dread that the deteriorating war situation would somehow enable Communists supposedly hidden within the army, IRAA, and universities to concoct a revolution in Japan.

With Yoshida's support, Konoe prepared a lengthy memorial and arranged to present it to the emperor on February 14, 1945. In his presentation, Konoe called the emperor's attention to the Soviet Union's successes in the European war and suggested "the considerable danger that the Soviet Union will eventually intervene in Japan's domestic affairs."[11] Moreover, the prince warned the emperor, on the "domestic scene I see all the conditions necessary to bring about a communist revolution": declining living standards, labor unrest, "a pro-Soviet mood," and "the secret maneuvers of leftist elements who are manipulating this from behind." The greatest danger, Konoe hinted darkly, came from the "many young military men who seem to believe that our *kokutai* and communism can coexist." The only way to save the situation, he counseled, was to end the war "as soon as possible."

Konoe's morose fears about Japan's fate did not spur the emperor to action in February, but in the spring, when Suzuki became prime minister, Konoe again materialized to offer his advice and service. With Japan encircled and its cities increasingly devastated, Suzuki and other moderates within his cabinet decided to ask the Soviet Union to broker a settlement with the United States, just as the United States itself had extended its good offices to mediate a peace agreement between Japan and Russia a generation earlier. In June the emperor signaled his support for the plan, thus indicting that he now desired to find an honorable way to end hostilities. Even though the Kremlin turned aside Japan's initial overtures, Suzuki remained hopeful, and in early July the prime minister asked Konoe to carry to Moscow a personal letter from the emperor stating His Majesty's heartfelt hopes for peace, an assignment the prince agreed to after a private meeting with the monarch.

Before Konoe could complete his arrangements to travel to Moscow, however, Stalin, Churchill, and Truman gathered at Potsdam, Germany, to discuss Japan's surrender. The American president was aware of Japan's peace feelers, but he doubted their sincerity and did not suggest pursuing them. Nor was Truman inclined to show any mercy toward Japan, especially after he received news of the successful test explosion of an atomic device at Alamogordo, New Mexico. On July 26 the Allies issued the Potsdam Declaration, demanding that Japan surrender "unconditionally" or face utter destruction. The declaration further called upon the Japanese government to purge itself of its militarist leaders, disarm its military, limit its sovereignty to the territorial borders established at the beginning of the Meiji period, and accept an Allied occupation of the country. Nothing was said about the fate of the emperor, the foundation of Japan's revered *kokutai*.

Suzuki was in a bind. The army still was determined to fight to the end. Moreover, no matter how much some members of the cabinet were inclined toward peace, they could not bring themselves to accept an open-ended surrender that would permit a foreign army of occupation to dismantle the imperial system and to indict Japan's reigning monarch as a common war criminal if it so chose. Suzuki, fearful that he would provoke Truman further if he rejected the Potsdam terms outright, announced that Japan simply would "ignore" the declaration. It was an unfortunate choice of words by the seventy-eight-year-old prime minister; his exact expression, "mokusatsu," carried the nuance of "to treat with silent contempt," and Truman responded by hurling unrestrained violence against a Japan that already was teetering on the brink of collapse.

On July 24 Truman authorized the U.S. Army Strategic Air Forces to use a "special bomb" against Japan if Suzuki rejected the Potsdam Declaration. With the war in Europe over and his country longing to return to the normal routines of life, the American chief executive was determined to end hostilities in the Pacific as quickly as possible. In addition to avoiding the further loss of American lives, the president had an eye on Russia. The Soviets were mustering forces along Manchukuo's borders and across the straits from Hokkaidō, and if Truman could end the Pacific war before Russia entered it, he would foreclose the possibility of a divided Japan and thus escape the sorts of problems that a partitioned Germany already was posing for postwar Europe.

Moreover, Truman was new to his office, and the project leading to the production of the atomic bomb had built up its own relentless momentum. Everyone involved expected the bomb to be used; that was why America had expended so much money and effort to develop it. Truman, still unsure of his presidential footing, saw no good reason to question that assumption or to consider at length alternatives to dropping the atomic bomb on the Japanese, such as setting off a demonstration blast over a deserted island or simply waiting for the combined effects of continued firebombings and an American naval blockade to persuade Japan to surrender. Additionally, he screened out any moral qualms he might have had about using the new weapon; he simply was employing the best available technology to end a horrible war on the soonest possible day. "Let there be no mistake about it," he wrote, "I regarded the bomb as a military weapon and never had any doubt that it should be used."[12]

Later Truman and his advisers claimed that using the atomic bomb saved lives. In 1947 Harry L. Stimson, secretary of war under Roosevelt and Truman, contributed a special essay to *Harper's Magazine* that became the administration's official, approved version of events. An invasion of Kyūshū in the fall of 1945 followed by landings on Honshū the next spring, Stimson wrote, would have "cost over a million casualties, to American forces alone."[13] The secretary apparently pulled that number out of thin air, however, for army estimates submitted to Truman in July 1945 predicted that the projected landing on Kyūshū would result in a maximum of 33,500 Americans killed, wounded, or missing. Against that number of U.S. military losses, Truman knew that when his air force dropped the new atomic bomb over an undefended Japanese city, the explosion "would inflict damage and casualties beyond imagination." Yet, in a war in which few people any longer regarded the other side as fellow human beings, Truman and Stimson judged such sacrifice to be reasonable and acceptable.

At eight-fifteen on the morning of August 6, a single B-29, *Enola Gay*, dropped "a special bomb," 9.8 feet long and 2.3 feet in diameter, on the men, women, and children of Hiroshima. The atomic device exploded about sixteen hundred feet aboveground, and the temperature at the hypocenter below reached more than seven thousand degrees Fahrenheit. Everything within a mile-and-a-quarter radius of the eruption burned, and all within that killing circle who were exposed to the heat waves died, their skin and internal organs ruptured by the incredible temperatures. A wall of shock waves spread out from the epicenter at the speed of sound, obliterating concrete buildings, blowing apart wooden structures, and tearing limbs from bodies. Radiation was everywhere. Firestorms ravaged the city, and moisture collecting on rising ash came back to earth as radioactive "black rain." There are no accurate figures for the number of dead at Hiroshima, although a 1977 government estimate set the number at between 130,000 and 140,000.

On August 8 Foreign Ministry monitors picked up a Soviet radio broadcast announcing that country's intent to declare war on Japan and to invade Manchuria, the Kuril Islands, and Korea. Just before noon on the following day, August 9, the Americans dropped a second atomic bomb on Nagasaki and killed another 60,000 to 70,000; in all, nearly 500,000 civilians now had perished in the bombing of Japanese cities. Through all that travail and agony, the army minister and the army and navy chiefs of staff refused to endorse Suzuki's pleas for surrender. Total defeat, they contended, still might be avoided somehow, and further resistance might yet win from the Americans a guarantee for the throne's postwar existence.

On the night of August 9–10 and again on the morning of August 14, Suzuki convened imperial conferences and asked the emperor to intervene and break the deadlock between the prime minister and the military. Each time the emperor spoke on behalf of peace, and in the second meeting he instructed the military to comply with his wishes. That evening he affixed his

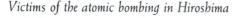

*Victims of the atomic bombing in Hiroshima*

seal to a rescript ending the war and then recorded the text for broadcast the next day. At noon on August 15 Japanese families huddled around their radios at home or gathered in front of loudspeakers hooked to a single village receiver to listen to the emperor's words. It was the first time in Japanese history that the semidivine monarch spoke directly to his subjects, and many had difficulty understanding his somewhat archaic phrasing as he praised the ideals for which the people of Japan had fought and suffered and then called upon them to "endure the unendurable" and accept defeat in order "to pave the way for a grand peace for all the future generations to come."

Across the war-weary country all Japanese, those who had welcomed the Greater East Asia War and those who had suffered its terrible consequences, contemplated the emperor's message about the nation's future. In Tokyo Vice Admiral Ōnishi, reassigned to the navy general staff, had spent the final hours of the war arguing that surrender was unthinkable. After listening to the emperor's broadcast, Ōnishi returned to his home and wrote an open letter to the youth of Japan. He expressed his appreciation to the spirits of the dead pilots of his inspiration, the Special Attack Corps, apologized for his failure to achieve victory, and called upon the nation's youth to abide by the emperor's words and strive for peace throughout the world. Ōnishi then unsheathed his sword and disemboweled himself with traditional crosswise cuts to the stomach. As he lay dying, his blood washing over the tatami flooring, he wrote a final poem:

Refreshed and clear, the moon now shines
After the fearful storm.[14]

Three hundred miles away, in the ancient city of Kyoto, Kawakami Hajime too listened to the emperor's words. Arrested for joining the underground Communist Party in the 1930s, his health broken in jail, the renowned academic economist and political activist emerged from his self-imposed seclusion to write two poems:

Ah, such happiness,
At somehow living long enough
To see this rare day
When the fighting has ceased.
Now I, too,
Will crawl out of my sickbed
To see the light
In the sky that is clearing.[15]

# PART V

# Contemporary Japan

私が、小学校五年の時だった。昼休みに、校庭で遊んでいたら、急に近所のやはり五年生の女の子が、私に向かって「朝鮮人！朝鮮人！」と叫び初めた。それで、回りで遊んでいた大勢の子供達は、何が起こったのかを思ってか、皆、二人に輪を作る様に寄って来た。その子は、その後を繰返し、朝鮮人！朝鮮人！と怒鳴りつづけた。私は、劣等感と怒りの混りあった気持で、いっぱいだった。まだ十才で、内気ではあったが、朝鮮人を怒鳴る声は大きくなり、もう我慢できなく、黙って思い切り、その子の左頬に、ピシャリと一発叩いた。朝鮮人って、何が悪いんだ。と強く心の中で思ったかどうしたものか、私は言えなかった。でも、教室に戻って行く間、私は、誇りと自信でいっぱいだった。それから四十年以上たった今でも、その頃、私の苗字は、長子であった。日本の占領時代、韓国人は皆日本から、名字に変えさせられた。それで、私の両親は、韓国名の子を長子に…たのである。その日帰国名の子・どうして私が、韓国人だって知っているんだ

# Chronology

**1945**

☐ *August 15* The emperor announces Japan's surrender

☐ *August 25* Ichikawa Fusae and other prominent women organize the Women's Committee on Postwar Countermeasures

☐ *August 30* MacArthur arrives in Japan

☐ *September 2* Japan signs the instrument of surrender

☐ *September 27* The emperor visits MacArthur at SCAP headquarters

☐ *October 11* MacArthur issues a statement calling for the emancipation of women, the encouragement of labor unionization, education reform, and the "democratization" of economic institutions

☐ *October 13* Prime Minister Shidehara appoints Matsumoto Jōji to chair a committee to consider constitutional revision

☐ *November 3* Ichikawa Fusae helps establish the New Japan Women's League

☐ *November 6* MacArthur accepts the Yasuda plan for "*zaibatsu* busting"

☐ *December 16* Konoe Fumimaro commits suicide

☐ *December 17* Women receive the right to vote

☐ *December 22* The Diet passes the Trade Union Law (implemented March 1, 1946)

**1946**

☐ *January 1* The emperor issues his "Declaration of Humanity"

☐ *January 4* SCAP distributes purge directives

☐ *February 3* MacArthur instructs GHQ to prepare a model constitution

☐ *February 13* SCAP presents its draft constitution to the Matsumoto committee

☐ *May 3* SCAP convenes the International Military Tribunal for the Far East

☐ *May 7* Ibuka Masaru and Morita Akio found Tōkyō Tsūshin Kyōgō (renamed as Sony on January 1, 1958)

☐ *September 27* The Labor Relations Adjustment Law takes effect

☐ *August 1* Japan Federation of Labor Unions holds inaugural meeting

☐ *August 16* Keidanren (Federation of Economic Organizations) begins operations

☐ *October 7* The Diet approves the new constitution

☐ *October 21* The Diet passes the Land Reform Bill

☐ *November 3* The emperor proclaims the new constitution

**1947**

☐ *January 31* MacArthur forbids a general strike scheduled for the next day

March 31 The Fundamental Law of Education is promulgated

April 14 The Diet passes the Anti-monopoly Law

May 3 The new constitution comes into effect

July MacArthur dissolves the Mitsubishi and Mitsui general trading companies

September 1 The Labor Standards Law takes effect, and the Ministry of Labor begins operations

December 18 The Diet passes the Law for the Elimination of Excessive Concentrations of Economic Power (Deconcentration Law)

December 22 The new Civil Code is promulgated (takes effect on January 1, 1948)

**1948**

November 12 The International Military Tribunal for the Far East renders its verdicts

December 23 Tōjō and six others sentenced to death by the International Military Tribunal for the Far East are hanged

**1949**

March 7 Joseph M. Dodge issues his economic prescriptions for Japan

May 24 MITI is created

October 1 The People's Republic of China comes into being

**1950**

May–December The "red purge" removes thousands of suspected communists from their jobs

June 25 The Korean War begins

July 8 MacArthur instructs the Japanese government to create the National Police Reserve

**1951**

April 11 Truman removes MacArthur from his position as SCAP and as commander of United Nations forces in Korea

September 8 Japan signs the San Francisco Peace Treaty and the United States–Japan Security Treaty

**1952**

April 28 The San Francisco Peace Treaty and the United States–Japan Security Treaty take effect

August 13 Japan joins the IMF and the World Bank

**1955**

July 20 The cabinet establishes the Economic Planning Agency

October 13 Parties on the left merge to form the Japan Socialist Party (JSP)

November 11 Conservative parties merge to form the Liberal Democratic Party (LDP)

The All-Japan Committee for Buraku Liberation, founded in 1946 as the successor to the prewar Suiheisha, changes its name to the Buraku Liberation League

The era of "high-speed growth" begins

**1956**

October 19 Officials from Moscow and Tokyo sign the Soviet–Japanese Joint Declaration

**1960**

May–June Demonstrations against the United States–Japan Security Treaty rack the country and force the resignation of Prime Minister Kishi

June 23 The Diet approves renewal of the United States–Japan Security Treaty

December 27 The Ikeda cabinet adopts the Income-Doubling Plan as official policy

**1964**

October 1 The Shinkansen "Bullet Trains" begin operations

October 10 The Tokyo Olympics opens

**1965**

June 22 Tokyo and Seoul conclude the Korea–Japan Treaty

August 3 The Pollution Countermeasures Basic Law takes effect

**1968**

October 17 Kawabata Yasunari receives the Nobel Prize in literature

Japan's output of goods and services surpasses that of West Germany and every other capitalist economy except that of the United States

**1969**

July 10 The government promulgates the Special Measures and Enterprise Law concerning Assimilation

**1972**

May 5 Okinawa reverts to Japan

September 29 Japan recognizes the PRC as the legitimate government of China

**1973**

The oil shock ends the era of "high-speed growth"

**1976**

February 4 The Lockheed scandal begins with allegations, voiced in the United States Senate, that former Prime Minister Tanaka and other Japanese politicians accepted bribes and kickbacks

**1978**

August 12 The China–Japan Peace and Friendship Treaty normalizes relations between the two governments

**1980**

December Nantonaku, kurisutaru ("Somehow, Crystal") becomes a best-seller

**1983**

January 26 Tanaka Kakuei is found guilty of accepting bribes and kickbacks from Lockheed

**1984**

May 27 The Utari Society drafts model legislation demanding greater civil rights for Ainu

**1985**

May 17 The Diet passes the Equal Employment Opportunity Law (implemented April 1, 1986)

September 22 Major trading nations agree on the Plaza Accord

**1986**

April 1 The Equal Employment Opportunity Law takes effect

**1987**

Per capita national income overtakes that of the United States

**1989**

January 7 The Shōwa Emperor dies

January 8 The monarchy formally proclaims Heisei as the new reign name

June 3 The Recruit Scandal brings down the Takeshita cabinet

June 26 The Korean Youth Association in Japan sends a letter to the United Nations Commission on Human Rights summarizing the leading demands of Koreans residing in Japan

**1990**

The Nikkei stock average falls by 40 percent from its closing high in December 1989, marking the onset of a decade of economic malaise

**1993**

March 27 Deputy Prime Minister Kanemaru Shin is arrested for accepting bribes

August 9 Hosokawa Morihiro becomes the first non-LDP prime minister since 1954

**1994**

December 10 Ōe Kenzaburō is presented with the Nobel Prize in Literature

⬜ The suicides of several middle-school students call public attention to the phenomena of schoolyard bullying

**1995**

⬜ *January 17* Thousands die when the Great Hanshin Earthquake rocks Kōbe and the surrounding area

**1997**

⬜ *November 3* Sanyo Securities, Japan's seventh-largest brokerage house, declares bankruptcy

⬜ *November 17* Burdened by nonperforming loans, the Hokkaidō Takushoku fails

⬜ *November 26* Yamaichi Securities, one of Japan's top four brokerages, announces it will voluntarily shut down

⬜ *December 15* The Bank of Japan's quarterly survey of business confidence indicates deep pessimism in the corporate sector about Japan's economic prospects

⬜ Juvenile crimes jump by 20 percent over the previous year, to a level not seen since 1975

# CHAPTER 15

# The Years of Occupation

On August 30, 1945, General Douglas MacArthur boarded his aircraft in the Philippines for the flight to Japan. During the journey MacArthur alternately napped and spoke with his adjutants about his hopes for the forthcoming occupation of his defeated enemy. These he phrased simply: to root out those elements of Japanese thought and behavior that had given birth to aggression and, in their place, nurture the growth of democracy. When his aircraft set down at 2:05 P.M. at Atsugi Air Base south of Tokyo, MacArthur demonstrated to the Japanese for the first time his uncanny ability to strike a dramatic gesture that would establish the tone for future action. The forward door of the aircraft came open, and General MacArthur, whose troops had brought the Empire of Japan to its knees, emerged unarmed and in shirtsleeves. He gazed slowly around him and then deliberately descended to the tarmac. "Melbourne to Tokyo; it was a long way" were MacArthur's first laconic words in Japan.[1]

MacArthur's landing—with no speeches, pageantry, or troops to review—simultaneously calmed apprehensions among those Japanese who feared a brutish military occupation and articulated the general's expectation that his former enemy would cooperate to democratize the country and return it to the rank of peaceful nations. MacArthur continued to communicate through gestures and symbols for the next several days. When Japanese and American representatives gathered on the USS *Missouri* in Tokyo Bay to sign the official instrument of surrender on September 2, the only ornamentation on the otherwise austere deck were two American flags. One had hung over the White House on the morning Pearl Harbor had been attacked, and the other was the thirty-one-star Old Glory that had flown from the mast of

Commodore Perry's ship when he sailed into the same bay nearly a century earlier and forced the shogunate to abandon its policy of national seclusion. We have prevailed, MacArthur signaled, and the second opening of Japan is about to begin.

## Americans and Japanese, MacArthur and Yoshida

On paper, the occupation of Japan was a joint Allied undertaking. The Far Eastern Commission, consisting of delegates from eleven (later thirteen) nations and headquartered in Washington, D.C., formulated general policy. Beneath the FEC came the Allied Council for Japan (ACJ in the alphabet soup nomenclature of the occupation years) and its agent, the Supreme Commander of the Allied Powers (SCAP), a term that referred to both the person and the office in charge of the day-to-day management of occupation business. Composed of representatives from the United States, the Soviet Union, China, and Australia, the Tokyo-based Allied Council for Japan functioned as the FEC's executive arm, meeting as circumstances dictated to discuss problems and advise SCAP about the best way to implement tactically the strategic measures mandated by the FEC.

Theory and praxis were two different matters, however. The United States had borne the brunt of the fighting in the Pacific, and it fully intended to assume exclusive responsibility for designing and managing the occupation of its former enemy. The State Department had begun planning for the occupation as early as 1942, even while American forces in the Pacific still were on the retreat. By the summer of 1945 American policy makers had agreed upon a set of priorities that they formally set down in the "United States Initial Post-Surrender Policy Relating to Japan." At the top of the docket were the dismemberment of the Japanese empire, constitutional revisions to strengthen the prerogatives of the Diet, dissolution of *zaibatsu* conglomerates, and severance of the linkages between Shinto and government. Having completed its preparations, the American government made certain that the FEC could do little more than rubber-stamp its policies. No FEC injunction, for instance, could take effect without the approval of the U.S. representative, and a further provision gave the United States the right to issue "unilateral interim directives" whenever the commission failed to act expeditiously, an action that the United States resorted to on several occasions.

Moreover, MacArthur turned the ACJ, which met in Tokyo on 162 occasions during the occupation, into a powerless debating society. Appointed

SCAP on August 14, 1945, MacArthur generally saw eye to eye with the early policy recommendations emanating from Washington, viewing them as the specific measures that would advance his own broadly defined goal of making Japan into a full-fledged democracy and a peaceful neighbor to all. Consequently, he habitually skipped ACJ meetings, and when he did attend, the general did not listen especially closely to what delegates said. Similarly, MacArthur routinely consigned ACJ memorandums to his circular file, preferring instead to send the council brief notes informing the delegates about measures that he already had undertaken on his own initiative. Before long he dropped even that courtesy. "SCAP directives came in writing in the early days; then they began to come verbally, and later not at all," recalled one official. In the end the ineffectual ACJ occupied little but the office where it convened its meetings.

With the FEC and ACJ pushed to the wings, MacArthur strode to center stage and seized every opportunity to stamp his personality on events. As SCAP, he did, in fact, wield astonishing powers, including the authority to dissolve the Diet, censor the press, disband political parties, and issue administrative directives that had the writ of law. He was, some said, the Blue-Eyed Shogun. MacArthur did nothing to dissuade the Japanese of that impression. Carefully, with symbol aforethought, he selected for his headquarters the Dai-Ichi Insurance Building. Situated just opposite the Imperial Palace, the Dai-Ichi was one of a very small number of Western-style structures left standing in bombed-out Tokyo, and its bold silhouette towered over the moat that encircled the emperor's residence. Moreover, when the throne's advisers raised the possibility of SCAP coming to the palace to meet the emperor, MacArthur instead summoned *him* to the general's personal residence in the former U.S. embassy building. The famous photograph of the occasion shows the lanky general, clad in an open-necked khaki shirt and without a necktie, towering over the diminutive monarch, who had carefully dressed in formal tails for the meeting. It was a graphic pairing of posture and clothing that left no doubt about who was the victor and who was the vanquished. "Tell the emperor . . ." began MacArthur through an interpreter.

For all MacArthur's grandiloquent language and exaggerated public posturing, however, he did not single-handedly determine the pace and direction of reform. Washington had decided that the occupation of Japan would be indirect. That is, the Japanese bureaucracy was left in place and took instructions from parallel agencies, or sections, within the Allied Powers General Headquarters (or, more commonly, GHQ), staffed by approximately five thousand Americans under MacArthur's command. MacArthur tended

*MacArthur and the emperor*

to treat GHQ personnel in much the same manner as he dealt with his battlefield commanders, assigning them tasks and then leaving it to them to
fight the battle. Happily for him, most key personnel shared his views about
what had led Japan into war and totalitarianism, and their enthusiasm and
hard work often carried the reforms forward faster than might otherwise
have been the case. Occupation lore is filled with such stories as that of
Lieutenant Ethel Weed, a member of the Civil Information and Education
Section of GHQ. That advocate of women's rights drove her jeep the length
of Japan in 1945 and 1946, meeting women of all ages and backgrounds,
sharing baths with them in rural hot springs, and urging them to take advantage of the new rights open to them. Japan, Lieutenant Weed's Japanese assistant noted, "was for her a piece of white cloth on which she was
free to paint to her heart's content."

Despite MacArthur's dominating personality and the energy of the U.S.
occupationaires, the Japanese also managed to assert their own will in the
immediate postwar years, and far from being passive objects manipulated
by American planners, they emerged as significant actors in their own right.
The Japanese bureaucracy was a powerful force that helped shove the occupation in certain directions. With the Japanese government continuing to
function, officials unsympathetic to SCAP had ample opportunity to derail

or at least hobble the intent of MacArthur's plans. Other ministers, however, rallied behind those occupation reforms that were similar to measures they and their predecessors had favored earlier, before the war intervened. Thus, as early as October 1945, activist bureaucrats within the Ministry of Agriculture and Forestry drafted a land reform bill, without any prodding or guidance from GHQ, that embodied many of the provisions put forward to deal with vexing tenancy problems in the prewar period.

If there was a symbolic counterpart to General MacArthur on the Japanese side, it was Yoshida Shigeru, who served as prime minister for a total of seven years between the spring of 1946, when he formed his first cabinet, and the late fall of 1954, when he stepped down from office. As a prewar diplomat Yoshida had held a variety of postings in China and the West, receiving his highest appointment as ambassador to Great Britain in 1936. Consistently throughout the 1920s and early 1930s, Yoshida had advocated a resolute policy toward China that would maintain peace and simultaneously permit Japan to expand its economic influence in northern Asia, yet he also had argued that cooperation with the West was necessary to win its approval for Japan's role in Asia. As a member of the "Anglo-American clique" within the Foreign Ministry Yoshida had strongly opposed the Tripartite Pact of 1940. Disgruntled with Japan's alliance with Germany, he sat out the war years as an ordinary citizen and in the spring of 1945 even spent two months in prison for his role in forming the YOHANSEN group.

Yoshida's record as an "internationalist" and his stint in jail won him a favorable reputation with SCAP, and occupation authorities encouraged him

---

**TABLE 15.1**  *Prime Ministers, 1945–1954*

| PRIME MINISTER | CABINET NUMBER | CABINET TERM |
| --- | --- | --- |
| Higashikuni Naruhiko | | August 17, 1945–October 9, 1945 |
| Shidehara Kijūrō | | October 9, 1945–May 22, 1946 |
| Yoshida Shigeru | First | May 22, 1946–May 24, 1947 |
| Katayama Tetsu | | May 24, 1947–March 10, 1948 |
| Ashida Hitoshi | | March 10, 1948–October 15, 1948 |
| Yoshida Shigeru | Second | October 15, 1948–February 16, 1949 |
| Yoshida Shigeru | Third | February 16, 1949–October 30, 1952 |
| Yoshida Shigeru | Fourth | October 30, 1952–May 21, 1953 |
| Yoshida Shigeru | Fifth | May 21, 1953–December 10, 1954 |

to serve as foreign minister in two early postwar cabinets, before he became prime minister. Perhaps because he was sixty-seven years old when he took that office for the first time, Yoshida had little patience with opposition to his policies, as suggested by his famous moniker One Man Yoshida. But his other nickname, the Pocket Churchill, more imaginatively captured his fondness not just for cigars and arrogant behavior but also for conservative politics and for an unyielding foreign policy that would best serve his nation's long-term economic interests. He came to the office of prime minister an unabashed patriot who believed that the 1930s and early 1940s were an aberration, a sad departure from the path of democracy and capitalism blazed by the enlightened leadership of the Meiji and Taishō periods. Moreover, he thought that the disgraces of the war years could be laid at the feet of a handful of militarists and fellow conspirators. Consequently, he argued, the occupation should consist of only a mild housecleaning, followed by an invigorating set of reforms that would rehabilitate the economy and reestablish Japan as a stable member of the international community of nations. Those views led him to oppose, and occasionally to work to overturn, some of SCAP's reforms, but it is doubtful whether Yoshida, any more than MacArthur, deserves quite as much credit for charting a course through the occupation years as his own rhetoric would suggest.

## Old Dreams, New Hopes, Ordinary People

Also bursting into excited activity during the autumn of 1945 were many of prewar Japan's dispossessed—women, labor leaders, and political activists on the left—who put forth their own plans for change, some of which they originally had formulated in the Taishō era and then set aside during "the period of national emergency." Consequently, Communists, many freed from years in prison on SCAP's orders, legally formed the Japan Communist Party in October 1945, and together with other leftists, who hailed the Americans as an "army of liberation" rather than as an "army of occupation," began organizing labor unions and advocating programs that, from their point of view, would help Japan transcend its militaristic, totalitarian past. Similarly, just days after the war ended, Ichikawa Fusae convened a Woman's Committee on Postwar Countermeasures, and later that year she organized and became president of the New Japan Women's League, an association that advocated the franchise and expansion of legal rights for women.

Many ordinary Japanese shared the desire to revive old dreams. Lieutenant Weed may have felt free to paint as she pleased when she began her

*Women voting in the Diet elections of 1946*

journey across Japan, but her images would have remained little more than meaningless scribbles if Japanese women themselves had not arranged them into a coherent view of the future. It was their support, nurtured by the leadership of women like Ichikawa and mindful of the legacy of struggle in the interwar era, that ensured success for a law, promulgated on December 17, 1945, that extended the right to vote to women. Of the 79 women who campaigned for seats in the House of Representatives in the first postwar election, held in April 1946, 39 emerged victorious. Women visited the polls in droves that April, when 67 percent of all eligible women cast ballots. This was less than the incredible 79 percent turnout rate for males, but because so many men had been killed in the war or were still overseas waiting to be mustered out of the service, more women (13.8 million) than men (12.8 million) voted in the House election.

If the aspirations of the past provided a beacon of inspiration, the trauma of war and defeat also had a profound impact on how men and women from all walks of life imagined a better future. For middle- and working-class families, everything was in short supply in the autumn of 1945: jobs, housing, food, and medicine, hopes and dreams most of all. According to SCAP's grim estimates, the war cost Japan one-third of its total wealth and one-half of its total potential income. Nearly six million servicemen and civilian expatriates returned to Japan by the end of 1947, touching off a ruthless scramble for jobs in an economy that stood on the brink of ruin. Inflation complicated matters. Even though the government placed price controls on a wide range of foods and commodities used in daily life, wholesale prices for such items rose by 539 percent in 1946 and 336 percent the next year. In the chaos of defeat, living standards plummeted to 65 percent of prewar levels in rural areas and to just 35 percent in cities.

It is difficult to exaggerate the bleakness of life in the first months, even years of peace. The Japanese called their cities *yaki-nohara* ("scorched fields"), and the first Americans to enter Tokyo were shocked by the devastation: "The little man suffered most," wrote one journalist, since the "terror bombing" razed "whole workers' districts."[2] Moreover, "Everything had been flattened for miles between Yokohama and Tokyo. Only thumbs stood up from the flatlands—the chimneys of bathhouses, heavy house safes and an occasional stout building with heavy iron shutters." Those fortunate enough to have a house left standing in the suburbs or nearby countryside took in relatives and friends, but in Japan's cities hastily constructed shantytowns became home to tens of thousands of families who crowded together in makeshift huts constructed from charred pieces of wood, tar paper, and other debris. The least fortunate, including war orphans and widows, took shelter in burned-out trolley cars and buses, the underground passageways of major train stations, and even caves burrowed into the urban rubble. In early 1947 Tōjō's younger brother was discovered among vagrants in Osaka, and as late as 1948 an astounding 3.7 million families still lacked housing of their own.

Poorly sheltered, the Japanese did not eat well either. The majority of civilians already were malnourished when the emperor announced Japan's surrender, and disastrous harvests in 1945 and 1947—a consequence of poor weather, broken-down transportation and distribution systems, insufficient fertilizer, worn-out equipment, and worn-out farmers—added to the misery. Just as they had done in the last year of the war, people relied on barley and potatoes rather than rice, mixed ground acorns and sawdust with flour when making dumplings and bread, and got what protein they could from worms, grasshoppers, rats, and frogs. The United States helped avert mass starvation during the winter of 1945–1946 by shipping emergency supplies of wheat, ground corn, powdered milk, and corned beef, but hunger shadowed everyone for a very long time. In 1947 the average family spent

*American occupationaries help feed the Japanese, 1945–1946*

70 percent of its income for food, nearly twice as much as poor urban laborers at the outbreak of the Manchurian Incident. Even so, most people
were surviving on approximately twelve hundred calories daily, about one-
half what the government said was sufficient for an ordinary adult.

Diseases flourished in the squalor and poverty of the middle and late
1940s. Between 1945 and 1948 some 650,000 people contracted cholera,
dysentery, typhoid fever, diphtheria, epidemic meningitis, polio, and other
communicable diseases. With the health care system in shambles and medicines in scarce supply, nearly 100,000 of them died. An old enemy, tuberculosis, carried off even more victims; in 1947 nearly 150,000 succumbed
to TB, and the disease claimed more than 100,000 lives annually until 1951.
In 1947 the infant mortality rate soared to 77 deaths per 1,000 births (compared to 5 per 1,000 forty years later). Nationwide, mortality rates reached
about 15 per 1,000 in 1947, versus 6 per 1,000 in the late 1980s.

For some, psychological trauma heaped more pain on top of illness and
material deprivation. Glorified in wartime rhetoric, widows of soldiers and
sailors discovered that government and society had little sympathy to spare
for their plight after 1945. Military paychecks no longer arrived in the mail,

and it was nearly impossible for women to compete with returning veterans for factory jobs. Her missing husband had abandoned the family business to "fight for the emperor," one woman complained in a letter to a major newspaper, but the world now merely turned a cold shoulder to her and her three children.[3] Public attitudes toward demobilized soldiers could be just as heartless. Ex-servicemen found themselves stigmatized as losers who had failed their nation or, as stories about wartime atrocities in China and Southeast Asia started to appear in the news media, even looked upon suspiciously as horrible creatures who had committed unspeakable acts. When he returned to Japan, one veteran wrote, "My house was burned, my wife and children missing. What little money I had quickly was consumed by high prices, and I was a pitiful figure. Not a single person gave me a kind word. Rather, they cast hostile glances my way."

In the midst of poverty, stories about large-scale corruption and individuals who bettered their lot at the expense of others proliferated, adding to the general sense of anguish and discontent. Coal, gasoline, cigarettes, lumber, cement, rolled steel, and other capital goods went missing by the tons as gangsters, corrupt industrialists, and greedy officers found a way to pilfer military stores. The pillage became so great that one government report, issued in July 1947, concluded that "the goods thus diverted from their proper channels and the individuals thus enriched are a cancer threatening the economy of this country." On a more intimate scale, everyone seemed to have heard about demobilized servicemen who smuggled home knapsacks stuffed with looted goods or scoundrels who furtively stripped clothing from the dead and stole blankets, some still stained with blood and sputum, from hospitals and sanitariums.

Such stories were not so farfetched, for a fair amount of illicit merchandise could be found on display in the seventeen thousand so-called blue-sky markets that sprang up around the country. Stall owners also sold and bartered legitimate goods: old clothing, pots and pans hammered out of used artillery casings, and food from the countryside. Thousands of families depended on the open-air markets for obtaining precious fresh vegetables and household wares that were not available anywhere else, but everything—whether it was acquired legally or simply had fallen off the wagon—was pricey. The vendors, many of whom were repatriated soldiers or discharged factory workers, mercilessly charged every yen they could get, while giving away as little as possible for things customers wanted to trade. One petty entrepreneur recalled treating an exhausted woman, her children in tow, with contempt, calling a treasured prewar kimono that she wanted to swap with him a moth-eaten rag in order to beat down the price.

They later may have regretted their tactics, but such marketers also remembered the thrill of making as much each day as an average white-collar worker earned in a month.

People responded to the dismal toughness of the postwar years in a variety of ways. Some retreated into a world of inebriation, while others entered the underworld in order to get enough money to live. Organized gangs preyed on the weak and vulnerable, homeless teenage boys peddled stolen food coupons and rolled drunks and vagrants, and women turned to prostitution. Some "women of the dark" prowled the streets together, such as the fifty members of the Blood Cherry Gang. More commonly, an individual woman struck up a relationship with a GI, a valuable source of cigarettes and liquor which she could barter on the black market, or simply sold the use of her body for food. "There were three consecutive days when I went without eating," remembered one young widow who lived in the bowels of a Tokyo train station in 1946. Then "a man I did not know gave me two rice balls. I devoured them. The following night he again brought me two rice balls. He then asked me to come to the park because he wanted to talk with me. I followed him. That is when I sank into the despised profession of being a 'woman of the dark.'"

As exhausted and despondent as they were, most Japanese gritted their teeth and tried to cope, to hold spirit and family together, despite how hopeless it might seem at times. As one housewife in the city of Kōfu wrote late in 1945, "With two children, one eleven and the other eight, ours is a family of four. For us, it is a forbidden spiritual luxury to think about our future. We are so preoccupied with daily life; our only concern is how to survive today—and hopefully tomorrow. We consume ten days' worth of rationed food in just five days. But we have to eat somehow and have no choice but to go and find food on the black market. My husband's monthly salary is ¥200, while our livelihood costs are about ¥600. To make ends meet, we sell everything we can. I know we cannot get along much longer this way."[4]

Such resilience eventually triumphed, and gradually, step by step, the Japanese began to rebuild their shattered lives and ruined country. As they revived old dreams and conjured up new hopes, they confronted the reforms being formulated by SCAP, and at the end of the day, the ordinary men and women of Japan emerged as potent agents for change. Whether it came to voting in elections, throwing their support behind the labor movement, enthusiastically endorsing land reform, or carefully scrutinizing proposals to amend the constitution, ultimately, few items on SCAP's agenda stood much chance of succeeding or enduring beyond the occupation years unless the Japanese people stood behind them.

## Demilitarization

Three *d*'s—demilitarization of Japanese society, democratization of the political process, and decentralization of wealth and power—spelled out the first phase of the occupation, conducted between 1945 and 1947. MacArthur arrived in Japan possessed of an unshakable belief that the Japanese military, *zaibatsu* conglomerates, and right-wing extremists had colluded to lead their country down the road to imperialistic conquest and ultimately to war with the United States and its allies. Japan's "feudalistic" nature, the general was fond of declaring, had propelled it into war, and a simple housecleaning thus would not be sufficient; the occupation needed to reform thoroughly both the Japanese state and Japanese society. MacArthur articulated his notion of how to accomplish that goal in a public statement released to Japanese newspapers on October 11, 1945, in which he stressed the need to rectify "the traditional social order under which the Japanese people for centuries have been subjugated." Specifically, he said, that effort must include the liberalization of the constitution, the emancipation of women, the encouragement of labor unionization, the opening of schools to more liberal education, and the "democratization" of Japanese economic institutions.

MacArthur began by dismantling Japan's colonial empire and destroying its potential to wage war. SCAP stripped Japan of Sakhalin, Manchuria, Korea, Taiwan, its Pacific mandate, and the territories it had seized in China, reducing the country to the four main islands that it had started with in 1868. In prompt fashion, occupation authorities abolished the army and navy and commenced the laborious task of demobilizing more than five million troops, nearly half of whom were still overseas, and overseeing the repatriation of three million civilians who lived in Japan's overseas possessions. As traumatic as that experience was for the returnees, from SCAP's perspective matters seemed to progress smoothly, just as MacArthur's shirt-sleeved landing at Atsugi Air Base suggested they would, and in January 1946 America withdrew one of its two armies of occupation.

Demilitarization segued into a ruthless purge, described in one newspaper headline as a "bloodless revolution." Just after the New Year's holidays of 1946, SCAP issued a directive with the ominous-sounding title "Removal and Exclusion of Undesirable Personnel from Public Office." The document disbanded ultranationalist groups and compelled the Japanese bureaucracy to form "screening committees" that would remove from public life all "active exponents of militarism and militant nationalism." The purge ran like an irresistible tide through Japanese society, and by the time it crested in the summer of 1948, more than 200,000 had lost their jobs. No level of society went unaffected. Former police officers turned in their badges, publishers and newspaper reporters emptied out their desks, and political figures by the score pounded the pavement searching for new ways to keep body and soul together. The purge even touched several prominent individuals who sympathized with SCAP reforms, such as Ichikawa Fusae, banished from public office for a time because of her association with state-sponsored women's organizations during the war.

The purge elicited various reactions. Thousands, horrified by what had befallen their county in the 1930s and 1940s, wrote letters denouncing the individuals they held responsible for the tragedy. Inside government, many officials thought that the purges went too far and victimized the innocent, and some bureaucrats sought ways to deflect the course of the purge and moderate its impact. Not surprisingly, the central bureaucracy itself emerged relatively unscathed since the civil servants who staffed the screening committees were predictably lenient toward themselves and fellow officials. Only 145 bureaucrats had to leave office, and 67 of them would have been spared if they had not belonged to the Budōkai (Martial Arts Club), an association of police administrators interested in judo and traditional Japanese fencing. But a GHQ official became alarmed after a translator misconstrued the club's name as the Military Virtues Association. When the same official later intercepted a letter one member sent to another, trying to cheer up his friend with the words "Let's not lose heart; we'll see better days," SCAP insisted that club members be added to the purge list.

No amount of bureaucratic cronyism, however, could save the men SCAP decided to prosecute as war criminals. During and after the war the Allies placed about six thousand Japanese on trial, primarily for atrocities committed in battle or against civilians in occupied countries, and executed more than nine hundred of them. On May 3, 1946, SCAP convened the International Military Tribunal for the Far East "for the just and prompt trial and punishment of the major war criminals in the Far East." The tribunal indicted twenty-eight former high-ranking government and military leaders, and in the subsequent months eleven judges, one each from the nine Allied countries that signed the instrument of surrender plus India and the Philippines, heard evidence that the accused conspired to plan Japan's aggression, waged war, or authorized or permitted atrocities.

Critics of the war crimes trials claimed that SCAP merely wanted "victors' justice." Participating in a nation's decision to wage war, they insisted, was not technically a war crime as defined by various conventions signed at The Hague and in Geneva. Furthermore, they regretted that the judges were not empowered to consider acts committed by Americans, an unpardonable omission for those who wanted to call Truman to task for dropping atomic bombs on Japanese cities. The judge from India agreed with that assessment. "The decision to use the atom bomb," he noted, caused "indiscriminate destruction of civilian life and property." Since "nothing of that magnitude could be traced to the accused," he argued, the twenty-eight Japanese defendants ought to be acquitted and released immediately.[5] Nevertheless, after nearly two years of deliberations, the tribunal sent seven men to the gallows, including Doihara Kenji and the former prime ministers Hirota Kōki and Tōjō Hideki. The ex-generals Araki Sadao, Koiso Kuniaki, and Minami Jirō were sentenced to life in prison, as were the former premier Hiranuma Kiichirō and Hashimoto Kingorō, founder of the Cherry Blossom Society. SCAP decided that Matsuoka Yōsuke was too ill to stand trial (he received final Catholic rites and died in Tokyo University Hospital in June 1946); it indicted but did not try Kishi Nobusuke and, for reasons that remain unclear, did not bring Ishiwara Kanji before the bar.

The emperor also escaped punishment. British and Soviet representatives to the FEC wanted to indict the monarch as a war criminal, seeing his participation in the imperial conferences as prima facie evidence that he had conspired to commit aggression and allowed atrocities to occur. Against that, some American planners in Washington, including the former ambas-

*Tōjō Hideki in the docket*

sador to Japan Joseph C. Grew, were more impressed by the emperor's role in ending the Two Twenty-six Incident; his caution in the autumn of 1941, when he instructed Tōjō to make a final diplomatic effort to salvage peace; and his decision to end hostilities in 1945. Moreover, they argued, if SCAP converted the imperial institution into a constitutional monarchy, the emperor could contribute to stability in the postwar era by ensuring the co-operation of the civil bureaucracy and helping hold together the social fabric of the nation. Without the throne, others feared, government and society might dissolve into chaos and open the door to a Communist takeover of Japan. MacArthur himself came down on the side of retaining the emperor as a symbol of state. Like Truman when the president contemplated using the bomb, MacArthur valued practical concerns over moral considerations. For centuries, the Blue-Eyed Shogun understood, the emperor had served as the protective umbrella legitimating those who ruled in his name, and the general appreciated the manner in which the monarch encouraged his people to accept SCAP directives. Lack of protection at the top, MacArthur believed, would threaten the success of the occupation.

## Democratization

SCAP permitted the emperor to stay, but America's insistence that Japan democratize its political process changed forever the monarch's position within the Japanese body politic. Prewar planning committees had proposed a massive restructuring of the Japanese political system, and in October 1945 the American secretary of state articulated the specific principles that SCAP should follow. The constitution had to be revised so that people enjoyed guaranteed civil liberties; the cabinet must answer to the legislature, not the emperor; and the Japanese government ultimately had to "derive its authority from and be responsible to the electorate."[6] MacArthur agreed wholeheartedly with those proposals. Quickly, he urged the prewar premier Konoe Fumimaro to take a leadership role in liberalizing the Japanese constitution and began to press the new prime minister, Shidehara Kijūrō, to name a committee to recommend specific restructuring measures.

Few of Japan's leaders, however, shared SCAP's belief that dramatic change was necessary. Shidehara initially balked at doing MacArthur's bidding, stating publicly that Japan could achieve democracy without altering the existing constitution. All that was needed, Shidehara claimed, was the passage of a few new laws, such as the expansion of the franchise to women. Minobe Tatsukichi added his support to the contention that democracy could flourish under the terms of the original 1889 constitution. Forced from the Diet and his university professorship in the 1930s for having advocated the organ theory of government, Minobe reentered public life in the post-war period as a distinguished constitutional expert and privy councillor. In a series of newspaper articles published in November 1945, Minobe stated his opposition to revisions "in this emergency situation." Konoe also skittered away from ideas about undertaking fundamental reforms. In late November he submitted a report to the emperor that strongly urged retaining the principle of imperial sovereignty, although it also recommended strengthening the role of the Diet. Even that modest suggestion died with the "well-meaning child of fate" in December, when Konoe committed suicide on the day of his scheduled arrest as a war criminal.

MacArthur, however, would not give up, and in response to SCAP prodding Shidehara appointed a committee of scholars and bureaucrats to consider the case for constitutional revision. Chaired by Matsumoto Jōji, a legal scholar and minister of commerce and industry for a brief time in the 1930s, the committee still was in the midst of its deliberations when the *Mainichi shinbun* newspaper on February 1, 1946, published what it billed as a draft constitution that the committee planned to submit to the cabinet and Diet for approval. The conservative bias of the document was clearly evident. On the one hand, it expanded civil rights and assigned the Diet broader duties, such as the responsibility for appointing cabinets. On the other hand, such concessions to SCAP's well-known preferences came only grudgingly. Human rights, as in the 1889 constitution, were not made absolute and could be restricted by legislation. Moreover, the Matsumoto committee reaffirmed the principle of imperial sovereignty, and it called for the retention of Japan's armed forces.

Reaction to the Matsumoto draft was swift, and overwhelmingly unfavorable. The popular press ridiculed the effort as too superficial and conservative, as did thousands of ordinary men and women across Japan, who wrote derisive letters to the editor. Whatever the nation's leaders felt about the need for constitutional revision, clearly vast segments of the war-weary Japanese population wanted more than a cosmetic make-over; they supported thoroughgoing reform that would remove militarists from power, expand personal liberties, and ensure that the disasters of the 1930s and early 1940s never be repeated. Indeed, even as the Matsumoto committee was deliberating during the winter months of 1945–1946, groups of politically aware Japanese were busy writing their own constitutions, just as ordinary citizens had done in the 1880s when Itō Hirobumi crafted Japan's first "fundamental law of the state." Most drafts circulated publicly at the beginning of 1946 were decidedly liberal and called for curtailing the prerogatives of the emperor, relocating sovereignty with the people, and guaranteeing civil rights.

Privately, MacArthur was irate with Matsumoto. The general considered the proposed constitutional changes utterly unacceptable, so trivial that they left Japan's political structure basically unaltered. On February 3, MacArthur instructed General Courtney Whitney, chief of the Government Section of GHQ, to prepare a model constitution that could serve as a "guide" for the Shidehara cabinet. For one extraordinary week, a task force of GHQ staff members—two dozen career officers and former civilians, including several lawyers, a smattering of professors and journalists, an ex-congressman, and a Wall Street investor—held their own constitutional convention in the sixth-floor ballroom of the Dai-Ichi Insurance Building. It was an incredible, audacious undertaking; never before had conquerors rewritten their enemy's national charter. Nevertheless, the drafting committee took up its assignment with idealism, confidence, and what one member called a humanistic spirit. As another participant recalled, at no time did she ever contemplate punishing the Japanese or even try to teach them something. Rather, she and her colleagues believed their responsibility was to write a document that would help create a more democratic and egalitarian Japan, the kind of society most Japanese desired but could not obtain from the country's current leadership.

After just six hectic days Whitney presented the draft of an entirely new constitution to General MacArthur. Pleased, the supreme commander instructed Whitney to present mimeographed copies of the so-called MacArthur constitution to Matsumoto's committee, symbolically enough, on February 13 (February 12 in the United States, Abraham Lincoln's birthday). It was a tense meeting. The Japanese representatives "appeared visibly surprised and disturbed" by many aspects of the MacArthur blueprint.[7] The emperor would continue to occupy the throne, but no longer would he play a direct role in the political process. Nor would he be considered "sacred and inviolable," as proclaimed in the 1889 constitution. Rather, the very first article in the MacArthur draft deprived the chrysanthemum throne of sovereignty and converted the monarch into "the symbol of the State and of the unity of the people, deriving his position from the will of the people with whom resides sovereign power."[8] Henceforth, the emperor's specific political duties would be limited to purely ceremonial functions, and even on these occasions he could act "only with the advice and approval of the Cabinet."

The MacArthur draft also disestablished Shinto and separated church from state by providing that "No religious organization shall receive any privileges from the State" and by declaring that "The State and its organs shall refrain from religious education or any other religious activity." That clause represented the culminating step in a protracted effort to strip the emperor of his divinity and dress him in new secular clothing. On December 15, 1945, SCAP had fired its opening salvo when it issued a decree ordering a cessation of state support for all shrines and prohibited "the dissemination of Shinto doctrines in any educational institution supported wholly or in part by public funds." Such practices, the document declared, had perverted "Shinto theory and beliefs into militaristic and ultra-nationalistic propaganda designed to delude the Japanese people and lead them into wars of aggression."[9]

The process of converting the throne into a civil, and ceremonial, monarchy moved a step forward on New Year's Day 1946, when the emperor released to the press a rescript that became popularly known as his Declaration of Humanity. Written chiefly in response to prompting from personnel in GHQ, the document stated in Japanese that the emperor should not be considered an *akitsu-mikami* ("manifest god"). The reliance on that esoteric and obscure circumlocution was significant, for while the term signified that the emperor was not a living son of God in a Western sense, it did not unequivocally repudiate his mythical and divine descent from Sun Goddess Amaterasu. To please SCAP, however, the official English translation rendered *akitsu-mikami* more loosely as "divine": "The ties between me and my people have always been formed by mutual trust and affection. They do not depend upon mere legends or myths. Nor are they predicated on the false conception that the emperor is divine, and that the Japanese are superior to other races and destined to rule the world."[10] The imprecise use of language did not trouble SCAP, whose officials blessed the rescript as the emperor's "renunciation of divinity," just as they later believed that MacArthur's constitution drove the final wedge between the throne and Shinto.

In addition to questions of imperial sovereignty and the role of the emperor in postwar Japan, the Matsumoto committee expressed its concern about Article 9, the famous "peace clause." In its final form, Article 9 stated that "the Japanese people forever renounce war as a sovereign right of the nation and the threat or use of force as a means of settling international disputes" and further pledged that "land, sea, and air forces, as well as other war potential, will never be maintained." It is not clear who first articulated the idea for a peace clause. The concept probably originated with MacArthur himself, although years later Shidehara claimed that he suggested it to the general during a meeting early in 1946. Whatever the genesis of the idea, its inclusion in the MacArthur draft startled members of the Matsumoto committee, for no other modern state ever had constitutionally renounced war as a "sovereign right" of the nation.

Other provisions in the MacArthur draft were less earthshaking, but they contributed just as greatly to an unambiguous reordering of Japan's political system. Very pointedly the GHQ document affirmed the principle of parliamentary supremacy by proclaiming the Diet to be "the highest organ of state power" and the "sole law-making organ of the State." Moreover, the new "fundamental law of the state" made the cabinet collectively responsible to the legislature. Specifically, it entrusted the Diet with appointing the prime minister and provided that the premier and his cabinet must resign en masse if the legislature passed a no-confidence resolution. The constitution further strengthened the Diet's role by abolishing all nonparliamentary agencies such as the Privy Council, which previously had shared decision-making powers with the cabinet and legislature.

Thirty-one articles in the MacArthur draft strengthened the fundamental civil rights of the Japanese populace. Significantly, these were to be "guaranteed" as "eternal and inviolate rights." That is, they were considered absolute, and not subject to limitation by law, as had been the case in the 1889 constitution and in the Matsumoto draft. Many, such as the "right to life, liberty, and the pursuit of happiness," were familiar to any student of the American constitutional system. One article provided for "universal adult suffrage," whereas other clauses promised freedom of assembly and the press, stated that no person could be arrested "without the immediate privilege of counsel," and decreed that people shall be secure in their homes against unreasonable search and seizure. Interestingly enough, the MacArthur draft was even more liberal than its American prototype, for it also provided for academic freedom, free universal education, the promotion of public health and social security, choice of occupation, marriage based on mutual consent, the right of workers to organize and bargain collectively, and the right of everyone "to maintain the minimum standards of wholesome and cultured living."

Alarmed at the implications of the document presented to him, Matsumoto at once huddled with Prime Minister Shidehara. When Whitney handed the GHQ draft to his committee, Matsumoto reported, the general made it abundantly clear that should the Japanese refuse to adopt the principles of the American document, SCAP "could not answer for whatever might happen to the emperor," implying that the monarch would be put on trial as a war criminal.[11] Think that over, Whitney suggested at one point, while he and his aides took a stroll in the garden to "enjoy some of your atomic sunshine," a cynicism that made it abundantly clear who was calling the shots. Moreover, the intense public debate about constitutionalism had drawn a tight circle around the prime minister's options. To turn a cold shoulder to MacArthur's draft would risk arousing even more stinging public criticism of the Matsumoto document, which contained few of the SCAP provisions that were likely to be very popular among the Japanese population, such as the lengthy list of personal rights and freedoms.

Shidehara sought a meeting with MacArthur to sound out the possibility of a compromise. A three-hour discussion between the two took place on February 22, 1946, and the general was unyielding. The supreme commander carefully spelled out once again his support for the basic principles articulated in the GHQ draft, and he repeated his belief that the British and Soviet representatives would insist upon abolishing the throne if liberalization of the constitution did not proceed forthwith. Shidehara caved in and instructed Matsumoto to reconvene his committee and revise its draft in accordance with the American model. The GHQ task force reviewed and approved the committee's new version on March 4, and Matsumoto submitted it to the Japanese cabinet the following day. Its essentials conformed very closely to the original MacArthur draft. The only substantial alteration was the provision for a bicameral Diet, agreed upon by MacArthur and Shidehara in the meeting on February 22.

Passage proceeded relatively smoothly. The cabinet released the text to the press on March 6, 1946, and all major political parties quickly came out in favor of the new constitution except for the Communist Party, which wished to indict the emperor as a war criminal and institute a Japanese People's Republic. The document then went to the Diet, which voted its approval on October 7, following some additional tinkering with vocabulary and sometimes heated objections by conservatives about relocating the locus of sovereignty and about the ways in which the new constitution might negatively affect the "national polity" (kokutai). Finally, on November 3, 1946—the ninety-fourth anniversary of the birth of Emperor Meiji—his grandson, the Shōwa emperor, promulgated the new constitution as an amendment to the original 1889 document. The new provisions about the separation of church and state notwithstanding, the emperor dutifully, in time-honored tradition, reported his actions to his ancestors in special commemorative ceremonies held at three major Shinto shrines, and the new constitution took effect on May 3, 1947.

## Decentralization

Another purpose of the American occupation of Japan was to blast apart the concentrations of wealth and power claimed by Japan's wartime elites, dismantle the structures through which they worked their supposedly evil ways, and encourage the growth of new constituencies that would support SCAP and its reform program. Thus, as 1945 turned into 1946, word went out from the Dai-Ichi Building to GHQ personnel instructing them to break up the *zaibatsu* conglomerates, foster the growth of labor unions, carry out a rural land reform program, remove control over education from the hands of the central bureaucracy, and rewrite the civil code.

As with so many other occupation initiatives, policy makers in Washington made the original decision to raze Japan's largest conglomerates, to engage in "*zaibatsu* busting," as it sometimes was called. According to official thinking, statistical evidence indicated that major *zaibatsu* dominated perhaps three-quarters of Japan's industrial and commercial activities. For many American planners, two suppositions flowed from the data. One was that the heads of those conglomerates had conspired with the military to enlarge Japan's overseas empire, thus bringing on war with China and the United States. The large *zaibatsu*, in the words of one famous American antimonopolist, were "the architects of Japan's irresponsible government."[12] The second assumption was that wealth of such magnitude inherently was antithetical to the growth of democracy. In words that brought nods of agreement from SCAP, the head of one State Department mission, dispatched to Japan late in 1945 to investigate big business, reported that the "concentration of economic control enabled the *zaibatsu* to continue a semifeudal relationship between themselves and their employees, suppress wages, and hinder the development of independent political ideologies. Thus the formation of the middle class, which was useful in opposing the militarist group in other democratic countries, was retarded."[13]

The Japanese were not oblivious of the intentions of the American occupation authorities. Business leaders recognized that some degree of *zaibatsu* dissolution was inevitable, and they hastily came forth with their own plans in the hopes of minimizing SCAP's ax wielding. Thus, early in November 1945 the Yasuda *zaibatsu* put forward a proposal for economic reform that immediately won the endorsement of the Mitsui, Mitsubishi, and Sumitomo conglomerates. Under the Yasuda plan, each of the four major *zaibatsu* holding companies would sell its stock to the public, whereupon the company directors, together with all *zaibatsu* family members employed in the enterprises, would resign their offices.

MacArthur accepted the Yasuda proposal on November 6, 1945, but with the proviso that SCAP reserved the right to undertake additional, more radical measures. Eventually, with support from the influential Whitney, MacArthur decided that the *zaibatsu* needed to be rid of more than just their top directors and family members. Consequently, beginning in January 1947, some six hundred corporate officers found their names added to the purge list. Hundreds of other managers resigned in anticipation of being driven from their posts, and ultimately a total of nearly fifteen hundred businessmen, including almost one in every four top-level executives, left their companies. To the mounting frustration of some GHQ officials, however, many of those men soon resurfaced in new corporate settings since they were banned only from employment in certain companies, not from working altogether. Thus, the ousted head of the Mitsui Bank became the chairman of the board of the fledgling Sony Company, which benefited greatly from his experience and personal contacts with Japan's other business elites.

SCAP stepped up its campaign against the *zaibatsu* in 1947. In April American occupation authorities pressured the Diet to pass the Antimonopoly Law, which prohibited cartels and monopolistic holding companies. As soon as the law went into effect in July, MacArthur rocked the Japanese business world by dramatically ordering the dissolution of two corporate giants, the Mitsubishi and Mitsui general trading companies. Subsequently, in the fall of 1947, MacArthur urged the Diet to pass the Law for the Elimination of Excessive Concentrations of Economic Power, which authorized dismantling any company that so dominated a particular market that potential newcomers were unlikely to survive. When GHQ estimated that the new legislation might be applied to more than one thousand Japanese firms, reaction within business circles was largely negative, and even many who tolerated the abolition of major *zaibatsu* spoke out against the new measure. But MacArthur had his way. In a hectic night session of the Diet on December 18, with SCAP supporters working every cloakroom and the clock turned back at 11:59 P.M. to delay the scheduled closure of that year's legislative session, both houses reluctantly approved the already infamous Deconcentration Law, as the bill was known for short.

MacArthur and his allies within GHQ also saw a vigorous labor union movement as essential to the decentralization of economic power. Many positive benefits, SCAP believed, would flow from striking a more equitable balance between labor and management. Specifically, the abolition of "feudal" relationships between employers and employees would correct the gross maldistribution of incomes that characterized the interwar period, contribute to the emergence of an industrial democracy, and guard against any future resurgence of militarism. At the same time, MacArthur hoped, improved working conditions and higher wages would create a constituency of middle-class wage earners who could be counted on to support SCAP's overall reform program.

Early in the fall of 1945 MacArthur declared his expectation that Japan elevate the status of workers by guaranteeing their right to organize, bargain collectively, and engage in strikes. To his delight, he found himself pushing against a door that already was beginning to open, for many Japanese bureaucrats championed greater rights for workers. Their attitudes reflected ideas advanced earlier by the "shepherds of the people" within the Home Ministry, who, during the Taishō decades, had lobbied for tougher factory legislation and favored workers' health insurance in hope of minimizing the kinds of conflicts that inevitably seemed to accompany industrialization in Western nations. As Japan had sunk deeper into the China bog in the 1930s, bureaucrats increasingly had redirected their efforts to regulating labor-management relations in a manner that served Japan's wartime mobilization, and the establishment of the government-controlled Sanpō in November 1940 spelled the demise of an independent labor movement. The new opportunities of the postwar years, however, reinvigorated labor's advocates within the bureaucracy, and allied with them were other Japanese who believed that it was necessary to promote trade union activities to prevent a total industrial breakdown. Thus, several days before MacArthur publicly identified economic democratization as one of SCAP's primary goals on October 11, 1945, the Japanese cabinet appointed a group of bureaucrats, scholars, and labor leaders to draft model labor legislation.

Impressed, SCAP remained largely on the sidelines as that deliberative body rapidly drew up the Trade Union Law, which the Diet passed in December 1945. To a great extent, the bill anticipated what the Japanese thought MacArthur wanted: It repeated provisions of the Wagner Act, passed in the United States in 1935, that guaranteed all workers in both the private and public sectors (excluding only firemen, police, and prison guards) the rights to organize, engage in collective bargaining, and participate in strikes. Alongside those foreign-inspired clauses, the Trade Union Law contained articles taken almost verbatim from measures drafted by Home Ministry bureaucrats in the interwar period (but not passed by the Diet), such as a provision that shielded unions from claims for damages arising from the legal exercise of their rights.

The Japanese government took the initiative in enacting two other important pieces of labor legislation in 1946 and 1947. The Labor Relations Adjustment Law also drew inspiration from the Wagner Act and prohibited unfair practices by management, such as refusing to recognize unions, discharging or otherwise discriminating against workers for union activities, and interfering in internal union affairs. To gain those legal protections, however, unions had to register with the government and demonstrate that they were "democratic" organizations whose purpose was to engage in collective bargaining, not in political activities. The Labor Standards Law, the last of the so-called three fundamental labor laws, dealt with minimum wages, maximum hours of work (eight hours a day, forty-eight in a week), paid holidays, plant safety, apprentice training, and the employment of women and children. Finally, to administer these laws, the Japanese government in 1947 established a Ministry of Labor, with Yamakawa Kikue, the prewar political activist, serving as chief of the section concerned with women and youth.

Heady with the new protections that surrounded their activities and eager to protect their jobs in precarious times, Japan's workers organized on an unprecedented scale. No factory worker carried a union card in August 1945, but by January 1946 nearly 1,200 unions had come into existence with a total membership of nearly 900,000 workers, more than double the prewar peak. The numbers quickly swelled to 4.8 million workers and 17,000 unions by the end of 1946 and to 6.7 million workers and 33,900 unions by mid-1948, when nearly one-half of the work force belonged to unions. Most of the new labor organizations were so-called enterprise unions. That is, rather than form industry-wide, horizontal unions that recruited all workers who possessed particular job skills and then establish subordinate chapters at several firms, postwar labor leaders favored company-specific, vertical unions that enrolled nearly all employees within a given firm—both white- and blue-collar workers, skilled as well as unskilled—excluding only the top echelons of management. Prewar rhetoric, which stressed the familylike nature of the firm, employee loyalty, and employer paternalism, had prepared the way for the growth of enterprise unions, and the perception, common in 1946 and 1947, that employment security depended on one's becoming permanently attached to a stable company encouraged their proliferation. Concurrently, labor leaders organized a few nationwide labor federations— notably the moderate Japan Federation of Labor Unions, re-created from the prewar Sōdōmei, and the more militant, Communist-led Congress of Industrial Labor Unions of Japan—to help keep company unions informed about developments elsewhere and to assist them in coordinating their activities.

Occupation authorities also regarded land reform as one of the primary means to promote democracy and prevent the resurgence of militarism. To

SCAP's way of thinking, high tenancy rates had intensified the rural depression of the interwar decades and turned villages into fertile breeding grounds for ultranationalism. When Japan surrendered in 1945, close to 50 percent of the country's population of seventy-two million still lived in agricultural villages, and about one-quarter of all farm families owned less than 10 percent of the land they cultivated. Fearing that continued rural poverty might generate unrest and derail the entire SCAP reform program, MacArthur on December 9, 1945, issued a public declaration informing the Japanese public and government about exactly what needed to be done: confiscate fields from landlords and sell them at affordable prices to tenants.

As straightforward as that proposal might seem, it is improbable that SCAP could have carried out such a fundamental reordering of society without the cooperation of the Japanese government and the participation of a substantial portion of the farming population itself. Indeed, before the war many Japanese had seen rural tenancy as a significant "social problem," and in 1945 some bureaucrats began to plan for land reform even before MacArthur announced his thoughts about the matter. A reform bill, drafted by officials within the Ministry of Agriculture and Forestry, passed the Diet in December 1945, but SCAP voiced its disappointment after its calculations showed that only about one-third of Japan's tenant families would be able to acquire enough land to support themselves. That set off a round of discussions among Japanese bureaucrats and GHQ officials, and when Yoshida Shigeru became prime minister in 1946, he put his weight behind a new measure, which passed the Diet on October 21.

The land reform bill of 1946 authorized the government to purchase all land belonging to absentee landlords. It also permitted resident landlords to keep only as much land as their families could cultivate (approximately 2.5 acres in most prefectures; 10 in Hokkaidō), plus an additional amount that they could rent out (about 5 acres in most cases). The state compensated landlords according to a complicated formula based on 1945 rice prices and production costs, and the government resold the land it acquired to former tenants at the purchase price. The buyers could either pay cash or take a thirty-year 3.2 percent mortgage.

By most measures, the land redistribution program was as dramatic and as filled with consequence as any reform undertaken during the occupation years. Nary a single family in all the villages of Japan went unaffected, as the government purchased several million acres of land from 2.3 million landowners and resold it to 4.7 million tenant farmers. Needless to say, many landlords felt that they had been deprived of their livelihoods unfairly. "My father's death, the land reforms, the heavy taxes, all reduced our family to penury," recalled one young man, filled with self-pity. "We had to bid farewell to the way of life that, from the time of our ancient ancestors, saw many tenants labor for our well-being. Now we had to use our own anemic arms to work the land ourselves."[14] In one especially gruesome case a former landlord, whose military unit finally was repatriated from China in 1946, killed three tenant families and set fire to six houses when he discovered that he would have to relinquish most of his land.

Families that were land-poor, by contrast, benefited enormously. Overnight, tenancy became a thing of the past. By 1950, when the land reform program was completed, only a minuscule number of farm families still owned less than 10 percent of the land they farmed, and resident-owners cultivated nearly 90 percent of all paddy. Moreover, they acquired their new holdings at incredibly low prices. By the final year of the program the hyperinflation of the postwar era had reduced the actual purchase price to approximately 5 percent of the yield of the land. Put another way, in 1950 a tenant could pay off the mortgage on a quarter acre of paddy for the cost of just thirteen packages of cigarettes, whereas the same piece of land in 1939 sold for an amount equivalent to a nine-year supply of cigarettes, a price far beyond the reach of an ordinary tenant family.

As landlords lost their wealth, they also bade farewell to their status as village elites, replaced by a broad class of independent farmers who, as SCAP hoped, prospered and became increasingly inclined to support the principles of democracy and capitalism. "Before the war," reminisced one farmer many years later, "you could work and work and work and you never saved money, could never eat delicious food, couldn't eat enough food. Now even without working your guts out you have money left over—well, not that much left over, but enough so that we don't feel in need—and our everyday life is sheer luxury compared with what it used to be."[15] Perhaps, for once, MacArthur was not outrageously guilty of vainglorious hyperbole when he declared that he knew of no more successful land reform program since the time of the Roman Empire.

The need for educational reform, another prominent example of decentralization, occupied the minds not only of SCAP but also of Japanese government authorities and the general public. In March 1946 a group of twenty-seven American educators arrived for a three-week whirlwind tour of Japan, and they confidently prepared a set of recommendations based on the principle that "control of the schools should be widely dispersed rather than highly centralized."[16] That autumn SCAP placed before a Japanese commission the full report, and the Japanese government soon transferred a great deal of jurisdiction over the school system from the Ministry of Education to popularly elected prefectural school boards empowered to select teachers, decide texts, and set the curriculum. The prewar multitrack system, considered elitist and thus undemocratic, was scrapped in favor of an American-style single-track system that included six years of elementary school, three years of junior high school, and three years of high school. At the same time, the government expanded the system of higher education by funding a number of four-year colleges.

In addition to structural changes, officials addressed questions of educational philosophy. Responding to criticisms that ultranationalistic values had corrupted the interwar curriculum, the government retired the Imperial Rescript on Education and in 1947 introduced the Fundamental Law of Education, which declared that the primary goal of the education system was to "esteem individual dignity and endeavor to bring up people who love truth and peace."[17] By that date schools already had dropped the prewar ethics courses, and educators were busy rewriting textbooks to emphasize the virtues of democracy and pacifism. The faculty in most public primary and secondary schools quickly embraced the new orthodoxy. Ashamed of their role in promoting militaristic values, grief-stricken over the deaths of so many of their students who had gone into battle clinging to the ideologies and repeating the slogans they had learned in the classroom, and appalled by the miserable living conditions of the postwar years, most teachers were only too happy to dedicate themselves to another objective set by the Fundamental Law of Education: "to contribute to the peace of the world and welfare of humanity by building a democratic and cultural state."

Determined to exterminate authoritarian concentrations of social power, SCAP urged Japanese authorities to revise the Meiji Civil Code. In particular, MacArthur wanted to abolish the "feudalistic" authority that male heads of family exerted over wives and children and revoke the privileged position accorded to eldest sons. Not all Japanese saw eye to eye with the supreme commander; conservatives such as the legal scholar Nakagawa Zennosuke extolled the old family system as "the very root of Oriental morality" and "the glory of the Japanese spirit." Nevertheless, as was the case with so many other occupation reforms, large numbers of Japanese were interested in the same ends as the Americans. In this case, women had harangued against the civil code for years before the war, and their discontent blazed forth in 1945 and 1946, as constitutional revision and expansion of the franchise augured a brave new world of gender equality. Consequently, the Justice Ministry appointed a review commission even before SCAP passed along word that it expected to see a new civil code, and in retrospect many Japanese involved in the effort tended to minimize SCAP's role. "Japan moved to abolish the family system of her own volition. Abolition was not forced on us by General MacArthur," was the way Okuno Ken'ichi, director of the Civil Affairs Bureau and later a Supreme Court justice, remembered it. Another member of the commission agreed, claiming that amending the chapters on inheritance and domestic relations were necessary in order to bring family law into conformity "with the new constitution's emphasis on the dignity of the individual and the equality of the sexes." Alfred Oppler, the SCAP member assigned to oversee proceedings, concurred with such assessments. His staff never ordered, or even urged, a completed revision of the old ordinance, Oppler wrote, and the commission "did a more thorough job than we had expected."[18]

## The Reverse Course

As rapid and consequential as SCAP's Herculean efforts to reform Japan were, time brought a shift in occupation policy, a modulation so distinct that many heralded it as a reverse course. The term was too simplistic, for MacArthur would never permit himself to do a complete about-face, but after 1947 the old soldier began to modify some reform measures and even acquiesced to the almost total overturning of others. No single reason inspired the reorientation of occupational policy, and no one person or agency choreographed its progression, but as the United States struggled to come to terms with its new global and strategic responsibilities in the postwar era, enthusiasm for further reform waned, and the *d*'s of 1945–1947 gave way to the *r*'s of reconstructing the economy, restraining labor, rehabilitating individuals who had been driven from their jobs and professions, rearming the military, and realigning Japan fully with the Western comity of nations.

Many who advocated turning in new directions were reacting to the specter of international communism, which seemed to them to cast an ever-lengthening shadow over East Asia in the late 1940s. The onset of the Cold War with the Soviet Union, the creation of Soviet satellite states in Eastern Europe, the growing realization that Mao Zedong was destined to prevail in China, and the increasingly bitter hostility between the two Koreas convinced many U.S. officials that their foreign policy required a stable, democratic Japan capable of standing as a bulwark against the further spread of communism in the Pacific region. Political stability in turn seemed to hinge on Japan's economic revival. In a widely quoted speech delivered in San Francisco on January 6, 1948, President Harry S. Truman's secretary of the army sounded those themes. "New developments were arising" in Asia, the secretary declared, that required Japan to have a "free government" and a "sound and self-supporting economy" so that it could "serve as a deterrent against any other totalitarian war threats."[19] Unequivocally, Japan was to become America's Pacific ally. The best way for SCAP to help Japan fulfill its new mission, other officials added, was to encourage economic revitalization by pulling a choke collar on a labor movement that had become too exuberant and by calling an end to *zaibatsu* busting, which, in the words of one SCAP critic, threatened to turn Japan into an impoverished nation of "mere shopkeepers."

The so-called Japan Lobby soon chimed in. Standing at the center of that group were ex-Ambassador Grew and several former State Department officials who had participated in wartime planning for the occupation. Even then they had argued that a healthy Japanese economy was a prerequisite for long-term peace in the Pacific. Moreover, they disagreed with the prevailing notion that the older *zaibatsu*, such as Mitsui and Mitsubishi, were militaristic. To be certain, the heads of such conglomerates were loyal patriots who had supported their country during the Greater East Asia War, and their companies had produced munitions for the army and navy. Nevertheless, according to the Japan Lobby, the old-line *zaibatsu* had not advocated military expansion in the 1930s, and abolishing them served no good purpose. Such views had lost out to more drastic ideas for reform in 1945 and 1946, but in the closing years of the decade the frustrated former planners rephrased their arguments for publication in *Newsweek*, the unofficial organ of the Japan Lobby, whose pages carried the complaint that the Deconcentration Law threatened to "atomize the Japanese business structure as effectively as the famous bomb destroyed Hiroshima."[20]

American businessmen fleshed out the ranks of the Japan Lobby, adding their voices to the call for a reverse course. After visiting Japan in the autumn of 1947 on a fact-finding mission for investment firms, James Lee Kauffman, whose law offices had represented many U.S. companies doing business in prewar Japan, compiled a lengthy report that had considerable impact on official thinking in Washington. In it, he cautioned America's most powerful corporations to hold off investing in Japan. To do so would be reckless, he declared, because "crackpots" within SCAP were promoting "socialism" and engineering reforms that would result in economic collapse, "much to the delight of severeal hundred Russians serving in the Soviet Embassy in Tokyo."[21]

As debate over SCAP's economic policies unfolded, elected officials discovered other reasons to assail MacArthur's policies. In Congress, prominent senators and representatives took the podium to express deep concern about what they regarded as dangerous Communist involvement in Japan's burgeoning labor movement, while others contended that the occupation simply was costing the U.S. Treasury too much. The United States spent nearly $600 million on salaries and food for SCAP personnel in the first two years of the occupation, and indirect costs were even more considerable. Japanese economic revitalization, the new argument went, would provide relief for the overburdened American taxpayer.

Stringent demands emanating from Japanese circles added to the crescendo of criticism. Perhaps SCAP's most vocal faultfinder was Yoshida Shigeru. Although he had supported some of MacArthur's initiatives during his first term as prime minister, from May 1946 until the spring of the following year, Yoshida more frequently disagreed with the supreme commander. Still, the premier had little choice but to bite his tongue as SCAP pursued the purge, broke up the *zaibatsu*, relocated the emperor within the constitutional system, and tilted the scales in favor of labor over management. In elections held in January 1949, however, Yoshida's Liberal Party won a stunning victory at the polls and established the parliamentary base for the Yoshida era, which was to last until One Man stepped down as prime minister late in 1954. As he sensed his grasp of the premiership becoming more secure during the late 1940s, Yoshida vigorously harangued SCAP to redirect its efforts toward advancing economic stabilization and reconstruction. In addition, he seized every opportunity to proclaim another of his views: Responsible bureaucrats, conservative party politicians, and business leaders must be left alone to implement their own designs for an independent, economically prosperous, and politically stable Japan.

At first MacArthur tried to deflect the criticism that fell upon SCAP from so many quarters, but during the late 1940s the occupation began to rotate, gear by single gear, toward new goals. Revision first came to labor policy, and events within Japan triggered the change. As workers flocked to their enterprise unions during the autumn of 1946, the contentious Congress of Industrial Labor Unions of Japan called for a nationwide labor offensive to win a "living wage" and permanent job security. In response, more than 2.6 million union members, including schoolteachers and other workers from the public sector, vowed to shut down the country in a strike scheduled for February 1, 1947. The overwhelming majority of those workers embraced bread-and-butter goals, voicing demands for higher pay and the assurance of a minimum wage. Pro-Communists within the congress provided organizational leadership for the strike, however, and they came armed with a political agenda. As the day of the strike neared, spokespersons called upon Yoshida, an impassioned anti-Communist, to resign the premiership, and they further insisted that a leftist coalition replace his cabinet.

One Man could scarcely restrain himself. Publicly the acerbic prime minister branded the congress a "gang of outlaws." Privately he negotiated for SCAP's help, requesting the Americans to intervene and forbid the strike. MacArthur was not unsympathetic. The general and his GHQ advisers had envisaged a labor movement dedicated to the ideals of industrial democracy, and they had no more tolerance than Yoshida for a politicized union movement. Dramatically, on the evening before the strike was to begin, MacArthur banned the demonstration, on the grounds that he could not permit such a disruptive strike, or countenance social chaos, when Japan's economy remained mired in a precarious state. To make certain that workers heeded his prohibition, the general ordered the head of the strike committee personally to broadcast the cancellation. "In light of the strict orders of the Supreme Commander for the Allied Powers," the labor leader announced in a trembling voice, "we have no option but to abandon the strike. I can only recall the saying: 'one step back, two steps forward.' Workers and peasants, banzai! Let us remain united."[22] The period of confrontation between labor and SCAP had begun.

When Yoshida named his second cabinet in October 1948, he began to overhaul labor legislation. MacArthur supported the initiative, having that summer sent a letter to the Japanese government inviting it to restrict the right of public employees to strike. The Ministry of Labor also showed itself willing to scuttle some earlier laws in favor of statutes crafted to undercut union militants and restore a balance of power between labor and management. Even before MacArthur's letter arrived in its hands, the ministry had drafted a statement defining its version of what a labor union ought to be: "With reference to the key objectives laid out in the Trade Union Law, a union has an obligation, first and foremost, to economic reconstruction."[23] As bureaucrats Ministry of Labor officials felt responsible for maintaining social order and for creating an environment that would permit the economy to realize its full potential. In 1945, when labor was weak, those overarching goals dictated that bureaucrats propose legislation favorable to labor. In 1948, after millions of workers had enrolled in politicized and bellicose unions, the bureaucracy tilted toward the side of capital to dampen the possibility of social unrest.

Yoshida moved to restrain labor radicalism in 1949 by sponsoring a revision of the Labor Relations Adjustment Law in order to give government-appointed commissions greater purview over the certification of unions, a maneuver designed to isolate unions from Communist influence. Yoshida capped those efforts in 1950, when, with SCAP's agreement, he launched the "red purge" to remove alleged Communists from government positions and the labor movement. Very quickly, the campaign spread to private businesses, and by the autumn of 1950 as many as twenty thousand "leftist" teachers, journalists, and factory workers found themselves unemployed. Cited as justification for those dismissals, ironically, was the old SCAP Directive 548, which prohibited people from engaging in "resistance or opposition to the Occupational Forces."

In 1948 MacArthur began to edge away from *zaibatsu* busting, revealing another aspect of the reverse course. Passage of the Deconcentration Law in December 1947 had unleashed a hailstorm of criticism from Japanese business leaders, who predicted economic ruin if SCAP persisted in dismantling or reorganizing upward of one thousand companies. At the same time, in Washington the Kauffman report aroused fears about the "crackpots" in GHQ, and George F. Kennan of the State Department Policy Planning Staff added his support to the notion that the Deconcentration Law would lead to economic disaster and result in near anarchy, leaving Japan vulnerable to a Communist takeover. In March 1948 the influential Kennan visited MacArthur to deliver Washington's message in person: SCAP must modify its programs and place a new priority on economic recovery and political stability so as to prepare the island nation to join the stand against international communism.

The pressure was too much even for MacArthur to bear. In April 1948 he consented to the creation of a Deconcentration Review Board to examine earlier plans to abolish companies powerful enough to prevent newcomers from entering their markets. Immediately the new board declared hundreds of companies outside the scope of the law's intent. When the review body first met, SCAP already had designated 325 Japanese companies for dismemberment or reorganization. The board quickly winnowed the number of targeted firms to 19 and then to just 9. Unusually subdued, MacArthur's staff announced that the deconcentration program had been brought to a satisfactory completion. At the same time, SCAP stood silent as Japanese appeal boards began to "depurge" thousands of former corporate managers.

Demilitarization was another early policy that was stood on its head as growing tensions with the Communist world prompted Americans to rethink Japan's possible defense role in East Asia. In November 1948 Washington authorized SCAP to create a paramilitary force of 150,000 inductees to supplement the regular Japanese police. Having fought his away across the Pacific, MacArthur harbored deep suspicions about the scheme, so he simply refused to implement it until 1950, when the outbreak of the Korean War forced his hand. As America's armed forces left Japan for the peninsula in the summer of 1950, MacArthur ordered the Japanese government to form a National Police Reserve of 75,000 men, whose ostensible purpose was to ensure domestic tranquillity. Those "police," however, were equipped with M-1 rifles, machine guns, mortars, flamethrowers, artillery, tanks, and American advisers, one of whom described the reserve as "a little American Army."

Rearmament had to be squared officially with Article 9 of the new constitution, which explicitly declared that "the Japanese people forever renounce war as a sovereign right of the nation" and clearly stated that Japan would never maintain land, sea, or air forces. At first, Yoshida supported a literal interpretation of that provision, even agreeing that it prohibited armament for self-defense. But the establishment of the National Police Reserve made it impossible for the prime minister to hold to that reading, and 48 percent of the Japanese public surveyed in an opinion poll in February 1952 responded that he was lying when he said that Japan was not rearming. No amateur in the game of semantic gymnastics, Yoshida ultimately adopted the thesis that Article 9 permitted Japan to maintain military forces as long as those units did not possess "war potential." Successor cabinets preferred to speak of "offensive potential," settling into the position that Japan, like other sovereign nations and in accordance with the United Nations Charter, possessed the inalienable right to defend itself and that maintenance of a military with solely defensive capabilities did not violate the spirit of the constitution.

## Independence

By 1950 Americans clearly were beginning to tire of the occupation; most Japanese long since had done so. From an early date, Yoshida enjoyed quipping that GHQ ought to stand for "go home quickly," but MacArthur became the first major figure to call for an end to the occupation when he suggested, during a news conference held on March 17, 1947, that it was time to conclude a formal peace treaty to replace the instrument of surrender signed aboard the USS *Missouri*. The initial two years of his stewardship, he explained, had proved enormously successful: Japan was disarmed, the institutional reforms necessary for democratic growth had been lifted into place, land reform was under way, and plans had been formulated to break up the concentrated wealth of malevolent capitalists. In his mind, the general had prepared the foundation for a peaceful future, and to drag out the occupation would serve no useful end.

Despite MacArthur's early, and to some surprising, advocacy of a peace treaty, fate did not tap him to negotiate such a document on behalf of the

United States. The task of putting together a treaty acceptable to Japan and the nearly fifty other nations expected to sign it fell to the prominent Republican John Foster Dulles, whom President Truman named as his chief intermediary on May 18, 1950. By that time MacArthur was on his way out of favor with the president in any case. Truman appointed MacArthur commander of UN forces in Korea when hostilities broke out there in June 1950, but after the general publicly disagreed with the president over military policy the next year, the feisty, no-nonsense Truman summarily relieved MacArthur of both his military command and his position as SCAP. To witness the civilian commander in chief remove the awesome Blue-Eyed Shogun from power, declared many Japanese, was the clearest object lesson in the meaning of democracy that they could expect to experience.

Dulles began by consulting with America's wartime allies. Some favored a charitable settlement. The vindictiveness of the Paris Peace Conference, they suggested, ultimately had spawned resentments that Adolf Hitler and the Nazi Party rode to power; to inflict similar humiliation upon the Japanese risked creating a legacy of bitterness that did not bode well for future generations. Others, however, lobbied for a tough treaty. The nations of Southeast Asia that had suffered the most from Japanese aggression wanted to exact heavy reparations from Japan, while Great Britain, fearful for its Asian markets, pushed for limitations on its future export potential. That debate, as well as the deepening Cold War with the Soviet Union and the blazing-hot war on the Korean peninsula, shaped Dulles's thinking about Japan's future global role. The treaty, he concluded with Truman's blessing, should establish a framework for Japan's continued economic recovery and political stability so as to lock Japan into the Western alliance, secure for the United States military prerogatives that would enable America to project its power forward into the Pacific, and enable Japan to rearm and contribute to regional self-defense.

Dulles's toughest negotiations lay with the crusty Japanese prime minister. Throughout the entire occupation, no goal obsessed Yoshida Shigeru more than the restoration of full sovereignty to his country. Diplomacy had been his career, and he signaled his determination to bring Japan back into the comity of nations by serving as his own foreign minister during his first three cabinets. Yoshida held strong, stubborn, and well-known views about what sort of treaty he considered appropriate. Never would he endorse a punitive settlement, and he bargained strongly for a nonrestrictive treaty that would place no limitations on Japan's economic or political future. Within that context, he favored alignment with the United States, which, he believed, would create a new version of the happier premilitarist era when the agreements concluded at the Washington Conference sheltered Japanese interests.

Despite his tenacious views on treaty negotiations, One Man was compelled to display at least some sensitivity to the opinions of others. His opponents on the Japanese political left drew up their own set of "peace principles": Japan must be neutral, not part of either Cold War camp; rearmament should not be tolerated; and U.S. forces must not be permitted to remain on Japanese soil. Yoshida, however, had no truck with neutrality. "The babbling of a sleepwalker," he called it, a diplomatic posture that made it as difficult to secure a peaceful future as it was "to pluck a flower from a mirror."[24] Nevertheless, the left's peace principles gained widespread support among the Japanese voting public, and Yoshida courted their displeasure only at the risk of losing the very office that cast him in the role of peace negotiator.

Caught in the crossfire of domestic politics, Yoshida maneuvered as best he could. He remained convinced that Japan's future security required a defensive alliance with the United States and that Japan had no choice but to allow the United States to station troops on its soil. But he adamantly resisted massive, large-scale rearmament. When Dulles put that demand on the table during a personal meeting in January 1951, suggesting that Japan plan for a ground force of 300,000 soldiers, Yoshida drew the arrows from his quiver: His country couldn't afford it; the public wouldn't tolerate it; the constitution prohibited it; Japan's neighbors would be horrified. To some extent, the barrage camouflaged other reasons: Although he was a staunch anti-Communist, Yoshida never did share America's paranoia about the threat of international communism, nor did he accept Dulles's contention that Japan was in imminent danger of Communist attack. Also, if the most secret of all truths be known, Yoshida did not trust the old generals who commanded the new National Police Reserve.

Proposals went back and forth during the spring and summer of 1951, before representatives from Japan, the United States, and nearly fifty other nations gathered in San Francisco for the formal peace conference. On September 8, 1951, Japan and forty-eight of its former enemies put their signatures to the San Francisco Peace Treaty (the Soviet Union, Poland, and Czechoslovakia walked out of the proceedings; China was not invited because of disagreement over whether the legitimate government was located in Beijing or Taipei). Yoshida got much of what he had sought, and most observers agreed that the terms of the settlement were reasonably generous and not vengeful. The treaty terminated the still-existing state of war, provided for the withdrawal of occupation personnel ninety days after the accord came into effect, restored Japan's sovereignty, and spelled out its right to self-defense. Finally, the document placed no limits on Japan's economy or trade. Instead, the signatories recognized the need to assist its economic reconstruction and even offered to support its future application for membership in the United Nations.

Mere hours after Japan signed the peace agreement, its representatives in San Francisco put their names to the United States–Japan Security Treaty. A genetic offspring of the Cold War, the document permitted the United States to station its troops in Japan indefinitely. Although public opinion polls later showed most Japanese supported the peace treaty, many objected that Yoshida ceded too much ground when he assented to the security accord. That agreement, his opponents feared, subordinated Japan's defense needs to U.S. policy and actually placed Japan's future at risk. Particularly annoying to them were the stipulations that U.S. troops stationed in Japan operated under a broad mandate to maintain peace throughout East Asia and that the United States was free to dispatch those forces anywhere, anytime, with no obligation to seek the permission of, or even consult with, the Japanese government. The danger seemed crystal clear: If the United States launched a military action from bases on Japanese soil, it might well drag Japan into a conflict that was solely a product of American foreign policy machinations and not at all in Japan's interests. Other critics hammered at Yoshida for agreeing to two other clauses that humiliated Japan, they charged, by compromising its rights as a sovereign nation. One of those authorized American soldiers to quell domestic riots and disturbances when so requested by Japanese officials, and the other prohibited Japan from granting bases or other military privileges to any third nation without first securing the consent of the United States. Yoshida, his detractors complained, had condemned Japan to "Subordinate Independence."

That sharp barb infuriated Yoshida, but the veteran of countless political battles outflanked his opponents and successfully guided the peace and security treaties through the Diet during the autumn of 1951. With Japan now unabashedly on America's side in the Cold War, the U.S. Senate ratified the peace and security treaties in March 1952, and the two agreements went into effect on April 28, 1952. Yoshida considered the implementation of the San Francisco System the greatest triumph of his career. Japan had regained its sovereignty, its long occupation by a foreign nation had come to a close, the country had cast its lot with the seemingly invincible Anglo-American bloc, and the island nation was assured of the economic assistance of the world's great industrialized powers. Yoshida had realized his version of Japan's postwar future.

The moment of Yoshida's most cherished personal victory also marked the beginning of his political demise. The Japanese public remained considerably ambivalent toward the San Francisco System, and slogans such as "Subordinate Independence" influenced the direction of public opinion; a poll conducted by the *Asahi shinbun* newspaper late in 1952 revealed that only 18 percent of all Japanese concurred that their country had become truly independent. By that time Yoshida's favorable rating had plunged to just 20 percent, down from 58 percent a year earlier. With his public support eroding, Yoshida became more caustic than ever, his corrosive sarcasm alienating many whose support would have been useful. When the president of the University of Tokyo criticized certain aspects of the proposed peace treaty, Yoshida branded him a "prostitute of learning" and then ignored advice to heal wounds by steadfastly refusing to apologize or even retract his outburst as an "inadvertent" remark.[25]

During Diet debates in February 1953, Yoshida lashed out at a socialist interlocutor, calling him a stupid idiot (*baka yarō*), and the sound of that expletive, seemingly mild in translation yet obscenely profane in actual usage, brought an immediate vote of no confidence. Yoshida managed to win the subsequent election, but he further damaged his reputation the next year by intervening in a case of suspected bribery, the tainted trading of political favors for campaign contributions, in order to forestall the arrest of his favorite protégé, the future prime minister Satō Eisaku. In the fall of 1954, still uncertain about the breadth of Japan's economic recovery, Yoshida traveled to the United States to plead personally for a Marshall Plan for Asia. Washington was totally unreceptive, and even conservatives at home turned against him. On December 10, 1954, the aging Yoshida Shigeru resigned as prime minister of Japan and took his place in occupation history alongside his old antagonist, the retired general Douglas MacArthur.

In 1945 these two towering figures shared common ground, each professing to envisage an independent, non-Communist, stable future for Japan. When looking backward, however, Yoshida and MacArthur saw two distinct Japanese histories that were fundamentally opposed to each other. In turn, those contrasting perceptions about the meaning of the Japanese past gave flower to radically different opinions about how to bring the postwar vision into focus. For Yoshida, the glories of the Meiji and Taishō periods—constitutionalism, industrialization, the rise to prominence on the world scene—constituted an honorable past, and all Japan needed to do was to pick itself up from a "historical stumble," the aberration of the 1930s, and get back on the path of certain progress. His agenda was straightforward: Preserve constitutional institutions under the imperial umbrella, ensure that the bureaucracy and conservative politicians had unchallenged leadership roles in the political process, nurture a capitalistic economy that would be pulled forward by powerful conglomerates, restrain radicalism, and return Japan to partnership with the Western powers. MacArthur had a less sanguine conception of the Meiji legacy. For him, that era constituted the genesis of Japan's later aggression, a period when cultural and psychological sores had begun to fester, only to secrete totalitarianism and militarism in the 1930s. To MacArthur's way of thinking, Japan did not just stumble; rather, its problems were an illness caused by its feudal past, and SCAP needed to initiate deep, structural reforms to root out the disease. Instead of resurrecting the past, Japan had to move forward into a demilitarized, democratized future that reserved an important place for new social forces.

MacArthur's version of reform predominated between 1945 and 1947, as SCAP demobilized Japan's military, demythologized the emperor, rewrote the constitution, broke up the largest of the business conglomerates, promoted unionism, confiscated and redistributed farmland, restructured the education system, and revised the civil code. The general would accept for this all the credit that came his way, and more; later he wrote, "I had to be an economist, a political scientist, an engineer, a manufacturing executive, a teacher, even a theologian of sorts."[26] None of SCAP's reforms, however, would have been possible had not a host of other people been pushing on the wheel with MacArthur. Planning experts in wartime Washington, occupationaires such as General Courtney Whitney and Lieutenant Ethel Weed, the Japanese bureaucrats who wished to adjust historical imbalances between management and labor and solve old problems such as rural poverty, and the new constituencies that benefited from the reforms: All added their contributions and made possible that which MacArthur never could have achieved on his own.

By the winter of 1947–1948, however, a new constellation of forces was taking shape. At its nucleus was Yoshida Shigeru. During his first term as prime minister, Yoshida had accepted many early reforms only grudgingly, his resistance futile until old-line bureaucrats and traditional party conservatives, who feared that SCAP had gone too far, came into his orbit. Surprisingly they discovered new allies in unexpected places: in the Japan Lobby and even in the White House and the halls of the U.S. Congress. Together, that unlikely group of political bedfellows began to push the occupation in new directions, placing the emphasis on recovery and reconstruction. "Rectifying excesses," Yoshida liked to call it. Important too were changing attitudes among the Japanese people. Devastated by the suffering of the war years, they were amazingly open and receptive to reform in 1946 and 1947.

The early measures proposed by MacArthur played to that sentiment and to a significant degree succeeded because of it. By the end of the decade, however, occupation weariness was replacing war weariness, and the voting public began to return to the Diet, in election after election, majorities that generally supported the new departures.

The first postwar decade was filled with the wonders of a great historical moment: powerful adversaries, shifting alliances, twists and turns of policy, inconsistencies on the part of many individuals. The occupation evolved in ways that were frequently tortured and oftentimes confusing even to those who lived through it, but the seven years between 1945 and 1952 altered forever the course of Japanese history. To be certain, many of the reforms, in either their original or "rectified" versions, accelerated developments whose beginnings could be traced back to the prewar past. The notions of party government and cabinet responsibility, Japan's alignment with the industrialized West, and the extension of the franchise to women all were ideas that the Japanese earlier had tried on for size. The lesson was clear: Those reforms that had their proponents in the years before the war or that found new constituencies to support them won quick passage and had the best chance of enduring beyond the postwar decades.

Still, it is difficult to imagine that anything less than the trauma of defeat and the disciplined intensity of a foreign occupation would have produced a constitution that moved sovereignty from the emperor to the people and guaranteed people's rights, a land reform program that touched virtually every rural family in the country, a military establishment limited to providing self-defense, and a labor movement that became as large and as energetic as could be found anywhere. In the full sweep of Japanese history the occupation years stand with the period of national reunification in the seventeenth century and the Meiji Restoration of the nineteenth century as one of the great turning points in the country's past, and the Japanese people in that short span of time experienced changes perhaps as profound and rapid as those found in any revolutionary epoch in modern world history.

CHAPTER 16

# Recovery and Affluence

On the afternoon of October 10, 1964, some seventy-five thousand spectators rose from their seats in Tokyo's Kasumigaoka National Stadium to hear the emperor declare the opening of the eighteenth Olympic Games of the modern era. As part of the festivities that day, jets of the Self-Defense Force inscribed the five Olympic rings in the brisk autumn sky, ten thousand five-color balloons floated upward, and children from a local primary school escorted into the stadium the mayor of Rome, host of the previous Olympiad. The march of participants included seven thousand athletes representing nearly ninety nations. The crowd cheered when the Cuban contingent gaily waved small Rising Sun flags as it passed the royal box, erupted in applause when the Japanese national team entered the stadium, and then stood in near reverential silence as Sakai Yoshinori, a nineteen-year-old university student who was born just outside Hiroshima on the morning of the world's first atomic bombing, came running into the stadium bearing the Olympic torch.

The Japanese organizing committee carefully and deliberately staged the Tokyo Olympics to celebrate the country's recovery from defeat and its reentry onto the world's stage. Chairing the committee was Yasukawa Daigorō, a businessman who had devoted himself to developing peaceful uses for atomic energy in Japan. As one who had made his own reconciliation with the past, Yasukawa proclaimed that his responsibility was to organize an Olympiad that would "not only be a display of sportsmanship by the world's athletes, but will also serve to highlight the continuing efforts of the Japanese people as a worthy member of the world family of nations."[1]

*The opening ceremonies of the 1964 Olympics*

Tokyo had been scheduled to host the 1940 games, only to have had them canceled when fighting broke out in Europe. In the eyes of the outside world, the emperor at that time personified Japan's unquenchable thirst for empire, its bellicose intentions, and its closed, elitist political system. In 1964 the emperor's very visible and well-publicized role as the official Patron of the Games portrayed him in a different light, placing him on the international stage as the dignified leader of a fully rehabilitated and peaceful Japan. Seated next to the monarch at the opening ceremonies was the prime minister, Ikeda Hayato, a silent reminder to all that Japan was democratic as well as peaceful and that the emperor, under the terms of the new constitution, symbolically represented the nation's popularly elected civilian government.

The planning committee for the 1964 games also responded to a strong desire voiced by many Japanese to show off, both to themselves and to visitors from abroad, the fruits of Japan's remarkable economic recovery. Approximately 80 percent of the government's total expenditures of 970 billion yen for the Olympics went into public works projects. Just as the youthful torchbearer represented Japan's indomitable spirit, its rise from the ashes of destruction, other visible examples of the nation's growing postwar prosperity impressed visitors: New and expanded subway lines ran beneath Tokyo, a modern expressway linked the capital with Nagoya, and the first blue and white "Bullet Train," the fastest in the world, pulled out of Tokyo Station on October 1 and whisked passengers the three hundred miles to Osaka in an unheard-of three hours and ten minutes. "Prosperity in Peace Time" became the refrain of the day, and private capital dressed Tokyo with smart hotels and mammoth apartment complexes that demonstrated a growing sense of achievement, optimism, and well-being.

A renewed pride in Japanese traditions also flourished during the Olympiad. With images of peace and prosperity replacing memories of war, many Japanese no longer feared reproach if they openly demonstrated respect for their nation's cultural past. Japanese athletes proudly competed in judo, a sport new to the Olympics that year, and entertained international audiences with exhibitions of kendo fencing. New Olympic buildings also helped, in Yasukawa's words, develop the games "in line with a distinctively Japanese image." Constructed as the venue for the judo competition and martial arts exhibitions, architects designed the steel and ferroconcrete Nippon Budōkan to resemble the Yumedono, the wooden Hall of Dreams that is part of the Temple Hōryūji, one of Japan's oldest centers of worship and situated just outside the ancient imperial capital of Nara. Like the Yumedono, the martial arts hall had an octagonal floor plan and was capped by a distinctive roof with a pointed orb placed at its center. For the Olympic fans who visited the Nippon Budōkan, its location beside the moats and ramparts of the Imperial Palace strengthened the association of past with present, tradition with modernity.

Most Japanese treasured the Olympic experience as a time of national bonding, a shining moment when the nation came together to affirm its political, economic, and spiritual recovery from the horrors of war and defeat. In his column for a major daily, a leading literary figure confessed that while "attending the opening ceremony I was overwhelmed by the thought that Japan had finally regained its national competency to the stage where it could manage to host such an ostentatious show."[2] In a similar vein, after watching the Japanese national team win the gold medal in women's volleyball, the novelist Ariyoshi Sawako, acclaimed for her sensitive treatment of contemporary social issues, articulated feelings that many of her generation held about the postwar era: "I could almost visually see fulfilled the sense of responsibility that had hovered above the heads of the weeping girls. They have striven so many years just for this moment. Thank you."

Not all Japanese wished to join in celebration, however. One noted architectural critic disapproved the symbolism inherent in the Nippon Budōkan, labeling the geometrically precise, hard-edged structure "an anti-modern exoticism," a "fascist building" that called to mind "the architecture of the Berlin Games during the Nazi Period."[3] Similarly, as the warm glow of the Olympics faded and the 1960s turned into the 1970s and 1980s, some Japanese began to reassess the experiences of the late Shōwa period. As they did so, certain critics began to disparage the particular style of democracy that emerged in the postwar decades, others pointed out that Japan's industrial resurgence, great as it was, had not brought equal benefits to all people of the nation, and some began to doubt that contemporary society and culture represented an improvement over the past.

## The LDP Rules

As Yoshida Shigeru's popularity skidded to new lows in 1953 and 1954, Japan's socialist parties began to scent the possibility of capturing a majority of seats in forthcoming Diet elections. To strengthen their hand, the two leading parties on the left in October 1955 formed the Nihon Shakaitō, known commonly as the JSP after the initials for its translated name, the Japan Socialist Party. In reaction, Yoshida's Liberal Party merged the following month with another conservative party, the Japan Democratic Party, to form the Jiyū Minshutō, or LDP (Liberal Democratic Party). The Liberal and Japan Democratic parties were successors to the prewar Seiyūkai and Minseitō, and just as those organizations had done during the Taishō period, the new LDP dominated party politics. Formed while Hatoyama Ichirō held the premiership, the LDP swept subsequent Diet elections, and for the next four decades, until the autumn of 1993, the party enjoyed a remarkable hold on power with fifteen leaders of the LDP serving consecutively as prime minister.

Organizationally the LDP functioned as a party of factions. Throughout its political heyday a half dozen or so major alliances jockeyed with one another for influence. Each faction constituted a separate entity that raised its own campaign funds, promoted the careers of its members, negotiated with other factions for control of high party and cabinet posts, and rotated the office of prime minister among themselves. Because of its coalitions, the LDP advocated an eclectic set of policies, even while projecting an image

**TABLE 16.1** *LDP Prime Ministers, 1954–1993*

| PRIME MINISTER | CABINET NUMBER | CABINET TERM |
|---|---|---|
| Hatoyama Ichirō | First | December 10, 1954–March 19, 1955 |
| Hatoyama Ichirō | Second | March 19, 1955–November 22, 1955 |
| Hatoyama Ichirō | Third | November 22, 1955–December 23, 1956 |
| Ishibashi Tanzan | | December 23, 1956–February 25, 1957 |
| Kishi Nobusuke | First | February 25, 1957–June 12, 1958 |
| Kishi Nobusuke | Second | June 12, 1958–July 19, 1960 |
| Ikeda Hayato | First | July 19, 1960–December 8, 1960 |
| Ikeda Hayato | Second | December 8, 1960–December 9, 1963 |
| Ikeda Hayato | Third | December 9, 1963–November 9, 1964 |
| Satō Eisaku | First | November 9, 1964–February 17, 1967 |
| Satō Eisaku | Second | February 17, 1967–January 14, 1970 |
| Satō Eisaku | Third | January 14, 1970–July 7, 1972 |
| Tanaka Kakuei | First | July 7, 1972–December 22, 1972 |
| Tanaka Kakuei | Second | December 22, 1972–December 9, 1974 |
| Miki Takeo | | December 9, 1974–December 24, 1976 |
| Fukuda Takeo | | December 24, 1976–December 7, 1978 |
| Ōhira Masayoshi | First | December 7, 1978–November 9, 1979 |
| Ōhira Masayoshi | Second | November 9, 1979–July 17, 1980 |
| Suzuki Zenkō | | July 17, 1980–November 27, 1982 |
| Nakasone Yasuhiro | First | November 27, 1982–December 27, 1983 |
| Nakasone Yasuhiro | Second | December 27, 1983–July 22, 1986 |
| Nakasone Yasuhiro | Third | July 22, 1986–November 6, 1987 |
| Takeshita Noboru | | November 6, 1987–June 3, 1989 |
| Uno Sōsuke | | June 3, 1989–August 10, 1989 |
| Kaifu Toshiki | First | August 10, 1989–February 28, 1990 |
| Kaifu Toshiki | Second | February 28, 1990–November 5, 1991 |
| Miyazawa Kiichi | | November 5, 1991–August 9, 1993 |

of conservative pragmatism. That is, the party consistently pledged fidelity to parliamentary democracy, the free enterprise system, the sanctity of private property, and such civic values as love of nation, respect for the family, and deference to law and order. At the same time, each faction endorsed specific policies that brought those values alive for its own particular group of supporters: guaranteed crop prices for farmers, expanded social welfare programs that contributed to the well-being of the elderly and those who ran their own retail shops, improved working conditions and a minimum wage for factory workers, and academic freedom for educators.

The success of LDP factions in reaching out to diverse constituencies was one reason behind its long-term ability to control the Diet and cabinet. So too was its predilection to embrace hot new issues, as when it called for all-out economic growth in the 1960s and then in the 1970s pushed for antipollution legislation and earmarked a larger portion of the national budget for parks, libraries, and other amenities to improve urban life. Cooperation with the bureaucracy also was important since those officials bore formal responsibility for implementing the laws passed by LDP legislators. Yoshida, himself a prewar member of the Foreign Ministry, nurtured good ties with the bureaucracy by encouraging leading officials to take up careers as LDP politicians. So close did the relationship become that three retired bureaucrats became heads of major factions within the LDP and served consecutively as prime minister from 1957 to 1972: Kishi Nobusuke, Ikeda Hayato, and Satō Eisaku (Kishi's younger brother, who in his youth had been adopted by a relative's family).

Despite its ability to dominate the political scene, the LDP occasionally ran into heavy turbulence. Haughty to begin with, Kishi Nobusuke toted some tattered historical baggage with him when he became prime minister in 1957. Many voters disapproved of his record as an official in Manchukuo and his service during the war first as minister of commerce and industry and later as deputy minister of munitions. Opposition politicians liked to call him War Criminal Kishi, a reference to his indictment by SCAP. When the minority opposition within the LDP-controlled Diet used filibusters and sit-ins to delay approval of a slightly revised United States–Japan Security Treaty in May 1960, Kishi resorted to unusually heavy-handed tactics to ram the bill through, at one point even inviting the police into the Diet to drag his opponents from the chambers and then calling a snap vote with only LDP members present. Incensed at the prime minister's disregard for democratic procedures, labor went on strike, and across Japan students by the hundreds of thousands swarmed into the streets in protest. The crisis reached a peak on June 10, 1960, when Dwight D. Eisenhower's press secretary, in Japan to arrange a prospective presidential visit, had to scramble aboard a helicopter to escape the wrath of demonstrators who surrounded his limousine and threatened to overturn it. When one young woman was crushed to death during a violent clash between students and riot police in Tokyo five days later, the firestorm of criticism intensi-

*Students and police clash during demonstrations opposing an extension of the United States–Japan Security Treaty*

fied, forcing Kishi to resign just days after the Diet had approved the treaty extension.

Money politics also became an especially sensitive issue with the electorate in the 1960s and 1970s. Diet members had enormous appetites for funds. Election campaigns were costly as candidates often showered inducements—trips to the Diet members' Tokyo offices, expensive presents, even cash "gifts"—upon influential supporters who could help turn out the vote. Once in office, legislators needed large sums to provide the care and feeding that voters in their home districts expected. LDP politicians in particular had reputations for fostering close ties with their constituents by contributing to local charities, providing funds to establish new businesses or prop up old ones, and sending gifts to weddings, funerals, and festivals. To meet their need for satchels stuffed with cash, politicians turned to large corporations and well-heeled individuals who were willing to make generous donations to campaign coffers, pay inflated honorariums for brief speeches, and shell out hundreds of thousands of yen to attend dinners and cocktail parties. The quid pro quo, everyone understood, was that the Diet member would give a sympathetic hearing to legislation favorable to his benefactors.

In the late 1960s and early 1970s, investigative reporters for leading newspapers and journals gave a thorough airing to the sometimes illicit, sometimes legal but unethical fund-raising practices that tainted the LDP in the eyes of many. As public dismay about political corruption mounted, Tanaka Kakuei's tenure as prime minister seemed to confirm everyone's worst fears about the pervasive, sinister nature of political financing. A hard-as-nails, self-made man who always seemed to wear a smirk on his face, Tanaka ran a construction company that earned him a fortune from government contracts during the war years. In 1947 the still-young Tanaka first won election to the Diet. He joined the LDP when it was formed in the 1950s and subsequently served as finance minister under Ikeda and Satō. Throughout his political career, Tanaka steadily built a reputation as an archmanipulator of under-the-table funding—indeed, during his very first term in the House of Representatives, prosecutors charged him with accepting bribes from owners of major coal mines—but he carefully lavished attention and largess upon his electoral district in his native Niigata Prefecture, and election after election voters returned him to his Diet seat.

As soon as Tanaka became prime minister in the summer of 1972, allegations about shady contributions from supporters in the real estate and construction businesses enveloped his administration in a quickening whirlwind of controversy. Almost daily, exposés appeared in leading newspapers and magazines. At one point, it was revealed, Tanaka had placed a twice-divorced ex-nightclub hostess in charge of his faction's campaign funds, the billions of yen that were used to lubricate the LDP political machine. Such machinations staggered the nation and eventually drove him from office in December 1974. Less than two years later Japanese police arrested him after a U.S. Senate investigation into the affairs of the Lockheed Aircraft Corporation alleged that he had accepted 500 million yen in bribes and secret kickbacks during his term as prime minister to "encourage" the state-owned All Nippon Airways to purchase Lockheed planes. After seven years of deliberations the Tokyo District Court found Tanaka guilty as charged, although drawn-out appeals and a near-fatal stroke saved him the embarrassment of a jail cell.

Several parties contested the LDP hegemony. On the left the Japan

*Ichikawa Fusae*

Communist Party, which into the 1980s typically controlled 20 or 30 of the 512 seats in the House of Representatives, advocated a peaceful transition to socialism and opposed the United States–Japan Security Treaty. The Japan Socialist Party (JSP), which enjoyed the backing of organized labor and sometimes elected more than 100 candidates to the Diet, lobbied for socialist economic programs and led the attack on Kishi in May and June 1960. The more centralist Kōmeitō, or Clean Government Party, entered the political fray in 1964 and soon thereafter won considerable public support for a platform that called for the elimination of political corruption, more generous funding for social welfare programs, and peaceful coexistence with all countries.

Several of Japan's most prominent women politicians also took exception with LDP policies and modes of operation and stood for office, either as independents or as members of an opposition party. Kamichika Ichiko, the prewar feminist and journalist who had spent two years in jail for stabbing her lover Ōsugi Sakae after he forsook her for Itō Noe, joined the postwar JSP and from 1953 to 1969 served in the House of Representatives, where she became a leading spokesperson for equality of the sexes and campaigned against legalized prostitution (finally abolished by the Prostitution Prevention Law of 1956). A notable independent was the venerable Ichikawa Fusae, who first won election to the upper house of the Diet in 1953 and for the next twenty-five years campaigned for human rights and railed against the corrosive influence of money politics.

The public's response to the LDP was ambivalent. Until well into the 1980s the constituencies that benefited most from LDP legislation faithfully supported the party; other Japanese, offended by continuous examples of corruption, criticized LDP politicians for lacking idealism and for placing personal advantage ahead of the best interests of the nation. At the same time, even alienated voters often were not willing to trust the country's fate to the minority parties; those politicians, it often was said, bickered endlessly among themselves over minor ideological principles and proposed economic programs that seemed hopelessly flawed. The electorate's ambivalence came out in public opinion polls, which throughout the 1970s indicated that large numbers, at times a majority, of respondents preferred that some party other than the LDP lead the country. Yet, throughout that decade and the next, voters continued to elect enough LDP representatives to the Diet that the party controlled the office of prime minister and held the overwhelming majority of cabinet portfolios. The ability of the LDP to retain its grasp on power reduced the role of the political opposition and evoked criticism that Japanese democracy was a dysfunctional single-party system.

## High-speed Growth and Government Priorities

The juxtaposition of economic conditions during the postwar decade against those prevailing in the 1980s startles the imagination. In 1945 and 1946 Japan was devastated, and a decade later the future still did not seem to hold much promise. In the mid-1950s, Japan's GNP still was just of one-fifteenth that of the United States, wages were only slightly higher than during the best of the prewar years, and in 1957 Edwin O. Reischauer, the distinguished Harvard professor who was acknowledged as the foremost Western scholar on Japan and who later served as the U.S. ambassador to that country, discouragingly observed: "The economic situation in Japan may be so fundamentally unsound that no policies, no matter how wise, can save her from slow economic starvation and all the concomitant political and social ills that situation would produce."[4]

Ironically, even as Reischauer wrote, Japan already was crossing the threshold into an era of economic growth that was to astound the world. By the beginning of the 1960s massive capital formation, accelerating investments in plants and equipment, and spirited competition for international markets had made Japan's GNP the fifth largest among the world's capitalist economies. Throughout the 1960s, the vintage years of high-speed

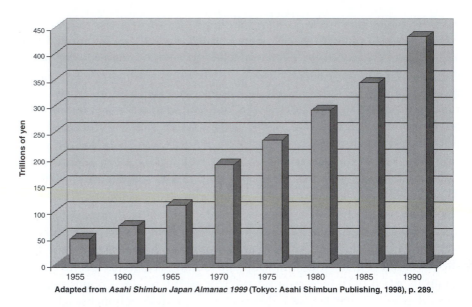

Adapted from *Asahi Shimbun Japan Almanac 1999* (Tokyo: Asahi Shimbun Publishing, 1998), p. 289.

**FIGURE 16.1**  *GNP, 1955–1990*

growth, the economy expanded at an average rate of more than 10 percent a year, and before the decade was over, Japan's output of goods and services surpassed that of West Germany—and every other free market economy in the world except that of the United States. After the "oil shock" of 1973, when the Organization of Petroleum Exporting Countries increased crude oil prices by nearly 70 percent, Japan's economy contracted temporarily before recovering a measure of its former dynamism. The breathtaking high-speed years were finished, but from 1975 through the 1980s the GNP grew a very enviable 3.5 to 5.5 percent a year, and in 1987 per capita GNP overtook that of the United States.

The unprecedented economic boom changed life dramatically for Japan's citizens. By the early 1970s a majority of Japanese were residing in cities where living standards rivaled those in other advanced nations; in rural Japan, real household income stood roughly four times higher than in 1955, and farm families enjoyed the same television programs, drove the same automobiles, and used the same refrigerators and washing machines as their urban counterparts. In the late 1980s the world watched in awe as jumbo jet after jumbo jet deposited Japanese tourists on the beaches of Hawaii, corporations flush with profits snapped up Rockefeller Center and other

American architectural landmarks, and well-heeled twenty-somethings rushed to Tokyo's international airport each November to sample the newly arrived Beaujolais.

The compelling image of a prostrate Japan turned economic Colossus prompted many to herald its postwar recovery as an "economic miracle." It was not, in terms of either time or causality. Despite the commonly held belief that Japan engineered a phoenixlike comeback from the desolation of the war, it actually took longer to return to prewar levels of per capita GNP there than it did in Germany and the rest of Western Europe, and any appearance of a rapidly paced turnaround stemmed largely from the fact that the scale of physical destruction was so great in Japan. Neither was there anything preternatural about the reasons for the country's return to the ranks of the industrially advanced nations of the globe. Rather, its resurgence was due to a legacy of past accomplishments, an indomitable determination to succeed in the quest for modernity, prodigious amounts of hard work, generally shrewd planning, and occasional injections of unanticipated stimulation, or what economists prefer to think of as exogenous events.

According to many experts, the implementation of the Dodge Line marked the beginning of Japan's economic recovery. Joseph M. Dodge, a cheerless Detroit banker who had overseen currency reforms in occupied Germany, arrived in Japan in February 1949 as President Truman's special adviser to SCAP on financial matters. A believer in classical economic theory, Dodge preached that tight money and government austerity were the only effective means to combat hyperinflation. Working closely with Ikeda Hayato, Japan's finance minister at the time and a future prime minister, Dodge measured out one bitter dose of medicine after another, insisting upon the need to balance the budget, reduce the money supply, and decrease the scope of government intervention in the economy by phasing out existing price controls and eliminating government subsidies to private companies. The Dodge Line was highly controversial. Some economists credited it with extinguishing the flames of Japan's postwar inflation, sweeping away economic deadwood, and clearing the fields for subsequent growth. The cost, however, was a severe recession that left Japanese labor furious as real wages shrank rapidly and 500,000 people in the public and private sectors lost their jobs.

However history ultimately judges the Dodge Line, the first statistically significant uptick in Japan's economic vital signs occurred during the Korean War. From 1950 to 1953 Japan served as a staging area and supply depot for UN forces fighting on the peninsula. As a consequence, Japanese companies received contracts worth nearly two billion dollars for textiles, lumber, paper, steel, and vehicles. It was a bonanza that inflated business profits, spurred investment in new plants and equipment, and returned the economy to full capacity. Beginning in the mid-1960s, a second exogenous event, the war in Vietnam, resulted in a new round of procurement orders from the U.S. military that provided another stimulating infusion to the Japanese economy.

Japan's ruling conservatives contributed to the country's postwar resurgence by assigning the nation's highest priority to economic growth. During his first term as prime minister, Yoshida Shigeru decided to channel special assistance to certain basic industries considered essential to resuscitating the economy. In December 1946 he and his cabinet endorsed the priority production program formulated by Arisawa Hiromi, the economist who in the 1930s had advocated greater state intervention in the economy. The basic thrust of Professor Arisawa's industrial targeting scheme was to allocate precious coal reserves and imported oil to steel manufacturers and then direct the increased production of steel to other key industries, such as shipbuilding and chemicals, that could lead Japan out of its economic depths by providing jobs and stimulating demand across many industrial sectors. Over the next year and a half, output in the targeted sectors rose substantially and prepared many companies to keep pace with the flood of orders that came their way during the Korean War.

Following the LDP's inception in the mid-1950s, Japan's conservative hegemony put the expression "high-speed growth" on everyone's tongue and translated GNP into a surrogate measurement for the nation's general well-being. Emblematic of the LDP's emphasis on economic development above all else was the creation of the Economic Planning Agency in 1955. A spiritual heir to interwar planning groups, the EPA is a cabinet-level council of economic and statistical experts who report to the prime minister. Its main tasks are to assess Japan's economic strengths, predict forthcoming trends, periodically recommend to the cabinet a comprehensive set of specific policies that address current problems and promise to exploit future opportunities, and offer advice to private enterprises about their business prospects.

Between 1955 and 1990 the EPA drafted eleven major economic plans, or visions, as they are known, including the celebrated Income-Doubling Plan that Prime Minister Ikeda Hayato adopted as official policy on December 27, 1960. That scheme boldly called for doubling national wealth during the 1960s by pumping investments into science and technology, extending special tax breaks and subsidized loans to industries that contributed the most to high-speed growth, and aggressively expanding international trade. Remarkably, the economy annually grew at an even faster pace than the ambitious 7.2 percent proposed in the plan, reaching a phenomenal 14.5 percent in 1961, and national income doubled in just seven short years.

Along with the EPA, the ministries of Finance, of Construction, and of Agriculture, Forestry, and Fisheries fleshed out what some called Japan's economic bureaucracy, helping formulate and execute plans to move the economy toward national goals. No government agency, however, maintained a higher profile during the era of high-speed growth than did the Ministry of International Trade and Industry, MITI for short. Created in May 1949 out of the old Ministry of Commerce and Industry (1925–1943; 1945–1949), MITI carried a full tool kit that it drew from to construct "industrial policy." Under Japanese law, its officials controlled import and export permits, which they distributed in a manner that funneled foreign technology and raw materials into preferred industrial sectors. Moreover, since MITI had the authority to license new plant construction and recommend specific firms for low-interest loans from the Japan Development Bank, founded in 1951 to supplement lending by private financial institutions, it had considerable influence over decision making by individual enterprises. MITI also provided specific companies with abundant amounts of its notorious "administrative guidance," requests and suggestions about actions a firm ought to undertake, as well as hints about what might happen should MITI's wisdom go unheeded. Facilitating the flow of administrative guidance was the practice of *amakudari* ("descents from heaven") that saw many MITI officials accept high-level executive positions with Japan's leading corporations after they elected to retire early from the bureaucracy, usually when they were barely in their fifties.

In the 1950s and early 1960s MITI used its influence to promote the favorites of Japan's "economic bureaucracy," shipbuilding and steel, so as to complete Japan's transition, begun in the interwar years, from an Asian-oriented producer of light industrials to a global competitor in heavy industry. During the 1960s MITI turned to other sectors that it believed could win foreign customers and thus serve as locomotives for Japan's further economic development. To that end, officials erected import barriers to protect the nascent automobile industry and directed investment funds to companies manufacturing petrochemicals and machine tools. Following the oil shock of 1973, MITI foresaw increased competition from developing nations in Latin America and along the Pacific Rim, which were building their own industrial infrastructures. To stay one step ahead in the game, ministry officials advocated that Japan become a "knowledge-intensive" society and shift its productive efforts toward such high-tech areas as robotics, fiber optics, computers, software, lasers, and biotechnology.

## The Business Community and the Postwar Recovery

Big business responded enthusiastically to the opportunities of the late Shōwa era. In the initial postwar decade, familiar shipbuilders, such as Ishikawajima Heavy Industries and Kawasaki Heavy Industries, took out government-backed loans, imported advanced technology from the West, introduced new techniques, such as electric welding and the automatic cutting of steel plates, and by the late 1950s had made Japan the world's leading shipbuilder. Toyota, whose plants had been reduced to rubble during the war, began a comeback in the early 1950s after earning handsome profits repairing and supplying parts for U.S. military vehicles during the Korean War. Quickly Toyota and other automotive firms, such as Nissan, hired innovative engineers, automated their new factories, installed robots on the assembly line, improved inventory control by coordinating parts production and delivery with subcontractors, signed up dealerships, and introduced such stylish new models as the Toyota Corona (1957) and the Nissan Bluebird (1959). The results were phenomenal. As indicated in Table 16.2, Japan's automakers sold just fifty thousand cars in 1953, while a mere seven years later drivers slipped ignition keys into ten times that many new autos. The oil shock of 1973 gave Japanese firms an opportunity to establish a foothold in the American market, as consumers there began to trade in their gas guzzlers for smaller, more fuel-efficient models. By 1980 Japan was producing more cars than any other country, three years later Toyota and Nissan ranked as the number two and three automakers in the world, and by the end of the decade Japanese manufacturers controlled nearly 25 percent of the U.S. market.

Sharing the spotlight were newly visible electronics manufacturers, such as Matsushita and Sony. Matsushita's roots went back to 1918, when Matsushita Kōnosuke, still in his early twenties, opened a small shop in Osaka, where he made and sold batteries for bicycle lamps. He began to produce small home appliances in the mid-1930s and named his operations the Matsushita Electric Industrial Company. In the 1950s the firm exploded onto the national scene. It linked up with N. V. Philip's Gloeilampenfabriken to gain access to the latest technology, introduced mass-production techniques to manufacture an ever-expanding line of electrical appliances for the home, and increased sales an amazing sevenfold between 1955 and 1960, as it aggressively marketed in Japan and overseas televisions, audio equipment, refrigerators, vacuum cleaners, and washing machines under the Matsushita, National, and Panasonic brand names.

One of Matsushita's strongest rivals in the audio and video area was the

**TABLE 16.2** *Japanese Automobile Production, 1953–1983*

| YEAR | AUTOMOBILES PRODUCED | NUMBER EXPORTED | PERCENT EXPORTED |
|------|---------------------|-----------------|------------------|
| 1953 | 49,778 | 0 | 0.0% |
| 1957 | 181,977 | 6,554 | 3.6 |
| 1960 | 481,551 | 38,809 | 8.1 |
| 1965 | 1,875,614 | 194,168 | 10.4 |
| 1970 | 5,289,157 | 1,086,776 | 20.5 |
| 1973 | 7,082,757 | 2,067,556 | 29.2 |
| 1980 | 11,042,884 | 5,966,961 | 54.0 |
| 1983 | 11,111,659 | 5,669,510 | 51.0 |

**TOP WORLD COMPANIES, 1983**

| | |
|---|---|
| General Motors | 5,098,000 |
| Toyota | 3,272,000 |
| Nissan | 2,483,000 |
| Ford | 2,476,000 |

Adapted from Michael A. Cusumano, *The Japanese Automobile Industry: Technology and Management at Nissan and Toyota* (Cambridge: Council on East Asian Studies, Harvard University, 1985), pp. 3–4.

Sony Corporation, founded in 1946 by Ibuka Masaru and Morita Akio. Ibuka was the firm's engineering genius, responsible in 1950 for developing the first tape recorders manufactured in Japan and later for inventing the transistor radio, after Sony acquired the patent rights for transistors from Western Electric in 1953. In the following years Ibuka spearheaded the development of numerous commercial applications for semiconductors, which Sony used to produce an array of smaller and more affordable televisions, videocassette recorders, and other new products. Morita, the finance and marketing specialist who lauded his colleague as having "a great genius for innovation," introduced Sony's products to world markets, established manufacturing plants overseas, and in 1970 saw Sony become the first Japanese company to be listed on the New York Stock Exchange. So great were Morita's accomplishments that *Time* magazine in 1997 selected him as one of the twenty "most influential business geniuses of the century," and when Morita died in 1999, the *New York Times* wrote that he had "changed the world's image of the term 'Made in Japan' from one of parasols and shoddy imitations to one of high technology and high reliability in miniature packages."[5]

Although Sony preferred to handle its own marketing arrangements, many Japanese firms relied on general trading companies, or *sōgō shōsha*, to speed their wares to retail shelves. General trading companies arrange both foreign and domestic marketing opportunities for their clients and provide them with a broad range of financial services, including loan guarantees, foreign exchange risk management, and equity participation. In the late 1980s the nine largest trading companies handled about half the country's imports and exports, and their total sales amounted to approximately 25 percent of Japan's gross national product. All nine had their origins in the prewar era, and many had familiar names: The Osaka-based Sumitomo Corporation distributed an impressive variety of industrial and consumer goods, about 10 percent of Japan's entire foreign trade in 1989 flowed through 150 overseas offices of Mitsui & Company, and with agents in more than eighty countries, the Mitsubishi Corporation engaged in general trading, arranged technology transfers for its customers, and was busy moving into such new areas as telecommunications and information processing.

Each of the largest general trading companies provided the nucleus for a group of affiliated enterprises that in some ways functioned like a prewar *zaibatsu*. Often referred to as *keiretsu*, the new corporate groupings came together after the occupation officially ended, and each usually included a bank, diverse manufacturing enterprises, engineering firms, and insurance companies. While the outward appearance between *zaibatsu* and *keiretsu* is arresting, there are significant differences: No holding companies coordinate activities, thousands of shareholders own each company's stock, and the core trading companies cannot legally compel allied firms to use their services exclusively. Nevertheless, the individual companies that constitute a corporate grouping do cooperate closely with one another in ways that make *keiretsu* powerful competitors on both the domestic and international scenes.

Influential business associations, such as Keidanren (the Federation of Economic Organizations), also exerted an impact on economic policy making by helping define economic goals and communicating them to the government. Formed in 1946, Keidanren in the 1980s included nearly one thousand individual corporations and more than one hundred industry-wide groups representing electronics firms, automobile manufacturers, financial institutions, and so forth. Blessed with ample financing, a large staff, and dozens of specialized research committees, Keidanren has formulated proposals about how to stimulate economic growth, built a consensus among members for its propositions, and transmitted specific recommendations to the government.

Since it is made up of Japan's leading companies and enterprise groups, it has been able to lobby effectively with the LDP on behalf of big business.

A government that made economic growth a national priority, bureaucrats who crafted industrial policy, the emergence of powerful companies and corporate alliances, and a consensual voice for big business: That congruity of seemingly common interests prompted some observers in the 1970s to popularize the term "Japan Incorporated" to suggest that a unique government–business relationship accounted for the country's postwar "economic miracle." As happens with many idioms, however, the underlying concept was too simplistic. For one thing, Japan never had a planned economy, only a penchant for economic planning. Moreover, conflict between MITI and other government agencies often crippled attempts to build a consensus behind certain projects. Such was the case in the 1970s and 1980s, when some parts of the bureaucracy—in particular the Ministry of Posts and Telecommunications, which had its own ideas about how to incubate a telecommunications industry—sabotaged most of MITI's efforts to promote high-tech consortia. In addition, MITI had almost no presence in some industrial sectors; beyond offering protections against foreign imports, for instance, it played no sustained, constructive role in developing the automotive industry. Finally, MITI's administrative guidance did not always carry much weight with major companies, which frequently preferred to act in ways that served their own specific interests. Thus, when it intruded into the circle of automakers to counsel Toyota not to challenge Isuzu's monopoly on diesel-powered trucks in 1956, reasoning that Japan did not need two such manufacturers, the chairman of Toyota fired back that "government has no right to tell us to stop. Toyota will continue selling diesel trucks even if the ministry is against it."[6]

Without anyone's denying that MITI and other segments of the economic bureaucracy played a role in promoting economic development during the era of high-speed growth in the 1960s and early 1970s, it is useful to distinguish between the mere act of drawing up plans and the more complex reality behind the country's overall economic success. In that context, major Japanese corporations deserve a greater share of the spotlight, for their efforts and initiatives were the major driving force behind Japan's stunning postwar recovery. Through the 1970s domestic consumer demand propelled the Japanese economy, and Sony bumped heads with Matsushita to obtain more shelf space in major retail centers, while Toyota and Nissan battled tooth and nail for domestic market share. As such companies built a customer base, refined technology purchased abroad, improved productivity, brought new state-of-the-art products to store shelves, and improved their balance sheets, they

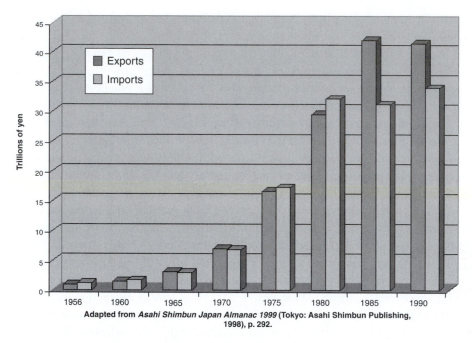

Adapted from *Asahi Shimbun Japan Almanac 1999* (Tokyo: Asahi Shimbun Publishing, 1998), p. 292.

**FIGURE 16.2** *Exports and Imports, 1956–1990*

made themselves into world-class competitors that could lead Japan's attempt to penetrate international markets, as shown in Figure 16.2

Small and medium-size enterprises also contributed greatly to the vigor of Japan's postwar economic recovery. Those businesses came in a variety of shapes: mom-and-pop retailers, family-owned restaurants and construction companies, regional wholesalers, and subcontractors for Japan's giant manufacturing corporations. The number of such firms increased rapidly during the era of high-speed growth and in 1989, constituted more than 90 percent of all registered companies in Japan. Such enterprises flourished for a variety of reasons. Entrepreneurs-to-be, an important influence on economic growth since the Meiji period, enthusiastically embraced innovative technology and production techniques to introduce popular new products to the consumer market, as Sony did in its infancy. Other small-scale operations filled an important niche in Japan's industrial structure; the presence of subcontractors allowed the Toyotas and Matsushitas of the world to have a reliable supply of quality parts without having to invest in plants themselves or expand their permanent work forces. The economic bureaucracy, fully aware of the role smaller firms played in growing the economy and achieving the goal of full employment, offered extensive assistance in the form of tax incentives, information about improving productivity, and an infrastructure of financial institutions, such as the Small Business Finance Corporation, established in 1953 to provide low-interest loans to buy equipment and modernize businesses.

Japan's relationship with its mentor, the United States, and a benign international environment also facilitated its recovery during the late Shōwa period. The capitalist countries were determined to replace the self-contained economic spheres of the prewar era with an open international economy in which goods, capital, and services could move freely across national borders. As part of that effort, the advanced nations of Western Europe and the Americas established the International Monetary Fund (IMF) and the World Bank with the intention of promoting international monetary cooperation and assisting with the reconstruction of postwar economies. In 1952 the United States sponsored Japan's membership in those two organizations and three years later arranged to have Japan join GATT, the General Agreement on Tariffs and Trade, whose goal was to reduce trade barriers. To assist its new ally in the Pacific further, the United States until 1971 tolerated a yen pegged at 360 to the dollar, a deliberate undervaluation that benefited Japanese exports enormously. Moreover, because of the United States–Japan Security Treaty, Japan could spend less than 1 percent of its national budget for defense, meaning that corporations, less burdened with taxes than otherwise would have been the case, were able to invest their profits in endeavors that had greater direct benefits for the economy. Finally, in the 1950s and 1960s the U.S. government did not object to Japanese restrictions on certain imports, such as automobiles, while it permitted Japanese manufacturers nearly unfettered access to the great American consumer market. In all, Japan reaped enormous advantages from a new economic order characterized by international cooperation, expanding trade opportunities, and stable commodity prices.

No single explanation can account adequately for Japan's postwar resurgence. More plausibly, as happened in the Meiji era, a number of factors came together to push the economic trend lines upward. Beyond the favorable international situation and the relationship with the United States, the legacy of the past projected an undeniable importance. A tradition of entrepreneurship, a labor pool filled with talented managers and blue-collar workers, and the experience of organizing successful large-scale enterprises all stood the country in good stead in the postwar era. The government helped by providing political stability, repairing and modernizing the country's infrastructure of transportation and communication, stabilizing the banking and currency systems, and crafting policies and bureaucratic agencies that promoted high-speed growth. Meanwhile, workers took up their tools and learned new skills, while corporate magnates and more humble entrepreneurs rebuilt old companies and invented new ones, adapted technology, and maneuvered to take advantage of domestic and international opportunities. Most men and women were happy with the results. Like the farmer who declared that his life was "sheer luxury" compared with the prewar years, when he "could never eat delicious food, couldn't eat enough food," nearly all Japanese came to enjoy an unprecedented level of physical comfort and even affluence in the closing decades of the Shōwa era.

## Affluence and the New Middle Class

High-speed economic growth accelerated the pace of urbanization as people gave up their lives as farmers, miners, foresters, and fishermen to take manufacturing jobs in and around urban centers. In 1950, 38 percent of the country's population lived in cities; 72 percent did so in 1972. By 1990 the redistribution of Japan's population had given rise to very large, densely populated conurbations. The million-plus cities of Fukuoka and Kita Kyūshū anchored a sprawling, expanding urban–industrial zone in northern Kyūshū. In central Japan the population of Nagoya proper, itself the nucleus of nearly forty commercial and industrialized satellite cities, zoomed past two million, and so tightly woven was the Kōbe–Osaka–Kyoto urban web, home to more than fifteen million, that travelers were hard put to discern the boundaries between cities. Farther to the north and east, thirty-nine million men and women jammed into the Tokyo Metropolitan Area. In total, nearly half of all Japanese lived within thirty miles of the three largest cities (Tokyo, Osaka, and Nagoya), squeezed into just 6 percent of the total land area of the country.

Within those great urban centers, the bleakness of the postwar years increasingly gave way to the good life. From the late 1950s Japan's economic boom translated into better housing, a richer and more varied diet, and more fashionable clothing. Everywhere remembrances wove themselves around a common theme: how poor we were then, how well off we are now. And who could deny the contrast? During the years of high-speed growth, bulldozers leveled lots for eleven million new houses and apartments, increasing the country's housing stock by nearly 70 percent. As quickly as

*Kita Kyūshū*

they could, people threw out the *monpe* and the darned clothing of the post-war years, packed away the family sewing machine, and began donning, as age, gender, and the passing decades dictated, a panoply of fashions: business suits and dark ties, miniskirts and imported sweaters, blue jeans with sweatshirts and sneakers, Liz Claiborne dresses and Gucci scarves. The diet also became more cosmopolitan as people ate more meat, bread, and pasta, drank more milk and fruit juices, relaxed at German-style beer halls, and dined in restaurants featuring American, French, Italian, Spanish, Russian, Greek, Korean, and Chinese cuisine.

Japan's urban centers were home to a broadly defined middle class that experienced the good life in different ways. The "new rich"—successful entrepreneurs, senior management in major corporations, and those lucky enough to inherit some farmland that they could sell to a developer before moving to town—might drive Mercedes-Benzes, vacation in San Francisco and Paris, and live in two-story residences containing separate living and dining rooms, a spacious tatami room opening onto a Japanese garden, a fully applianced kitchen, a modern bath with a space-age electronic toilet, and enough bedrooms for the parents and all the children to enjoy some privacy. Down the street, blue-collar workers, middle managers in small firms, and young families just starting out in life crowded into blocks of walk-up apartments, each household making do with a 2DK—two small tatami rooms, a combination dining room–kitchen, and a tiny bath that in total seldom spread over more than four or five hundred square feet. For such families, cars and vacations were more likely to be domestic than foreign.

Between the two extremes, a new cultural icon defined the expectations for many members of the urban middle class. During the 1960s and 1970s university-educated males aspired more than anything else to become salaried, white-collared office workers for major corporations, or a *sararī-man*, as the media dubbed the epitome of the so-called New Middle Class lifestyle. Such careers were not easy, since the *sararī-man* totally committed his soul and energies to the company, accepted temporary transfers to regional branch offices without complaint, took few vacations, cheerfully worked overtime almost every day, and once or twice a week (though perhaps tired and out of sorts) joined his colleagues for after-hours snacks and drinks. Moreover, his superiors expected him to continue to work hard and

*Salarymen troupe off to work*

faithfully discharge his responsibilities even if he eventually became a "window watcher," a *sararī-man* who had climbed the corporate ladder as high as his talents merited and who thus could expect no further promotions.

The payoffs for making such sacrifices were handsome. The salaryman basked in the assurance of lifetime employment, knew that his company would not lay him off even if his health or the economy took a turn for the worse, received an annual pay raise (even after promotion became only a remote possibility), spent his weekends and holidays playing golf with his friends and relaxing with his family, and banked a settlement equivalent to three or four years' worth of income upon retirement. In all, according to one scholar, the salaryman served as a model for other Japanese since his lifestyle was "within the range of realistic hopes and modern enough to be worthy of their highest aspirations."[7]

A typical salaryman hoped to marry a woman for whom he felt a romantic attachment and who comported herself in a manner that recalled the "good wife, wise mother" of an earlier generation. Since the husband's income was sufficient to take care of the family's needs, the main task of the housewife was to provide a comfortable home environment and serve her family. If the *sararī-man* breadwinner was able to carve out a better than average career, the family might live in a modest three-bedroom suburban house with a small garden; if not, then in a "mansion," a modern condominium whose amenities, but not floor space, rivaled those found in a single-family house. In either case, the wife spent her days cleaning, doing the marketing and cooking, gardening, and sometimes socializing with her friends in the neighborhood or from college days. She also was expected to manage household expenses, pay the bills on time, keep everyone well fed and neatly clothed, and carefully set aside enough to take care of both budgeted and unanticipated future expenses.

A mother as well as wife, she also had to raise the (ideally, two) children, sometimes almost single-handedly since father was at the office so much. In particular, in her persona as an "education mother" (*kyōiku mama*), she was supposed to hover over the kids nightly, making certain that they completed their homework assignments so that they could successfully scale the education ladder from local elementary school to a respected high school and then an appropriate college. The New Middle Class life brought women both frustration and gratification. Few housewives regarded cleaning and washing as anything but dull, and some regretted that their husbands had to spend so much time at the office. "I don't know why Japanese men marry," wondered one woman, "if they are never going to be home."[8] Nevertheless, according to most accounts in the mass media, the typical housewife–mother

*A middle-class Tokyo neighborhood in the 1950s*

also found a great deal of satisfaction in her life: She was married to a man for whom she felt both affection and respect, enjoyed financial security, relished her free moments and the time she spent with her family, and took pride in nurturing the futures of her husband and children. Society reciprocated by honoring the modern version of a good wife and wise mother, and as one expert noted, "Japanese women perceive their work as wives and mothers as important because it is socially valued."[9]

The New Middle Class lifestyle also imposed expectations upon youth. The sons and daughters of *sararī-man* fathers and education mothers could not expect to inherit family businesses or farms, but they could follow in their parents' footsteps. For boys, that meant studying especially hard, perhaps even spending a year or so after high school graduation in special cram schools so that they could pass the rigorous entrance examinations that guarded the portals to Japan's elite colleges. Girls could anticipate walking a different path to adulthood. For them, many parents considered junior college the suitable end point for higher education, since few corporate boardrooms, bureaucratic offices, or professional societies set out welcome

mats for career women. When the children were graduated, mother and father encouraged the sons to seek the security and prestige of a salaryman's
life. The received wisdom called upon young women to work for a couple
of years as an OL, a pink-collar "office lady" who did menial clerical work;
to take lessons in assorted polite arts, such as flower arranging and the tea
ceremony; and then to settle down with Mr. Right in an ideal union described in one ironic expression as *ie tsuki, kā tsuki, baba nuki* ("having a house,
a car, and no mother-in-law").

## Farm Families and the Good Life

The reverse side of rapid urbanization was a massive rural exodus as the
promise of well-paying jobs and the excitement of bright lights lured millions of young men and women into Japan's burgeoning cities. The speed
of the transition was astounding. In 1950 fully half of all graduates from
middle and high schools went into agriculture. A mere decade later, in 1960,
only 10 percent did so, and even that figure fell by half over the next five
years. Between 1950 and 1970 Japan's total farm population dropped from
thirty-six million to twenty-three million, and by 1990 only 3 to 5 percent
of the country's working population was toiling in the fields, compared with
almost 50 percent when the occupation had come to an end.

*A woman in a* monpe *threshes barley, 1946*

*A farmer transplants rice mechanically, 1974*

Although depopulation cast a pall over Japan's more remote regions, especially in the northeast and along the coast of the Sea of Japan, in the long run rapid mechanization enabled most families that stayed on the farm to enjoy less onerous, more productive, and increasingly prosperous lives. Throughout the 1960s and 1970s the growing affordability of domestically manufactured power-driven tillers (89,000 in use in 1955; 3.5 million in 1970), plows, and planters eliminated much of the grueling, backbreaking labor of spring planting; hand-held sprayers and new chemical insecticides kept summer pests at bay; and threshers, grain dryers, and minitrucks helped farmers gather the harvest and deliver it to market. As a result, Japan's total rice crop increased from about ten million to slightly more than fourteen million tons between 1950 and 1975. Such productivity gains meant that farmers could grow all the rice consumed in the country and still set aside some time and land for other high-income endeavors, such as raising fruits and vegetables, growing cut flowers, and fattening up expensive, hand-massaged beef cattle for urban consumers.

Mechanization also affected lifestyles. The proliferation of laborsaving devices released men from full-time duty in the fields. Some commuted daily to permanent jobs in nearby sawmills and foundries or found employment as taxi drivers and salesmen in regional towns; others moved away from home for several months during the slack winter season, taking temporary jobs as construction workers in major cities. More and more, farm work gravitated into the hands of the *san-chan*, a reference to stay-at-home wives, grandfathers, grandmothers, made by combining the word "three" (*san*) with the diminutive form of the honorific customarily attached to names and titles (also pronounced *san* but transposed here to the more affectionate *chan*). Yet woman's work apparently was never done, since the majority of farm wives and nearly all unmarried daughters supplemented family incomes whenever possible by clerking in local shops and government offices, doing piecework part-time in local pajama and glove factories, and even working on construction projects.

*San-chan* farming placed heavy physical and psychological strains on women, especially the wives who worked outside the home and feared that they were neglecting their children and husbands. One explained:

When a couple works together in the fields, they can understand each other's hardships and pleasures, but it is difficult to understand another's feelings when you work in different places. After you return home from work, you have housework to do. You should be womanly, but after working outside as hard as a man, it is not easy suddenly to become womanly. Many times when I return home tired, I forget to say even a word of comfort to my husband. When the woman, too, is busy, she often neglects even to straighten up the house. When her husband reproaches her, she flies into a rage. At such times she should apologize, but she wants to reply, "I haven't been playing around all day, you know."[10]

Whatever the social costs imposed by the modernization of agriculture, increasing productivity and greater access to nonfarm income made for a much wealthier countryside. Farm incomes exploded, multiplying 700 percent between 1960 and 1979 and then nearly doubling again during the 1980s, as shown in Figure 16.3. Remarkably, in 1973 average farm family income was 7 percent, and in 1990 nearly 20 percent, higher than for the families of urban workers. Almost as surprising, by 1990 only one in eight of Japan's farm families pursued agriculture on a full-time basis, and most rural families earned a whopping 70 percent of their incomes from nonfarm activities.

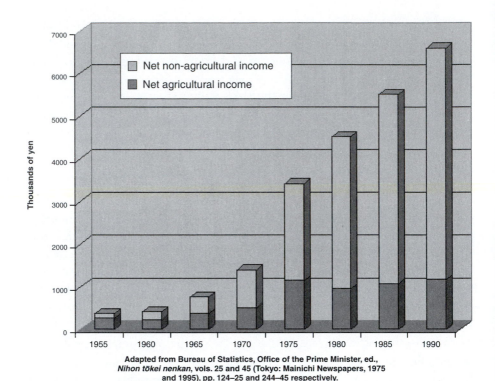

Adapted from Bureau of Statistics, Office of the Prime Minister, ed.,
*Nihon tōkei nenkan*, vols. 25 and 45 (Tokyo: Mainichi Newspapers, 1975
and 1995), pp. 124–25 and 244–45 respectively.

**FIGURE 16.3**  *Annual Income for Farm Households, 1955–1990*

The newly affluent farm families participated fully and enthusiastically
in Japan's vibrant consumer society. They drove the same Toyotas, preferred
the same blue jeans, built the same up-to-date houses, and stuffed them with
the same array of electric appliances as did their middle-class city cousins.
Playfully, in both city and village, people reshaped the three sacred imperial regalia (the mirror, sword, and jewel) to create imaginative symbols for
their new affluence. In the late 1950s, it was said, everyone wanted the three
s's—a *senpūki*, *sentaku*, and *suihanki* (electric household fan, electric washing
machine, and electric rice cooker). A few years later consumer desires turned
to the three k's—*kā*, *kūrā*, and *karā terebi* (car, home air conditioner, and color
television)—while a more chic triad of j's—jewels, jet vacations overseas,
and a *jūtaku* (a splendid modern house)—set the tone for the 1970s.

The mixed blessings of the late Shōwa era left many farm families perplexed about the future. Few would give up the laborsaving equipment and

material well-being that had come their way, but most were uneasy, even discontented, about how the changing nature of agriculture had buffeted their lives. One common reaction was to cast a wistful eye toward the lifestyle of the urban family. Given the rigors facing them, it was not unusual that many farm women dreamed of being "just a housewife," and many rural families even deposited their incomes from farming and part-time jobs with the local agricultural cooperative and then withdrew it monthly, "just like a salaryman." But emulating the urban New Middle Class could not erase anxieties about the future. Many a farmer doubted that the social circumstances of rural life would improve anytime soon, and almost every farm couple wondered if they should encourage their children to stay with the land or counsel them toward other work. Education statistics indicated that a growing number of daughters and second and third sons were seeking college degrees and the comfort of city jobs. Apparently many farm families approved such a change in life course, even while regretting that college graduation would take their children to far-off places for career and marriage. As one scholar observed, for the late Shōwa farm youth "getting ahead and staying put are not easily reconciled."[11]

## Critiquing the Experiences of the Late Shōwa Era

Whatever clouds obscured the future of agriculture, many Japanese wholeheartedly applauded the changes that swept the country between the mid-1950s and the mid-1980s, hailing them as the triumphal climax of Japan's quest for modernity. Not unexpectedly, positive assessments credited the economic miracle for moving the nation to the apex of the modern, industrialized world and for creating a mass society in which most people, according to one prominent social scientist, were "reasonably well-to-do, well educated, and proud of their values and lifestyle."[12] Many experts and public commentators credited the LDP and the central bureaucracy for providing Japan with an era of prosperity, internal stability, and international peace unprecedented in its modern history. After noting the close relationship that existed between politicians and bureaucrats, one pundit especially credited the "higher civil service" for "initiating important social and economic policies" that enabled Japan to achieve its "remarkable success."[13]

Foreign observers joined in lauding Japan's postwar recovery and growing affluence. In *Japan as Number One*, published in 1979 and a best seller in Japan and the United States, a distinguished sociologist acknowledged that Japanese society had its fair share of shortcomings but concluded that on balance "Japan has dealt more successfully with more of the basic problems of postindustrial society than any other country."[14] At the same time, Edwin O. Reischauer, so pessimistic twenty-five years earlier, called Japan the "best organized and most dynamic of all major nations."[15] So impressed was the prominent futurologist Herman Kahn with Japan's economic performance that he saw Japan as America's heir apparent and declared that the twenty-first century would belong to the island nation.

Many ordinary Japanese expressed a general contentment with the way events had unfolded in the late Shōwa period by cultivating a self-satisfied sense of homogeneity and middle-class inclusiveness. Despite obvious differences in income levels, for nearly twenty years, from the early 1970s through the late 1980s, more than 90 percent of all Japanese—male and female, farmer and big-city resident, *sararī-man* and OL—identified themselves as belonging to the "middle class" in the annual survey of Japanese society conducted by the prime minister's office and in spot polls taken by news organizations.

A shared consumerism and a common desire to own the most up-to-date material goods contributed greatly to the notion that Japan was a one-class nation. Similar fashions and food, seen and eaten in every town and prefecture, further encouraged a sense of homogeneity. So too did television. By 1960 half of all households had a TV receiver, more than 90 percent watched the Olympics on their own black-and-white sets, and a similar percentage enjoyed color TV in their homes in 1975. With the average person tuning in for nearly four hours a day, news broadcasts, serialized dramas, cooking shows, sportscasts, and TV "events," such as the enormously popular "Red and White Singing Contest," a three-hour program aired live on NHK each New Year's Eve that featured leading singers performing their hits from the past year, created the impression that everyone participated in a uniform national culture. Even regional dialects, in prewar Japan simultaneously a stigma and source of local pride for those from the "sticks," were heard less and less frequently as "NHK-Japanese" became the nation's standard.

Furthermore, after the occupation ended, the government returned control over primary and secondary schooling to the Ministry of Education. Beginning in the late 1950s, bureaucrats in Tokyo set curricular guidelines for schools nationwide and zealously exercised their authority to review and authorize textbooks, with the consequence that children across the country once again learned virtually identical lessons, often on the same day. The approved texts generally spread the message that an enlightened Meiji leadership had set Japan on the road to modernity; that the 1930s and 1940s were an aberration, best passed over quickly and discussed in bland vocabulary that had Japan "intruding into" rather than "invading" China; and that the later Shōwa decades witnessed a return to the expected course of peace and progress. Meanwhile, ethics courses, reintroduced in elementary and middle schools in 1958, provided an opportunity for students to discuss family relationships, social obligations, and national values.

Despite the standardization of education, mass culture, and material standards of living, the concept of a single middle class did not accurately describe the reality of family, school, and work, as suggested by the life histories of Japanese farm families. Moreover, even within the country's major cities, where so many persons subscribed to the aspirations of the *sararī-man* lifestyle, fewer than one-quarter of all workers were white-collar employees who enjoyed lifetime employment, and just slightly more than 50 percent of high school graduates continued to college (and only a small fraction of those passed the entrance exams into elite universities). The notion of homogeneity papered over the persistence of variations—between city and countryside, male and female, young and old—and, as the Shōwa period drew to a close, the diverse experiences of more than 100 million Japanese added a rainbow of unflattering hues to the emerging critique of the late Shōwa experience.

While some Japanese showered profuse accolades upon the economic miracle, others blamed a fixation with the rising GNP and all-out economic growth for inflicting unjustified social costs on the ordinary men, women, and children of the country. Few would deny that living standards in general had improved in the postwar decades or that beneficiaries far outnumbered the victims of high-speed growth. Nevertheless, overcrowding, long commutes between home and office, and undersized housing continued to plague urban dwellers. Moreover, unbridled industrialization had turned Japan into "a polluters' paradise," in the phrase of one observer, where toxic wastes poisoned the food chain, contaminated effluents wiped out coastal fishing, and automobile exhaust mixed with smokestack gases to produce clouds of suffocating photochemical smog.[16]

During the late 1950s and 1960s thousands of residents in industrial cities, such as Yokkaichi in Mie Prefecture, suffered from asthma and other respiratory diseases, cadmium poisoning crippled villagers and townspeople living along the Jinzū River in Toyama Prefecture, and in western Japan arsenic-contaminated powdered milk sold by the Morinaga Milk Industry Company caused diarrhea, fever, and leukemia among 12,000 infants, 130 of whom died. The most notorious case of environmental pollution occurred at the city of Minamata in Kumamoto Prefecture, where mercury compounds

*Victims of Minamata disease*

discharged into local fishing waters by the Chisso Corporation touched off a massive outbreak of a degenerative disease that progressed from numbness of the extremities to constriction of vision and hearing, loss of bodily control, and mental incapacity. The disease first appeared in the 1950s, and by 1979 more than 300 residents of Minamata had died, while another 1,200 suffered from various symptoms.

Eventually the LDP and the bureaucracy responded by enacting some of the toughest antipollution legislation in the world. But they did not move nearly quickly enough for many skeptics, who launched grassroots protests against what they considered inadequate government responses to their concerns. In 1958 the victims and their relatives at Minamata were among the first to organize a citizens' movement, and elsewhere farmers, fishermen, and other ordinary Japanese also banded together to demonstrate against industrial pollution and environmental destruction. Activist lawyers and sympathetic doctors, scientists, and journalists offered help and tactical advice about how to file legal suits for damages. By 1967, when the Diet finally passed the comprehensive Pollution Countermeasures Basic Law, courts had handed down several landmark judgments in the plaintiffs' favor.

The success of the antipollution actions inspired other kinds of citizens' movements. During the late 1960s and 1970s activists blocked the construction of a new airport in Okinawa Prefecture that would have destroyed irreplaceable species of coral, and residents in several prefectures successfully thwarted government plans to build nuclear reactors near their homes.

A particular feature of the new activism was the appearance of voluntary associations organized by stay-at-home housewives. Employing what they called a mother's logic, those women campaigned against rising food prices, traffic congestion and accidents, and inadequate garbage disposal. The typical citizens' movement tended to see itself as a nonpolitical, nonpartisan alliance that came together on a temporary basis to achieve a specific goal. Even so, the actions of the various protest groups constituted a stinging rebuke of certain LDP policies and damned those who would elevate economic growth above any concerns.

Other critics of the late Shōwa experience drew a bead on the extravagant excesses of the New Consumerism practiced by Japan's nouveau riche and the more affluent members of the middle class. Well-to-do Japanese might prefer to see themselves as enlightened consumers whose liberated consumption patterns freed them from outdated, restrictive norms of hierarchy and class. For their detractors, however, expensive tennis lessons, hundred-dollar melons, top-of-the-line automobiles that were driven only on Sundays, and memberships in exclusive golf clubs that ran into the tens of thousands of dollars represented not an exciting new lifestyle but rather a cri de coeur that suggested just how thoroughly boredom and spiritual emptiness pervaded life in Japan's suburbs and wealthier urban neighborhoods.

For many, Nantonaku, kurisutaru ("Somehow, Crystal") exemplified the nightmare of young, well-to-do Tokyoites committed to a price-is-no-object lifestyle. A prize-winning first novel by a university student that quickly sold 800,000 copies after it appeared in December 1980, Nantonaku, kurisutaru depicted two weeks in the life of a college student who had a casual affair with a young man she met at a disco while her musician boyfriend was away on tour. The plot, however, was secondary to the more than four hundred notes that accompanied the text and informed the reader about the pleasures of the "crystal" life, a term the author coined to describe the nihilistic attitudes of his materialistic generation. "If you feel like cake in the middle of the night," the author instructed, "the place to go is Chianti's* in Aoyama 3-chōme,* where you can have your cake with a glass of white wine. Afterwards, go for ice cream at Swensen's,* a shop with San Francisco flavors on 'Killer' Avenue*," with each asterisk referring the reader to a detailed note extolling the virtues of a chic retailing district, shop, or brand name.[17] Particularly galling to critics of unrestrained consumerism were the facile sophistication and mocking arrogance of many passages: "Buying a Courrèges summer sweater and carrying if off in a Courrèges shopping bag: it's the snobbery* I wanted to cherish" and "It's o.k. to have espresso with cake, but once in a while, you want to have it French style, with white wine: it's the affectation I wanted to cherish."

For those repelled by the "affectation" and "snobbery" of the fictional characters in *Nantonaku, kurisutaru*, it was a short step to attacking the real-life "nuclearized" family that was coming to typify middle-class urban life in general. Although the transformation toward smaller families had taken longer than the rhetoric suggested, it had been dramatic: In the 1920s, more than 30 percent of all Japanese households had three or more generations sharing the same hearth; in 1985, 61 percent were nuclear families, 18 percent were single-person households, and just 15 percent had three generations living together under the same roof. For conservative commentators, changing household composition signaled an erosion of traditional values. Isolated in their small house or cramped condominium, the *sararī-man* and his wife could not easily care for elderly parents, thus raising the specter of older persons "dying alone and unwanted."[18] Moreover, the salaryman father was absent from the home too much and did not discipline his children nearly enough. The leisured middle-class mother did not help matters either. Already excessively obsessed with material objects, she spent too much time playing tennis with a small coterie of friends and then carving the sugar cubes into fancy designs for afternoon tea, with the consequence that she lost her "natural child-rearing instincts." Not surprisingly, in the eyes of such critics, Japanese children studied hard, but they were growing up introverted and withdrawn, spineless and weak-willed, selfish and egotistical.

The families of *shitamachi* offered a real-life, self-conscious critique of the New Middle Class lifestyle. Often translated as "downtown," *shitamachi* refers to urban neighborhoods filled cheek by jowl with small shopkeepers and artisans. A typical "downtown" district might include a bakery, rice dealer, bookstore, barbershop, beauty parlor, flower store, and a couple of small restaurants and coffee shops with a few tables each; family workshops making tofu, noodles, tatami mats, kimonos, plastic bottles, and machine parts; and retailers specializing in vegetables, fruits, fish, groceries, toys, stationary, sporting goods, electrical appliances, beer and sake, and futon and other bedding. Frequently the families of *shitamachi*, most of whom lived in apartments above their shops, boasted that their cultural values and social identities derived from traditional merchant life in Japan's preindustrial castle towns.

Although such assertions relied on a highly selective reading of the past, the people of *shitamachi* did lead lives and interact with their neighbors in ways that contrasted sharply with the stereotypical middle-class family. One anthropological study identified the "Onuma household" as epitomizing the *shitamachi* ideal. The father, mother, and adult son and his wife ran the family business, which employed about half a dozen other people and handled the silk brocades that went into expensive wedding kimonos. Grandmother Onuma helped out by packing boxes, answering the telephone, cooking meals, and keeping an eye on the grandchildren. It was a lifestyle that merged family and business, home and workplace, with three generations cooperating to maintain an enterprise that could be passed intact to the fourth, still in the toddler stage. Moreover, self-employed shopkeepers like the Onumas, who worked according to their own schedules, socialized with their neighbors in ways that office workers never could, participating in everything from political clubs to volunteer fire-fighting brigades and sports teams. Gathered around the family table in the evening, the Onumas drew comfort from the warmth of community ties, took pride in the autonomy that came from running one's own business, and felt "smug" when comparing themselves with the "drudges" who worked as salarymen.[19]

## Popular Nostalgia

The valorization of the *shitamachi* family and community was part of a nostalgic longing for the values of the past that began to sweep across Japan during the 1970s and then intensified in the 1980s. After decades of rapid change—of defeat, occupation, and recovery; of industrialization, urbanization, affluence, and the standardization of cultural norms—many Japanese had a sad sense that something valuable was about to slip from their hands and disappear forever. For them, the consummate *shitamachi* multigenerational family represented the reincarnation of traditional personal relationships in a way that neither the truncated *sararī-man* family nor the modern farm household, itself undergoing radical change and threatened with extinction, could ever emulate.

The Japan National Railway's "Discover Japan" campaign cast up romantic visions of things past and now nearly lost. Launched to promote ridership to scenic spots by vacationing families and small groups of friends, the wildly successful slogan, according to one scholar, "came to symbolize a generation's desire to escape to its origins."[20] Large color posters, displayed prominently in the windows of travel bureaus and at JNR stations, featured young people—often one or two city women still in their early twenties, obviously single, and dressed in blue jeans—encountering some aspect of a more authentic, almost forgotten Japaneseness: village girls raking autumn leaves at a local Shinto shrine, a weathered farmer carrying vegetables, a solitary Buddhist monk praying at a lonely mountain temple, a woman gathering seaweed along a rocky shore. The locales for the miniature dramas of self-discovery were not usually Japan's famous tourist meccas but, rather, were unnamed landscapes, at once familiar yet still remote enough to represent a purer time and place. With uncanny perception, each "Discover Japan" poster transformed a single scene, glimpsed in a fleeting moment, into a timeless, universal depiction of what it should mean to be and to feel Japanese.

Somewhat ironically, although the farm family itself was no longer what it had been, the "Discover Japan" campaign helped ignite a *furusato būmu* ("home village boom") that further romanticized country life and made rural folk into shining exemplars of Japanese tradition. A *furusato* is one's hometown or ancestral village, the place, in the words of one Japanese, "where one can return whenever the urge strikes; a place where one's heart finds repose and where the routines of daily life are grounded in compassion; a place where customs are highly valued."[21] Thus, in the 1980s urban dwellers trooped back to the rural heartland to find their roots, and villagers made a pitch for domestic sightseers (and, not incidentally, their tourist yen) by sponsoring handicraft exhibitions and harvesttime contests, hosting amateur puppet plays and folk Kabuki, and reviving old festivals (and inventing new ones). Like the persons who sought to "Discover Japan," those who celebrated the *furusato* hoped to capture a moment out of time where the honest integrity of farm work, the bonds of family and community, and the memory of quaint, thatched-roof farmhouses still counted for something.

Popular nostalgia is a way to use the verities of yesteryear to prepare for the uncertainties of tomorrow. When different worlds touch, the comforts and solace of the past can ease the anxieties of the present and provide a moral compass to carry forward into the unknown future. With the Shōwa epoch drawing to a close, Japanese pondered their circumstances, wondering if economic growth was a blessing or curse, if the government was friend or foe, and if new ways of life could be as satisfying as the old. As they did so, several events of considerable consequence, lurking unseen over the horizon, were about to break the LDP hegemony, throw the golden economy into deep recession, and create a new world order. As the Japanese found themselves venturing into the uncharted waters of the 1990s, the critiques of the late Shōwa era transformed themselves into an extended discussion about how Japan might employ the lessons of the past to move forward into another new century and a new millennium.

CHAPTER 17

# Another New Century

On January 7, 1989, the Shōwa emperor died, and his elaborate obsequies recalled the grand farewell that the nation paid his grandfather, Emperor Meiji, in 1912. At the beginning of the century the booming of the funeral cannon sounded to the novelist Natsume Sōseki "like the last lament for the passing of an age." At century's end the death of the Shōwa emperor likewise signaled to many Japanese the conclusion to another momentous period in their history. The Shōwa emperor had assumed the throne in the 1920s, when political parties first claimed a leading role in policy formation, *mobo* and *moga* defined new cultural norms, and Japan was a friend to the capitalist nations of the West. Twenty years into his reign, Japan was a defeated nation, condemned in the eyes of the world for militaristic policies and an insular mentality, its future bleak and unpromising. Some four decades later, at the end of the longest imperial reign in Japan's recorded history, the country had regained its international standing, surprised everyone with its economic prowess, become a more open and egalitarian society, and affirmed its status as one of the most advanced, modern nations on the face of the globe. With the death of the Shōwa emperor, there was much to pause and reflect upon, and to many, Japan seemed to have completed its quest for modernity.

The Shōwa emperor's son and successor, Crown Prince Akihito, choose Heisei for his reign title. Taken from passages in the Chinese classics *Shi ji* ("Book of History") and *Shu jing* ("Book of Documents"), the era name expressed a hope for achieving peace everywhere, in heaven and on earth, at home and abroad. Japan's new monarch soon discovered, however, that peace was not synonymous with serenity and tranquillity. During the first Heisei decade

Japan's apparently unstoppable economy hit an abrupt speed bump and then broke down in recession, the LDP watched power slip from its grasp, a younger generation questioned the relevance of middle-class values, discontented minorities challenged the validity of an imagined cultural homogeneity, and the collapse of the Soviet Union reordered the international landscape.

The upheavals of the 1990s opened up questions about plotting the future course of democracy in Japan, renewing economic growth, discovering a way to maintain social cohesion while encouraging individual self-fulfillment, and interacting with the outside world. Suddenly, rather than being the pursuit of a fixed, achievable goal, the quest for modernity seemed more like a journey on a turbulent river that flowed on forever, always changing, never ending. Nearly one hundred years earlier, at the juncture of the Meiji and Taishō eras, Japan looked back on a half century of rapid change, put aside nostalgia for the past, and began to take up the challenges and explore the opportunities of a new century. It was time to do so once again.

## Bursting Bubbles

Enriched by an excessively strong dollar, in the early 1980s Americans feasted on a rich diet of goods purchased from Japan and other exporting nations. In quick order, America's ravenous appetite for foreign products led to chronic trade imbalances, and protectionists began to call for import restrictions and other measures to insulate U.S. manufacturers against foreign competition. Concerned that such sentiments for trade limitations ultimately might endanger the free trade system of the postwar era, representatives from the leading industrial powers met at New York's Plaza Hotel in September 1985 and decided to intervene in foreign exchange markets in order to bolster the yen and weaken the dollar. Such monetary engineering, experts concurred, would right the balance of trade by dampening demand in the United States for suddenly expensive foreign goods and encouraging America's trading partners to purchase cheaper U.S. manufactures. In addition, Japan and other major exporting nations agreed to stimulate domestic demand as a way of encouraging imports from the United States. As a consequence of the so-called Plaza Accord, the value of the Japanese yen quickly doubled in value, while at home the Japanese government boosted consumption by sponsoring a stimulus package that included lower taxes, reduced interest rates, and easier credit.

The Plaza Accord did not achieve its intended results, however. The robust yen permitted Japanese firms to import raw materials at cheaper prices than before and to invest in modern new plants, with the ironic consequence that lower costs of production fueled a renewed spurt in Japanese exports; between 1985 and 1987 Japan's annual trade surplus with the United States skyrocketed from forty-nine to eighty-seven billion dollars. Awash with profits, Japanese firms expanded abroad. From 1986 to 1991 Japanese overseas investment amounted to more than 200 billion dollars, as the Sony Corporation laid out a massive sum to buy Columbia Pictures, and Matsushita purchased MCA, making those two Japanese companies proud competitors in the global entertainment market. Meanwhile, Honda and other automobile manufacturers opened production facilities in the American heartland, and Japanese real estate firms snapped up famous golf courses and luxury hotels in Hawaii and California. At home full employment, higher wages, and growing corporate investments climaxed in a frenzy of speculation; the Nikkei index of leading stocks tripled from just under thirteen thousand points in January 1986 to nearly thirty-nine thousand in December 1989, while housing and land prices in major urban centers spiraled upward at the same dizzy pace.

The air rushed out of Japan's overheated "bubble economy" in 1989. A recession in Western industrial nations and intense competition from developing countries in Southeast Asia, Latin America, and Eastern Europe trimmed corporate sales. With profits slumping, the Nikkei went into a nosedive, plummeting by nearly 40 percent, from thirty-nine thousand to twenty-four thousand points, between December 1989 and the end of 1990, before shedding another ten thousand points to close at the fourteen thousand level in August 1992, a loss of nearly 65 percent from its peak. At the same time, companies tabled their expansion plans, home buyers hesitated, and the real estate market collapsed, wiping out paper assets worth hundreds of trillions of yen.

With the pricking of the speculative bubble, the 1990s turned into a decade of declining consumption, business retrenchment, stagnation, pessimism, and finally a stubborn, disheartening recession. Between 1992 and 1995, real rates of economic growth crept along at barely 1 percent per annum, the most anemic performance of the postwar era, and an embarrassed Matsushita sold MCA at a bargain-basement price, while Sony swallowed heavy operating losses in order to hang on to Columbia Pictures. Worse was still ahead. As the economy slid into the doldrums, speculators who had taken out bank loans to finance their stock and real estate acquisitions could not meet repayment schedules, nor could they sell their rapidly deflating assets to pay off their obligations. By some estimates, Japan's banks were stuck with the equivalent of one trillion dollars' worth of nonperforming loans, and as they cut back on their lending in the mid-1990s, a severe credit crunch added to the nation's economic woes.

Its banking sector in crisis, Japan could not avoid being drawn into the pan-Asian recession triggered by the collapse of the Thai currency in the summer of 1997. By early fall, Japan's unemployment rate and the number of business bankruptcies reached new highs for the postwar era. In November, Sanyo and Yamaichi Securities, two of the country's leading brokerage houses, and Hokkaidō Takushoku, a large bank in northern Japan, went under, making that month "one of the most troubled in the annals of Japanese financial history," according to one analyst, and conjuring up frightful comparisons to the banking crisis of the late 1920s.[1] A year later, in the autumn of 1998, some optimists averred that Japan's economic fundamentals were solid and foresaw an eventual turnaround, only to hear the head of the Economic Planning Agency announce that the nation's economy had contracted by −0.7 percent in fiscal 1997 (April 1, 1997–March 31, 1998) and then predict that the numbers would worsen as it headed toward the new millennium. Indeed, the gross domestic product fell by 1.4 percent in the fiscal quarter of October–December 1999, and in the spring of 2000 the unemployment rate stood at 4.9 percent, a postwar high.

The LDP's political bubble also burst at the beginning of the Heisei era. In the spring of 1989, Prime Minister Takeshita Noboru, who had taken over Tanaka Kakuei's faction within the LDP, resigned his office after the public learned that he had accepted 150 million yen in illegal donations from Recruit Cosmo, a publishing and real estate company. The LDP suffered further embarrassment when news leaked out that Takeshita's successor, Uno Sōsuke, had been paying for a geisha's favors and then slipped her hush money to keep quiet about the tawdry details of their long-running affair. Uno stepped down in disgrace after just six weeks in office, and the LDP turned over the party presidency, and thus the office of prime minister, to Kaifu Toshiki, a little-known Diet member whose chief virtue was that he had not been tarred by any scandal. Although Kaifu proved to be unexpectedly popular with the Japanese public, when his second term expired, the LDP reverted to the norm and tapped an old-time insider, Miyazawa Kiichi, to lead the party and the nation. It was not a happy choice. In March 1993 Kanemaru Shin—Takeshita's successor as head of the old Tanaka faction and Miyazawa's deputy prime minister—was arrested for taking illegal contributions from Sagawa Kyūbin, a parcel delivery service, when police raids uncovered one billion yen's worth of gold bars secreted in his office and under the floorboards of his home.

The Recruit and Sagawa scandals, together with the LDP's inability to deal effectively with Japan's economic woes, undermined confidence in the

**TABLE 17.1**   *Prime Ministers in the First Decade of the Heisei Era*

| PRIME MINISTER | PARTY AFFILIATION | CABINET NUMBER | CABINET TERM |
|---|---|---|---|
| Takeshita Noboru | LDP | | November 6, 1987–June 3, 1989 |
| Uno Sōsuke | LDP | | June 3, 1989–August 10, 1989 |
| Kaifu Toshiki | LDP | First | August 10, 1989–February 28, 1990 |
| Kaifu Toshiki | LDP | Second | February 28, 1990–November 5, 1991 |
| Miyazawa Kiichi | LDP | | November 5, 1991–August 9, 1993 |
| Hosokawa Morihiro | JNP | | August 9, 1993–April 25, 1994 |
| Hata Tsutomu | JRP | | April 25, 1994–June 30, 1994 |
| Murayama Tomiichi | SDPJ | | June 30, 1994–January 11, 1996 |
| Hashimoto Ryūtarō | LDP | First | January 11, 1996–November 7, 1996 |
| Hashimoto Ryūtarō | LDP | Second | November 7, 1996–July 30, 1998 |
| Obuchi Keizō | LDP | | July 30, 1998–April 5, 2000 |

LDP denotes affiliation with the Liberal Democratic Party.

JNP denotes affiliation with the Japan New Party.

JRP denotes affiliation with the Japan Renewal Party.

SDPJ denotes affiliation with the Social Democratic Party of Japan (previously, Japan Socialist Party).

party and ushered in a period of political instability. Disillusioned with their elders, a number of younger politicians defected from the LDP and formed several independent parties, including the Japan New Party, the Japan Renewal Party (Shinseitō), and the New Party Harbinger (Shintō Sakigake). Voters also shunned the LDP, which lost control of the House of Representatives in elections held in July 1993. After elaborate negotiations, Hosokawa Morihiro, head of the Japan New Party, cobbled together a seven-party coalition and on August 9, 1993, became the first non-LDP prime minister since the party was formed in 1955. When it came to light that he too had suspect dealings with Sagawa Kyūbin, Hosokawa resigned, to be followed by two other non-LDP prime ministers before the Liberal Democrats regained control of the cabinet under the leadership of Hashimoto Ryūtarō.

The future of the LDP remained unclear, however, as Japan headed into the new century. The public showed little confidence in Hashimoto's successor, Obuchi Keizō, who professed himself to be a "mild-mannered and plodding" individual.[2] When Obuchi suffered a stroke that left him hospitalized and brain-dead in April 2000, LDP veteran Mori Yoshirō took over the helm of state and announced that his administration would work for the "Rebirth of Japan" by creating a society, "rich in spirit," where people "live in security," realize their "dreams for the future," and engender "the trust of the world."[3] As lofty as those goals appeared, public opinion polls indicated that most Japanese had little faith in the ability of any politician to lead Japan out of its economic and political wasteland.

## Assessing Blame and Finding Cures for the End-of-the-Millennium Blues

As Mori's sloganeering suggested, the events of the early Heisei era evoked serious discussion about the economic and political future of Japan. On the political side of the ledger, the decade of the 1990s opened with calls for the return of "rugged" statesmen in the tradition of Itō Hirobumi and Yoshida Shigeru, who frequently were portrayed as "farsighted and courageous" leaders with great "strength of character."[4] Within the ranks of the LDP itself, Hashimoto Ryūtarō and other politicians who maneuvered to grasp power liked to bill themselves as "new leaders" who would bring fresh perspectives and renewed energy to the governing process. In that spirit, Hashimoto's cabinet in December 1997 announced plans for a comprehensive reform of Japan's financial system, nicknamed the Japanese Big Bang after the sweeping deregulation of the British securities industry undertaken by Prime Minister Margaret Thatcher in 1986. However, the inability of the cabinet to translate such talk into specific measures that would "rescue the nation from a slump that seems to have no end," in the words of one commentator, left most Japanese unimpressed.[5] In July 1998 voters handed the LDP a humiliating defeat in the election for the House of Councillors, prompting Hashimoto's resignation. The elevation of the uninspiring Obuchi and Mori to the nation's highest political office left many Japanese wondering aloud about just how to attract more capable individuals into politics.

Rather than focus on individual personalities, other critics posed systemic questions, asking whether Japan should move toward a two-party or multiparty system. Decades of single-party rule by the LDP, some charged, had encouraged money politics, tempted party leaders to ignore popular opinion and make decisions behind closed doors, and brought about an unfortunate state of affairs in which timid "politicians deal with little problems but not with the greater issues."[6] More open competition between two or more parties, in that view, would unleash a "meaningful rivalry of ideas" that could generate vigorous and substantive public debate, result in the formulation of more imaginative policy alternatives, and compel the prime minister and Diet members to serve the public in a more responsible manner.[7]

In that context, speculation arose about whether the LDP could, or even should, survive a shift to a more pluralistic system. Election results clearly demonstrated that a vast proportion of the Japanese public had exhausted its patience with the LDP, and surprisingly, party regulars themselves were divided on the question. Some politicians, like Hashimoto and Obuchi, clearly hoped to recapture the glory of the past, but others thought "it would be a relief if the LDP just dissolved," as one old-timer said. "We oldsters should hang up our gloves and retire from the ring, taking pride in what we accomplished. The youngsters should be out there forming a new party—or they can join another party, if that's what they want. The thing is, sooner or later the party is going to break up. If that's the case, I'd rather it cut loose its ballast and relaunch itself now while the time is ripe instead of waiting for the entire ship to sink."[8]

Others who surveyed the wreckage of the 1990s turned the spotlight on the bureaucracy. With a few vocal exceptions, almost everyone agreed that during the late Meiji and Taishō periods, and then again for the half century that stretched from the occupation until the twilight of the Shōwa epoch, the national ministries were the preserve of Japan's "best and brightest," home to capable and conscientious professionals who crafted economic programs, designed educational systems, and authored social legislation that won worldwide respect. But somehow, something had gone wrong, and Kasumigaseki, the area of downtown Tokyo where most major ministries were headquartered, had turned into a bog inhabited by unimaginative, arrogant, rigid-thinking dullards who merely were "obsessed with maintaining the status quo" and "protecting vested interests." As a result of such shortcomings, some claimed, "the entire government" was "losing dynamism" and no longer was able to respond nimbly to emergency situations.[9]

Popular discontent with bureaucratic ineptitude reached a crescendo in the wake of the Great Kanshin Earthquake, which rocked Kōbe and neighboring areas on January 17, 1995, killing more than 5,000, damaging over 100,000 buildings, and leaving 400,000 people homeless. Officials monitoring the situation from their perches at Kasumigaseki grossly misjudged the extent of the catastrophe, and the prime minister was slow to mobilize the Self-Defense Force and the national Fire Defense Agency. Because of the "shameful inaction, indecision, and inertia" on the part of the officialdom, critics charged, fires raged for days after they should have been extinguished, and hundreds trapped in the rubble died unnecessarily.[10] As public dismay over the calamity mounted, Prime Minister Murayama acknowledged the government's failure to act expeditiously, but that April angry citizens threw his words back at him as children continued to carry drinking water and emergency food to school, damaged tracks still prevented travel by Bullet Trains from Osaka to Kōbe and points west, and the Diet sat around endlessly debating funding bills for relief and rehabilitation.

The role of the bureaucracy also moved to the center of debates about the economic malaise. According to some experts, the economic bubble had become dangerously large and then exploded because the "mandarins" in Kasumigaseki turned a blind eye to reckless practices by banks and brokerage houses. At the heart of the problem, it was said, were "cozy ties between regulators and those being regulated."[11] The notion that the Ministry of Finance had "become a hotbed of corruption" took on a sharper edge in 1995 and 1996 after officials in the ministry were found guilty of accepting handouts from the very financial institutions they were supposed to be overseeing. Such transgressions led to the arrests of 4 high-ranking MOF officials, while 112 subordinates received some form of "administrative punishment," ranging from written reprimands to suspensions and pay cuts. It all made for a bleak future. "As long as incompetent bureaucrats remain at the helm, refusing to relinquish their power," one particularly irate critic wrote, "our prospects are too dismal even to consider."[12]

Few were shy about offering solutions to overcoming bureaucratic corruption and lassitude. Everyone hoped to attract more talented and ethical individuals to government service, and most watchdogs also agreed that it was wise to reduce the size of what was judged to be an overstaffed, and therefore clumsy and unresponsive, bureaucracy. Thus, when the Administrative Reform Council, a body of experts especially convened by Prime Minister Hashimoto, in December 1997 recommended consolidating the existing twenty-two ministries and cabinet-level agencies to just twelve ministries and a Cabinet Office, the premier received applause for recognizing the need "to perform much-needed liposuction on a grossly obese bureaucracy."[13] Others put forth a different argument, declaring that the key to the future was to restore "constitutional balance"—that is, to reestablish the right of the Diet and the cabinet to control the mandarins who ran the ministries. Consequently, when Obuchi assumed office in July 1998, he admitted that "public mistrust of politics has risen to a truly high level" and called for "a restoration of political authority," by which he meant that it was "essential" for elected officials "to exercise true political leadership" by "unambiguously reversing the power balance between political leaders and bureaucrats."[14]

Although bankers and the heads of other financial institutions came under fire in the 1990s, most other corporate leaders moved through the decade with their dignity and public respect intact. As the ongoing recession and recurring financial crises took their toll, supporters of the business community put forth proposals about how to revitalize the economy. In plotting future economic directions, some analysts urged Japan to try to outdo the United States in the development of new computer and software industries. Others suggested that the best choice was to continue on course as a manufacturing nation. After all, as one observer pointed out, the "recession has not sapped the nation's manufacturing strength," and in the words of another, Japanese should remember that "making things is what their country does best."[15]

Events at the turn of the century provoked a great deal of skepticism about those prescriptions, however. In the summer of 2000 shareholders of the tire maker Bridgestone watched the value of their holdings plunge by half after people worldwide initiated legal action against its wholly owned U.S. subsidiary, Firestone, for design and manufacturing mistakes that caused fifty deaths and hundreds of injuries. At virtually the same time public confidence in a once-proud automaker evaporated when prosecutors twice in a single week raided the headquarters of Mitsubishi Motors to seize evidence concerning the company's systematic cover-up of manufacturing defects. Not long thereafter, fifteen thousand people fell ill after consuming contaminated products distributed by Snow Brand, a leading dairy firm. An investigation revealed that the company routinely falsified certificates of freshness and recycled old milk returned from stores. That scandal touched off a wave of consumer complaints against other food companies, and the mass media soon had more stories than they could carry about flies in canned juices and dead lizards in potato chips.

The crisis of the nineties—the "lost decade," in the words of many—hung over the future of all Japanese, and the debates about how to overcome the end-of-the-millennium blues were heated and noisy. Still, it was important to listen to silences and to remember what went unsaid. However much discord scarred the initial decade of the Heisei period, few Japanese voiced any doubt that democracy and capitalism were the appropriate roads to follow as they prepared to step forward into another new century. Despite the sluggish, disappointing economic performance of the 1990s, and despite having endured a succession of lackluster prime ministers whose apparent incompetence threatened to paralyze the nation, there were no serious calls to abandon parliamentary democracy or the private enterprise system. Rather, the belief that Japan's successes during the twentieth century came when party government and market-based capitalism flourished, and that failures mounted when the nation turned in other directions, was almost universal. As the Heisei era folded itself into the new century, then, the questions revolved around how to promote a better-functioning constitutional system and free market economy based on the private ownership of business.

## Japan in the Global Community

Japanese foreign policy rested on several axioms in the late Shōwa period. The first, hand-wrought by Yoshida Shigeru and reaffirmed by successive LDP cabinets with varying degrees of enthusiasm, was that Japan place an absolute priority on its relationship with the United States. The United States–Japan Security Treaty, agreed to in 1951 and amended in 1960, set the parameters for that alliance by committing Japan to strategic dependence upon the United States and economic interdependence with its new Pacific ally. In practice, that meant Japan would align its economy with the capitalistic nations of the West, rely on the United States to protect it militarily, and not resist overtly the lead of its mentor when major world crises erupted.

Attempts to repair diplomatic relations with neighbors in Asia constituted the second hallmark of postwar Japanese foreign policy. Cold War tensions and Tokyo's decision to take shelter under the wing of the American eagle, however, created a number of complications. America froze China out of the negotiations that culminated in the San Francisco System after Mao Zedong marched triumphantly into Beijing and established the People's Republic of China (PRC) in October 1949. Consequently, on the same afternoon that Japan signed the peace agreement in September 1951, Tokyo concluded a separate treaty with Taiwan and joined the United States in recognizing that island regime as the official government of China. Those actions did not sit easy with many Japanese, who believed that in the long run Japan needed to be on good terms with China proper, whatever its government's political orientation. That possibility materialized only in the early 1970s, when the United Nations admitted the PRC to its ranks and the United States did an abrupt about-face on the China question. Shortly thereafter, in September 1972, Prime Minister Tanaka traveled to Beijing and signed a joint communiqué whose clauses provided for the exchange of consular officials, recognized the PRC as "the sole legal government of China," and specified Japan's "full understanding" that Taiwan constituted "an inalienable part" of the sovereign territory of China. Finally, on August 12, 1978, Tokyo and Beijing signed the China–Japan Peace and Friendship Treaty to reaffirm their earlier agreement and completely normalize relations.

Tokyo and Seoul required prolonged negotiations before representatives of those two nations finally signed the Korea–Japan Treaty in June 1965. That accord, together with a set of supplementary agreements, recognized the Republic of Korea as the only legitimate government on the peninsula, established diplomatic and consular relations, and called for cultural cooperation. Left in a state of limbo was Japan's relationship with the Democratic People's Republic of Korea. Branded a pariah nation by the United States after the outbreak of the Korean War in 1951, North Korea remained almost a noncountry in Japan's eyes as well throughout the late Shōwa period.

Japan's attempts to put a new keel under its relations with the Soviet Union involved more heavy lifting. The two old foes signed the Soviet–Japanese Joint Declaration on October 19, 1956, ending the state of war that had existed since August 9, 1945, and restoring official diplomatic linkages. Nevertheless, Japan's inclusion in the defense perimeter that America was building around the USSR and the so-called Northern Territories issue—irreconcilable counterclaims by Moscow and Tokyo to rights of sovereignty over four small islands lying off the northern coast of Hokkaidō—combined with a long history of mistrust to make friendly ties nearly impossible.

Within the limitations imposed by the San Francisco System, the third guiding principle for Japanese policy makers was to decouple politics from commerce as far as possible so that Japan could become a trading friend to the world. Such efforts encountered no insurmountable obstacles in Western Europe or the Americas, even after Japan's escalating trade surpluses brought forth charges of unfair competition and an emotional, self-indulgent round of Japan bashing by Western politicians and businesspeople in the late 1980s. In 1990, West Germany, the United Kingdom, Canada, France, and Italy were among Japan's top ten trading partners, and incredibly, the amount of Japan's enormous import and export trade with the United States approached that of the other nine nations combined, as seen in Table 17.2.

In Asia the rebuilt diplomatic structure opened up ample commercial opportunities for Japanese corporations across the region, North Korea excepted. As early as 1952 Japan concluded the first in a series of trade agreements with the PRC that enabled bilateral trade to grow to U.S. $1.2 billion

**TABLE 17.2** *Japan's Leading Trading Partners, 1970–1990*
(in millions of U.S. dollars)

|  | 1970 | | 1980 | | 1990 | |
|---|---|---|---|---|---|---|
|  | JAPANESE EXPORTS | JAPANESE IMPORTS | JAPANESE EXPORTS | JAPANESE IMPORTS | JAPANESE EXPORTS | JAPANESE IMPORTS |
| United States | 5,940 | 5,560 | 31,367 | 24,408 | 90,322 | 52,369 |
| West Germany | 550 | 617 | 5,756 | 2,501 | 17,782 | 11,487 |
| South Korea | 818 | 229 | 5,363 | 2,996 | 17,457 | 11,707 |
| Australia | 589 | 1,598 | 3,389 | 6,982 | 6,900 | 12,369 |
| China | 569 | 254 | 5,078 | 4,323 | 6,130 | 12,054 |
| United Kingdom | 480 | 395 | 3,782 | 1,954 | 10,786 | 5,239 |
| Canada | 563 | 929 | 2,437 | 4,724 | 6,727 | 8,392 |
| France | 127 | 186 | 2,021 | 1,296 | 6,128 | 7,590 |
| Italy | 192 | 143 | 955 | 939 | 3,407 | 5,008 |
| Soviet Union | 341 | 481 | 2,778 | 1,860 | 2,563 | 3,351 |

Adapted from *Japan: An Illustrated Encyclopedia*, vol. 1 (Tokyo: Kodansha, 1993), p. 399.

by the time relations were regularized in 1972 and then to U.S. $18.1 billion by 1990. In addition, so-called private trade with Taiwan continued to expand even after Tokyo severed official diplomatic ties, and had the "private trade" been entered into official ledgers, in 1990 Taiwan would have been Japan's fourth-largest trading partner, importing U.S. $15.4 billion of Japanese goods and sending U.S. $8.5 billion worth in return. Trade with the Republic of Korea grew even more rapidly: In 1990 Japan's imports from Korea totaled U.S. $11.7 billion, and its exports U.S. $17.5 billion, figures that made Japan Korea's third-largest trading partner. Japan-USSR trade remained at much lower levels, but Russia was a major market for Japan's steel producers and construction industries, while the Siberian provinces sold oil, lumber, and metals, such as platinum and nickel, to Japanese firms.

Not surprisingly, trade issues tended to shape interactions with the nations of Southeast Asia, most of which signed diplomatic accords with Japan in the 1950s. During the 1960s Japanese corporate outposts and billboards advertising everything from Hondas to Sonys sprouted up along city horizons from Manila to Singapore. By the late Shōwa period Japan had become a regular customer for Indonesian oil and the products of light industry from other countries, while flooding the region with appliances, automobiles, machine tools, steel, and so forth. In 1990 Japanese trade with the nations of Southeast Asia topped U.S. $50 billion, although every country except Indonesia ran a significant trade deficit with Asia's economic titan.

Throughout the late Shōwa decades the Japanese debated the merits of the San Francisco System. Some believed that "subordinate independence" served their country reasonably well. Businesspeople could see clearly how economic imbrication with Europe and the Americas and the restoration of peace with Asia contributed in multiple ways to high-speed growth and the impressive domestic prosperity that the Japanese had come to enjoy. Anti-Communists appreciated the safeguards erected against Japan's old nemesis, the Soviet Union. Meanwhile, those who abhorred their country's aggression in the 1930s and 1940s felt some assurance that the reduced size of its armed forces, when considered with the provisions of Article 9 in the constitution, had made any possible resurgence of militarism unlikely.

Critics were quick to note, however, that there had been enormous trade-offs. Psychologically the subordination of Japan's national interests to those of another country, its conqueror, constantly ate at Japanese pride. That sense of humiliation deepened when the security treaty signed in 1951 authorized the United States to administer Okinawa directly, recognizing only Japan's "residual sovereignty" over the prefecture. Until those islands reverted to Japan in 1972, the U.S. government ran affairs there almost as if the prefecture were a colonial possession, and its military built so many bases that Okinawa, in the view of some, resembled a gigantic American aircraft carrier. Moreover, some Japanese remained forever skeptical about claims that U.S. forces stationed on bases in Okinawa and across Japan would deter external threats to Japan. Rather, they feared that the presence of those foreign troops might embroil Japan in an unwanted conflict or even place it in the path of a horrible nuclear showdown between Cold War foes. Finally, resentments over the San Francisco System caused considerable domestic unrest: In 1960, millions protested the renewal of the security treaty and toppled the Kishi government, and during the anti–Vietnam War movement of 1967 to 1970, eighteen million Japanese took to the streets to demonstrate against the war and demand the immediate reversion of Okinawa.

The fall of the Berlin Wall in 1989 and the implosion of the Soviet Union in December 1991 punctuated the flow of history. Just as in Europe, those events marked the end of the Cold War era in Asia, and to many Japanese they further suggested that the San Francisco System had become an archaism. If the death of the Shōwa emperor and the bursting of the economic and political bubbles spurred Japanese to reconsider their domestic futures, the early 1990s also presented a fresh opportunity to evaluate foreign policy tenets and objectives. Near the top of almost everyone's agenda was a reexamination of the relationship with the United States, and not far behind was a reconsideration of Japan's future role in Asia and on the world stage.

The new international environment, according to some political figures who traditionally had criticized the San Francisco System, represented a long-awaited chance for Japan to disentangle itself from the alliance with the United States and stake out a more autonomous foreign policy. Other important government officials and influential media pundits, however, were not so ready to separate past from future. Rather, they argued, Japan needed to stay close to America, if for no other reason than that the complex economic interrelationships linking the two countries made mutual cooperation a prerequisite to the future prosperity of both. Moreover, while the USSR no longer posed the threat it once had, the remnants of the Cold War persisted more stubbornly in East Asia than elsewhere in the world: The Korean peninsula remained bitterly divided, tensions between China and Russia occasionally approached the flash point, and the new Russian Federation showed no inclination to settle the Northern Territories dispute. Given those unstable conditions, many still considered a military alliance with the United States the surest guarantee that a local conflict would not expand and wrap its tentacles around Japan.

Among the leading politicians and officials in Kasumigaseki who wanted Japan to stay tethered to the United States, many wished their country to assume a role on the world stage more commensurate with its economic standing. At the beginning of the Heisei period one prominent academic noted that Japan was a "financial power" with a GNP 50 percent greater than that of a united Germany. "For a country of this size to remain a minor player politically and militarily," he wrote, "is no longer acceptable."[16] Such rhetoric was not intended to imply that Japan ought to become a military superpower. Rather, it supported the view that the country should contribute to global security by participating in what some called collective self-defense. Unpacked, that phrase signified that Article 9 should be interpreted as allowing the Self-Defense Force to join operations organized by Japan's allies or the United Nations to maintain international stability.

Finally, some Japanese urged their country to exert its influence more in Asia. For many members of the LDP, that meant emphasizing security issues. "As an Asian country," one of the party's position papers noted, "Japan must strive to preserve peace and maintain stability in the Asian region, always seeking the understanding and support of other Asian countries."[17] What one writer termed "the problem of Japan's past," however, made it difficult for his country to win much sympathy for its position.[18] In particular, the Japanese government's stubborn refusal to express remorse to former "comfort women" or to pay compensation to the victims who survived that terrible indignity aroused anger across Asia. In addition, Japan's neighbors never completely accepted official expressions of contrition for the war. When leaders of the People's Republic of China visited Tokyo in April 1989, the Heisei emperor personally apologized for Japan's wartime activities in China, and at a state banquet that May, he rose to tell the president of Korea, "I think of the sufferings your people underwent during this unfortunate period, which was brought about by my country, and cannot but feel the greatest regret."[19] Many Asians were not persuaded of the sincerity of such words, however, and the Chinese president Jiang Zemin cast a pall over his state visit in November 1998, when he pointedly and repeatedly called upon Japan to offer more heartfelt expressions of remorse. "In Japan," he stated in a press conference, "there are still people in high positions who constantly distort history and try to beautify aggression. It is important that the Japanese squarely face history and learn a lesson from it."[20] Sometimes, it seemed to some, no amount of apologizing, of expressing regret for the past, would ever be acceptable to the generation of Asians who had suffered so much at the hands of the Japanese military.

As Japan stood on the brink of the new century, an evolutionary reorientation of its foreign policy seemed to be taking recognizable form. At home the government reaffirmed its commitment to the security alliance with the United States. On the world stage Japan's profile still cast a lesser shadow than those of many other leading world powers, but Japanese delegates were assuming more leadership roles in the United Nations and international financial organizations. Simultaneously, Tokyo began to move toward collective security. It sent minesweepers to the Persian Gulf following the conclusion of the Gulf War in 1991, and in September 1992 it dispatched Self-Defense personnel to Cambodia as part of a UN peacekeeping mission. Within Asia, Japan tried to rebuild its image by beefing up foreign aid assistance and funding scholarship programs that enabled tens of thousands of Asian students to learn Japanese and study at Japanese universities.

## Social Obligation, Self-Fulfillment

New social realities also filled the first decade of the Heisei era. Japan, many began to realize, rapidly was becoming a "gray society." In the year 2000 somewhat more than 10 percent of the population was sixty-five years of age or older; by 2025 the sixty-five–plus share of the population would reach 27 percent, or more than thirty million people, giving Japan the world's most top-heavy population pyramid. Juxtaposed against the image of an elderly, infirm Japan was the figure of an energetic, articulate, and more autonomous woman who was establishing a place for herself in corporate and professional offices at century's end and forging new kinds of relationships with the men in her life. Youth also pushed its way into the picture, too often, many believed, by adopting behaviors that undermined traditional social covenants and by committing crimes that horrified society. Bewildering and disturbing to some, exhilarating and filled with promise for others, the changes reshaping society at the turn of the millennium opened the door to bold, new discussions about gender, family, the workplace, and school.

The challenge of caring for the elderly, especially the 5.5 million expected to be either mentally incapacitated or bedridden in 2025, renewed a national debate about the role of women. From one perspective, the changing demographics plucked the strings of the familiar refrain, nearly as old as Japan's quest for modernity itself, that society's needs required housewives to stay home and care for their families. To a degree that surprised some observers, such rhetoric continued to define a comfortable role for many middle-class homemakers, who derived gratification and a sense of self-esteem from the creative nurturing of family. It was fortunate for the country that they did so, for while most elderly claimed they did not want to live with their children, few alternatives were available, and the daughter or daughter-in-law remained the primary caregiver as Japan headed into the twenty-first century. Overall, in 1990, one of every fifteen nonworking women in her forties was providing home care for the elderly, and predictions put that share at one in five in 2005 and an astounding one in two in 2025, barring massive government investments in nursing homes and other facilities.

Other social critics took a contrary view of women, arguing that daughters and wives had to get out of the house and into the workplace. Projections suggested that in 2025 each retired person would be supported by just 2.3 people of working age (those between fifteen and sixty-four), down from 5.8 in 1990. Compounding the problem was another new social reality: In the 1990s women were not as quick to marry as those of previous generations, and they were choosing to have fewer children. According to the Ministry of Health and Welfare, in 1994 the fertility rate, a measure of the birthrate for women of childbearing age, had fallen to a historic low of 1.46, a decline of nearly 30 percent from 1975 and well below the level needed to sustain the population at a stable level. Very clearly, in the calculations of many social scientists, more women had to take jobs and pay taxes if

Japan were to honor its social obligation to provide the aging population with adequate pensions and medical benefits.

New conceptions of self-worth and a stronger emphasis on the self-fulfillment of the individual prompted women themselves to consider employment and the workplace from fresh perspectives. Increasingly, female activists questioned the inevitability of a preordained domestic destiny and insisted that women had the right to select from a menu of life choices. In that spirit, Atsumi Ikuko, scholar and founder of the journal *Feminisuto* ("Feminist"), wrote that "men's role has been the production of materials outside, and women's role has lain in the production of life at home. Japanese feminist theory considers that both are equally important. Men should be more involved in the production of life, and women in the production of materials. The current feminist movement," Atsumi added, in words that echoed the ideals of the Taishō period activist Yosano Akiko, "aims at the kind of society in which a woman can not only be economically independent but also be free to choose the way she wants to live. In such a society, if she wants to be a housewife, it's all right, but a woman who wants to work can do so without being discriminated against. The movement seeks to change roles not only in the family but also in society."[21]

The Equal Employment Opportunity Law (EEOL) of 1986 further altered contemporary realities and remolded future visions. It called on businesses to "endeavor to give women equal opportunity" to compete with men for any job and stipulated that everyone should receive equal pay for comparable work. Two years later revisions to the Labor Standards Law eliminated restrictions that dated to the Taishō era on women's overtime and work deemed dangerous to their health and safety. Some critics complained that the laws did not achieve their intended effect. A decade after the enactment of the EEOL Japanese women still earned just over half of what men did (compared with about 75 percent in the United States and 90 percent in Australia), and one graduating senior at a prestigious university in Kyoto bristled when the company official interviewing her for a position with a major newspaper asked, "Are you sure you won't quit after you marry? We wouldn't want to take such a risk."[22] Nevertheless, the EEOL and the new labor standards legitimized women's aspirations and raised public consciousness about work and gender.

In combination, the mix of changing demographics, new social ideals, and revised legal norms drew increasing numbers of women into the workplace. At the dawn of the twenty-first century, full-time female employees outnumbered full-time housewives, and fully half of all mothers with school-age children worked. To be certain, women remained especially visible in small, family businesses and service industries, and in large corporations the overwhelming majority still were compartmentalized as pink-collar OLs or stuck in dead-end jobs on the production line. At the same time, however, unprecedented numbers of women were invading previously all-male domains to become engineers, architects, and doctors; in 1998, 200 of the 932 engineers joining the electronics giant NEC were women. Even in the corporate offices of major companies, dressed-for-success career women could be seen leaping aboard executive elevators in ever-increasing numbers; the number of white-collar women managers doubled, to about 8 percent of all executives, in the decade following the implementation of the EEOL. Still, success did not come easy. "In Japan," one young female manager noted, "glass ceilings are barely centimeters off the floor."[23]

Working women challenged companies to reform themselves to meet the needs of a more diverse work force. With increasing boldness, women demanded equal pay and treatment, as provided by the EEOL, and *sekuhara* ("sexual harassment") entered the Japanese vocabulary as women came forward to complain about offensive and discriminatory behavior by male coworkers and employers. Working mothers added other items to the reform agenda. In particular, they insisted that companies provide such amenities as flex time schedules, family care leave time, holidays coordinated with school vacations, job sharing, and on-site day care. The vision of the future advanced by such women included rewarding jobs, fair pay, and the opportunity to be good mothers, in Japanese terms. They did not want to be clones of male workers, they claimed; rather, drawing on the legacy of Yosano Akiko, they wanted recognition of the many diverse roles they performed in life.

Japanese women also put gender relations and marriage on the table for discussion in the 1990s. As single women explored the greater career opportunities available to them, many discovered that they could support themselves without having to rely on a man, either financially or psychologically, and they began to delay marriage and celebrate the single life. In 1993 the average age at marriage for Japanese women had risen to twenty-seven years, up by nearly five years since the 1950s and second highest in the world to Swedish women. Moreover, at the turn of the century more than 8 percent of women in Tokyo who had passed through the so-called marriageable years (ages eighteen to forty-four) had never wed, suggesting that the single life gradually was emerging as an acceptable option in the country's larger cities. Self-reliant and autonomous from male dominance, greater numbers of single women created for themselves liberated lifestyles that recalled the openness of Japan's urban centers in the 1920s. According to one newspaper account, young women in the 1990s wanted "to live independently, self-sufficiently, take on lovers and have relationships based on equality."[24]

Whatever the lure of the not-married-for-life alternative, most single women in their twenties—94 percent according to one government poll conducted in 1992—assumed that eventually they would wed, manage households, and raise children. But those women too cast up new visions about an ideal marriage. In one startling twist, nearly 90 percent of the single women employed at the time of the 1992 survey declared that they intended to keep on working after marriage. Such women, it seemed, wanted it all—the self-satisfaction of a career and the self-fulfillment of family—and they posed another challenge to government and private enterprise to help women find a way to balance the responsibilities of work and home.

As matters turned out, the reality of meeting the heavy demands of career and family life proved considerably more daunting than most women expected before they married, and in the early Heisei period about half of all wives left the work force when children came along. The fact that Japanese society continued to honor the "separate sphere" of the housewife and to give full credit to women for what they did as mothers eased the transition from office to home and helped homebound women feel fulfilled. Nevertheless, many full-time housewives endorsed the emerging vision of a more egalitarian, caring relationship with their spouses. More than ever before, married women, whether they worked outside the house or not, felt it important for their husbands to participate substantially in family life and to share wholeheartedly such responsibilities as child care and housework.

In addition to the availability of jobs, women used new notions about divorce to gain a certain leverage in pressing their demands. The divorce rate in Japan approximately doubled between 1970 and 1995, and at century's end there were about twenty-four divorces for every hundred new marriages, compared with thirty-two in France, forty-two in Great Britain, and fifty-five in the United States. As in the West, women in Japan who had the temperament and skills to move into full-time jobs were especially apt to consider divorce if their marriage turned sour. As one expert noted, if a middle-aged salaryman came home drunk and his wife greeted him with the announcement "I've decided to start working," he had better have a glass of water, compose himself, and ask, "Full-time or part-time?" If the answer was "full-time," he must recognize that the situation was "dangerous."[25]

Change is seldom easy, and in provincial Japan men of the older generation had a particularly difficult time accepting new ideas about marriage. Asked if he loved his wife of thirty-three years, one cattle farmer in a small town nestled in the rolling hills of Mie Peninsula some two hundred miles southwest of Tokyo, furrowed his brow, looked perplexed, and replied, "Yeah, so-so, I guess. She's like air or water. You couldn't live without it, but most of the time, you're not conscious of its existence."[26] A seventy-two-year-old neighbor, Uemura Yuri, reported, "There was never any love between me and my husband," and revealed sadly that her mate of forty-plus years had never told her that he liked her, complimented her on a meal, held her hand, given her a present, or shown her affection in any way. He even used to beat her, Mrs. Uemura recalled, "But, well, we survived."

Younger males in Japan's larger population centers were quicker to come to grips with the new realities, but even there some could be heard muttering, "This is a terrible time to be a man."[27] Epitomizing the new low for urban middle-class husbands and fathers was the television advertisement for a double-binned clothes washer that showed a neatly dressed housewife, nose wrinkled in disgust, picking up her husband's underwear with a pair of extralong chopsticks and tossing them into the heavy-duty bin as her young daughter said, "Let's keep Dad's yucky stuff separate." Still, whatever media images abounded in the early Heisei period, a considerable number of younger men accepted and even welcomed the new trends in marriage. In one 1987 survey 52 percent of men (and 37 percent of women) agreed with the statement "Men work outside of the home while women work in the home." In the middle of the 1990s just 35 percent of men and 25 percent of women held the same view.

To a significant degree, the willingness of both younger men and women to enter the new-style marriage was intertwined with the continuing evolution of household patterns. Across Japan the nuclear household, which to a noticeable extent had defined the middle-class ideal during the late Shōwa era, almost entirely had replaced the multigenerational extended family by the end of the twentieth century. Under the older arrangements, most marriages were arranged, and friends, family, and society expected couples like the Uemuras to set aside personal feelings about their spouses and make a go of the union for the sake of the household. Within the smaller, "couples-oriented" nuclear household of the early Heisei era, the private, horizontal relationship between husband and wife took precedence over the vertical relationships across generations. As a consequence, young men and women in the 1990s, even more so than the New Middle Class of the 1970s and 1980s, saw conjugal love as the primary reason to get married. By the mid-1990s three-quarters of all weddings were self-declared "love marriages," compared with about one-half in the early 1960s, and modern couples preferred more romance in their relationships than had been typical for the older generation.

As new attitudes took hold at the turn of the century, more and more young men could be seen strolling the supermarket aisles with their wives, taking a turn doing the dishes and diapering the baby, and treating the family to a Sunday drive and dinner at a "family restaurant." Despite the raising divorce rate, most women seemed to agree that the couples-oriented lifestyle resulted in happier marriages and a more contented homelife. As indicated in Table 17.3, in the 1990s the majority of Japanese women, far more so than their American counterparts, believed circumstances had improved for wives and mothers over the past two decades. Even Mrs. Uemura said that her husband was treating her better. "The other day, he tried to pour me a cup of tea," she remarked excitedly. "It was a big change. I told all my friends."

Male views about company life also were changing. As early as the mid-1980s some social commentators noted the appearance of the *shinjinrui*, a "new breed" of young Japanese workers, according to the newsperson who coined the term, "that the older generation finds impossible to comprehend or communicate with."[28] The new generation, critics claimed, scorned the maxim, expounded by the Tokugawa period thinker Ishida Baigan and repeated by many thereafter, that the meaning of life is found in the discipline of work. In sharp contrast with that received wisdom, observers noted, blue-collar workers in the 1990s refused to take the *k* jobs, employment they considered *kitanai, kitsui, kiken* ("dirty, difficult, dangerous"). Recent college graduates interviewing for white-collar positions, meanwhile, wanted plenty of holidays, no overtime, and generous salaries right away, while they

**TABLE 17.3** *Women's Attitudes in Japan and the United States toward Marriage and Family, 1990*

Percent of women who responded to the question, "How have things changed for women since 1970?"

|  | MARRIAGE | | ROLE AS MOTHER | | ROLE AS HOMEMAKER | |
|---|---|---|---|---|---|---|
|  | JAPAN | U.S. | JAPAN | U.S. | JAPAN | U.S. |
| Improved | 59 | 34 | 50 | 36 | 56 | 37 |
| Haven't changed | 28 | 16 | 31 | 20 | 33 | 23 |
| Gotten worse | 10 | 45 | 17 | 41 | 10 | 37 |

Adapted from Iwao Sumiko, "Japanese and American Women Today: A Comparison," *Japan Echo* 20:3 (Autumn 1993), p. 70.

were still young, rather than have to wait until they climbed their way to the top of a particular firm's seniority ladder. Confirming the new attitudes, even Japan's most prestigious companies became distressed by the growing number of young white-collar employees who quit after just three or four years on the job, and a government white paper on labor issued in July 1990 revealed that young workers in Japan were less satisfied than those in the United States and Britain with their wages, working hours, chances for promotion, and opportunities to utilize their own individual talents.

Some social commentators saw the younger generation's desire for more leisure time, better pay, and more comfortable working conditions as a reaction against the overemphasis on single-minded dedication to the job that major companies had imposed upon white-collar workaholics in the late Shōwa period. Others blamed society. Salarymen, one high-placed official noted, "are no longer respected as noble corporate warriors" and, as a consequence, "have grown ashamed of their habitual devotion to the job."[29] Still others vented their anger at the younger people themselves. Since they had been "brought up amid material indulgence" and "raised in an environment of leniency," one observer concluded, it was only natural that Generation Xers wanted "to take life easy" and exploit a tight job market for their own selfish ends.[30] However one assigned responsibility, all agreed that the evolving attitudes posed grave challenges for the new century. Some foresaw the end of the lifetime employment system, while others, more alarmist, believed the new antiwork ethic meant that eventually "society will languish, and Japan, deprived of the industriousness of its labor force, will become a second-rate country."

## Youth in Trouble, Schools under Fire

Adolescents and children also made headlines at the beginning of the Heisei period. Few social critics would dispute that the majority of Japanese young people were sensible, cheerful, and well adjusted, and in public opinion surveys teenagers demonstrated a keener sense of social responsibility than their elders regarding such issues as the need to become good global citizens, preserve the environment, and improve the quality of life, even at the expense of economic growth. Nevertheless, during the 1990s the older generation grew increasingly troubled by an elusive, but to them readily apparent, breakdown in social morality, manifested in their children's estrangement from parents and siblings, eating disorders, teenage promiscuity, and recreational drug use.

Persistent bullying, or *ijime*, also scandalized the nation. Part of the schoolyard scene from the early 1970s, bullies typically ridiculed, humiliated, and beat their victims almost daily. In one case the culprits forced a classmate to run constant errands, doodled mustaches on his face with felt markers, forced him to climb a tree and sing the school song as other kids looked on, and even staged his mock funeral. Analysts were not surprised to learn that perpetrators of *ijime* often came from dysfunctional families in which alcoholism and spousal violence was commonplace, but they could scarcely fathom the mentality of the more ordinary students who meekly acquiesced to their own victimization. After classmate thugs repeatedly squeezed him for large sums of money, including an impossible demand for 120,000 yen, Ōkōcho Kiyoteru, an eighth grader in Aichi Prefecture, hanged himself on November 27, 1994, one of several distraught youths who committed suicide that year after being bullied. Kiyoteru's lengthy suicide note was filled with relentless phrases of self-blame and a painful sense of guilt about every aspect of his young life. "If I had just refused to pay the money," he wrote, "nothing like this would have ever happened. I am really sorry. Please do not blame the people who took the money. I should be blamed because I was the one who gave the money so willingly." To his parents, he added, "I am really sorry that I have always been the cause of worry for you. I was such a selfish child. It must have been really difficult to have me as your son."[31]

A spurt in the number of adolescents charged with criminal misconduct added to society's unease. During the postwar decades, crime rates had trended downward, and between 1986 and 1996 the number of teenagers classified as delinquents by the police plunged from 1.6 million to just over 800,000. Then, in 1997, juvenile crimes jumped by 20 percent over the previous year. Moreover, in 1997 youths aged fourteen to nineteen, who constituted just 9 percent of Japan's population, committed 34 percent of all murders and robberies and fully 45 percent of violent crimes, such as assault and battery. Included in that latter number were twenty-five hundred muggings of middle-aged men, what young ruffians called *oyaji-gari* ("old-man hunting").

For many pundits, the fact that most young delinquents came from the middle class was even more worrisome than the spike in crime rates itself. One might understand why poor kids would go old-man hunting in the immediate postwar years, when ten thousand muggings a year were commonplace, and in 1955 about half of Japan's juvenile offenders came from impoverished or dysfunctional families. By the mid-1990s, however, nearly four-fifths of young miscreants lived with both parents, and about 90 percent could be described as thoroughly middle class. To the shock of most adults, adolescents arrested for theft reported that their main motive simply was to get money for entertainment. As the Japanese became materially affluent, the social commentators cried, they seemed to become spiritually bankrupt.

A surge in teenage prostitution, euphemistically called subsidized friendship, seemed to confirm that judgment. Middle-aged men infatuated with younger girls only had to dial commercial voice mail services to screen such messages as "I am a sixteen-year-old high school girl. I am looking for someone to meet me tomorrow for some subsidized friendship. I am 165 centimeters tall and weight forty-nine kilograms. I think I am pretty cute. My price is '5' [50,000 yen] for about two hours."[32] Beeped through, the man might meet a chirpy, well-dressed, and to all outward appearances ordinary student, who engaged in sex simply because she wanted 100,000-yen designer handbags and other brand name luxuries that she could not afford from her family allowance. In 1995 the National Police Agency placed under protective custody more than five thousand female minors for prostitution and other sex-related crimes, and 4 percent of the high school girls questioned in a survey conducted by the Tokyo Metropolitan Government in October 1996 claimed they had engaged in friendship for pay.

As juvenile delinquents and teenage prostitutes multiplied in number, the education system came under fire for failing the country's youth. Perhaps the chief reason that juvenile crime so horrified the nation was that there existed, as one expert put it, a "national consensus that Japan's most important resource is its children, and the nation's most important job is their education."[33] Thus arrows of reproach crisscrossed the air. Some parents criticized teachers for being too lax, while others claimed that the school system's overly severe treatment of their children led to pent-up stresses that found relief in criminal conduct. Teachers pointed the finger back at parents. "A large portion of the blame for the emergence of students who are selfish and stubborn," wrote one teacher, "must lie with the way adults have raised them. Children have been left to their own devices: The goal of child-rearing is no longer to prepare an independent member of society, but to emphasize individuality."[34] Another blamed parents for having "no moral structure in their lives" and coddling children, even to the extent of protesting teachers' evaluations, "calling up on the phone and saying, 'I know he's better than that!,'" in the irate words of one eighth-grade instructor.[35]

Those entrusted with educating students in the 1990s had to contend with two differing traditions. On the one hand, from the late Meiji period through the Greater East Asia War, educational policy had placed a strong emphasis on moral training and on preparing individuals to be loyal, responsible citizens who would support their government. On the other hand, at the end of the nineteenth century Japanese such as Miyake Setsurei and Ueki Emori had argued that education should "encourage and nourish the development of man's naturally given abilities" in order to create an enlightened and autonomous citizenry that would help advance world culture. Similarly, the SCAP-sanctioned Fundamental Law of Education, promulgated in 1947, declared that the basic objective of the education system was to help each child reach his or her full potential as an individual so that s/he could "contribute to the peace of the world and welfare of humanity by building a democratic and cultural state."

The dual legacies of the past weighed heavily on teachers in the early Heisei period. Not surprisingly, some members of the profession urged fellow educators to bring the creativity inherent in each child to full flower, while others clung to the notion that "The real challenge for schoolteachers," as one declared at a roundtable discussion, "isn't academic instruction. It's guidance—teaching kids how to behave in school and society."[36] The debates on education repeated the concerns about adjusting marriage, family, and the workplace to the realities of the new century. In all those cases, social obligation and individual self-fulfillment stood as opposite poles that seemed to define the range of future possibilities.

## Challenges from Minorities

The sense of middle-class homogeneity that pervaded the 1970s and 1980s was the grandchild of efforts to inculcate a sense of common national community that extended back to the Meiji era. At that time partisans for the new order spoke about a distinctive Japanese personality, forged over aeons, and defined a code of civil ethics that drew on an idealized mythohistory in order to mold kokumin ("citizens") who embraced collective goals and aspirations. The rhetoric of the war years heightened the feeling that the Japanese were a "special race" whose members descended from a common ancestry, spoke a single language, and ascribed to a specific set of religious beliefs and cultural practices that distinguished them not only from Westerners but also from their neighbors in Asia.

In the 1970s, after two decades of rapid change, some intellectuals and social commentators produced a vast literature under the rubric of Nihonjin ron ("debates on being Japanese") that set out once again to discover the essential features of a unique Japanese culture and singular national character.

Some analysts produced serious and insightful works; others advanced outrageous claims. Among them was the agricultural minister who maintained that Japan should not import Australian beef since the intestines of his countrymen were shorter than those of Westerners and therefore ill suited to digesting meat and other Western staples. However fanciful and narcissistic the *Nihonjin ron* debates became in the late Shōwa era, however, they contributed to the emerging notion that everyone who lived on the Japanese islands belonged to a particular race-culture. Indeed, when Japan ratified the United Nations' International Covenant on Civil and Political Rights in 1979, its representative reported, "The right of any person to enjoy his own culture, to profess and practice his religion or to use his own language is ensured under Japanese law. However, minorities of the kind mentioned in the Covenant do not exist in Japan."[37]

*Burakumin* and members of other minority communities in Japan saw matters differently. In the late Shōwa decades, the Buraku Liberation League, successor to the prewar Suiheisha, rekindled the old fight for equality. In the 1950s and 1960s the league waged "administrative struggles" against local governments to better the living environment in *burakumin* neighborhoods by improving housing, paving streets, and supplying purer water. That campaign bore fruit in 1969, when the national government issued the Special Measures and Enterprise Law concerning Assimilation that served as the basis for a series of community development projects. Between 1969 and 1993 the national and local governments spent nearly fourteen billion yen to lay sewer systems, upgrade streetlighting and fire-fighting services, construct high-rise apartment buildings, and build schools, medical clinics, and community centers in specially designated target areas.

Although government efforts narrowed many of the gaps between *burakumin* neighborhoods and mainstream society, the Special Measures Law did not provide legal sanctions against many guileful forms of discrimination. Consequently, in the late Shōwa period, activists campaigned for unequivocal statutory regulations banning all forms of social intolerance. Concurrently, some community leaders revived the older tactics of denunciation in order to combat subtle expressions of prejudice. In one particularly prominent incident in Hyōgo Prefecture, supporters of the Buraku Liberation League confined fifty-two teachers to school premises and threatened to keep them there until they signed statements of self-criticism and promised to establish a study group on *burakumin* problems at the school. When the teachers refused, the *burakumin* protesters subjected them to intense verbal harassment that put forty-three emotionally exhausted teachers in the hospital, thirteen of them for as long as six weeks.

Japan's Ainu population also regarded pronouncements about an all-embracing homogeneity as dangerously misleading. Throughout the middle decades of the twentieth century, Ainu communities remained mired in poverty, children continued to encounter negative stereotypes and overt discrimination in the integrated schools that the prewar Ainu Society had struggled for, and adults ran into stubborn prejudice when they tried to find jobs or marry outside Ainu circles. Matters began to change only in the 1970s, when a new generation aggressively began to confront society's hostility. Some activists drew inspiration from the efforts of *burakumin* to overcome marginalization, while the emergence of indigenous people's movements worldwide stimulated activity by other groups of young Ainu. Domestic events, especially the celebrations held in Sapporo in 1968 to mark the centennial of the Meiji Restoration and one hundred years of "Hokkaidō History," also had their effect. Attended by the emperor, and mounted at considerable public expense, those festivities scarcely mentioned the Ainu, and planners made no place for them at either the newly constructed Pioneer Village or Museum of Development, except to depict them as guides or coolies for early explorers.

All Ainu resented the historical amnesia of 1968, which seemed to deny their very existence. In reaction, some groups such as the Utari ["Our People"] Society, successor to the Ainu Society, pressured the central government to finance twelve billion yen in development projects similar to those being undertaken in *burakumin* communities. More radical, and usually younger, Ainu borrowed the tactics of denunciation from the *burakumin* and successfully forced the cancellation of television programs that portrayed them in a negative manner, extracted public apologies from magazines that printed discriminatory cartoons, and took on the country's largest travel agency after it advertised a tour to visit a "real Ainu village" and experience "the ancient customs and culture of the famed hairy Ainu."[38]

The increasingly positive sense of self-identity evident in the 1970s and 1980s sparked a rapidly growing interest in Ainu history and culture. In ever-greater numbers, communities hosted festivals that featured prayers in the Ainu language, recitations of oral literature, performances of re-created dances, and displays of traditional embroidered costumes. Activists even created new symbols of "Ainuness." An Ainu flag appeared in 1973, and people began to speak wistfully of the *Ainu Moshiri* ("the quiet earth where humans dwell"), both a mythological golden age and physical space where Ainu had lived communally and in idealized harmony with nature before being overrun by Japanese colonizers. As self-perceptions changed, the Utari Society, which claimed to represent half of Japan's seventeen thousand Ainu, articulated its aspirations for the future in a proposal it issued on May 27, 1984. Entitled the New Ainu Law, the document set forth model legislation that would recognize the ethnic and economic "self-reliance" of Japan's indigenous people, allow them to preserve their language and culture, abolish all forms of racial discrimination, and guarantee them basic human rights and full participation in the political process.

Koreans made up Japan's largest ethnic minority at century's end. About 90 percent of the approximately 700,000 Koreans resident in Japan then were the children, grandchildren, and, increasingly, great-grandchildren of the men and women who had come to Japan, voluntarily or otherwise, during the colonial period. Japan had extended certain prerogatives of citizenship to Koreans, such as the privilege of seeking employment throughout the empire, after the annexation in 1910. When the San Francisco Peace Treaty went into effect, however, the Japanese government totally disenfranchised the Koreans remaining in the country, demoting them to the status of resident aliens and leaving them only a legally precarious right to live in Japan permanently. Since Japan confers citizenship on the basis of parental nationality (*jus sanguinis*, "law of blood," as opposed to *jus soli*, "law of soil"), and since the naturalization process was a technically complicated process made more dreadful by steely-eyed, acid-tongued bureaucrats who took pride in intimidating applicants, most Koreans who chose to stay in Japan after 1952 lived there without full rights of citizenship. So too have their descendants, despite the fact that the overwhelming majority were born in Japan, have spent their entire lives there, have been graduated from Japanese schools, and speak only Japanese.

In addition to living in legal uncertainty, the Korean minority has had to endure the same burdens of social and economic discrimination as other marginalized groups: schoolyard taunts, whispers in supermarket aisles, vacant apartments suddenly rented out, engagements broken when parental disapproval became too great to bear, hermetically sealed doors at major corporations, removal from blue-collar jobs after concealed identities came to light, and pressure on successful athletes and entertainers to pretend they were Japanese. Sometimes the lack of legal standing combined with social prejudice to place Koreans in particularly galling and frustrating straits. In August 1945 an estimated total of seventy thousand Koreans were in Hiroshima and Nagasaki, many conscripted to work in factories producing war matériel. Approximately forty thousand of those Koreans died in the atomic bombings or within a year from bombing-related diseases and injuries. In 1959 and again in 1968 the Japanese government passed legislation that extended special medical services, health care allowances, and tax exemptions

to those who suffered disabilities or illness as a result of the atomic bombings. Although neither of those laws contained a nationality requirement, a
full twenty years later fewer than five hundred of the seven thousand or so
Korean survivors of the bombings who were still alive and residing in Japan
had received any benefits, largely because of legal difficulties in proving
that they were in Hiroshima or Nagasaki at the time of the bombings. Denied compensation, they endured further anguish when municipal authorities refused them permission to erect a cenotaph to stand alongside a
memorial to Japanese victims at the Hiroshima Peace Park.

Like other minorities, Koreans joined the struggle against discrimination and prejudice in the late Shōwa era: Community leaders demanded that
Korean neighborhoods be included among the target areas for public works
projects, citizen groups publicized examples of egregious intolerance, and
individuals sued companies over discrimination. In 1989 the Korean Youth
Association in Japan sent to the UN Commission on Human Rights a letter that summarized the leading demands of the Korean minority. Prominent among them were guaranteed human rights for Koreans as "indisputably
constituent members of Japanese society," freedom "in the selection of employment and the pursuit of economic activities," access to social security
benefits, the right to vote in local government elections and run for local
office, and relief measures for Korean atomic bomb victims.

Regardless of the distress experienced by marginalized groups, even the
most radical activists would acknowledge that protest, remonstration, and
the cultivation of more positive self-images combined to improve the situation for minorities over the final decades of the twentieth century. For *burakumin*, Ainu, and Koreans—as well as the ethnic Chinese, Okinawans,
repatriated descendants of Japanese emigrants, and resident aliens from other
parts of Asia who formed Japan's other sizable minority groups—living conditions became more comfortable, discrimination less blatant, and opportunities for advancement and self-fulfillment more plentiful. More specifically,
by the mid-1990s, 62.7 percent of *burakumin* families owned their own homes
(compared with a national average of 59.8 percent), the proportion of *burakumin* children entering high school approached that of the mainstream
population, and 20 percent of all *burakumin* adolescents (versus 28 percent
of other Japanese) attended college, whereas only 2 percent had done so in
the 1960s. Ainu efforts to develop a political voice paid off internationally
in 1992, when they were invited to participate in the opening ceremonies
for the United Nations International Year of the World's Indigenous People, and domestically in 1994, when Kayano Shigeru became the first Ainu
elected to the Diet.

The attitudes of government officials also seemed to be changing. In the 1990s the city of Nagasaki allocated a significant part of its budget to assist Korean victims of the atomic bombings, and the mayor of Hiroshima finally authorized the construction of a Korean memorial inside the Peace Park. By that time the national government had opened positions in education and local government service to Koreans and extended to most of them the same social security benefits enjoyed by Japanese citizens. Even the naturalization service apparently was experiencing a change of heart as one leading bureaucrat wrote: "It goes without saying that sharing the same nationality does not require people to have a homogeneous culture and lifestyle. Only when naturalized persons become able to say 'I am Japanese of such and such origin' without hiding their previous nationality will Japanese society be said to have internationalized from within."[39]

Despite the changes evident in the 1990s, observers concurred that much remained to be done in the twenty-first century. Prejudice in marriage and employment was still rife, and some observers contended that Japanese authorities overlooked new and increasingly subtle and insidious forms of discrimination. Nevertheless, the burgeoning and very visible demand for minority rights had laid to rest any notion that Japan was a one-dimensional, ethnically homogeneous society. Similarly, minorities had challenged Japanese society to become more open and pluralistic, just as critics of one-party government had issued a call for a more pluralistic, less elitist political system. Moreover, the insistence of the *burakumin* and other minorities that they could contribute to the well-being of the social whole even as they acquired greater opportunities for self-fulfillment roughly paralleled the claims of younger mainstream men and women for more egalitarian marriages and for work relationships that respected the needs of the individual while still doing honor to what were considered legitimate social obligations.

## Of Time and Self

At the beginning of the twentieth century many Japanese looked forward to living in a society that was becoming increasingly democratic and industrialized. At the same time, they hoped that Japan eventually would become part of a global community, a "province of the world" where even people like Henrik Ibsen and Leo Tolstoy were "no longer foreigners." In a manner anticipated by no one at the century's dawn, the Great Depression and Manchurian Incident churned up a tsunami that nearly drowned such dreams and ambitions. Yet out of the destruction of the Greater East Asia War emerged a renewed commitment to old aspirations, and by century's end the island nation on the far rim of the Pacific had embraced political and economic systems that were not fundamentally dissimilar from the categories of parliamentary democracy and industrial capitalism found elsewhere. Moreover, Japan clearly had absorbed the world. From the range of commodities sold in small-town shopping arcades to the architectural forms found in their major cities, the Japanese shared a common material culture with the citizens of other advanced nations, and they also had internalized the music, art, and literature of Western societies.

Somewhat surprisingly, the celebration of New Year's 2000 paid scant attention to the quantum changes that had profoundly transformed Japan during the twentieth century. Instead, the nation focused its attention inward on the problems of the present. In its New Year's Day editorial the *Japan Times* noted that "the last ten years have been a dismal experience. In the economic sphere Japan has degenerated from the pinnacle of world success to a fumbling giant; the art of governance is in shambles; and the nation has seen the rise of a moral vacuum as classrooms have turned into battlefields and teenagers sell their bodies in the name of 'subsidized friendship.' "[40] No one, however, seemed able to offer any stirring, inspirational formula for overcoming the end-of-the-century malaise. Nebulous platitudes about finding "a new sense of purpose" and "charting a new course for the century" filled the newspapers, and when Prime Minister Obuchi addressed the nation at one o'clock on the morning of January 1, he blandly reported that Japan was experiencing no serious computer-related Y2K problems. Most Japanese approached the new century in the same low-key manner: Some visited Buddhist temples, where the ringing of bells signified the casting aside of the sins of the past year, others went to Shinto shrines to purchase auspicious talismans and ask the blessing of the gods for the coming year, and across the country families gathered together to enjoy special foods and watch the "Red and White Singing Contest."

The absence of any clarion call for dramatic political change suggested perhaps that most Japanese were satisfied that the tools and principles of parliamentary democracy eventually would return good governance and economic prosperity to their country. Elsewhere, however, some individuals wanted to blaze a new cultural path into the future. If most men and women celebrated New Year's 2000 in a way that seemed somehow so Japanese at century's end, others were calling for a new cosmopolitanism. In contrast with the older notion, prevalent at the beginning of the century, that Japan should learn from others and become a country where Ibsen and Tolstoy were no longer strangers, the new internationalism of the late twentieth and early twenty-first centuries implied a responsibility to transcend nationality, look beyond the difficulties of the moment, and contribute something to world culture.

One notable practitioner of the new culturalism was the architect and city planner Tange Kenzō, who designed the Hiroshima Peace Memorial Hall in 1955, at the beginning of his career. A decade later he orchestrated the reconstruction of Skopje, Yugoslavia, after an earthquake destroyed that city, and he was the lead architect for Tokyo's stunning new metropolitan office complex, completed in 1991. Reviewing that lifework, many critics lauded Tange for using asymmetry and other traditional principles of Japanese design to shape modern materials into original, boldly imagined buildings that turned the architectural world on its head by separating functionalism from a rigid geometrical style.

Working in another medium, the avant-garde fashion designer Issey Miyake hoped to participate in world culture as just another individual, devoid of any particular national identity. "Away from the home country, living and working in Paris," he once reminisced, "I looked at myself very hard and asked, 'what could I do as a Japanese fashion designer?' Then I realized that my very disadvantage, lack of Western heritage, would also be my advantage. The lack of Western tradition," he continued, "was the very thing I needed to create contemporary and universal fashion. But as a Japanese I come from a heritage rich in tradition. I realized these two wonderful advantages I enjoy," Miyake concluded, "and that was when I started to experiment creating a new genre of clothing, neither Western nor Japanese but beyond nationality."[41] Finally, at long last, at the junction of two centuries, at the union of two millennia, it seemed possible to be both Japanese and modern, even to transcend national identity.

Increasingly in the late Shōwa and early Heisei periods, the world was warming to things Japanese. Around the globe, people ate sushi, bought packages of instant ramen noodles in local food markets, practiced judo and karate, and sang tunes to the accompaniment of karaoke music. Expressions of Japanese values and behavior also piqued the curiosity of people everywhere and often won their appreciation as well. When the Nobel Prize committee in the 1960s first decided to honor a Japanese writer, it selected Kawabata Yasunari, a "purely Japanese" novelist whose works were thought to express a typical Japanese melancholy as they explored the sensuous yet fragile and precarious nature of love and human existence. Closer to the end of the century, films like *Tanpopo* ("Dandelion") and *Shall we dansu?* ("Shall We Dance?")—one a string of humorous vignettes about Japanese and food;

the other a sensitive portrayal of how one middle-aged salaryman confronted the loneliness of his existence by gliding into a budding relationship with a beautiful ballroom dance instructor that never quite became airborne and of how his wife reacted to the threat of adultery—played to packed theaters in Japan and abroad.

In other instances people outside Japan were intrigued by how specific depictions of Japanese lifestyles and values might contain some universal meaning. Thus, even while Tange's buildings were winning international applause, the second Japanese to receive the Nobel Prize in literature was Ōe Kenzaburō, whose books examined the Hiroshima experience, antagonisms between mountain villagers on the island of Shikoku and the central government in Tokyo, and a father's life with his disabled son. Although Ōe anchored his novels in the particular experiences of the late Shōwa period, he forged, in the view of one prominent literary critic, "a connection between specific circumstances and a universal outlook." Ōe's approach, he continued, "focuses not on how distant Japan is but how close. Ōe writes of Japan's anguish, and thus of the anguish of all contemporary humanity."[42]

Employing different sorts of images, the serialized TV drama *Oshin* also attracted a large international following in the forty-one countries where it was broadcast. Presumably many of those viewers tuned in to learn something about the life of ordinary Japanese as they followed the story of Oshin, a woman who spent her childhood in a poor farming village in northern Japan, took a job as a live-in maid, and overcame a series of obstacles to become the owner of a supermarket in Tokyo. But the real secret of *Oshin*'s international popularity, according to one analyst, was that the leading character exhibited values that transcended linguistic and cultural barriers: "strength of character, warm-heartedness, perseverance, courage, and industriousness."[43] As for Miyake, *Elle* awarded him the highest accolade the French fashion industry can bestow: *Son style dépasse les modes* ("His style goes beyond fashion").

The future course of the new cosmopolitanism is not clear. Nor was it possible in the early light of a new century to know when, or even if, Japan would find a way to overcome its economic and political malaise. Some eight hundred years earlier, at the beginning of the thirteenth century, the poet Kamo no Chōmei had become disgusted at a world that for him was too filled with misfortune and calamity. Seeking a more tranquil life, he abandoned the capital of Kyoto to live in a small hut in the nearby hills. There he wrote *Hōjōki*, a short commentary on the nature of existence. "Ceaselessly," Chōmei began his essay, "the river flows, and yet the water is never the same, while in the still pools the shifting foam gathers and is gone, never staying for a moment. Even so is man and his habitation."[44] A reflection on the Buddhist precept about the impermanence of life, Chōmei's thought stands as an appropriate metaphor for the present. Just as his river was ever churning, creating bubbles that quickly disappeared and then reformed again, still recognizable but reconstituted in different patterns, so today do notions about what it means to be modern and what it means to be Japanese endlessly transform themselves in reaction to the swirl of surrounding historical events.

In their wake, changing conceptions of identity produce diversity, contention, and a multiplicity of views about the future of politics, the economy, and society. Over the course of the modern era Japanese notions about who they are and how they ought to coexist with the other peoples of the world have changed enormously. Visions of self and nation continue to transform themselves today, and the Japanese have no single answer to the questions and challenges that face them as they step forward into the new century. Historians, for their part, often prefer to see change as accumulative and evolutionary, but history itself has taught that the flow of time also encounters waterfalls, discontinuities that break the past from the present and make the future always unpredictable.

# Notes

## CHAPTER 1: THE TOKUGAWA POLITY

1 Adapted from Helen Craig McCullough, tr., *Genji and Heike: Selections from* The Tale of Genji *and* The Tale of the Heike (Stanford: Stanford University Press, 1994), p. 265, and A. L. Sadler, tr., *The Ten Foot Square Hut and Tales of the Heike* (Rutland, Vt.: Charles E. Tuttle, 1972), p. 22.

2 The quotations by Europeans are from Michael Cooper, S.J., ed., *They Came to Japan: An Anthology of European Reports on Japan, 1543–1640* (Berkeley: University of California Press, 1965), pp. 4–7 (modified).

3 Joan R. Piggott, *The Emergence of Japanese Kingship* (Stanford: Stanford University Press, 1997), p. 210 (modified).

4 *The Man'yōshū*: The Nippon Gakujutsu Shinkōkai Translation of *One Thousand Poems* (New York: Columbia University Press, 1969), pp. 282–83.

5 Lee A. Butler, "Court and Bakufu in Early 17th Century Japan" (Ph.D. dissertation, Princeton University, 1991), pp. 113–14.

6 "Laws of Military Households (Buke Shohatto), 1615," in David J. Lu, ed., *Japan: A Documentary History* (Armonk, N.Y.: M. E. Sharpe, 1997), pp. 206–8 (modified).

7 This observation and the subsequent quote about the regional lords are from Harold Bolitho, "The Han," in John W.

Hall et al., gen. eds., *The Cambridge History of Japan*, vol. 4: Hall, ed., *Early Modern Japan* (Cambridge: Cambridge University Press, 1991), p. 200.

8 Herman Ooms, *Tokugawa Village Practice: Class, Status, Power, and Law* (Berkeley: University of California Press, 1996), pp. 363–73, and Maruyama Masao, *Studies in the Intellectual History of Tokugawa Japan*, tr. Mikiso Hane (Princeton: Princeton University Press, 1974), p. 127.

9 Herman Ooms, "Neo-Confucianism and the Formation of Early Tokugawa Ideology: Contours of a Problem," in Peter Nosco, ed., *Confucianism and Tokugawa Culture* (Princeton: Princeton University Press, 1984), pp. 28–29 (modified).

10 W. J. Boot, "The Religious Background of the Deification of Tokugawa Ieyasu," in Andriana Boscaro, Franco Gatti, and Massimo Raveri, eds., *Rethinking Japan*, vol. 2: *Social Sciences, Ideology and Thought* (Sandgate, Folkestone, Kent: Japan Library, 1990), p. 335.

11 Naomi Okawa, *Edo Architecture: Katsura and Nikko*, tr. Alan Woodhull and Akito Miyamoto (New York: Weatherhill/Heibonsha, 1975), p. 16 (modified).

12 Shigeru Matsumoto, *Motoori Norinaga, 1730–1801* (Cambridge: Harvard University Press, 1970), p. 84 (modified).

13 Engelbert Kaempfer, *The History of Japan, Together with a Description of the Kingdom of Siam, 1690–1692*, tr. J. G. Scheuchzer, F.R.S., vol. 2 (Glasgow: James MacLehose and Sons, 1906), p. 331.

14 For Keinen's diary entries, see Jurgis Elisonas, "The Regime of the Unifiers," in Wm. Theodore de Bary et al. comp., *Sources of the Japanese Tradition*, vol. 1: *From Earliest Times to 1600* (New York: Columbia University Press, 2001, 2nd ed.), pp. 468–69 and 471, and "The Inseparable Trinity: Japan's Relations with China and Korea," in *The Cambridge History of Japan*, vol. 4, p. 293.

15 Jurgis Elisonas, "Christianity and the Daimyo," in *The Cambridge History of Japan*, vol. 4, p. 367.

16 Charles MacFarlane, *Japan: An Account, Geographical and Historical* (New York: George P. Putnam, 1852), p. 18 (modified).

17 Cooper, ed., *They Came to Japan*, p. 401.

18 Ronald P. Toby, *State and Diplomacy in Early Modern Japan* (Princeton: Princeton University Press, 1984), p. 101.

19 Based on Engelbert Kaempfer, *Kaempfer's Japan: Tokugawa Culture Observed*, ed., tr., and annot. by Beatrice M. Bodart-Bailey (Honolulu: University of Hawai'i Press, 1999), pp. 360–68, and Kaempfer, *The History of Japan*, pp. 85–94.

## CHAPTER 2: CITIES, COMMERCE, AND LIFESTYLES

1 James L. McClain, "Space, Power, Wealth, and Status in Seventeenth-Century Osaka," in McClain and Wakita Osamu, eds., *Osaka: The Merchants' Capital of Early Modern Japan* (Ithaca: Cornell University Press, 1999), pp. 55–56 (modified).

2 Tessa Morris-Suzuki, *The Technological Transformation of Japan: From the Seventeenth to the Twenty-first Century* (Cambridge: Cambridge University Press, 1994), p. 29.

3 Thomas C. Smith, "Premodern Economic Growth: Japan and the West," in Smith, *Native Sources of Japanese Industrialization, 1750–1920* (Berkeley: University of California Press, 1988), p. 29.

4 Tessa Morris-Suzuki, *Re-Inventing Japan: Time, Space, Nation* (Armonk, N.Y.: M. E. Sharpe, 1998), p. 13.

5 Takeuchi Makoto, "Festivals and Fights: The Law and the People of Edo," in James L. McClain, John M. Merriman, and Ugawa Kaoru, eds., *Edo and Paris: Urban Life and the State in the Early Modern Era* (Ithaca: Cornell University Press, 1994), pp. 404–05 (modified).

6 James L. McClain, *Kanazawa: A Seventeenth-Century Japanese Castle Town* (New Haven: Yale University Press, 1982), p. 94.

7 Nishiyama Matsunosuke, *Edo Culture: Daily Life and Diversions in Urban Japan, 1600–1868*, tr. and ed. Gerald Groemer (Honolulu: University of Hawai'i Press, 1997), p. 160 (modified).

8 Smith, "Premodern Economic Growth," p. 27.

9 For the quotations by Bird, see Susan B. Hanley, *Everyday Things in Premodern Japan: The Hidden Legacy of Material Culture* (Berkeley: University of California Press, 1997), p. 188; Isabella Lucy Bird, *Unbeaten Tracks in Japan* (Rutland, Vt.: Charles E. Tuttle, 1973, reprint edition), pp. 49–53; and Bird, *The Englishwoman in America* (Madison: University of Wisconsin Press, 1966, rep. ed.), pp. 148–49.

## CHAPTER 3: SELF AND SOCIETY

1 Jippensha Ikku, *Shanks' Mare*, tr. Thomas Satchell (Rutland, Vt.: Charles E. Tuttle, 1960), p. 237 (modified).

2 Helen Craig McCullough, ed., *Genji and Heike: Selections from* The Tale of Genji *and*

The Tale of the Heike (Stanford: Stanford University Press, 1994), pp. 394–95.

3 *Kodansha Encyclopedia of Japan*, vol. 2 (Tokyo: Kodansha, 1983), s.v. Martin Collcutt, "Miyamoto Musashi," p. 222 (modified).

4 Miyamoto Musashi, *The Book of Five Rings*, tr. Thomas Cleary (Boston: Shambhala, 1993), pp. 38 and 46 (modified).

5 Ryusaku Tsunoda, Wm. Theodore de Bary, and Donald Keene, comps., *Sources of Japanese Tradition* (New York: Columbia University Press, 1958), p. 395.

6 Eiko Ikegami, *The Taming of the Samurai: Honorific Individualism and the Making of Modern Japan* (Cambridge: Harvard University Press, 1995), p. 218.

7 Unless otherwise noted, quotations from "In the Shadow of Leaves" are based on Yamamoto Tsunetomo, *Hagakure: The Book of the Samurai*, tr. William Scott Wilson (New York: Avon, 1979), pp. 37, 51, 41, 66, 17, and 84.

8 Ikegami, *The Taming of the Samurai*, p. 289.

9 Ivan Morris, *The Nobility of Failure: Tragic Heroes in the History of Japan* (New York: New American Library, 1975), p. 316 (modified).

10 Moriya Katsuhisa, "Urban Networks and Information Networks," tr. Ronald P. Toby, in Nakane Chie and Ōishi Shinzaburō, eds., *Tokugawa Japan: The Social and Economic Antecedents of Modern Japan*, tr. ed. Conrad Totman (Tokyo: University of Tokyo Press, 1990), p. 120 (modified).

11 Donald H. Shively, "Popular Culture," in John W. Hall et al., gen. eds., *The Cambridge History of Japan*, vol. 4: Hall, ed., *Early Modern Japan* (Cambridge: Cambridge University Press, 1991), p. 765.

12 Tetsuo Najita, *Visions of Virtue in Tokugawa Japan: The Kaitokudō Merchant Academy of Osaka* (Chicago: University of Chicago Press, 1987), p. 255.

13 Quotations attributed to Ishida are based on Robert N. Bellah, *Tokugawa Religion: The Values of Pre-Industrial Japan* (Boston: Beacon Press, 1957), p. 158; Ishikawa Ken, "Baigan Ishida's *Shingaku* Doctrine," tr. Takeo Katow, *Philosophical Studies of Japan* 6 (1965), pp. 26–27; and Eiji Takemura, *The Perception of Work in Tokugawa Japan: A Study of Ishida Baigan and Ninomiya Sontoku* (Lanham, Md.: University Press of America, 1997), p. 65.

14 Bellah, *Tokugawa Religion*, p. 149.

15 Unless otherwise noted, the quotations from household codes are based on J. Mark Ramseyer, "Thrift and Diligence: House Codes of Tokugawa Merchant Families," *Monumenta Nipponica* 34:2 (Summer 1979), pp. 210, 213, 216, 214, 215, 212, and 217.

16 Quotations attributed to Mitsui Takafusa are from E. Sydney Crawcour, "Some Observations on Merchants: A Translation of Mitsui Takafusa's *Chōnin Kōken Roku*," *Transactions of the Asiatic Society of Japan*, 3d series, vol. 8 (December 1961), pp. 87, 107, 119, and 121, and Mitsui Takahara, "Chōnin's Life under Feudalism," *Cultural Nippon* 8:2 (June 1940) as reprinted by Nippon Bunka Chūō Renmei (Tokyo: 1940), pp. 1–32.

17 Miyamoto, *The Book of Five Rings*, p. 6.

18 Bellah, *Tokugawa Religion*, p. 157.

19 Quotations attributed to Ninomiya are based on Takemura, *The Perception of Work in Tokugawa Japan*, pp. 129–31 and 120, and *Sources of the Japanese Tradition*, pp. 585, 578, and 582.

20 Quotations from *Onna daigaku* are based on translations in Basil Hall Chamberlain, *Things Japanese* (London: Kegan Paul, Trench, Trübner & Co., 1890), pp. 370, 371, 369, 372, 374, and 367; Sakai

Atsuharu, "Kaibara Ekken and 'Onna Daigaku,'" *Cultural Nippon* 7:4 (1939), pp. 51–55; and Joyce Ackroyd, "Women in Feudal Japan," *Transactions of the Asiatic Society of Japan*, 3d series, vol. 7 (November 1959), p. 53.

21 "A Sermon by Hosoi Heishū," in Michiko Y. Aoki and Margaret B. Dardess, comps. and eds., *As the Japanese See It: Past and Present* (Honolulu: University of Hawaii Press, 1981), p. 65.

22 Jennifer Robertson, "The Shingaku Woman: Straight from the Heart," in Gail Lee Bernstein, ed., *Recreating Japanese Women, 1600–1945* (Berkeley: University of California Press, 1991), pp. 97 and 94.

23 Kate Wildman Nakai, "Introduction," in Yamakawa Kikue, *Women of Mito Domain: Recollections of Samurai Family Life*, tr. Nakai (Tokyo: University of Tokyo Press, 1992), p. xxiii (modified).

24 Anne Walthall, "The Life Cycle of Farm Women in Tokugawa Japan," in Bernstein, ed., *Recreating Japanese Women, 1600–1945*, p. 58.

25 Gary P. Leupp, *Servants, Shophands, and Laborers in the Cities of Tokugawa Japan* (Princeton: Princeton University Press, 1992), p. 85 (modified).

26 Yamakawa, *Women of Mito Domain*, pp. 170–71.

27 Uchida Kusuo, "Protest and the Tactics of Direct Remonstration: Osaka's Merchants Make Their Voices Heard," in James L. McClain and Wakita Osamu, *Osaka: The Merchants' Capital of Early Modern Japan* (Ithaca: Cornell University Press, 1999), p. 89.

28 Mark Ravina, *Land and Lordship in Early Modern Japan* (Stanford: Stanford University Press, 1999), p. 1 (modified).

29 Fukuzawa Yukichi, *An Outline of a Theory of Civilization*, tr. David A. Dilworth and G. Cameron Hurst (Tokyo: Sophia University, 1973), p. 160.

30 Constantine N. Vaporis, "To Edo and Back: Alternate Attendance and Japanese Culture in the Early Modern Period," *Journal of Japanese Studies* 23:1 (Winter 1997), p. 39.

31 George Elison, *Deus Destroyed: The Image of Christianity in Early Modern Japan* (Cambridge: Council on East Asian Studies, Harvard University, 1988, 2d printing), p. 321 (modified).

32 Ronald P. Toby, "The 'Indianness' of Iberia and Changing Japanese Iconographies of the Other," in Stuart B. Schwartz, ed., *Implicit Understandings: Observing, Reporting, and Reflecting on the Encounters between Europeans and Other Peoples in the Early Modern Era* (Cambridge: Cambridge University Press, 1994), p. 342.

33 Richard Siddle, *Race, Resistance and the Ainu of Japan* (London: Routledge, 1996), p. 42.

34 Quotations of Bashō's poetry are from *Bashō: The Narrow Road to the Deep North and Other Travel Sketches*, tr. Nobuyuki Yuasa (Baltimore: Penguin Books, 1966), pp. 118–23.

35 Ihara Saikaku, *Some Final Words of Advice*, tr. Peter Nosco (Rutland, Vt.: Charles E. Tuttle, 1980), p. 128.

## CHAPTER 4: THE MEIJI RESTORATION

1 Nakai Nobuhiko and James L. McClain, "Commercial Change and Urban Growth in Early Modern Japan," in John W. Hall et al., gen. eds., *The Cambridge History of Japan*, vol. 4: Hall, ed., *Early Modern Japan* (Cambridge: Cambridge University Press, 1991), p. 594 (modified).

2 James L. McClain, "Failed Expectations: Kaga Domain on the Eve of the Meiji Restoration," *Journal of Japanese Studies* 14:2 (Winter 1988), p. 415.

3 Kozo Yamamura, *A Study of Samurai Income and Entrepreneurship: Quantitative Analyses of Economic and Social Aspects of the Samurai in Tokugawa and Meiji Japan* (Cambridge: Harvard University Press, 1974), p. 132 (modified).

4 Susan B. Hanley and Kozo Yamamura, *Economic and Demographic Change in Preindustrial Japan 1600–1868* (Princeton: Princeton University Press, 1977), p. 147 (modified).

5 Harold Bolitho, "The Tempō Crisis," in Hall et al., *The Cambridge History of Japan*, vol. 5: Marius B. Jansen, ed., *The Nineteenth Century* (Cambridge: Cambridge University Press, 1989), p. 230.

6 Anne Walthall, *Social Protest and Popular Culture in Eighteenth-Century Japan* (Tucson: University of Arizona Press, 1986), pp. 214–15.

7 Quotations by Mabuchi and Norinaga are from Peter Nosco, *Remembering Paradise: Nativism and Nostalgia in Eighteenth-Century Japan* (Cambridge: Council on East Asian Studies, Harvard University, 1990), pp. 123 and 199–200 (modified).

8 Tetsuo Najita, "Ambiguous Encounters: Ogata Kōan and International Studies in Late Tokugawa Japan," in James L. McClain and Wakita Osamu, eds., *Osaka: The Merchants' Capital of Early Modern Japan* (Ithaca: Cornell University Press, 1999), p. 221 (modified).

9 Quotations by Sugita are from Hirakawa Sukehiro, "Japan's Turn to the West," tr. Bob Tadashi Wakabayashi, in *The Cambridge History of Japan*, vol. 5, pp. 438 (modified) and 437.

10 Carmen Blacker, "Millenarian Aspects of New Religions," in Donald Shively, ed., *Tradition and Modernization in Japanese Culture* (Princeton: Princeton University Press, 1971), p. 575.

11 H. D. Harootunian, "Late Tokugawa Culture and Thought," in *The Cambridge History of Japan*, vol. 5, p. 230.

12 The shogunate's communication and the inscription on the Russian plate are from George Alexander Lensen, *The Russian Push toward Japan: Russo-Japanese Relations 1697–1875* (Princeton: Princeton University Press, 1959), pp. 154–55 (modified).

13 W. G. Beasley, *Great Britain and the Opening of Japan 1834–1858* (London: Luzac, 1951), p. 15.

14 Unless otherwise noted, quotations by Aizawa are taken from Bob Tadashi Wakabayashi, *Anti-Foreignism and Western Learning in Early-Modern Japan* (Cambridge: Council on East Asian Studies, Harvard University, 1991, 2d ed.), pp. 90, 165, 125 (modified), and 276.

15 J. Victor Koschmann, *The Mito Ideology: Discourse, Reform, and Insurrection in Late Tokugawa Japan, 1790–1864* (Berkeley: University of California Press, 1987), p. 57 (modified).

16 Tessa Morris-Suzuki, "The Frontiers of Japanese Identity," in Stein Tønnesson and Hans Antlöv, eds., *Asian Forms of the Nation* (Richmond, Surrey: Nordic Institute of Asian Studies in cooperation with Curzon Press, 1996), p. 54.

17 Richard Siddle, *Race, Resistance and the Ainu of Japan* (London: Routledge, 1996), p. 40 (modified).

18 D. C. Greene, "Correspondence between William II of Holland and the Shogun of Japan A.D. 1844," *Transactions of the Asiatic Society of Japan* 39 (1907), pp. 110–15.

19 Centre for East Asian Cultural Studies, comp. and publ., *Meiji Japan through Contemporary Sources*, vol. 2 (Tokyo: 1970), pp. 6–8.

20 Arthur Walworth, *Black Ships off Japan: The Story of Commodore Perry's Expedition* (New York: Knopf, 1946), p. 39 (modified).

21 Allen Burnett Cole, "The Dynamics of American Expansion toward Japan,

1791–1860" (Ph.D. dissertation, University of Chicago, 1940), pp. 143–44.

22 Francis L. Hawks, comp., *Narrative of the Expedition of an American Squadron to the China Seas and Japan: Performed in the Years 1852, 1853, and 1854, under the Command of Commodore M. C. Perry, United States Navy, by Order of the Government of the United States* (New York: D. Appleton, 1856), pp. 296–97.

23 Walworth, *Black Ships off Japan*, pp. 240–46 (modified).

24 Hawks, *Narrative of the Expedition of an American Squadron to the China Seas and Japan*, pp. 299–301.

25 *Meiji Japan through Contemporary Sources*, vol. 2, pp. 18–19.

26 Ibid., pp. 31–35 (modified).

27 W. G. Beasley, tr. and ed., *Select Documents on Japanese Foreign Policy 1853–1868* (London: Oxford University Press, 1955), p. 181.

28 W. G. Beasley, *The Meiji Restoration* (Stanford: Stanford University Press, 1972), p. 121 (modified).

29 *Select Documents on Japanese Foreign Policy 1853–1868*, p. 180 (modified).

30 Anne Walthall, "Off with Their Heads!: The Hirata Disciples and the Ashikaga Shoguns," *Monumenta Nipponica* 50:2 (Summer 1995), p. 158 (modified).

31 M. William Steele, "Goemon's New World View: Popular Representations of the Opening of Japan," *Asian Cultural Studies* 17 (March 1989), p. 80.

32 Anne Walthall, "Edo Riots," in James L. McClain, John M. Merriman, and Ugawa Kaoru, eds., *Edo and Paris: Urban Life and the State in the Early Modern Period* (Ithaca: Cornell University Press, 1994), pp. 425–27, for this and the following quote (modified).

33 Stephen Vlastos, *Peasant Protests and Uprisings in Tokugawa Japan* (Berkeley: University of California Press, 1986), p. 114.

34 Beasley, *The Meiji Restoration*, pp. 258–59.

35 Charles L. Yates, *Saigō Takamori: The Man behind the Myth* (London: Kegan Paul, 1995), p. 81 (modified).

36 The quotes by Kido and Iwakura are from Beasley, *The Meiji Restoration*, pp. 266–67 (modified).

37 George M. Wilson, *Patriots and Redeemers in Japan: Motives in the Meiji Restoration* (Chicago: University of Chicago Press, 1992), p. 103.

## CHAPTER 5: "NEW BEGINNINGS"

1 Based on Ishii Ryosuke, ed., *Japanese Legislation in the Meiji Era*, tr. William J. Chambliss (Tokyo: Pan-Pacific Press, 1958), p. 145, and Robert M. Spaulding, Jr., "The Intent of the Charter Oath," in Richard K. Beasley, *Studies in Japanese History and Politics* (Ann Arbor: University of Michigan Press, 1967), pp. 6–26.

2 Roger F. Hackett, "The Meiji Leaders and Modernization: The Case of Yamagata Aritomo," in Marius B. Jansen, ed., *Changing Japanese Attitudes toward Modernization* (Princeton: Princeton University Press, 1972, 3d print.), p. 244.

3 Charles Lanman, ed., *The Japanese in America* (Tokyo: Japan Advertiser Press, 1926, rep. ed.), p. 22.

4 Itō Hirobumi, "Some Reminiscences of the Grant of the New Constitution," in Count Shigenobu Ōkuma, comp., *Fifty Years of New Japan*, vol. 1, ed. Marcus B. Huish (London: Smith, Elder, & Company, 1910), pp. 125–26.

5 William Elliot Griffis, *The Mikado's Empire* (New York: Harper & Brothers, 1890), p. 526, and Iwata Masakazu, *Ōkubo Toshimichi: The Bismarck of Japan* (Berkeley: University of California Press, 1964), pp. 143–44.

6 *Japanese Legislation in the Meiji Era*, pp. 723–24.

7 Ibid., p. 722.

8 W. G. Beasley, *The Meiji Restoration* (Stanford: Stanford University Press, 1972), p. 374.

9 The poem and quotations concerning Saigō are from Ivan Morris, *The Nobility of Failure: Tragic Heroes in the History of Japan* (New York: New American Library, 1975), pp. 258–66.

10 Hirakawa Sukehiro, "Japan's Turn to the West," tr. Bob Tadashi Wakabayashi, in John W. Hall et al., gen. eds., *The Cambridge History of Japan*, vol. 5: Marius B. Jansen, ed., *The Nineteenth Century* (Cambridge: Cambridge University Press, 1989), p. 448.

11 Walt Whitman, "A Broadway Pageant," in *The First Japanese Embassy: Japan-U.S. Centennial 1860–1960* (New York: Information Office, Consulate General of Japan, 1960), np.

12 Hirakawa, "Japan's Turn to the West," p. 463.

13 Beasley, *The Meiji Restoration*, pp. 369–70.

14 Eugene Soviak, "On the Nature of Western Progress: The Journal of the Iwakura Embassy," in Donald H. Shively, ed., *Tradition and Modernization in Japanese Culture* (Princeton: Princeton University Press, 1971), p. 15.

15 Marlene Mayo, "Rationality in the Meiji Restoration: The Iwakura Embassy," in Bernard S. Silberman and Harry D. Harootunian, eds., *Modern Japanese Leadership: Transition and Change* (Tucson: University of Arizona Press, 1966), pp. 357–58 (modified).

16 Beasley, *The Meiji Restoration*, p. 370 (modified).

17 Hirakawa, "Japan's Turn to the West," p. 455.

18 Ibid., p. 482 (modified).

19 Albert M. Craig, "Fukuzawa Yukichi: The Philosophical Foundations of Meiji Nationalism," in Robert E. Ward, ed., *Political Development in Modern Japan* (Princeton: Princeton University Press, 1968), pp. 120–21 (modified).

20 Edward Seidensticker, *Low City, High City: Tokyo from Edo to the Earthquake: How the Shogun's Ancient Capital Became a Great Modern City, 1867–1923* (New York: Knopf, 1983), p. 35.

21 Carmen Blacker, *The Japanese Enlightenment: A Study of the Writings of Fukuzawa Yukichi* (Cambridge: Cambridge University Press, 1964), p. 31 (modified).

22 Lanman, ed., *The Japanese in America*, pp. 31–32 (modified).

23 Tokutomi Kenjirō [Roka], *Footprints in the Snow*, tr. Kenneth Strong (Tokyo: Charles E. Tuttle, 1970), p. 110 (modified).

24 Donald H. Shively, "The Japanization of the Middle Meiji," in Shively, ed., *Tradition and Modernization in Japanese Culture*, pp. 92–93.

## CHAPTER 6: CRAFTING A CONSTITUTIONAL POLITY

1 An eyewitness account of the ceremony can be found in Toku Baelz, ed., *Awakening Japan: The Diary of a German Doctor, Erwin Baelz* (Bloomington: Indiana University Press, 1974), pp. 81–83.

2 The quotation by Yamagata and the subsequent quotation from Itō are from George M. Beckmann, *The Making of the Meiji Constitution: The Oligarchs and the Constitutional Development of Japan, 1868–1891* (Lawrence: University of Kansas Publications, Social Science Studies, 1957), pp. 126–30.

3 Walter W. McLaren, ed., "Japanese Government Documents," *Transactions of*

the *Asiatic Society of Japan*, vol. 42, part 1 (1914), pp. 426–32.

4 Stephen Vlastos, "Opposition Movements in Early Meiji, 1868–1885," in John W. Hall et al., gen. eds., *The Cambridge History of Japan*, vol. 5: Marius B. Jansen, ed., *The Nineteenth Century* (Cambridge: Cambridge University Press, 1989), p. 407 (modified).

5 Ishii Ryosuke, ed., *Japanese Legislation in the Meiji Era*, tr. William J. Chambliss (Tokyo: Pan-Pacific Press, 1958), pp. 720–21.

6 "Japanese Government Documents," pp. 502–4.

7 Itō Hirobumi, "Some Reminiscences of the Grant of the New Constitution," in Count Shigenobu Ōkuma, comp., *Fifty Years of New Japan*, vol. 1, ed. Marcus B. Huish (London: Smith, Elder, & Company, 1910), p. 127.

8 "Japanese Government Documents," pp. 88–90 (modified).

9 Roger F. Hackett, *Yamagata Aritomo in the Rise of Modern Japan, 1838–1922* (Cambridge: Harvard University Press, 1971), p. 110 (modified).

10 Itō, "Some Reminiscences of the Grant of the New Constitution," pp. 124–25.

11 Carol Gluck, *Japan's Modern Myths: Ideology in the Late Meiji Period* (Princeton: Princeton University Press, 1985), p. 74.

12 Takahashi Fujitani, *Splendid Monarchy: Power and Pageantry in Modern Japan* (Berkeley: University of California Press, 1996), p. 53 (modified).

13 Gluck, *Japan's Modern Myths*, p. 75.

14 James L. Huffman, *Politics of the Meiji Press: The Life of Fukuchi Gen'ichirō* (Honolulu: University of Hawaii Press, 1980), pp. 139–54.

15 Richard H. Miner, *Japanese Tradition and Western Law: Emperor, State, and Law in the*

*Thought of Hozumi Yatsuka* (Cambridge: Harvard University Press, 1970), p. 25.

16 Gluck, *Japan's Modern Myths*, p. 105.

17 Donald H. Shively, "Nishimura Shigeki: A Confucian View of Modernization," in Marius B. Jansen, ed., *Changing Japanese Attitudes toward Modernization* (Princeton: Princeton University Press, 1972, 3d print.), p. 213.

18 George Akita and Hirose Yoshihiro, "The British Model: Inoue Kowashi and the Ideal Monarchical System," *Monumenta Nipponica* 49:4 (Winter 1994), p. 417.

19 Itō, "Some Reminiscences of the Grant of the New Constitution," p. 128 (modified).

20 Centre for East Asian Cultural Studies, comp. and publ., *Meiji Japan through Contemporary Sources*, vol. 3 (Tokyo: 1972), pp. 235–41.

21 Ian Reader, with Esben Andreasen and Finn Stefánsson, *Japanese Religions: Past and Present* (Sandgate, Folkestone, Kent: Japan Library, 1993), p. 71.

22 The official text of the emperor's message to his ancestors is contained in Itō Hirobumi, *Commentaries on the Constitution of the Empire of Japan*, tr. Itō Miyoji (Tokyo: Chūō Daigaku, 1906, 2d ed.), pp. 167–68.

23 The constitution is available in *Japan: An Illustrated Encyclopedia*, vol. 1 (Tokyo: Kodansha, 1993), "Constitution of the Empire of Japan, 1889," pp. 232–35; *Japanese Legislation in the Meiji Era*, pp. 725–33; and Beckmann, *The Making of the Meiji Constitution*, pp. 151–56.

24 Itō, *Commentaries on the Constitution of the Empire of Japan*, pp. 64–65.

25 Roger F. Hackett, "The Meiji Leaders and Modernization: The Case of Yamagata Aritomo," in Jansen, ed., *Changing Japanese Attitudes toward Modernization*, p. 244.

26 Itō, *Commentaries on the Constitution of the Empire of Japan*, p. 131.

## CHAPTER 7: TOWARD AN INDUSTRIAL FUTURE

1 Thomas C. Smith, *Political Change and Industrial Development in Japan: Government Enterprise, 1868–1880* (Stanford: Stanford University Press, 1955), p. 26.

2 Masakazu Iwata, *Ōkubo Toshimichi: The Bismarck of Japan* (Berkeley: University of California Press, 1964), p. 236.

3 Shibusawa Keizō, comp. and ed., *Japanese Society in the Meiji Era*, tr. and adapt. Aora H. Culbertson and Kimura Michiko (Tokyo: Ōbunsha, 1958), p. 378.

4 Steven W. McCallion, "Trial and Error: The Model Filature at Tomioka," in William D. Wray, *Managing Industrial Enterprise: Cases from Japan's Prewar Experience* (Cambridge: Council on East Asian Studies, Harvard University, 1989), p. 90.

5 Smith, *Political Change and Industrial Development in Japan*, p. 42.

6 Matsukata Masayoshi, *Report on the Adoption of the Gold Standard in Japan* (Tokyo: Japanese Government Press, 1899), p. 54 (modified).

7 Kyugoro Obata, *An Interpretation of the Life of Viscount Shibusawa* (Tokyo: Tokyo Printing Company, 1937), pp. 136–39 (modified).

8 Johannes Hirschmeier, *The Origins of Entrepreneurship in Meiji Japan* (Cambridge: Harvard University Press, 1964), p. 232 (modified).

9 Nimura Kazuo, *The Ashio Riot of 1907: A Social History of Mining in Japan*, ed. Andrew Gordon, tr. Terry Boardman and Gordon (Durham: Duke University Press, 1997), p. 38 (modified).

10 F. G. Notehelfer, "Japan's First Pollution Incident," *Journal of Japanese Studies* 1:2 (Spring 1975), p. 364 (modified).

11 Kenneth Strong, "Tanaka Shōzō: Meiji Hero and Pioneer against Pollution," *Japan Society Bulletin* (London) 67 (June 1972), p. 10 (modified).

12 Kenneth Strong, *Ox against the Storm: A Biography of Tanaka Shozo—Japan's Conservationist Pioneer* (Sandgate, Folkestone, Kent: Japan Library, 1995), p. 74.

## CHAPTER 8: LIVING THE MEIJI DREAM

1 E. Patricia Tsurumi, *Factory Girls: Women in the Thread Mills of Meiji Japan* (Princeton: Princeton University Press, 1990), p. 54.

2 Kazuo Okochi, *Labor in Modern Japan* (Tokyo: Science Council of Japan, 1958), p. 7.

3 Tsurumi, *Factory Girls*, pp. 194–95.

4 Mikiso Hane, *Peasants, Rebels, and Outcastes: The Underside of Modern Japan* (New York: Pantheon Books, 1982), pp. 190–91 (modified).

5 The songs are from Tsurumi, *Factory Girls*, pp. 91, 84, 97, and 197.

6 Ibid., p. 56.

7 Sumiya Mikio, "The Development of Japanese Labour-Relations," *Developing Economies* 4:4 (December 1966), p. 506.

8 Ibid., p. 501.

9 Carol Gluck, *Japan's Modern Myths: Ideology in the Late Meiji Period* (Princeton: Princeton University Press, 1985), p. 111.

10 Hozumi Nobushige, "The New Japanese Civil Code, as Material for the Study of Comparative Jurisprudence: A Paper Read at the International Congress of Arts and Science, at the Universal Exposition, Saint Louis 1904" (Tokyo: Tokyo Printing Company, 1904), p. 4.

11 Ueno Chizuko, "Genesis of the Urban Housewife," *Japan Quarterly* 34:2 (April–June 1987), p. 136.

12 Motoyama Yukihiko, "The Political Background of Early Meiji Educational Policy: The Central Government," tr. Richard Rubinger, in Motoyama, *Proliferating Talent: Essays on Politics, Thought, and Education in the Meiji Era*, ed. J. S. A. Elisonas and Rubinger (Honolulu: University of Hawai'i Press, 1997), pp. 116–17.

13 Byron K. Marshall, *Learning to be Modern: Japanese Political Discourse on Education* (Boulder: Westview Press, 1994), p. 53.

14 Gluck, *Japan's Modern Myths*, pp. 118–19.

15 Ian Reader, with Esben Andreasen and Finn Stefánsson, *Japanese Religions: Past and Present* (Sandgate, Folkestone, Kent: Japan Library, 1993), p. 71.

16 Horio Teruhisa, *Educational Thought and Ideology in Modern Japan*, tr. and ed. Steven Platzer (Tokyo: University of Tokyo Press, 1988), p. 69.

17 Ivan Parker Hall, *Mori Arinori* (Cambridge: Harvard University Press, 1973), pp. 411–12.

18 Donald Roden, *Schooldays in Imperial Japan: A Study in the Culture of a Student Elite* (Berkeley: University of California Press, 1980), p. 40 (modified).

19 Horio, *Educational Thought and Ideology in Modern Japan*, pp. 35 and 37.

20 Motoyama Yukihiko, "Thought and Education in the Late Meiji Era," tr. J. Dusenbury, in Motoyama, *Proliferating Talent*, p. 358.

21 Notto R. Thelle, *Buddhism and Christianity in Japan: From Conflict to Dialogue, 1854–1899* (Honolulu: University of Hawaii Press, 1987), p. 99 (modified).

22 The quotations from *Ono ga tsumi* are taken from the analysis in Kathryn Ragsdale, "Marriage, the Newspaper Business, and the Nation-State: Ideology in the Late Meiji Serialized *Katei Shōsetsu*," *Journal of Japanese Studies* 24:2 (Summer 1998), pp. 249, 250, 250–51, and 252.

## CHAPTER 9: THE ACQUISITION OF EMPIRE

1 *New York Times*, September 8, 1905, p. 8 (modified), and September 10, 1905, p. 6.

2 Shumpei Okamoto, *The Japanese Oligarchy and the Russo-Japanese War* (New York: Columbia University Press, 1970), p. 208.

3 This and the subsequent quotation are from Richard Siddle, *Race, Resistance and the Ainu of Japan* (London: Routledge, 1996), pp. 61 (modified) and 56.

4 Centre for East Asian Cultural Studies, comp. and publ., *Meiji Japan through Contemporary Sources*, vol. 2 (Tokyo: 1970), pp. 122–26.

5 This and the subsequent quote by Yamagata are from Roger F. Hackett, *Yamagata Aritomo in the Rise of Modern Japan, 1838–1922* (Cambridge: Harvard University Press, 1971), p. 138.

6 The quotations of Fukuzawa (some modified) are from Carmen Blacker, *The Japanese Enlightenment: A Study of the Writings of Fukuzawa Yukichi* (Cambridge: Cambridge University Press, 1964), pp. 124–36 passim.

7 This and subsequent quotes by Tokutomi are from John D. Pierson, *Tokutomi Sohō, 1863–1957: A Journalist for Modern Japan* (Princeton: Princeton University Press, 1980), pp. 229–37 passim.

8 Peter Duus, "Economic Dimensions of Meiji Imperialism: The Case of Korea, 1895–1910," in Ramon H. Myers and Mark R. Peattie, eds., *The Japanese Colonial Empire, 1895–1945* (Princeton: Princeton University Press, 1984), p. 138 (modified).

9 William G. Beasley, *Japanese Imperialism 1894–1945* (Oxford: Clarendon Press, 1991), p. 48.

10 Hilary Conroy, *The Japanese Seizure of Korea: 1868–1910: A Study of Realism and Ide-

alism in International Relations (Philadelphia: University of Pennsylvania Press, 1960), p. 255 (modified).

11 Donald Keene, "The Sino-Japanese War of 1894–95 and Japanese Culture," in Keene, Landscapes and Portraits (Tokyo: Kodansha International, 1971), pp. 269–70 (modified).

12 Bruce Cumings, Korea's Place in the Sun: A Modern History (New York: W. W. Norton, 1997), p. 135.

13 Beasley, Japanese Imperialism 1894–1945, p. 89.

14 Marlene Mayo, "Attitudes toward Asia and the Beginnings of Japanese Empire," in Grant K. Goodman, comp., Imperial Japan: A Reassessment (New York: Occasional Papers of the East Asian Institute, Columbia University, 1967), p. 18.

## CHAPTER 10: NEW AWAKENINGS, NEW MODERNITIES

1 Natsume Sōseki, Kokoro, tr. Edwin McClellan (Chicago: Gateway Editions, 1957), p. 246.

2 Robert Jay Lifton, Shūichi Katō, and Michael R. Reich, Six Lives, Six Deaths: Portraits from Modern Japan (New Haven: Yale University Press, 1979), p. 31.

3 Carol Gluck, Japan's Modern Myths: Ideology in the Late Meiji Period (Princeton: Princeton University Press, 1985), p. 217.

4 Junji Banno, The Establishment of the Japanese Constitutional System, tr. J. A. A. Stockwin (London: Routledge, 1992), p. 9.

5 George Akita, Foundations of Constitutional Government in Modern Japan 1868–1900 (Cambridge: Harvard University Press, 1967), p. 84.

6 Quotations concerning the riots of 1918 are from Michael Lewis, Rioters and Citizens: Mass Protest in Imperial Japan (Berkeley: University of California Press, 1990), pp. 111 and 133 (modified).

7 Thorstein Veblen, Essays in Our Changing Order, ed. Leon Ardzrooni (New York: Viking Press, 1943), p. 257.

8 John Dewey set forth his observations about Japan in the essays "Liberalism in Japan" and "On the Two Sides of the Eastern Sea," reprinted in his Characters and Events: Popular Essays in Social and Political Philosophy, vol. 1, ed. Joseph Ratner (New York: Henry Holt, 1929), pp. 149–71.

9 Ryusaku Tsunoda, Wm. Theodore de Bary, and Donald Keene, comps., Sources of Japanese Tradition (New York: Columbia University Press, 1958), p. 744.

10 Mitani Taichirō, "The Establishment of Party Cabinets, 1898–1932," tr. Peter Duus, in John W. Hall et al., gen. eds., The Cambridge History of Japan, vol. 6: Duus, ed., The Twentieth Century (Cambridge: Cambridge University Press, 1988), pp. 87 and 56.

11 Morinosuke Kajima, The Diplomacy of Japan, 1894–1922, vol. 3 (Tokyo: Kajima Institute of International Peace, 1980), p. 528.

12 Mark R. Peattie, "The Japanese Colonial Empire, 1895–1945," in The Cambridge History of Japan, vol. 6, p. 239.

13 Mark R. Peattie, "Japanese Attitudes toward Colonialism, 1895–1945," in Ramon H. Myers and Peattie, eds., The Japanese Colonial Empire, 1895–1945 (Princeton: Princeton University Press, 1984), p. 106.

14 Ibid., p. 107 (modified).

15 The text of Nitobe's talk appears under the title "Japanese Colonization" in Asiatic Review 16:45 (January 1920), pp. 113–21.

16 Junius B. Wood, "Japan's Mandate in the Pacific," Asia: The American Magazine on

*the Orient* 21:7 (July 1921), p. 751, and George Trumbull Ladd, "The Annexation of Korea: An Essay in 'Benevolent Assimilation,'" *Yale Review*, new series 1:4 (July 1912), p. 644 (modified).

17 Bruce Cumings, *Korea's Place in the Sun: A Modern History* (New York: W. W. Norton, 1997), p. 157.

18 Margit Nagy, "Middle-Class Working Women during the Interwar Years," in Gail Lee Bernstein, ed., *Recreating Japanese Women, 1600–1945* (Berkeley: University of California Press, 1991), p. 207 (modified).

19 This and other quotations by Hani are from her "Stories of My Life," tr. Chiko Irie Mulhern, in Mulhern, ed., *Heroic with Grace: Legendary Women of Japan* (Armonk, N.Y.: M. E. Sharpe, 1991), pp. 236–64.

20 Christine R. Yano, "Defining the Modern Nation in Japanese Popular Song, 1914–1932," in Sharon A. Minichiello, ed., *Japan's Competing Modernities: Issues in Culture and Democracy, 1900–1930* (Honolulu: University of Hawai'i Press, 1998), p. 254.

21 Harris I. Martin, "Popular Music and Social Change in Prewar Japan," *Japan Interpreter: A Journal of Social and Political Ideas* 7:3–4 (Summer–Autumn 1974), p. 342 (modified).

22 Miriam Silverberg, "The Modern Girl as Militant," in Bernstein, ed., *Recreating Japanese Women, 1600–1945*, p. 241 (modified).

## CHAPTER 11: THE TUMULTUOUS TWENTIES

1 Thomas C. Smith, *Native Sources of Japanese Industrialization, 1750–1920* (Berkeley: University of California Press, 1988), p. 242, n. 15.

2 Koji Taira, "Economic Development, Labor Markets, and Industrial Relations in Japan, 1905–1955," in John W. Hall et al., gen. eds., *The Cambridge History of Japan*, vol. 6: Peter Duus, ed., *The Twentieth Century* (Cambridge: Cambridge University Press, 1988), pp. 631–32.

3 Andrew Gordon, *Labor and Imperial Democracy in Prewar Japan* (Berkeley: University of California Press, 1991), p. 81, n. 3.

4 Bryon K. Marshall, *Capitalism and Nationalism in Prewar Japan: The Ideology of the Business Elite* (Stanford: Stanford University Press, 1967), p. 72 (modified).

5 George Elison, "Kōtoku Shūsui: The Change in Thought," *Monumenta Nipponica* 32:3–4 (1967), p. 445.

6 Quotations by Kanno are from Mikiso Hane, ed. and tr., *Reflections on the Way to the Gallows: Rebel Women in Prewar Japan* (Berkeley: University of California Press and Pantheon Books, 1988), pp. 55–56 and 61 (modified).

7 Germaine A. Hoston, *The State, Identity, and the National Question in China and Japan* (Princeton: Princeton University Press, 1994), p. 148 (modified).

8 George Oakley Totten, III, *The Social Democratic Movement in Prewar Japan* (New Haven: Yale University Press, 1966), pp. 207–8 (modified).

9 Robert A. Scalapino, *The Early Japanese Labor Movement: Labor and Politics in a Developing Society* (Berkeley: Institute of East Asian Studies, University of California, 1983), p. 243, n. 34.

10 Sharon L. Sievers, *Flowers in Salt: The Beginnings of Feminist Consciousness in Modern Japan* (Stanford: Stanford University Press, 1983), p. 163.

11 Laurel Rasplica Rodd, "Yosano Akiko and the Taishō Debate over the 'New Woman,'" in Gail Lee Bernstein, ed., *Recreating Japanese Women, 1600–1945* (Berkeley: University of California Press, 1991), p. 180.

12 Vera Mackie, *Creating Socialist Women in Japan: Gender, Labour and Activism, 1900–1937* (Cambridge: Cambridge University Press, 1997), p. 96 (modified).

13 Vera Mackie, "Writing and the Making of Socialist Women in Japan," in Elise K. Tipton, ed., *Society and the State in Interwar Japan* (London: Routledge, 1997), pp. 134–35 (modified).

14 Henry D. Smith II, *Japan's First Student Radicals* (Cambridge: Harvard University Press, 1972), p. 56 (modified).

15 Nitobe Inazō, *The Japanese Nation: Its Land, Its People, Its Life; with Special Consideration to Its Relations with the United States* (New York: G. P. Putnam's Sons, 1912), pp. 86–87 (modified).

16 Richard Siddle, *Race, Resistance and the Ainu of Japan* (London: Routledge, 1996), p. 127.

17 Shigeki Ninomiya, "An Inquiry Concerning the Origin, Development, and Present Situation of the *Eta* in Relation to the History of the Social Classes in Japan," *Transactions of the Asiatic Society of Japan*, 2d series, vol. 10 (December 1933), p. 109.

18 Ian Neary, *Political Protest and Social Control in Pre-War Japan: The Origins of Buraku Liberation* (Atlantic Highlands, N.J.: Humanities Press International, 1989), p. 68.

19 Michael Weiner, *The Origins of the Korean Community in Japan, 1910–1923* (Atlantic Highlands, N.J.: Humanities Press International, 1989), p. 85.

20 Ibid., p. 107.

21 Emily Groszos Ooms, *Women and Millenarian Protest in Meiji Japan: Deguchi Nao and Ōmotokyō* (Ithaca: Cornell University Press, 1993), p. 109.

22 Mark J. McNeal, S.J., "The Destruction of Tokyo: Impressions of an Eyewitness," *Catholic World* 118 (December 1923), pp. 311 and 308.

23 Kim San and Nym Wales, *Song of Ariran: The Life Story of a Korean Rebel* (New York: John Day, 1941), p. 37.

24 David J. Lu, ed., *Japan: A Documentary History* (Armonk, N.Y.: M. E. Sharpe, 1997), p. 397.

25 Sheldon Garon, *Molding Japanese Minds: The State in Everyday Life* (Princeton: Princeton University Press, 1997), p. 16.

26 Thomas R. H. Havens, *Farm and Nation in Modern Japan: Agrarian Nationalism, 1870–1940* (Princeton: Princeton University Press, 1974), p. 106 (modified).

27 Mariko Asano Tamanoi, "The City and the Countryside: Competing Taishō 'Modernities' on Gender," in Sharon A. Minichiello, ed., *Japan's Competing Modernities: Issues in Culture and Democracy, 1900–1930* (Honolulu: University of Hawai'i Press, 1998), p. 93 (modified).

28 Stephen Vlastos, "Agrarianism without Tradition: The Radical Critique of Prewar Japanese Modernity," in Vlastos, ed., *Mirror of Modernity: Invented Traditions of Modern Japan* (Berkeley: University of California Press, 1998), p. 83 (modified).

29 Mark R. Peattie, "Japanese Attitudes toward Colonialism, 1895–1945," in Ramon H. Myers and Peattie, eds., *The Japanese Colonial Empire, 1895–1945* (Princeton: Princeton University Press, 1984), p. 117.

30 Okakura Kakuzō, *The Ideals of the East, with Special Reference to the Art of Japan* (Rutland, Vt.: Charles E. Tuttle, 1970), p. 1 (modified).

31 Oka Yoshitake, *Konoe Fumimaro: A Political Biography*, tr. Shumpei Okamoto and Patricia Murray (Lanham, Md.: Madison Books, 1992), p. 12.

32 Ikuhiko Hata, "Continental Expansion, 1905–1941," in *The Cambridge History of Japan*, vol. 6, p. 290.

33 Akira Iriye, *After Imperialism: The Search for a New Order in the Far East, 1921–1931* (New York: Atheneum, 1969), p. 146.

# CHAPTER 12: "A PERIOD OF NATIONAL EMERGENCY"

1 Seki Hiroharu, "The Manchurian Incident, 1931," tr. with an Introduction by Marius B. Jansen, in James W. Morley, ed., *Japan's Road to the Pacific War*, vol. 1: *Japan Erupts: The London Naval Conference and the Manchurian Incident, 1928–1932* (New York: Columbia University Press, 1984), p. 228 (modified).

2 Kerry Smith, *A Time of Crisis: Japan, the Great Depression, and Rural Revitalization* (Cambridge: Harvard University Asia Center, 2001), p. 72.

3 Mark R. Peattie, *Ishiwara Kanji and Japan's Confrontation with the West* (Princeton: Princeton University Press, 1975), p. 118.

4 This and the subsequent quote by the prime minister are from Takehiko Yoshihashi, *Conspiracy at Mukden: The Rise of the Japanese Military* (New Haven: Yale University Press, 1963), pp. 9 and 7.

5 Kakegawa Tomiko, "The Press and Public Opinion in Japan, 1931–1941," in Dorothy Borg and Shumpei Okamoto, with the assistance of Dale K. A. Finlayson, eds., *Pearl Harbor as History: Japanese-American Relations 1931–1941* (New York: Columbia University Press, 1973), p. 537 (modified).

6 John N. Penlington, *The Mukden Mandate: Acts and Aims in Manchuria* (Tokyo: Maruzen, 1932), pp. 23–25.

7 Sadako N. Ogata, *Defiance in Manchuria: The Making of Japanese Foreign Policy, 1931–1932* (Berkeley: University of California Press, 1964), pp. 30–31 (modified).

8 Mainichi Daily News, *Fifty Years of Light and Dark: The Hirohito Era* (Tokyo: Mainichi Newspapers, 1975), p. 56 (modified).

9 Tessa Morris-Suzuki, *Shōwa: An Inside History of Hirohito's Japan* (New York: Schocken Books, 1985), p. 20.

10 "Address Delivered by Yosuke Matsuoka, Chief Japanese Delegate, at the Seventeenth Plenary Meeting of the Special Assembly of the League of Nations," in Matsuoka, *Japan's Case in the Sino-Japanese Dispute* (Geneva: Japanese Delegation to the League of Nations, 1933), pp. 49–61 passim (modified).

11 Shimada Toshihiko, "Designs on North China, 1933–1937," tr. with an Introduction by James B. Crowley, in Morley, ed., *Japan's Road to the Pacific War*, vol. 2: *The China Quagmire: Japan's Expansion on the Asian Continent, 1933–1941* (New York: Columbia University Press, 1983), p. 58.

12 Herbert P. Bix, *Hirohito and the Making of Modern Japan* (New York: HarperCollins, 2000), pp. 253–54.

13 Sandra Wilson, "Angry Young Men and the Japanese State," in Elise K. Tipton, ed., *Society and the State in Interwar Japan* (London: Routledge, 1997), p.109.

14 Yoshino Sakuzō, "Fascism in Japan," *Contemporary Japan*, 1:2 (September 1932), p. 185.

15 Vera Mackie, *Creating Socialist Women in Japan: Gender, Labour and Activism, 1900–1937* (Cambridge: Cambridge University Press, 1997), p. 60.

16 Louise Young, *Japan's Total Empire: Manchuria and the Culture of Wartime Imperialism* (Berkeley: University of California Press, 1998), p. 84.

17 Ian Reader, with Esben Andreasen and Finn Stefánsson, *Japanese Religions: Past and Present* (Sandgate, Folkestone, Kent: Japan Library, 1993), p. 71.

18 Ogata Sadako, "The Role of Liberal Nongovernmental Organizations in Japan," in Borg and Okamoto, eds., *Pearl Harbor as History*, p. 472.

19 Richard J. Smethurst, "The Military Reserve Association and the Minobe Crisis of 1935," in George M. Wilson, ed., *Crisis Politics in Prewar Japan: Institutional and*

*Ideological Problems of the 1930s* (Tokyo: Sophia University, 1970), p. 8 (modified).

20 Frank O. Miller, *Minobe Tatsukichi: Interpreter of Constitutionalism in Japan* (Berkeley: University of California Press, 1965), p. 227.

21 Patricia G. Steinhoff, *Tenkō: Ideology and Societal Integration in Prewar Japan* (New York: Garland, 1991), p. 55.

22 George M. Beckmann, "The Radical Left and the Failure of Communism," in James W. Morley, ed., *Dilemmas of Growth in Prewar Japan* (Princeton: Princeton University Press, 1971), pp. 165–69 (modified).

23 John R. Stewart, *Manchuria since 1931* (New York: Secretariat, Institute of Pacific Relations, 1936), p. 37.

24 Ben-Ami Shillony, *Revolt in Japan: The Young Officers and the February 26, 1936 Incident* (Princeton: Princeton University Press, 1973), p. 122.

25 George M. Wilson, *Radical Nationalist in Japan: Kita Ikki 1883–1937* (Cambridge: Harvard University Press, 1969), p. 69.

26 James B. Crowley, *Japan's Quest for Autonomy: National Security and Foreign Policy, 1930–1938* (Princeton: Princeton University Press, 1966), pp. 270–71 (modified).

27 Based on Bix, *Hirohito and the Making of Modern Japan*, p. 723, n. 56, and Shillony, *Revolt in Japan*, p. 173.

28 *The Diary of a Japanese Innkeeper's Daughter*, tr. Miwa Kai, ed. and annot. Robert J. Smith and Kazuko Smith (Ithaca: East Asia Program, Cornell University, 1984, 2d print.), p. 164.

## CHAPTER 13: IN PURSUIT OF A NEW ORDER

1 The quotations from the law and subsequent Home Ministry directive are from Gregory J. Kasza, *The State and the*

*Mass Media in Japan, 1918–1945* (Berkeley: University of California Press, 1988), pp. 235 and 237 (modified).

2 Mark R. Peattie, *Ishiwara Kanji and Japan's Confrontation with the West* (Princeton: Princeton University Press, 1975), p. 301.

3 James B. Crowley, *Japan's Quest for Autonomy: National Security and Foreign Policy 1930–1938* (Princeton: Princeton University Press, 1966), p. 335.

4 James B. Crowley, "A Reconsideration of the Marco Polo Bridge Incident," *Journal of Asian Studies* 22:3 (May 1963), p. 289.

5 Haruko Taya Cook and Theodore F. Cook, *Japan at War: An Oral History* (New York: New Press, 1992), pp. 164–65.

6 Robert J. C. Butow, *Tojo and the Coming of the War* (Stanford: Stanford University Press, 1961), p. 111.

7 Gordon M. Berger, "Three-Dimensional Empire: Japanese Attitudes and the New Order in Asia, 1937–1945," *Japan Interpreter* 12:3–4 (1979), p. 368.

8 William Miles Fletcher III, *The Search for a New Order: Intellectuals and Fascism in Prewar Japan* (Chapel Hill: University of North Carolina Press, 1982), p. 137.

9 Yoshino Sakuzō, "Fascism in Japan," *Contemporary Japan: A Review of Far Eastern Affairs* 1:2 (1932), p. 185.

10 The Arisawa quotations are from Bai Gao, *Economic Ideology and Japanese Industrial Policy: Developmentism from 1931 to 1965* (London: Cambridge University Press, 1997), pp. 24 and 75 (modified).

11 "On the National Mobilization Law," *Tokyo Gazette* (May 1938), p. 2.

12 Nakamura Takafusa, *Economic Growth in Prewar Japan*, tr. Robert A. Feldman (New Haven: Yale University Press, 1983), p. 298.

13 This and the subsequent criticism of the plan are from Fletcher, *The Search for a New Order*, p. 152.

14 Shiota Shōbei, "A 'Ravaged' People: The Koreans in World War II," tr. John H. Boyle, *Japan Interpreter* 7:1 (Winter 1971), p. 43 (modified).

15 Harris I. Martin, "Popular Music and Social Change in Prewar Japan," *Japan Interpreter: A Journal of Social and Political Ideas* 7:3–4 (Summer–Autumn 1974), p. 348.

16 Japanese Ministry of Education, *Kokutai no hongi: Cardinal Principles of the National Entity of Japan*, tr. John O. Gauntlett and ed. Robert K. Hall (Cambridge: Harvard University Press, 1937), p. 183 (modified).

17 Andrew Gordon, *Labor and Imperial Democracy in Prewar Japan* (Berkeley: University of California Press, 1991), p. 259.

18 Dorothy Robins-Mowry, *The Hidden Sun: Women of Modern Japan* (Boulder: Westview Press, 1983), p. 81.

19 Ian Neary, "Tenkō of an Organization: The Suiheisha in the Late 1930's," *Proceedings of the British Association for Japanese Studies* 2:2 (1977), pp. 64–76.

20 Hull and the consul general are quoted in Jonathan Marshall, *To Have and Have Not: Southeast Asian Raw Materials and the Origins of the Pacific War* (Berkeley: University of California Press, 1995), pp. 65–66 and 62.

21 Hata Ikuhiko, "The Army's Move into Northern Indochina," tr. Robert A. Scalapino, in James W. Morley, ed., *Japan's Road to the Pacific War*, vol. 4: *The Fateful Choice: Japan's Advance into Southeast Asia, 1939–1941* (New York: Columbia University Press, 1980), p. 172.

22 Akira Iriye, *The Origins of the Second World War in Asia and the Pacific* (London: Longman, 1987), p. 153.

23 Unless otherwise noted, quotations by participants in liaison and imperial conferences are from Nobutaka Ike, tr. and ed., *Japan's Decision for War: Records of the 1941 Policy Conferences* (Stanford: Stanford

University Press, 1967), pp. 135–36, 180, 186, and 281–82 (some modified).

24 Based on Herbert P. Bix, *Hirohito and the Making of Modern Japan* (New York: HarperCollins, 2000), p. 414.

25 Tsunoda Jun, "The Decision for War," tr. David A. Titus, in Morley, ed., *Japan's Road to the Pacific War*, vol. 5: *The Final Confrontation: Japan's Negotiations with the United States, 1941* (New York: Columbia University Press, 1994), pp. 264–65 (modified).

26 Ibid., p. 321.

27 Akira Iriye, *Pearl Harbor and the Coming of the Pacific War: A Brief History with Documents and Essays* (Boston: Bedford/St. Martin's, 1999), p. 94 (modified).

## CHAPTER 14: THE GREATER EAST ASIA WAR

1 Herbert P. Bix, *Hirohito and the Making of Modern Japan* (Tokyo: HarperCollins, 2000), p. 437.

2 Dan Kurzman, *Kishi and Japan: The Search for the Sun* (New York: Ivan Obolensky, 1960), p. 185 n.

3 Regine Mathias, "Women and the War Economy in Japan," in Erich Pauer, ed., *Japan's War Economy* (London: Routledge, 1999), p. 68.

4 Gregory J. Kasza, *The Conscription Society: Administered Mass Organizations* (New Haven: Yale University Press, 1995), p. 19 (modified).

5 Mariko Asano Tamanoi, "Knowledge, Power, and Radical Classifications: The 'Japanese' in 'Manchuria,' " *Journal of Asian Studies* 59:2 (May 2000), p. 260 (modified).

6 Ienaga Saburō, *The Pacific War, 1931–1945*, tr. Frank Baldwin (New York: Pantheon, 1978), p. 155.

7 Ba Maw, *Breakthrough in Burma: Memoirs of a Revolution, 1939–1946* (New Haven: Yale University Press, 1968), p. 185.

8 Quotations by kamikaze pilots are from Ivan Morris, *The Nobility of Failure: Tragic Heroes in the History of Japan* (New York: New American Library, 1975), pp. 309 and 313 (modified).

9 General Curtis E. LeMay, with MacKinlay Kantor, *Mission with LeMay: My Story* (Garden City, N.Y.: Doubleday, 1965), p. 387.

10 John W. Dower, *Japan in War and Peace: Selected Essays* (New York: New Press, 1993), pp. 124–26, 130, and 133.

11 John W. Dower, *Empire and Aftermath: Yoshida Shigeru and the Japanese Experience, 1878–1954* (Cambridge: Council on East Asian Studies, Harvard University, 1988, 2d print.), pp. 260–64.

12 Harry S. Truman, *Memoirs*, vol. 1: *Year of Decisions* (Garden City, N.Y.: Doubleday, 1955), p. 419.

13 Harry L. Stimson, "The Decision to Use the Atomic Bomb," *Harper's Magazine* 194:1161 (February 1947), p. 102.

14 Morris, *The Nobility of Failure*, p. 332.

15 Robert Jay Lifton, Shūichi Katō, and Michael R. Reich, *Six Lives Six Deaths: Portraits from Modern Japan* (New Haven: Yale University Press, 1979), p. 155.

## CHAPTER 15: THE YEARS OF OCCUPATION

1 Unless otherwise noted, quotations concerning American occupation personnel and policies are from articles published serially in the *Asahi shinbun* newspaper and translated into English as *The Pacific Rivals: A Japanese View of Japanese-American Relations* (New York: Weatherhill and Asahi Shimbun-sha, 1972), esp. pp. 117–28 and 161–64.

2 Russell Brines, *MacArthur's Japan* (Philadelphia: J. B. Lippincott, 1948), p. 40 (modified).

3 Unless otherwise specified, quotations in this section are from John W. Dower, *Embracing Defeat: Japan in the Wake of World War II* (New York: W. W. Norton, 2000, paperback ed.), pp. 64, 60, and 117 (modified).

4 Mainichi Daily News, *Fifty Years of Light and Dark: The Hirohito Era* (Tokyo: Mainichi Newspapers, 1975), p. 211 (modified).

5 Richard H. Minear, *Victors' Justice: The Tokyo War Crimes Trial* (Princeton: Princeton University Press, 1971), pp. 100–101 (modified).

6 Theodore McNelly, "The Japanese Constitution: Child of the Cold War," *Political Science Quarterly* 74 (1979), pp. 179–80.

7 Supreme Commander for the Allied Powers, Government Section, *Political Reorientation of Japan: September 1945 to September 1948* (Washington, D.C.: Government Printing Office, 1949), p. 105.

8 The MacArthur draft is included in Satō Tatsuo, "The Origin and Development of the Draft Constitution of Japan," *Contemporary Japan* 24:4–6 (1956), pp. 188–99; the new constitution as promulgated on November 3, 1946, appears in *Japan: An Illustrated Encyclopedia*, vol. 1 (Tokyo: Kodansha, 1993), pp. 229–32.

9 Mark R. Mullins, Shimazono Susumu, and Paul L. Swanson, eds., *Religion and Society in Modern Japan: Selected Readings* (Berkeley: Asian Humanities Press, 1993), p. 173.

10 Dower, *Embracing Defeat*, p. 314.

11 Richard B. Finn, *Winners in Peace: MacArthur, Yoshida, and Postwar Japan* (Berkeley: University of California Press, 1992), p. 97.

12 Marlene J. Mayo, "American Wartime Planning for Occupied Japan: The Role of Experts," in Robert Wolfe, ed., *Americans as Proconsuls* (Carbondale: Southern Illinois University Press, 1984), p. 36.

13 Howard B. Schonberger, "Zaibatsu Dissolution and the American Restoration of Japan," *Bulletin of Concerned Asian Scholars* 5:2 (September 1973), pp. 16–31 (modified).

14 Mikiso Hane, *Peasants, Rebels, and Outcasts: The Underside of Modern Japan* (New York: Pantheon Books, 1982), p. 250.

15 Ronald P. Dore, *Shinohata: A Portrait of a Japanese Village* (New York: Pantheon Books, 1978), p. 65.

16 "Report of the [First] U.S. Education Mission: Digest," in Edward R. Beauchamp and James M. Vardaman, Jr., eds., *Japanese Education since 1945: A Documentary Study* (Armonk, N.Y.: M. E. Sharpe, 1994), p. 87.

17 "Fundamental Law of Education, 1947," in Herbert Passim, ed., *Society and Education in Japan* (Teachers College and East Asian Institute, Columbia University, 1965), pp. 302 and 301.

18 Alfred C. Oppler, *Legal Reform in Occupied Japan: A Participant Looks Back* (Princeton: Princeton University Press, 1976), p. 117.

19 Vidya Prakash Dutt, ed., *East Asia: China, Korea, Japan, 1947–50* (London: Oxford University Press, 1958), pp. 631–37.

20 "Japan: Confidentially, Some Confidential Shades of FEC-230," *Newsweek* (December 29, 1947), p. 31.

21 Schonberger, "Zaibatsu Dissolution and the American Restoration of Japan," pp. 22–26 (modified).

22 Tessa Morris-Suzuki, *Shōwa: An Inside History of Hirohito's Japan* (New York: Schocken Books, 1985), pp. 247–48.

23 Sheldon Garon, *The State and Labor in Modern Japan* (Berkeley: University of California Press, 1987), p. 239.

24 John W. Dower, *Empire and Aftermath: Yoshida Shigeru and the Japanese Experience, 1878–1954* (Cambridge: Council on East Asian Studies, Harvard University, 1988), p. 371.

25 *The Pacific Rivals*, p. 107.

26 Douglas MacArthur, *Reminiscences* (New York: McGraw-Hill, 1964), pp. 281–82.

## CHAPTER 16: RECOVERY AND AFFLUENCE

1 The quotations by Yasukawa are from his "Message from Tokyo Olympic Committee," *Contemporary Japan* (October 1963), pp. 638–41.

2 Quotations in this paragraph are from Mainichi Daily News, *Fifty Years of Light and Dark: The Hirohito Era* (Tokyo: Mainichi Newspapers, 1975), pp. 341–42.

3 James L. McClain, "Cultural Chauvinism and the Olympiads of East Asia," *International Journal of the History of Sport* 7:3 (December 1990), p. 395.

4 Edwin O. Reischauer, *The United States and Japan* (Cambridge: Harvard University Press, 1957, rev. ed.), p. 51.

5 Nick Lyons, *The Sony Vision* (New York: Crown, 1976), p. 41, and Hanada Hideji, "If Morita Akio Had Become Japan's 'Business Premier,'" *Japan Echo* 27:1 (February 2000), Internet edition, no pagination (tr. and ab. from " 'Zaikai sōri' shūnin mokuzen ni taoreta Sonī Morita Akio no munen," *Ekonomisuto*, October 26, 1999, pp. 68–70).

6 Dennis B. Smith, *Japan since 1945: The Rise of an Economic Superpower* (New York: St. Martin's Press, 1995), p. 109.

7 Ezra F. Vogel, *Japan's New Middle Class* (Berkeley: University of California Press, 1963, 2d ed.), p. 268.

8 Anne E. Imamura, *Urban Japanese Housewives: At Home and in the Community* (Honolulu: University of Hawaii Press, 1987), p. 67.

9 Merry White, "The Virtue of Japanese Mothers: Cultural Definitions of Women's Lives," *Daedalus* 116:3 (Summer 1987), p. 153.

10 Gail Lee Bernstein, "Women in Rural Japan," in Joyce Lebra, Joy Paulson, and Elizabeth Powers, eds., *Women in Changing Japan* (Boulder: Westview Press, 1976), p. 44 (modified) and p. 45.

11 William W. Kelly, "Finding a Place in Metropolitan Japan: Ideologies, Institutions, and Everyday Life," in Andrew Gordon, ed., *Postwar Japan as History* (Berkeley: University of California Press, 1993), p. 215.

12 Murakami Yasusuke, "The Age of New Middle Mass Politics: The Case of Japan," *Journal of Japanese Studies* 8:1 (Winter 1982), p. 36 (modified).

13 Kubota Akira, "The Political Influence of the Japanese Higher Civil Service," *Japan Quarterly* 28:1 (January–March 1981), p. 45 (modified).

14 Ezra F. Vogel, *Japan as Number One: Lessons for America* (Cambridge: Harvard University Press, 1979), p. viii.

15 Edwin O. Reischauer as quoted on the back cover of the Harper Colophon edition of Vogel's *Japan as Number One* (New York: 1980).

16 Koji Taira, "Dialectics of Economic Growth, National Power, and Distributive Struggles," in Gordon, ed., *Postwar Japan as History*, p. 171.

17 Norma Field, "*Somehow*: The Postmodern as Atmosphere," in Masao Miyoshi and H. D. Harootunian, eds., *Postmodernism and Japan* (Durham: Duke University Press, 1989), pp. 172–79.

18 Margaret Lock, "Restoring Order to the House of Japan," *Wilson Quarterly* 14:4 (Autumn 1990), pp. 46–47.

19 Theodore C. Bestor, "Tokyo Mom-and-Pop," *Wilson Quarterly* 14:4 (Autumn 1990), pp. 28–31.

20 Marilyn Ivy, "Tradition and Difference in the Japanese Mass Media," *Public Culture* 1:1 (Fall 1988), p. 21.

21 Jennifer Robertson, *Native and Newcomer: Making and Remaking a Japanese City* (Berkeley: University of California Press, 1991), p. 23 (modified).

## CHAPTER 17: ANOTHER NEW CENTURY

1 Fujiwara Sakuya, "Japan's Financial Woes and the Hopes for Big Bang," *Japan Echo* 25:1 (February 1998), Internet edition, no pagination (modified).

2 Obuchi Keizō, "From Foreign Minister to Prime Minister," *Japan Echo* 25:5 (October 1998), Internet edition, no pagination.

3 "Prime Minister Mori: A Full Life of Encounters with Remarkable People," news release from the Consulate General of Japan, Boston, July 24, 2000.

4 Tokuyama Jirō, "The Leaderless State," *Japan Echo* 18:4 (Winter 1991), pp. 35–41 (tr. and abr. from "Rīdā naki kuni wa horobu," *Chūō Kōron* [October 1991], pp. 124–40).

5 Masuzoe Yōichi, "The LDP's Electoral Setback," *Japan Echo* 25:5 (October 1998), Internet edition, no pagination.

6 Masamura Kimihiro et al., "The LDP in Crisis," *Japan Echo* 16:3 (Autumn 1989), p. 17 (tr. and abr. from "Jimintō ittō shihai wa owaru ka," *Ekonomisuto* [July 3, 1989], pp. 12–21).

7 Noguchi Yukio, "The Persistence of the 1940 Slump," *Japan Echo* 24: Special Issue (1997), Internet edition, no pagination (translated from *1940 taisei, saraba senji keizai* [Tokyo: Tōyō Keizai, 1995], pp. 133–50 and 177–99).

8 Iwami Takao, "Japanese Politics in an Age of Realignment," *Japan Echo* 21:1 (Spring 1994), p. 9 (modified; tr. and abr.

from "Jimintō wa ikinokoreru ka," *Bungei Shunjū* [January 1994], pp. 104–10).

9 Noda Nobuo, "The Built-in Defects of Japanese Government," *Japan Echo* 18:4 (Winter 1991), pp. 44–45 (tr. and abr. from "Sabakareru 'han'ei kyōdōtai,' " *Shokun* [October 1991], pp. 26–38).

10 Sassa Atsuyuki, "Fault Lines in Our Emergency Management System," *Japan Echo* 22:2 (Summer 1995), p. 23 (tr. and abr. from " 'Gominkan' ga inakatta sōri kantei," *Chūō Kōron* [April 1995], pp. 62–73).

11 Kishi Nobuhito, "Is MOF to Blame for Japan's 'Second Defeat'?," *Japan Echo* 25:5 (October 1998), Internet edition, no pagination.

12 Sakaiya Taichi, "The Myth of the Competent Bureaucrat," *Japan Echo* 25:1 (February 1998), Internet edition, no pagination (tr. and abr. from "Gendai kanryō 'chō' munōron," *Bungei Shunjū* [October 1997], pp. 94–103).

13 Yoshida Katsuji, "The Administrative Reform Debacle—Hashimoto's Nemesis," *Japan Quarterly* 45:1 (January–March 1998), p. 30.

14 Obuchi, "From Foreign Minister to Prime Minister" (modified).

15 Fujiwara, "Japan's Financial Woes and the Hope for Big Bang," and Takeuchi Yasuo, "Revitalizing Japanese Manufacturing," *Japan Echo* 23:4 (Winter 1996), Internet edition, no pagination.

16 Satō Seizaburō, "Time for a Review of Japan's Security Policy," *Japan Echo* 17:4 (Winter 1990), p. 23.

17 "Japan's Role in the International Community: Draft Report," *Japan Echo* 19:2 (Summer 1992), p. 52.

18 Ikeda Tadashi, "Toward an Open-Ended Asia Policy," *Japan Echo* 22:1 (Spring 1995), p. 21 (tr. from " 'Ajia-shugi' de nai Ajia gaikō o," *Gaikō Forum* [February 1994], pp. 52–60).

19 David A. Titus, "Accessing the World: Palace and Foreign Policy in Post-Occupation Japan," in Gerald L. Curtis, ed., *Japan's Foreign Policy after the Cold War: Coping with Change* (Armonk, N.Y.: M. E. Sharpe, 1993), p. 67.

20 "Chinese President Slaps Japan over Apology for WWII Actions," *Providence Sunday Journal*, November 29, 1998, p. A6.

21 Kathleen S. Uno, "The Death of 'Good Wife, Wise Mother'?," in Andrew Gordon, ed., *Postwar Japan as History* (Berkeley: University of California Press, 1993), p. 314 (modified).

22 Suzuki Kazue, "Equal Job Opportunity for Whom?," *Japan Quarterly* 43:3 (July–September 1996), p. 54.

23 Jean R. Renshaw, *Kimono in the Boardroom* (New York: Oxford University Press, 1999), p. 132.

24 Merry White, "Home Truths: Women and Social Change in Japan," *Daedalus* 121:4 (Fall 1992), p. 70.

25 Ogawa Naohiro, "When the Baby Boomers Grow Old," *Japan Echo* 23: Special Issue (1996), p. 19 (tr. and abr. from " 'Dankai kōreika' no kyōfu," *Sansāra* [October 1995], pp. 160–67).

26 Nicholas D. Kristof, "Who Needs Love? In Japan, Many Couples Don't," *New York Times*, February 11, 1996, Internet edition, no pagination.

27 White, "Home Truths," p. 70.

28 Chikushi Tetsuya, "Young People as a New Human Race," *Japan Quarterly* 33:3 (July–September 1986), p. 291.

29 Sugahara Mariko, "Five Fatal Symptoms of the Japanese Disease," *Japan Echo* 21:2 (Summer 1994), p. 69 (tr. from " 'Nihon byō' itsutsu no shōjō," *Chūō Kōron* [April 1994], pp. 108–16).

30 Ijiri Kazuo, "The Breakdown of the Japanese Work Ethic," *Japan Echo* 17:4

(Winter 1990), pp. 38–40 (modified; tr. and abr. from "Rikurūto no mō hitotsu no hanzai," *Shokun* [October 1990], pp. 174–84).

31 Nishiyama Akira, "Among Friends: The Seductive Power of Bullying," *Japan Quarterly* 43:4 (October–December 1996), pp. 51–57.

32 Mark Schreiber, "Juvenile Crime in the 1990s," *Japan Quarterly* 44:2 (April–June 1997), pp. 84–85.

33 Merry White, "The Virtue of Japanese Mothers: Cultural Definitions of Women's Lives," *Daedalus* 116:3 (Summer 1987), p. 154.

34 Kawakami Ryōichi, "A Teacher's Diary," *Japan Echo* 25:1 (February 1998), Internet edition, no pagination (modified; tr. and abr. from " 'Okosamakyō' ga koko made gakkō o dame ni shita," *Bungei Shunjū* [October 1997], pp. 300–316).

35 "Crisis in the Schools," *Japan Echo* 25:3 (June 1998), Internet edition, no pagination.

36 Ibid.

37 Richard Siddle, *Race, Resistance and the Ainu of Japan* (London: Routledge, 1996), p. 179.

38 Richard Siddle, "Ainu: Japan's Indigenous People," in Michael Weiner, ed., *Japan's Minorities: The Illusion of Homogeneity* (London: Routledge, 1997), p. 32.

39 Chikako Kashiwazaki, "The Politics of Legal Status: The Equation of Nationality with Ethnonational Identity," in Sonia Ryang, ed., *Koreans in Japan: Critical Voices from the Margins* (London: Routledge, 2000), p. 29 (modified).

40 "Let's Make a New Start," *Japan Times*, January 1, 2000, Internet edition, no pagination (modified).

41 Dorinne Kondo, "The Aesthetics and Politics of Japanese Identity in the Fashion Industry," in Joseph J. Tobin, ed., *Re-Made in Japan: Everyday Life and Consumer Taste in a Changing Society* (New Haven: Yale University Press, 1992), pp. 179 (modified) and 194.

42 Katō Shūichi, "Ōe Kenzaburō and the Nobel Prize," *Japan Echo* 22:1 (Spring 1995), pp. 78–79 (modified; tr. from "Kawabata Yasunari kara Ōe Kenzaburō e," *Asahi shinbun*, evening edition, October 20, 1994, p. 15).

43 Iwao Sumiko, "Popular Culture Goes Regional," *Japan Echo* 21:4 (Winter 1994), p. 74.

44 Translated by A. L. Sadler in *The Ten Foot Square Hut and Tales of the Heike* (Rutledge, Vt.: Charles E. Tuttle, 1972), p. 1.

# Glossary

**Ainu:**   Indigenous peoples who inhabited Ezochi (Hokkaidō, nearby islands of the Kuril chain, and southern Sakhalin); became citizens of Japan after the Meiji Restoration.

**alternate attendance (sankin kōtai 参勤交代) system:**   The practice of requiring daimyo to reside periodically in Edo (generally every other year) and to leave their legal wives, immediate heirs, and appropriate retinues of service personnel in the city at all times.

**Amaterasu Ōmikami 天照大神：**   The Sun Goddess; the progenitor deity of Japan's line of Heavenly Sovereigns.

**bakufu 幕府：**   The "tent government" of the shogun; the Tokugawa shogunate presided over affairs of the nation from 1603 to 1868.

**bunmei kaika 文明開化：**   "Civilization and Enlightenment"; a phrase popular among those who wished to introduce Western culture and ideas to Japan in the 1870s.

**burakumin 部落民：**   The name applied to descendants of outcasts after the terms *eta* and *hinin* were legally abolished in 1871.

**bushi 武士：**   A warrior; see also samurai.

**Bushidō 武士道：**   "The Way of the Warrior"; a code of ethics designed to mold the beliefs and behavior of the warrior estate.

**chōnin 町人：**   Used in various contexts to mean (1) merchant and artisan landholders—that is, people who were entitled to possess, rent out, sell, and bequeath specified parcels of land, and who paid taxes and levies on those plots—(2) merchants and artisans in general; and (3) all nonsamurai who lived in cities.

**Chōnindō 町人道：**   "The Way of the Merchant"; a code of ethics designed to mold the beliefs and behavior of merchant and artisan families.

**daimyo (daimyō 大名):**   Territorial lords who ruled over holdings with an assessed productive capacity of ten thousand or more koku of rice during the early modern era.

**Dajōkan:**   The Grand Council of State; the central administrative organ of government following its establishment as part of the Taika Reforms; the highest executive organ for oligarchic government from 1868 to 1885.

A22

**(Rikken) Dōshikai:**   One of two mainstream political parties in the prewar era; founded in 1913 and later renamed Kenseikai (1916) and Minseitō (1927); generally more liberal than its rival, the Seiyūkai, the party favored universal manhood suffrage, sponsored social legislation, and reduced military budgets in the 1920s.

**Dutch Studies, Dutch Learning:**   A general name for the study of Western science, medicine, and mathematics in the eighteenth and early nineteenth centuries; most texts available to Japanese were written in Dutch or translated from other European languages into Dutch.

**Emishi 蝦夷：**   Peoples in northern Honshū who resisted the imposition of Yamato rule; later referred to as Ezo.

**eta 穢多：**   Hereditary outcast families that tanned animal hides and fashioned them into equipment used by samurai in the early modern period; lived in segregated communities, often on the outskirts of a castle town; preferred to be known as *kawata* (leather workers).

**Ezochi 蝦夷地：**   The Ainu homeland, consisting of Hokkaidō, nearby islands of the Kuril chain, and southern Sakhalin.

**Fukuzawa Yukichi (1835–1901):**   A lower-ranking samurai from western Japan, Fukuzawa studied Dutch and Western sciences at Nagasaki, opened a school (today's Keiō University) in Edo in 1858, taught himself English, traveled to Europe and America three times in the 1860s; as a prominent educator and author, he emerged as a leading proponent of Civilization and Enlightenment and as Japan's most vocal advocate of learning from the West in the 1870s and 1880s.

**genrō 元老：**   "Elder statesmen" who advised the emperor on political matters during the late Meiji and Taishō periods.

**Gotō Shinpei (1857–1929):**   Born in northern Japan, Gotō entered the Home Ministry in 1883 and supervised several public health projects; headed the civil administration of Taiwan from 1898 to 1906, when he became the first president of the South Manchuria Railway Company and oversaw Japanese colonization efforts in the Kwantung Leased Territory; appointed mayor of Tokyo in 1920 and home minister in 1923, he played a major role in rebuilding the city after the 1923 earthquake.

**Greater East Asia Coprosperity Sphere:**   A concept articulated in the summer of 1940 to express the ambition to create a politically and economically integrated Asia free from Western domination.

**Hara Takashi (1856–1921):**   A native of northern Japan, Hara became a journalist before entering government service in 1882; he helped found the Seiyūkai political party in 1900 and, as home minister on several occasions between 1906 and 1914, used pork-barrel politics to expand the party's influence; after the rice riots in 1918, Hara became the first prime minister to hold a seat in the lower house, have the majority of ministerial posts filled by party members, and govern when the Diet was in session.

**Hibiya Park:** Opened in 1903 on the site of former daimyo mansions, the park soon became a "public space" where demonstrators met to protest the Treaty of Portsmouth in September 1905; later, middle-class families included the park in their Sunday outings, and the government organized mass meetings there in the late 1930s and 1940s to support the fighting in China and the Pacific.

**hinin 非人:** "Nonhumans"; outcasts who entertained and begged for a living in the early modern era; the shogunate enlisted some to carry out such tasks as assisting at executions and caring for victims of contagious diseases.

**Hokkaidō Colonization Office:** Opened by the government in 1869 to promote the settlement and economic development of Hokkaidō; although it achieved only modest success, its activities deprived the indigenous Ainu of their land rights; abolished in 1882 after a major scandal erupted over the proposed sale of the office's assets at a nominal price to private individuals with insider connections.

**Home Ministry:** Established in 1873 with powers to import technology from abroad and organize the manufacturing effort at home, the Home Ministry later supervised prefectural and local government agencies, controlled the police, and oversaw elections; was abolished in 1947.

**Ichikawa Fusae (1893–1981):** A native of Nagoya, Ichikawa was a schoolteacher and journalist before joining with the noted feminist Hiratsuka Raichō to form the New Woman's Association in 1920; in 1924 organized the Women's Suffrage League to spur interest in extending voting rights to women and remained a leading suffragette until 1940; after the war she organized the New Japan Women's League, which advocated expanded legal rights for women, and was elected five times to the House of Councillors, the upper house of the Diet.

**ie 家:** The household, as it exists through generations, including living members, their deceased predecessors, and future successors; the primary unit of social organization among samurai and prosperous merchant families in the early modern era.

**imperial conferences:** Formal meetings in the presence of the emperor at which decisions previously reached at liaison conferences were approved and sanctioned.

**Imperial Rescript on Education:** Promulgated in October 1890, the rescript promoted patriotism, loyalty to the emperor, traditional Confucian-based values, and the notion that the country existed as a single family under the headship of the emperor; students at schools across Japan participated in periodic, ceremonial readings of the rescript until 1945; was rescinded officially in June 1948.

**Imperial Rule Assistance Association:** A mass political association established in October 1940 to promote the goals of the New Order Movement; conservatives opposed the IRAA, on the ground that it violated the spirit of the Meiji constitution, and the Home Ministry eventually gained control over the organization and used it to mobilize popular support for the Greater East Asia War.

**Instructions of the Keian Era:**   Issued by the shogunate in 1649, the thirty-two articles included in the compilation enjoined peasants to be hardworking, frugal, self-sufficient, and obedient.

**Ise Shrine:**   The collective name for an assemblage of important Shinto shrines; the Inner Shrine at Ise, said to date to the third century C.E., enshrines Amaterasu Ōmikami; located in Mie Prefecture.

**ishin 維新:**   A phrase from classical Chinese thought that signifies a renewal, a new beginning of all things, to be accomplished by harnessing together the energies of all segments of society; translated as "restoration" in *Meiji ishin*.

**Ishiwara Kanji (1889–1949):**   A career army officer, Ishiwara joined the staff of the Kwantung Army in 1928 and played a leading role in formulating the Manchurian Incident; in 1937 he became chief of the operations division at the general staff, but differences with other generals about Japan's China policy isolated him, and he retired in 1941.

**Itō Hirobumi (1841–1909):**   Born in Chōshū domain, Itō became an active member of the *sonnō jōi* movement; studied in England in the 1860s and advocated signing treaties with Western nations after his return to Japan; a leading oligarch, he supervised the drafting of the constitution; completed three terms as prime minister, founded the Seiyūkai political party in 1890, represented Japan in the negotiations that produced the Treaty of Shimonoseki in 1895, and served as Japan's first resident general in Korea; assassinated by a Korean nationalist in 1909.

**Itō Noe (1895–1923):**   Born in Kyūshū, Itō attended high school in Tokyo and in 1915 became editor of the feminist journal "Bluestocking" (*Seitō*); a dedicated anarchist, she became a founding member of the Red Wave Society, a socialist women's group, in 1921; together with her lover and fellow anarchist Ōsugi Sakae, she was killed by police in the aftermath of the Great Kantō Earthquake.

**Iwakura Mission:**   A delegation of important government leaders and students, organized and led by Iwakura Tomomi, that visited the United States and Europe from 1871 to 1873 in an effort to secure treaty revision and to study the political and economic systems of the West.

**Iwakura Tomomi (1825–1883):**   A courtier, Iwakura became a leader of the antishogunate movement and arranged for the surrender of the Imperial Palace in Kyoto to loyalist forces on January 3, 1868; led the Iwakura Mission to the West in 1871 and tapped Itō to draft a constitution.

**junshi 殉死:**   The suicide of a warrior upon the death of his master.

**kaikoku 開国:**   An "open country"; a phrase popular among those willing to establish treaty relations with Western nations in the 1850s.

**kami 神:**   Divine spirits that reside on the High Celestial Plain or in natural phenomena; usually worshiped at Shinto shrines, the deities generally act benevolently toward the human population.

**kamikaze 神風:**   The "divine winds" that twice destroyed invading Mongol fleets in the late thirteenth century, reinforcing the belief that Shinto deities protected Japan.

**kamikaze pilots:**   Young volunteers who attempted to defend Japan in the final stages of the Greater East Asia War by diving their planes into American ships.

**Kansai region:**   Western Japan; traditionally, the area around Kyoto and Osaka, including the provinces of Ōmi, Yamashiro, Tanba, Tango, Izumi, Kawachi, Yamato, Kii, Ise, Iga, Tajima, Settsu, Harima, and Awaji.

**Kantō region:**   Eastern Japan; traditionally, the area bounded by the seven provinces of Hitachi, Shimotsuke, Kōzuke, Musashi, Shimōsa, Kazusa, and Awa, to which Sagami is sometimes added to make the Eight Kantō Provinces.

**Kawakami Hajime (1879–1946):**   A graduate of Tokyo University, Kawakami became known as an authority on classical economics while teaching there and at Kyoto University; concerned with the persistence of poverty, he began to study socialist thought and eventually gravitated toward Marxist economics; joined the underground Japan Communist Party in 1932 and was arrested the next year and imprisoned; released from jail in 1937, his health broken, he retired to Kyoto.

**kawata 皮田:**   See *eta*.

**keiretsu 系列:**   A group of affiliated business enterprises in the postwar era; several *keiretsu* were assemblages of the subsidiaries of former *zaibatsu*.

**Kido Takayoshi (1833–1877):**   A low-ranking samurai from Chōshū domain, Kido participated in the *sonnō jōi* movement and arranged for the Chōshū-Satsuma alliance that toppled the shogunate; after the restoration, he drafted the Charter Oath, directed the abolition of domains, and was a member of the Iwakura Mission.

**Kinai region:**   The area immediately around Kyoto; traditionally, the five so-called Capital Provinces of Yamato, Yamashiro, Kawachi, Settsu, and Izumi.

**Kishi Nobusuke (1896–1987):**   A graduate of Tokyo University, Kishi entered the Ministry of Agriculture and Commerce and became a leading renovationist bureaucrat; played a key role in formulating economic policy in Manchukuo in the late 1930s and from 1941 to 1944 directed Japan's economic mobilization as a member of Tōjō's cabinet; arrested as a war criminal, Kishi escaped prosecution and won election to the House of Representatives in 1953; he served two terms as prime minister from February 1957 to July 1960; the elder brother of three-time prime minister Satō Eisaku.

**koku 石:**   A measure of volume equal to approximately five bushels; theoretically enough rice to feed one person for one year; used to calculate samurai stipends as well as the productive capacity of villages and daimyo domains.

**kokumin 国民:**   "National citizens"; a term coined in the Meiji period to describe a citizenry that would be unquestioningly loyal to the new state and bonded together by common political values.

**kokutai 国体：** Usually rendered as "national essence," the term connoted a harmonious and unique amalgam of government and religion that presumably had infused Japanese political life from the golden days of antiquity as Heavenly Sovereigns conducted rites of governance and looked over the welfare of the people.

**Konoe Fumimaro (1891–1945):** The son of a Kyoto aristocrat, Konoe was appointed to the House of Peers in 1916, joined the Japanese delegation to the Paris Peace Conference, and became a well-known pan-Asianist in the 1920s; served as prime minister three times between June 1937 and October 1941; while prime minister, Konoe presided over the widening of the fighting in China, launched the New Order Movement, created the Imperial Rule Assistance Association, and urged the establishment of a Greater East Asia Coprosperity Sphere.

**Kuroda Kiyotaka (1840–1900):** A native of Satsuma domain, Kuroda participated in the antishogunate movement in the 1860s and was appointed director of the Hokkaidō Colonization Office in 1874; tapped to negotiate a treaty with Korea, in January 1876 he sent a flotilla of modern warships into Korean waters and forced that country to sign the humiliating Treaty of Kanghwa; after being implicated in the scandal concerning the Hokkaidō Colonization Office in 1881, he reemerged as prime minister in 1888 and later became a *genrō*.

**Kwantung Army:** A unit of the Japanese Army created in 1906 and assigned the responsibility to safeguard the Kwantung Territory and the railway zone in Liaodong Peninsula; in the 1920s politicized young officers in the Kwantung Army advanced arguments about the need to separate Manchuria from China and create a Japanese zone of control in northern Asia; members of the unit initiated the Manchurian Incident, and its officers dominated affairs of state in Manchukuo.

**Kwantung Territory:** The name given to the Japanese-occupied strategic zone at the southern tip of the Liaodong Peninsula, containing the great port of Dairen and the major fortress and ice-free naval base at Port Arthur; acquired from Russia under terms of the Portsmouth Treaty.

**liaison conferences:** Meetings between key cabinet members and representatives from the military supreme command; held from late 1937 for the purpose of discussing policy issues.

**makoto 誠：** Sincerity; in Chinese Confucianism, sincerity was considered the cardinal virtue that ought to govern relationships between individuals; in the Japanese Shinto tradition, *makoto* developed its own cluster of nuances, signifying that which was true, genuine, pure, and honest.

**Matsukata Masayoshi (1835–1924):** A samurai from Satsuma domain, Matsukata participated in the antishogunate movement in the 1860s; after 1868 became a prefectural governor; later joined the government in Edo, helped implement the land tax reform of 1873, served as finance minister, and completed two terms as prime minister.

**Matsuoka Yōsuke (1880–1946):** Born in Yamaguchi Prefecture, Matsuoka was graduated from the University of Oregon School of Law in 1900 and returned to Japan to join the diplomatic corps; in the late 1920s became a vice-president of the South Manchuria Railway Company and in 1930 was elected to the Diet, where he became a vocal opponent of Shidehara's policy of cooperative imperialism; as Japan's delegate to the League of Nations, he orchestrated his country's withdrawal from that organization in the wake of the Manchurian Incident; served as a cabinet adviser from 1937 to 1940 and as foreign minister in 1940 and 1941, when he was instrumental in formulating the goals of the Greater East Asia Coprosperity Sphere, oversaw Japan's move into Southeast Asia, and linked Japan diplomatically with Germany and Italy; arrested as a war criminal, he was judged too ill to stand trial; died in June 1946.

**Minami Jirō (1874–1955):** A career military officer, Minami joined the Wakatsuki cabinet as army minister in 1931, was named commander of the Kwantung Army and ambassador to Manchukuo in 1934, and later served as governor-general of Korea; indicted as a war criminal, he was sentenced to life imprisonment.

**Minobe Tatsukichi (1873–1948):** A professor at Tokyo University, Minobe was a leading proponent of the organ theory of government, which held that the emperor was only one "organ" within the larger state and that other organs—the Diet, bureaucracy, cabinet, and so forth—were constitutionally entitled to exercise specific governing prerogatives; in the 1930s rightists attacked Minobe's ideas as lèse majesté, forced him to resign from the House of Peers, and caused his books to be banned; wounded in an assassination attempt in 1936, Minobe retired from public life until 1946, when he advised the cabinet on the drafting of the postwar constitution.

**MITI (Ministry of International Trade and Industry):** Created in 1949 out of the prewar Ministry of Commerce and Industry (1925–1943; 1945–1949), MITI sought to promote rapid economic growth; it was empowered to introduce new technology and direct financing and natural resources to selected industries, and many observers credited its bureaucrats with designing an effective industrial policy.

**naiyū gaikan 内憂外患:** A Confucian phrase signifying "troubles from within and without"; invoked at chaotic times when the course of a nation's history seemed to be cascading toward a major watershed.

**narikin 成金:** A nouveau riche.

**National General Mobilization Law:** Decreed on April 1, 1938, this legislation authorized the government to ration labor among industrial sectors, organize all industries into cartels that would implement government planning goals, and seize factories and land for wartime production purposes; abolished by U.S. occupation authorities in 1945.

**National Learning:** A scholarly movement that emerged in the eighteenth century; leading members included Kamo no Mabuchi and Motoori Norinaga, who wished to discover the essence of the Japanese tradition through a rigorous analysis of ancient texts.

**New Order Movement:** Proclaimed in 1940 by Konoe Fumimaro, who envisaged a reorganization of Japan's political and economic systems as a bulwark against the dual menace of Western imperialism and Communism; included calls for a planned economy and the establishment of a mass political organization, the Imperial Rule Assistance Association, to support the government.

**new religions:** Religious movements that developed independently of organized Shinto or Buddhism but drew on previous religious traditions; promised believers help in the here and now and tended to be popular among those who lived on the economic margins of society; the first wave of new religions, including the Kurozumi and Tenri sects, arose in the early nineteenth century, and more were founded in the late Meiji and Taishō periods.

**NHK (Nihon Hōsō Kyōkai):** Established in 1926, the Japan Broadcasting Corporation came under the control of the Communications Ministry and had a monopoly on all radio broadcasting; in 1950 new laws authorized commercial broadcasting, and reorganized NHK as a public corporation; financed through mandatory monthly subscription fees paid by individual households, NHK added television outlets in 1953 and today specializes in educational programming.

**Nihonbashi:** The leading merchant district in Edo; the neighborhood took the name of a bridge constructed in 1603, the starting point for the Tōkaidō Highway; flourished as a commercial district in the late nineteenth and twentieth centuries.

**Ninomiya Sontoku (1787–1856):** A proponent of rural development who organized programs to improve agricultural productivity in several domains; the Peasant Sage, as Ninomiya became known, wrote more than thirty volumes of practical and moral advice for farmers; urged people to "repay virtue" (*hōtoku*)—that is, to work hard, be frugal, and help others as a way of repaying the deities for their blessings—and praised as an exemplar of virtue in school textbooks in the 1930s.

**Nitobe Inazō (1862–1933):** A graduate of Sapporo Agricultural College, Nitobe studied in Germany and the United States and became a Quaker; later was a professor of colonial policy at Tokyo University and served as the undersecretary-general of the League of Nations; prided himself on being an internationalist and opponent of militarism but was an outspoken supporter of the government's policies toward the Ainu and a staunch defender of Japan's colonization of Korea.

**Oguri Tadamasa (1827–1868):** A leading official in the shogunate and member of the 1860 mission to the United States; directed the shogunate's military and economic reforms from 1864 to 1868 and favored punishing dissident domains in the 1860s; the only shogunal official to be executed after the restoration.

**Ōkubo Toshimichi (1830–1878):** A samurai from Satsuma domain who participated in the antishogunate movement in the 1860s; as a leading oligarch after 1868 he was the chief architect of the land tax reform of 1873 and worked to promote industrialization; commanded troops that helped put down the rebellion of Saigō Takamori and was assassinated by Saigō sympathizers in 1878.

**Ōkuma Shigenobu (1838–1922):** A samurai from Mizen domain, Ōkuma joined the Meiji government in 1868 and helped establish a modern currency and national mint; founded the Rikken Kaishintō political party in 1882 and in 1898 became the first head of a political party to be named prime minister; in 1882 founded a school that became Waseda University.

**Popular Rights Movement:** A nationwide political movement that flourished in the late 1870s and 1880s; most participants advocated a more liberal constitution and more broad-based participation in the anticipated parliamentary system than the Meiji leadership was willing to countenance.

**Public Order and Police Law of 1900:** Promulgated by the cabinet of Yamagata Aritomo in March 1900, the act aimed to restrain the activities of antigovernment groups, especially the nascent labor movement; specific articles restricted the rights of workers to organize and strike, banned political activity by women, soldiers, and priests, and underscored the right of the police to forbid or disband any meeting or demonstration; restraints on labor organizations were relaxed in 1919, the provision barring women from joining political associations was removed in 1922, and the law itself was abolished by U.S. occupation authorities in November 1945.

**Regulations concerning Warrior Households:** Regulations defining the conduct of the daimyo lords and the direct retainers of the shogun; included restrictions on marriage, naming heirs, and castle construction; promulgated in 1615 and revised periodically thereafter.

**rōnin 浪人:** A "floating man"; a masterless samurai.

**ryōsai kenbo 良妻賢母:** "Good wife, wise mother"; a term coined in the late nineteenth century to describe a social model that kept women in the private sphere but accorded them respect as the moral foundation of the family.

**Ryūkyū Islands:** An archipelago south of Kyūshū, of which the largest island is Okinawa; during the early modern period the island chain was simultaneously an autonomous kingdom, a tributary state of China, and a dependency of Satsuma domain; the Meiji government claimed sovereignty over the islands and incorporated them into Japan proper as Okinawa Prefecture in 1879.

**Saigō Takamori (1827–1877):** A samurai from Satsuma domain, Saigō helped arrange the Chōshū–Satsuma alliance and led loyalist armies in fighting against shogunal forces in 1868; resigned from the new government after other oligarchs vetoed his idea for an expedition against Korea in 1873; led a failed counterrebellion against the Meiji government in 1877.

**Saionji Kinmochi (1849–1940):** The scion of an aristocratic family in Kyoto, Saionji studied law, forged a close friendship with Itō Hirobumi, helped found the Seiyūkai, and completed two terms as prime minister between 1906 and 1912; remained influential as a *genrō* until his death.

**samurai 侍:**   A warrior; more specifically, a warrior with the privilege of personal attendance upon his lord.

**Seiyūkai:**   Founded by Itō Hirobumi in 1900, the Seiyūkai became one of Japan's two mainstream political parties; maintained a conservative orientation and, under the presidency of Tanaka Giichi, became identified with an assertive foreign policy and antagonism toward the political left; dissolved in 1940.

**Sengoku age:**   The period from the Ōnin War of 1467–1477 until the conclusion of the wars of reunification at the end of the sixteenth century, when constant strife made Japan "A Country at War."

**Shibusawa Eiichi (1841–1931):**   The son of a prosperous farm family, Shibusawa joined the Meiji government in 1869, assisted in tax and currency reforms, and played a key role in establishing the Tomioka silk filature; resigned office in 1873 to enter private business and subsequently founded the First National Bank, helped organize nearly three hundred industrial and commercial enterprises, and advanced the ideal of the unselfish businessperson whose only ambition was to contribute to the nation's well-being.

**Shidehara Kijūrō (1872–1951):**   A native of Osaka, Shidehara joined the Foreign Ministry after graduation from Tokyo University and was named ambassador to the United States in 1919; served as Japan's representative to the Washington Conference and as foreign minister in Kenseikai–Minseitō cabinets from 1924 to 1927 and again from 1929 to 1931; believed that Japan could best promote its interests in Asia by cooperating with other imperialist powers to maintain a balance of power in the region; named prime minister in October 1945; his cabinet presided over the promulgation of the new constitution.

**Shinpū Tokubetsu Kōgekitai 神風特別攻撃隊:**   "Divine Wind Special Attack Corps"; see *kamikaze pilots.*

**Shinto (Shintō 神道):**   "The Way of the Gods"; Japan's indigenous religion.

**shishi 志士:**   Radical young samurai, self-styled "men of high purpose," who advocated *sonnō jōi* and countenanced violence in the late 1850s and early 1860s in order to drive foreigners out of Japan and foster imperial-based rule.

**shōen 荘園:**   Private landed estates that paid dues to aristocratic and religious proprietors; disappeared as daimyo consolidated their authority over the countryside in the sixteenth century.

**shogun:**   An abbreviation of *seii tai shōgun* (**征夷大将軍**; "Great Barbarian-Subduing Field Marshal"); from the medieval period, the Heavenly Sovereign entrusted the shogun to head a *bakufu* ("tent government"; shogunate) that wielded military and police powers designed to complement civil authority; the Tokugawa family held the post from 1603 to 1868 and expanded the powers of the office so that the shogun became a national hegemon who administered the affairs of the nation on behalf of the Heavenly Sovereign.

**shogunate:**   See *bakufu.*

**Shōwa Restoration:**   A slogan popular with the radical right in the early 1930s; suggested the need for righteous young men to replicate the feat of the *shishi*, the "men of high purpose" of the 1860s, by overthrowing a corrupt political and economic system, this one dominated by party politicians and capitalists, thus paving the way for wise, enlightened ministers to rule in the name of a benevolent emperor.

**sonnō jōi 尊王攘夷：**   "Revere the Heavenly Sovereign, Expel the Barbarians"; slogan popular among those who wished to overthrow the shogunate in the late 1850s and early 1860s.

**South Manchuria Railway Company:**   Established by Imperial Ordinance in 1906 to manage Japan's economic interests in southern Manchuria; also carried out functions of a state agency, such as operating utilities and managing civil organs related to law, security, education, and public health.

**Suiheisha (Levelers' Society):**   A national organization founded in 1922 by outcast groups to advocate equal political and social rights and the improvement of living conditions.

**Sun Goddess:**   See Amaterasu Ōmikami.

**tennō 天皇：**   The Heavenly Sovereign, or emperor; the titular head of the national government and sacerdotal chief of the indigenous Shinto religion.

**terakoya 寺子屋：**   A "temple school"; a privately run school in the early modern era.

**The Three Metropoles:**   Edo, Kyoto, and Osaka, the leading cities of the early modern period.

**Tōhoku region:**   Northern Japan; traditionally, the area corresponding to the ancient provinces of Dewa and Mutsu.

**Tōkaidō Highway:**   "Eastern Sea Road"; the highway that ran along the Pacific Coast for nearly three hundred miles from Edo to Kyoto, with an extension to Osaka; fifty-three post towns along the Tōkaidō Highway offered services to travelers.

**Ugaki Kazushige (1868–1956):**   A career army officer who served as army minister in several cabinets in the 1920s and early 1930s, when he emerged as a hero of the radical right; as governor-general of Korea from 1931 to 1936 Ugaki encouraged the growth of heavy and military industries and ruthlessly suppressed Korean opposition to the Japanese occupation of their country; purged by the U.S. occupation, he later was rehabilitated and in 1953 was elected to the upper house of the Diet.

**Washington Conference:**   Held between November 1921 and February 1922, the conference produced several agreements, notably the Four-Power Treaty, the Washington Naval Treaty, and the Nine-Power Treaty, which attempted to reduce international tensions and rivalries by creating a naval balance of power in the Pacific and preserving the territorial integrity of China.

**Yamagata Aritomo (1838–1922):** A low-ranking samurai from Chōshū domain, Yamagata became a radical advocate of *sonnō jōi* ideology; after the restoration, he spearheaded the effort to create a conscript army and led troops to suppress the rebellion of Saigō Takamori; played a key role in developing the system of local government enacted in the late 1880s; completed two terms as prime minister, served as chief of the general staff during the Russo-Japanese War, and was an influential *genrō*.

**Yamakawa Kikue (1890–1980):** Born in Tokyo, Yamakawa became active in the women's movement and in 1920 founded the Red Wave Society, a socialist organization for women; in 1947 she became the first head of the Women's and Minors' Bureau in the Ministry of Labor.

**Yosano Akiko (1878–1942):** Born near Osaka, Yosano established her literary reputation with the publication in 1901 of *Midaregami* ("Tangled Hair"), a collection of nearly four hundred passionate and sensuous poems; later became a leading feminist, publishing many volumes of poetry and social commentary.

**Yoshida Shōin (1830–1859):** A leading advocate of *sonnō jōi*; opened a school in his native Chōshū and included Itō Hirobumi and Yamagata Aritomo among his students; executed after being implicated in a plot to assassinate a high-ranking member of the shogunate.

**Yoshino Sakuzō (1878–1933):** A professor at Tokyo University, Yoshino was a leading spokesperson for liberal democratic ideals in the Taishō period; favored what he called *minpon shugi* ("democracy based upon the people"), by which he meant that party cabinets were an appropriate governing mechanism since they permitted ordinary people to shape their own political destinies.

**zaibatsu 財閥:** Large-scale conglomerates composed of banking, industrial, and commercial companies; played a key role in the development of the Japanese economy from the late Meiji period through the Greater East Asia War.

# Further Readings

## General

Allinson, Gary D. *Japanese Urbanism: Industry and Politics in Kariya, 1872–1972*. Berkeley: University of California Press, 1975.

Barnhart, Michael A. *Japan and the World since 1868*. New York: Edward Arnold, 1995.

Bartholomew, James R. *The Formation of Science in Japan*. New Haven: Yale University Press, 1989.

Beasley, William. G. *Japanese Imperialism 1894–1945*. Oxford: Clarendon Press, 1991.

Bernstein, Gail Lee. *Recreating Japanese Women, 1600–1945*. Berkeley: University of California Press, 1991.

————, and Haruhiro Fukui, eds. *Japan and the World: Essays in Japanese History and Politics*. New York: St. Martin's Press, 1988.

Boscaro, Adriana; Franco Gatti; and Massimo Raveri, eds. *Rethinking Japan*. 2 vols. Sandgate, Folkestone, Kent: Japan Library, 1990.

Brownlee, John S. *Japanese Historians and the National Myths, 1600–1945: The Age of the Gods and Emperor Jimmu*. Vancouver: University of British Columbia Press, 1997.

Coaldrake, William H. *Architecture and Authority in Japan*. London: Routledge, 1996.

Davis, Darrell William. *Picturing Japaneseness: Monumental Style, National Identity, Japanese Film*. New York: Columbia University Press, 1996.

De Vos, George. *Japan's Minorities: Burakumin, Koreans, Ainu, Okinawans*. London: Minority Rights Group, 1983.

Denoon, Donald, et al., eds. *Multicultural Japan: Palaeolithic to Postmodern*. Cambridge: Cambridge University Press, 1996.

Dower, John W. *Japan in War and Peace: Selected Essays*. New York: New Press, 1993.

Eisenstadt, S. N. *Japanese Civilization: A Comparative View*. Chicago: University of Chicago Press, 1996.

Fogel, Joshua A. *The Cultural Dimensions of Sino-Japanese Relations: Essays on the Interactions between China and Japan in the Nineteenth and Twentieth Centuries*. Armonk, N.Y.: M. E. Sharpe, 1994.

Francks, Penelope. *Japanese Economic Development: Theory and Practice*. London: Routledge, 1992.

Garon, Sheldon. *Molding Japanese Minds: The State in Everyday Life.* Princeton: Princeton University Press, 1997.

———. *The State and Labor in Modern Japan.* Berkeley: University of California Press, 1987.

Giffard, Sydney. *Japan among the Powers, 1890–1990.* New Haven: Yale University Press, 1994.

Gordon, Andrew. *The Evolution of Labor Relations in Japan: Heavy Industry, 1853–1955.* Cambridge: Council on East Asian Studies, Harvard University, 1985.

Hall, John W., et al., gen. eds. *The Cambridge History of Japan.* Cambridge: Cambridge University Press.

Vol. 4:  Hall, ed. *Early Modern Japan* (1991).

Vol. 5:  Marius B. Jansen, ed. *The Nineteenth Century* (1989).

Vol. 6:  Peter Duus, ed. *The Twentieth Century* (1988).

Hane, Mikiso. *Peasants, Rebels, and Outcastes: The Underside of Modern Japan.* New York: Pantheon Books, 1982.

Hardacre, Helen. *Kurozumikyō and the New Religions of Japan.* Princeton: Princeton University Press, 1986.

———. *Shintō and the State, 1868–1988.* Princeton: Princeton University Press, 1989.

Havens, Thomas R. H. *Architects of Affluence: The Tsutsumi Family and the Seibu-Saison Enterprises in Twentieth-Century Japan.* Cambridge: Council on East Asian Studies, Harvard University, 1994.

Heisig, James W., and John C. Maraldo, eds. *Rude Awakenings: Zen, the Kyoto School, and the Question of Nationalism.* Honolulu: University of Hawai'i Press, 1995.

Hopper, Helen M. *A New Woman of Japan: A Political Biography of Katō Shidzue.* Boulder: Westview Press, 1996.

Howe, Christopher. *The Origins of Japanese Trade Supremacy: Development and Technology in Asia from 1540 to the Pacific War.* Chicago: University of Chicago Press, 1996.

Hunter, Janet, ed. *Japanese Women Working.* London: Routledge, 1995.

Imamura, Anne E., ed. *Re-Imaging Japanese Women.* Berkeley: University of California Press, 1996.

Irokawa Daikichi. *The Age of Hirohito: In Search of Modern Japan.* Tr. Mikiso Hane and John K. Urda. New York: Free Press, 1995.

Johnson, Chalmers A. *MITI and the Japanese Miracle: The Growth of Industrial Policy, 1925–1975.* Stanford: Stanford University Press, 1982.

Johnston, William. *The Modern Epidemic: A History of Tuberculosis in Japan.* Cambridge: Council on East Asian Studies, Harvard University, 1995.

Lee, Changsoo, and George De Vos. *Koreans in Japan: Ethnic Conflict and Accommodation.* Berkeley: University of California Press, 1981.

Linhart, Sepp, and Sabina Frühstück, eds. *The Culture of Japan as Seen through Its Leisure.* New York: State University of New York Press, 1998.

Marshall, Bryon K. *Academic Freedom and the Japanese Imperial University, 1868–1939.* Berkeley: University of California Press, 1992.

Maruyama Masao. *Thought and Behaviour in Modern Japanese Politics.* Ed. Ivan Morris. London: Oxford University Press, 1963.

McCormack, Gavan, and Yoshio Sugimoto, eds. *The Japanese Trajectory: Modernization and Beyond.* Cambridge: Cambridge University Press, 1988.

Minami Ryōshin. *The Economic Development of Japan: A Quantitative Study.* Tr. Ralph Thompson and Minami with assistance from David Merriman. New York: St. Martin's Press, 1994, 2d ed.

Morikawa Hidemasa. *Zaibatsu: The Rise and Fall of Family Enterprise Groups in Japan.* Tokyo: University of Tokyo Press, 1992.

Morris-Suzuki, Tessa. *A History of Japanese Economic Thought.* London: Routledge, 1989.

———. *Re-Inventing Japan: Time, Space, Nation.* Armonk, N.Y.: M. E. Sharpe, 1998.

———. *The Technological Transformation of Japan: From the Seventeenth to the Twenty-first Century.* Cambridge: Cambridge University Press, 1994.

Mulhern, Chieko Irie, ed. *Heroic with Grace: Legendary Women of Japan.* Armonk, N.Y.: M. E. Sharpe, 1991.

Mullins, Mark R.; Shimazono Susumu; and Paul L. Swanson, eds. *Religion and Society in Modern Japan.* Berkeley: Asian Humanities Press, 1993.

Najita, Tetsuo, and J. Victor Koschmann, eds. *Conflict in Modern Japanese History: The Neglected Tradition.* Princeton: Princeton University Press, 1982.

Nakamura Masanori, ed. *Technology Change and Female Labour in Modern Japan.* Tokyo: United Nations University Press, 1994.

Nakamura Takafusa. *Economic Growth in Prewar Japan.* Tr. Robert A. Feldman. New Haven: Yale University Press, 1983.

Ortolani, Benito. *The Japanese Theatre: From Shamanistic Ritual to Contemporary Pluralism.* Leiden: E. J. Brill, 1990.

Pflugfelder, Gregory M. *Cartographies of Desire: Male-Male Sexuality in Japanese Discourse, 1600–1950.* Berkeley: University of California Press, 1999.

Samuels, Richard J. *The Business of the Japanese State: Energy Markets in Comparative and Historical Perspective.* Ithaca: Cornell University Press, 1987.

Seidensticker, Edward. *Low City, High City: Tokyo from Edo to the Earthquake: How the Shogun's Ancient Capital Became a Great Modern City, 1867–1923.* New York: Knopf, 1983.

———. *Tokyo Rising: The City since the Great Earthquake.* New York: Knopf, 1990.

Siddle, Richard. *Race, Resistance and the Ainu of Japan.* London: Routledge, 1996.

Smethurst, Richard J. *Agricultural Development and Tenancy Disputes in Japan, 1870–1940.* Princeton: Princeton University Press, 1986.

Smith, Thomas C. *Native Sources of Japanese Industrialization, 1750–1920*. Berkeley: University of California Press, 1988.

Steenstrup, Carl. *A History of Law in Japan until 1868*. Leiden: E. J. Brill, 1996.

Takeuchi Johzen. *The Role of Labour-Intensive Sectors in Japanese Industrialization*. Tr. Hiromichi Matsui. Tokyo: United Nations University Press, 1991.

Tanaka, Stefan. *Japan's Orient: Rendering Pasts as History*. Berkeley: University of California Press, 1993.

Tonomura, Hitomi; Anne Walthall; and Wakita Haruko, eds. *Women and Class in Japanese History*. Ann Arbor: Center for Japanese Studies, University of Michigan, 1999.

Vlastos, Stephen, ed. *Mirror of Modernity: Invented Traditions of Modern Japan*. Berkeley: University of California Press, 1998.

Wakita Haruko, Anne Bouchy, and Ueno Chizuko, eds. *Gender and Japanese History*. Tr. ed. Gerry Yokota-Murakami. 2 vols. Osaka: Osaka University Press, 1999.

Weiner, Michael, ed. *Japan's Minorities: The Illusion of Homogeneity*. London: Routledge, 1997.

White, James W.; Michio Umegaki; and Thomas R. H. Havens, eds. *The Ambivalence of Nationalism: Modern Japan between East and West*. Lanham, Md.: University Press of America, 1990.

Wray, William D., ed. *Managing Industrial Enterprise: Cases from Japan's Prewar Experience*. Cambridge: Council on East Asian Studies, Harvard University, 1989.

## Part I: Traditional Japan

Bellah, Robert N. *Tokugawa Religion: The Values of Pre-Industrial Japan*. Boston: Beacon Press, 1957.

Bix, Herbert P. *Peasant Protest in Japan, 1590–1884*. New Haven: Yale University Press, 1986.

Bolitho, Harold. *Treasures among Men: The Fudai Daimyo in Tokugawa Japan*. New Haven: Yale University Press, 1974.

Brown, Philip C. *Central Authority and Local Autonomy in the Formation of Early Modern Japan: The Case of Kaga Domain*. Stanford: Stanford University Press, 1993.

Coaldrake, A. Kimi. *Women's Gidayū and the Japanese Theatre Tradition*. London: Routledge, 1997.

Cooper, Michael. *They Came to Japan: An Anthology of European Reports on Japan, 1543–1640*. Berkeley: University of California Press, 1965.

De Poorter, Erika, ed. *As the Twig is Bent . . . Essays in Honour of Frits Vos*. Amsterdam: J. C. Gieben, 1990.

Dore, Ronald P. *Education in Tokugawa Japan*. Berkeley: University of California Press, 1965.

Dunn, Charles J. *Everyday Life in Traditional Japan*. Tokyo: Charles E. Tuttle, 1972.

Elison, George. *Deus Destroyed: The Image of Christianity in Early Modern Japan*. Cambridge: Council on East Asian Studies, Harvard University, 1988, 2d print.

————, and Bardwell L. Smith, eds. *Warlords, Artists, and Commoners: Japan in the Sixteenth Century*. Honolulu: University of Hawaii Press, 1981.

Gerhart, Karen M. *The Eyes of Power: Art and Early Tokugawa Authority*. Honolulu: University of Hawai'i Press, 1999.

Gerstle, C. Andrew, ed. *18th Century Japan: Culture and Society*. Sydney: Allen & Unwin, 1989.

Hanley, Susan B. *Everyday Things in Premodern Japan: The Hidden Legacy of Material Culture*. Berkeley: University of California Press, 1997.

————, and Kozo Yamamura. *Economic and Demographic Change in Preindustrial Japan, 1600–1868*. Princeton: Princeton University Press, 1977.

Harootunian, Harry D. *Things Seen and Unseen: Discourse and Ideology in Tokugawa Nativism*. Chicago: University of Chicago Press, 1988.

Hauser, William B. *Economic Institutional Change in Tokugawa Japan: Osaka and the Kinai Cotton Trade*. Cambridge: Cambridge University Press, 1974.

Howell, David L. *Capitalism from Within: Economy, Society, and the State in a Japanese Fishery*. Berkeley: University of California Press, 1995.

Ikegami, Eiko. *The Taming of the Samurai: Honorific Individualism and the Making of Modern Japan*. Cambridge: Harvard University Press, 1995.

Jannetta, Ann Bowman. *Epidemics and Morality in Early Modern Japan*. Princeton: Princeton University Press, 1987.

Kalland, Arne. *Fishing Villages in Tokugawa Japan*. Honolulu: University of Hawai'i Press, 1995.

Kaempfer, Engelbert. *Kaempfer's Japan: Tokugawa Culture Observed*. Ed., tr., and annot. Beatrice M. Bodart-Bailey. Honolulu: University of Hawai'i Press, 1999.

Kassel, Marleen. *Tokugawa Confucian Education: The Kangian Academy of Hirose Tansō (1782–1856)*. Albany: State University of New York Press, 1996.

Kelly, William W. *Deference and Defiance in Nineteenth-Century Japan*. Princeton: Princeton University Press, 1985.

Kornicki, P. F., and I. J. McMullen, eds. *Religion in Japan: Arrows to Heaven and Earth*. Cambridge: Cambridge University Press, 1996.

Leupp, Gary P. *Male Colors: The Construction of Homosexuality in Tokugawa Japan*. Berkeley: University of California Press, 1995.

————. *Servants, Shophands, and Laborers in the Cities of Tokugawa Japan*. Princeton: Princeton University Press, 1992.

Massarella, Derek. *A World Elsewhere: Europe's Encounter with Japan in the Sixteenth and Seventeenth Centuries*. New Haven: Yale University Press, 1990.

————, and Beatrice Bodart-Bailey, eds. *The Furthest Goal: Engelbert Kaempfer's Encounter with Tokugawa Japan*. Sandgate, Folkestone, Kent: Japan Library, 1995.

McClain, James L. *Kanazawa: A Castle Town in Seventeenth-Century Japan*. New Haven: Yale University Press, 1982.

————, John M. Merriman, and Ugawa Kaoru, eds. *Edo and Paris: Urban Life and the State in the Early Modern Era*. Ithaca: Cornell University Press, 1994.

————, and Wakita Osamu, eds. *Osaka: The Merchants' Capital of Early Modern Japan*. Ithaca: Cornell University Press, 1999.

McMullen, I. J. *Genji gaiden: The Origins of Kumazawa Banzan's Commentary on the Tale of Genji*. Oxford: Ithaca Press, Oxford Oriental Institute, 1991.

McMullin, Neil. *Buddhism and the State in Sixteenth-Century Japan*. Princeton: Princeton University Press, 1984.

Najita, Tetsuo, ed. *Tokugawa Political Writings*. Cambridge: Cambridge University Press, 1998.

————. *Visions of Virtue in Tokugawa Japan: The Kaitokudō Merchant Academy of Osaka*. Chicago: University of Chicago Press, 1987.

Nakai, Kate Wildman. *Shogunal Politics: Arai Hakuseki and the Premises of Tokugawa Rule*. Cambridge: Council on East Asian Studies, Harvard University, 1988.

Nakane Chie and Ōishi Shinzaburō, eds. *Tokugawa Japan: The Social and Economic Antecedents of Modern Japan*. Ed. Conrad Totman. Tokyo: University of Tokyo Press, 1988.

Nishiyama Matsunosuke. *Edo Culture: Daily Life and Diversions in Urban Japan, 1600–1868*. Tr. and ed. Gerald Groemer. Honolulu: University of Hawai'i Press, 1997.

Nosco, Peter, ed. *Confucianism and Tokugawa Culture*. Princeton: Princeton University Press, 1984.

————. *Remembering Paradise: Nativism and Nostalgia in Eighteenth-Century Japan*. Cambridge: Council on East Asian Studies, Harvard University, 1990.

Ooms, Herman. *Charismatic Bureaucrat: A Political Biography of Matsudaira Sadanobu 1758–1829*. Chicago: University of Chicago Press, 1975.

————. *Tokugawa Ideology: Early Constructs, 1570–1680*. Princeton: Princeton University Press, 1985.

————. *Tokugawa Village Practice: Class, Status, Power, Law*. Berkeley: University of California Press, 1996.

Ravina, Mark. *Land and Lordship in Early Modern Japan*. Stanford: Stanford University Press, 1999.

Roberts, Luke S. *Mercantilism in a Japanese Domain: The Merchant Origins of Economic Nationalism in 18th-Century Tosa*. Cambridge: Cambridge University Press, 1998.

Rubinger, Richard. *Private Academies of Tokugawa Japan*. Princeton: Princeton University Press, 1982.

Sakai, Naoki. *Voices of the Past: The Status of Language in Eighteenth-Century Japanese Discourse*. Ithaca: Cornell University Press, 1992.

Sawada, Janine Anderson. *Confucian Values and Popular Zen: Sekimon Shingaku in Eighteenth-Century Japan*. Honolulu: University of Hawai'i Press, 1993.

Seigle, Cecilia Segawa. *Yoshiwara: The Glittering World of the Japanese Courtesan*. Honolulu: University of Hawai'i Press, 1993.

Smith, Thomas C. *The Agrarian Origins of Modern Japan*. Stanford: Stanford University Press, 1959.

Smits, Gregory. *Visions of Ryukyu: Identity and Ideology in Early-Modern Thought and Politics*. Honolulu: University of Hawai'i Press, 1999.

Takemura Eiji. *The Perception of Work in Tokugawa Japan: A Study of Ishida Baigan and Ninomiya Sontoku*. Lanham, Md.: University Press of America, 1997.

Toby, Ronald P. *State and Diplomacy in Early Modern Japan: Asia in the Development of the Tokugawa Bakufu*. Princeton: Princeton University Press, 1984.

Totman, Conrad. *The Lumber Industry in Early Modern Japan*. Honolulu: University of Hawai'i Press, 1995.

———. *Politics in the Tokugawa Bakufu, 1600–1843*. Cambridge: Harvard University Press, 1967.

Tucker, Mary Evelyn. *Moral and Spiritual Cultivation in Japanese Neo-Confucianism: The Life and Thought of Kaibara Ekken, 1630–1740*. Albany: State University of New York Press, 1989.

Vaporis, Constantine Nomikos. *Breaking Barriers: Travel and the State in Early Modern Japan*. Cambridge: Council on East Asian Studies, Harvard University, 1994.

Vlastos, Stephen. *Peasant Protests and Uprisings in Tokugawa Japan*. Berkeley: University of California Press, 1986.

Wakabayashi, Bob Tadashi. *Japanese Loyalism Reconstructed: Yamagata Daini's Ryūshi Shinron of 1759*. Honolulu: University of Hawai'i Press, 1995.

Walker, Brett L. *The Conquest of the Ainu: Ecology and Culture in Japanese Expansion, 1590–1800*. Berkeley: University of California Press, 2001.

Walthall, Anne, ed. and tr. *Peasant Uprisings in Japan: A Critical Anthology of Peasant Histories*. Chicago: University of Chicago Press, 1991.

———. *Social Protest and Popular Culture in Eighteenth-Century Japan*. Tucson: University of Arizona Press, 1986.

White, James W. *Ikki: Social Conflict and Political Protest in Early Modern Japan*. Ithaca: Cornell University Press, 1995.

Wigen, Kären. *The Making of a Japanese Periphery, 1750–1920*. Berkeley: University of California Press, 1995.

# Part II: Japan in Revolutionary Times

Akita, George. *Foundations of Constitutional Government in Modern Japan, 1868–1900.* Cambridge: Harvard University Press, 1967.

Baxter, James C. *The Meiji Unification through the Lens of Ishikawa Prefecture.* Cambridge: Council on East Asian Studies, Harvard University, 1994.

Beasley, W. G. *Japan Encounters the Barbarian: Japanese Travellers in America and Europe.* New Haven: Yale University Press, 1995.

———. *The Meiji Restoration.* Stanford: Stanford University Press, 1972.

Blacker, Carmen. *The Japanese Enlightenment: A Study of the Writing of Fukuzawa Yukichi.* Cambridge: Cambridge University Press, 1964.

Bowen, Roger. *Rebellion and Democracy in Meiji Japan: A Study of Commoners in the Popular Rights Movement.* Berkeley: University of California Press, 1980.

Conroy, Hilary; Sandra T. W. Davis; and Wayne Peterson, eds. *Japan in Transition: Thought and Action in the Meiji Era, 1868–1912.* Rutherford: Fairleigh Dickinson University Press, 1984.

Craig, Albert. *Chōshū in the Meiji Restoration.* Cambridge: Harvard University Press, 1961.

Duus, Peter. *The Japanese Discovery of America: A Brief History with Documents.* Boston: Bedford Books, 1997.

Ericson, Steven J. *The Sound of the Whistle: Railroads and the State in Meiji Japan.* Cambridge: Council on East Asian Studies, Harvard University, 1996.

Esenbel, Selçuk. *Even the Gods Rebel: The Peasants of Takaino and the 1871 Nakano Uprising in Japan.* Ann Arbor: Association for Asian Studies, 1998.

Frost, Peter. *The Bakamatsu Currency Crisis.* Cambridge: East Asian Research Center, Harvard University, 1970.

Fujitani, Takashi. *Splendid Monarchy: Power and Pageantry in Modern Japan.* Berkeley: University of California Press, 1996.

Gluck, Carol. *Japan's Modern Myths: Ideology in the Late Meiji Period.* Princeton: Princeton University Press, 1985.

Guth, Christine M. E. *Art, Tea, and Industry: Masuda Takashi and the Mitsui Circle.* Princeton: Princeton University Press, 1993.

Hackett, Roger F. *Yamagata Aritomo in the Rise of Modern Japan, 1838–1922.* Cambridge: Harvard University Press, 1971.

Harootunian, Harry D. *Toward Restoration: The Growth of Political Consciousness in Tokugawa Japan.* Berkeley: University of California Press, 1991, rev. ed.

Huber, Thomas M. *The Revolutionary Origins of Modern Japan.* Stanford: Stanford University Press, 1981.

Huffman, James L. *Creating a Public: People and Press in Meiji Japan.* Honolulu: University of Hawai'i Press, 1997.

————. *Politics of the Meiji Press: The Life of Fukuchi Gen'ichirō*. Honolulu: University Press of Hawaii, 1980.

Ketelaar, James Edward. *Of Heretics and Martyrs in Meiji Japan: Buddhism and Its Persecution*. Princeton: Princeton University Press, 1990.

Kidd, Yasue Aoki. *Women Workers in the Japanese Cotton Mills: 1800–1920*. Ithaca: China-Japan Program, Cornell University, 1978.

Kinmonth, Earl H. *The Self-Made Man in Meiji Japanese Thought: From Samurai to Salary Man*. Berkeley: University of California Press, 1981.

Koschmann, J. Victor. *The Mito Ideology: Discourse, Reform, and Insurrection in Late Tokugawa Japan, 1790–1864*. Berkeley: University of California Press, 1987.

Jansen, Marius B. *Sakamoto Ryōma and the Meiji Restoration*. Princeton: Princeton University Press, 1961.

Lewis, Michael L. *Becoming Apart: Natural Power and Local Politics in Toyama, 1868–1945*. Cambridge: Harvard University Asia Center, 2000.

Lincicome, Mark E. *Principle, Praxis, and the Politics of Educational Reform in Meiji Japan*. Honolulu: University of Hawai'i Press, 1995.

Marshall, Byron K. *Learning to Be Modern: Japanese Political Discourse on Education*. Boulder: Westview Press, 1994.

Motoyama Yukihiko. *Proliferating Talent: Essays on Politics, Thought, and Education in the Meiji Era*. Ed. J. S. A. Elisonas and Richard Rubinger. Honolulu: University of Hawai'i Press, 1997.

Nimura Kazuo. *The Ashio Riot of 1907: A Social History of Mining in Japan*. Ed. Andrew Gordon. Tr. Terry Boardman and Gordon. Durham: Duke University Press, 1997.

Nish, Ian, ed. *The Iwakura Mission to America and Europe: A New Assessment*. Richmond, Surrey: Japan Library, 1998.

Ooms, Emily Groszos. *Women and Millenarian Protest in Meiji Japan: Deguchi Nao and Ōmotokyō*. Ithaca: East Asia Program, Cornell University, 1993.

Peattie, Mark R. *Nanyō: The Rise and Fall of the Japanese in Micronesia, 1885–1945*. Honolulu: University of Hawaii Press, 1988.

Ramseyer, J. Mark, and Francis M. Rosenbluth. *The Politics of Oligarchy: Institutional Choice in Imperial Japan*. Cambridge: Cambridge University Press, 1995.

Reader, Ian, with Esben Andreasen and Finn Stefánsson, eds. *Japanese Religions: Past and Present*. Sandgate, Folkestone, Kent: Japan Library, 1993.

Roden, Donald. *School Days in Imperial Japan: A Study in the Culture of a Student Elite*. Berkeley: University of California Press, 1980.

Rose, Barbara. *Tsuda Umeko and Women's Education in Japan*. New Haven: Yale University Press, 1992.

Sievers, Sharon. *Flowers of Salt: The Beginnings of Feminist Consciousness in Modern Japan*. Stanford: Stanford University Press, 1983.

Smith, Thomas C. *Political Change and Industrial Development in Japan: Government Enterprise, 1868–1880*. Stanford: Stanford University Press, 1955.

Strong, Kenneth. *Ox against the Storm: A Biography of Tanaka Shozo—Japan's Conservationist Pioneer*. Sandgate, Folkestone, Kent: Japan Library, 1995.

Sugiyama Shinya. *Japan's Industrialization in the World Economy, 1859–1899*. London: Athlone Press, 1988.

Thelle, Notto R. *Buddhism and Christianity in Japan: From Conflict to Dialogue, 1854–1899*. Honolulu: University of Hawaii Press, 1987.

Totman, Conrad. *The Collapse of the Tokugawa Bakufu, 1862–1868*. Honolulu: University of Hawaii Press, 1980.

Tsurumi, E. Patricia. *Factory Girls: Women in the Thread Mills of Meiji Japan*. Princeton: Princeton University Press, 1990.

Umegaki, Michio. *After the Restoration: The Beginning of Japan's Modern State*. New York: New York University Press, 1988.

Uno, Kathleen S. *Passages to Modernity: Motherhood, Childhood, and Social Reform in Early Twentieth Century Japan*. Honolulu: University of Hawai'i Press, 1999.

Wakabayshi, Bob Tadashi. *Anti-Foreignism and Western Learning in Early Modern Japan: The New Theses of 1825*. Cambridge: Council on East Asian Studies, Harvard University, 1983.

Walthall, Anne. *The Weak Body of a Useless Woman: Matsuo Taseko and the Meiji Restoration*. Chicago: University of Chicago Press, 1998.

Waters, Neil. *Japan's Local Pragmatists: The Transition from Bakamatsu to Meiji in the Kawasaki Region*. Cambridge: Council on East Asian Studies, Harvard University, 1983.

Westney, D. Eleanor. *Imitation and Innovation: The Transfer of Western Organizational Patterns to Meiji Japan*. Cambridge: Harvard University Press, 1987.

Whitney, Clara A. N. *Clara's Diary: An American Girl in Meiji Japan*. Ed. M. William Steele and Tamiko Ichimata. Tokyo: Kodansha, 1978.

Wilson, George. *Patriots and Redeemers in Japan: Motives in the Meiji Restoration*. Chicago: University of Chicago Press, 1992.

Wray, William D. *Mitsubishi and the N.Y.K., 1870–1914: Business Strategy in the Japanese Shipping Industry*. Cambridge: Council on East Asian Studies, Harvard University, 1984.

Yamamoto Hirofumi, ed. *Technological Innovation and the Development of Transportation in Japan*. Tokyo: United Nations University Press, 1993.

# Part III: Japan in the New Century

Banno Junji. *The Establishment of the Japanese Constitutionalism System*. Tr. J. A. A. Stockwin. London: Routledge, 1992.

Bernstein, Gail Lee. *Japanese Marxist: A Portrait of Kawakami Hajime, 1879–1946.* Cambridge: Harvard University Press, 1976.

Brook, Timothy, and Bob Tadashi Wakabayashi, eds. *Opium Regimes: China, Britain, and Japan, 1839–1952.* Berkeley: University of California Press, 2000.

Ching, Leo. *Becoming Japanese: Colonial Taiwan and the Politics of Identity Formation.* Berkeley: University of California Press, 2001.

Crump, John. *Hatta Shuzo and Pure Anarchism in Interwar Japan.* Basingstoke: Macmillan, 1993.

Duus, Peter. *The Abacus and the Sword: The Japanese Penetration of Korea, 1895–1910.* Berkeley: University of California Press, 1995.

———. *Party Rivalry and Political Change in Taishō Japan.* Cambridge: Harvard University Press, 1968.

———, Ramon H. Myers, and Mark R. Peattie, eds. *The Japanese Informal Empire in China, 1895–1937.* Princeton: Princeton University Press, 1989.

Fletcher, William Miles, III. *The Japanese Business Community and National Trade Policy, 1920–1942.* Chapel Hill: University of North Carolina Press, 1989.

Fraser, Andrew; R. H. P. Mason; and Philip Mitchell. *Japan's Early Parliaments, 1890–1905: Structure, Issues, and Trends.* London: Routledge, 1995.

Gordon, Andrew. *Labor and Imperial Democracy in Prewar Japan.* Berkeley: University of California Press, 1991.

Hane, Mikiso, tr. and ed. *Reflections on the Way to the Gallows: Rebel Women in Prewar Japan.* Berkeley: University of California Press and Pantheon Books, 1988.

Harootunian, H. D., and Bernard S. Silberman, eds. *Japan in Crisis: Essays on Taishō Democracy.* Princeton: Princeton University Press, 1974.

Hastings, Sally Ann. *Neighborhood and Nation in Tokyo, 1905–1937.* Pittsburgh: University of Pittsburgh Press, 1995.

Hirai, Atsuko. *Individualism and Socialism: Kawai Eijiro's Life and Thought (1891–1944).* Cambridge: Council on East Asian Studies, Harvard University, 1987.

Hoston, Germaine A. *Marxism and the Crisis of Development in Prewar Japan.* Princeton: Princeton University Press, 1986.

———. *The State, Identity, and the National Question in China and Japan.* Princeton: Princeton University Press, 1994.

Howes, John F., ed. *Nitobe Inazō: Japan's Bridge across the Pacific.* Boulder: Westview Press, 1995.

Kaneko Fumiko. *The Prison Memoirs of a Japanese Woman.* Tr. Jean Inglis. Intro. Mikiso Hane. Armonk, N.Y.: M. E. Sharpe, 1991.

Kinzley, W. Dean. *Industrial Harmony in Modern Japan: The Invention of a Tradition.* London: Routledge, 1991.

Large, Stephen S. *Organized Workers and Socialist Politics in Inter-war Japan*. Cambridge: Cambridge University Press, 1981.

———. *The Rise of Labor in Japan: The Yūaikai, 1912–1919*. Tokyo: Sophia University, 1972.

Lewis, Michael L. *Rioters and Citizens: Mass Protest in Imperial Japan*. Berkeley: University of California Press, 1990.

Li, Lincoln. *The China Factor in Modern Japanese Thought: The Case of Tachibana Shiraki, 1881–1945*. Albany: State University of New York Press, 1996.

Lone, Stewart. *Japan's First Modern War: Army and Society in the Conflict with China 1894–95*. New York: St. Martin's Press, 1994.

Mackie, Vera. *Creating Socialist Women in Japan: Gender, Labour, and Activism, 1900–1937*. Cambridge: Cambridge University Press, 1997.

———. *Imagining Liberation: Feminism and Socialism in Early Twentieth Century Japan*. Nepean, N. S. W.: Women's Research Centre, University of Western Sydney, 1995.

Marsland, Stephen E. *The Birth of the Japanese Labor Movement: Takano Fusatarō and the Rōdō Kumiai Kiseikai*. Honolulu: University of Hawaii Press, 1989.

Minichiello, Sharon, ed. *Japan's Competing Modernities: Issues in Culture and Democracy, 1900–1930*. Honolulu: University of Hawai'i Press, 1998.

Miwa Kimitada. *Nitobe Inazō and the Development of Colonial Theories and Practices in Prewar Japan*. Tokyo: Institute of International Relations, Sophia University, 1987.

Molony, Barbara. *Technology and Investment: The Prewar Japanese Chemical Industry*. Cambridge: Council on East Asian Studies, Harvard University Press, 1990.

Myers, Ramon H., and Mark R. Peattie, eds. *The Japanese Colonial Empire, 1895–1945*. Princeton: Princeton University Press, 1984.

Najita, Tetsuo. *Hara Kei in the Politics of Compromise, 1905–1915*. Cambridge: Harvard University Press, 1967.

Neary, Ian. *Political Protest and Social Control in Pre-War Japan: The Origins of Buraku Liberation*. Atlantic Highlands, N.J.: Humanities Press International, 1989.

Nolte, Sharon. *Liberalism in Modern Japan: Ishibashi Tanzan and His Teachers, 1905–1960*. Berkeley: University of California Press, 1987.

Notehelfer, F. G. *Kōtoku Shūsui: Portrait of a Japanese Radical*. Cambridge: Cambridge University Press, 1971.

Raddeker, Hélène Bowen. *Treacherous Women of Imperial Japan*. London: Routledge, 1997.

Shimazu, Naoko. *Japan, Race and Equality: The Racial Equality Proposal of 1919*. London: Routledge, 1998.

Smith, Kerry. *A Time of Crisis: Japan, the Great Depression, and Rural Revitalization*. Cambridge: Harvard University Asia Center, 2001.

Stanley, Thomas A. *Ōsugi Sakae: Anarchist in Taishō Japan: The Creativity of the Ego.* Cambridge: Council on East Asian Studies, Harvard University, 1982.

Teow, See Heng. *Japan's Cultural Policy toward China, 1918–1931.* Cambridge: Harvard University Asia Center, 1999.

Tipton, Elise, ed. *Society and State in Interwar Japan.* London: Routledge, 1997.

Waswo, Ann. *Japanese Landlords: The Decline of a Rural Elite.* Berkeley: University of California Press, 1977.

Weiner, Michael. *The Origins of the Korean Community in Japan, 1910–1923.* Atlantic Highlands, N.J.: Humanities Press International, 1989.

———. *Race and Migration in Imperial Japan.* London: Routledge, 1994.

## Part IV: Japan at War

Barnhart, Michael A. *Japan Prepares for Total War: The Search for Economic Security, 1919–1941.* Ithaca: Cornell University Press, 1987.

Barshay, Andrew E. *State and Intellectual in Imperial Japan: The Public Man in Crisis.* Berkeley: University of California Press, 1988.

Berger, Gordon Mark. *Parties Out of Power in Japan, 1931–1941.* Princeton: Princeton University Press, 1977.

Brooker, Paul. *The Faces of Fraternalism: Nazi Germany, Fascist Italy, and Imperial Japan.* Oxford: Clarendon Press, 1991.

Connors, Lesley. *The Emperor's Advisor: Saionji Kinmochi and Pre-War Japanese Politics.* Beckenham, Kent: Croom Helm, 1987.

Crowley, James B. *Japan's Quest for Autonomy: National Security and Foreign Policy, 1930–1938.* Princeton: Princeton University Press, 1966.

Dower, John W. *War without Mercy: Race and Power in the Pacific War.* New York: Pantheon Books, 1986.

Duus, Peter; Ramon H. Myers; and Mark Peattie. *The Japanese Wartime Empire, 1931–1945.* Princeton: Princeton University Press, 1996.

Fletcher, William Miles, III. *The Search for a New World Order: Intellectuals and Fascism in Prewar Japan.* Chapel Hill: University of North Carolina Press, 1983.

Gao, Bai. *Economic Ideology and Industrial Policy in Japan: Developmentalism from 1931 to 1965.* Cambridge: Cambridge University Press, 1997.

Gluck, Carol, and Stephen R. Graubard, eds. *Showa: The Japan of Hirohito.* New York: W. W. Norton, 1992.

Harris, Sheldon H. *Factories of Death: Japanese Biological Warfare, 1932–45, and the American Cover-up.* London: Routledge, 1994.

Havens, Thomas R. H. *Valley of Darkness: The Japanese People and World War Two*. New York: W. W. Norton, 1978.

Hogan, Michael J. *Hiroshima in History and Memory*. Cambridge: Cambridge University Press, 1996.

Ienaga Saburō. *The Pacific War, 1931–1945*. Tr. Frank Baldwin. New York: Pantheon, 1978.

Iriye, Akira. *After Imperialism: The Search for a New Order in the Far East, 1931–1941*. Cambridge: Harvard University Press, 1965.

———. *The Origins of the Second World War in Asia and the Pacific*. London: Longman, 1987.

———. *Pearl Harbor and the Coming of the Pacific War: A Brief History with Documents and Essays*. Boston: Bedford/St. Martin's, 1999.

———. *Power and Culture: The Japanese-American War, 1941–1945*. Cambridge: Harvard University Press, 1981.

Kasza, Gregory J. *The Conscription Society: Administered Mass Organizations*. New Haven: Yale University Press, 1995.

———. *The State and the Mass Media in Japan, 1918–1945*. Berkeley: University of California Press, 1988.

Kiyosawa Kiyoshi. *The Wartime Diary of Kiyosawa Kiyoshi*. Ed. Eugene Soviak. Tr. Soviak and Kamiyama Tamie. Princeton: Princeton University Press, 1999.

Large, Stephen. *Emperor Hirohito and Shōwa Japan: A Political Bibliography*. London: Routledge, 1992.

Marshall, Jonathan. *To Have and Have Not: Southeast Asian Raw Materials and the Origins of the Pacific War*. Berkeley: University of California Press, 1995.

Minichiello, Sharon. *Retreat from Reform: Patterns of Political Behavior in Interwar Japan*. Honolulu: University of Hawaii Press, 1984.

Mitchell, Richard H. *Censorship in Imperial Japan*. Princeton: Princeton University Press, 1984.

———. *Janus-Faced Justice: Political Criminals in Imperial Japan*. Honolulu: University of Hawai'i Press, 1992.

Morley, James W., ed. *Japan's Road to the Pacific War*. New York: Columbia University Press.

Vol. 1: *Japan Erupts: The London Naval Conference and the Manchurian Incident, 1928–32* (1984).

Vol. 2: *The China Quagmire: Japan's Expansion on the Asian Continent, 1933–1941* (1983).

Vol. 3: *Deterrent Diplomacy: Japan, Germany, and the USSR, 1935–1940* (1976).

Vol. 4: *The Fateful Choice: Japan's Advance into Southeast Asia, 1939–1941* (1980).

Vol. 5: *The Final Confrontation: Japan's Negotiations with the United States* (1994).

Myers, Ramon H. *The Japanese Economic Development of Manchuria, 1932 to 1945.* New York: Garland, 1982.

Nakamura Masanori. *The Japanese Monarchy: Ambassador Grew and the Making of the "Symbol Emperor System," 1931–1991.* Tr. Herbert P. Bix, Jonathan Baker-Bates, and Derek Bowen. Armonk, N.Y.: M. E. Sharpe, 1992.

Nakamura Takafusa. *A History of Shōwa Japan, 1926–1989.* Tr. Edwin Whenmouth. Tokyo: University of Tokyo Press, 1998.

Ogata, Sadako N. *Defiance in Manchuria: The Making of Japanese Foreign Policy, 1931–1932.* Berkeley: University of California Press, 1964.

Pauer, Erich, ed. *Japan's War Economy.* London: Routledge, 1999.

Peattie, Mark R. *Ishiwara Kanji and Japan's Confrontation with the West.* Princeton: Princeton University Press, 1975.

Pincus, Leslie. *Authenticating Culture in Imperial Japan: Kuki Shuzo and the Rise of National Aesthetics.* Berkeley: University of California Press, 1995.

Rimer, J. Thomas. *Culture and Identity: Japanese Intellectuals during the Interwar Years.* Princeton: Princeton University Press, 1990.

Selden, Kyoko, and Mark Selden, trs. and eds. *The Atomic Bomb: Voices from Hiroshima and Nagasaki.* Armonk, N.Y.: M. E. Sharpe, 1989.

Shillony, Ben-Ami. *Politics and Culture in Wartime Japan.* Oxford: Clarendon Press, 1981.

———. *Revolt in Japan: The Young Officers and the February 26, 1936 Incident.* Princeton: Princeton University Press, 1973.

Silverberg, Miriam. *Changing Song: The Marxist Manifestos of Nakano Shigeharu.* Princeton: Princeton University Press, 1990.

Tanaka Yuki. *Hidden Horrors: Japanese War Crimes in World War II.* Boulder: Westview Press, 1996.

Tipton, Elise K. *The Police State: The Tokkō in Interwar Japan.* Honolulu: University of Hawai'i Press, 1990.

Titus, David A. *Palace and Politics in Prewar Politics.* New York: Columbia University Press, 1974.

Tsurumi Shunsuke. *An Intellectual History of Wartime Japan, 1931–1945.* London: KPI, 1986.

Wetzler, Peter. *Hirohito and War: Imperial Tradition and Military Decision Making in Prewar Japan.* Honolulu: University of Hawai'i Press, 1998.

Williams, Peter, and David Wallace. *Unit 731: Japan's Secret Biological Warfare in World War II.* New York: Free Press, 1989.

Yamanouchi, Yasushi; J. Victor Koschmann; and Ryūichi Narira, eds. *Total War and "Modernization."* Ithaca: East Asia Program, Cornell University, 1998.

Young, Louise. *Japan's Total Empire: Manchuria and the Culture of Wartime Imperialism*. Berkeley: University of California Press, 1998.


## Part V: Contemporary Japan

Aldous, Christopher. *The Police in Occupation Japan: Control, Corruption, and Resistance to Reform*. London: Routledge, 1997.

Allen, Matthew. *Undermining the Japanese Miracle: Work and Conflict in a Coalmining Community*. Cambridge: Cambridge University Press, 1994.

Allinson, Gary D. *Suburban Tokyo: A Comparative Study in Politics and Social Change*. Berkeley: University of California Press, 1979.

————, and Yasunori Sone, eds. *Political Dynamics in Contemporary Japan*. Ithaca: Cornell University Press, 1993.

Aoki Masahiko and Ronald P. Dore, eds. *The Japanese Firm: Sources of Competitive Strength*. Oxford: Oxford University Press, 1994.

Bailey, Jackson H. *Ordinary People, Extraordinary Lives: Political and Economic Change in a Tōhoku Village*. Honolulu: University of Hawai'i Press, 1991.

Bernstein, Gail Lee. *Haruko's World: A Japanese Farm Woman and Her Community*. Stanford: Stanford University Press, 1983.

Bestor, Theodore C. *Neighborhood Tokyo*. Stanford: Stanford University Press, 1989.

Bix, Herbert P. *Hirohito and the Making of Modern Japan*. Tokyo: HarperCollins, 2000.

Braw, Monica. *The Atomic Bomb Suppressed: American Censorship in Occupied Japan*. Armonk, N.Y.: M. E. Sharpe, 1991.

Brinton, Mary C. *Women and the Economic Miracle: Gender and Work in Postwar Japan*. Berkeley: University of California Press, 1992.

Buckley, Roger. *US-Japan Alliance Diplomacy 1945–1990*. Cambridge: Cambridge University Press, 1992.

Buruma, Ian. *The Wages of Guilt: Memories of War in Germany and Japan*. New York: Farrar, Straus, and Giroux, 1994.

Campbell, John Creighton. *How Policies Change: The Japanese Government and the Aging Society*. Princeton: Princeton University Press, 1992.

Calder, Kent E. *Crisis and Compensation: Public Policy and Political Stability in Japan, 1949–1986*. Princeton: Princeton University Press, 1988.

————. *Pacific Defense: Arms, Energy, and America's Future in Asia*. New York: Willliam Morrow, 1996.

————. *Strategic Capitalism: Private Business and Public Purpose in Japanese Industrial Finance*. Princeton: Princeton University Press, 1993.

Callon, Scott. *Divided Sun: MITI and the Breakdown of Japanese High-Tech Industrial Policy, 1975–1993.* Stanford: Stanford University Press, 1995.

Chalmers, Norma J. *Industrial Relations in Japan: The Peripheral Workforce.* London: Routledge, 1989.

Curtis, Gerald L. *The Japanese Way of Politics.* New York: Columbia University Press, 1988.

————, ed. *Japan's Foreign Policy after the Cold War: Coping with Change.* Armonk, N.Y.: M. E. Sharpe, 1993.

Cusumano, Michael A. *The Japanese Automobile Industry: Technology and Management at Nissan and Toyota.* Cambridge: Council on East Asian Studies, Harvard University, 1985.

————. *Japan's Software Factories: A Challenge to U.S. Management.* New York: Oxford University Press, 1991.

Dale, Peter N. *The Myth of Japanese Uniqueness.* New York: St. Martin's, 1986.

Davis, Winston B. *Japanese Religion and Society: Paradigms of Structure and Change.* Albany: State University of New York Press, 1992.

Dees, Bowen C. *The Allied Occupation and Japan's Economic Miracle: Building the Foundations of Japanese Science and Technology, 1945–52.* Richmond, Surrey: Japan Library, 1997.

Dore, Ronald P. *British Factory–Japanese Factory: The Origins of National Diversity in Industrial Relations.* Berkeley: University of California Press, 1973.

————. *City Life in Japan: A Study of a Tokyo Ward.* Berkeley: University of California Press, 1958.

————. *Japan, Internationalism and the UN.* London: Routledge, 1997.

————. *Land Reform in Japan.* London: Oxford University Press, 1959.

————. *Shinohata: A Portrait of a Japanese Village.* New York: Pantheon Books, 1978.

Dower, John. *Embracing Defeat: Japan in the Wake of World War II.* New York: W. W. Norton, 1999.

————. *Empire and Aftermath: Yoshida Shigeru and the Japanese Experience, 1878–1954.* Cambridge: Council on East Asian Studies, Harvard University, 1979.

Edwards, Walter. *Modern Japan through Its Weddings: Gender, Person, and Society in Ritual Portrayal.* Stanford: Stanford University Press, 1989.

Finn, Richard B. *Winners in Peace: MacArthur, Yoshida, and Postwar Japan.* Berkeley: University of California Press, 1992.

Glaubitz, Joachim. *Between Tokyo and Moscow: The History of an Uneasy Relationship, 1972–1990s.* Honolulu: University of Hawai'i Press, 1995.

Gordon, Andrew, ed. *Postwar Japan as History.* Berkeley: University of California Press, 1993.

————, ed. *The Wages of Affluence.* Cambridge: Harvard University Press, 1998.

Green, Michael J. *Arming Japan: Defense Production, Alliance Politics, and the Post-War Search for Autonomy*. New York: Columbia University Press, 1995.

Greenfeld, Karl Taro. *Speed Tribes: Days and Nights with Japan's Next Generation*. New York: HarperCollins, 1995.

Haley, John Owen. *Authority without Power: Law and the Japanese Paradox*. New York: Oxford University Press, 1991.

Harries, Meirion, and Susie Harries. *Sheathing the Sword: The Demilitarization of Postwar Japan*. New York: Macmillan, 1987.

Hatch, Walter, and Kozo Yamamura. *Asia in Japan's Embrace: Building a Regional Production Alliance*. Cambridge: Cambridge University Press, 1996.

Havens, Thomas R. H. *Fire across the Sea: The Vietnam War and Japan, 1965–1975*. Princeton: Princeton University Press, 1987.

Hein, Laura E. *Fueling Growth: The Energy Revolution and Economic Policy in Postwar Japan*. Cambridge: Council on East Asian Studies, Harvard University, 1990.

———, and Mark Selden, eds. *Censoring History: Citizenship and Memory in Japan, Germany, and the United States*. Armonk, N.Y.: M. E. Sharpe, 2000.

Hosoya Chihiro et al., eds. *The Tokyo War Crimes Trial: An International Symposium*. Tokyo: Kodansha, 1986.

Imamura, Anne E. *Urban Japanese Housewives: At Home and in the Community*. Honolulu: University of Hawaii Press, 1987.

Inoguchi Takashi. *Japan's Foreign Policy in an Era of Global Change*. New York: St. Martin's Press, 1993.

Inoue Kyoko. *MacArthur's Japanese Constitution: A Linguistic and Cultural Study of its Making*. Chicago: University of Chicago Press, 1991.

Ishida Takeshi and Ellis S. Krauss, eds. *Democracy in Japan*. Pittsburgh: University of Pittsburgh Press, 1989.

Iwao Sumiko. *The Japanese Woman: Traditional Image and Changing Reality*. New York: Free Press, 1992.

Ivy, Marilyn. *Discourses of the Vanishing: Modernity, Phantasm, Japan*. Chicago: University of Chicago Press, 1995.

Janssens, Rudolf V. A. *"What Future for Japan?" U.S. Wartime Planning for the Postwar Era*. Amsterdam: Rodopi, 1995.

Johnson, Chalmers A. *Japan, Who Governs? The Rise of the Developmental State*. New York: W. W. Norton, 1995.

Kataoka Tetsuya, ed. *Creating Single-Party Democracy: Japan's Postwar Political System*. Stanford: Hoover Institution Press, Stanford University, 1992.

———. *The Price of a Constitution: The Origin of Japan's Postwar Politics*. New York: Crane Russak, 1991.

Katō Shūichi. *A Sheep's Song: A Writer's Reminiscences of Japan and the World*. Berkeley: University of California Press, 1999.

Kersten, Rikki. *Democracy in Postwar Japan: Maruyama Masao and the Search for Autonomy*. London: Routledge, 1996.

Kohno, Masaru. *Japan's Postwar Party Politics*. Princeton: Princeton University Press, 1997.

Kondo, Dorinne K. *Crafting Selves: Power, Gender, and Discourses of Identity in a Japanese Workplace*. Chicago: University of Chicago Press, 1990.

Kōsai Yutaka. *The Era of High-Speed Growth: Notes on the Postwar Japanese Economy*. Tr. Jacqueline Kaminski. Tokyo: University of Tokyo Press, 1986.

Koschmann, J. Victor. *Revolution and Subjectivity in Postwar Japan*. Chicago: University of Chicago Press, 1996.

Koshiro Yukiko. *Trans-Pacific Racisms and the U.S. Occupation of Japan*. New York: Columbia University Press, 1999.

Kumazawa Makoto. *Portraits of the Japanese Workplace: Labor Movements, Workers, and Managers*. Tr. Andrew Gordon and Mikiso Hane. Boulder: Westview Press, 1996.

Lam, Alice C. L. *Women and Japanese Management: Discrimination and Reform*. London: Routledge, 1992.

LeBlanc, Robin M. *Bicycle Citizens: The Political World of the Japanese Housewife*. Berkeley: University of California Press, 1999.

Lebra, Takie. *Above the Clouds: Status Culture of the Modern Japanese Nobility*. Berkeley: University of California Press, 1992.

———. *Japanese Women: Constraint and Fulfillment*. Honolulu: University of Hawaii Press, 1984.

Lincoln, Edward J. *Japan: Facing Economic Maturity*. Washington, D.C.: Brookings Institution, 1988.

———. *Japan's New Global Role*. Washington, D.C.: Brookings Institution, 1993.

Lincoln, James R., and Arne L. Kalleberg. *Culture, Control, and Commitment: A Study of Work Organization and Work Attitudes in the United States and Japan*. Cambridge: Cambridge University Press, 1990.

Masumi Junnosuke. *Contemporary Politics in Japan*. Tr. Lonny E. Carlile. Berkeley: University of California Press, 1995.

Mathews, Gordon. *What Makes Life Worth Living? How Japanese and Americans Make Sense of Their Worlds*. Berkeley: University of California Press, 1996.

McCormack, Gavan. *The Emptiness of Japanese Affluence*. Armonk, N.Y.: M. E. Sharpe, 1996.

McKean, Margaret A. *Environmental Protest and Citizen Politics in Japan*. Berkeley: University of California Press, 1981.

McNamara, Dennis L. *Textiles and Industrial Transition in Japan*. Ithaca: Cornell University Press, 1995.

Mendl, Wolf. *Japan's Asia Policy: Regional Security and Global Interests*. New York: Routledge, 1997.

Milly, Deborah J. *Poverty, Equality, and Growth: The Politics of Economic Need in Postwar Japan*. Cambridge: Harvard University Asia Center, 1999.

Minear, Richard. *Victors' Justice: The Tokyo War Crimes Trial*. Princeton: Princeton University Press, 1971.

Miyoshi, Masao. *Off Center: Power and Culture Relations between Japan and the United States*. Cambridge: Harvard University Press, 1991.

————, and H. D. Harootunian, eds. *Japan in the World*. Durham: Duke University Press, 1993.

Moore, Joe. *Japanese Workers and the Struggle for Power*. Madison: University of Wisconsin Press, 1983.

Morris-Suzuki, Tessa. *Beyond Computopia: Information, Automation, and Democracy in Japan*. London: Kegan Paul International, 1988.

Mouer, Ross E., and Yoshio Sugimoto. *Images of Japanese Society: A Study in the Structure of Social Reality*. London: Kegan Paul International, 1986.

Nakamura Takafusa. *The Postwar Japanese Economy: Its Development and Structure, 1937–1994*. Tokyo: University of Tokyo Press, 1995.

Ogasawara Yuko. *Office Ladies and Salaried Men: Power, Gender, and Work in Japanese Companies*. Berkeley: University of California Press, 1998.

Ohnuki-Tierney, Emiko. *Illness and Culture in Contemporary Japan*. Cambridge: Cambridge University Press, 1984.

Okita Saburo, ed. *The Postwar Reconstruction of the Japanese Economy*. Tokyo: University of Tokyo Press, 1992.

Patrick, Hugh, ed. *Japan's High Technology Industries: Lessons and Limitations of Industrial Policy*. Seattle: University of Washington Press, 1986.

————, and Henry Rosovsky, eds. *Asia's New Giant: How the Japanese Economy Works*. Washington, D.C.: Brookings Institution, 1976.

Pempel, T. J. *Uncommon Democracies: The One-Party Dominant Regimes*. Ithaca: Cornell University Press, 1990.

Pharr, Susan J. *Political Women in Japan: The Search for a Place in Political Life*. Berkeley: University of California Press, 1981.

————. *Losing Face: Status Politics in Japan*. Berkeley: University of California Press, 1990.

————, and Ellis S. Krauss, eds. *Media and Politics in Japan*. Honolulu: University of Hawai'i Press, 1996.

Plath, David W. *The After Hours: Modern Japan and the Search for Enjoyment.* Berkeley: University of Calfornia Press, 1964.

———, ed. *Work and Lifecourse in Japan.* Albany: State University of New York Press, 1983.

Pyle, Kenneth B. *The Japanese Question: Power and Purpose in a New Era.* Washington, D.C.: American Enterprise Institute Press, 1992.

Reed, Steven. *Making Common Sense of Japan.* Pittsburgh: University of Pittsburgh Press, 1993.

Renshaw, Jean R. *Kimono in the Boardroom: The Invisible Evolution of Japanese Women Managers.* New York: Oxford University Press, 1999.

Richardson, Bradley M. *Japanese Democracy: Power, Coordination, and Performance.* New Haven: Yale University Press, 1997.

Roberson, James E. *Japanese Working Class: An Ethnographic Study of Factory Workers.* London: Routledge, 1998.

Roberts, Glenda S. *Staying on the Line: Blue-Collar Women in Contemporary Japan.* Honolulu: University of Hawai'i Press, 1994.

Robertson, Jennifer E. *Native and Newcomer: Making and Remaking a Japanese City.* Berkeley: University of California Press, 1991.

———. *Takarazuka: Sexual Politics and Popular Culture in Modern Japan.* Berkeley: University of California Press, 1998.

Rosenbluth, Francis McCall. *Financial Politics in Contemporary Japan.* Ithaca: Cornell University Press, 1989.

Ryang, Sonia, ed. *Koreans in Japan: Critical Voices from the Margins.* London: Routledge, 2000.

Schaller, Michael. *Altered States: The United States and Japan since the Occupation.* New York: Oxford University Press, 1997.

———. *The American Occupation of Japan: The Origins of the Cold War in Asia.* New York: Oxford University Press, 1985.

Schilling, Mark. *The Encyclopedia of Japanese Pop Culture.* New York: Weatherhill, 1997.

Schonberger, Howard B. *Aftermath of War: Americans and the Remaking of Japan, 1945–1952.* Kent: Kent State University Press, 1989.

Schoppa, Leonard J. *Education Reform in Japan: A Case of Immobilist Politics.* London: Routledge, 1991.

Smith, Robert J. *Kurusu: The Price of Progress in a Japanese Village, 1951–1975.* Stanford: Stanford University Press, 1978.

Stevens, Carolyn S. *On the Margins of Japanese Society: Volunteers and the Welfare of the Urban Underclass.* London: Routledge, 1997.

Stockwin, J. A. A. *Japan: Divided Politics in a Growth Economy.* New York: W. W. Norton, 1975.

Tabb, William K. *The Postwar Japanese System: Cultural Economy and Economic Transformation.* New York: Oxford University Press, 1995.

Tilton, Mark. *Restrained Trade: Cartels in Japan's Basic Materials Industries: Confronting Economic Change in Japan.* Ithaca: Cornell University Press, 1996.

Tobin, Joseph J., ed. *Re-Made in Japan: Everyday Life and Consumer Taste in a Changing Society.* New Haven: Yale University Press, 1992.

Tsuchimochi, Gary H. *Education Reform in Postwar Japan: The 1946 U.S. Education Mission.* Tokyo: University of Tokyo Press, 1993.

Tsuru Shigeto. *Japan's Capitalism: Creative Defeat and Beyond.* Foreword by John Kenneth Galbraith. Cambridge: Cambridge University Press, 1993.

Tsurumi Shunsuke. *A Cultural History of Postwar Japan 1945–1980.* London: KPI, 1987.

Uriu, Robert M. *Troubled Industries: Confronting Economic Change in Japan.* Ithaca: Cornell University Press, 1996.

Vogel, Ezra F. *Japan's New Middle Class: The Salary Man and His Family.* Berkeley: University of California, 1963.

White, Merry I. *The Japanese Educational Challenge: A Commitment to Children.* New York: Free Press, 1987.

———. *The Material Child: Coming of Age in Japan and America.* New York: Free Press, 1993.

———, and Kristina R. Huber. *Challenging Tradition: Women in Japan.* New York: Japan Society, 1991.

———, and Barbara Molony, eds. *Proceedings of the Tokyo Symposium on Women.* Tokyo: International Group for the Study of Women, 1979.

Whittaker, D. H. *Small Firms in the Japanese Economy.* Cambridge: Cambridge University Press, 1997.

Yoneyama, Lisa. *Hiroshima Traces: Time, Space, and the Dialectics of Memory.* Berkeley: University of California Press, 1998.

Yoshino Kosaku. *Cultural Nationalism in Contemporary Japan: A Sociological Enquiry.* London: Routledge, 1992.

# Credits

# *Photographs*

Chicago.; p. 64: *Southern Barbarians* (Namban Byobu). Japan, Momoyama or early Edo period, c. 1600–1650. One of a pair of six-fold screens, ink, color, and gold on paper, 159.3 × 351.2 cm. © The Cleveland Museum of Art, 2001, Leonard C. Hanna Bequest, 1960.193.1; p. 84: Courtesy of Roger Keyes; p. 105: National Diet Library, Tokyo; p. 106: Museum of Art, Rhode Island School of Design; gift of Mrs. John D. Rockefeller, Jr; photography by Erik Gould; p. 108: Collection of the Tokyo National Museum; p. 109: Collection of the Kyoto National Museum; p. 113: From an announcement of expositions, courtesy of Roger Keyes; p. 158: Asahi Shimbun Photo Service; p. 170: Robert Dennis Collection of Stereoscopic Views, Photography Collection, Miriam & Ira D. Wallach Division of Art, Prints & Photographs, The New York Public Library; p. 172: © Hoshun Yamaguchi Memorial Hall; p. 176: Kyodo News; p. 180: Scala/Art Resource, NY; p. 184: © Bettmann/Corbis; p. 199: © Bettmann/Corbis; p. 228: Kyodo News; p. 244: Courtesy of the Russian Geographical Society; p. 250: The Mainichi Newspapers; p. 263: The Mainichi Newspapers; p. 271: courtesy of Shido-Bunko, Institute of Oriental Classics, Keio University; p. 277: From the journal *Ie no hikari*, courtesy of Kerry Smith; p. 297: Museum of Art, Rhode Island School of Design; gift of Roger S. Keyes and Elizabeth Coombs; photography by Erik Gould; p. 308: © Corbis; p. 320: © Bettmann/Corbis; p. 337: Kyodo News; p. 340: The Mainichi Newspapers; p. 342: The Mainichi Newspapers; p. 345: Asahi Shimbun Photo Service; p. 346: From Edward Seidensticker, *Low City, High City*, New York: Knopf, 1983; p. 350: From Edward Seidensticker, *Low City, High City*, New York: Knopf, 1983; p. 352: Yumeji Takehisa print from *The Sun*, Autumn 1977, no. 20, p. 41; p. 353: From Edward Seidensticker, *Low City, High City*, New York: Knopf, 1983; p. 354: Kyodo News; p. 363: From Sheldon Garon, *Molding Japanese Minds*, Princeton, N.J.: Princeton University Press, 1997; p. 369: The Mainichi Newspapers; p. 371: The Mainichi Newspapers; p. 377: The Mainichi Newspapers; p. 380: Nihon Kindai Bungakukan—The Museum of Modern Japanese Literature; p. 390: Kyodo News; p. 399: From a farmer's diary, courtesy of Nishida Yoshiaki; p. 413: © Bettmann/Corbis; p. 418: The Mainichi Newspapers; p. 437: © Bettmann/Corbis; p. 443: Kyodo News; p. 450: Museum of Art, Rhode Island School of Design; gift of Colonel Marcellus and Emily Duffy; photography by Del Bogart; p. 452: © Bettmann/Corbis; p. 465: The Mainichi Newspapers; p. 488: Asahi Shimbun Photo Service; p. 504: The Mainichi Newspapers; p. 506: The Mainichi Newspapers; p. 514: The Mainichi Newspapers; p. 517: Courtesy of Jung-Kang McClain; p. 525: © Corbis; p. 529: © Bettmann/Corbis; p. 531: Kyodo News; p. 536: Courtesy of the National Archives and Records Administration—Central Plains Region (Kansas City); p. 563: Asahi Shimbun Photo Service; p. 567: © Bettmann/Corbis; p. 570: Kyodo News; p. 583: Kyodo News; p. 584: Kyodo News; p. 586: from R. P. Dore, *City Life in Japan*, Berkeley and Los Angeles: University of California Press, 1958; p. 587: © Horace Bristol/Corbis; p. 588: Courtesy of Gail Lee Bernstein; p. 594: © Michael S. Yamashita/Corbis.

Every effort has been made to contact the copyright holders of the selections. Rights holders of any selections not credited should contact W. W. Norton & Company, Inc., 500 Fifth Avenue, New York, NY 10110, in order for a correction to be made in the next reprinting of our work.

# Index